RESEARCH METHODS IN THE SOCIAL SCIENCES

Sixth Edition

RESEARCH METHODS
IN THE SOCIAL SCIENCES

Sixth Edition

CHAVA FRANKFORT-NACHMIAS
University of Wisconsin, Milwaukee

DAVID NACHMIAS
Tel Aviv University and
Israel Democracy Institute

WORTH PUBLISHERS

To our daughters, Anat and Talia

Research Methods in the Social Sciences, Sixth Edition
© 2000, 1996 by Worth Publishers and St. Martins Press

Printed in the United States of America.

ISBN-13: 978-1-57259-794-5
ISBN-10: 1-57259-794-1

Sixth Printing

Executive Editor: Alan McClare
Project Director: Scott Hitchcock
Marketing Manager: Renee Ortbals
Art Director: Barbara Reingold
Text and Cover Design: Barbara Reingold
Production Editor: Margaret Comaskey
Production Manager: Barbara Seixas
Composition: Progressive Information Technologies, Inc.
Printing and Binding: R. R. Donnelley & Sons Company

Acknowledgments can be found at the back of the book on page 527, which constitutes an extension of the copyright page.

Library of Congress Cataloging-in-Publication Data

Nachmias, Chava.
   Research methods in the social sciences : Chava Frankfort-Nachmias, David
   Nachmias. –6th ed.
         p. cm.
   Includes bibliographical references and index.
   1.   Social sciences—Methodology. 2. Social sciences—Research. I. Title. II.
         Nachmias, David

H61 .N25 1999
300'.7'2 21-dc21

Worth Publishers
41 Madison Avenue
New York, New York 10010
www.worthpublishers.com

CONTENTS IN BRIEF

Detailed Contents   •

PREFACE

The goal of the Sixth Edition of *Research Methods in the Social Sciences,* as in the previous editions, is to offer a comprehensive, systematic presentation of the scientific approach within the context of the social sciences. We emphasize the relationship between theory, research, and practice, and integrate research activities in an orderly framework so that the reader can more easily learn about the nature of social science research.

In our view, social science research is a cyclical, self-correcting process consisting of seven major interrelated stages: definition of the research problem, statement of the hypothesis, research design, measurement, data collection, data analysis, and generalization. Each of these stages is interrelated with theory in that it both affects and is affected by it. The text leads the reader through each stage of this process.

THE NEW EDITION

The Sixth Edition incorporates the following revisions:

—+ Appendix A, "Introduction to SPSS" has been updated to SPSS version 9.0 for Windows. Appendix A serves to assist students in preparing and executing computerized data analysis using this widely available and often-used software package. It includes step-by-step instructions covering basic and intermediate procedures normally required for management and analysis of survey data. The step-by-step instructions are illustrated with the appropriate window screens. Demonstrations of the various procedures are integrated into the Appendix using the GSS 1996 data set.

—+ New SPSS problems were developed for the following chapters: 3, 7, 8, 10, 11, 14, 15, 16, 17, 18, and 19. The new problems fully utilize the GSS 1996 data set and have a rich substantive context.

—+ Appendix B has been expanded to include guidelines on how to conduct a literature search successfully.

The new edition continues to blend a broad range of classic social science research studies with up-to-date examples of contemporary social science issues. The additions and changes reflect the concerns and developments that have surfaced in the field since the publication of the previous edition. The text has also benefitted from the constructive criticism offered by instructors, both users and nonusers, in research methods courses taught across the global village. Following their advice, we have revised the prose to make the tone less formal and the concepts even more accessible for students.

THE PLAN OF THE BOOK

The book's organization progresses logically from the conceptual and theoretical building blocks of the research process to data analysis and computer applications, offering students a comprehensive and systematic foundation for comprehending the breadth and depth of social science research. The book's self-contained yet integrated chapters promote flexibility in structuring courses, depending upon the individual instructor's needs and interests. The text adapts easily to two kinds of courses: a basic methods course or one that covers methods and statistics sequentially.

Chapter 1 examines the foundations of knowledge, the objectives of scientific research, and the basic assumptions of the scientific approach. Chapters 2 and 3 discuss the basic issues of empirical research and the relationship between theory and research.

They cover the topics of concept formation, the roles and types of theories, models, variables, and the various sources for research problems and for the construction of hypotheses. Chapter 4 focuses on ethical concerns in social science research and proposes ways to ensure the rights and the welfare of research participants, including the right to privacy.

Chapters 5 and 6 present the research design stage. A research design is a strategy that guides investigators; it is a logical model for inferring causal relations. Experimental designs are discussed and illustrated in Chapter 5, and quasi- and pre-experimental designs are examined in Chapter 6. Chapter 7 is concerned with measurement and quantification. The issues of validity and reliability—inseparable from measurement theory— are also reviewed here, together with the issue of measurement error. In Chapter 8, we present the principles of sampling theory, the most frequently used sampling designs, and the methods for estimating sample size.

In Chapters 9 through 13, we present and illustrate the various methods of data collection available to social scientists. Observational methods, laboratory experiments, and field experimentation are the subjects of Chapter 9. Survey research—particularly the mail questionnaire, the personal interview, and the telephone interview—is examined in Chapter 10. Chapter 11 describes and illustrates methods of questionnaire construction: the content of questions, types of questions, question format, and the sequence of questions. The discussion of the pitfalls of questionnaire construction addresses the issue of bias. Chapter 12 is devoted to the theory and practice of qualitative research, with a particular emphasis on participant observation and field research. In Chapter 13 we discuss major issues of secondary data analysis—the census, unobtrusive data as private and public documents, and content analysis.

The next five chapters are concerned with data processing and analysis. In Chapter 14 we present the latest techniques of codebook construction, coding schemes and devices, ways to prepare data for computer processing, the use of computers in social science research, and communication network linkages. Chapter 15 introduces the univariate distribution, measures of central tendency and dispersion, and various types of frequency distributions. Chapter 16 examines the central concept of bivariate analysis, concentrating on several measures of nominal, ordinal, and interval relationships, which are discussed and compared. The major topics of multivariate analysis, statistical techniques of control and interpretation, causal inferences, and path analysis are the subjects of Chapter 17. Chapter 18 presents common techniques used in constructing indexes and scales; and in Chapter 19 we discuss strategies of hypothesis testing, the level of significance, the region of rejection, and several parametric and nonparametric tests of significance.

This text, together with the supporting materials, will help readers move through the major stages of the research process.

ANCILLARY MATERIALS

Research Methods in the Social Sciences is accompanied by several useful ancillaries:

- → A *Study Guide* by Kenrick S. Thompson of Arkansas State University Mountain Home, which lists chapter objectives, key terms and concepts, and main points in the chapters, and provides self-evaluation exercises, review tests, and exercises and projects.

- → An *Instructor's Manual/Test Bank,* also by Kenrick S. Thompson, that provides chapter abstracts, objectives, main points, lists of key terms, suggested research projects;

and essay, discussion, and multiple-choice questions for each chapter, as well as transparency masters of selected summary boxes and figures.

—+ *Computer Software,* in the form of two data sets taken from the General Social Survey for 1996, conducted by the National Opinion Research Center. The first data set—gss96worth—includes 119 variables and 950 cases and can be used with the full version of SPSS. The second data set—gss96student—has 44 variables and 950 cases and can be used with the SPSS student version. These data are keyed to new SPSS exercises at the ends of 11 chapters.

—+ A computerized test item file, which provides the test items from the *Instructor's Manual Test Bank* in either Macintosh or IBM formats.

ACKNOWLEDGMENTS

Our literary debts are testified to throughout the text. Many students, instructors, reviewers, and colleagues have offered useful ideas and comments since the First Edition was published in 1976.

We are particularly grateful to Michael Baer, Bruce S. Bowen, Jeffery Brudney, Gary T. Henry, and Allen Rubin. We are also grateful to the Literary Executor of the late Sir Ronald A. Fisher, F.R.S., to Dr. Frank Yates, F.R.S., to Longman Group Ltd., London, for permission to reprint appendixes from their book *Statistical Tables for Biological, Agricultural, and Medical Research,* Sixth Edition (1974), and to the reviewers of the Fifth Edition: Lydia Andrade, San Jose State University; Claire L. Felbinger, American University; Richard Nagasawa, Arizona State University; Marcellina Offoha, Ithaca College; Alfred Powell, University of Texas at San Antonio; John K. Price, Louisiana Tech University; Jules J. Wanderer, University of Colorado at Boulder; and David G. Wegge, St. Norbert College.

We are grateful to Nina Reshef of The Public Policy Program, Tel-Aviv University, who assisted David Nachmias, and whose significant contribution is evident throughout the text; and to Pat Pawasarat, who assisted Chava Frankfort-Nachmias in the revision of the text.

Finally, we wish to express our indebtedness to the staff of Worth Publishers, especially to Scott Hitchcock, who has ably assisted in the revision of the Sixth Edition. We also extend our sincere thanks to Margaret Comaskey, Barbara Rusin, and Barbara Seixas for their patience and support throughout the project.

Chava Frankfort-Nachmias
David Nachmias

THE SCIENTIFIC APPROACH

ient's confidence in the response. Those who wish to discredit or delegitimize the authority of such a knowledge producer must not only thoroughly refute his or her claims, they must also provide an alternate source of knowledge.

Mystical Mode

In the mystical mode, knowledge or what is considered to be truth is obtained from authorities on the supernatural: prophets, diviners, mediums, and the like. In its reliance on knowledge producers, the mystical mode is similar to the authoritarian mode. However, unlike other modes of knowledge, mysticism depends on the appearance of supernatural events and on the psychological and physical state (the receptivity) of the knowledge "consumer." This helps to explain why the mystical mode depends, to a large extent, on the use of ritual and ceremony. For example, the rites surrounding astrological prophecy are aimed at persuading the layperson of the astrologer's supernatural powers.

Moreover, under conditions of acute depression, helplessness, or various types of intoxication, the knowledge "consumer" may be more willing to accept the knowledge produced by the mystical mode. Confidence in the knowledge produced in this manner decreases as the number of refutations increases, as the educational level of a society rises, or as one's psychological state improves.

Rationalistic Mode

According to the school of philosophy known as **rationalism,** all knowledge can be obtained by strict adherence to the forms and rules of logic. The underlying assumptions of rationalism are (1) the human mind can understand the world independent of its observable phenomena, and (2) forms of knowledge exist that are independent of our personal experiences. In other words, the rationalistic mode is concerned with knowledge that is true in principle as well as logically possible and permissible; that is, knowledge is true a priori.

To the rationalist, in order to think scientifically, the models of abstract formal logic must be followed. As such, rationalism is a *normative* master science—following its rules makes it possible to distinguish unsound thinking from sound scientific claims. According to classical rationalists, the Greek philosopher Aristotle (384–322 B.C.E.) developed the definitive framework for the world of logic and, hence, the structure of knowledge and truth.

With respect to the work of Aristotle, the German philosopher Immanuel Kant (1724–1804) argued:

> Since Aristotle it [i.e., the study of logic] has not had to retrace a single step, unless we choose to consider as improvements the removal of some unnecessary subtleties, or the clearer definition of its matter, both of which refer to the elegance rather than to the solidity of the science. It is remarkable also, that to the present day, it has not been able to make one step in advance, so that, to all appearances, it may be considered as completed and perfect.[3]

The view that knowledge exists a priori and that it is independent of human experience is still held, long after the period of classical rationalism. In contemporary science, pure mathematics represents the supreme embodiment of rationalism. Pure mathematics consists of statements that are universally valid, certain, and independent of the empirical world. For example, the statements of pure geometry are considered to be true by

---

3. Immanuel Kant, *Critique of Pure Reason*, trans. Max Muller (London: Macmillan, 1881), p. 688.

definition. Pure geometry says little about reality; its propositions are **tautological,** that is, true solely by virtue of their logical form. Although pure mathematics and formal logic are essential ingredients in the scientific approach, their value for the social sciences "exists only in so far as they serve as means to fruitful progress in the subject matter, and they should be applied, as complex tools always should, only when and where they can help and do not hinder progress." [4]

BASIC ASSUMPTIONS OF SCIENCE ●

The scientific approach is grounded on a set of basic **assumptions,** fundamental premises considered to be unproven and unprovable. These assumptions are necessary prerequisites for conducting the scientific discourse. **Epistemology,** the study of the foundations of knowledge, examines the nature of these premises and how they work. Reviewing these assumptions can help us to understand better the scientific approach and the claim that this approach to knowledge about the natural world is superior to other approaches.

   1.   *Nature is orderly.* The most basic assumption of the scientific approach is that there is a recognizable regularity and order in the natural world; events do not just occur. Scientists assume that some relationships and structure continue to exist even within rapidly changing environments. They also assume that change is patterned and, therefore, can be understood.

   The scientific conception of nature excludes omnipotent or supernatural forces as the sources of the order assumed to exist. For scientists, nature is the term used for all empirically observable objects, conditions, and events that exist independent of human intervention, including human beings as biological systems. What they call the "laws of nature" do not prescribe the order of events; rather, they describe what is actually happening. However, order and regularity are necessarily inherent in the phenomena. For example, there is no logically compelling reason why the seasons should follow each other as they do, with winter following autumn, autumn summer, and so on. But because winter always follows autumn, despite variations in temperatures or snowfalls, for example, scientists conclude that other regularities may underlie other observable phenomena.

   2.   *We can know nature.* The assumption that we can know nature is no more provable than are the assumptions that nature is orderly and that the laws of nature do exist. This assumption expresses the basic conviction that human beings are just as much a part of nature as any other object, condition, or event. In addition, although each of us possesses unique and distinctive characteristics, as human beings we can be understood and explained by the same methodology used to study other natural phenomena. That is, individuals and social phenomena exhibit sufficient recurrent, orderly, and empirically demonstrable patterns to be amenable to scientific investigation. Put simply, the human mind is capable of knowing not only nature but also itself and the minds of others.

   3.   *All natural phenomena have natural causes.* The assumption that all natural phenomena have natural causes (or antecedents) lies at the core of the scientific revolution. By rejecting the belief that forces other than those found in nature cause natural events, the scientific approach opposes fundamentalist religion as well as spiritualism and magic. Importantly, until scientists can explain the occurrence of phenomena in natural terms, they reject other arguments, including supernatural ones. Once empirical

4. Kurt Lewin, *Field Theory in Social Science* (Westport, CT: Greenwood Press, 1975), p. 12.

regularities are discovered and established, they can serve as evidence for the existence of cause-and-effect relationships.

4. *Nothing is self-evident.* Scientific knowledge is not self-evident; claims for truth must be demonstrated objectively. Scientists cannot rely on tradition, subjective beliefs, and cultural norms to verify scientific knowledge. They admit that possibilities for error are always present; hence, even the simplest claims call for objective verification. Because of this characteristic, scientific thinking is skeptical and critical.

5. *Knowledge is based on experience.* If science is to help us understand the real world, it must be **empirical;** that is, it must rely on our perceptions, experience, and observations. Perception is a fundamental tool of the scientific approach, and it is achieved through our senses:

> Science assumes that a communication tie between man and the external universe is maintained through his own sense impressions. Knowledge is held to be a product of one's experiences, as facets of the physical, biological, and social world play upon the senses.[5]

However, knowledge is not acquired only through the perceptions transmitted by the five senses of touch, smell, taste, hearing, and sight. Many phenomena cannot be experienced or observed directly. Observation is required to back up what we have perceived. Observation, as a mental activity, is neither self-evident nor entirely detached from the scientific terms, concepts, and theories employed by scientists. As the distinguished philosopher of science Sir Karl Popper (1902–1994) wrote:

> The naive empiricist . . . thinks that we begin by collecting and arranging our experiences, and so ascend the ladder of science. . . . But if I am ordered: "Record what you are experiencing," I shall hardly know how to obey this ambiguous order. Am I to report that I am writing; that I hear a bell ringing; a newsboy shouting; a loudspeaker droning; or am I to report, perhaps, that these noises irritate me? . . . A science needs points of view, and theoretical problems.[6]

Historically, the assumption that scientific knowledge should be based solely on empirical observation was a reaction against the belief that knowledge is innate in human beings, or that pure reason alone is sufficient to produce verifiable knowledge.

6. *Knowledge is superior to ignorance.* Closely related to the assumption that we can know ourselves as well as we can know nature is the belief that knowledge should be pursued for its own sake as well as for its contribution to improving the human condition. The contention that knowledge is superior to ignorance does not, however, imply that everything in nature can or will be known. Scientists assume that all knowledge is tentative and changing. Things that we did not know in the past we know now, and what we consider to be knowledge today may be modified in the future. Truth in science is always dependent on the evidence, methods, and theories employed, and it is always open to review.

The belief that relative knowledge is better than ignorance is diametrically opposed to the position taken by approaches based on absolute truth. As Gideon Sjoberg and Roger Nett put it:

> Certainly the ideal that human dignity is enhanced when man is restless, inquiring, and "soul searching" conflicts with a variety of belief systems that would strive toward a closed

---

5. Gideon Sjoberg and Roger Nett, *A Methodology for Social Research* (New York: Harper & Row, 1968), p. 26.

6. Karl R. Popper, *The Logic of Scientific Discovery* (New York: Science Editions, 1961), p. 106.

system, one based on absolute truth. The history of modern science and its clash with absolute systems bears testimony to this proposition.[7]

True believers already "know" all there is to know. In contrast, scientific knowledge threatens the old ways of seeing and doing things; it challenges dogma, stability, and the status quo. In return, the scientific approach can offer only tentative truth, whose validity is relative to the existing state of knowledge. The strengths and weaknesses of the scientific approach rest on the provisional and relative nature of truth:

> It is a strength in the sense that rational man will in the long run act to correct his own errors. It is a weakness in that scientists, not being so confident of the validity of their own assertions as is the general public, may, in those frequent periods when social crises threaten public security, be overturned by absolutists. Science is often temporarily helpless when its bastions are stormed by overzealous proponents of absolute systems of belief.[8]

AIMS OF THE SOCIAL SCIENCES ●

Having discussed the assumptions of science, we are now in a position to address the question raised earlier: What does science have to offer people who take an interest in society's problems? The ultimate goal of the social and all other sciences is to produce a cumulative body of verifiable knowledge. Such knowledge enables us to *explain, predict,* and *understand* the empirical phenomena of interest to us. We believe that a substantial body of knowledge can be used to improve the human condition. But what are scientific explanations? When can we make predictions? When are we justified in claiming that we understand empirical phenomena?

Scientific Explanation

Why are government expenditures per capita higher in Great Britain than in the United States? One response could be that the British want their government to spend more. Such an explanation might satisfy the layperson but it would not satisfy social scientists unless the same reasoning explained the level of government expenditures per capita in other countries. In fact, despite reports that most Britons want their government to spend more, government expenditures per capita in Great Britain declined after the Conservative Party returned to power in the 1980s.

The social scientist's aim is to provide general explanations for "Why?" questions. When scientists ask for an explanation of why a given event or behavior has occurred, they are in fact asking for a systematic and empirical analysis of the antecedent factors that caused the event or behavior.

Ever since the Scottish philosopher David Hume (1711–1776) expounded his theories on scientific thinking, the term **explanation** has been applied to the process of relating the phenomenon to be explained to other phenomena by means of *general laws*. General laws comprise the framework in which particular explanations are derived. In the words of Richard Braithwaite:

> The function of science . . . is to establish general laws covering the behavior of empirical events or objects with which the science in question is concerned, and thereby to enable us to connect together our knowledge of the separately known events, and to make

---

7. Sjoberg and Nett, *A Methodology for Social Research*, p. 25.
8. Ibid., p. 26.

reliable predictions of events as yet unknown. . . . If science is in a highly developed state, . . . the laws which have been established will form a hierarchy in which special laws appear as logical consequences of a small number of highly general laws. . . . If the science is in an early stage of development, . . . the laws may be merely the generalizations involved in classifying things into various classes.[9]

As scientific disciplines progress, the types of the explanations they provide change. Carl Hempel made an important distinction between the two basic types of scientific explanation: **deductive** and **probabilistic.** This classification is based on the kinds of generalizations that the explanation employs.[10]

DEDUCTIVE EXPLANATIONS. A deductive explanation calls for (1) a universal generalization, (2) a statement of the conditions under which the generalization holds true, (3) an event to be explained, and (4) the rules of formal logic. When using deductive explanation, a scientist explains a phenomenon by showing that it follows from an established universal law. For example, a scientific explanation for the return to earth of an object thrown into the air is based on the law of gravity. This law states that if all objects exercise a mutual attraction on one another, any particular object is expected to behave in the same way with reference to the earth. The essential condition for a universal law, then, is that it embraces all the cases of the same type within its domain.

In deductive reasoning, the premises lead, by necessity, to the conclusion; that is, if and only if the premises are true, the conclusion must be true. However, if the premises are not true, the conclusion will not be true. To illustrate this type of reasoning, let's say that in democracies, all elected officials seek reelection (untrue premise); John Brown is an elected official; therefore, John Brown will seek reelection (untrue conclusion). Our example illustrates why deductive explanations are the most powerful type of scientific explanation: Conclusions are considered to be true *only so long as* their premises are true. This also means that their premises are considered true until someone proves that they are not. In addition, because they cover all the cases of a single type, they explain unique as well as common events.

PROBABILISTIC EXPLANATIONS.   Not all scientific explanations are based on universal laws. This is particularly so in the case of the social sciences because few, if any, meaningful universal generalizations can be made. Instead, social scientists, as a rule, use *probabilistic* or *inductive* explanations. For example, a political scientist might explain a particular increase in government expenditures in the United States by suggesting that the rise was a response to adverse economic conditions because, in the past, increased expenditures have followed severe economic conditions. This explanation links the phenomenon to be explained to an event that occurred earlier—the country's economic difficulties. A scientist may propose such an explanation because it has been found that there is a relationship between economic conditions and government expenditures. The relationship cannot be expressed by a universal law because not every case of adverse economic conditions brings about an increase in government expenditures. The social scientist can only suggest that there is a high probability that severe economic conditions will induce increases in government expenditures, or that, in a large percentage of all the cases investigated, severe economic conditions led to increases in government expenditures. Explanations of this type are referred to as probabilistic or inductive explanations

9. Richard B. Braithwaite, *Scientific Explanation* (New York: Harper & Row, 1960), p. 1.

10. Carl G. Hempel, *Philosophy of Natural Science* (Englewood Cliffs, NJ: Prentice-Hall, 1966), ch. 5.

because they are derived from probabilistic generalizations. In other words, a probabilistic explanation uses generalizations that express either an arithmetic relationship between phenomena (*n* percent of *X = Y*) or a tendency for such events to take place (*X* tends to cause *Y*). (Inference, the process of deriving logical conclusions from premises known or assumed to be true, will be discussed further with respect to its role in social research in Chapter 19.)

When compared to universal laws, the major limitation of probabilistic or inductive generalizations is that conclusions about specific cases cannot be drawn with complete certainty. If, for instance, you know that 70 percent of the members of an ethnic group voted for the Democratic Party in elections for the House of Representatives over the past 20 years, you still cannot conclude with absolute certainty that a particular ethnic group member voted Democratic with the probability of .70. Factors other than membership in the specific group may have influenced the vote of the individual in question. Perhaps that person is a member of a social club with a long tradition of Republican political attachments. This membership may outweigh the influence of his or her ethnic identification when voting, even though the group's voting pattern may remain the same.

Prediction

Deductive and probabilistic explanations are essential components of scientific knowledge. **Prediction** constitutes another. In fact, the ability to make correct predictions is regarded as the outstanding characteristic of science. If knowledge is deficient, prediction is impossible. For example, if you know that 2 times 6 is 12, you can predict the outcome of a count of any two groups of six objects. If you know that the freezing point of water is 32°F or 0°C, you can predict what will happen to your car during the winter if you forget to add antifreeze to the water in the radiator. If you know that governments tend to spend more during economic recessions, you can predict that future recessions will bring about increases in government spending. If you know that job placement programs help to solve unemployment problems, you can predict that unemployment rates will decline after such programs are successfully implemented.

The expectation that scientific knowledge should lead to accurate predictions is based on the argument that if you know that *X* causes *Y* and that *X* is present, *you can then predict* that *Y* will occur. Underlying this argument is the assumption that if a universal law or a probabilistic generalization is *both* established and true—that is, the antecedent conditions required for the outcome have been fulfilled—then the only reasons for failing to make an accurate prediction are (1) that the law or the generalization is not in fact true, or (2) that the antecedent conditions have been identified incorrectly. Returning to one of our previous examples, let's say that the problem of unemployment continues after establishing job placement programs. We might then say that by measuring the unemployment rate we have shown that the original prediction was incorrect. Either the generalization that job placement programs solve unemployment problems is untrue, or job placement programs have been erroneously identified as the only activities that reduce unemployment.

Recalling the deductive mode of explanation, we can see that the process of prediction is, logically speaking, the *reverse* of the process of explanation. When making predictions, the antecedent observations are used merely to point out whether or not the initial conditions required for the event to take place are in fact present. Universal laws or probabilistic generalizations are then used to substantiate the prediction that if these conditions are present, they will be followed by specific consequences. Stated differently, prediction requires that we make sure that all the conditions required to cause an event are present, whereas universal laws or probabilistic generations justify the predictions we then make.

The logical structure of scientific explanations and predictions can now be summarized.[11] This structure consists of the following parts:

1. A statement E describing the specific phenomenon or event to be explained

2. A set of statements A to A_n describing the specific relevant conditions that are antecedent or causally related to the phenomenon to be described by E

3. A set of universal laws or probabilistic generalizations L to L_n that state: "Whenever events of the kind described by A_1 to A_n take place, an event of the kind described by E occurs."

For these three parts to constitute an explanation of the event or the behavior, they must fulfill at least two conditions:

1. Statement E must be deducible from statements A and L taken together but not from either set of statements taken separately.

2. Statements A and L must be true.

The following is a symbolic presentation of the logical structure of scientific explanations and predictions.

$$A_1, \ldots, A_n,$$

Therefore, E

The logical structure of explanation is identical to that of prediction. The difference between them lies in the perspective of the scientist. In the case of explanation, E is a past event relative to the scientist's current point of view, and he or she seeks the appropriate L's and A's from which to deduce the explanation of the event; in the case of prediction, the scientist already knows the L's and A's and seeks the future event implied by the former.

Understanding

The third essential component of social scientific knowledge is *understanding.* The term understanding is used in two radically different ways—**Verstehen** (or empathic understanding) and predictive understanding. These different usages evolved as the social sciences progressed as sciences. Most important, the terms reflect the subject matter of the social sciences—human behavior—and the fact that social scientists are more than mere observers: They are also participants in the behavior they explore. In the words of Hans Zetterberg:

> Symbols are the stuff out of which cultures and societies are made. . . . For example, a sequence of conception, birth, nursing and weaning represents the biological reality of parenthood. But in analyzing human parenthood we find, in addition to the biological reality, a complex of symbols [e.g., values, norms] dealing with the license to have children, responsibilities for their care and schooling, rights to make some decisions on their behalf, obligations to launch them by certain social rituals. . . . Our language thus contains codifications

11. The following discussion draws on Richard S. Rudner, *Philosophy of Social Science* (Englewood Cliffs, NJ: Prentice-Hall, 1966), p. 60.

of what parents are and what they shall do and what shall be done to them, and all these sentences in our language represent the social reality of parenthood. Social reality, in this as in other cases, consists of symbols.[12]

But are symbols and, by implication, human behavior amenable to investigation by the same methodology used in the natural sciences? Is the subject matter of the social sciences so complex and distinctive that a unique methodology is required for its study? Do social scientists, unlike natural scientists, have to "get inside" their subject matter in order to understand it?

THE *VERSTEHEN* TRADITION. According to the *Verstehen* (the German term meaning "empathy") tradition, the natural and social sciences are separate bodies of knowledge because the nature of their subject matter is different.

Adherents to the *Verstehen* tradition contend that natural and social scientists must employ different methods of research. For example, unlike the natural scientist, the social scientist must grasp both the historical dimension of human behavior and the subjective aspects of human experience. The German sociologist Max Weber (1864–1930) argued that if social scientists want to understand the behavior of individuals and groups, they must "put themselves into the place of the subject of inquiry." This means that they must comprehend the other's view of reality, the way that reality is expressed in symbols, as well as the values and attitudes that underlie that view.[13]

More recently, the **interpretive approach** has emerged as an outgrowth of the *Verstehen* tradition. Kenneth Gergen, one of the major proponents of this approach, stated that:

> A fundamental difference exists between the bulk of the phenomena of concern to the natural as opposed to the sociobehavioral scientist. There is ample reason to believe that the phenomena of focal concern to the latter are far less stable (enduring, reliable, or replicable) than those of interest to the former.[14]

Those who follow the interpretive approach realize that not only is their subject matter different but, because of this difference, the credibility of the findings and explanatory principles they propose is considered to be less than that attributed to the natural sciences. The methodology of *Verstehen* and its approaches is elaborated in Chapter 12.

PREDICTIVE UNDERSTANDING. In contrast to the *Verstehen* tradition, **logical empiricists** take the position that social scientists can attain objective knowledge when studying the social as well as the natural world. They contend that the two sciences can be investigated by the same methodology. Furthermore, although logical empiricists accept empathic understanding as a helpful route to making discoveries, they demand that these discoveries be validated by empirical observation before they are integrated into the body of scientific knowledge. (The idea of discovery versus validation is discussed in greater detail later in this chapter.)

---

12. Hans L. Zetterberg, *On Theory and Verification in Sociology*, 3d enlarged ed. (Totowa, NJ: Bedminster Press, 1965), pp. 1–2. See also Kenneth J. Gergen, *Toward Transformation of Social Knowledge* (New York: Springer-Verlag, 1982).

13. Max Weber, *The Theory of Social and Economic Organization*, trans. A. M. Henderson and Talcott Parsons (New York: Free Press, 1964).

14. Gergen, *Toward Transformation of Social Knowledge*, p. 12.

THE ROLES OF METHODOLOGY ●

The sciences, then, are not united by their subject matter but rather by their methodology. What sets the scientific approach apart from other modes of acquiring knowledge is the assumptions on which it is based and its methodology.

A scientific **methodology** is a system of explicit rules and procedures. It provides the foundations for conducting research and evaluating claims for knowledge. This system is neither static nor infallible. Rather, these rules and procedures are constantly being reviewed and improved as scientists look for new means of observation, analysis, logical **inference** (i.e., the process of deriving logical conclusions based on premises known to be true or on evidence gathered), and generalization. Once these procedures are found to be compatible with the underlying assumptions of the scientific approach, they are incorporated into the system of rules, the "logic of inquiry," that govern scientific methodology. Hence, scientific methodology is first and foremost self-correcting:

> Science does not desire to obtain conviction for its propositions at *any* price. . . . [A] proposition must be supported by logically acceptable evidence, which must be weighed carefully and tested by the well-known canons of necessary and probable inference. It follows that the *method* of science is more stable, and more important to men of science, than any particular result achieved by its means. In virtue of its method, the scientific enterprise is a self-corrective process. It appeals to no special revelation or authority whose deliverances are indubitable and final. It claims no infallibility, but relies upon the methods of developing and testing hypotheses for assured conclusions. The canons of inquiry are themselves discovered in the process of reflection, and may themselves become modified in the course of study. The method makes possible the noting and correction of errors by continued application of itself.[15]

The methodology of the social sciences continues to evolve slowly and carefully. During its evolution, the continuous exchange of ideas, information, and criticism makes it possible to establish firmly, or institutionalize, commonly accepted rules and procedures and to develop the corresponding methods and techniques. This system of rules and procedures represents the *normative* framework of scientific methodology. Scientific norms set the standards to be followed in scientific research and analysis; they define the "rules of the scientific game." The rules, in turn, enable communication, promote constructive criticism, and enhance progress.

Methodology Provides Rules for Communication

Anatol Rapoport illustrated the general problem of communication that exists between two people who have not shared a common experience by means of the following anecdote:

> A blind man asked someone to explain the meaning of "white."
>
> "White is a color," he was told, "as, for example, white snow."
>
> "I understand," said the blind man. "It is a cold and damp color."
>
> "No, it doesn't have to be cold and damp. Forget about snow. Paper, for instance, is white."
>
> "So it rustles?" asked the blind man.
>
> "No, indeed, it need not rustle. It is like the fur of an albino rabbit."

---

15. Morris R. Cohen and Ernest Nagel, *An Introduction to Logic and Scientific Method* (Orlando, FL: Harcourt Brace Jovanovich, 1962), pp. 395–396.

this reason, a dominant paradigm tends to remain the accepted paradigm long after it fails to be congruent with empirical observations.

A Logic of Discovery?

In Kuhn's view, there can be no logic of discovery, only a sociopsychology of discovery: Anomalies and inconsistencies always abound in science, but a dominant paradigm covers up the doubts aroused by puzzle-solving activities until a crisis causes it to be overthrown. This process nevertheless raises several questions: Is there a rational cause for the appearance of a crisis? What makes scientists suddenly aware of one? Exactly how is a rival paradigm constructed? Kuhn's thesis unfortunately does not address these questions. To repeat, for him there is no logic of discovery but rather a process motivated by group struggle within a scientific community.

In sharp contrast to Kuhn's descriptive view of science as a sociopsychological as well as intellectual activity is Karl Popper's *prescriptive,* normative theory. Popper argues that a scientific community ought to be and, to a considerable degree, actually is an "open society" in which no dominant paradigm is ever sacred. Popper states that science should be in a state of permanent revolution, that criticism lies at the heart of any scientific enterprise. For him, refutations of claims for knowledge constitute the essence of its revolutions:

> In my view the "normal" scientist, as Kuhn describes him, is a person one ought to be sorry for. . . . The "normal" scientist . . . has been badly taught. He has been taught in a dogmatic spirit: he is a victim of indoctrination. He has learned a technique which can be applied without asking for the reason why. . . . [25]

Popper does admit, however, that at any given moment, scientists are "prisoners" caught in their paradigms, expectations, past experiences, and language—with one important qualification:

> We are prisoners in a Pickwickian sense: if we try, we can break out of our framework at any time. Admittedly, we shall find ourselves again in a framework, but it will be a better and roomier one; and we can at any moment break out of it again.[26]

In order to place these two points of view into perspective, we need to distinguish between the two contexts of scientific activities: *justification* and *discovery.*[27] The **context of justification** refers to the situation in which scientists perform specific activities that help them to validate claims for knowledge logically and empirically. Scientific method is one of the basic tools used in this context; it provides scientists with the logic of justification regardless of how they arrive at their insights into the subjects they study. In contrast, the **context of discovery** represents the situation in which insights are actually made, unconstrained by methodology. Scientific methodologies may facilitate making discoveries but, at the initial stages of exploration, no formal rules or logic can operate as guides. This is the point where creativity, insight, imagination, and inspiration are enormously important. Although these can be nurtured, they cannot be reduced to rules: As John Stuart Mill (1806–1873) said, "There is no science which will enable man to bethink himself of that which will suit his purpose."[28]

25. Karl R. Popper, "Normal Science and Its Dangers," in *Criticism and the Growth of Knowledge,* ed. Imre Lakatos and Alan Musgrave (New York: Cambridge University Press, 1970), p. 53.

26. Ibid., p. 56.

27. See Kaplan, *The Conduct of Inquiry,* pp. 12–18.

28. Quoted in Kaplan, ibid., p. 16.

THE RESEARCH PROCESS

Scientific knowledge is knowledge grounded in both reason and experience (observation). Scientists employ the criteria of logical validity and empirical verifiability to assess claims for knowledge. These two criteria are translated into scientific research through the **research process.** The research process is the overall scheme of activities in which scientists engage in order to produce knowledge; it is the paradigm of scientific inquiry.

As illustrated in Figure 1.1, the research process consists of seven fundamental stages: *problem definition, hypothesis construction, research design, measurement, data collection, data analysis,* and *generalization.* Each stage influences the development of *theory* and is influenced by it in turn. In this book, we will discuss extensively each stage, as well as the transitions between them. For the moment, we will limit ourselves to a general overview of the process.

The most characteristic feature of the research process is its *cyclical nature.* It usually starts with a problem and ends with a tentative empirical generalization. The generalization ending one cycle serves as the beginning of the next cycle. This cyclical process continues indefinitely, reflecting the progress of a scientific discipline and the growth of scientific knowledge.

Figure 1.1

The Main Stages of the Research Process

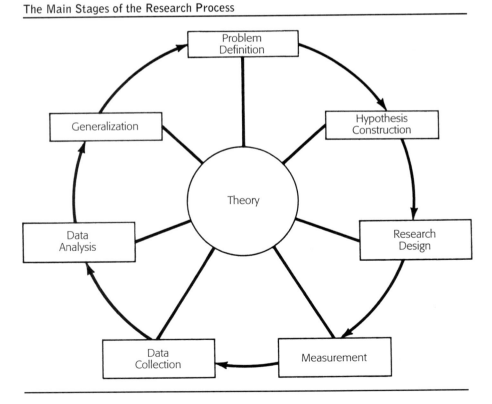

The research process is also *self-correcting*. Scientists test tentative generalizations—hypotheses—about research problems both logically and empirically. If they reject these generalizations, they formulate and test new ones. In the process, scientists reevaluate all the research operations they have performed because a tentative generalization may be rejected not only because it is invalid but also because of errors in how the research was conducted. For example, a researcher will reject the generalization that economic crises lead to increased government spending if it cannot be logically validated and empirically verified. That is, a generalization can be rejected, *even if it is true,* if the procedures for validation and verification (e.g., research design, measurement, or data analysis) are deficient. To minimize the risk of rejecting true generalizations, a scientist reexamines each stage of the research process before revising old or suggesting new generalizations. This is why scientific methodology is said to be self-correcting. Ideas and theories, by themselves, do not provide the tools for reexamining their basic claims or the conclusions they are meant to support.

Finally, you should be aware that the research process as presented here is somewhat idealized; that is, it is a rational reconstruction of scientific practice:

> The reconstruction idealizes the logic of science only in showing us what it would be if it were extracted and refined to utmost purity. . . . [But] not even the greatest of scientists has a cognitive style which is wholly and perfectly logical, and the most brilliant piece of research still betrays its all-too-human divagations.[29]

In practice, the research process occurs

> (1) sometimes quickly, sometimes slowly; (2) sometimes with a very high degree of formalization and vigor, sometimes quite informally, unself-consciously, and intuitively; (3) sometimes through the interaction of several scientists in distinct roles (of, say, "theorist," "research director," "interviewer," "methodologist," "sampling expert," "statistician," etc.), sometimes through the efforts of a single scientist; and (4) sometimes only in the scientist's imagination, sometimes in actual fact.[30]

Therefore, our idealized reconstruction of the research process is not intended to be rigid; it is meant to convey the underlying themes of social science research.

THE PLAN OF THIS BOOK ●

This book is organized so as to follow the major stages of the research process. Chapters 2 and 3 cover the conceptual foundations of empirical research and the relationships between theory and research. They focus on the fundamental elements of research: concepts, definitions, the functions and structures of theories, models, relations, variables, and the construction of research hypotheses.

Chapter 4 is concerned with the ethical and moral questions confronted by social scientists. In this chapter we discuss issues relating to the rights of research participants, the obligations of scientists, the interactions between participants and scientists, and professional codes of ethics. The have become increasingly important in planning and executing research projects.

In Chapters 5 and 6, we focus on the research design stage. A research design is the strategy that guides the investigator throughout the process of research. It is a logical model of proof that allows the researcher to draw inferences concerning the causal

---

29. Ibid., pp. 10–11.

30. Wallace, *The Logic of Science in Sociology,* p. 19.

relations that may be found among the phenomena under investigation. As you will see, there are various types of research designs, each of which includes the conditions for accepting or rejecting causal inferences.

Chapter 7 is concerned with the measurement stage of research. At this stage, researchers systematically assign symbols, usually numbers, to empirical observations. These numbers and their relations are amenable to quantitative analyses capable of revealing information that could not have been discerned without them. Numbers, because they can be added, subtracted, percentaged, and correlated, are used for describing, explaining, and predicting social phenomena.

Typically, scientific generalizations are not based on all the measured observations that might be obtained but on a relatively small number of cases—a sample. In Chapter 8, we cover the major topics involved with sampling theory: methods for choosing representative samples, sample size, and sample designs.

The five subsequent chapters cover the data collection stage. This is the stage where researchers make and record empirical observations. Data (observations) can be collected by various methods, including structured observation, nonstructured observation, personal interviews, impersonal surveys, public records, or private records. No data collection method is foolproof, nor will any one method suit all research problems. Different problems call for different methods, and each method has inherent advantages as well as limitations.

Chapter 14 focuses on the major aspects of data processing, the link between data collection and data analysis. During data processing, the observations researchers have gathered in the data collection stage are transformed into a system of conceptual categories. These categories are then translated into coding schemes that also lend themselves to quantitative analysis. These codes can then be recorded and processed by computers. The central issues involved in coding and automatic data processing are also covered in this chapter.

In the next stage of the research process, scientists conduct quantitative, statistical analyses. Statistics are numbers that can be used to summarize, analyze, or evaluate a body of information. It is useful to distinguish between two categories of statistics according to their different functions: *descriptive statistics* and *inferential statistics*. Researchers use descriptive statistical procedures to organize, describe, and summarize data. Chapter 15 covers descriptive univariate distributions; Chapter 16, bivariate distributions; and Chapter 17, multivariate data analysis techniques. In Chapter 18, we present methods of index construction and scaling. The second category of statistics, inferential or inductive statistics, makes it possible for researchers to generalize beyond the data in hand, to evaluate differences among groups, and to estimate unknown values. These methods, discussed in Chapter 19, facilitate the conduct of systematic inquiry.

SUMMARY

1. The sciences are united by their methodology, not by their subject matter. What sets the scientific approach apart from other ways of acquiring knowledge is the assumptions on which it is grounded in addition to its methodology.

2. The assumptions of the scientific approach are as follows: Nature is orderly, we can know nature, natural phenomena have natural causes, nothing is self-evident, knowledge is derived from the acquisition of experience, and while knowledge is tentative, it is superior to ignorance.

3. The methodology of the scientific approach serves three major purposes: It pro-

vides rules for communication, rules for logical and valid reasoning, and rules for intersubjectivity (the ability to share knowledge). These three systems of rules allow us to understand, explain, and predict human behavior and events in our environments in a manner that other modes for producing knowledge (authoritarian, mystical, rationalistic) cannot do.

4. Scientific knowledge is knowledge that can be validated by *both* reason and experience or sensory evidence (empirical observations). The scientific method requires strict adherence to the rules of logic and observation. Such adherence discourages dogma because it maintains that the research process is cyclical and self-correcting. Rational criticism should be at the heart of the scientific enterprise, and science ought to be in permanent change. Obviously, scientific communities, like other professional communities, are involved in internal power struggles that are not always conducive to the progress of science. Such power struggles are inevitable. However, claims for knowledge are ultimately accepted only insofar as they are congruent with the assumptions and methodology of science.

KEY TERMS FOR REVIEW ●

assumptions of science (p. 5)
constructive criticism (p. 13)
context of discovery (p. 17)
context of justification (p. 17)
deductive explanation (p. 8)
empirical observation (p. 6)
epistemology (p. 5)
explanation (p. 7)
inference (p. 12)
interpretive approach (p. 11)
intersubjectivity (p. 14)
logic (p. 13)
logical empiricists (p. 11)

methodology (p. 12)
normal science (p. 15)
paradigm (p. 15)
prediction (p. 9)
probabilistic explanation (p. 8)
rationalism (p. 4)
replication (p. 13)
research process (p. 18)
revolutionary science (p. 16)
science (p. 2)
tautological (p. 5)
Verstehen (p. 10)

STUDY QUESTIONS ●

1. Compare and contrast the scientific approach with the authoritarian, mystical, and rationalistic modes of knowing.
2. Discuss the assumptions underlying the scientific approach.
3. What are the aims of science as a knowledge-producing enterprise?
4. Describe the research process and its stages.
5. How is science actually carried out, both as a cyclical process of reasoning and observation and as a social institution?

ADDITIONAL READINGS ●

Agnew, Neil M., and Sandra W. Pyke. *The Science Game: An Introduction to Research in the Behavioral Sciences,* 6th ed. Englewood Cliffs, NJ: Prentice-Hall, 1994.

Boulding, Kenneth E. "Science: Our Common Heritage." *Science,* 207 (1980): 831–836.

Cohen, I. Bernard. *Revolution in Science.* Cambridge, MA: Belknap Press, 1985.

Fiske, Donald W., and Richard A. Shweder, eds. *Metatheory in Social Science: Pluralisms and Subjectivities.* Chicago: University of Chicago Press, 1986.

Kruskal, William H., ed. *The Social Sciences: Their Nature and Uses.* Chicago: University of Chicago Press, 1986.

O'Hear, Anthony. *An Introduction to the Philosophy of Science.* New York: Oxford University Press, 1989.

Popper, Karl R. In W. W. Bartley, III, ed. *Realism and the Aim of Science,* Lanham, MD: Rowman & Littlefield, 1992.

Scheffler, Israel. *Science and Subjectivity.* 2d ed. Indianapolis: Hackett, 1982.

Taylor, Charles. *Philosophy and the Human Sciences.* New York: Cambridge University Press, 1985.

CONCEPTUAL FOUNDATIONS OF RESEARCH

Can the discovery of an ancient Roman water-driven flour mill in southern France challenge how we conceptualize and subsequently research the life cycles of civilizations? A. Trevor Hodge, a classicist and archeologist, believes that it can. Archeologists and historians have traditionally considered slavery to be the cause of the technological decline of the Roman Empire. However, Hodge contends that the mill's size and sophisticated use of waterpower point in another direction. Instead of slavery, he would put greater emphasis on purely technological factors—in this case, the absence of horseshoes and inadequate harnesses—to explain the arrest in Rome's technological advance and its underutilization of natural resources in the ancient Roman economy.[1]

•| **IN THIS CHAPTER** we first discuss concepts, the building blocks of theoretical systems. After reviewing the functions of concepts, we discuss first conceptual and then operational definitions, and how they relate to the research process. We then distinguish among the four levels of theory and explain how the models represent different aspects of the real world. We close this chapter by reviewing the debate over theory-then-research or research-then-theory as the appropriate strategy to adopt when doing research in the social sciences.

As we saw in Chapter 1, scientific knowledge is validated by both reason and experience. This implies that social scientists operate at two distinct but interrelated levels: the conceptual–theoretical and the observational–empirical. Social science research is the outcome of the interaction between these two levels. In this chapter we concentrate on the conceptual–theoretical level and the relationships that exist between its components and empirical research.|

CONCEPTS •

Thinking involves the use of language. Language itself is a system of communication composed of symbols and the rules that permit us to combine these symbols in different ways. One of the most significant symbols in a language, especially as it relates to research, is the *concept.* A **concept,** like other symbols, is an abstraction, a representation of an object, or one of that object's properties, or a behavioral phenomenon. Scientists begin the process of research by forming concepts as "shorthand" descriptions of the empirical world. Each scientific discipline develops its unique set of concepts. For example, "social status," "role," "power," "bureaucracy," "community," "relative deprivation," and "cohort" are common concepts in political science and sociology, whereas "intelligence," "perception," and "learning" are common in psychology. To scientists, concepts and symbols constitute a professional language. Thus, when a social scientist uses the word "cohort," other social scientists immediately know what it represents: a group of people sharing a demographic characteristic such as age. For people who are untrained in the social sciences, "cohort" might be "gibberish," because the term has no meaning for them.

Functions of Concepts

Concepts are heuristic devices; as such, they fulfill several important functions in social science research. First and foremost, they provide the tools for communication. Without

---

1. A. Trevor Hodge, "A Roman Factory," *Scientific American,* 263(5) (1990): 106–111.

a set of agreed-upon concepts, scientists could not communicate their findings or replicate each others' studies. Communication based on the intersubjective sharing of knowledge and understanding would be impossible. It is important to remember that concepts are abstractions; they are based on sensory perceptions and used to convey information in a very concise manner. Concepts, therefore, do not actually exist as empirical phenomena—they are abstract *symbols* of phenomena, not the phenomena themselves. Treating concepts as though they were the concrete phenomena that they represent leads to the **fallacy of reification:** the error of regarding abstractions as real rather than the product of human thought. For example speaking or writing about the concept " the presidency " as if the term itself has drives, needs, or instincts is an error despite the tendency to do so.

Second, concepts allow us to develop a *perspective*—a way of looking at empirical phenomena that can be shared with others: "Through scientific conceptualization the perceptual world is given an order and coherence that could not be perceived before conceptualization."[2] Concepts enable scientists to focus on some aspect of reality by defining its components and then by attempting to discover whether that aspect is shared by different phenomenon in the real world:

> It permits the scientist, in a community of other scientists, to lift his own idiosyncratic experiences to the level of consensual meaning [i.e., intersubjectivity]. It also enables him to carry on an interaction with his environment; he indicates to himself what a concept means and acts toward the designation of that meaning. The concept thus acts as a sensitizer of experience and perception, opening new realms of observation, closing others.[3]

Third, concepts allow scientists to classify and generalize. In other words, scientists use concepts to structure, categorize, order, and universalize their experiences and observations. As John McKinney puts it:

> All phenomena are unique in their concrete occurrence; therefore no phenomena actually recur in their concrete wholeness. The meaning of identity is always "identical for the purpose in hand." To introduce order with its various scientific implications, including prediction, the scientist necessarily ignores the unique, the extraneous, and [the] nonrecurring, and thereby departs from perceptual experience. This departure is the necessary price he must pay for the achievement of abstract generality. To conceptualize means to generalize to some degree. To generalize means to reduce the number of objects by conceiving of some of them as being identical.[4]

For example, the concept "tree" enables us to overlook the ways in which pine, oak, spruce, fir, palm, and apple differ from one another and grasp how they resemble each other—their generic qualities. "Tree" is the general concept that enables us to perceive a large number of unique characteristics such as color, height, or age, and comprehend them in an orderly fashion. "Tree" is also an abstract concept in the sense that the unique attributes of our examples, the pine, oak, spruce, fir, palm, and apple, are "lost" in the process of conceptualization. Abstraction and generalization are, therefore, processes that enable scientists to isolate and then delineate the main attributes of the empirical phenomena of interest. However, in describing the process we are not implying that, once formed, a concept is a perfect, fully encompassing symbol of what it represents— its content is inevitably limited to the attributes *the scientist* considers essential. This

---

2. Norman K. Denzin, *The Research Act*, 3d ed. (Englewood Cliffs, NJ: Prentice-Hall, 1989), p. 38.

3. Ibid.

4. John C. McKinney, *Constructive Typology and Social Theory* (Norwalk, CT: Appleton & Lang, 1966), p. 9.

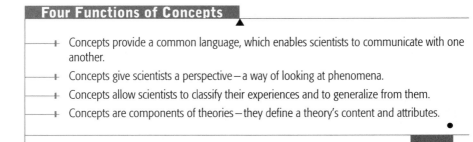

Four Functions of Concepts

+ Concepts provide a common language, which enables scientists to communicate with one another.
+ Concepts give scientists a perspective — a way of looking at phenomena.
+ Concepts allow scientists to classify their experiences and to generalize from them.
+ Concepts are components of theories — they define a theory's content and attributes.

means that concepts can change as new evidence is gathered. In addition, how they were formed is reviewed during the process of inquiry.

Fourth, concepts serve as components of theories; they are the key elements of explanations and predictions. Concepts, when linked in a systematic and logical way, lead to theories. They are the critical elements in any theory because they define its content and attributes. For example, the concepts "power" and "legitimacy" define the substance of theories of governance. The concepts "individualism" and "Protestantism" define and shape Durkheim's theory of suicide, which predicts suicide rates in many Western societies as a function of the relationships between individualism and religion. The concept "relative deprivation" is central to theories of revolution, while "supply" and "demand" are the pillars of economic theory. These examples illustrate the close relationship between concept formation and theory construction.

DEFINITIONS

If concepts are to serve the functions of communication, organization of experience, generalization, and theory construction, they have to be clear, precise, and agreed upon. Everyday language, however, is often vague or ambiguous. Concepts such as "power," "bureaucracy," "discrimination," and "satisfaction" mean different things to different people and are used in different contexts to designate various things. Usually, this does not create major problems in ordinary conversations. Science, however, cannot progress with an ambiguous and imprecise language.

Because of this need for precision, every scientific discipline is concerned with its vocabulary. Social scientists have likewise attempted to establish a clear and precise body of concepts (abstractions) to characterize their subject matter. Those elements of the subject matter that can be measured empirically are called variables, and will be discussed in Chapter 3. Although many concepts have been invented, used, refined, and discarded, others remain ambiguous and inconsistent. This should not be too surprising: Social scientists face the difficult problem of distinguishing their concepts from those commonly used by the subjects they want to study. As the social sciences progress, so will their vocabulary. To help them in achieving the desired clarity and precision during research, scientists employ two major types of definitions: *conceptual* and *operational*. The difference between them is important, for they help the scientist decide how variables are to be measured.

Conceptual Definitions

Definitions that describe concepts by using other concepts are called **conceptual definitions.** In certain cases, these may be used as variables in the research process. For example, "power" has been conceptually defined as the ability of an actor (e.g., an individual, a group, the state) to get another actor to do something that the latter would not otherwise do. The conceptual definition of "relative deprivation" is an actor's perception of a discrepancy between his or her "value expectations" and his or her "value capabilities." [5]

In these two examples, the variables "value expectations" and "value capabilities" are themselves concepts: We cannot sense value expectations empirically, we can only conceive of them through intellectual processes of abstraction. However, the process of definition need not stop here. In the case of "relative deprivation," a person who is unfamiliar with the theory is likely to ask, "What are 'values,' 'capabilities,' 'expectations,' and 'perceptions'?" These concepts call for further clarification. "Expectations," for instance, have been defined as manifestations of the prevailing norms found in the immediate economic, social, cultural, and political environments. But what is meant by "norms," "immediate," "economic," "social," "cultural," and "political"? These are also concepts that need to be defined by still other concepts, and so on.

At a certain point in this process, scientists encounter concepts that cannot be defined by other concepts. These are called **primitive terms.** For example, colors, sounds, smells, and tastes are primitive terms. Primitive terms are unambiguous and usually conveyed by clear-cut empirical examples. Scientists and laypersons agree on their meaning, which simplifies communication among researchers and the difficulties involved in planning research and interpreting research findings. For example, a scientist can point to a real-life behavior and define it as "voting." The word "voting" represents a set of easily observable behaviors that can be described or operationalized as a series of steps (such as going to a voting booth) but need not be. As such, "voting" can be used as a primitive term in theorizing and research.

Conceptual definitions, therefore, consist of primitive terms and derived terms. **Derived terms** are those terms that can be defined by using primitive terms. If agreement exists on the meanings of the primitive terms "individual," "interact," and "regularly," we can define the concept "group" (derived term) as two or more individuals who interact regularly. Derived terms make it possible to refer to increasingly complex phenomena simply and efficiently. Obviously, derived terms are easier to use than primitive terms; think of how troublesome it would be constantly to repeat the primitive terms that comprise the definition of "group." [6]

Finally, a crucial point to remember with respect to conceptual definitions is that they are neither true nor false. As pointed out earlier, concepts are symbols that permit communication. Thus, conceptual definitions are either useful for communication and research, or they are not. Although you can criticize the intelligibility of a conceptual definition or question whether it is being used consistently, there is no point in criticizing such a definition for not being true. Put simply, the definition is what the definer says it is.

To summarize, conceptual definitions share the following essential attributes:

—+ They point out the unique elements or qualities of whatever is defined. A definition must include all cases it covers and exclude all cases not covered.

—+ They should not be circular; that is, conceptual definitions must not contain any element of the phenomenon or object being defined. Defining "bureaucracy" as an organization that has bureaucratic qualities or "power" as a quality shared by powerful people does not enhance communication.

5. Ted R. Gurr, *Why Men Rebel* (Princeton, NJ: Princeton University Press, 1970), p. 24.

6. Paul D. Reynolds, *A Primer in Theory Construction* (New York: Macmillan, 1971), pp. 45–48.

—+ They should be stated positively. Defining "intelligence" as a property that lacks color, weight, and character obviously does not enhance communication because there are many other properties that lack color, weight, and character. Positive definitions point explicitly to those attributes that are unique to the concept they define.

—+ They should use clear terms, whose meaning is agreed upon by everyone. A term such as "sexual harassment," for example, means different things to different people; therefore, it should not be used in a definition.

Operational Definitions

Often, as we have already indicated, the empirical attributes or events represented by concepts and certain variables cannot be observed directly. Examples include the concepts "power," "relative deprivation," "intelligence," and "satisfaction" and, generally, nonbehavioral properties such as perceptions, values, and attitudes. In such cases, researchers have to infer the empirical existence of the concept. They make inferences of this kind by using operational definitions, definitions that provide concepts with empirical referents.

Operational definitions bridge the conceptual–theoretical and empirical–observational levels. An operational definition delineates a set of procedures that describe the activities a researcher needs to perform to establish empirically the existence, or degree of existence, of the phenomenon described by a concept. That is, operational definitions define *what to do* and *what to observe* in order to make the phenomenon studied perceivable and understandable. They do so through making the meanings of concepts concrete by laying out the measuring procedures that provide the empirical criteria necessary for scientifically applying concepts that have no directly observable characteristics. Operational definitions, therefore, make it possible to confirm the existence of those concepts.

The idea of operational definitions was developed by the operational school of thought, exemplified in the works of the physicist P. W. Bridgman. Bridgman's main idea is that the meaning of every scientific concept must be made observable through the use of a set of procedures (operations) that test the criteria for applying the specific concept. Stated differently, the meaning of a concept is fully and exclusively determined by its operational definition. Bridgman explains:

> The concept of length is therefore fixed when the operations by which length is measured are fixed: that is, the concept of length involves as much as and nothing more than the set of operations by which length is determined. In general, we mean by any concept nothing more than a set of operations; *the concept is synonymous with the corresponding set of operations.*[7]

Thus, an operational definition of "length" would specify a procedure involving the use of a ruler for determining the distance between two points. Similarly, the term "harder" as applied, say, to minerals, might be operationally defined as follows: "To determine whether mineral M_4 is harder than mineral M_5, draw a sharp point of a piece of M_4 under pressure across the surface of a piece of M_5 (test operation); M_4 will be said to be harder than M_5 only if a scratch is produced (specific test result)."[8] Similarly, an operational definition of "intelligence" consists of a test to be administered in a certain way

7. Percy W. Bridgman, *The Logic of Modern Physics* (New York: Ayer, 1980), p. 5.

8. Carl G. Hempel, *Philosophy of Natural Science* (Englewood Cliffs, NJ: Prentice-Hall, 1966), p. 89 (edited slightly).

Theory means different things to different people. Some social scientists would identify theory with any kind of conceptualization. Concepts such as "power," "social status," "democracy," "bureaucracy," and "deviance," when defined and used in explanations of empirical phenomena, are sometimes equated with theories. In this broad sense, any conceptualization, as opposed to any observation, can be viewed as theory. Other social scientists equate theory with the "history of ideas." Still others view theory in a narrow sense: as a *logical–deductive* system consisting of a set of interrelated concepts from which testable propositions can be derived deductively. Before we discuss what theory is and what types of theory are prevalent in the social sciences, it is useful to point out some common misconceptions about theory.

What Theory Is Not

The layperson usually contrasts "theory" with "practice." The claim that something is "all right in theory but won't work in practice" conveys the idea that theory is impractical. As Arnold Brecht put it, "The relation between practice and theory is well indicated in the popular saying that we learn best through 'trial and error.' Trial is practice; error refers to theory. When theory miscarries in practical trials it needs correction." [13] In principle, theory should not be contrasted to practice. Rather, theory relates to practice; that is, scientists accept a theory (and its practical applications) only when the methodology for using it is logically and explicitly pointed out. A credible theory provides the conceptual foundations for reliable knowledge; theories help us explain and predict the phenomena of interest to us and, in consequence, assist us in making intelligent practical decisions.

Another misconception about theory results from people substituting the term "theory" for "philosophy." Thus the writings of classical scholars such as Plato, Aristotle, Locke, Marx, and Pareto are often identified with "theory." In fact, prior to World War II, theory in the social sciences was comprised almost exclusively of philosophy in its various forms, with particular emphasis on moral philosophy, that is, ideas of how things *ought* to be. Plato's exposition of the ideal just polity, in which the absolute knowledge of the philosopher-king is the guide for political and social behavior, is a familiar example.

We should bear in mind when comparing theories with philosophies that moral philosophies state value judgments: They are neither true nor false, because they are not empirically verifiable. If you believe strongly that socialism is the best of all economic systems, no amount of empirical evidence will prove or disprove that belief. Unlike philosophical works, however, scientific theories are abstractions representing certain aspects of the empirical world; they are concerned with the *how* and *why* of empirical phenomena, not with the *should be.*

Types of Theories

There is no one simple definition of theory on which all social scientists would agree because there are many different kinds of theories, each serving a different purpose. David Easton, for example, suggested that theories can be classified according to their *scope*—whether they are macro or micro theories; according to their *function*—whether they seek to deal with static or dynamic phenomena, with structure or process; according to their *internal structure*—whether they are logical systems of thought with closely knit interrelationships or a more loosely defined set of propositions; or according to their *level*—"by the relationship of the behavioral systems to which they refer as ranked on

---

13. Arnold Brecht, *Political Theory* (Princeton, NJ: Princeton University Press, 1959), p. 19.

some hierarchical scale."[14] Our classification, however, is based on the distinction Parsons and Shils made among four *levels* of theory: ad-hoc classificatory systems, taxonomies, conceptual frameworks, and theoretical systems.[15]

AD-HOC CLASSIFICATORY SYSTEMS. The lowest level of theorizing is the **ad-hoc classificatory system.** It consists of arbitrary categories constructed in order to organize and summarize empirical observations. For example, a researcher might classify responses to the questionnaire item, "All groups can live in harmony in this country without changing the system in any way," into four categories: "Strongly agree," "Agree," "Strongly disagree," and "Disagree." These categories constitute an ad-hoc classificatory system because they simply arrange observations; they are not derived from a more general theory of social order.

TAXONOMIES. The second level of theory is the categorical system, or **taxonomy.** A taxonomy consists of a system of logically related categories constructed to fit empirical observations in such a way that relationships among the categories can be defined. The categories, therefore, reflect the interdependence of the reality they describe. Talcott Parsons's analysis of social action exemplifies this level of theory. He suggests that behavior has four attributes: It is goal-oriented, occurs in group situations, is normatively regulated, and involves an expenditure of energy. When behavior displays all these attributes, it constitutes a social system. Furthermore, social systems take three forms: personality systems, cultural systems, and social structures.[16] Parsons carefully defined these seven categories and then explained their interrelations. Ever since Parsons formulated this taxonomy, researchers have assigned empirical observations to these categories.

Taxonomies basically perform two important functions in social science research. The first, which is related to the precise definitions of their categories, is to specify the unit of empirical reality to be analyzed and indicate how that unit may be described (e.g., in Parsons's taxonomy, social systems). The goal of a taxonomy is to provide

> . . . an orderly schema for classification and description. . . . When faced with any subject of research, [one] can immediately identify its crucial aspects or variables by using his taxonomy as a kind of a "shopping list." To "test" his taxonomy, he takes a fresh look at subject *X* and shows that the general terms defining his dimensions have identifiable counterparts in *X*.[17]

The second function of the taxonomy is to "summarize and inspire descriptive studies,"[18] such as those concerned with the empirical distribution of one or more categories comprising the taxonomy. However, taxonomies do not provide explanations; they only describe empirical phenomena by fitting them into their categories. Knowledge of the concepts that represent specific phenomena (e.g., "government spending") and their distributions (e.g., how much is spent on various programs) is not equivalent to explaining or predicting those same phenomena (e.g., why some governments spend more on defense than on education).

14. David Easton, "Alternative Strategies in Theoretical Research," in *Varieties of Political Theory*, ed. David Easton (Englewood Cliffs, NJ: Prentice-Hall, 1966), pp. 1–13.

15. Talcott Parsons and Edward A. Shils, *Toward a General Theory of Action* (New York: Harper & Row, 1962), pp. 50–51.

16. Ibid., pp. 247–275.

17. Hans L. Zetterberg, *On Theory and Verification in Sociology*, 3d enlarged ed. (Totowa, NJ: Bedminster Press, 1965), p. 26.

18. Ibid.

Figure 2.2

A Conceptual Framework of Political Systems

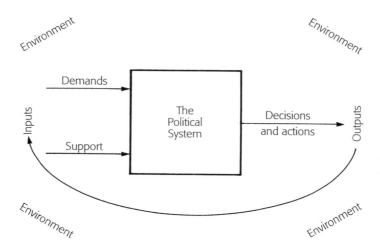

From David Easton, *A System Analysis of Political Life* (Chicago: University of Chicago Press, 1979)

CONCEPTUAL FRAMEWORKS. The third level of theory is the **conceptual framework.** In a conceptual framework, descriptive categories are systematically placed in a broad structure of explicit propositions—statements of relationships between two or more empirical properties—which are to be accepted or rejected. Easton's conceptualization of politics is a fruitful example of a conceptual framework. Easton identifies the major functions of political systems as the "authoritative allocation of values." [19] All political systems, whatever their form of government (democracies as well as dictatorships), allocate values authoritatively. Easton uses concepts such as "inputs," "outputs," "environment," and "feedback" (Figure 2.2) to describe and explain empirical observations. These concepts are then interrelated, with "feedback" performing the functions of continuity or change. Easton also offers a variety of propositions to explain how "inputs" (differentiated into "demands" and "supports") are generated, how political decision makers react to "inputs," how the "environment" influences "inputs" and decision makers, and how "outputs" (differentiated into "decisions" and "actions"), through "feedback," change or preserve the nature of "inputs."

This conceptual framework belongs to a higher level than a taxonomy because its propositions summarize behaviors as well as provide explanations and predictions for vast numbers of empirical observations. Much of what is considered theory in the social sciences consists of conceptual frameworks, which can be used to direct systematic empirical research. However, the propositions derived from conceptual frameworks are not established deductively, that is, from an a-priori set of universal generalizations. Their

19. David Easton, *A System Analysis of Political Life* (Chicago: University of Chicago Press, 1979), pp. 21–32; see also David Easton, *A Framework for Political Analysis* (Chicago: University of Chicago Press, 1979).

dependence on empirical observation in the earlier stages of theorizing and research limits their explanatory and predictive powers of conceptual frameworks and impairs their usefulness for future research.

THEORETICAL SYSTEMS. **Theoretical systems** combine taxonomies and conceptual frameworks by relating descriptions, explanations, and predictions in a systematic manner. This is the highest level of theory and requires the most rigorous definition: A theoretical system is comprised of propositions that are interrelated in a way that permits some propositions to be derived from others. When such a theoretical system exists, social scientists can claim to have explained and predicted the phenomenon they have studied.

A theoretical system, such as Durkheim's classic theory of suicide, provides a framework for the inclusive explanation of empirical phenomena; its scope is not limited to one particular aspect of the event to be explained. It consists of a set of *concepts,* which indicate what the theory is about, some of which are abstract (e.g., "anomie"), whereas others are measurable (e.g., "suicide rates"). These measurable empirical properties are termed *variables.* (A detailed discussion of variables and their types is found in Chapter 3.)

A theoretical system also consists of a set of *propositions.* However, contrary to their status within a conceptual framework, these propositions form a *deductive system.* In other words, this set of propositions forms a *calculus* (a method of analysis or calculation using special symbolic notation). Therefore, by following the rules established for manipulating them, scientists can deduce some propositions from others. When propositions are formulated on the basis of other propositions, they are said to be explanatory as well as predictive statements.

Durkheim's theory of suicide, as restated by George Homans, provides a classic example of a theoretical system:[20]

1. In any social group, the suicide rate varies directly with the degree of individualism.

2. The degree of individualism varies with the incidence of Protestantism.

3. Therefore, the suicide rate varies with the incidence of Protestantism.

4. The incidence of Protestantism in Spain is low.

5. Therefore, the suicide rate in Spain is low.

In this example, proposition 3 is deduced from propositions I and 2, and proposition 5 is deduced from 3 and 4. Accordingly, for example, if you did not know the suicide rate in Bulgaria but did know that there were few Protestants in the country (i. e., a low incidence of Protestantism), this information, together with proposition 3, would allow you to predict a low rate of suicide in Bulgaria. Thus, Durkheim's theoretical system provides both an explanation and a prediction of suicide rates.

Finally, some of the propositions of a theoretical system must be *contingent,* that is, dependent on empirical reality in the sense that "experience is relevant to their truth or falsity or to that of propositions derived from them."[21] Indeed, acceptance of a theoretical system depends ultimately on whether scientists are able to verify empirically those of its propositions whose validity depends on the evidence gathered by means of scientific methodologies.

20. Homans, "Contemporary Theory in Sociology," p. 959.

21. Ibid.

Figure 2.3

A Model of the Policy Implementation Process

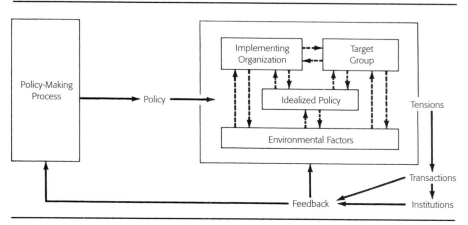

ating force in society: Implementation causes strain and conflicts among the implemen-
tors of the policy as well as the people affected by it. Tensions lead to *transactions*,
Smith's term for the responses to these tensions and conflicts. The feedback initiated by
transactions and institutions influences the four components of the implementation
process as well as future policy making.

Models, then, are tools for explanation and prediction. If they are well designed, they
approximate reality faithfully; but the models themselves are never the reality. Indeed,
models are often changed to represent reality more accurately and to incorporate new
knowledge. Thus, the critical attribute of a scientific model is that it can be tested empirically; it can be proved false and changed or discarded.

THEORY, MODELS, AND EMPIRICAL RESEARCH   ●

The social sciences, as scientific disciplines, rest on two major components: theory and
empirical research. Social scientists, as scientists, operate in two "worlds," the world of
observation and experience, and the world of ideas, theories, and models. Establishing
systematic links between these two worlds improves the prospects for achieving the
goals of the social sciences—understanding, explanation, and accurate predictions of social phenomena. How can we create these links? Should we first construct theories and
models and then move to the world of empirical research? Or should theory follow empirical research?

Theory Before Research

According to one major school of thought, theory should come first, to be followed by
research; this is often referred to as the **theory-then-research strategy.** Karl Popper
(1902–1994) was the most systematic exponent of this strategy. He argued that scientific knowledge progresses most rapidly when scientists develop ideas (conjectures) and

then attempt to refute them through empirical research (refutations).[29] Popper denied the systematic bearing of empirical research on theorizing. He believed that research seldom generates new theories, or that it can serve as a logical basis for theory construction. Theories "can only be reached by intuition, based upon something like an intellectual love of the objects of experience." [30]

The theory-then-research strategy, in a highly simplified form, involves the following five stages[31]:

1. Construct an explicit theory or model.

2. Select a proposition derived from the theory or model for empirical investigation.

3. Design a research project to test the proposition.

4. If the proposition derived from the theory is rejected by the empirical data, make changes in the theory or the research project (for example, research, design, measurement; see Figure 1.1) and return to stage 2.

5. If the proposition is not rejected, select other propositions for testing or attempt to improve the theory.

Research Before Theory

In sharp contrast to Karl Popper, Robert Merton, a proponent of the **research-then-theory strategy,** argues as follows:

> It is my central thesis that empirical research goes far beyond the passive role of verifying and testing theory; it does more than confirm or refute hypotheses. Research plays an active role: it performs at least four major functions which help shape the development of theory. It initiates, it reformulates, it deflects, and it clarifies theory.[32]

According to this view, empirical research suggests new problems for theory, calls for new theoretical formulations, leads to the refinement of existing theories, and provides verification. The research-then-theory strategy, again in highly simplified form, consists of the following four stages[33]:

1. Investigate a phenomenon and delineate its attributes.

2. Measure the attributes in a variety of situations. (Measurement and measuring procedures are discussed in Chapter 7.)

3. Analyze the resulting data to determine if there are systematic patterns of variation.

4. Once systematic patterns are discovered, construct a theory. The theory may be of any of the types discussed earlier, although a theoretical system is preferred.

Clearly, both strategies regard theory construction and refinement as the foremost manifestation of scientific progress. The real dilemma is over the place of theory in the total research process. We contend that no dogmatic commitment to either strategy is neces-

29. Karl R. Popper, *Conjectures and Refutations: The Growth of Scientific Knowledge* (New York: Harper & Row, 1968).

30. Karl R. Popper, *The Logic of Scientific Discovery* (New York: Science Editions, 1961).

31. Reynolds, *A Primer in Theory Construction*, pp. 140–144.

32. Robert K. Merton, *Social Theory and Social Structure*, rev. and enlarged ed. (New York: The Free Press, 1968), p. 103.

33. Reynolds, *A Primer in Theory Construction*, pp. 140–144.

sary for the conduct of research. The social sciences have progressed in spite of this controversy, and scientific research has been pursued under both strategies. In effect, theory and research continuously interact, as suggested by Figure 1.1. As Ernest Nagel maintains, the contrast between the two strategies is more apparent than real:

> Distinguished scientists have repeatedly claimed that theories are "free creations of the mind." Such claims obviously do not mean that theories may not be *suggested* by observational materials or that theories do not require support from observational evidence. What such claims do rightly assert is that the basic terms of a theory need not possess meanings which are fixed by definite experimental procedures, and that a theory may be adequate and fruitful despite the fact that the evidence for it is necessarily indirect.[34]

SUMMARY

1. One of the most significant symbols in science is the concept. Science begins by forming concepts to describe the empirical world and advances by connecting these concepts into theoretical systems. Concepts enable effective communication, introduce a point of view, provide the means for classification and generalization, and serve as the building blocks of propositions, theories, and hypotheses.

2. To serve their functions effectively, concepts have to be clear, precise, and agreed upon. These qualities are achieved by means of conceptual and operational definitions. A conceptual definition describes concepts using primitive and derived terms. Operational definitions state the procedures and activities that researchers should perform in order to observe empirically the phenomena represented by concepts. Hence, operational definitions link the conceptual–theoretical level with the empirical–observational level.

3. Although social scientists agree that theory is the ultimate achievement of scientific activities, there are divergent views concerning the meaning and structure of theory. At present, scientists distinguish four levels of theory: ad-hoc classificatory systems, taxonomies, conceptual frameworks, and theoretical systems. One major type of theoretical system is axiomatic theory. An axiomatic theory contains a set of concepts and definitions, a set of statements, a set of relational statements divided into axioms and theorems, and a logical system used to relate concepts within the statements as well as to deduce theorems from axioms and other theorems.

4. Scientists use models to represent systematically certain aspects of the real world. Models are abstractions that serve the purpose of ordering and simplifying our view of reality while representing its essential attributes. Scientists also use models to gain insight into phenomena that cannot be observed directly, such as an economic system.

5. Scientists have established systematic links between the empirical and the conceptual worlds with the assistance of two general strategies: theory-then-research and research-then-theory. Although there is a lively controversy as to which strategy is most fruitful for enhancing scientific progress, our position is that theory and research should interact continuously and that the contrast between the two strategies is more apparent than real.

---

34. Ernest Nagel, *The Structure of Science* (New York: Heckett, 1979), p. 86.

KEY TERMS FOR REVIEW ●

ad-hoc classificatory system (p. 34)
axiomatic theory (p. 37)
concept (p. 24)
conceptual definition (p. 26)
conceptual framework (p. 35)
congruence (p. 36)
derived term (p. 27)
fallacy of reification (p. 25)

model (p. 39)
operational definition (p. 28)
primitive term (p. 27)
research-then-theory strategy (p. 42)
taxonomy (p. 34)
theoretical import (p. 32)
theoretical system (p. 36)
theory-then-research strategy (p. 41)

STUDY QUESTIONS ●

1. Discuss the four functions of concepts in social science research.
2. Distinguish between conceptual definitions and operational definitions, and give an example of each from one of the social sciences you have studied.
3. Discuss the common misconceptions regarding theories. Can you think of any others?
4. Describe and explain the use of models in social science research. Can you give examples from other courses?
5. Discuss the controversy of theory-then-research versus research-then-theory. Which strategy do you think more accurately reflects the process of scientific research? Why?

ADDITIONAL READINGS ●

Banting, Keith, Stuart S. Blume, Michael Carley, and Carol Weiss. *Research Utilization.* Urbana, IL: Policy Studies Organization, 1976.

Bartholomew, David J. *Mathematical Models in Social Science,* reprint. New York: Wiley, 1981.

Blalock, Hubert M., Jr. *Basic Dilemmas in the Social Sciences.* Beverly Hills, CA: Sage, 1984.

Braithwaite, Richard B. "Models in Empirical Science." In *Readings in the Philosophy of Science,* 2d ed., ed. Baruch A. Grody. Paramus, NJ: Prentice-Hall, 1989, pp. 268–293.

Bulmer, Martin. *Social Science and Social Policy.* London: Allen & Unwin, 1987.

Isaak, Alan C. *Scope and Methods of Political Science,* 4th ed. San Diego, CA: Harcourt Brace, 1988.

Krathwohl, David R. *Social and Behavioral Science Research.* San Francisco: Jossey-Bass, 1985.

Lave, Charles A., and James G. March. *An Introduction to Models in the Social Sciences,* reprint. Lanham, MD: University Press of America, 1991.

Rubinstein, Moshe F., and Kenneth Pfeiffer. *Concepts in Problem Solving.* Paramus, NJ: Prentice-Hall, 1980.

Simon, Herbert A. *Sciences of the Artificial,* 3d ed. Cambridge, MA: MIT Press, 1996.

Stinchcombe, Arthur L. *Constructing Social Theories.* New York: Harcourt Brace Jovanovich, 1968.

Stinchcombe, Arthur L. *Theoretical Methods in Social History.* New York: Academic Press, 1978.

Wagner, Peter, Carol H. Weiss, Bjorn Wittrock, and Hellmut Wolman. *Social Sciences and Modern States: National Experiences and Theoretical Crossroads.* New York: Cambridge University Press, 1991.

Weiss, Carol. *Social Science Research and Decision-Making.* New York: Columbia University Press, 1980.

statements on democracy and then use this percentage as an indicator of the degree to which the political system in the country is democratic, he or she could be making the individualistic fallacy. For instance, a political system can have an authoritarian regime even if most of its citizens share democratic values. Furthermore, the concept "democratic" does not mean the same thing at the two levels of analysis. Applied to the individual, it refers to values, attitudes, and behavior; applied to the political system, the concept refers to the system's structure, institutions, and method of decision making. We cannot explain or predict the political system's structure or behavior only from knowledge about the members of its population.

VARIABLES ●

Research problems are conveyed by a set of concepts. We saw in Chapter 2 that concepts are abstractions representing empirical phenomena. In order to move from the conceptual to the empirical level, concepts are converted into *variables*. **Variable** refers to the properties or attributes that can be clearly identified and measured in some way. We use variables in place of concepts for constructing and testing hypotheses.

Concepts are converted into variables by *translating* or *mapping* them into a set of values. For example, when researchers assign numbers to attributes or properties, they are locating those properties within a set of values. This means that a variable is an empirical property that can take on two or more values. If a property can change, either in quantity or quality, and that change can be measured, the property can be considered a variable. For example, "social class" is a variable because it can be differentiated into a number of distinct values, such as lower, lower middle, middle, upper middle, and upper. Similarly, "expectations" is a variable because it can be assigned at least two values: "high" and "low."

Variables have numerous characteristics that determine their place in the research design and the types of measurement techniques that are to be used. Variables can be distinguished analytically by whether they are treated as dependent, independent, or control variables (which indicates their place in the explanatory scheme of the research). Variables can also be distinguished by whether they are continuous or discrete variables (which determines how they will be measured). A variable (e.g., gender) that can be assigned only two values is called a *dichotomous variable.*

Dependent and Independent Variables

When researchers ask questions, they are basically trying to explain something that has been observed either by themselves or by others. Their explanations, if they are to be considered valid according to the requirements of scientific methodology, have to rely on the ability to measure changes in the phenomenon they want to explain. The variable whose changes the researcher wishes to explain is termed the **dependent variable,** whereas the variable the researcher thinks induces or explains the change is the **independent variable.** For this reason, the independent variable is also called the **explanatory variable.** (Dependent variables are also referred to as *criterion variables,* and independent variables as *predictor variables.*)

Relationships between variables are often expressed as equations. In the language of mathematics, the symbol for the dependent variable appears on the left-hand side of an equation. For example, if we write $Y = f(X)$, we are considering Y to be the dependent variable and X the independent variable. As written, we are simply saying that Y is a *function* (indicated by *f*) of *X*—that is, changes in the values of *X* are associated with changes in the values of *Y*, or *X* explains or predicts *Y*.

For example, a researcher might want to explain why some young people participate more than others in risky sexual activity. Based on the chosen model of risk taking, the researcher may suggest that the more an individual is exposed to factors that increase the risk of facing a number of personal problems, such as low parental supervision, the more that young person is liable to participate in risky sexual activity. In this case, the researcher may hypothesize that unsafe sex (the dependent variable, *Y*) is the outcome of exposure to risk factors. In this illustration, low parental supervision (the independent variable, *X*) is hypothesized to be one of the risk factors that leads to variations in a young person's participation in unsafe sex.[3]

In the real world, variables are neither dependent nor independent: The researcher decides how to view them, and that decision is based on the research objective. An independent variable in one investigation may be a dependent variable in another, and the same researcher, working on different projects, may classify the same variables in different ways. To continue with the above example, if you want to explain variations in risky sexual behavior, risky sexual behavior will be the dependent variable, and parental supervision will be the independent variable. But if you want to explain changes in parental supervision (or why some parents supervise their children more closely than others do), parental supervision will be regarded as the dependent variable and the child's risk behavior will be one of the independent variables.

Most of the phenomena that social scientists investigate require them to assess the effects of several independent variables on one or more dependent variables. This is the natural outcome of the complexity of social phenomena. One independent variable usually explains only a certain amount of the change in the values observed in the dependent variable; hence, additional independent variables have to be introduced in order to explain more of that variation. For example, when risky sexual activity among youth is studied as a dependent variable, parental supervision explains why some young people participate in unsafe sex more than others. This explanation is incomplete, however, because other factors contribute to explaining the observed behavior. Among these additional factors (i.e., other independent variables) are age, gender, educational attainment, living in a distressed neighborhood, and peer-group influence.[4]

Control Variables

In order to establish definitive relations among the phenomena observed, it may not be sufficient to specify only independent and dependent variables. Scientists often introduce **control variables** into their research methodology to reduce the risk of wrongly attributing explanatory power to the independent variable(s) they have selected. More specifically, control variables are used to test the possibility that an empirically observed relation between two variables has not been caused by the independent variable identified in the hypothesis. Such a relation is called a **spurious relation,** that is, a relation that can be explained by variables other than those stated in the hypothesis. In other words, if the researcher can eliminate (or control for) the influence of all the other possible variables and still obtain an empirical relation between the independent and the dependent

---

3. Daniel F. Perkins, Tom Luster, Francisco A. Villarruel, and Stephen Small, "An Ecological, Risk-Factor Examination of Adolescents' Sexual Activity in Three Ethnic Groups," *Journal of Marriage and the Family* 60(3) (1998): 660–673.

4. Ibid.

Figure 3.1

Importance of a Control Variable

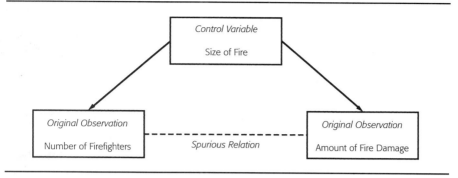

variables, the relation is nonspurious. In effect, the researcher uses control variables to ensure that there is a causal link between the variables stated in the hypothesis, and that the observed relation is not based on some other factor.

Suppose you have noticed, on the basis of various news reports, that the greater the damage caused by a fire, the larger the number of firefighters present at the site. You might then hypothesize that the larger the number of firefighters appearing at the site of a fire (the independent variable), the greater the extent of fire damage (the dependent variable). Generally, firefighters are not considered to be the direct cause of fire damage. Accordingly, the amount of fire damage should not be explained by the number of firefighters at the site but by another variable, namely, the size of the fire. Large fires prompt the appearance of a larger number of firefighters and also cause more damage. Thus the original observed relation between the number of firefighters at the fire site and the amount of fire damage is spurious because a third variable, the size of the fire, is what really explains the results. In order to make sure that the relation you have hypothesized is real, you can use size of the fire as a control variable when testing the relation (Figure 3.1).

Let us consider another example to illustrate the significance of control variables in validating an empirically observed relation. It has frequently been argued that the level of political participation has an influence on government expenditures. You would like to test the hypothesis that the amount of government expenditures (dependent variable) is caused by the extent of political participation (independent variable), which appears to be a valid relation. However, a significant body of research has shown that the empirical relation between political participation and government expenditures vanishes when economic development is introduced as a control variable.[5] After introducing this other variable, you would find that the level of economic development influences *both* government expenditures and political participation. If you had not considered the influence of the variable economic development, the relation observed between political participation and government expenditures would continue to appear valid. Control variables thus serve the important purpose of helping us test whether or not the observed relations

5. For the first breakthrough study on this issue, see Hayward R. Alker, *Mathematics and Politics* (New York: Macmillan, 1965).

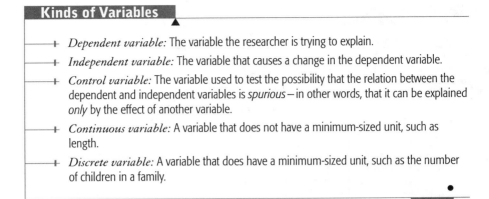

Kinds of Variables

+ *Dependent variable:* The variable the researcher is trying to explain.

+ *Independent variable:* The variable that causes a change in the dependent variable.

+ *Control variable:* The variable used to test the possibility that the relation between the dependent and independent variables is *spurious* — in other words, that it can be explained *only* by the effect of another variable.

+ *Continuous variable:* A variable that does not have a minimum-sized unit, such as length.

+ *Discrete variable:* A variable that does have a minimum-sized unit, such as the number of children in a family.

between independent and dependent variables are spurious (for more on spurious and nonspurious relations, see Chapter 5).

Continuous and Discrete Variables

Another important property of variables is whether or not they are continuous or discrete. This property, as we shall see in later chapters, directly affects research operations, particularly measurement procedures, data analysis, and methods of statistical inference and generalization.

A **continuous variable** does not have a minimum-sized unit by definition. Length is an example of a continuous variable because there is no minimum unit of length that can be found in nature, which means there is no inherent, clear internal division of the variable into precise units. Time is another example of such a continuous variable. When these variables are measured, the measurement unit is imposed by using some instrument, such as a ruler or a clock. A particular object may be at least 10 inches long, it may be 10.5 inches long, or it may be 10.5431697 inches long. In principle, we can speak of a tenth of an inch, a ten-thousandth of an inch, or a ten-trillionth of an inch. Although we cannot measure all possible lengths with absolute accuracy (some values will be too small for any measuring instrument to register), it is conceptually possible for objects to have an infinite number of lengths.

Unlike continuous variables, **discrete variables** do have a minimum-sized unit, which means that one unit can be clearly differentiated from another. The amount of money in your bank account at any given moment is an example of a discrete variable because currency has a minimum unit. You can have $101.21 or $101.22, but not $101.21843. Different amounts of money cannot differ by less than the minimum-sized unit, in this case, one cent. The number of children in a family is another example of a discrete variable because the minimum unit is one child. Families may have 3 or 4 children but not, say, 3.5 children. If some unit of a variable cannot be subdivided, the variable is, again, discrete. This should be borne in mind when you read, for instance, that the average American family has, say, 2.2 children or 1.8 cars — these figures do not mean that the discrete units of analysis, children or automobiles, can be divided in real life. The numbers 2.2 and 1.8 are, after all, statistics — products of arithmetical calculations — and not real units of measurement (see Chapters 7 and 14 for further explanations).

RELATIONS

In earlier chapters, we saw that scientific explanations and predictions involve how we *relate* the phenomenon to be explained (dependent variable) to other phenomena (explanatory or independent variables) by means of general laws or theories. But what is a relation?

A **relation** in scientific research always refers to a connection that exists between two or more variables. When we say that variable *X* and variable *Y* are related, we mean that something is *shared,* held in common, by both variables. For example, if we say that education and income are related, we mean that the two "go together," that they covary, or change together in a systematic way. **Covariation** is what education and income have in common: Individuals with higher education have higher incomes. For social scientists, establishing a relation consists of determining whether the values of one variable covary with values of one or more other variables, and of measuring those values. That is, the researcher systematically pairs the values obtained for one variable with values obtained for other variables. Table 3.1 illustrates this process. The two columns display two sets of observations, each reporting the values of education (operationally defined by years of schooling) and income for six individuals. The table expresses a relation because the two sets of values are seen as connected in an orderly way, that is, they covary: Higher education is linked with higher income and lower education with lower income.

Kinds of Relations

Two variables are related when changes in the values of one systematically bring about changes in the values of the other. In the last example, changes in years of schooling brought about changes in income. The way these variables covary can be described by the properties of that relationship, the most fundamental of which are direction and magnitude.

DIRECTION.   When we speak of **direction of a relation,** we mean that the relations between the variables are either positive or negative. A **positive relation** means that as values of one variable increase, values of the other also increase. For example, the relation between education and income is positive because increases in years of schooling lead to higher income in the future. There is also a positive relation between interest in politics and political participation: As individuals become more interested in politics, they

Table 3.1

Relation Between Education and Income

Observations	Years of Schooling	Income
Dan	16	$35,000
Ann	15	30,000
Marie	14	27,000
Jacob	13	19,000
Philip	12	15,000
Suzanne	11	12,000

science research to discover empirical relations between phenomena and to measure them as accurately as possible in terms of their magnitude. (Precise measures of magnitude, such as coefficients of correlations, are discussed in Chapters 16 and 17.)

Having discussed variables and relations, the basic ingredients of the research problem, we can now turn to the subject of hypotheses and their characteristics.

HYPOTHESES •

A **hypothesis** is a tentative answer to a research problem, expressed in the form of a clearly stated relation between independent and dependent variables. Hypotheses are *tentative* answers because they describe relations meant to be tested through the process of research; that is, hypotheses are considered to be credible answers to research problems only *after* they have been tested empirically. When constructing a hypothesis, the researcher does not know whether it will indeed be verified. If the hypothesis is rejected, another one is put forward; if it is accepted, it is incorporated into the body of scientific knowledge.

Researchers derive hypotheses deductively from theories, inductively on the basis of direct observations, on the basis of their experience and intuition, or by using a combination of these approaches. In terms of the scientific research process, the sources from which hypotheses are derived are of little significance; what is crucial is the way in which they are rejected or accepted as descriptions of the empirical world. To illustrate, some believe that Pythagoras (6th century B.C.E.) derived his theory of octaves and the relationship between music and mathematics after observing that the different sounds coming from a blacksmith's anvils were related to their weight.[6] Another example is taken from this scene broadcast as part of the television movie *And the Band Played On:* Dr. Don Francis of the Center for Disease Control arrives at an insight into how the HIV virus invades receptor cells in the blood by watching his colleague, Dr. Harold Jaffe, play PacMan.[7] However, neither of these episodes, despite their imaginative appeal, led scientists to accept the hypotheses they may have inspired—acceptance came only after they were supported by empirical data.

Research hypotheses share four common characteristics, all of which are related to their role in the research process. Hypotheses are *clear, specific, amenable to empirical testing with the available research methods,* and *value-free.* Examining these characteristics in greater detail will help you understand how to construct your own hypotheses and evaluate the hypotheses of others.

1. *Hypotheses must be clear.* In order to test a hypothesis empirically, one has to define all the variables included. Conceptual and operational definitions, as discussed in Chapter 2, help clarify the variables used to construct the hypotheses. The professional literature and experts' opinions can be of great help in this respect. Suppose your hypothesis states that alienation (your independent variable) is inversely related to political participation, your dependent variable. By examining the professional literature, you can discover how other researchers defined the variables. Among these definitions, you are likely to find one suitable for your own research hypothesis. If not, you can always build on others' experience when defining the variables in a way more appropriate to your

---

6. R. J. Stewart, *Music and the Elemental Psyche* (Wellingborough, UK.: 1987), pp. 121–122.

7. John D. Piette, "Review Symposium, 'Playing It Safe,'" *Journal of Health Politics, Policy and Law*, 19(2) (1994): 453.

research needs. In any case, your operational definitions must be clear and precise enough to make observation, measurement, and replication possible.

2. *Hypotheses are specific.* Investigators have to point out the relations expected to be found among the variables in terms of direction (positive or negative) and the conditions under which the relations will hold. A hypothesis stating that *X* is related to *Y* is too general. The relation between *X* and *Y* can be positive or negative. Importantly, because relations are not independent of time, space, or the unit of analysis, these must also be specified. As we saw earlier, the observed relations between variables may vanish when we change the unit of analysis (as the result of the ecological fallacy, for instance). Thus, although the relations between, say, education and political participation can be studied at the individual, group, or electoral district level, conceptual and operational definitions appropriate to each level must be specified for the hypothesis to be meaningful as a guide to research.

The hypothesis should also state explicitly the conditions under which the relations will be observed. For instance, in order to predict the relation between alienation and political participation, is it more appropriate to conduct survey research, observe a mass rally, or count how often a person views televised interviews of political candidates? Here theory becomes especially important, for it helps the researcher generate researchable and fruitful hypotheses.

3. *Hypotheses are testable with available methods.* A researcher can arrive at clear and specific hypotheses yet find that there are no research methods to test them. How, for example, are we to test the hypothesis that object A is 3 inches longer than object B without a ruler? How are we to test the hypothesis that the secretions of microbe C have a positive relation to disease D without an instrument permitting the identification of the antibodies released when a microbe invades the body? Or how are we to test the relation between education and political participation without the appropriate methods for observing these variables?

The simplicity of these examples should emphasize the point that scientists cannot test hypotheses unless they have methods for testing them. Indeed, progress in science is as dependent on the development of new research methods for observation, data collection, and data analysis—and on the availability of those methods to as many researchers as possible—as it is on conceptualizing variables and theorizing.

Some social scientists belittle the value of methods for fear of being enslaved by them. Investigators can, of course, become entrapped by one method of research if they employ it dogmatically, without regard to the research problem at hand, or if they regard methodology as an end rather than a means. Hypotheses that lack methods of testing may still have a place in the scientific approach if they are innovative or stimulate creative research. However, their verification depends on the ability to test them, a task that depends on the availability of methods of research.

4. *Scientific hypotheses are value-free.* In principle, the researcher's own values, biases, and subjective preferences have no place in scientific research, which is based on the objective observation of empirical data. In the real world, however, because research in the social sciences is, to a certain extent, a social activity affected by its milieu, researchers must be aware of their personal biases. By making those biases explicit, scientists provide one set of tools for differentiating between their personal views and their empirical findings; as a result, their research findings and the subsequent interpretations of the findings can be assessed with the maximum objectivity possible. As Gunnar Myrdal wrote in the classic study of prejudice:

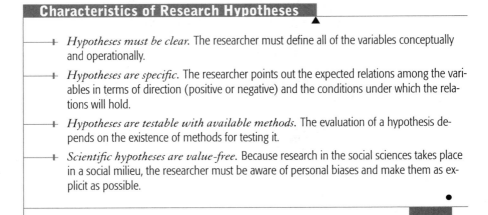

Characteristics of Research Hypotheses

+ *Hypotheses must be clear.* The researcher must define all of the variables conceptually and operationally.

+ *Hypotheses are specific.* The researcher points out the expected relations among the variables in terms of direction (positive or negative) and the conditions under which the relations will hold.

+ *Hypotheses are testable with available methods.* The evaluation of a hypothesis depends on the existence of methods for testing it.

+ *Scientific hypotheses are value-free.* Because research in the social sciences takes place in a social milieu, the researcher must be aware of personal biases and make them as explicit as possible.

The attempt to eradicate biases . . . is a hopeless and misdirected venture. . . . There is no other device for excluding biases in the social sciences than to face the valuations and to introduce them as explicitly stated, specific, and sufficiently concretized value premises.[8]

PROBLEMS AND HYPOTHESES: SOME EXAMPLES ●

Problems raise general questions about relations among variables; hypotheses suggest tentative, concrete, and testable answers. A few examples should clarify the distinction between problems and hypotheses and illustrate how hypotheses are constructed and expressed.

We first list some examples of research questions derived from more general political, economic, and social problems:

—+ Who makes public policy in the United States?

—+ What causes inflation?

—+ Does bureaucracy threaten democracy?

—+ Are affirmative action programs achieving their objectives?

—+ Does school integration enhance educational attainment?

—+ What factors determine urbanization?

—+ What causes political violence?

The research process requires that the scientist operationalize such general questions into a series of hypotheses—in order to investigate them. For example, Ted Gurr offered a set of hypotheses, including the following, as tentative answers to the question on political violence:[9]

—+ The potential for group violence increases as the intensity and scope of relative deprivation among members of a group increases.

8. Gunnar Myrdal, *The American Dilemma* (New York: Harper, 1944), p. 1043.

9. Ted R. Gurr, *Why Men Rebel* (Princeton, NJ: Princeton University Press, 1970), pp. 360–367.

—+ The potential for political violence varies strongly with the intensity and scope of normative justifications [i.e., justifications provided by commonly held moral standards] for political violence among members of a group.

—+ The potential for political violence in any specific case varies strongly with the potential for group violence generally.

—+ The magnitude of political violence varies strongly with the potential for political violence.

Another example of hypothesis construction is from the oft-cited Gibbs and Martin study on the causes of urbanization.[10] The authors advanced these hypotheses:

—+ The degree of urbanization in a society varies directly with the dispersion [i.e., distribution over a wide physical area] of objects of consumption.

—+ The degree of urbanization in a society varies directly with the division of labor.

—+ The division of labor in a society varies directly with the dispersion of objects of consumption.

—+ The degree of urbanization in a society varies directly with technological development.

—+ Technological development in a society varies directly with the dispersion of objects of consumption.

Gerald Hage's attempt to synthesize theory and research in the field of complex organizations is an excellent illustration of hypotheses arrived at deductively.[11] Hage transformed some key ideas in Max Weber's theory of bureaucracy into variables. For example, Hage restated the concept of "hierarchy of authority" as the variable "degree of organizational centralization" and restated the concept of "rules and procedures" as the variable "degree of formalization" (how much the behavior involved with every job is codified into rules and regulations). This enabled him to construct three major hypotheses:

—+ The greater the centralization in organizations, the greater the volume of production, and vice versa.

—+ The greater the centralization, the greater the efficiency, and vice versa.

—+ The greater the centralization, the greater the formalization, and vice versa.

SOURCES FOR RESEARCH AND HYPOTHESES   ●

Research problems and hypotheses can be derived in many ways—from theories, directly from observation, intuitively—singly or in combination. Probably the best source for stimulating the statement of research problems and hypotheses is the professional literature. A critical review of the professional literature familiarizes the researcher with the current state of knowledge; with concepts, theories, major variables, and conceptual and operational definitions; with problems and hypotheses that others have studied; and

---

10. Jack P. Gibbs and Walter T. Martin, "Urbanization, Technology, and the Division of Labor: International Patterns," in *Urbanism, Urbanization and Change*, 2d ed., ed. Paul Meadows and Ephraim H. Mizruchi. (Reading, MA: Addison-Wesley, 1976), pp. 132–145.

11. Gerald Hage, *Theories of Organizations: Forms, Process, and Transformation* (New York: Wiley-Interscience, 1980), pp. 36–40.

with the research methods used. Basing new research on the knowledge described in the professional literature also contributes to the accumulation of scientific knowledge.

Due to the expanding quantity and complexity of the material available, reviewing the professional literature is no longer a simple task. This is true for the professional researcher as well as for the student. Inasmuch as thousands of articles and books in the social sciences are published every year, it is best to begin any search with one of the guides to published literature. These guides, which include bibliographies, indexes, and abstracts, are increasingly becoming computerized. The Appendix on Report Writing (Appendix B) will present some ideas on how to incorporate past research into your own presentation of hypothesis and research findings. This appendix also provides techniques for assessing how appropriate the report is to your own research.

Bibliographies, Indexes, and Abstracts

The following are useful basic reference books, bibliographies, and indexes of the published professional social science literature. Libraries are increasingly purchasing computerized reference material in the form of CD-ROMs (Compact Disk-Read Only Memory) or subscribing to on-line databases such as DIALOG. CD-ROMs are similar in their hardware configuration to music CDs. Consequently, adjustments must be made to the hardware and programming of the standard PC in order to use them. These electronic media store massive amounts of information in a highly accessible manner. The terms "on-line," "CD-ROM," and "microfiche" after a title indicate the nonprint availability of the sources indicated. The references below index articles published in journals by author's last name, specialization, or a key word in the title.

→ Balay, Robert, ed. *Guide to Reference Books, Supplement to the 10th ed.* Chicago: American Library Association, 1992.

→ Balay, Robert, Murray S. Martin, and Vee F. Carrington, eds., *Guide to Reference Books,* 11th ed. Chicago: American Library Association, 1996.

→ The library card catalog and subject guide. (The majority of universities have computerized their card catalogs with on-line database programs. If your university has done so, you can use a terminal to check bibliographic information and to find out whether the library owns the item.)

→ The following reference works list the publication information necessary to find the book or article you seek. All are available in print format.

Biography Index	*International Bibliography of the*
(also: on-line, CD-ROM)	*Social Sciences*
Book Review Index	(also: on-line)
(also: microfiche, on-line)	*National Union Catalog*
Cumulative Book Index	(also: microfiche)
(also: on-line, CD-ROM)	*PAIS International*
Education Index	(also: on-line, CD-ROM)
(also: on-line, CD-ROM)	*Social Sciences Citation Index* (SSCI)
Index of Economic Articles in Journals	(also: on-line, CD-ROM)
and Collective Volumes	*Social Sciences Index*
(also: on-line)	(also: on-line, CD-ROM)

→ Abstracts contain short summaries of the works cited.

3. For purposes of research, scientists make a distinction between independent, dependent, and control variables. An independent variable is the presumed cause of the dependent variable, and a dependent variable is the presumed outcome of the changes in the independent variable. Researchers use control variables to test whether the observed relations between independent and dependent variables are spurious. Variables can be continuous or discrete. A discrete variable has a minimum-sized unit; a continuous variable does not have a minimum-sized unit.

4. A relation in empirical research always refers to an association between two or more variables. When we say that two variables are related, we mean that there they have something in common. Researchers establish the presence of a relation by determining whether values of one variable covary with values of other variables. Two properties of relations should be stressed: direction and magnitude. When we speak of direction, we mean that the relation between the variables is either positive or negative. The magnitude of a relation is the extent to which variables covary positively or negatively.

5. Hypotheses are tentative answers to research problems. They are expressed in the form of a relation between dependent and independent variables. Research hypotheses have to be clear, specific, and amenable to empirical testing with the available research methods.

6. Research problems and hypotheses can be derived deductively from theories, or directly from observation or intuition. The best source for learning about research problems and hypotheses is the professional literature. The social scientist should be informed of the major guides to published research, including reference books, bibliographies, indexes, abstracts, journals, and statistical sourcebooks. Most university libraries now offer on-line (computerized) database search services.

KEY TERMS FOR REVIEW ●

continuous variable (p. 52)
control variable (p. 50)
covariation (p. 53)
dependent variable (p. 49)
direction of a relation (p. 53)
discrete variable (p. 52)
ecological fallacy (p. 48)
explanatory variable (p. 49)
hypothesis (p. 56)
independent variable (p. 49)

individualistic fallacy (p. 48)
magnitude of a relation (p. 55)
negative relation (p. 54)
positive relation (p. 53)
relation (p. 53)
research problem (p. 46)
spurious relation (p. 50)
unit of analysis (p. 47)
variable (p. 49)

STUDY QUESTIONS ●

1. Identify two empirical social science problems.
2. What is the ecological fallacy? What is the individualistic fallacy? How can a researcher avoid these fallacies?
3. Write three researchable hypotheses and identify their independent, dependent, and control variables.
4. Using the same three hypotheses, clearly indicate expected changes in the magnitude and direction of the relations between the dependent and independent variables.

5. What are some major sources of information regarding the research problems identified in Question 1?

SPSS PROBLEMS

For an introduction to the Statistical Package for Social Sciences (SPSS), turn to Appendix A.
1. Browse the file **gss96worth** by clicking on **Utilities** and **Variables.** Identify the variables dealing with abortion attitudes. Then identify the variables for education, income, and race.
   a. From these variables formulate at least three hypotheses. For each hypothesis identify the independent and the dependent variable.
   b. Perform a literature search and find one to three articles dealing with your hypotheses. Summarize the findings in the article(s). Do these findings support your hypotheses?
2. Construct potential hypotheses to relate the following variables from the **gss96worth** file. For each hypothesis indicate the independent and dependent variables. If appropriate, specify the hypothesized direction of the relationship. Write a brief statement explaining why you believe there is a relationship between the variables as specified in your hypotheses. (Note: you will need to examine these variables through the **Utilities-Variables** functions before you can answer these questions.
   a. "educ" and "aidcol"   d. "class" and "cappun"
   b. "educ" and "attend"   e. "class" and "equincome"
   c. "attend" and "bible"

ADDITIONAL READINGS

Alker, Hayward R. "A Typology of Ecological Fallacies." In *Quantitative Analysis in the Social Sciences*, ed. Mattei N. Dogan and Stein Rokkam. New York: Cambridge University Press, 1969.

Bailey, Kenneth D. *Typologies & Taxonomies: An Introduction to Classification Techniques.* Thousand Oaks, CA: Sage, 1994.

Bailey, Kenneth D. *Methods of Social Research*, 4th ed. New York: The Free Press, 1994.

Bronowski, Jacob. *The Origins of Knowledge and Imagination*. New Haven, CT: Yale University Press, 1979.

Gilreath, Charles L. *Computerized Literature Searching: Research Strategies and Data Bases*. Boulder, CO: Westview Press, 1984.

Harris, Cooper M. *Integrating Research: A Guide to Literature Review*. Newbury Park, CA: Sage, 1989.

Johnson, Janet B. *Political Science Research Methods*, 2d ed. Washington, DC: CQ Press, 1991.

Kramer, Jerald H. "The Ecological Fallacy Revisited: Aggregate Versus Individual Level Findings on Economics and Elections and Sociotropic Voting." *American Political Science Review*, 77 (1983): 92–111.

Reason, Peter, and John Rowan, eds. *Human Inquiry: Developments in New Paradigm Research.* Thousand Oaks. CA: Sage, 1989.

Suchowski, Amy R. *CD-ROMS in Print, An International Guide to CD-ROM, CD-I, 3DO, MMCD, CD32, Multimedia and Electronic Products.* Detroit, London: Gale Publishing, 1998.

Williams, Martha E., Lawrence Lannon, and Carolyn G. Robins, eds. *Computer-Readable Databases: A Directory and Data Sourcebook*. Ann Arbor, MI: Books on Demand, a Division of University Microfilms, 1985.

ETHICS IN SOCIAL SCIENCE RESEARCH

Focus groups are becoming an increasingly popular data collection method among social scientists and pollsters because of the nature of the information that can be gathered. When using this method, the research brings together a group of individuals, usually chosen on the basis of similar age, social status, or some other characteristic important for the goals of the research. The participants are then encouraged to interact among themselves (and sometimes with the moderator) while expressing their opinions on a selected topic. The freedom with which they interact, and the immediacy of the information they may relay, makes this a useful method for exploratory research regarding topics ranging from attitudes toward new products, such as automobile models, to the efficacy of health education programs. Focus groups are often used for the purpose of creating change in the attitudes or behavior of the participants and the groups they represent, for example, political party preference.

The advantages of the method are clear: The researcher has access to more personally articulated accounts of feelings and experiences as well as to the language and concepts ordinarily used by the participants. Moreover, in such an egalitarian atmosphere, participants can raise issues that are truly of concern to them in a more straightforward way.[1]

Because of the openness of the research situation, the focus group method can raise some important ethical issues for the social scientist. These issues concern the confidentiality of the information communicated and the anonymity of the participants in the groups. For example, how is the researcher to deal with the spontaneously offered information sometimes revealed by minors about their high-risk sexual behaviors? Given that the conversations are usually transcribed and often filmed, how is the identity of the participants to be protected, particularly when sensitive issues are discussed? In addition, how can the researcher weigh the benefits of the method against the participants' right to privacy?

These ethical problems are not unique to the focus group method—they can arise in any number of research settings (e.g., experiments) using a range of data collection methods. In this chapter, we review these issues and some of the techniques used to protect research participants.

•I IN THIS CHAPTER we discuss the ethics of conducting social science research. We describe the major ethical problems involved and mention several of the ways that have been devised to protect the rights and welfare of participants in the social scientific studies. We begin by presenting three well-known case studies—on obedience to authority, police behavior, and the attitudes of college students—as examples of how research methodology can raise ethical issues. We then discuss the core ethical dilemma of social scientists—the conflict between the right to conduct research and the right of research participants to self-determination, privacy, and dignity. A cost–benefit framework is offered as a guideline for making ethical decisions in specific situations. The importance of informed consent, as well as its dimensions, are explained. The right to privacy is reviewed, followed by how we can ensure anonymity of the participants and confidentiality of the information revealed. Finally, we present a composite code of ethics developed for social scientists.

1. Based on Sue Wilkinson, "Focus Group Methodology: A Review," *International Journal of Social Research Methodology*, 1 (1998): 181–203.

physical or emotional injury, invasion of privacy, or physical or psychological stress, or when they are asked to surrender their autonomy temporarily (e.g., in drug research). Participants should know that their involvement is voluntary at all times, and they should receive, beforehand, a thorough explanation of the benefits, rights, risks, and dangers involved in their participation in the research project.

The Reasons for Informed Consent

The idea of informed consent derives from both cultural values and legal considerations. It is rooted in the high value we attach to freedom and self-determination. We believe that people should be free to determine their own behavior because freedom is a cherished value. Advocates of this view might even argue, like John Locke, that freedom is a natural right, and that restrictions on freedom must be carefully justified and agreed to. Regulations and laws have been enacted in order to guarantee that individual freedom is preserved. A research procedure, however, may limit the expression of that freedom in some way, because research tries to manipulate behavior or the context of behavior. When the individuals involved in research risk limitation of their freedom, they must be asked to agree to this limitation because of this basic value as well as because of legal constraints.

Furthermore, asking individuals whether they wish to participate in a research project reflects respect for the right of self-determination. One reason for advocating informed consent is the argument that informed individuals are best able to promote their own well-being. Because people tend to protect their own interests, allowing them freedom of choice about their participation after they have been properly informed about the research is one way to safeguard against the use of hazardous research procedures.[10] Finally, from the researcher's perspective, informed consent shifts part of the responsibility to the participants for any negative effects they may experience in the course of the study. At the same time, it reduces the legal liability of the researcher because participants will have voluntarily agreed to take part in the research project.

The Meaning of Informed Consent

Although the principle of informed consent enjoys widespread acceptance, researchers have yet to implement it consistently. This situation is mainly a result of disagreements over what informed consent means in specific situations. Questions like "What is an informed participant?" "How do we know that a person understands the information given?" "How much information should be given?" "What if it is extremely important that participants do not know whether they are in the experimental or control group?" are obviously difficult, and there are no standard answers. It is possible and useful, however, to clarify the intent of informed consent. We do so in order to point out its major elements and to discuss some of the issues involved in its implementation.

Eduard Diener and Rick Crandall define informed consent as "the procedure in which individuals choose whether to participate in an investigation after being informed of facts that would be likely to influence their decision."[11] Thus, informed consent involves four elements: competence, voluntarism, full information, and comprehension.

COMPETENCE. Competence, the assumption underlying the principle of informed consent, implies that any decision made by a responsible, mature individual *who has*

---

10. Diener and Crandall, *Ethics in Social and Behavioral Research*, p. 36.

11. Ibid., p. 34.

been given the relevant information will be the correct decision. However, because many people may not be mature or responsible, the problem becomes one of systematically identifying those who belong to this category.

In general, people are incapable of providing consent if they have impaired mental capacity or a questionable ability to exercise self-determination. Persons generally considered incompetent to exercise this right include young children, comatose medical patients, and mental patients. When participation in a research project (e.g., tests of a therapeutic treatment) may provide direct benefits to the subjects, it is considered appropriate for the guardians, parents, and others responsible for such individuals to make these decisions for them. When direct benefits are not expected and there is some risk of negative effects, many suggest that the research should be prohibited altogether.[12]

VOLUNTARISM.   A social scientist who complies with the principle of informed consent ensures the freedom of participants to choose whether or not to take part in a research project and guarantees that exposure to known risks is undertaken voluntarily. However, establishing the conditions under which individuals can freely decide to do so is a complex task. In research situations that involve institutional settings (e.g., prisons, mental institutions, hospitals, or public schools), persons in positions of authority exercise substantial influence over the participants. For example, a patient in the care of a physician-researcher may consent to a treatment because he or she is physically weak or is under the influence of the physician in some way. Although the ethics of medical experimentation emphasize voluntary consent, researchers were not confronted with the major implications of infringements on **voluntarism** until after World War II. The *Nuremberg Code,* devised after the gruesome evidence of Nazi medical experimentation came to light, delineates the researcher's responsibility to explain carefully the conditions of the research as a prerequisite to receiving truly voluntary consent:

> This means that the person involved should have legal capacity to give consent; [the person] should be so situated as to be able to exercise free power of choice, without the intervention of any element of force, fraud, deceit, over-reaching, or other ulterior form of constraint or coercion.[13]

In order to establish the conditions conducive to voluntary consent, some observers have suggested that the researcher establish an egalitarian relationship with the participants and view the research endeavor as a joint adventure in the exploration of the unknown.[14] Other scientists have proposed that the presence of a neutral third party when informing the participant will minimize possibilities for coercion. Still others advise that participants be allowed to consult with others after a request for consent is made but before a decision is reached.

FULL INFORMATION.   To be acceptable, consent must be *voluntary and informed.* Consent may be uninformed yet given voluntarily or fully informed yet involuntary.

In practice, it is impossible to obtain fully informed consent, as this would require the researcher to communicate numerous technical and statistical details, including some

---

12. Paul D. Reynolds, *Ethical Dilemmas and Social Science Research* (San Francisco: Jossey-Bass, 1979), p. 91.

13. Ibid., p. 436.

14. Ibid., p. 93.

that might undermine the usefulness of a study or an experiment. Frequently, scientists themselves do not have full information about the consequences of the research procedures. If, in Paul Reynolds's words, "there were full information, there would be no reason to conduct the research—research is only of value when there is ambiguity about a phenomenon."[15] This does not imply that the informed consent principle is totally inapplicable. As a means of confronting the practical difficulties, scientists have adopted the strategy of **reasonably informed consent.**

Federal guidelines are based on the idea of reasonably informed consent. The guidelines call for researchers to communicate six basic elements of information in order for consent to be reasonably informed:[16]

1. A fair explanation of the procedures to be followed and their purposes
2. A description of the attendant discomforts and risks reasonably to be expected
3. A description of the benefits reasonably to be expected
4. A disclosure of appropriate alternative procedures that might be advantageous to the participant
5. An offer to answer any inquiries concerning the procedures
6. An instruction that the person is free to withdraw consent and to discontinue participation in the project at any time without prejudicing the status of the participant

Some of the elements of information included in these guidelines are obviously controversial. For example, disclosure of the research purpose could invalidate the findings; this was the case in the Milgram experiments and the Reiss study. Scientists also disagree over how much information must be disclosed. In fact, a study by H. R. Resnick and T. Schwartz illustrates a research situation where providing complete information can be undesirable. Resnick and Schwartz told potential participants in a verbal conditioning study everything about the experiment before it began, giving them a lengthy, detailed explanation about the research procedures. Many participants never showed up for the study. And, contrary to the findings from other similar studies, those who did participate did not learn. This case illustrates how detrimental giving participants too much information can be for research outcomes.[17]

The criteria for deciding what information should be given to participants have become crucial. One criterion is the legal framework of what a "reasonable and prudent person" would want to know. Researchers must fully disclose all aspects of the study that a person concerned about his or her own welfare would need to know before making a decision. This is especially true if there is any risk of negative physical or psychological consequences being felt or if any rights are to be infringed during the study.

A more easily applied method for determining what information may be relevant to participants is to let a committee representing potential participants or both investigators and participants select what is to be transmitted. Another procedure is to interview surrogate participants systematically, and allow them to determine the relevant information.[18]

15. Ibid., p. 95.

16. HEW, *Institutional Guide to D. H. E. W. Policy,* p. 7.

17. H. R. Resnick and T. Schwartz, "Ethical Standards as an Independent Variable in Psychological Research," *American Psychologist,* 28 (1973): 134–139.

18. For this and other procedures, see Reynolds, *Ethical Dilemmas and Social Science Research,* pp. 95–96.

COMPREHENSION. The fourth element of informed consent, **comprehension,** refers to our "confidence that the participant has provided knowing consent when the research procedure is associated with complex or subtle risks." [19] Clearly, it may be difficult for the participant to comprehend an elaborate description of the project fully, even if it is provided in nontechnical language.

A number of ways have been suggested to ensure complete comprehension. These include the use of highly educated participants, who are most likely to understand the information; the availability of a consultant to discuss the study with the participant; and a time lag between the request for participation and the decision to take part in the study. A common procedure used to assess comprehension consists of questioning the participants directly or asking them to respond to questionnaires that test whether they understand the information they have received.[20]

The Responsibility of the Scientist

Ensuring informed consent is the most general solution to the problem of how to promote social science research without encroaching on the participants' rights and welfare. If all the conditions associated with informed consent—competence, voluntarism, full information, and comprehension—are observed, the scientist can be relatively confident that the rights and welfare of research participants have received appropriate attention.

The principle of informed consent should not, however, be made a universal requirement for all social science research. Although desirable, it is not an absolute necessity in studies where no danger or risk is involved. The more serious the risk to research participants, the greater the obligation to obtain informed consent. At the same time, investigators have the primary responsibility for possible negative effects on participants, even if the latter have consented to take part in the research.

PRIVACY •

Invasions of privacy are of great concern to us all, especially in an era when computerized databanks, both governmental and commercial, are so accessible to outside interests. The **right to privacy**—"the freedom of the individual to pick and choose for himself the time and circumstances under which, and most importantly, the extent to which, his attitudes, beliefs, behavior, and opinions are to be shared with or withheld from others" [21]—may easily be violated during a study or after its completion.

In the investigation of the attitudes of college students conducted by the American Council on Education, we saw that respondents were requested to give private, sensitive information that could have been used by campus administrators and government authorities to identify campus activists. The data were placed in computer storage and made available to anyone willing to pay a small user's fee, a practice that is more and more common today. To protect their research participants, the researchers separated the identity of the participants from their responses in the databank. At the time, however, the possibility that authorities might subpoena the information was quite real. In this study, the researchers requested private information from students, but they could

---

19. Ibid., p. 97.

20. Ibid.

21. M. O. Ruebhausen and Oliver G. Brim, "Privacy and Behavioral Research," *American Psychologist,* 21 (1966): 432.

not guarantee confidentiality in the pervading political climate. In order to protect their privacy, the researchers subsequently made the sensitive information "subpoena-free" by storing the code that linked the data to the individual respondents in a separate file. Although this technique has been implemented in many scientific studies, the protection of the respondent's privacy is still problematic. As new methods become widespread (such as focus group research) and the frequency of public opinion surveys increases (especially for marketing research and in the period prior to elections), the issue is becoming more sensitive.

Dimensions of Privacy

Three different dimensions of privacy have been identified: the sensitivity of information being given, the setting in which observations are made, and dissemination of the information.[22] Before discussing a few methods for safeguarding privacy, it is useful to discuss each of the three dimensions separately.

SENSITIVITY OF INFORMATION. **Sensitivity of information** refers to how personal or potentially threatening the information is that the researcher wishes to collect. As a report by the American Psychological Association states: "Religious preferences, sexual practices, income, racial prejudices, and other personal attributes such as intelligence, honesty, and courage are more sensitive items than 'name, rank, and serial number.'"[23] The greater the sensitivity of the information, the more researchers are obligated to provide safeguards to protect the privacy of the research participants. For example, until the November 1993 Joseph Steffan decision, Pentagon policy universally barred gay people from serving as soldiers and sailors.[24] If information about a soldier's sexual preferences had been transmitted during a research project before that decision was reached, the investigators would have had to be doubly scrupulous in ensuring his or her privacy.

SETTING IN WHICH OBSERVATIONS ARE MADE. The setting of a research project may vary from very private to completely public. For example, the home is considered one of the most private settings in our culture, and intrusions into people's homes without their consent are forbidden by law. However, the extent to which a particular setting is public or private is not always self-evident and may lead to ethical controversies. For example, in order to study the nature of the activities of male homosexuals engaging in brief, impersonal sexual encounters in public locations (restrooms), Laud Humphreys assumed the role of a covert observer. He adopted the voyeuristic role of a "watch queen" (warning participants of approaching police, teenagers, or heterosexual males), thus gaining the confidence of the participants and access to a setting in which they could be observed. He also recorded the license plate numbers of 134 vehicles used by the participants and interviewed 50 of these people in their homes as part of a legitimate public health survey conducted one year later.[25] Critics charged that although the study was conducted in a public restroom, the participants did not initiate sexual activities ("private

22. Diener and Crandall, *Ethics in Social and Behavioral Research*, pp. 55–57.

23. American Psychological Association, *Ethical Principles in the Conduct of Research with Human Subjects* (Washington, DC: Ad Hoc Committee on Ethical Standards in Psychological Research, American Psychological Association, 1973), p. 87.

24. David A. Kaplan and Daniel Glick, "'Into the Hands of Bigots'," *Newsweek*, November 29, 1993, p. 43.

25. Laud Humphreys, *Tearoom Trade: Impersonal Sex in Public Places* (Hawthorne, NY: Aldine, 1975).

acts") until they were assured that the public setting was temporarily "private." Humphreys was, therefore, accused of invading their privacy.

DISSEMINATION OF INFORMATION.   The third aspect of privacy concerns the ability to match personal information with the identity of research participants. For example, information about income remains relatively private if only the investigator has access to it. But when such information, including amounts and names, is publicized, especially through the media, privacy is seriously invaded. The greater the number of people who can learn details of the information, the more concern there must be about privacy.

Fictionalizing the names of research participants does not always protect privacy if other details are available. For example, in *Small Town in Mass Society*, Arthur Vidich and Joseph Bensman described the intimate and sometimes embarrassing details of the lives of the residents of a small town in upstate New York.[26] Although the town and its inhabitants were given fictitious names in the book, the individual descriptions were easily recognized by those involved. Not only was this aspect of the study severely criticized,[27] the townspeople staged a parade in which each wore a mask bearing the fictitious name given to him or her by the researchers—a clear indication that the whole town knew the identities of the characters in the published study. At the tail end of the parade came a manure spreader, with an effigy of the researcher looking into the manure.[28]

Researchers must consider all three aspects—sensitivity of the information, the setting in which observations are made, and the extent of the dissemination of information obtained—when deciding how private certain information is and what safeguards must be used to protect research participants.

Nevertheless, like most rights, privacy can be voluntarily relinquished. Research participants may voluntarily allow a researcher access to sensitive information and settings, or they may agree to being identified by name in the research report. In the latter case, the informed consent of the participants is absolutely necessary.

ANONYMITY AND CONFIDENTIALITY ●

Two common methods used to protect participants are anonymity and confidentiality. The obligation to protect the anonymity of research participants and to keep research data confidential is all-inclusive. It should be fulfilled at all costs unless the researcher makes advance arrangements to the contrary with the participants. As in the case of privacy, the spread of computer networks such as the Internet and advanced satellite communications is making the safeguarding of anonymity and confidentiality more technically complicated and morally necessary.

Anonymity

Researchers provide **anonymity** by separating the identity of individuals from the information they give. A participant is considered anonymous when the researcher or other persons cannot identify any specific bit of information with a particular participant. That is, if information is given anonymously, the researcher is unable to associate a name with

26. Arthur J. Vidich and Joseph Bensman, *Small Town in Mass Society* (Garden City, NY: Doubleday, 1960).

27. Urie Bronfenbrenner, "Freedom and Responsibility in Research: Comments," *Human Organization*, 18 (1959): 49–52.

28. Diener and Crandall, *Ethics in Social and Behavioral Research*, p. 62.

the data; the identity of the participant is thereby secured even though sensitive information may be revealed. For example, researchers can maintain anonymity in a mail survey (discussed in Chapter 10) by removing identification numbers from questionnaires after they are returned. On the other hand, a respondent to a personal interview cannot be considered anonymous because the respondent is known to the interviewer.

One procedure for ensuring anonymity is simply not to request names and other means of identifying participants in a research project. Alternatively, researchers may ask participants to use an alias of their own choosing or to alter well-remembered identification numbers (e.g., by subtracting the numerals of their birthday from their Social Security number). Anonymity may be enhanced if names and other identifiers are linked to the information by a code number. While preparing the data for analysis, researchers can also maintain anonymity by separating identifying information from the data itself—for instance, by not entering these details into the main data file. Further safeguards include forbidding duplication of records, use of passwords to control access to data, and automatic monitoring of file use.[29]

Confidentiality

Participants in social science research are often told that the information they provide will be treated as confidential, that is, although the researchers are able to link the information obtained with some participant, they will not reveal it publicly. Despite the strict moral and professional obligation to keep the promise of *confidentiality* made to a project participant, there are circumstances in which it may be difficult or even impossible to do so. One of the most important of these situations arises when information is subpoenaed by judicial authorities or legislative committees.

In the data collection stage, researchers should clearly and accurately inform study participants about the meaning and limits of confidentiality, preferably by written documents. The greater the danger posed by the information itself and the greater the chances of subpoena or audit of that data, the more explicit the explanation given to participants should be. Donald Campbell and his co-authors offer suggestions for wording these explanations. However, when the material collected involves no obvious jeopardy to the participants, a general promise of confidentiality is sufficient:

> These interviews will be summarized in group statistics so that no one will learn of your individual answers. All interviews will be kept confidential. There is a remote chance that you will be contacted later to verify the fact that I actually conducted this interview and have conducted it completely and honestly.[30]

Where full and honest answers to research questions could jeopardize a respondent's interests, the respondent should be so informed, for example:

> These interviews are being made to provide average statistical evidence in which individual answers will not be identified or identifiable. We will do everything in our power to keep your answer completely confidential. Only if so ordered by Court and Judge would we turn over individually identified interviews to any other group or government agency.[31]

29. For an excellent discussion of these and other procedures, see Reynolds, *Ethical Dilemmas and Social Science Research*, pp. 167–174.

30. Donald T. Campbell et al., "Protection of the Rights and Interests of Human Subjects in Program Evaluation, Social Indicators, Social Experimentation, and Statistical Analyses Based upon Administrative Records: Preliminary Sketch." Northwestern University (Evanston, IL) mimeographed, 1976.

31. Ibid.

In order to permit outsiders' access to data without compromising the confidentiality requirement, a number of techniques have been developed. These include the following:[32]

1. *Deletion of identifiers*—for example, names, Social Security numbers, and street addresses—from the data released on individuals

2. *Crude report categories*—for example, releasing county rather than neighborhood (or Census tract) data, year of birth rather than specific date, profession but not professional specialization, and so on

3. *Microaggregation*—that is, constructing "average persons" from data gathered and releasing these data rather than the original data on individual participants

4. *Error inoculation*—deliberately introducing errors into the identifying information on individual records while leaving the aggregate data unchanged

PROFESSIONAL CODES OF ETHICS ●

Regulations guiding social science research now exist at several levels. Legal statutes, ethics review committees at research universities and institutions, professional codes of ethics, and the personal ethics of the individual researcher are all important regulatory mechanisms. We will concentrate on the issue of professional codes of ethics and present a composite ethical code prepared for researchers in the social sciences.

The major professional societies have developed **codes of ethics** to assist their members in making these decisions. Ethical codes are written to cover the specific problems and issues that scientists frequently encounter during the research carried out within a particular profession. They help the individual researcher because they state and explain what is required and what is forbidden. Codes sensitize researchers to their obligations and to those problematic areas where agreement exists over the proper ethical behavior to be practiced. These codes therefore reflect the operating consensus within the profession.

Paul Reynolds has put together a useful composite code of ethics based on statements appearing in 24 separate codes related to the conduct of social science research. Most of the individual codes have been adopted by national associations of social scientists. Reynolds's composite code is reported in Exhibit 4.1. (The figure after each item indicates how many of the 24 ethical codes included such a statement.)

Exhibit 4.1
A CODE OF ETHICS FOR SOCIAL SCIENTISTS

Principles

General Issues Related to the Code of Ethics

1. The social scientist(s) in charge of a research project is (are) responsible for all decisions regarding procedural matters and ethical issues related to the project whether made by themselves or subordinates (7).

32. See Henry W. Riecken and Robert F. Boruch, *Social Experimentation* (Orlando, FL: Academic Press, 1979), pp. 258–269.

2. Teachers are responsible for all decisions made by their students related to ethical issues involved in research (1).

3. All actions conducted as part of the research should be consistent with the ethical standards of both the home and host community (1).

4. Ethical issues should be considered from the perspective of the participant's society (2).

5. If unresolved or difficult ethical dilemmas arise, assistance or consultation should be sought with colleagues or appropriate committees sponsored by professional associations (2).

6. Any deviation from established principles suggests: (a) that a greater degree of responsibility is being accepted by the investigator, (b) a more serious obligation to seek outside counsel and advice, and (c) the need for additional safeguards to protect the rights and welfare of the research participants (2).

Decision to Conduct the Research

7. Research should be conducted in such a way as to maintain the integrity of the research enterprise and not to diminish the potential for conducting research in the future (3).

8. Investigators should use their best scientific judgment for selection of issues for empirical investigation (1).

9. The decision to conduct research with human subjects should involve evaluation of the potential benefits to the participant and society in relation to the risks to be borne by the participant(s)—a risk–benefit analysis (2).

10. Any study which involves human subjects must be related to an important intellectual question (4).

11. Any study which involves human subjects must be related to an important intellectual question with humanitarian implications, and there should be no other way to resolve the intellectual question (2).

12. Any study which involves human participants must be related to a very important intellectual question if there is a risk of permanent, negative effects on the participants (2).

13. Any study involving risks as well as potential therapeutic effects must be justified in terms of benefits to the client or patient (2).

14. There should be no prior reason to believe that major permanent negative effects will occur for the participants (1).

15. If the conduct of the research may permanently damage the participants, their community, or institutions within their community (such as indigenous social scientists), the research may not be justified and might be abandoned (2).

Conduct of the Research

16. All research should be conducted in a competent fashion, as an objective, scientific project (4).

17. All research personnel should be qualified to use any procedures employed in the project (7).

18. Competent personnel and adequate facilities should be available if any drugs are involved (4).

19. There should be no bias in the design, conduct, or reporting of the research—it should be as objective as possible (4).

Exhibit 4.1 (*continued*)

Effects on and Relationships with the Participants

Informed Consent

General

20. Informed consent should be used in obtaining participants for all research; investigators should honor all commitments associated with such agreements (10).

21. Participants should be in a position to give informed consent; otherwise it should be given by those responsible for the participant (2).

22. Informed consent should be used if the potential effects on participants are ambiguous or potentially hazardous (7).

23. If possible, informed consent should be obtained in writing (1).

24. Seek official permission to use any government data, no matter how it was obtained (1).

Provision of Information

25. Purposes, procedures, and risks of research (including possible hazards to physical and psychological well-being and jeopardization of social position) should be explained to the participants in such a way that they can understand (7).

26. Participants should be aware of the possible consequences, if any, for the group or community from which they are selected in advance of their decision to participate (1).

27. The procedure used to obtain the participant's name should be described to him or her (1).

28. Sponsorship, financial and otherwise, should be specified to the potential participants (2).

29. The identity of those conducting the research should be fully revealed to the potential participants (2).

30. Names and addresses of research personnel should be left with participants so that the research personnel can be traced subsequently (1).

31. Participants should be fully aware of all data gathering techniques (tape and video recordings, photographic devices, physiological measures, and so forth), the capacities of such techniques, and the extent to which participants will remain anonymous and data confidential (2).

32. In projects of considerable duration, participants should be periodically informed of the progress of the research (1).

33. When recording videotapes or film, subjects should have the right to approve the material to be made public (by viewing it and giving specific approval to each segment) as well as the nature of the audiences (1).

Voluntary Consent

34. Individuals should have the option to refuse to participate and know this (1).

35. Participants should be able to terminate involvement at any time and know that they have this option (3).

36. No coercion, explicit or overt, should be used to encourage individuals to participate in a research project (6).

Protection of Rights and Welfare of Participants

General Issues

37. The dignity, privacy, and interests of the participants should be respected and protected (8).

38. The participants should not be harmed; welfare of the participants should take priority over all other concerns (10).

39. Damage and suffering to the participants should be minimized through procedural mechanisms and termination of risky studies as soon as possible; such effects are justified only when the problem cannot be studied in any other fashion (8).

40. Potential problems should be anticipated, no matter how remote the probability of occurrence, to ensure that the unexpected does not lead to major negative effects on the participants (1).

41. Any harmful aftereffects should be eliminated (4).

42. The hopes or anxieties of potential participants should not be raised (1).

43. Research should be terminated if danger to the participants arises (3).

44. The use of clients seeking professional assistance for research purposes is justified only to the extent that they may derive direct benefits as clients (1).

Deception

45. Deceit of the participants should only be used if it is absolutely necessary, there being no other way to study the problem (3).

46. Deception may be utilized (1).

47. If deceit is involved in a research procedure, additional precautions should be taken to protect the rights and welfare of the participants (2).

48. After being involved in a study using deception, all participants should be given a thorough, complete, and honest description of the study and the need for deception (5).

49. If deception is not revealed to the participants, for humane or scientific reasons, the investigator has a special obligation to protect the interests and welfare of the participants (1).

Confidentiality and Anonymity

50. Research data should be confidential and all participants should remain anonymous, unless they (or their legal guardians) have given permission for release of their identity (15).

51. If confidentiality or anonymity cannot be guaranteed, the participants should be aware of this and its possible consequences before involvement in the research (4).

52. Persons in official positions (studied as part of a research project) should provide written descriptions of their official roles, duties, and so forth (which need not be treated as confidential information) and be provided with a copy of the final report on the research (1).

53. Studies designed to provide descriptions of aggregates or collectivities should always guarantee anonymity to individual respondents (1).

54. "Privacy" should always be considered from the perspective of the participant and the participant's culture (1).

Exhibit 4.1 (*continued*)

55. Material stored in databanks should not be used without the permission of the investigator who originally gathered the data (1).

56. If promises of confidentiality are honored, investigators need not withhold information on misconduct of participants or organizations (1).

57. Specific procedures should be developed for organizing data to ensure anonymity of participants (1).

Benefits to Participants

58. A fair return should be offered for all services of participants (1).

59. Increased self-knowledge, as a benefit to the participants, should be incorporated as a major part of the research design or procedures (1).

60. Copies or explanations of the research should be provided to all participants (2).

61. Studies of aggregates or cultural subgroups should produce knowledge which will benefit them (1).

Effects on Aggregates or Communities

62. Investigators should be familiar with, and respect, the host cultures in which studies are conducted (1).

63. Investigators should cooperate with members of the host society (1).

64. Investigators should consider, in advance, the potential effects of the research on the social structure of the host community and the potential changes in influence of various groups or individuals by virtue of the conduct of the study (1).

65. Investigators should consider, in advance, the potential effects of the research and the report on the population or subgroup from which participants are drawn (1).

66. Participants should be aware, in advance, of potential effects upon aggregates or cultural subgroups which they represent (1).

67. The interests of collectivities and social systems of all kinds should be considered by the investigator (1).

Interpretations and Reporting of the Results of the Research

68. All reports of research should be public documents, freely available to all (4).

69. Research procedures should be described fully and accurately in reports, including all evidence regardless of the support it provides for the research hypotheses; conclusions should be objective and unbiased (14).

70. Full and complete interpretations should be provided for all data and attempts made to prevent misrepresentations in writing research reports (6).

71. Sponsorship, purpose, sources of financial support, and investigators responsible for the research should be made clear in all publications related thereto (3).

72. If publication may jeopardize or damage the population studied and complete disguise is impossible, publication should be delayed (2).

73. Cross-cultural studies should be published in the language and journals of the host society, in addition to publication in other languages and other societies (2).

74. Appropriate credit should be given to all parties contributing to the research (9).

75. Full, accurate disclosure of all published sources bearing on or contributing to the work is expected (8).

76. Publication of research findings on cultural subgroups should include a description in terms understood by the participants (2).

77. Whenever requested, raw data or other original documentation should be made available to qualified investigators (1).

78. Research with scientific merit should always be submitted for publication and not withheld from public presentation unless the quality of research or analysis is inadequate (1).

Reprinted with permission from Paul Davidson Reynolds, *Ethical Dilemmas and Social Science Research* (San Francisco: Jossey-Bass, 1979), pp. 443–448.

SUMMARY

1. Because the social sciences are both scientific and humanistic, a fundamental ethical dilemma exists: How are we to develop systematic, verifiable knowledge when research procedures may infringe on the rights and welfare of individuals? There are no absolute right or wrong answers to this dilemma.

2. The values that we attach to the potential benefits and costs of social science research depend on our backgrounds, convictions, and experience. The ethical researcher is educated about ethical guidelines, thoroughly examines the potential benefits and costs of the research project, exercises judgment in each situation, and accepts responsibility for his or her choice.

3. Within this ethical decision-making framework, the two most common issues are informed consent and privacy. Informed consent is the most general solution to the problem of how to promote social science research without encroaching on individual rights and welfare. By thoroughly informing potential participants about the purpose of the research and the procedures to be used, we enable individuals to make informed choices regarding their participation in a research project. Informed consent involves four basic aspects: competence, voluntarism, full information, and comprehension. The more serious the risk to the welfare or freedom of the research participants, the greater the researcher's obligation to obtain informed consent.

4. The right to privacy can be easily violated during a study or after its completion. In deciding how private the given information is, researchers consider three criteria: the sensitivity of the information, the setting in which the observations are made, and the extent to which the information is disseminated. Two common ways to protect the privacy of research participants are to maintain their anonymity and to keep the data confidential.

5. A broad consensus regarding ethical issues is emerging. Evidence for this trend is found in the adoption of ethical codes by professional societies. These codes state what is required and what is forbidden within the context of research. Although these codes sensitize researchers to their obligations and to those problematic areas where agreement has been reached about proper ethical practice, there is still no substitute for the individual investigator's personal code of ethics.

KEY TERMS FOR REVIEW

anonymity (p. 78)
codes of ethics (p. 80)
competence (p. 73)
comprehension (p. 76)
confidentiality (p. 71)
deception (p. 71)

ethical dilemma (p. 72)
informed consent (p. 72)
reasonably informed consent (p. 75)
right to privacy (p. 76)
sensitivity of information (p. 77)
voluntarism (p. 74)

STUDY QUESTIONS

1. Why do ethical concerns often arise in the conduct of research? Do you think there is a way of avoiding them in social science research?
2. List several costs and benefits of research that an investigator must weigh in deciding whether the benefits of a research project outweigh its costs to participants. Relate these costs and benefits to a specific research topic.
3. Discuss in detail the nature of informed consent. Have you participated in a research project that required informed consent? If so, how did you make your decision?
4. How can we protect the privacy of individuals when dealing with sensitive research topics? Do you have additional suggestions?
5. Distinguish between the issues of anonymity and confidentiality. Which of the two do you consider to be more problematic for the social science researcher?

ADDITIONAL READINGS

Beauchamp, Tom L., Ruth R. Faden, R. Jay Wallace, Jr., and LeRoy Walters, eds. *Ethical Issues in Social Science Research.* Baltimore: Johns Hopkins University Press, 1982. ·

Faden, Ruth R., Tom L. Beauchamp, and Nancy M. King. *A History and Theory of Informed Consent.* New York: Oxford University Press, 1986.

Gubrium, Jaber F., ed. *The Politics of Field Research: Beyond Enlightenment.* Newbury Park, CA: Sage, 1989.

Kallen, Allan J. *Ethical Issues in Behavioral Research.* Malden, ME: Blackwell, 1996.

Kimmel, Allan J. *Ethics and Values in Applied Social Research.* Newbury Park, CA: Sage, 1988.

Lappe, M. "Accountability in Science." *Science,* 187 (1975): 696–698.

Lee, Raymond M., *Doing Research on Sensitive Topics.* Thousand Oaks, CA: Sage, 1993.

Mastroianni, Anna C., Ruth R. Faden, Daniel Federman, and Institute of Medicine Staff. *Women and Health Research: Ethical and Legal Issues of Including Women in Clinical Studies,* Vols. 1 and 2. Washington, DC: National Academy Press, 1994.

Morris, Karen, Diana Woodward, and Eleanor Peters. "'Whose Side Are You On?' Dilemmas in Conducting Feminist Ethnographic Research With Young Women." *International Journal of Social Research Methodology, 1* (3), (1998): 217–230.

Punch, Maurice. *The Politics and Ethics of Field Work.* Thousand Oaks, CA: Sage, 1985.

Sieber, Joan E. *Planning Ethically Responsible Research: A Guide for Social Science Students.* Newbury Park, CA: Sage, 1992.

Sieber, Joan E., ed. *The Ethics of Social Research.* New York: Springer-Verlag, 1992.

RESEARCH DESIGNS: EXPERIMENTS

"Who Are the Whites?" [1] This is the question guiding a 1992 study of color classifications in the 1980 Brazilian census. Unlike the United States, where race is defined through lines of descent, in Brazil individuals classify themselves by color using a combination of physical and socioeconomic characteristics. Thus children may be classified differently than their parents or siblings. The researchers in this study noted that the forced-choice, four-category color question on the Brazilian census used an obscure term for the mixed-color, or "brown," category. They argued that the use of this term caused people to reject the mixed-color option and identify themselves as either black or white, inflating the number of people counted in these categories (the fourth category, yellow, was seldom chosen). They hypothesized that if the obscure term were changed to a term more commonly used, more people would identify themselves as being of mixed color, reducing the number of both blacks and whites and more accurately reflecting the way individuals would classify themselves in a free-choice description of their color. The researchers tested a sample of the population using a pretest–posttest design and found support for their hypothesis. Based on their findings, they argued that studies using 1980 census data to compare the life experiences of Brazilian blacks and whites are flawed because many people of mixed color are included in both the black and white census categories. In turn, researchers who have used census data in their studies will be examining the design and implementation of the color-classification study to evaluate the validity of the findings. The design and implementation of such experimental studies and the factors that influence validity are the subjects of this chapter.

●| **IN THIS CHAPTER** we discuss the research design as a logical model of causal inference and distinguish among several research designs. In the first section, we give an example of how an experimental research design is implemented. In the second section, we explain the structure of experimental designs. We then examine the four components of research designs: comparison, manipulation, control, and generalizability. Finally, we present some commonly used experimental designs.

Once the research objectives have been determined, the hypotheses explained, and the variables defined, the researcher confronts the problem of constructing a research design that will make it possible to test the hypotheses. A research design is the program that guides the investigator as he or she collects, analyzes, and interprets observations. It is a logical model of proof that allows the researcher to draw inferences concerning causal relations among the variables under investigation. The research design also defines the domain of generalizability, that is, whether the obtained interpretations can be generalized to a larger population or to different situations.|

THE RESEARCH DESIGN: AN EXAMPLE   ●

Any researcher who is about to test a hypothesis faces some fundamental problems that must be solved before the project can be started: Whom shall we study? What shall we observe? When will observations be made? How will the data be collected? The

---

1. Marvin Harris, Josildeth Gomes Consorte, Joseph Lang, and Bryan Byrne, "Who Are the Whites?: Imposed Census Categories and the Racial Demography of Brazil," *Social Forces,* 72 (1993): 451–462.

research design is the "blueprint" that enables the investigator to come up with solutions to these problems and guides him or her in the various stages of the research.

Our purpose here is to describe the processes involved in designing a study and to demonstrate how the specific research design that a scientist decides to use helps to structure the collection, analysis, and interpretation of data. We will describe research based on an experimental design summarized in the book *Pygmalion in the Classroom* by Robert Rosenthal and Lenore Jacobson.[2] This study was an attempt to test the effect that others' expectations have on a person's behavior. The central idea of the study was that one person's expectations for another's behavior may serve as a self-fulfilling prophecy. This is not a new idea, and we can find many anecdotes and theories to support it. The most notable example is George Bernard Shaw's play *Pygmalion* (1916), which was later adapted as the musical *My Fair Lady.* To use Shaw's own words:

> You see, really and truly, apart from the things anyone can pick up (the dressing and the proper way of speaking, and so on), the difference between a lady and a flower girl is not how she behaves, but how she's treated. I shall always be a flower girl to Professor Higgins, because he always treats me as a flower girl, and always will; but I know I can be a lady to you, because you always treat me as a lady, and always will.

Many studies of animal behavior support Shaw's shrewd observations. In these studies, when experimenters believed their animal subjects were genetically inferior, the animals performed poorly. However, when the experimenters thought the animals were genetically superior, the animals excelled in their performance. In reality, there were no genetic differences between the two groups of animals.

Rosenthal and Jacobson, who conducted the *Pygmalion in the Classroom* study, argued that if animal subjects believed to be brighter actually became brighter because of their trainers' expectations, then it might also be true that schoolchildren believed by their teachers to be brighter would indeed become brighter because of their teachers' expectations.

To test this hypothesis, the investigators selected one school—Oak School—as a laboratory in which the experiment would be carried out. Oak was a public elementary school in a lower-class community. On theoretical grounds, the study should have examined the effects of teachers' favorable or unfavorable expectations on their pupils' intellectual competence. However, because of ethical concerns, only the hypothesis that teachers' favorable expectations will lead to an increase in intellectual competence was tested.

The independent variable of the study was the expectations held by the teachers. The investigators manipulated the expectations by using the purported results of a standard nonverbal test of intelligence. This test was described to the teachers as one that would predict intellectual "blooming." At the beginning of the school year, following schoolwide pretesting, the teachers were given the names of the students in their classrooms who were among the 20 percent of Oak School's children who in the academic year ahead would supposedly show dramatic intellectual growth. These predictions were allegedly made on the basis of the children's scores on the "intellectual blooming" test. However, the names of the potential bloomers were actually chosen randomly. Thus the difference between the potential bloomers and their classmates was only in the mind of the teacher.

---

2. Robert Rosenthal and Lenore Jacobson, *Pygmalion in the Classroom* (New York: Holt, Rinehart and Winston, 1968); see also E. Y. Babad, J. Inbar, and R. Rosenthal, "Pygmalion, Galatea, and the Golem: Investigations of Biased and Unbiased Teachers," *Journal of Educational Psychology*, 74 (1982): 459–474.

Participants in both the experimental and control groups were told that they would be playing the role of purchasing executives reviewing proposals for a new airborne reconnaissance system. Each individual was instructed to read the request for proposals and study proposals submitted by three fictitious companies. Groups then discussed the proposals and attempted to reach consensus regarding the proposal ranking. After reaching a decision, a postexperimental questionnaire was administered. The questionnaire included a measure of subjective mental workload as well as a number of items assessing each member's impression of the group. The experimental and control group were compared in terms of their final proposal ranking, time to decision, and subjective mental workload.

Teams in the electronic chat condition were significantly less accurate in proposal rankings and took much longer to decide than groups in the face-to-face communication conditions. Moreover, groups in the electronic chat condition experienced significantly higher mental workload levels than groups in the control condition. The results of the study indicate that organizations trying to remain on the cutting age by using computer-mediated communication may overlook the fact that it may actually reduce group effectiveness in decision making.

Why Study Experiments?

The classic experimental design is usually associated with research in the biological and physical sciences. We are used to associating experiments with studies in the natural sciences rather than with the study of social phenomena such as discrimination, gang behavior, religion, or social attraction. Why, then, do we spend considerable time discussing experiments in the social sciences? The reasons are twofold. First, the classic experimental design helps us understand the logic of *all* research designs; it is a model against which we can evaluate other designs. Second, an experiment allows the investigator to draw causal inferences and observe, with relatively little difficulty, whether or not the independent variable caused changes in the dependent variable. With other research designs, this causal relation cannot be easily determined. Thus, when we understand the structure and logic of the classic experimental design, we can also understand the limitations of other designs.

Generally, social scientists use the experiment less widely than natural scientists, primarily because its rigid structure often cannot be adapted to social science research. Thus, social scientists frequently use designs that are weaker for drawing causal inferences but are more appropriate to the type of problems they examine. Designs identified as quasi-experiments (discussed in Chapter 6) are more common in social science research.

Yet, as we see from the *Pygmalion* and electronic information sharing examples, experiments certainly are used in the social sciences. As a matter of fact, in some social science fields such as social psychology, experiments are the predominant design. Moreover, the use of experiments has become more widespread in policy analysis and evaluation research.

CAUSAL INFERENCES ●

Both the *Pygmalion* experiment and the electronic information sharing experiment are tests of causal hypotheses. Indeed, at the heart of all scientific explanations is the idea of causality; that is, an independent variable is expected to produce a change in the dependent variable in the direction and of the magnitude specified by the theory. However, if a scientist observes that whenever the independent variable varies, the dependent variable varies too, it does not necessarily mean that a cause-and-effect relationship exists.

Consider, for instance, crime control policies. A major objective of such policies is to deter crime. Now, does the observation that a person does not commit a crime imply that he or she has been effectively deterred from doing so by a government policy? The answer depends on whether the individual was inclined to engage in criminal behavior in the first place. Furthermore, even if the person was inclined to commit a crime, was he or she deterred by the possibility of apprehension and punishment, or by other factors such as the lack of opportunity or peer-group influence? Accordingly, even if researchers observe that when the government enacts more aggressive crime control policies, the frequency of crimes actually committed declines, they cannot safely conclude that the two are causally related.

In practice, the demonstration of causality involves three distinct operations: demonstrating covariation, eliminating spurious relations, and establishing the time order of the occurrences.

Covariation

Covariation simply means that two or more phenomena vary together. For example, if a change in the level of education is accompanied by a change in the level of income, you can say that education covaries with income, that is, that individuals with higher levels of education have higher incomes than individuals with lower levels of education. Conversely, if a change in the level of education is not accompanied by a change in the level of income, education does not covary with income. In scientific research, the notion of covariation is expressed through measures of relations commonly referred to as *correlations* or *associations.* Thus in order to infer that one phenomenon causes another, a researcher must find evidence of a correlation between phenomena. For example, if poverty is not correlated (does not covary) with violence, it cannot be the cause of violence.

Nonspuriousness

The second operation requires the researcher to demonstrate that the covariation he or she has observed is *nonspurious.* As explained in Chapter 3, a nonspurious relation is a relation between two variables that cannot be explained by a third variable. If the effects of all relevant variables are controlled for and the relation between the original two variables is maintained, the relation is nonspurious. When researchers establish that a relation is nonspurious, they have strong evidence that there is an inherent causal link between variables and that the observed covariation is not based on an accidental connection with some associated phenomena. As we saw in Figure 3.1, the observed covariation between the number of firefighters at a fire and the amount of fire damage is spurious because a third variable—the size of the fire—explains the covariation.

Time Order

The third operation, *time order,* requires the researcher to demonstrate that the assumed cause occurs first or changes prior to the assumed effect.

For example, a number of studies have shown that the covariation between urbanization and democratic political development is nonspurious. To establish that urbanization is causally related to democratic development, a researcher must also demonstrate that the former precedes the latter. The implicit assumption here is that phenomena in the future cannot determine phenomena in the present or the past. It is usually not

The Logical Model of Proof: Three Necessary Components

- *Covariation:* Two or more phenomena vary together.
- *Nonspuriousness:* The effects of all relevant variables are controlled for and the relation between the original two variables is maintained.
- *Time order:* The assumed cause occurs first or changes prior to the assumed effect.

difficult to determine the time order of phenomena. The status of parents influences the educational expectations of their children, and not vice versa; an interest in politics precedes political participation; and depression precedes suicide. In other cases, however, the time order is harder to determine. Does urbanization precede political development, or does political development occur prior to urbanization? Does achievement follow motivation, or does a change in the level of motivation follow achievement? We shall discuss the methods employed to determine the time order of events in Chapters 6 and 17, but at this point we merely want to stress the significance of the time order criterion when formulating causal explanations.

COMPONENTS OF A RESEARCH DESIGN

The classic research design consists of four components: comparison, manipulation, control, and generalization. The first three are necessary to establish that the independent and dependent variables are causally related. Comparison allows us to demonstrate covariation, manipulation helps in establishing the time order of events, and control enables us to determine that the observed covariation is nonspurious. Generalization, the fourth component, concerns the extent to which the research findings can be applied to larger populations and different settings.

Comparison

The process of comparison underlies the concept of covariation or correlation. A **comparison** is an operation required to demonstrate that two variables are correlated. Suppose that we wanted to demonstrate a correlation between cigarette smoking and lung cancer: that the smoking of cigarettes is associated with a greater risk of getting lung cancer. To examine this, a researcher might compare the frequency of cancer cases among smokers and nonsmokers or, alternatively, compare the number of cancer cases in a population of smokers before and after they started smoking. Or suppose that we believe that television viewing contributes to sexist views of the roles of men and women among adolescents. We should then expect to find covariation of television viewing with sexist attitudes. That is, adolescents who spend more time watching television will exhibit traditional sex role stereotypes. To estimate the covariation of television viewing and sex role conceptions, we could compare groups of light and heavy viewers, or we could compare one group's sex role conception before and after viewing a television program that portrays traditional sex role images. In other words, to assess covariation, we evaluate the adolescents' scores on the dependent variables before and after the introduction of the independent variable, or we compare a group that is exposed to the independent variable with one that is not. In the former case, a group is compared with itself; in the latter case, an experimental group is compared with a control group.

Manipulation

The notion of causality implies that if *Y* is caused by *X*, then an induced change in *X* will be followed by a change in *Y*. It is hypothesized that the relations are asymmetrical: that one variable is the determining force and the other is a determined response. In order to establish causality, the induced change in *X* would have to occur prior to the change in *Y*, for what follows cannot be the determining variable. For example, if a researcher is attempting to prove that participation in an alcohol treatment group decreases denial of drinking problems, he or she must demonstrate that a decrease in denial took place after participation in the treatment group. The researcher needs to establish some form of control over (**manipulation** of) the assignment to the treatment group so that he or she can measure the level of denial of drinking problems before and after participation in the group. In experimental settings, especially in laboratory experiments, researchers can introduce the experimental treatment themselves; in natural settings, however, this level of control is not always possible. In both cases, the major evidence required to determine the time sequence of events—that is, that the independent variable precedes the dependent variable—is that a change occurred only after the activation of the independent variable.

Control: The Internal Validity of Research Designs

Control, the third criterion of causality, requires that the researcher rule out other factors as rival explanations of the observed association between the variables under investigation. Such factors could invalidate the inference that the variables are causally related. Donald Campbell and Julian Stanley have termed this issue the problem of **internal validity.** In order to establish internal validity, a researcher must answer the question of whether changes in the independent variable did, in fact, cause the dependent variable to change.[5] The effort to attain internal validity is the guiding force behind the design and implementation of a research project.

The factors that may jeopardize internal validity can be classified as those that occur prior to the research operation—extrinsic factors—and those that are intrinsic to it and impinge on the results during the study period.

EXTRINSIC FACTORS. Ethical considerations and issues of practicality sometimes prevent the random assignment of research participants to the experimental and control groups in social science research. When researchers must use some other means of assignment, possible biases—selection effects—can be introduced into the experiment because **extrinsic factors** may have produced differences between the experimental and control groups *prior to* the research operation. When the two groups differ at the outset of the experiment, it is difficult for researchers to separate selection effects from the effects of the independent variable. For example, in an evaluation of the effectiveness of employment programs for welfare recipients, the Manpower Demonstration Research Corporation compared welfare recipients who participated in federal job programs with other welfare recipients. They found that these programs increased the employment and earnings of participants and reduced welfare costs for taxpayers. However, a rival explanation for the observed changes in employment and earnings is that the program participants were initially different from other welfare recipients; perhaps they differed in their

---

5. Donald T. Campbell and Julian C. Stanley, *Experimental and Quasi-Experimental Designs for Research* (Skokie, IL: Rand McNally, 1963), p. 3.

motivation to seek employment, and this initial difference could have accounted for their high level of employment and earnings.

Selection effects are especially problematic in cases in which the individuals themselves decide whether to participate in an experiment. In such cases, the investigator cannot tell whether the independent variable itself caused the observed differences between the experimental and control groups or whether other factors related to the selection procedures were responsible for the observed effects. In fact, many social programs are available on a self-selection basis to a larger target population. Researchers find it difficult to assess the effectiveness of such programs because of selection effects, among other things. Selection factors must be controlled before the investigator can rule them out as rival explanations. Later in this chapter we discuss methods for controlling selection factors.

INTRINSIC FACTORS. **Intrinsic factors** include changes in the individuals or the units studied that occur during the study period, changes in the measuring instrument, or the reactive effect of the observation itself. The following are the major intrinsic factors that might invalidate a causal interpretation given to research findings.[6]

1. *History.* **History** refers to all events that occurred during the time of the study that might affect the individuals studied and provide a rival explanation for the change in the dependent variable. For example, in a study attempting to assess the effect of an election campaign on voting behavior, the hypothesis might be that information about a candidate to which voters are exposed during the campaign is likely to influence their voting. Investigators compare the voting intentions of individuals before and after exposure to the information. Differences in the voting intentions of the two groups—the one that has been exposed to information and the other that has not—could be the result of differential exposure to the information or, alternatively, of events that occurred during this period. Perhaps a governmental conflict has happened, an international crisis has erupted, the rate of inflation has increased, or an incumbent has proposed additional taxes. The longer the time lapse between the pretest and the posttest, the higher the probability that events other than the independent variable will become potential rival hypotheses.

2. *Maturation.* **Maturation** involves biological, psychological, or social processes that produce changes in the individuals or units studied with the passage of time. These changes could possibly influence the dependent variable and lead to erroneous inferences. Suppose that one wants to evaluate the effect of a specific teaching method on student achievement and records the students' achievement before and after the method was introduced. Between the pretest and the posttest, students have gotten older and perhaps wiser; this change, unrelated to the teaching method, could possibly explain the difference between the two tests. Maturation, like history, is a serious threat to the validity of causal inferences.

3. *Experimental mortality.* **Experimental mortality** refers to dropout problems that prevent the researcher from obtaining complete information on all cases. When individuals drop out selectively from the experimental or control group, the final sample on which complete information is available may be biased. In a study of the effect of the media on prejudice, for instance, if most dropouts were prejudiced individuals, the results could give the impression that exposure to media reduced prejudice, whereas in

---

6. Ibid.

fact it was the effect of experimental mortality that produced the observed shift in opinion.

4. *Instrumentation.* **Instrumentation** designates changes in the measuring instruments between the pretest and the posttest. To associate the difference between posttest and pretest scores with the independent variable, researchers have to show that repeated measurements with the same measurement instrument under unchanged conditions will yield the same result. If they cannot show the same result, the observed differences could be attributed to the change in the measurement instrument and not necessarily to the independent variable. The stability of measurement is also referred to as *reliability,* and its absence can be a threat to the validity of experiments (see Chapter 7). For example, if a program to improve cognitive skills were evaluated by comparing preprogram and postprogram ratings by psychologists, any changes in the psychologists' standard of judgment that occurred between testing periods would bias the findings.

5. *Testing.* The possible reactivity of measurement is a major problem in social science research. In other words, the process of testing may itself change the phenomena being measured. The effect of being pretested might sensitize individuals and improve their scoring on the posttest. A difference between posttest and pretest scores could thus be attributed not necessarily to the independent variable but rather to the experience gained by individuals while taking the pretest. It is known, for example, that individuals may improve their scores on intelligence tests by taking them often. Similarly, when they take a pretest, individuals may learn the socially accepted responses either through the wording of the questions or by discussing the results with friends. They might then answer in the expected direction on the posttest.

6. *Regression artifact.* The **regression artifact** is a threat that occurs when individuals have been assigned to the experimental group on the basis of their extreme scores on the pretest that measures dependent variables. When this happens and measures are unreliable, individuals who scored below average on the pretest will appear to have improved upon retesting. Conversely, individuals who scored above average on the pretest would appear to have done less well upon retesting. We are all familiar with this problem from our own experience in test taking. Most of us have sometimes performed below our expectations on an academic test because of factors beyond our control that had nothing to do with our academic ability. We may have had a sleepless night just before taking the test or been distracted by some serious personal problems. It is very likely that if we were to take the test again, our performance would improve without any additional studying. Viewed more generally, regression artifact can become a threat to the validity of a study whenever the treatment is expected to produce a change in individuals whose scores on the dependent variable are extreme to begin with.

For example, the Job Corps is considered a successful program for disadvantaged out-of-school youth, providing remedial education, vocational training, and health care. But if enrollees were chosen to participate in the program on the basis of their extremely low scores on an unreliable test, it is possible that they will show improvement when retested even without being directly affected by the program, simply because the unreliability of the test would cause their scores to change and they cannot get any worse. There is a risk, then, that their improvement will be erroneously attributed to the effect of the program.

7. *Interactions with selection.* Many of the intrinsic factors that pose a threat to the internal validity of experiments can interact with selection factors and present added threats to the validity of the study. The factors that are most commonly cited are *selection–history* and *selection–maturation.*

proportion of males and females. As Figure 5.2 shows, the two groups are matched separately for each extrinsic factor. Although it is somewhat less precise, frequency distribution matching is much easier to execute than precision matching and enables the investigator to control for several factors without having to discard a large number of cases.

The most basic problem in using matching as a method of control is that ordinarily the investigator does not know which of *all* the relevant factors are critical in terms of explaining the independent–dependent variable relationship. Furthermore, researchers can never be certain that they have considered all relevant factors.

RANDOMIZATION.   Matching is a method of controlling for a limited number of predefined extrinsic factors. However, even if it were possible to eliminate the effects of all the factors, investigators can never be sure that all of them have been isolated. Other factors of which the investigator is unaware may lead to erroneous causal interpretations. Researchers avoid this problem by using **randomization,** another process whereby cases are assigned to the experimental and control groups. Randomization can be accomplished by flipping a coin, by using a table of random digits, or by any other method that ensures that any of the cases has an equal probability of being assigned to either the experimental group or the control group.

Suppose that a researcher is examining the hypothesis that the participation of workers in the decision-making process of their place of work is conducive to production. Workers are divided into experimental and control groups; the experimental group is allowed to participate in decisions concerning the work schedule and its organization. The production level of both groups is measured at the beginning and at the end of the experiment. The objective is to see whether workers who took part in the decisions are significantly more productive than workers in the control group. However, a difference in the production level can be accounted for by numerous factors other than participation in the decision-making process, the factor whose effect is being examined. Obviously, a number of personal factors, such as age, physical fitness, intelligence, and motivation, could account for the difference. The highly motivated, the more intelligent, the more physically fit, and the younger workers could be more productive. Without a controlled assignment of the workers to the groups, perhaps the most motivated, intelligent, and fit among the younger participants would volunteer for the experimental group, a fact that might account for the improved production level.

One way to counteract the effect of these variables is by pairwise matching (Figure 5.1). Another is to randomize the groups by flipping a coin or using a table of random digits (see Appendix D) to decide which workers are assigned to the experimental group and which to the control group. Coin flipping is a simple process whereby the heads go into one group and the tails into another. A table of random digits may be used in many ways for different purposes—see page 169 for a description of how the table works. Randomization ensures that motivation, intelligence, physical fitness, and average age will have similar distributions in the two groups. Consequently, any difference in production between the groups can be attributed to the fact that workers in the experimental group participated in the decision-making process. In other words, randomization cancels out the effect of any systematic error due to extrinsic variables that may be associated with either the dependent variable (productivity) or the independent variable (participation in decision making). The advantage of this method is that it controls for numerous factors simultaneously even when the researcher is unaware of what they are. With this method, the investigator can equalize the experimental and control groups on *all* initial differences between them.

THE CONTROL GROUP.   Researchers control intrinsic factors by using a control group from which they withhold the experimental stimulus. Ideally, the control and experimental groups have been selected randomly or by matching so that they will have exactly the same characteristics. The groups also experience identical conditions during the study except for their differential exposure to the independent variable. Thus features of the experimental situation or external events that occur during the experiment are likely to influence the two groups equally and will not be confounded with the effect of the independent variable.

By using a control group, the researcher controls most of the intrinsic factors that could threaten the validity of the experiment. History does not become a rival hypothesis because the control and experimental groups are both exposed to the same events during the experiment. Similarly, maturation is neutralized because the two groups undergo the same changes. Including a control group does not necessarily avoid the mortality problem, because one group might lose more cases than the other and bias the results. The acceptable procedure is for researchers to include in the final sample only cases for which complete information is available, provide information on mortality, and discuss its implications. Researchers can also avoid the influence of instrument change by using a control group; if the change between posttest and pretest scores is a result of the instrument's unreliability, this will be reflected in both groups. Only when the groups are exposed to identical testing conditions does this method of control provide a solution to the instrumentation problem, however. Using a control group is also an answer to the matter of testing. The reactive effect of measurement, if present, is reflected in both groups and leaves no grounds for misinterpretation.

The use of a control group will help in counteracting the effects of factors that interact with selection (e.g., selection–maturation, selection–history, and other interactions) only if researchers use it in conjunction with methods that control for extrinsic factors, such as matching and randomization. Such methods assure that the group being treated and the control group have the same properties and that they experience identical conditions during the experiment.

Generalizability: External Validity

While internal validity is indeed a crucial aspect of social research, an additional significant question concerns the extent to which the research findings can be generalized to larger populations and applied to different social or political settings. Most research is concerned not only with the effect of one variable on another in the particular setting studied but also with its effect in other natural settings and on larger populations. This concern is termed the **external validity** of research designs. The two main issues of external validity are the representativeness of the sample and the reactive arrangements in the research procedure.

REPRESENTATIVENESS OF THE SAMPLE.   To ensure the external validity of a study, the characteristics of the subjects must reflect the characteristics of the population the researcher is investigating. Although randomization contributes to the internal validity of a study, it does not necessarily ensure that the sample is representative of the population of interest. Results that prove to be internally valid might be specific to the group selected for the particular study. This possibility becomes likely in situations where it is difficult to recruit cases to the study. Consider an experiment on college students that is carefully planned yet is based on volunteers. Investigators cannot assume that this group is representative of the student body, let alone the general population. To make possible

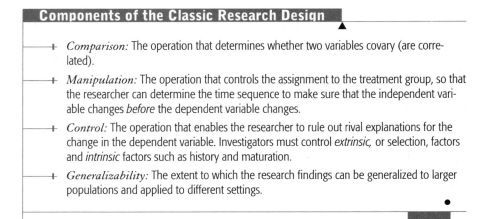

Components of the Classic Research Design

- *Comparison:* The operation that determines whether two variables covary (are correlated).
- *Manipulation:* The operation that controls the assignment to the treatment group, so that the researcher can determine the time sequence to make sure that the independent variable changes *before* the dependent variable changes.
- *Control:* The operation that enables the researcher to rule out rival explanations for the change in the dependent variable. Investigators must control *extrinsic,* or selection, factors and *intrinsic* factors such as history and maturation.
- *Generalizability:* The extent to which the research findings can be generalized to larger populations and applied to different settings.

generalizations beyond the limited scope of the specific study, researchers must take care to select the sample using a sampling method that assures representativeness. Probability methods such as random sampling make generalizations to larger and clearly defined populations possible, as discussed in Chapter 8. In theory, the experimental and control groups should each constitute a probability sample of the population. In practice, however, drawing a probability sample for an experiment often involves problems such as high cost and a high rate of refusal to cooperate.

REACTIVE ARRANGEMENTS. External validity can be compromised when the experimental setting or the experimental situation does not reflect the natural setting or situation to which researchers wish to generalize. When a study is carried out in a highly artificial and contrived situation, such as a laboratory, features of the setting might influence the subjects' response. For example, Muzafer Sherif designed a well-known study to examine how group norms—guidelines for behavior—influence individuals placed in an unstable

The Internal Validity of Research Designs

Extrinsic factors
- Selection

Intrinsic factors
- History
- Maturation
- Experimental mortality
- Instrumentation
- Testing
- Regression artifact
- Interaction with selection

The External Validity of Research Designs

▲

- Representativeness of the sample
- Reactive arrangements

●

situation in which all external bases of comparison are absent.[7] Sherif created the unstable situation and removed external bases of comparison experimentally by using the autokinetic effect, which occurs when a single stationary ray of light is introduced into a completely dark room. The ray of light seems to move erratically from place to place because of the lack of external reference points. Sherif found that participants' reports of movement were influenced by the responses of other group members. However, it can be claimed that an experimental situation in which persons are placed in a dark room and are required to respond to a ray of light does not represent ordinary social situations and that the observed results might very well be specific to the artificial situation.

Various other features in the setting might be reactive and affect the external validity of the study. For example, the pretest may influence the way individuals respond to the experimental stimulus; its observed effect would thus be specific to a population that has been pretested. The attitude or behavior of an experimenter can influence the way subjects respond because subjects generally desire to give the response they think the experimenter expects. In survey research it is particularly important to develop questions that are neutrally worded to avoid influencing responses (see Chapter 11).

DESIGN TYPES   ●

Research designs can be classified by the extent to which they meet the criteria we have discussed so far. Some designs allow researchers to manipulate variables but fail to employ methods of control or to provide an adequate sampling plan; others may include control groups but give the researcher no control over the manipulation of the independent variable. Accordingly, four major design types can be distinguished: *experimental, quasi-experimental, cross-sectional,* and *preexperimental.* In experimental designs, individuals or other units of analysis are randomly assigned to the experimental and control groups and the independent variable is introduced only to the experimental group. Such designs allow for comparison, control, manipulation, and, usually, generalizability. Quasi-experimental and cross-sectional designs ordinarily include combinations of some of these elements but not all of them. Typically, these designs lack possibilities for manipulation and randomization. Preexperimental designs include even fewer safeguards than quasi-experimental and cross-sectional designs, and in this sense they provide the least credibility in determining whether two or more variables are causally related. Some commonly used experimental designs are discussed in this chapter; preexperimental, quasi-experimental, and cross-sectional designs will be presented in Chapter 6.

Controlled Experimentation

The classic experimental design presented in Table 5.1 is one of the strongest logical models for inferring causal relations. The design allows for pretest, posttest, and control

7. Muzafer Sherif, "An Experimental Approach to the Study of Attitudes," *Sociometry,* 1 (1937): 90–98.

Table 5.2

The Solomon Four-Group Design

	Pretest		Posttest
R	O_1	X	O_2
R	O_3		O_4
R		X	O_5
R			O_6

group–experimental group comparisons; it permits the manipulation of the independent variable and thus the determination of the time sequence; and most significant, by including randomized groups, it controls for most sources of internal validity. However, the external validity of this design is weak, and it does not allow researchers to make generalizations to nontested populations. Two variations of the classic experimental design are stronger in this respect: the Solomon four-group design and the posttest-only control group design.

The Solomon Four-Group Design

The pretest in an experimental setting has advantages as well as disadvantages. Although pretesting provides an assessment of the time sequence as well as a basis of comparison, it can have severe reactive effects. By sensitizing the sampled population, a pretest might in and of itself affect posttest scores. For example, measuring public attitudes toward a government policy before its implementation may sensitize individuals to respond differently on a posttest from nonpretested persons because the pretest may have caused them to consider and research the possible implications of policy implementation. Furthermore, there are circumstances under which a premeasurement period is not practical. In education, for instance, researchers often experiment with entirely new methods of teaching for which pretests are impossible.

The Solomon four-group design, presented in Table 5.2, contains the same features as the classic design plus an additional set of control and experimental groups that are not pretested. Therefore, the reactive effect of testing can be measured directly, by comparing the two experimental groups (O_2 and O_5) and the two control groups (O_4 and O_6). These comparisons will indicate whether X has an independent effect on groups that were not sensitized by a pretest. If the comparisons show that the independent variable had an effect even with the absence of the pretest, the results can be generalized to populations that were not measured before being exposed to X. Moreover, as Campbell and Stanley suggest,

> not only is generalizability increased, but in addition, the effect of X is replicated in four different fashions: $O_2 > O_1$, $O_2 > O_4$, $O_5 > O_6$, and $O_1 > O_3$. The actual instabilities of experimentation are such that if these comparisons are in agreement, the strength of the inference is greatly increased.[8]

AN EXAMPLE: *THE SELLING OF THE PENTAGON.* An interesting application of the four-group design was a study on the effect of public affairs television in politics.[9]

---

8. Campbell and Stanley, *Experimental and Quasi-Experimental Designs*, p. 25.

9. Michael J. Robinson, "Public Affairs Television and the Growth of Political Malaise: The Case of 'The Selling of the Pentagon,'" *American Political Science Review*, 70 (1976): 409–432.

in small firms with low decentralization. Or, decentralization may significantly improve morale in large firms but have little effect in small firms. Factorial designs, then, increase the external validity of experiments because, as Ronald A. Fisher has suggested:

> Any conclusion . . . has a wider inductive basis when inferred from an experiment in which the quantities of other ingredients have been varied than it would have from any amount of experimentation in which these had been kept strictly constant. The exact standardization of experimental conditions, which is often thoughtlessly advocated as a panacea, always carries with it the real disadvantage that a highly standardized experiment supplies direct information only in respect of the narrow range of conditions achieved by standardization. Standardization, therefore, weakens rather than strengthens our ground for inferring a like result, when, as is invariably the case in practice, these conditions are somewhat varied.[11]

INTERACTION EFFECTS IN FACTORIAL DESIGNS. Another advantage of the factorial design is that it allows us to assess systematically how two (or more) independent variables interact. Variables interact when the effect of one independent variable on the dependent variable depends on the value of the second independent variable.

For example, if large organizational size is associated with low morale of members *only* in organizations that are low on decentralization, it means that size and decentralization interact. Conversely, if large size leads to lowered morale whether or not the organization is more or less decentralized, the effect of size on morale is independent of decentralization, and there is no interaction. The test for interaction makes it possible to expand greatly our understanding of the effect of independent variables on the dependent variable. It allows us to qualify our conclusions about their effects in an important way because we study the simultaneous operation of the two independent variables.

SUMMARY

1. The research design is the program that guides the investigator in the process of collecting, analyzing, and interpreting observations. It allows inferences concerning causal relations and defines the domain of generalizability.

2. The classic research design consists of four components: comparison, manipulation, control, and generalization. Comparison is an operation that enables researchers to demonstrate that the independent and dependent variables are related. Manipulation involves some form of control over the introduction of the independent variables, so that the investigator can determine the time order of the variables. The control component allows researchers to rule out other factors as rival explanations of the observed associations between the independent and dependent variables. The four component, generalization, requires that the findings of research be applicable to the natural settings and populations the researcher is investigating.

3. The process of control is related to the internal validity of the research design. To establish internal validity the researcher must rule out rival explanations for the change occurring in the dependent variable. Factors that may jeopardize internal validity are intrinsic or extrinsic to the research operation. Extrinsic factors are called

---

11. Ronald A. Fisher, *The Design of Experiments*, 8th ed. (New York: Hafner Press, 1971), p. 106.

selection effects. They are biases resulting from the differential recruitment of respondents to the experimental and control groups. Intrinsic factors are history, maturation, experimental mortality, instrumentation, testing, regression artifact, and factors that interact with the selection effects caused by differential assignment of subjects to the experimental and control groups.

4. Two methods of control are employed to counteract the effect of extrinsic factors. Matching allows investigators to control for variables that are known to them prior to the research operation, and randomization helps to offset the effects of foreseen as well as unforeseen factors. Intrinsic factors are controlled by using a control group.

5. Generalization addresses the problem of the external validity of research designs. It concerns the extent to which the research findings can be generalized to larger populations and applied to different settings.

6. Experimental research designs are the strongest models of proof because they permit the manipulation of the independent variables and provide maximum control over intrinsic and extrinsic factors. Two variations of the classic experimental design are the Solomon four-group design and the posttest-only control group design. Other designs allow the study of effects extended in time, and factorial designs permit researchers to examine the effects of more than one independent variable. The advantage of factorial designs is that they strengthen the external validity of the study and allow the investigator to assess the interaction between the independent variables.

KEY TERMS FOR REVIEW •

classic experimental design (p. 90)
comparison (p. 94)
control (p. 95)
control group (p. 90)
covariation (p. 93)
experimental group (p. 90)
experimental mortality (p. 96)
external validity (p. 101)
extrinsic factors (p. 95)
factorial design (p. 108)
history (p. 96)

instrumentation (p. 97)
internal validity (p. 95)
intrinsic factors (p. 96)
manipulation (p. 95)
matching (p. 99)
maturation (p. 96)
posttest (p. 90)
pretest (p. 90)
randomization (p. 100)
regression artifact (p. 97)
research design (p. 89)

STUDY QUESTIONS •

1. Describe the elements of the classic experimental design.
2. Distinguish between external and internal validity.
3. What operations are involved in the demonstration of causality?
4. List and describe the different methods of controlling threats to the internal validity of research.
5. What are three important variants of the classic experimental design? What are their advantages and disadvantages?

ADDITIONAL READINGS

Berkowitz, L., and E. Donnerstein. "External Validity Is More Than Skin Deep: Some Answers to Criticisms of Laboratory Experiments." *American Psychologist,* 37 (1982): 245–257.

Campbell, Donald T., and Thomas D. Cook. *Quasi-Experimentation.* Skokie, IL: Rand McNally, 1979.

Cobb, George W. *Introduction to Design and Analysis of Experiments.* New York: Springer, 1998.

Depoy, Elizabeth. *Introduction to Research: Understanding and Applying Multiple Strategies,* 2d ed. St. Louis: Mosby, 1998.

Martin, David W. *Doing Psychology Experiments,* 4th ed. Pacific Grove, CA: Brooks/Cole, 1996.

Ray, William, and Richard Ravizza. *Methods Toward a Science of Behavior and Experience,* 2d ed. Belmont, CA: Wadsworth, 1993.

Figure 6.1

The Simplest Design

After

Because of the nature of the variables being investigated—political orientations and

public opinions about economic reform within this changing environment. Their analysis focuses primarily on the extent to which opinions about reform are influenced by orientations toward the president and the ruling party.

Kaufman and Zuckerman's study is based on a probability sample of households selected initially by the Mexican government, which conducted a national survey. At each household, an interview of about 45 to 60 minutes was conducted with one respondent selected at random, with about an equal proportion of men and women. Respondents were asked a variety of questions, including questions about their attitudes toward economic reform and their orientations toward the president and the ruling party.

Because of the nature of the variables being investigated—political orientations and attitudes—the researcher cannot manipulate the independent variable and make before-and-after comparisons. Thus this research is not amenable to experimental investigation. Moreover, the time interval in which political orientations may shape attitudes toward economic reform extends over a relatively long period. Because of these limitations, it would be difficult to incorporate into a research design the components of manipulation and control, which are necessary to establish causality. This design may be diagrammed as in Figure 6.1, where the dashed X indicates political orientations and O_1 indicates attitudes toward economic reform. Obviously, such a design would suffer from serious methodological limitations, especially with regard to its internal validity.

To overcome the methodological limitations of cross-sectional designs, researchers use statistical analysis to approximate some of the operations that are naturally built into an experimental design. In their study, Kaufman and Zuckerman first needed to establish that political orientations—for example, orientations toward the ruling party—and attitudes toward economic reform are interrelated. Table 6.1 presents the results of a

Table 6.1

Attitudes Toward Economic Reform and Political Orientations

Support for Economic Reform	Agreement with the President (%)	
	Agree	Disagree
Agree	46.7	14.5
Agree in part	25.4	20.2
Disagree	27.9	65.3
Total	100.0	100.0

Figure 6.2

The Cross-Sectional Design

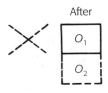

statistical analysis designed to assess the relationship between these two variables. By using statistics to organize, describe, and summarize the observations, the researchers are able to show that 46.7 percent of Mexicans who agree with the president but only 14.5 percent of those who disagree with the president support economic reform in Mexico. This observation is based on data analysis techniques called *cross-tabulation* and *bivariate percentage analysis,* which will be discussed in detail in Chapter 16.

By using these data analysis techniques, we have improved our design to approximate the posttest-only control group design (described in Chapter 5). This improved cross-sectional design is diagrammed in Figure 6.2. The dashed-cell O_2 indicates extra information we obtained during the data analysis stage. When the data are organized and summarized by category, as in Table 6.1, we are able to make a number of comparisons between the different groups.

Though the cross-sectional design as presented in Figure 6.2 would allow us to assess the relation between support for economic reform in Mexico and agreement with the president, we cannot conclude that these two variables are causally related. There are a number of possible explanations for the observed relation; for example, those who agree with the president may have higher incomes and thus be less vulnerable to the impact of economic reform and more likely to support it.

QUASI-EXPERIMENTAL DESIGNS   •

Using the classic experimental design as a model of logical proof, scientists have developed a number of quasi-experimental designs. As in cross-sectional designs, these designs are weaker on internal validity than experimental designs, and researchers must depend on data analysis techniques as a method of control. Quasi-experimental designs often allow researchers to select random samples from the population, but they do not require the random assignment of individual cases to the comparison groups. They are superior, however, to cross-sectional designs because they usually involve the study of more than one sample, often over an extended period of time. In the following sections we explore the most important quasi-experimental designs in current use.

Contrasted-Groups Designs

A common problem in social science research is that in many cases the researcher cannot randomly assign individuals or other units of analysis to comparison groups. For example, researchers cannot assign individuals to a race, gender, social class, or religion. At times, researchers use intact comparison groups either at the pretest phase only or at the posttest phase only. Causal inferences concerning the independent variables are especially vulnerable when researchers cannot use randomization to assign cases to groups that are known to differ in some important attributes; for example, when they are comparing poor communities with relatively well-to-do ones, groups from different ethnic backgrounds, or males with females. If a researcher uses a posttest-only design with such contrasted groups, differences on the posttest measures are likely to be due to initial differences between the groups rather than to the impact of the independent variable. Nevertheless, when researchers need to assess differences among such contrasted groups, several possible modifications in the research design can act as safeguards against the intrusion of influences other than that of the independent variable.

The least elaborate design for **contrasted groups** is one in which individuals or other units of analysis are regarded as members of *categoric groups*. Categoric group members share some attribute that assigns them to an identifiable category, such as males, Democrats, or Catholics. Members of each group are measured with respect to the dependent variables. For example, a researcher could compare the reading performances of children residing in different communities. This design can be symbolized in the following way, where $O_1, \ldots, O_k$ represent measures on the dependent variable by grouping category:

O_1

O_2

O_3

O_4

.

.

.

O_k

Researchers can perform straightforward comparative statistical analyses on the differences in measurement scores obtained for the k groups. For example, they can examine the difference between means—average scores—of the groups. However, because contrasted groups differ from one another in many ways, difficulties arise when researchers attempt to assess the causes for the observed differences. Relatedly, the groups might differ because of problems with the measurement procedures rather than because of any real differences among them. For instance, studies have shown repeatedly that measurements based solely on personal interviews are affected by the interviewers' backgrounds and that black and white interviewers elicit different answers from black respondents. (A more detailed discussion of this and other problems with interviews appears in Chapter 10.)

Researchers can reduce the risk of being wrong when making causal inferences based on contrasted-groups designs by obtaining supplementary evidence over time regarding the differences they have predicted in their hypothesis. If they obtain the same finding in other settings and make comparisons on a number of measures concerning the dependent variables, such supplementary evidence can increase the inferential powers of a contrasted-groups design.

A more elaborate design for contrasted groups is one in which researchers compare two or more intact groups before and after the introduction of the treatment variable. In this design—the nonequivalent control group design—statistical techniques are used to test for comparability between the contrasted groups before causal inferences are drawn.

Table 6.2

A Nonequivalent Control Group Design

Pretest		Posttest
O_1	X	O_2
O_3		O_4

A recent study evaluating the efficacy of a university-level remedial writing program provides an example of this design.[4] The researchers set out to evaluate the effectiveness, in improving writing skills, of a remedial English course followed by standard freshman English composition, compared with the standard English composition course alone. All participants in the study were students whose ACT scores fell below 16 (or 380 or below for SAT scores). The experimental groups consisted of students who enrolled in a remedial writing course in the fall semester followed by the standard English composition course in the spring. The control group consisted of students exempted from the remedial course and enrolled in the standard English composition course in the spring.

The writing competency of students in both classes was evaluated by a direct assessment in the form of a written essay and by an indirect assessment in the form of an objective test of knowledge of written expression. Both assessments were given before (pretest) and after (posttest) participation in the standard English composition course. The design used in this study is shown in Table 6.2. Since students were not randomly assigned to the experimental and control groups, the evaluation of the course's impact had significant methodological limitations. A critical issue, for example, was the fact that the experimental and the control group took the standard English composition course during different semesters. Differences in student capability in English across semesters might have led to differential instruction, grading, or both. Therefore, the researchers had to make special efforts to approximate comparability between the experimental and control groups. One strategy was to compare students with similar characteristics who took the standard English course during different semesters. This comparison served as a test of institutional variation across semesters. In addition, the researchers equated the experimental and control groups on their writing ability (the pretest), thus ruling out the alternative explanation that preexisting differences in writing ability accounted for differences between the two groups on the posttest.

The results of the study indicate that, compared to remedial students who took the one-semester standard English composition course, those students who took a remedial course followed by standard English composition exhibited superior performance on the objective test, with almost no benefit on the writing sample. We must stress again, however, the limitation of this design. Because of the absence of random assignment of students to the experimental and control groups, the internal validity of the study is jeopardized.

In some cases in which social scientists compare contrasted groups, measures are available on a number of occasions before and after the introduction of the independent

4. Adapted from Leona S. Aiken, Stephen G. West, David E. Schwalm, James L. Carrol, and Shenghwa Hsiung, "Comparison of a Randomized and Two Quasi-Experimental Designs in a Single Outcome Evaluation," *Evaluation Review*, 22 (1998): 207–244.

variable. In such cases, researchers can obtain multiple measures before and/or after exposure. Such supplementary data provide a measure of the amount of normal variation in the dependent variable from time to time, regardless of the independent variable's impact. Suppose that researchers wish to evaluate the effectiveness of a new approach to teaching reading implemented through the fifth grade in school E. They can compare achievement test scores in reading for children in the third through seventh grades in that school and in another school (C) in the same community that did not use the new approach. The study is conducted retroactively for students who are currently in the seventh grade and have remained in the school from the third grade up to that time. Because schools administer achievement tests each year, the researchers can obtain comparable measures for each of the five years. Evidence for a program effect when there are multiple measures over time consists of a sharp difference in the level of the dependent variable from before to after implementation of the program for the units being compared, as illustrated in Figure 6.3. Notice that the scores on the dependent variable increase steadily for school C—the school where the program was not implemented. In contrast, the scores for school E rise sharply between the fourth and fifth year and then level off.

Unlike the hypothetical results in Figure 6.3, the findings shown in Figure 6.4 indicate that the independent variable had no effect at all on the individuals in group E beyond what could be expected from the usual course of events, as evidenced in group C. The apparent change in group E is illusory because it is matched by a proportional change in group C.

Figure 6.3

Comparison of Two Contrasted Groups Indicating That the Independent Variable Had a Definite Effect

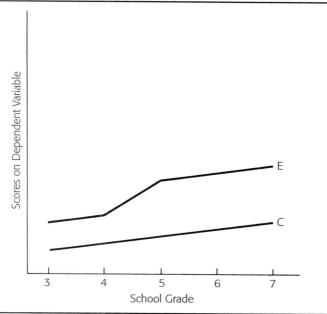

Figure 6.4

Comparison of Two Contrasted Groups Indicating That an Independent Variable Had No Effect

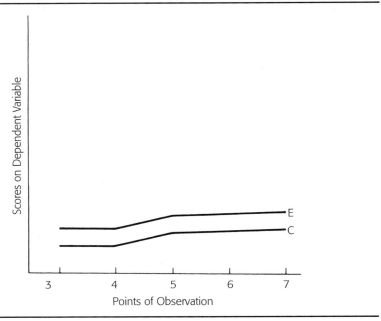

Planned Variation Designs

When researchers used **planned variation** designs, they expose individuals to stimuli that have been systematically varied in order to assess their causal effects. The Head Start Planned Variation (HSPV) is an excellent policy-relevant example of such a design. HSPV was a three-year investigation designed to compare the effects that different kinds of Head Start centers were having on the development of the academic skills of children from relatively poor families. The study was developed on the assumption that by select-ing a number of "sponsors"—schools, agencies, or voluntary organizations that took on management responsibilities—for different types of programs, and by systematically vary-ing the kinds of programs offered to children, the researchers could discover which kinds of programs most benefited which kinds of children.[5]

The sponsors selected to participate in the investigation varied substantially in terms of their goals and their teaching programs. During the 1971–1972 academic year, 11 sponsors were distributed over a total of 28 neighborhood sites scattered throughout the country. For purposes of comparison, 11 of the 28 sites also had "nonsponsored" class-rooms managed directly by Head Start staff. In addition, three sites had comparison groups of children who were not enrolled in any program. Children selected for this

---

5. The following account draws on Herbert I. Weisberg, *Short-Term Cognitive Effects of Head Start Programs: A Report on the Third Year of Planned Variation, 1971–1972* (Cambridge, MA: Huron Institute, 1973).

comparison group were contacted by direct recruitment and from Head Start waiting lists. Each sponsor operated two, three, or four sites. Each site had a different number of classrooms run by the specific sponsor. Some sites contained both sponsored and regular, nonsponsored Head Start classrooms; other sites had only sponsored classrooms.

One major shortcoming of this research design was that a number of important variables were not equally distributed across the sponsored sites. As Herbert I. Weisberg pointed out, race, age, prior preschool experience, and socioeconomic background were all unequally distributed. For example, one sponsor had almost no black children at his site, whereas another sponsor had almost no white children. In spite of this serious source of reduced validity, the researchers drew three general inferences: (1) Overall, both the sponsors' programs and the regular Head Start programs tended to accelerate certain kinds of specific academic performance, such as number and letter recognition; (2) pooling the 11 sponsored sets of classrooms and comparing them with the regular, nonsponsored Head Start classrooms showed no large differences; and (3) when the sponsored sets of classrooms were compared among themselves, some differences in performance emerged on several of the cognitive tests the children were given. In other words, certain types of curricula seemed to enhance different kinds of cognitive development.

Obviously, as we have implied, these conclusions are suggestive at best because of the unequal distributions of important variables across the sponsors. That is, because important variables were present in an unsystematic way, the researchers could not claim a high degree of validity or consequent applicability of the conclusions they drew. This example demonstrates that researchers can increase confidence in the findings obtained with planned variation designs when they can guarantee that important variables are equally distributed among the test groups, and if the dependent variables are measured on a number of occasions both before and after exposure to an independent variable.

Panels and Time-Series Designs

Some quasi-experiments are extended over time to allow researchers to examine changes in the dependent variable. Time poses a dilemma for social scientists for the following reasons. First and foremost, humans and the social environment are not static entities. They change in response to internal processes and external events, few of which can be willfully controlled by the researcher. Therefore, the variables the scientist wishes to investigate may be modified over time. This tendency may undermine the appropriateness or accuracy of the researcher's procedures and the validity of his or her conclusions. Methodologically, then, as time cannot be controlled in real life, methods must be adopted to control for its effects on the empirical data. We shall discuss two major designs that incorporate time: *panels* and *time-series designs.*

PANELS. A more rigorous solution to the time dilemma in cross-sectional studies and correlational designs is the **panel,** in which the same sample is examined at two or more time intervals. Panel studies allow researchers to approximate the before–after condition of experimental designs more closely by studying a group at two or more points in time. One of the most well known panel studies is the Michigan Panel Study of Income Dynamics (PSID).[6] The PSID began in 1968 with a sample of approximately 4,800 families drawn from the U.S. noninstitutional population. Since 1968, families have been interviewed annually on a wide variety of socioeconomic indicators. The PSID allows investigators to examine

---

6. John Fitzgerald, Peter Gottschalk, and Robert Moffitt, "An Analysis of Sample Attrition in Panel Data," *Journal of Human Resources,* 33 (1998): 251–299.

the dynamic aspect of economic behavior and to assess relationships between characteristics such as education, family dynamics, and socioeconomic behavior. The main advantage of the PSID as well as other panel designs is that it enables researchers to determine the direction of causation. That is, by comparing measures taken among the same respondents over time, it is possible to ascertain whether economic behavior is a cause or a result of sociodemographic characteristics. By comparing economic and sociodemographic measures of the same respondents over time, researchers could determine the order of influence.

The main problem with panels is obtaining an initial representative sample of respondents who are willing to be interviewed at set intervals over an extended period. Moreover, even if a researcher succeeds in obtaining their commitment, some respondents usually drop out, either because they refuse to continue to cooperate or because difficulties arise in tracing those who move or change jobs. A serious consequence of this decline in participation is that the researcher cannot determine if these respondents changed in a way different from those who remained in the study. This uncertainty may affect the representativeness and validity of the findings. Another problem occurring when investigators repeatedly interview the same group is *panel conditioning*—the risk that repeated measurements may sensitize the respondents to give a given set of answers. For example, members of a panel may try to appear consistent in the views they express on consecutive occasions. In such cases, the panel may become atypical of the population it was selected to represent. One possible safeguard to panel conditioning is to give members of a panel only a limited panel life (i.e., participation period) and then to replace them with persons taken randomly from a reserve list of the same general population.[7]

TIME-SERIES DESIGNS.   In cases when no comparison or control group is available for assessing cause-and-effect relations, investigators can use **time-series designs**—research designs in which pretest and posttest measures are available on a number of occasions before and after the activation of an independent variable. Usually, the investigator attempts to obtain at least three sets of measures before and three sets after the introduction of the independent variable. A typical time-series design can be represented as follows:

$$O_1 \quad O_2 \quad O_3 \quad X \quad O_4 \quad O_5 \quad O_6$$

By employing a time-series design, researchers can separate reactive measurement effects (see Chapter 5) from the effects of an independent variable. A time-series design also enables the researcher to see whether an independent variable has an effect over and above the reactive effects. If the reactive effect shows itself at O_3, this measure can be compared with O_4. An increase at O_4 above the increase at O_3 can be attributed to the independent variable. Researchers can also estimate whether the changes caused by introducing the independent variable are greater than those due to the passage of time, thus guarding against the maturation source of invalidity.

A classic illustration of the advantages as well as the problems involved with time-series designs is Campbell's evaluation study of the Connecticut crackdown on speeding following a record number of traffic fatalities in 1955.[8] At the end of 1956, a total of 284 traffic deaths were registered in Connecticut, compared with 324 the year before, a reduction of 12.3 percent. The results are displayed graphically in Figure 6.5, which intentionally magnifies the differences. Referring to these data, the authorities concluded that "the pro-

---

7. For a detailed analysis of the advantages and disadvantages of panels, see Robert F. Boruch and Robert W. Pearson, "Assessing the Quality of Longitudinal Surveys," *Evaluation Review*, 12 (1988): 3–58.

8. Donald T. Campbell, "Reforms as Experiments," *American Psychologist*, 24 (1969): 409–429.

Advantages and Disadvantages of Research Designs Used in the Social Sciences

EXPERIMENTAL DESIGNS

Advantages

+ Experiments enable researchers to exert a great deal of control over extrinsic and intrinsic variables, strengthening the validity of causal inferences (internal validity).

+ Experiments enable researchers to control the introduction of the independent variable so they may determine the direction of causation.

Disadvantages

+ External validity is weak because experimental designs do not allow researchers to replicate real-life social situations.

+ Researchers must often rely on volunteer or self-selected subjects for their samples. Therefore, the sample may not be representative of the population of interest, preventing researchers from generalizing to the population and limiting the scope of their findings.

CROSS-SECTIONAL AND QUASI-EXPERIMENTAL DESIGNS

Advantages

+ They allow researchers to carry out studies in natural, real-life settings using probability samples, thus increasing the external validity of their studies.

+ They do not require the random assignment of individual cases to comparison groups. While this limits the internal validity of studies employing these designs, it does enable researchers to study situations where the assignment of individuals to either a control or an experimental group might be unethical or impossible.

Disadvantages

+ The lack of adequate control over rival explanations makes it difficult for researchers to make unambiguous inferences.

+ Because researchers often cannot manipulate the independent variable, the direction of causation must be logically or theoretically inferred.

PREEXPERIMENTAL DESIGNS

Advantages

+ They may allow researchers to gather information when no other research design can be applied, or may allow researchers to show that further, more valid, research would be valuable.

Disadvantages

+ They are very weak on both internal and external validity and do not allow researchers to make causal inferences.

that are weak on internal validity, such as the one-shot case study, are, by definition, also weak on external validity because without internal validity, no generalizations can be made.

Perhaps the most serious threat to the internal validity of research designs is the lack of adequate control of extrinsic and intrinsic factors. In order for the results of a study to be generalizable, the design must allow researchers to study a sample that accurately represents the population in a real social setting or situation. External validity is sometimes increased by increasing the heterogeneity of the sample and of the experimental situation. However, as researchers increase realism and heterogeneity, they may be forced to sacrifice control.

This is the point where we can compare the weaknesses and advantages of the various designs. Whereas experiments are strong on control and weak on representation, quasi-experiments and cross-sectional designs are strong on representation but weak on control. Experiments have several advantages. First and foremost, they enable scientists to make valid causal inferences by exerting a great deal of control—particularly through randomization—over extrinsic and intrinsic variables. The second advantage is that experiments allow researchers to control the introduction of the independent variable, thus permitting them to determine the direction of causation. The major shortcomings of quasi-experiments, cross-sectional designs, and especially preexperiments are that they do not provide these advantages. Lack of adequate control over rival explanations and difficulties in manipulating the independent variable prevent the researcher from drawing unambiguous inferences.

However, although the experiment is accepted as the scientific method par excellence, it too has several shortcomings. The most frequent criticism of experiments, especially laboratory experiments, is that they are artificial and removed from real-life situations. Critics maintain, as we shall see in Chapter 9, that reality cannot be replicated in experimental settings and, hence, that important issues cannot be analyzed there. A second problem concerns the sample design. In experimental designs, it is difficult to represent a specified population. Many experiments include volunteers or have an incidental sample at best. Nonrepresentative samples prevent the investigator from generalizing to populations of interest and limit the scope of the findings. Conversely, most cross-sectional designs are carried out in natural settings and permit the employment of probability samples. This allows scientists to make statistical inferences to broader populations and permits them to generalize their findings to real-life situations.

Because no design can solve the problems of control and representation simultaneously, the investigator faces a difficult choice. Although in practice the nature of the study dictates this choice, scientists generally accept the rule that the attainment of internal validity is more crucial than the attainment of external validity. Still, experiments, cross-sectional studies, and quasi-experiments can be improved. Scientists using experiments can increase external validity by clearly defining the population to be studied and by drawing sampling units from this population following a probability sample design. Scientists using cross-sectional studies and quasi-experiments can greatly improve internal validity by including auxiliary information as a control against rival hypotheses. Moreover, by using more sophisticated statistical techniques such as path or causal analysis, researchers using cross-sectional studies and quasi-experiments can improve the quality of causal inferences.

SUMMARY

1. Randomization, together with careful experimental control, gives scientific research strength and persuasiveness that cannot ordinarily be obtained by other means. However, property—disposition relations are not readily amenable to experimenta-

tion, and social, political, and ethical considerations may discourage or prevent the use of experimental designs with stimulus–response relations.

2. Cross-sectional designs, most predominant in survey research, are used to examine relations between properties and dispositions and attempt to approximate the posttest-only control group design by using statistical data analysis techniques.

3. Quasi-experimental designs are similar to cross-sectional designs in that they are weaker on internal validity than experimental designs and depend on statistical data analysis techniques as a method of control. They are superior to cross-sectional designs, however, because they usually involve the study of more than one sample, often over an extended period of time. Contrasted-groups designs and planned variation designs are quasi-experiments; panel and time-series designs are quasi-experiments that are extended over time.

4. Traditionally, preexperimental research designs, such as the one-shot case study, were used when experimentation was impossible. Preexperiments are the weakest research designs since researchers cannot control for most of the sources of internal and external validity.

KEY TERMS FOR REVIEW ●

combined designs (p. 129)
contrasted groups (p. 119)
control-series design (p. 128)
cross-sectional design (p. 116)
extended time-series design (p. 125)
one-shot case study (p. 131)

panel (p. 123)
planned variation (p. 122)
property–disposition relationship
(p. 115)
stimulus–response relationship (p. 115)
time-series design (p. 125)

STUDY QUESTIONS ●

1. Describe the kinds of relationships that lend themselves to study with experimental or quasi-experimental designs. Provide an example of each kind.

2. Develop a quasi-experimental design to study the effect of sex education programs on teenage pregnancy rates. Be sure to explain your logic and the advantages and disadvantages of your research design.

3. Differentiate among combined designs, cross-sectional designs, and panel designs in terms of their strengths and weaknesses.

4. Discuss the limitations of preexperimental designs.

5. Discuss why designs with high internal validity tend to have low external validity.

ADDITIONAL READINGS ●

Bijleveld, Catrien C. J. H., and Leo Van Der Kamp. *Longitudinal Data Analysis.* Newbury Park, CA: Sage, 1998.

Black, Thomas. *Doing Quantitative Research in the Social Sciences.* Newbury Park, CA: Sage, 1999.

Cook, Thomas D., and Donald T. Campbell. *Quasi-Experimentation.* Skokie, IL: Rand McNally, 1979.

Hedrick, Terry E., Leonard Bickman, and Debra J. Rog. *Applied Research Design: A Practical Guide.* Newbury Park, CA: Sage, 1993.

Nachmias, David. *Public Policy Evaluation: A Systematic Approach,* 5th ed. Newbury Park, CA: Sage, 1993.

Figure 7.2

Assignment in Application of a Rule

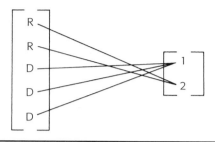

places. However, this does not undermine the significance of measurement in the research process—without measurement, we would have no science of social behavior.

Structure of Measurement

Measurement, then, is the assignment of numerals or numbers to objects, events, or variables according to rules. Rules are the most significant component of the measurement process because they determine the quality of the measures taken. For measurement to be meaningful, it must have an empirical basis. The function of rules is to tie the measurement process to an empirical basis, to reality. For example, suppose you are measuring the softness of three objects. Your rule for measuring softness states that the softer the object, the higher the number assigned to that object. Thus, if object A can scratch B but not vice versa, then B is softer than A; consequently, A will be assigned the number 1, and B the number 2. Similarly, if A can scratch B and B can scratch C, then A can probably scratch C. You would then deduce that object C is softer than objects A and B; hence, object C is assigned the number 3. As these are observable conditions, you can assign numbers to indicate the degree of softness that each object holds after performing a few scratch tests. In this case, the measurement procedure and the number system are isomorphic to reality; hence, the rule defining the measurement procedure is appropriate and valid. As such, the measurement procedure can be incorporated into the research process.

Isomorphism means "similarity or identity of structure." In determining whether a measurement procedure is isomorphic, the crucial question pertains to how similar in structure the numerical system used is to the structure of the concepts being measured. In the natural sciences, the problem of isomorphism is often of secondary concern because the relation between the concepts being observed and the numbers assigned to the observations is quite direct. In contrast, the social scientist must always be alert to the fact that this relation is usually indirect and not clear-cut:

> In order for him to be able to make certain operations with numbers that have been assigned to observations, the structure of his method of mapping numbers to observations must be isomorphic to some numerical structure which includes these operations.[3]

3. Sidney N. Siegel, *Nonparametric Statistics for the Behavioral Sciences* (New York: McGraw-Hill, 1988), p. 22.

When we say that two systems are isomorphic, we mean that they have similar structures and that the relations among their internal elements, or the operations in which they can be used, are also similar. Thus, when a researcher assigns numbers to objects or systems and then manipulates these numbers by, say, adding them, he or she is implying that the structure of this system of measurement is isomorphic to the relationships within, or between, the phenomena under study. Suppose we wanted to measure the success of affirmative action policies. We might want to follow the percentage of Hispanic women hired for, let us say, top managerial positions, over the years since passage of the respective laws and regulations, and compare that percentage to the number of Hispanic women college graduates majoring in business administration. This measure would be isomorphic to the phenomenon we are investigating—that is, obedience to affirmative action laws—if our theory or hypothesis suggested that the mere counting of the number of Hispanic women CEOs represented the intent of the law. We would probably not count the number of Hispanic women CEOs if we wanted to measure attitudes toward affirmative action, because a simple numerical measurement procedure is not isomorphic to the phenomenon of having attitudes.

Frequently, social scientists measure **indicators** of concepts rather than the concepts themselves. Concepts such as democracy, motivation, hostility, and power are complex ideas that cannot be observed directly; researchers must infer their presence by measuring the empirical, observable behaviors that indicate the extent of their presence. These behaviors are called indicators and represent operational definitions of the concept. Thus, if elections are held regularly in a country, a political scientist may suggest that holding elections is one indicator that the country has a democratic political system. If someone achieves a certain score on a motivation test (the operational definition), a psychologist may infer something about this person's level of motivation. In these examples, some identifiable behavior, which can be observed and measured, is used as an indicator of a concept.

Often, researchers must develop multiple indicators to represent the same abstract concept. Because the important concepts in the social sciences relate to phenomena that are complicated and multifaceted, the use of multiple indicators, each reflecting a distinctive aspect of the concept involved, is required. To return to democracy, a democratic political system entails much more than elections: The fairness of those elections, the degree of competition between parties, the freedom of the press, the freedom to organize, and the rights of minorities are other essential attributes of democracy. Consequently, the regularity of elections is, by itself, insufficient as an indicator of the degree of democracy found in a society. Each of the other attributes mentioned serves as an additional indicator of the total phenomenon and each attribute can be measured.

Indicators, however, cannot be selected arbitrarily. The choice of indicators should be grounded in both theory and empirical observation. The indicators used to measure democracy in the previous example derive from theories of democracy and the structure of political systems as well as observations of the actual behavior of existing political systems. Although the procedure for measuring directly observable concepts is identical to the one for measuring indicators of concepts, the rules for measuring indicators are more difficult to formulate because the process calls for a greater degree of inference about the connection between the concept and the indicators. The validity of the inferences made depends, in turn, on the theory that guides the research and the methodology used to conduct the research.

In sum, indicators are specified by operational definitions; after researchers observe the indicators, they assign numerals or numbers representing the extent to which the indicators are present in the observed behavior and subsequently perform quantitative analyses using those values. As in the case of measuring variables, the mathematical structure of the instrument measuring indicators must also be isomorphic.

LEVELS OF MEASUREMENT   ●

Because of the requirement of isomorphism between the measuring instruments and the empirical properties (or indicators) measured, scientists can distinguish different ways of measuring or, in technical terminology, distinct levels of measurement, according to the properties of the instrument. (The term *scales* is sometimes used instead of *levels of measurement*. A scale may be thought of as a tool for measuring: a speedometer is a scale, as is a ruler or a questionnaire.) The specific mathematical and statistical operations that a researcher can perform on a given set of numbers are related to the level of measurement. We will discuss the four principal levels of measurement—nominal, ordinal, interval, and ratio—and the mathematical operations we can perform at each level.

Nominal Level

The lowest level of measurement is the **nominal level.** At this level, numbers or other symbols are used to classify objects or events into categories that are names, classes of qualitative characteristics. As a rule, when a set of objects or events can be classified into categories that are *exhaustive* (that is, they include all cases of that type) and *mutually exclusive* (that is, no case can be classified as belonging to more than one category), a nominal level of measurement is attained. A different symbol is then used to represent each category. Gender, nationality, ethnicity, religion, marital status, place of residence (e.g., urban or rural), and party identification are all examples of nominal variables. Thus, when we assign the symbols 1 and 2 to the male and female members of a population, respectively, we are only saying that it is possible to classify a given population into males and females. The same population can be classified by religion: Christians might be represented by the numeral 6, Jews by 7, and Muslims by 8. In the first case, the population was classified into two categories; in the second, into three. At the nominal level, scientists can classify objects by utilizing any set of symbols. They can also change the symbols without altering any information, if they do so consistently and completely.

Mathematically, the basic property of the nominal level of measurement is that the characteristics of the cases found in any one category are assumed to be identical for all the cases covered by that category, and that there is no mathematical relationship between the categories. For example, all the residents of Canada and the United States are considered to be members of the nominal category "residents of the North American continent," regardless of their citizenship. Similarly, all the citizens of the 50 states belong to the same nominal category "U.S. citizens" for purposes of federal tax collection; their specific address determines whether they can be included in other nominal categories, such as state or city residents, for other tax rolls. Accordingly, at the nominal level, it is permissible to use only those mathematical manipulations or statistics that remain unchanged by such assignment of cases to different categories. The statistics used include frequency distributions, measures of qualitative variation, and appropriate measures of covariation, as discussed in Chapters 15 and 16.

Ordinal Level

Many of the variables studied by social scientists are not only classifiable, they also exhibit some kind of relation. Typical relations are "higher," "greater," "more desired," "more difficult," and so on. Such relations may be designated by the symbol >, which means "greater than." In reference to particular properties, > may be used to designate "is higher than," "is greater than," "is more desired than," and so forth (the symbol < means the opposite, i.e., "less than," etc.). For instance, consider the hypothesis that France is more democratic than Russia but less so than England. This can be expressed as a ranking of the degree of the variable democracy found in each country: France > Russia, France < England. In general, if the "greater than" (or "less than") relation covers all the observations that can be compared in this way (e.g., from "the most" to "the least," otherwise known as a complete ranking of objects), we have an example of the **ordinal level** of measurement. Ordinal measurement also requires that the equivalence relation holds for all the cases in the same rank, whereas the > relation holds between any pair of ranks.

The relationships between the ranks of the ordinal level of measurement display certain logical properties. These properties are important to remember when constructing hypotheses and arriving at conclusions with respect to ordinal variables. The > relation is irreflexive, asymmetrical, and transitive. Irreflexivity means that for any a, it is not true that $a > a$. Asymmetry means that if $a > b$, then $b \not> a$. Transitivity means that if $a > b$ and $b > c$, then $a > c$. In other words, if a variable such as "conservatism" is measured on the ordinal level, no individual classified as belonging to type A conservatism is more (or less) conservative than anyone else belonging to the same group; if the members of group A conservatism are more conservative that the members of group B conservatism, the opposite cannot be true (i.e., members of group B cannot be more conservative than members of group A); and we can infer that if a person in group A is more conservative than a person in group B, and if group B is more conservative than group C, then a person in group A is more conservative than a person in group C. Thus, the > relation (or, alternatively, the < relation) is maintained with regard to all the individuals in each of the three groups.

As an example of measurement at the ordinal level, consider the measurement of attitudes. Public opinion survey researchers usually measure attitudes by means of a series of questions; the possible answers to those questions are ranked in ascending or descending order. For instance, one of the statements used to measure political alienation is "People like me have a lot of influence on government decisions." A respondent is then asked to mark the number representing his or her degree of agreement (or disagreement) with this statement. Table 7.2 illustrates how the possible answers are ranked with their corresponding numbers. Several questions relating to the same attitude are often presented to the respondent; the researcher can then rank each respondent on the variable "alienation" by adding the numerical values (called "scores") of all the responses given by that respondent to all the statements.

Table 7.2

Ordinal Ranking Scale

Rank	Value
1	Agree strongly
2	Agree
3	Disagree
4	Disagree strongly

cate not only real differences but also *artifact differences,* variations produced by the measurement procedure itself. Those differences in scores that are due to anything other than real differences are termed **measurement errors.**

There are several common sources of measurement errors. First, the scores obtained may not be related to the attribute the researcher intended to measure but to another associated attribute. For example, in order to interpret and answer a question measuring moral development, respondents may require a certain level of intelligence and social awareness. The responses to this question will, in effect, reflect real differences in moral development, but they may also reveal the effect of differences in intelligence and social awareness. The influence of associated attributes leads to measurement error. Second, measurement errors may result from temporary differences in conditions, such as health or mood, which may affect a person's responses or behavior. Third, differences in the setting in which the measure is used can contribute to measurement errors. To illustrate, the age, race, and gender of interviewers influence the answers given by survey respondents. Fourth, differences in the administration of the measuring instrument (e.g., poor lighting, noise, tired interviewers) can lead to measurement errors. Fifth, measurement errors also result from differences in processing (e.g., different coders can introduce inconsistencies when coding similar answers to a question). The last major source of distortion occurs when different people interpret the measuring instrument in different ways.

The errors that arise from these sources can be either systematic or random errors. *Systematic errors* occur whenever the measuring instrument is used, and they appear consistently, with all cases and studies. They consistently introduce a degree of invalidity to the findings. *Random errors,* by contrast, affect each instance of the measuring instrument's use in a different way. The seriousness of the issues of validity and reliability prompted the development of techniques for reducing measurement errors.

VALIDITY ●

Validity is concerned with the question "Am I measuring what I intend to measure?" Measurement in the social sciences is, with very few exceptions, indirect. Under such circumstances, researchers are never completely certain that they are measuring the variable for which they designed their measurement procedure. The problem of the validity of the measurement is an outgrowth of the nature of the variables studied. For example, does voter turnout truly measure political alienation? If a respondent agrees with the statement "This world is run by a few people in power, and there is not much the little guy can do about it," is his or her response a genuine indicator of the presence of the variable "alienation"? Again, is a change in the incidence of venereal disease a result of changing morals or a change in the general health of the population? To answer such questions, the researcher must provide supporting evidence that a measuring instrument does, in fact, measure the variable that it appears to be measuring. The validity of measurement can, as a result, influence the validity of the conclusions drawn after testing hypotheses.

This brings us to the three basic types of validity, each of which is concerned with a different aspect of measurement: content validity, empirical validity, and construct validity. Each type of validity relates to a distinctive type of evidence and has a unique value under specific conditions.

Content Validity

Content validity means that the measurement instrument covers all the attributes of the concept you are trying to measure—that nothing relevant to the phenomenon under investigation is left out. There are two common types of content validity: face validity and sampling validity.

Face validity rests on the investigator's subjective evaluation of the appropriateness of the instrument for measuring the concept rather than whether the instrument measures what the researcher wishes to measure. For example, suppose an investigator wants to test the effects of the variable "sexual harassment" on the mental and physical health of victims of this type of behavior.[5] Testing hypotheses regarding the relation of sexual harassment to health requires a measuring instrument, such as a questionnaire, that can accurately describe not only behaviors considered harassing but also the severity of that harassment. These questions might refer to behaviors such as sexual comments about a person's body made by supervisors or co-workers and the assignment of unpleasant tasks on the basis of a person's sex. After constructing the questionnaire, the researcher is required to assess the face validity of the questions, that is, to determine that they capture the variable of sexual harassment accurately. If they do not, the ranking of the behaviors will not be meaningful. In order to do this, the questions can be compared to other questionnaires on the subject. In addition, a number of specialists ("judges") in the field might be consulted. If there is agreement among the judges that the questions capture all the elements of the phenomenon, the researcher can be reasonably sure that the questionnaire has face validity, that it indeed measures "sexual harassment." If the judges disagree, however, their lack of consensus would make it impossible to claim face validity for a measuring instrument. This means that the researcher cannot use the instrument with confidence.

The main problem with face validity is that there are no precise, replicable procedures for evaluating this type of content validity. As it is extremely difficult to repeat the evaluation procedure precisely, the researcher has to rely entirely on subjective judgments. For this reason, the choice of judges and other source questions is critical for the conduct of the research and the significance of the findings.

The primary concern of **sampling validity,** on the other hand, is whether a given population (i.e., the total set of cases belonging to a category representing the variable in the real world) is adequately sampled by the measuring instrument in question. In other words, do the statements, questions, or indicators that comprise the measuring instrument adequately represent the property being measured? The underlying assumption of sampling validity is that every variable has a content population consisting of a large number of items that can be expressed as statements, questions, or indicators; a highly valid instrument is composed of a representative sample of these items. In practice, problems arise when defining a content population for this is a theoretical, not an empirical, issue. In practice, sampling problems may impair the effectiveness of sampling validity as a test of an instrument's overall validity. However, ascertaining sampling validity serves an important function: It calls for familiarity with all the items describing the content population. Hence, sampling validity is especially useful in exploratory research, when investigators attempt to construct instruments and employ them for the first time.

Empirical Validity

Empirical validity is concerned with the relationship between a measuring instrument and the measured outcomes. Scientists assume that if a measuring instrument is valid, the results produced by applying the instrument and the relationships existing among the variables measured in the real world should be quite similar. For example, an educa-

---

5. Maureen Murdoch and Paul G. McGovern, "Measuring Sexual Harassment: Development and Validation of the Sexual Harassment Inventory," *Violence and Victims,* 13(3) (1998): 203–215.

tor might want to know if the scores obtained by the IQ test he or she is using really reflect the intelligence of the person assessed. In order to do so, evidence is gathered to support the existence of a relation between the test results and the variable of intelligence through the use of measures of correlation appropriate to the IQ test's level of measurement. (A correlation coefficient is an index of how much two measures or variables are related; details can be found in Chapter 16.) Of the various tests designed to evaluate the empirical validity of measuring instruments, predictive validity is the most widely used. For this reason, we shall discuss it at some length.

Researchers estimate **predictive validity** by assessing the results they expect to obtain against some other, external measure, referred to as an *external criterion* (or simply *criterion*), and by comparing their measuring instrument's outcomes with outcomes obtained by other measuring instruments with respect to this criterion. In other words, predictive validity is the degree of correlation, known as the correlation coefficient, between the results of a given measurement and an external criterion. For example, an investigator can validate an intelligence test by first obtaining the test scores of a group of college students and then obtaining the grade-point averages that these students achieved in their first year of college (the criterion). The researcher then computes a correlation coefficient between the two sets of measurements. The resulting correlation coefficient is called the predictive *validity coefficient.* Other criteria that could be used to validate intelligence tests are the various performance ratings used by educators and psychologists.

Figure 7.3 illustrates the process by which the predictive validity of an instrument is assessed. A variable (*V*) is measured by a certain measuring instrument (*I*). To assess the predictive validity of the instrument, the researcher employs a valid external criterion (*C*). The results obtained by *I* are correlated with the results obtained by *C*. The size of the validity coefficient (r_{IC}) indicates the predictive validity of the instrument.

In order to apply the test of predictive validity, researchers need to consider two general issues. One concerns the use of a measuring instrument rather than the criterion as a means of validation; for example, most colleges compare SAT scores (the measuring instrument) to past grade averages (the criterion) to predict the future achievement of potential students. The other issue relates to the validity of the criterion.

Regarding the first issue, a problem may arise if the criterion is too difficult or expensive to use. For instance, testing the quality of every computer board that comes off the assembly line is very expensive; therefore, only a sample is tested. In other cases, investigators may have to make initial measurements of a variable before deciding upon and then applying a specific criterion. Scholastic ability is such a variable—it must first be measured before being selected as a criterion for success in a course of study.

Figure 7.3

Assessing Predictive Validity

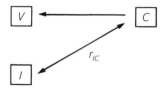

As far as the second issue is concerned, two common methods are used to establish the validity of the criterion. One method relies on the agreement among researchers that a certain criterion is valid for evaluating a measuring instrument. This agreement is subject to tests of face validity and sampling validity. A somewhat different method involves determining the percentage of individuals (or other units of analysis) who would be classified correctly by the instrument according to their known characteristics and expressing the relationship between the instrument's measured outcomes and the criterion in terms of a percentage.[6]

Suppose that a researcher needs to evaluate the validity of an instrument designed to measure political conservatism. If there are theoretically sound reasons for arguing that lower-class people are more conservative than middle-class people, the researcher can compare membership in the two classes as counted by the measuring instrument as a check of predictive validity. In this case, social class serves as an indirect criterion for the predictive validity of the instrument. If, however, the empirical findings reveal that lower-class persons are as conservative as middle-class persons, the measurement instrument lacks predictive validity. Conversely, a relatively strong relation between social class and conservatism would validate the instrument. However, a strong relation is a necessary but not a sufficient condition to establish the predictive validity of an instrument because the indirect criterion (social class) may also be related to variables other than political conservatism (e.g., education). That is, the instrument might be measuring variables other than political conservatism per se. An indirect criterion, then, is more useful for revealing that an instrument is not valid than it is for validating it.

Construct Validity

For the findings of measurement to be meaningful in more than a purely descriptive sense, the instrument must display **construct validity.** Researchers establish construct validity by relating a measuring instrument to the general theoretical framework within which they conduct their studies in order to determine whether the instrument is logically and empirically tied to the concepts and theoretical assumptions they are employing. Lee J. Cronbach, an early proponent of construct validity, observed that "whenever a tester asks what a score means psychologically or what causes a person to get a certain test score, he is asking what concepts may properly be used to interpret the test performance." [7] Theoretical expectations about the variable being measured lead the investigator to postulate various kinds and degrees of relationships between the particular variable and other specified variables. To demonstrate the construct validity of a measuring instrument, an investigator has to show that these relationships can be recognized and measured by their instrument. We shall illustrate the utility of construct validity through Milton Rokeach's well-known research on dogmatism.[8]

On the basis of theoretical reasoning, Rokeach constructed a dogmatism questionnaire. This instrument consisted of questions assumed to measure close-mindedness, a personality trait associated with strict adherence to any belief system or ideology, regardless of its content. Rokeach argued that ideological orientations are related to personality, thought processes, and behavior. Consequently, he predicted, among other things, that dogmatism is related to being strongly opinionated. Rokeach conducted a number of

---

6. C. G. Helmstadter, *Research Concepts in Human Behavior* (Englewood Cliffs, NJ: Prentice-Hall, 1970).

7. Lee J. Cronbach, *Essentials of Psychological Testing*, 4th ed. (New York: Harper & Row, 1984), p. 121.

8. Milton Rokeach, *The Open and the Closed Mind* (New York: Basic Books, 1960).

questions for one set and the even-numbered questions for the other. Each of the two sets of questions is treated as a separate questionnaire and scored accordingly. The results of the two sets are then correlated, with the correlation coefficient taken as an estimate of reliability. To adjust the correlation coefficient obtained between the two halves, the following formula, known as the Spearman–Brown prophecy formula, may be applied:

$$r_{xx'} = \frac{2r_{oe}}{1 + r_{oe}} \qquad (7.4)$$

where $r_{xx'}$ = the reliability of the original test

r_{oe} = the reliability coefficient obtained by correlating the scores of the odd statements with the scores of the even statements

This correction assumes that an instrument that is $2n$ questions long will be more reliable than an instrument that is n questions long. Because the length of the instrument has been halved by dividing it according to its odd- and even-numbered items, and each part has been scored separately, the complete instrument will have a higher reliability than either half could obtain had it been applied alone.

Cronbach, Rajaratnam, and Glesser introduced a revision to the traditional concept of reliability.[14] They argue that the chief concern of reliability theory is to answer the question "To what universe of potential measurements do we wish to generalize?" Thus, instead of reliability, they introduced the idea of generalizability. **Generalizability** implies that what scientists really want to know about is to what extent, and with respect to what properties, one set of measurements is like another sets of measurements that researchers might have taken from a given universe of potential measurements. The same applies to differences among the sets of measurements that might be selected from that universe of potential measurements. When scientists ask questions about the likeness or difference of potential measurements, they are asking about the limits of their ability to generalize based on the results of any one set of measurements. Whether we consider a particular relation among measurements to be evidence of reliability or generalizability depends on how we choose to define the likeness and difference of conditions and measures. The particular way that researchers construct lists of items or properties that are the same or different in each set of measurements depends, of course, on the research problem.[15]

SUMMARY   ●

1. Measurement is the assignment of numerals to variables, properties, or events according to rules. The most significant concept in this definition is "rules." The function of a rule is to tie the measurement procedure to reality, that is, to establish isomorphism between a certain numerical structure and the structure of the

14. Lee J. Cronbach, Nageswars Rajaratnam, and Goldine C. Glesser, "A Theory of Generalizability: A Liberalization of Reliability Theory," *British Journal of Statistical Psychology*, 16 (1963): 137–163.

15. For the statistical expression of the generalizability index, see ibid., and Goldine C. Glesser, Lee J. Cronbach, and Nageswars Rajaratnam, "Generalizability of Scores Influenced by Multiple Scores of Variance," *Psychometrika*, 30 (1965): 395–418.

variables being measured. If they can establish isomorphism, researchers can perform quantitative analyses with the numerals that stand for the properties.

2. Isomorphism between numerical systems and empirical properties enables the researcher to distinguish among four levels of measurement: nominal, ordinal, interval, and ratio. In general, the level of measurement determines which quantitative analyses can be performed on a given set of numbers.

3. Measurement procedures are highly sensitive to data transformation and measurement error. Properties that can be measured at a higher level of precision can also be measured at a lower level, but not vice versa. That is, some data can be transformed from the ratio level to the nominal level, but not all data can be transformed from the nominal to the ratio level.

4. Measurement error relates to the accuracy and consequent consistency of the measuring instrument itself. The source of the error may lie in a misunderstanding of what is actually being measured (e.g., intelligence rather than attitudes) or in the measure's sensitivity to the measurement setting (e.g., a respondent's ability to concentrate in a noisy testing room). In any case, measurement error reflects problems of measurement, not real differences in the variable being measured.

5. The concepts of validity and reliability are inseparable from measurement. They underlie the sources of measurement error. Validity is concerned with the question of whether researchers are measuring what they think they are measuring. Traditionally, three basic types of validity have been distinguished, each of which relates to a different aspect of the measurement situation: content validity, empirical validity, and construct validity. To validate a certain measuring instrument, the researcher must look for information appropriate to each of these three types of validity.

6. Reliability indicates the extent to which a measure contains variable errors. Operationally, it is assumed that any measure consists of a true component and an error component; the proportion of the amount of variation in the true component to the total variation indicates the measure's reliability. Researchers estimate reliability by one or more of the following methods: test–retest, parallel-forms, and split-half. The notion of generalizability implies that the main concern of reliability is with the extent to which a set of measurements is similar to other sets of measurements that might have been drawn from a given universe of potential measurements.

KEY TERMS FOR REVIEW ●

construct validity (p. 152)
content validity (p. 149)
empirical validity (p. 150)
face validity (p. 150)
generalizability (p. 157)
indicator (p. 142)
interval level (p. 146)
isomorphism (p. 141)
known-groups technique (p. 153)
measurement (p. 138)
measurement errors (p. 149)

nominal level (p. 143)
ordinal level (p. 144)
parallel-forms technique (p. 156)
predictive validity (p. 151)
ratio level (p. 147)
reliability (p. 154)
reliability measure (p. 155)
sampling validity (p. 150)
split-half method (p. 156)
test–retest method (p. 155)
validity (p. 149)

STUDY QUESTIONS

1. Define measurement and explain why measurement is important to scientific research.
2. What are the various levels of measurement? Why are the differences between the levels of measurement important? Give an example of data that can be transformed from one level to another, and another example of data that cannot be so transformed.
3. Define the concept "validity" and explain how to distinguish among the three major types of validity. Give concrete examples of when and how each type of validity is used.
4. Define the concept "reliability" and discuss the ways of assessing it.
5. How is validity related to reliability? Can you give an example?

SPSS PROBLEMS

1. Determine the level of measurement for each of these variables from the **gss96worth** file:
   a. "abhealth"
   b. "age"
   c. "aidold"
   d. "childs"
   e. "fear"
   f. "hrs 1"
   g. "income"
2. For each of the variables in Problem 1 that you classified as interval or ratio, indicate whether it is discrete or continuous.
3. For each of the following variables from the **gss96worth** data file find the measurement used in the GSS survey (Hint: you can examine the question for each variable either by clicking on **Utilities** and **Variables** or on **Utilities** and **File Info**). For each variable suggest procedures to evaluate its content validity and empirical validity.
   a. "health"
   b. "govtpow"
   c. "income91"
   d. "libath"
   e. "marital"

ADDITIONAL READINGS

Achen, Christopher H. "Toward Theories of Data: The State of Political Methodology." In *Political Science: The State of the Discipline*, rev. ed., ed. Ada Finifter. Washington, DC: American Political Science Association, 1993.

Blalock, Hubert M., Jr. *Conceptualization and Measurement in the Social Sciences.* Newbury Park, CA: Sage, 1982.

Blalock, Hubert M., Jr. *Causal Models in the Social Sciences*, 2d ed. Hawthorne, NY: Aldine de Gruyter, 1985.

Bohrnstedt, George W., and David Knoke. *Statistics for Social Data Analysis*, 2d ed. Itasca, IL: F. E. Peacock, 1991.

Bohrnstedt, George W., and David Knoke. *Strategies for Social Data Collection*, 3d ed. Itasca, IL: F. E. Peacock, no date indicated.

Judd, Charles M., Eliot D. Smith, and Louise H. Kidder. *Research Methods in Social Relations*, 6th ed. Forth Worth, TX: Harcourt Brace, 1991.

Schwartz, Norbert, Barbel Knauper, Hans-J. Hippler, Elisabeth Noelle-Neumann, and Leslie Clark. "Rating Scales: Numeric Values May Change the Meaning of Scale Labels." *Public Opinion Quarterly*, Winter (1991): 570–582.

Shively, W. Phillips. *The Craft of Political Research*, 4th ed. Paramus, NJ: Prentice-Hall, 1998.

SAMPLING AND SAMPLE DESIGNS

"Trial heat" polls for predicting the outcomes of elections before the official voting date have been popular for some time. During the 1992 presidential campaign, these polls greatly overestimated the margin of Bill Clinton's victory while they greatly underestimated Ross Perot's strength as a candidate. What do these inaccurate estimates say about polling and the sampling procedures used? By investigating how these trial heat polls were conducted, Richard Lau has come to some important methodological conclusions about polling in general.[1] According to Lau, variations in results, as well as errors, occur because of inconsistent sample sizes; the specific population included in the sampling frame, for example, "registered voters" versus "likely voters"; inconsistencies in determining nonresponse rates (the time of day or day of the week on which the poll is conducted effectively limits the inclusion of certain groups); the proportion of "undecideds"; and the precise number of days before the election that the poll is conducted. If these factors influence the results of trial heat polls, do they also influence the results obtained about other topics that researchers want to investigate with the use of samples?

The factors that Lau isolated all relate to the problems involved with obtaining a sample that represents the population a researcher is interested in studying. Those problems—and how to solve them—are the subject of this chapter.

• **IN THIS CHAPTER** we cover the fundamentals of sampling theory, the how and why of sample selection. In the first section we discuss the aims of sampling. We then move on to definitions and a discussion of fundamental concepts of sampling theory—population, the sampling unit, sampling frame, and the sample—as well as the construction of probability and nonprobability sampling designs. Next, we discuss the factors relevant to our determination of the appropriate sample size. Finally, we present procedures for estimating nonsampling errors.

Researchers collect data in order to test hypotheses and to provide empirical support for explanations and predictions. Once investigators have constructed their measuring instruments and collected sufficient data for investigating the research problem, their explanations and predictions supported by the data must be capable of being generalized to be of scientific value. As we emphasized in Chapter 1 (Figure 1.1), generalization constitutes a major stage of the research process. Generalizations are important not only for testing hypotheses but also for descriptive purposes. For example, questions such as "How much trust do Americans place in their elected representatives in Congress?" or "Are voters more concerned with the environment now than they were a decade ago?" or "Is there a difference between men and women in how they perceive the courts' treatment of sex offenders?" all call for descriptive generalizations.

Typically, generalizations are not based on data collected from all the observations, all the respondents, or all the events covered by the research problem. Instead, researchers use a relatively small number of cases (a sample) as the basis for making inferences about all the cases (a population). Election polls are a familiar example. Based on the responses of a relatively small group of respondents, pollsters forecast how the entire population of voters would vote if the election were held at the time the poll was

---

1. Richard R. Lau, "An Analysis of the Accuracy of 'Trial Heat' Polls During the 1992 Presidential Election," *Public Opinion Quarterly*, 58 (1994): 2–20.

taken; they also attempt to predict how those voters will vote when the actual election is held. Like pollsters, social scientists use various criteria in selecting the samples to be used when conducting their research. These criteria have direct bearing on the inferences they can make about the population represented by the chosen sample.

AIMS OF SAMPLING ●

Empirically supported generalizations are usually based on partial information because it is often impossible, impractical, or extremely expensive to collect data from all the individuals—or other units of analysis—covered by the research problem. Researchers can draw fairly precise inferences on all those units (a set) based on a relatively small number of units (a subset) when the subsets accurately represent the relevant attributes of the entire set. Marketing researchers, for example, use the preferences expressed by a small subset of households to develop and promote new products targeted at millions of customers. The U.S. Environmental Protection Agency uses a small number of automobiles to obtain data on the performance of a class of models. The data collected from this subset are used to define and impose the performance standards required of all automobiles.

The complete set of relevant units of analysis, or data, is called the **population.** When the data serving as the basis for generalizations is collected from a subset of the population, that subset is called a **sample.** When an attribute found in the population, such as median income or level of formal education, can be measured, it is called a **parameter;** its counterpart in the sample is termed a **statistic.** The major objective of sampling theory is to provide the conceptual basis for making accurate estimates of the unknown values of the parameters based on calculated sample statistics.

To estimate unknown parameters accurately from known statistics, researchers have to resolve three major problems: (1) the definition of the population, (2) the sample design, and (3) the size of the sample.

THE POPULATION ●

Methodologically speaking, a population is the "aggregate of all cases that conform to some designated set of specifications." [2] For example, the specifications "people" and "residing in Britain" are used to define the population consisting of all the individuals who live in Britain. Similarly, by employing the specifications "students" and "enrolled in state universities in the United States," we can define a population consisting of all the people enrolled in one type of university found in the United States. By using the same logic of selecting the relevant characteristics, you can define all the households living in a given community, all the registered voters in a particular district, or all the books in a public library. Those populations may be composed of all the residents in a certain neighborhood, members of the state legislature, two-story houses, cellular telephones per household, and so on. The specific nature of the population depends on the research problem. Thus, if you are investigating consumer behavior in a particular city, you might define the population as all the households in that city. Or, if you are focusing on a particular product—say, dog food—your population would be composed only of those people who have dogs as pets.

2. Isidor Chein, "An Introduction to Sampling," in Claire Selltiz et al. (eds.), *Research Methods in Social Relations*, 4th ed. (New York: Holt, Rinehart and Winston, 1981), p. 419.

Therefore, one of the first problems facing a researcher who wishes to estimate a population value (i.e., parameter) from a sample value (i.e., a statistic) is how to determine the population involved. Political scientists interested in voting behavior in Britain and wishing to draw a sample so as to predict how an election will turn out will select a sample that excludes anyone under 18 because those individuals do not have the right to vote. However, "all British residents 18 years of age or older" is an inadequate definition of the population of voters because British residents also have to meet certain legal requirements, other than age, before they are permitted to vote. Individuals who do not meet those criteria are not eligible to vote and should be excluded from the population to be sampled (i.e., the *sampling population*). The population, then, has to be defined in terms of (1) content, (2) extent, and (3) time: for example, (a) all individuals over 18 years of age living in permanent residential units, (b) in Britain, (c) as of May 1, 1999.

The Sampling Unit

A single member of a sampling population (e.g., a voter, a household, an event) is referred to as a **sampling unit.** Usually, sampling units have numerous attributes, one or more of which are relevant to the research problem. For example, if the population is defined as all third graders in a given town who attend public schools on a particular day, the sampling units are all third graders. Third graders, however, have many traits (variables), including grades, habits, gender, and ethnic background. A research project may examine only one variable, such as arithmetic grades, or relations among several variables, such as arithmetic grades, gender, and the level of formal education attained by parents.

A sampling unit is not necessarily an individual. It can be an event, a university, a city, a nation, or documents. For example, in a classic study of political conflict on the national level, Rudolph J. Rummel collected data on 22 measures of foreign and domestic conflict behavior (e.g., assassinations, guerrilla warfare, purges, riots, revolutions, military actions, wars) for 77 nations over a three-year period.[3] Although the sampling units were nations, not all nations were selected for his study. The sampling units had to meet two criteria to be included in the study: (1) national sovereignty for at least two years, as evidenced by diplomatic relations with other countries and the existence of a foreign ministry, and (2) a minimum population of 800,000.

For most researchers, especially beginners, a document represents one of the most common sampling units. One example of a document (or, more specifically in this case, the paragraphs in a document) used as a sampling unit can be found in a study of whether state-level political parties are ideologically inclined, as opposed to being practical and goal-oriented (the latter traits characterize political party machines). In order to do so, Joel W. Paddock ranked the paragraphs found in the platforms of the Republican and Democratic parties of 20 U.S. states on a five-point scale.[4] (The seven items in the scale represent the salient issues affecting voters, e.g., internal sovereignty and defense). The sample of party platforms was chosen according to a number of criteria, one of which was whether their home states' party committees displayed characteristics of what Mayhew has termed "traditional party organizations," or TPOs. A TPO can be defined by its hierarchical structure and the material incentives it offers its supporters, traits used to predict

---

3. Rudolph J. Rummel, "Dimensions of Conflict Behavior Within and Between Nations," in *Macroquantitative Analysis: Conflict, Development and Democratization,* ed. J. V. Gillespie and B. A. Nesvold (Newbury Park, CA: Sage, 1971).

4. Joel W. Paddock, "Explaining State Variation in Interparty Ideological Differences," *Political Research Quarterly,* 51(3) (1998): 765–780.

how political parties will respond to policy issues. In the present case, the methodology Paddock used to obtain the rankings involved content analysis of the paragraphs.

Finite and Infinite Populations

A population may be finite or infinite, depending on whether the sampling units are finite or infinite. By definition, a *finite population* contains a countable number of sampling units—for example, all the registered voters in a particular city in a given year. An *infinite population* consists of an endless number of sampling units, such as an unlimited number of coin tosses. Sampling designed to produce information about particular characteristics of a finite population is usually termed *survey sampling.*

Sampling Frame

Once researchers have defined the population of interest, they draw a sample that represents that population adequately. The actual procedures involve selecting a sample from a **sampling frame** comprised of a complete listing of sampling units. Ideally, the sampling frame should include all the sampling units in the given population. In practice, such information is rarely available; hence, researchers usually have to use substitute lists that contain the same information but that may not be comprehensive. For example, in large nationwide studies, it is impossible to obtain a complete and accurate listing of all the individuals residing in the United States. This difficulty is commonly encountered even by major research organizations, such as the Bureau of the Census, which regularly collect data about the entire nation. The 1990 Census of households, which cost an estimated $2.6 billion, required 277 million forms. The Bureau of the Census collected an estimated 3.3 billion individual answers, which were processed by nearly 480,000 staff members over the period 1988–1991. This staff compiled and checked address lists in order to gather and process vital information on approximately 250 million people in the United States. The Bureau of the Census hired 35,000 temporary staff to go door-to-door during 1988–1989, based on a list they had compiled of the addresses of about 43 million housing units, many outside metropolitan areas. In addition, the Census purchased about 55 million residential addresses located in large metropolitan areas from commercial mailing list companies. Census and U.S. Postal Service workers checked and updated the address lists before producing mailing labels for the questionnaire envelopes.[5] Yet, for all its efforts, it is estimated that the Census omitted at least 5 million of the nation's residents. One important cause for this oversight is the mobile lifestyle that is characteristic of the United States, which makes it difficult to compile a complete mailing list.

In smaller-scale studies, the sampling frame may be based on telephone directories, city directories, or membership lists of private and public organizations.

The researcher has to ensure that there is a high degree of correspondence between a sampling frame and the sampling population. The accuracy of the sample depends, first and foremost, on the sampling frame, because every aspect of the sample design—the population covered, the stages of sampling, and the actual selection process—is influenced by it. Before selecting a sample, the researcher has to evaluate the sampling frame for potential problems. Leslie Kish has provided a useful classification of the typical problems found in sampling frames: incomplete frames, clusters of elements, and blank foreign elements.[6]

---

5. From *Census '90 Basics* (Bureau of the Census, U.S. Department of Commerce, December 1985), p. 1.

6. Leslie Kish, *Survey Sampling* (New York: Wiley, 1965), sec. 2.7.

INCOMPLETE FRAMES. The problem of incomplete sampling frames arises when sampling units found in the population are missing from the list. For example, if the population includes all new residents in a community, a sampling frame based on a community's real estate multiple-listing service would be incomplete because the service registers new homeowners (sellers and buyers) but not renters.

When the sampling frame is incomplete, one option that might be available is the use of supplemental lists. For example, it may be possible to compile a list of all new renters in the community by using the city directory if the directory identifies new residents as homeowners or renters.

CLUSTERS OF ELEMENTS. The second potential type of problem with sampling frames is clusters of elements. This problem occurs when the sampling units are listed in groups rather than individually. For example, the sampling frame may consist of city blocks, whereas the study focuses on individuals. One possible solution to this problem is for the investigator to take a sample of blocks and then list all the individual households in each of the selected blocks. The researcher then selects individuals from each household (most households include more than one person) according to specific criteria, such as only individuals over 18 or only heads of households.

BLANK FOREIGN ELEMENTS. The problem of blank foreign elements is quite common. It occurs when some of the sampling units in the sampling frame are not part of the research population, such as the case where the research population is defined as eligible voters whereas the sampling frame includes individuals who are too young to vote. This problem often occurs when outdated lists are used as the sampling frame. Another example, one that is often encountered when using city directories, results when the directory lists an address but not its residents. In these cases, the individuals living at an address may have moved away, leaving the house or apartment empty. These cases should be treated as blanks and *simply omitted* from the sample. For these reasons, it is good practice to select a slightly larger sample initially, in order to compensate for such omissions.

Errors in Sampling Frames: The 1936 Presidential Election

Our discussion of errors in sampling frames would not be complete without mentioning a classic example of sampling failure, the 1936 *Reader's Digest* presidential poll. In 1936, Franklin Delano Roosevelt, completing his first term of office as president of the United States, was running against Alf Landon of Kansas, the Republican candidate. *Reader's Digest* magazine, in a poll consisting of about 2.4 million individuals, the largest in history, predicted a victory for Landon, forecasting that he would receive 57 percent of the vote to Roosevelt's 43 percent. Contrary to the poll's outcome, Roosevelt won the election by a huge landslide—62 percent to Landon's 38 percent.[7]

Despite the extremely large sample size, the error was enormous, the largest ever made by any polling organization. The major reason for the error was found in the sampling frame. The *Digest* had mailed questionnaires to 10 million people whose names and addresses were taken from sources such as telephone directories and club membership lists. In 1936, however, few poor people had telephones, nor were they likely to belong to clubs. Thus the sampling frame was incomplete, as it systematically excluded

---

7. David Freedman, Robert Pisani, and Roger Purves, *Statistics* (New York: Norton, 1978), pp. 302–307.

the poor. That is, the sampling frame did not reflect the actual voter population accurately. This omission was particularly significant because in that year, 1936, the poor voted overwhelmingly for Roosevelt, whereas the well-to-do voted mainly for Landon.[8]

SAMPLE DESIGNS ●

In the previous section, we discussed sampling problems in relation to the definition of the population and the sampling frame. Here, we discuss the second major sampling problem that arises when researchers attempt to secure a **representative sample.** The essential requirement of any sample is that it be as representative as possible of the population from which it is drawn. A sample is considered to be representative if the analyses made using the sampling units produce results similar to those that would be obtained had the entire population been analyzed.

Probability and Nonprobability Sampling

In modern sampling theory, a basic distinction is made between probability and nonprobability sampling. A **probability sample** is distinguished by the ability to specify the probability at which each sampling unit of the population will be included in the sample. In the simplest case, all units of a population have the same probability of being included in the sample. Accordingly, only probability sampling can be used in representative sampling designs. In a **nonprobability sample,** there is no way of specifying the probability of each unit's inclusion in the sample, and there is no assurance that every unit has some chance of being included. If a set of units has no chance of being included in the sample (e.g., those voters omitted from the *Reader's Digest* sample), this implies that the definition of the population is qualified or restricted; that is, if the traits of this set of units remain unknown, then the precise nature of the population cannot be known.[9] Alternatively, we can say that nonprobability samples are not fully representative of the sampling population. Returning to the 1936 election forecast, the voting intentions of the poor were unknown. Therefore, the *Reader's Digest* poll can be considered a clear case of nonprobability sampling.

A well-designed sample ensures that if a study were to be repeated on a number of different samples drawn from the same population, the findings obtained from each sample would not differ from the population parameters by more than a specified amount. A probability sample design thus makes it possible for researchers to estimate the degree to which the findings based on one sample are likely to differ from those obtained by studying the entire population. When a researcher is using a probability sample design, it is possible for him or her to estimate the population's parameters on the basis of the calculated sample statistics.

Although accurate estimates of the population's parameters can be calculated only with probability samples, social scientists often use nonprobability samples in their research. They do so when, under certain circumstances (e.g., exploratory research), convenience and economy outweigh the advantages of using probability sampling. Social scientists also use nonprobability samples when a sampling population cannot be defined precisely or when a list of the sampling population is unavailable. For example, no list has yet been compiled of all the drug addicts or all the illegal residents living in the United States.

---

8. Ibid.

9. Chein, "An Introduction to Sampling," p. 421.

Nonprobability Sample Designs

The three major designs utilizing nonprobability samples that are employed by social scientists are convenience samples, purposive samples, and quota samples.

CONVENIENCE SAMPLES. Researchers obtain a convenience sample by selecting whatever sampling units are conveniently available. A college professor may select the students in a class; or a researcher may take the first 200 people encountered on the street who are willing to be interviewed. Because researchers have no way of estimating how representative of the population the convenience sample is, they cannot estimate the population's parameters from the values of the characteristic obtained from the sample.

PURPOSIVE SAMPLES. When obtaining purposive samples (occasionally referred to as "judgment samples"), researchers use their subjective judgment and attempt to select sampling units that appear to be representative of the population. In other words, the chance that a particular sampling unit will be included in the sample depends primarily on the researcher's subjective judgment. Because it is usually difficult to determine why a researcher judges the sampling unit selected as being representative of the sample, it is difficult to determine the probability of the inclusion of any specific sampling unit in the sample. Nevertheless, social scientists have used purposive samples with some success when, for example, attempting to forecast election turnout. In the United States, pollsters select a number of small election districts in which election returns approximate overall state returns from previous years. All the eligible voters in the selected districts are interviewed as to their intentions to vote, and forecasts are made on the basis of these reports. The underlying (and indeed risky) assumption is that the selected districts continue to be representative of their respective states over the years.

QUOTA SAMPLES. The chief reason for using a quota sample is to select a sample that is as similar as possible to the sampling population. For example, if it is known that the population being researched has equal numbers of males and females, equal numbers of males and females are selected for the sample. If it is known that 15 percent of the population is composed of African Americans, 15 percent of the total sample will be African American. In quota sampling, groups characterized by specific variables such as gender, age, place of residence, and ethnicity are interviewed. For instance, an interviewer may be instructed to interview fourteen individuals, seven of whom live in the suburbs and seven in the central city. Seven have to be men and seven women; of the seven men, exactly three should be married and four single. The same would apply for women. From the example, it is obvious that a lack of similarity between the sample and the population is likely to occur with respect to those variables—such as age—that are not specified in the interviewers' quotas. As with other nonprobability samples, we cannot estimate the population's parameters accurately from our findings.

Pollsters frequently used quota samples in forecasting the outcomes of presidential elections until 1948, when three major polls predicted erroneously that Thomas E. Dewey would be elected president.[10] On Election Day, President Harry S Truman won with almost 50 percent of the popular vote, whereas Dewey received just over 45 percent.

10. Freedman et al., *Statistics*, pp. 302–307.

All three polls used quota samples whose sampling units represented the variables that the pollsters assumed influenced voting, such as place of residence, gender, age, ethnicity, and income. Although their assumptions about the importance of these variables were reasonable, many other factors also influenced voting in that election. Most significantly, no quota was set on whether the respondents identified with the Republican or Democratic party, because the distribution of party identification was exactly what these polling organizations did not know and were trying to find out. Perhaps the most serious problem in the 1948 polls was the fact that the interviewers were free to choose whomever they pleased within the assigned quotas. This left considerable room for interviewer choice, which, in turn, introduced a significant source of bias.[11]

Probability Sample Designs

We pointed out earlier that in contrast to nonprobability sampling, probability sample designs permit the researcher to specify the probability of each sampling unit's inclusion in the sample in a single draw from the population. Here we present four common probability sample designs: simple random sampling, systematic sampling, stratified sampling, and cluster sampling.

SIMPLE RANDOM SAMPLES. Simple random sampling is the basic probability sampling design, and it is incorporated into all the more elaborate probability sampling designs. **Simple random sampling** is a procedure that assigns to each of the sampling units of the population (denoted by the letter N) an equal and known nonzero probability in being selected. For example, when you toss a perfect coin, the probability that you will get heads or tails is equal and known (50 percent), and each subsequent outcome is independent of previous outcomes.

Scientists usually use computer programs or tables of random digits to select random samples. A table of random digits is reproduced in Appendix D. These tables are quite simple to use. First, list each sampling unit of the population and give it a number, from 1 to n. Then, start reading the table of random digits at some random starting point. Each digit that appears in the table is read in order (up, down, or across; the direction does not matter as long as it is consistent). Whenever a digit that appears in the table of random digits corresponds to the number of a sampling unit in your list, select that sampling unit for your sample. Continue this process until you reach the desired sample size. When using this method, the selection of any given sampling unit is random, that is, independent of the selection of previous sampling units. By doing so, you have eliminated systematic bias from the selection procedure. You can then estimate parameters with the confidence that the findings you obtain from your sample are representative of the real values you would find in the total population.

Random selection procedures ensure that every sampling unit of the population has an equal and known probability of being included in the sample; this probability is n/N, where n stands for the size of the sample and N for the size of the population.[12] For example, if the population consists of 50,389 eligible voters in a town and a simple random sample of 1,800 is to be drawn, the probability that each sampling unit in the population will be included in the sample is 1,800/50,389, or .0357 (see Exhibit 8.1).

---

11. Ibid., pp. 305–307.

12. For the mathematical reasoning, see Kish, *Survey Sampling*, pp. 39–40.

Exhibit 8.1

HOW TO DRAW A RANDOM SAMPLE

The Problem

In a cost-containment study of a regional hospital, patients' records are to be examined. There are $N = 100$ patients' records from which a simple random sample of $n = 10$ is to be drawn.

1. We number the accounts, beginning with 001 for the first account and ending with 100 for the one-hundredth account. Notice that we have assigned a three-digit number to each record in our population. If the total number of records were 1,250, we would need four-digit numbers. In this case, we need to select three-digit random numbers in order to give every record the same known chance of selection.

2. Now refer to Appendix D. Notice that each column contains five-digit numbers. If we drop the last two digits of each number and proceed down column 1, we obtain the following three-digit numbers:

104	854	521	007*
223	289	070*	053*
241	635	486	919
421	094*	541	005*
375	103	326	007
779	071*	293	690
995	510	024*	259
963	023*	815	097*
895	010*	296	

The last number listed is 097 from line 35 (column 1). We do not need to list more numbers because we have already found 10 different numbers that qualify for our sample (007 appears twice but is selected only once). The starred numbers are the numbers of the records chosen for our sample because they are the only numbers that fall in the range we specified, 001 – 100.

We now have 10 records in our simple random sample:

094	070	005
071	024	097
023	007	
010	053	

3. We need not start with the first row of column 1. We can select any starting point, such as the seventh row of column 2. We can also choose to progress in any way we want—down the columns, across them, or diagonally—as long as we decide ahead of time how we will proceed.

Exhibit 8.2

HOW TO DRAW A SYSTEMATIC SAMPLE

The Problem

A social scientist is interested in investigating the relationship between parents' occupations and the grade-point averages of their children, students on a large urban campus ($N = 35,000$). As the information needed can be obtained from the students' records, a sample of $n = 700$ records will be selected. Although we could select a simple random sample (see Exhibit 8.1), this would require a great deal of work. Alternatively, we could use the following procedure.

1. The first step is to determine the sampling interval, K. As $N = 35,000$ and the sample size $n = 700$, K is $35,000/700$; that is, $K = 50$.

2. We now select the first record at random from the first $K = 50$ records listed and then select every fiftieth record thereafter until we have reached a sample size of 700. This method is called a "1-in-50 systematic sample."

SYSTEMATIC SAMPLES. **Systematic sampling** consists of selecting every Kth sampling unit of the population after the first sampling unit is selected at random from the total of sampling units. Thus, if you wish to select a sample of 100 persons from a population of 10,000, you would take every hundredth individual ($K = N/n = 10,000/100 = 100$). The first selection is determined by some random process, such as the use of a table of random digits. Suppose that the fourteenth person were selected; the sample would then consist of individuals numbered 14, 114, 214, 314, 414, and so on.

Systematic sampling is more convenient than simple random sampling. When interviewers who are not trained in sampling techniques have to conduct sampling in the field, it is much simpler to instruct them to select every Kth person from a list than to have them use a table of random digits. Systematic samples are also easier to use with very large populations or when large samples are to be selected (see Exhibit 8.2).

With systematic sampling, each sampling unit in the population has a $1/K$ probability of being included in the sample. However, there may be a pattern in the data that occurs systematically at every Kth unit. The phenomenon represented by the pattern will bias the sample. For example, you may be doing a study of the average size of one-family homes in a city, and the first house chosen is a corner house. However, you may not be aware that every Kth house on your list is also a corner house. This might introduce a bias, since corner houses tend to be larger. If you are aware of a systematic pattern in the population of sampling units, and if you can shuffle the list thoroughly first, you can minimize potential problems.[13]

STRATIFIED SAMPLES. Researchers use **stratified sampling** primarily to ensure that different groups of a population are represented adequately in the sample so as to increase the level of accuracy when estimating parameters. Furthermore, all other things

13. For some other procedures for avoiding problems caused by systematic patterns in populations, see William Cochran, *Sampling Techniques*, 3d ed. (New York: Wiley, 1977).

being equal, stratified sampling considerably reduces the cost of executing the research. The underlying idea in stratified sampling is to use available information on the population "to divide it into groups such that the elements within each group are more alike than are the elements in the population as a whole." [14] That is, you create a set of homogeneous samples based on the variables you are interested in studying. If a series of homogeneous groups can be sampled in such a way that when the samples are combined they constitute a sample of a more heterogeneous population, you will increase the accuracy of your population estimates.

For example, suppose that it is known that there are 700 whites, 200 African Americans, and 100 Mexican Americans in a given population. If a random sample of 100 persons were drawn, we would probably not get exactly 70 whites, 20 African Americans, and 10 Mexican Americans; the proportion of Mexican Americans in particular might be too small. A stratified sample of 70 whites, 20 African Americans, and 10 Mexican Americans would ensure better representation of these groups. The stratification procedure does not violate the principle of random selection because a probability sample is subsequently drawn within each stratum or specific group.

The fundamental principle applied when dividing a sample into homogeneous strata is that the criteria on which the division is based be related to the variable the researcher is studying. Another important consideration is that when using these criteria, the ensuing number of subsamples do not, taken together, increase the total size of the sample beyond what would be required by a simple random sample. Suppose you want to estimate the median family income of a small town and you know the major characteristics of the families residing there. Because prior research has already established that income correlates with occupation, education, ethnicity, age, and gender, these criteria are sound bases for stratifying your sample. However, if all these criteria were in fact used, the value of the stratified sample would diminish because the number of subsamples required would become enormous.

Consider what would happen if there were four categories of occupation, three of education, three of ethnicity, three of age, and two of gender. The number of subsamples would then equal $4 \times 3 \times 3 \times 3 \times 2$, or 216. Because the minimum number of cases in each cell cannot be less than 10 to meet the statistical requirements of the analysis, you would need a minimum of 2,160 cases, that is, at least 10 cases in each cell. No one would consider such a sample size to be appropriate for studying the population of a small town. To solve this problem, we assume that many stratification criteria occur as associated factors (i.e., characteristics that appear together). Hence, if social status is chosen as the variable representing occupation, education, and ethnicity as well, the number of subsamples can be reduced to 4 (social status groups) $\times$ 3 (age groups) $\times$ 2 (gender groups) = 24 subsamples with a total of 240 cases. This is a more reasonable sampling design, and it would represent the population better than a simple random sample.

Sampling from the different strata can be either proportional or disproportional. If the number of sampling units taken from each stratum is of the same proportion within the total sample as the proportion of the stratum within the total population—a uniform sampling fraction (n/N)—you obtain a *proportionate stratified sample*. However, if proportion of the sampling units from each stratum included in the total sample is either above or below the proportion of the total number (N) in each stratum within the popu-

14. Morris H. Hansen, William N. Hurwitz, and William G. Madow, *Sample Survey Methods and Theory* (New York: Wiley, 1953), p. 40.

Exhibit 8.3

HOW TO DRAW A STRATIFIED SAMPLE

The Problem

In a study of revitalization in an urban neighborhood, we plan to examine the attitudes of new residents toward their community. We anticipate that the attitudes of homeowners may differ from those of renters. Therefore, as a means of ensuring the proper representation of both groups, we will use a proportional stratified random sample with two strata: new homeowners and renters.

1. The population consists of $N = N_1 + N_2$, with N_1 denoting new homeowners and N_2 renters. $N_1 = 200$ and $N_2 = 300$. Therefore, $N = 500$. We decide to select a proportional sampling fraction of $1/10$ from each stratum. Thus $N_1 = 20$ homeowners and $N_2 = 30$ renters will be included in the sample.

2. We then apply the simple random sampling procedure (see Exhibit 8.1) to each list separately.

---

lation—that is, if the sampling fractions vary—the sample is a *disproportionate stratified sample.* In other words, when the total number of people characterized by each variable (or stratum) fluctuates within the population, we need to choose the size of each sample for each stratum according to our research requirements. This choice is influenced by the likelihood of obtaining a sufficient number of sampling units from each stratum within the final sample. As a rule, disproportionate stratified samples are used either to compare two or more particular strata or to analyze one stratum intensively. When researchers use a disproportionate stratified sample, they have to weight the estimates of the population's parameters by the number of units belonging to each stratum[15] (see Exhibit 8.3).

CLUSTER SAMPLES. The fourth type of probability sampling used by social scientists is cluster sampling. It is frequently used in large-scale studies because it is the least expensive sample design. **Cluster sampling** involves first selecting larger groupings, called *clusters,* and then selecting the sampling units from the clusters. The clusters are selected by simple random sampling or by stratified sampling. Depending on the research problem, researchers can include all the sampling units in these clusters in the sample or select a number of units from within the clusters, using simple or stratified sampling procedures.

Suppose that the research objective is to study adults' attitudes regarding passage of a property tax bill in the various election districts of a city. No single list containing the names of all the adult residents is available, and it is too expensive to compile such a list. However, a map of the election districts does exist. First, we can randomly select a number of election districts from the list (first-stage cluster sampling). Then, within each of the districts, we can select blocks at random (second-stage cluster sampling) and interview all the persons on these blocks. We may also use a simple random sample within each block selected. In such a case, we would be constructing a three-stage cluster sample. (This sampling method is also called *area probability sampling* or just *area sampling.*) Similarly, a survey of urban households may use a sample of cities, a sample of

---

15. See Kish, *Survey Sampling,* pp. 77–82, for methods of weighting.

Exhibit 8.4

HOW TO DRAW A CLUSTER SAMPLE

The Problem

The purpose of the study is to interview residents of an urban community. No list of adult residents is available, and thus cluster sampling is used as the sampling design.

Stage 1

1. Define the area to be covered using an up-to-date map. Boundaries are marked; areas that do not include dwelling units are excluded.
2. Divide the entire area into blocks. Boundary lines should not divide buildings and should be easily identifiable by the interviewers.
3. Next, number the blocks, preferably serially and in winding fashion.
4. Finally, select a simple random or systematic sample of blocks, using the appropriate procedure.

Stage 2

1. List and number all dwelling units in each of the selected blocks. This sometimes requires interviewers to ensure that all new structures are listed.
2. Select a simple random or systematic sample of dwelling units.
3. Finally, interview selected individuals within each selected dwelling unit. The selection is usually made according to specific guidelines.

Based in part on Matilda White Riley, *Sociological Research: Exercises and Manual* (Orlando, FL: Harcourt Brace Jovanovich, 1963), vol. 2, p. 172.

districts within each city selected, and a sample of households within each selected district (see Exhibit 8.4).

The choice of clusters depends on the research objectives and the resources available for the study. Households, blocks, schools, districts, and cities have all been used as clusters. In fact, as Leslie Kish points out:

The population of the United States may be alternatively regarded as an aggregate of units which are entire counties; or of cities, towns, and townships; or of area segments and blocks; or of dwellings; or, finally, as individual persons. Indeed, all those sampling units are employed in turn for area samples of the United States.[16]

Probability Sampling: Summary

The four probability sampling designs that we have described are the designs most commonly used by social scientists. However, they do not exhaust the range of probability sampling procedures; you may consult the Additional Readings at the end of this chapter for further information. By way of a summary, the box on page 175 gives a brief description of the four designs.

16. Ibid., p. 150.

Probability Sampling: An Example

To illustrate the entire sampling process, we will review the procedures employed by the University of Michigan's Institute for Social Research (ISR) in its national surveys.[17] The sampling procedure involves three sampling designs: cluster sampling, stratified sampling, and simple random sampling.

ISR is among the largest university-based social science research organizations in the United States. Research projects conducted by the institute are sponsored by government agencies, private business, and public service organizations. Many of the studies involve large nationwide samples. The steps listed here approximate those followed by the ISR when drawing a national sample[18] (see Figure 8.1 on page 176).

1. The entire geographic area of the United States is divided into smaller areas, each called a *primary sampling unit* (PSU). The PSUs are generally counties or metropolitan areas. Out of the entire list of PSUs, researchers select 74 PSUs by stratified random sampling to ensure that rural areas, large and middle-sized cities, and regions are represented adequately.

2. Each of the selected 74 PSUs is further subdivided into smaller areas; for example, for a hypothetical PSU consisting of two large cities, six medium-sized towns, and the remaining rural portions of the county, the PSU is divided into three strata: (a) large cities, (b) smaller cities and towns, and (c) rural areas. Units within these strata are called *sample places*. One or more sample places are selected within each stratum.

3. Each sample place is further divided into *chunks*. A chunk is defined as an area having identifiable boundaries: For example, in urban areas, a chunk is

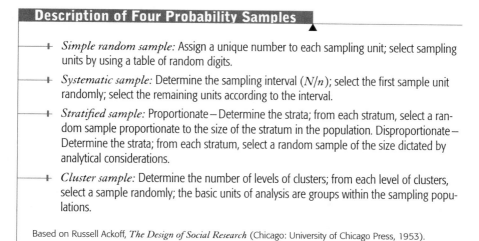

Description of Four Probability Samples

Simple random sample: Assign a unique number to each sampling unit; select sampling units by using a table of random digits.

Systematic sample: Determine the sampling interval (N/n); select the first sample unit randomly; select the remaining units according to the interval.

Stratified sample: Proportionate — Determine the strata; from each stratum, select a random sample proportionate to the size of the stratum in the population. Disproportionate — Determine the strata; from each stratum, select a random sample of the size dictated by analytical considerations.

Cluster sample: Determine the number of levels of clusters; from each level of clusters, select a sample randomly; the basic units of analysis are groups within the sampling populations.

Based on Russell Ackoff, *The Design of Social Research* (Chicago: University of Chicago Press, 1953).

---

17. Survey Research Center, *Interviewers Manual*, rev. ed. (Ann Arbor: Institute for Social Research, University of Michigan, 1976), chap. 8.

18. Ibid.

Figure 8.1

Drawing a National Sample

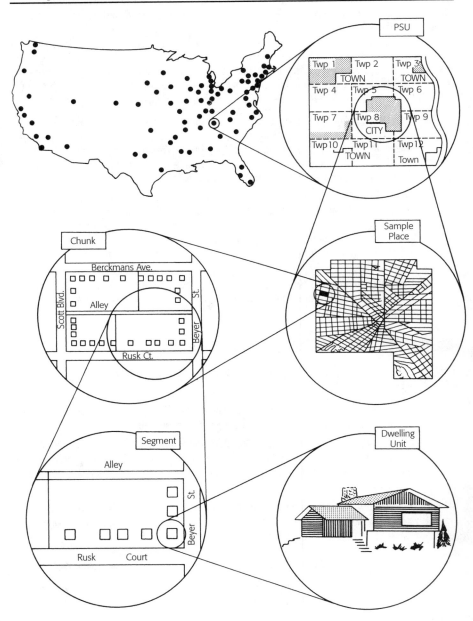

From Survey Research Center, *Interviewer's Manual*, rev. ed. (Ann Arbor: Institute for Social Research, University of Michigan, 1976), p. 8-2.

equivalent to a block; in rural areas, it is defined by roads or county lines. Within each sample place, chunks are randomly selected.

4. At this stage, the interviewers play a major role in the sampling process. They visit each chunk, list all the dwelling units, and suggest how the chunk can be divided into areas containing four to twelve dwelling units each. These areas are called *segments*. Segments are then randomly selected from each chunk.

5. At the last stage, researchers select the dwelling units to be included in the final sample from each segment. The procedure for selecting dwelling units varies. When a segment includes only a few dwelling units, all are included in the study. If the segment contains many dwelling units, only a specified fraction of the dwellings in that segment are included in the study.

SAMPLE SIZE ●

A *sample* is any subset of sampling units from a population. A **subset** is any combination of sampling units that does not include the entire set of sampling units that has been defined as the population. A sample may include only one sampling unit, all but one sampling unit, or any number in between. How do we determine the size of a sample?

There are several fallacies concerning the necessary size of a sample. One is that the sample size must be a certain proportion (often set at 5 percent) of the population; another is that an adequate sample size is about 2,000 cases; still another misconception is that any increase in the sample size will increase the precision of the sample results. These claims are incorrect because they are not based on sampling theory. To determine the size of a sample properly, researchers need to determine what level of accuracy is expected of their estimates—that is, the size of the standard error acceptable to them.

Standard Error

The concept of **standard error** (some researchers use the terms *error margin* or *sampling error*) is central to sampling theory and to determining the size of a sample. It is one of the statistical measures that indicates how closely the sample results reflect the true values of a parameter. We will illustrate the idea of standard error by making some computations based on simple random samples drawn from a small hypothetical population.

Our hypothetical population consists of five students earning $500, $650, $400, $700, and $600 per month; this means that the population's mean monthly income (denoted by μ) is $570.[19] Say that we draw a random sample of two with the purpose of estimating μ, and that the two students selected earn $500 and $400, respectively. The sample mean ($\bar{x}$) is therefore ($500 + $400)/2 = $450, which we take as the estimate of μ, the population mean. Since we already know that the population mean is $570, we can easily see that the estimate of $450 is inaccurate. Had we selected the two students earning $650 and $700, the sample mean would have been $675, which is also an inaccurate estimate of the population mean. In a similar manner, we can draw all the possible samples of size $n = 2$ from this population.

Table 8.1 presents the 10 possible samples and their means, the estimates of μ derived from each. None of these samples estimate μ accurately. However, some sample

19. See Chapter 15 for a discussion of the mean and the standard deviation.

| Table 8.1 |

Estimates of the Population's Mean

Possible Samples of $n = 2$ (incomes of students selected, in \$)	$\bar{x}$ (estimate of μ, in \$)
500 and 650	575
500 and 400	450
500 and 700	600
500 and 600	550
650 and 400	525
650 and 700	675
650 and 600	625
400 and 700	550
400 and 600	500
700 and 600	650
Total	5,700

means (for example, \$500 and \$650) are closer to the population mean than are others. If we continue to draw samples of $n = 2$ indefinitely, each of the samples in Table 8.1 will be selected more than once. We can then plot the distribution of all the sample means. The distribution that results from the value of the sample mean ($\bar{x}$) derived from an *infinite* number of samples is termed *the sampling distribution of the mean* or *mean distribution.* In our example, each of the 10 samples has an equal probability of being drawn (it is a simple random sample), and if we continue the selection indefinitely, each sample will be drawn an equal number of times. Consequently, the mean of the estimates derived from *all* the possible samples is 5,700/10 = 570, which equals the population mean.

In general, the mean distribution of an infinite number of samples is assumed to equal the mean of the population. The more that sample mean values deviate from the population mean, the greater is the variability of findings obtained from each sample, and the greater is the risk of making a large error in estimating a parameter of the population from one or a limited number of samples.

Because the population in our hypothetical example was small, we knew the population mean and could compare it with the means obtained from the samples. In reality, the population mean is unknown, and the researcher draws only a single sample (not an infinite number of samples) in order to estimate the population parameter. The distribution of the values obtained from a single sample serves as an indicator of the entire sampling distribution; the dispersion of those values within the single sample is measured by the standard deviation, s (see Chapter 15). The distribution of all the sample means about the mean of the total of these samples is termed the standard error (*SE*).

We calculate the standard deviation and then estimate the *SE* (see Chapter 15 for a detailed discussion of the standard error). We cannot calculate the *SE* directly because we cannot draw the infinite number of samples required for its calculation. Underlying this procedure is the assumption that the dispersion of the variable's value within a single randomly selected and representative sample indicates its dispersion within the sampling population.

The standard deviation of the sampling distribution in our example is calculated as follows:

$$[(575 - 570)^2 + (450 - 570)^2 + (600 - 570)^2 + (550 - 570)^2$$
$$+ (525 - 570)^2 + (675 - 570)^2 + (625 - 570)^2 + (550 - 570)^2$$
$$+ (500 - 570)^2 + (650 - 570)^2]/10 = \sqrt{4,350} = 65.95$$

We then estimate the *SE* by dividing the standard deviation of the sample by the square root of the sample size (*n*):

$$SE = \frac{s}{\sqrt{n}}$$

where s = standard deviation

n = sample size

If the population is small, the factor $1 - n/N$, a statistical procedure called the finite population correction, has to be included in the equation:

$$SE = \sqrt{\frac{s^2}{n}\left(1 - \frac{n}{N}\right)}$$

where s^2 = sample variance

n = sample size

N = population size

In this formula, the value of n/N is subtracted from 1 because the population is small. In our example, $N = 5$ and $n = 2$, so

$$s^2 = \frac{\begin{array}{c}(500 - 570)^2 + (650 - 570)^2 \\ + (400 - 570)^2 + (700 - 570)'(600 + 570)^2\end{array}}{4}$$

$$= \frac{58,000}{4} = 14,500$$

Therefore, the standard error of the sample means is calculated as

$$SE\ (\bar{x}\cdot)\ \sqrt{\left(\frac{14,500}{2}\right)\left(\frac{5 - 2}{5}\right)} = \sqrt{4,350} = 65.95$$

which is identical to the previous result.

Confidence Intervals

Before presenting the method for determining the sample size, we need to discuss one more concept, the **confidence interval.** We have pointed out that the population mean

Figure 8.2

Normal Curve: Percentage of Area from the Mean in Specified Standard Error Distances

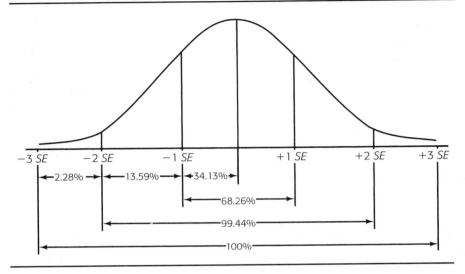

equals the mean of all the sample means that can be drawn from a population and that we can compute the standard deviation of these sample means. If the distribution of the sample means is normal or approximates normality, we can use the properties of the normal curve to estimate the location of the population mean.[20] If we knew the mean of all sample means (the population mean) and the standard deviation of these sample means (standard error of the mean), we could compute Z scores and determine the range within which any percentage of the sample means can be found. Between $-1Z$ and $+1Z$, we would expect to find 68 percent of all sample means; between $-1.96Z$ and $+1.96Z$, we would expect to find about 95 percent of all sample means; and between $-2.58Z$ and $+2.58Z$, we would expect to find 99 percent of all sample means. However, as we do not know the mean of the population, we have to estimate that mean on the basis of a single sample.

We can use the normal curve for this purpose (see Figure 8.2). A sample mean that is $+1.96Z$ scores, or approximately 2.0 standard errors above the population mean, has .025 probability of occurring; in other words, 95.5 percent of all sample means will deviate by less than $\pm 1.96Z$ from the mean. If it is unlikely for a sample mean to be $1.96Z$ or more than 2.0 standard errors above the population mean, it is just as unlikely for the population mean to be 2.0 standard errors below a given sample mean (i.e., $-1.96Z$). We do not know whether the sample mean is larger or smaller than the true mean of the population, but if we construct an interval of $-1.96Z$ to $+1.96Z$ about the sample mean, we can be confident that 95.5 percent of the population is located within that interval. We do not expect that the sample mean will in fact be as far as ± 2.0 standard

20. The concept of normality, expressed in the normal curve, points to assumptions about the distribution of a variable in the general population. See pages 344–345 for a detailed discussion of the normal curve and its properties.

errors away from the population mean, and we are quite certain that the population mean is no farther than this interval from the sample mean.

If we construct a confidence interval of $\pm 1.96Z$ scores, or approximately 2.0 standard errors from the mean about the sample mean, we expect the population mean to lie within this interval with about 95 percent confidence. This means that there is a 5 percent chance that we are wrong; that is, there is a 5 percent chance that the population mean does not fall within the interval. If you do not wish to take such a risk of being incorrect, you can use a different confidence interval. The chance that the population mean will be within $+2.58Z$ and $-2.58Z$, or approximately 3.0 standard errors from the sample mean, is 99 out of 100; this is termed the 99 percent confidence interval. (In Figure 8.2, for illustrative purposes, we indicate that 3 standard errors cover 100 percent of the sample when the sample population is large.) The width of the confidence interval around the sample mean employed is chosen by the researcher on the basis of the required level of predictive accuracy. In other words, the width of the confidence interval is determined by how much the researcher is willing to risk being wrong. The researcher could even use an interval of ± 0.68 standard errors of the mean and face only a 50 percent chance of being correct in assuming that the population mean does lie within that interval.

To sum up, if a given sampling distribution is known to be approximately normal, we can infer that about 68 percent of the sample estimates of which it is comprised will lie between its mean and 1 standard error, and about 95 percent between its mean and 2.0 standard errors. Confidence levels and standard errors are used routinely in surveys and opinion polls. Without these statistical checks pollsters, for example, would never be confident that their election forecasts were accurate, nor could marketing executives be confident of the degree of a new product's success.

Determining the Sample Size

Now we can estimate the size of the sample to be drawn. If cost and other practical limitations do not enter into the decision about sample size, there is no difficulty in determining the desired size. Recall the formula for the standard error of the mean:

$$SE = \frac{s}{\sqrt{n}}$$

where s = standard deviation of the variable under study

n = sample size

Inverting, we then have

$$n = \frac{s^2}{SE^2}$$

To calculate the sample size n, we have to have some idea of the standard deviation in the population. We also have decide how large a standard error to allow. If, for example, a random sample is to be drawn from a population consisting of 10,000 sampling units, $s^2 = .20$, and the desired $SE = .016$, the estimated sample size is

$$n = \frac{.20}{.000256} = 781.25$$

If the sample size turns out to be too large relative to the population, the finite population correction is added. In this case, n/N is added to 1. The final sample size is thereby calculated by

$$n' = \frac{n}{1 + (n/N)}$$

where N = population size

n = sample size

n' = optimal sample size

In our example, if $N = 10,000$, then

$$n' = \frac{781.25}{1 + \dfrac{781.25}{10,000}} \approx 725$$

In practice, decisions concerning the sample size are more complicated. First of all, researchers must decide how precise they want their sample results to be, that is, how large a standard error is acceptable. Second, they must decide how the results will be analyzed. Some data analysis techniques require larger samples than the one we originally planned. Third, if more than one variable is being examined, the researchers should decide whether a sample size satisfactory for one variable is adequate for the other variables.[21]

NONSAMPLING ERRORS

Sampling theory is concerned with the error introduced by using a sampling procedure. In a perfect sampling design, this type of error is minimized for any particular sample. At the same time, an error in our estimates calls attention to the difference between what is expected in the long run and what can be achieved if a researcher follows a particular set of procedures throughout a study. However, even if the sampling error is very small, there are other sources of error, for example, measurement error (see Chapter 7). In survey research, the most common error is **nonresponse error.** Nonresponses are defined as observations missing for reasons such as the refusal to be interviewed, an individual's absence from the home, and misplaced forms. Nonresponse can introduce substantial bias into the findings.

Recall the *Reader's Digest* poll of 1936: We discussed the errors made by the *Digest* in the process of selecting the sampling frame. But the *Digest* made an additional important error later on when it based its estimates on a very low response rate. The results of the poll were based on responses from 2.4 million out of the 10 million people originally included in the sample.[22] This biased the results considerably because, during the polling, evidence appeared indicating that the nonrespondents tended to vote for Roosevelt whereas, among the respondents, over half favored Landon.

---

21. For further details, see Kish, *Survey Sampling;* and C. A. Moser and Graham Kalton, *Survey Methods in Social Investigation,* 2d ed. (New York: Basic Books, 1972).

22. Freedman et al., *Statistics,* pp. 302–307.

Generally, the amount and kind of bias is related to the following conditions:

1. The greater the rate of nonresponse, the greater the bias introduced. The *response rate* can be calculated as follows:

$$R = 1 - \frac{n - r}{n}$$

where R = response rate

n = sample size

For example, if the original sample size is 1,200, and 1,000 responses are actually obtained, the response rate is $1 - (1,200 - 1,000)/1,200 = .83$ and the nonresponse rate is .17, or 17 percent.

2. The seriousness of the bias depends on the extent to which the population mean of the nonresponse stratum in the sample differs from that of the response stratum.[23]

3. Each of the following types of nonresponse influences the sample results in a different way. (These types of nonresponse apply to entire interview schedules as well as to parts of an interview or questionnaire and single questions).[24]

→ *Uninterviewables:* People who are ill, illiterate, or have language barriers.

→ *Not found:* People who have moved or are inaccessible; for instance, those with whom the interviewer cannot make an appointment.

→ *Not-at-homes:* People who are out when the interviewer calls but are reached later, and their responses are subsequently added.

→ *Refusals:* People who refuse to cooperate or to answer all the survey questions. Refusals may vary with the type of question being asked.

The proportion of nonrespondents depends on factors such as the nature of the population, the data collection method, the kinds of questions asked, the skill of the interviewers, and the number of callbacks that can be made. A poorly designed and/or administered interview schedule will result in a very high nonresponse rate.

To estimate the effect of nonresponse, an interviewer can collect information about the nonrespondents on callbacks, and then make certain estimates. Suppose that voters in a small community are surveyed to estimate the proportions of the population identifying with one political party or another, and that the survey has a 10 percent nonresponse rate. This information can be corrected with additional information gathered on the level of education, income, or ethnic background of the nonrespondents. Suppose that a 10 percent nonresponse rate amounts to 300 voters. Using other sources, you can estimate that 70 percent have incomes of about $75,000 a year. If you know that, in general, 90 percent of the people in this income bracket vote Republican, you might estimate that 189 of the nonrespondents are Republicans $(.70 \times 300 \times .90 = 189)$. However, because you have no way of ascertaining the possible error of this estimate, such estimates should be used to correct for nonresponses only if the nonresponse rate is relatively low.

23. Moser and Kalton, *Survey Methods in Social Investigation,* pp. 166–167.

24. Dennis J. Palumbo, *Statistics in Political and Behavioral Science,* rev. ed. (New York: Columbia University Press, 1977), p. 296.

SUMMARY

1. In this chapter, we focused on how we draw population estimates from sample statistics. To arrive at accurate estimates of parameters, the researcher has to resolve three major problems effectively: (a) definition of the population, (b) selection of a representative sample, and (c) determination of the sample size.
2. A population has to be defined in terms of content, extent, and time. A sample is any subset of sampling units taken from the population. A sample may range from one sampling unit to all but one sampling unit, or any number in between.
3. After defining the population and estimating the size of the sample, a representative sampling design has to be selected. A sample is representative if the analyses made on its units produce results identical to those that would be obtained had the entire population been analyzed. Researchers use probability sampling designs in situations where they can specify the probability of each unit of the population's being included in the sample. The characteristics of four basic probability samples—simple random, systematic, stratified, and cluster—are summarized in the box on page 175.
4. The determination of the sample size is directly dependent on the value of the standard error and on the width of the confidence interval set by the researcher. The confidence interval can be made extremely narrow if the researcher is willing to take a high risk of being wrong, or very wide if the researcher decides to take a small risk.
5. In survey research, nonresponse error is pervasive. Nonresponse is defined as measurements that are not performed because of refusal to answer, respondent absence, lost forms, and so on. Nonresponse can introduce a substantial bias into the findings. Consequently, if the nonresponse rate is low, researchers use one of the techniques discussed to compensate for the bias introduced.

KEY TERMS FOR REVIEW

cluster sampling (p. 173)
confidence interval (p. 179)
nonprobability sample (p. 167)
nonresponse error (p. 182)
parameter (p. 163)
population (p. 163)
probability sample (p. 167)
representative sample (p. 167)
sample (p. 163)

sampling frame (p. 165)
sampling unit (p. 164)
simple random sampling (p. 169)
standard error (p. 177)
statistic (p. 163)
stratified sampling (p. 171)
subset (p. 177)
systematic sampling (p. 171)

STUDY QUESTIONS

1. Why are samples used to study populations? List the different types of samples and give examples.
2. Distinguish between probability and nonprobability sampling, and explain the advantages and disadvantages of each. What sorts of social problems can be investigated with the use of the different sampling procedures?

3. Discuss the idea of sampling error and how it helps researchers to construct confidence intervals around their sample estimates. Give examples of how this information could influence your anticipated survey results.

4. What factors could introduce nonsampling error into a survey?

SPSS PROBLEMS

1. In this problem you are going to learn about the effect of sampling and sample size on obtaining estimates. For that purpose you will use the variable "income-91," for which you will calculate the mean and the standard error of the mean.

   a. Obtain the mean and the standard error of the mean for the variable "income91." Click on **Analyze → Summarize → Descriptive** and place "income91" in the variable list. Click on the **Options** box and select **Mean** and S.E. mean; click **Continue** and **OK** to calculate the statistics. Record the value of the mean and the standard error for "income91."

   b. Select a random sample of 10 percent from the **gss96worth file.** To use the sample procedure click on **Data → Select Cases.** The opening dialog box has four choices for selecting cases. Click on the **Random Sample of Cases** and then on **Sample.** In the next dialog box click on **Approximately** and type 10 in the box to ask for 10 percent of the original sample (you can always return to the full data file by selecting **All Cases**). Repeat the procedure described in 1a.

   c. Select random samples of 20, 35, and 50 percent each time, repeating the procedure described in 1a.

   d. How closely does the mean for "income91" from each random sample match that for the full sample? Does the estimate improve as you increase the sample size? What happens to the standard error of the mean as you increase the sample size? Explain.

ADDITIONAL READINGS

Alreck, Pamela L., and Robert B. Settle. *The Survey Research Handbook,* 2d ed. Blacklick, OH: McGraw-Hill, 1995.

Granovettes, Mark. "Network Sampling: Some First Steps." *American Journal of Sociology,* 81 (1976): 1287–1303.

Hess, Irene. *Sampling for Social Research Surveys, 1947–1980.* Ann Arbor: Institute for Social Research, University of Michigan, 1985.

Jaeger, Richard M. *Statistics: A Spectator Sport.* Thousand Oaks, CA: Sage, 1990.

Kalton, Graham. *Introduction to Survey Sampling.* Thousand Oaks, CA: Sage, 1983.

Rosenfeld, Paul, Jack W. Edwards, Marie D. Thomas, and Stephanie Booth-Kewley. *How to Conduct Organization Surveys: A Step-by-Step Guide.* Thousand Oaks, CA: Sage, 1998.

Salant, Priscilla, and Don A. Dillman. *How to Conduct Your Own Survey.* New York: Wiley, 1994.

Stuart, Alan. *The Ideas of Sampling,* 3d ed. New York: Oxford University Press, 1987.

Templeton, Jane F. *The Focus Group, A Strategic Guide to Organizing, Conducting and Analyzing the Focus Group Interview.* Blacklick, OH: McGraw-Hill, 1996.

Wainer, Howard, and Henry Braun (eds.). *Test Validity.* Mahwah, NJ: Erlbaum, 1988.

Yates, Frank. *Sampling Methods for Censuses and Surveys,* 4th ed. London: Griffin, 1987.

OBSERVATIONAL METHODS

The fragrance industry and the studies conducted in the new field of aromatherapy are based on the assumption that people respond to pleasing aromas in a positive way. Few of us have paid much systematic attention to how fragrances influence the way we feel or act, but Drs. Robert Baron and Marna Bronfen[1] have done just that. In a recent study, they investigated whether introducing pleasant fragrances into the work setting increases task performance (productivity) while reducing stress. Baron and Bronfen set up two controlled experimental situations in which a task, a fragrance, and a gift were manipulated experimentally. Their study raises two methodological issues every experimenter has to face: First, is experimental realism truly evoked within the laboratory setting? That is, is the situation experienced as real and meaningful by the participants in the experiment? Second, does the experiment reflect mundane realism? That is, does it contain elements similar to what the participants are likely to experience in the real world? In other words, Baron and Bronfen's work, like other experiments, asks us to consider the connection between the laboratory and real life, and whether the quality of the relationship between the two affects the validity of a researcher's findings.

● **IN THIS CHAPTER** we first discuss the four major methods of data collection used in the social sciences and illustrate the idea of triangulation—the practice of using more than one method of data collection as a strategy to test the same hypothesis. Next we discuss the role of observation in social science research. We then review the types of behavior that researchers observe and describe the main strategies for observing and recording data. The chapter closes with a discussion of controlled observation in the laboratory and in the field.

After deciding on the *what* and the *how* of the research design, we can proceed to the data collection stage. Social science data are obtained when researchers interested in investigating an event record observations of the phenomena. Four general methods of data collection may be distinguished: direct observation, survey research, secondary data analysis, and qualitative research. Social scientists employ a number of distinctive methods for each type of research, the most common of which are discussed in the following chapters. It should be emphasized at the outset, however, that each of the four fundamental methods has certain unique advantages but also some inherent limitations. For example, if a researcher asks members of a team to identity the most influential individual in their group by answering a questionnaire (survey research), the method may yield findings quite different from those that could be obtained through direct observation of the same work group. This example points to the fact that there is a certain degree of "method specificity" in each data collection method used. Consequently, researchers find it advantageous to triangulate whenever feasible—that is, they try to combine different methods of data collection to test the same hypothesis and corroborate their findings.

---

1. Robert A. Baron and Marna I. Bronfen, "A Whiff of Reality: Empirical Evidence Concerning the Effects of Pleasant Fragrances on Work-Related Behavior," *Journal of Applied Social Psychology*, 24 (1994): 1179–1203.

TRIANGULATION ●

Data in the social sciences are obtained in either formal or informal settings and involve verbal (oral and written) or nonverbal acts or responses. The combination of the two settings and the two types of responses results in the four major methods of data collection: observational methods, survey research (personal interviews and questionnaires, discussed in Chapters 10 and 11), qualitative research (discussed in Chapter 12), and secondary data analyses (such as the analysis of existing documents, a method discussed in Chapter 13). At one extreme, when researchers wish to study nonverbal actions in informal settings, they often use participant observation, a method of qualitative research. At the other extreme, when researchers focus on verbal (oral and written) acts in structured settings, the most commonly used methods of data collection are laboratory experiments and structured questionnaires.

As we pointed out previously, each data collection method has certain advantages as well as limitations. For example, if we observe behavior as it occurs (direct observation), we may miss the reasons for its occurrence, which may be better understood from the answers that respondents give to structured questionnaires. Similarly, if we ask respondents to report verbally on their behavior (interviewing), we have no guarantee that their actual behavior (studied by direct observation or by examining existing records) will be identical to their reported behavior. For example, in a study aimed at ascertaining the validity of welfare mothers' responses to interview questions about their voting habits, Carol Weiss reported:

> On the voting and registration questions, 82 percent of the welfare mothers answered accurately. Sixteen percent overreported their registration and 2 percent underreported. The amount and direction of response error are similar to those of the largely middle-class populations whose voting self-reports have been validated in previous studies.[2]

In voting behavior as in other behavior, discrepancies often appear between individuals' verbal reports and their actual behavior.

To a certain degree, research findings are affected by the nature of the data collection method used. Those research findings that are very strongly affected by the method used could be artifacts (i.e., findings that are a product of the data analysis method used; see below and Chapter 5) specific to the method used rather than empirical facts. As Donald Fiske points out:

> Knowledge in social science is fragmented, is composed of multiple discrete parcels. . . . The separateness or specificity of those bodies of knowledge is a consequence, not only of different objects of inquiry, but also of method specificity. Each method is one basis for knowing, one discriminable way of knowing.[3]

To minimize the degree of specificity or dependence on particular methods that might limit the validity or scope of the findings, a researcher can use two or more methods of data collection to test hypotheses and measure variables: This is the essence of **triangulation.** For example, a structured survey questionnaire might be supplemented with in-depth interviewing, existing records, or direct observation. If the findings obtained

2. Carol Weiss, "Validity of Welfare Mothers' Interview Responses," *Public Opinion Quarterly*, 32 (1968): 622–633.

3. Donald W. Fiske, "Specificity of Method and Knowledge in Social Science," in *Metalurgy in Social Science*, ed. Donald W. Fiske and Richard A. Shweder (Chicago: University of Chicago Press, 1986), p. 62.

by the different data collection methods are consistent, the validity of the findings increases. If not, then the hypotheses and research design call for reexamination. In addition, as a research strategy, triangulation has the benefit of increasing objectivity by raising social scientists "above the personal biases that stem from single methodologies. By combining methods in the same study, observers can partially overcome the deficiencies that flow from employing one single research or one method." [4]

ROLES OF OBSERVATION

Research in the social sciences is rooted in empirical observation, with each discipline specializing in a particular set of events and phenomena. For instance, political scientists observe the behavior of occupants of political offices; anthropologists observe rituals in simple rural as well as complex urban societies; and social psychologists observe interactions in small groups. In a sense, all social science research begins and ends with empirical observation.

The main advantage of observation is its *directness;* it enables researchers to study behavior in real time, as it occurs. The researcher does not have to ask people about their own behavior and the actions of others; he or she can simply watch them act and speak. This enables the researcher to collect data firsthand, thereby preventing "contamination" or distortion of the data by factors or events standing between him or her and the object of research. For example, when people are asked to report their past behavior, distortions in memory may influence the findings significantly, whereas memory has no effect on the behavioral data collected through observational methods.

Moreover, whereas other data collection methods introduce elements of artificiality into the research environment, observation describes phenomena as they occur in their *natural settings.* An interview, for example, is a method of data collection that involves face-to-face interaction. As such, interviewing is subject to unique problems because the agreed-upon roles of interviewer and interviewee may be violated. In situations where a lack of agreement prevails, interviewees may behave in an uncharacteristic manner (see Chapter 10). Such artificiality can be reduced if not entirely avoided in observational studies, especially when the research participants are not aware that they are being observed, or when they become accustomed to the observer and no longer regard him or her as an outsider.

Some studies focus on individuals who are unable to give verbal reports or to articulate in a meaningful way. For example, most studies of children require researchers to use methods of observation because it is difficult for children to be introspective, to verbalize, and to remain attentive to the lengthy tasks that are sometimes required by the research. David Riesman and Jeanne Watson, in an intriguing sociability study, used observational methods because the individuals studied "had no language for discussing sociable encounters, no vocabulary for describing parties except to say that they were 'good' or 'bad,' no way of answering the question 'What do you do for fun?' " [5]

Researchers can also use observational methods when individuals are unwilling to express themselves verbally. Compared to verbal reports, observation demands a lower level of active involvement from those being studied. Furthermore, through observation,

---

4. Norman K. Denzin, *The Research Act: A Theoretical Introduction to Sociological Methods,* 3d ed. (Englewood Cliffs, NJ: Prentice-Hall, 1989), p. 236.

5. David Riesman and Jeanne Watson, "The Sociability Project: A Chronicle of Frustration and Achievement," in *Sociologists at Work,* ed. Phillip E. Hammond (New York: Basic Books, 1964), p. 313.

researchers can validate verbal reports by comparing them with actual behavior. Finally, because the relationship between an individual and his or her environment is not altered in studies using observation, the researcher can detect the impact the environment has on the persons being studied. This facilitates analysis of the *contextual background* of the behavior observed.

It is important to remember that observation, as a method of data collection, uses many techniques. It can include casual experiences as well as sophisticated laboratory devices such as one-way mirrors and video cameras. Such diversity makes observation a suitable method for a variety of research purposes: Researchers employ observational methods in exploratory research in order to gain insights that will subsequently be tested as hypotheses; when collecting supplementary data for interpreting or validating findings obtained by other methods; or as primary methods of data collection in descriptive studies.

Observation, therefore, is a very versatile method. It can take place in natural settings, which enables studying phenomena, such as learning, as they occur in real-life situations (e.g., the classroom or the playground) or in the controlled experimental settings found in the laboratory. The choice of a procedure is guided by the requirements of the research. While the use of observation is determined by the state of knowledge about a general problem, the procedures used may be quite flexible. Alternatively, these procedures may be very specific and may use structured instruments designed in advance for unique contexts. For instance, when conducting participant observation, researchers can themselves participate in the activities of the group they are observing; they may be viewed as members of the group but minimize their participation; they may assume the role of an observer without being part of the group; or their presence may be concealed entirely from the people they are observing. Nevertheless, whatever the purpose of the study or the observational procedure used, researchers must effectively answer four major questions to ensure that the data obtained are systematic and meaningful: *What* will be observed? *Where and when* will the observations take place? *How* will the data be recorded? *How much* inference is required?

TYPES OF BEHAVIOR ●

The first significant issue concerns *what* to observe. Suppose a social scientist interested in studying the relationship between frustration and aggression hypothesizes that frustration leads to aggression. To test this hypothesis, the scientist must first observe frustration and aggression. To make observation possible, clear and precise operational definitions of the two variables have to be formulated. The operational definitions will determine how the variables will be measured, and whether that measurement will be based on nonverbal, spatial, extralinguistic, or linguistic behavior.[6]

Nonverbal Behavior

Nonverbal behavior is defined as "the body movements of the organism" and "consists of motor expressions . . . [that] may originate in various parts of the body."[7] Facial expressions in particular convey a whole range of emotions, including fear, surprise, anger,

---

6. The following discussion draws from Karl E. Weick, "Systematic Observational Methods," in *The Handbook of Social Psychology*, 3d ed., ed. Gardner Lindzey and Elliot Aronson (New York: Random House, 1985).

7. Paul Ekman, "A Methodological Discussion of Nonverbal Behavior," *Journal of Psychology*, 43 (1957): 141–149.

disgust, and sadness. Social scientists have studied nonverbal behavior extensively; their studies have repeatedly shown such behavior to be valid indicators of social, political, and psychological processes experienced by individuals and groups. Paul Ekman has suggested that observations of nonverbal behavior generate data that can serve "to repeat, contradict, or substitute for a verbal message, as well as accent certain words, maintain the communicative flow, reflect changes in the relationship in association with particular verbal messages and indicate a person's feeling about his verbal statement." [8] Scientists, therefore, often study nonverbal behavior as a means of validating other responses made by the respondents in the research situation.

Spatial Behavior

Spatial behavior refers to the actions taken by individuals as they structure the physical space around them. For example, people can move toward or away from a person or object; they can maintain closeness or distance in various contexts. For example, violations of personal space frequently produce stress, a condition in which people report feeling tense and anxious. The outcomes of stress lead to physiological symptoms: changes in galvanic skin response, pulse rate, and blood pressure, and so forth.[9] The range, frequency, and very outcomes of spatial behavior provide significant data for a variety of research aims. Scientists can then use these responses as indicators of, culturally determined spatial norms when conducting research on interpersonal behavior in a number of physical settings, such as crowds.

Observation of spatial behavior has taught us that there are distinct patterns in the way people use the space immediately surrounding them when they interact with others. Every culture develops unique unwritten codes regulating how closely individuals can approach each other: South Americans have narrower personal spaces than do North Americans, Germans, and the English. Cultural variations in personal space can have significant implications for behavior in culturally diverse cities and societies. An individual from a German background may find it uncomfortable to interact with a South American because each of them has difficulty establishing a satisfactory interpersonal space with the other. Friction may develop between the two as they try to establish a space defined as comfortable and acceptable in their respective cultures but as rude in terms of the other. Such differences in norms can even vary within one society. Aiello and Thompson found that among African American children, a greater degree of physical proximity is permitted than would be acceptable among Caucasians. However, adolescent African Americans maintain greater distances between themselves than do adolescent Caucasians.[10]

Linguistic Behavior

Linguistic behavior refers to words, the manifest content of speech, and the various attributes of verbal communication. The study of these characteristics can be applied to a

8. Paul Ekman, "Communication Through Nonverbal Behavior: A Source of Information About Interpersonal Relationship," in *Affect, Cognition, and Personality,* ed. Silvan S. Tomkins and Carroll E. Izard (New York: Springer, 1965), p. 441, and Paul Ekman and W. Friesen, "The Repertoire of Nonverbal Behavior: Categories, Origins, Usage and Coding," *Semiotica,* 1 (1969): 1–20.

9. S. Worchel and C. Teddlie, "The Experience of Crowding: A Two-Factor Theory," *Journal of Personality and Social Psychology,* 34 (1976): 30–40.

10. A. J. Aiello and E. D. Thompson, "Personal Space, Crowding, and Spatial Behavior in a Cultural Context," in *Human Behavior and Environment,* ed. I. Altman et al. (New York: Plenum, 1980).

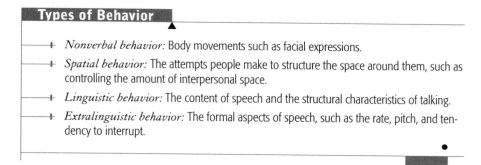

Types of Behavior

- *Nonverbal behavior:* Body movements such as facial expressions.
- *Spatial behavior:* The attempts people make to structure the space around them, such as controlling the amount of interpersonal space.
- *Linguistic behavior:* The content of speech and the structural characteristics of talking.
- *Extralinguistic behavior:* The formal aspects of speech, such as the rate, pitch, and tendency to interrupt.

number of research goals. Extensive use of measures of linguistic behavior has been made particularly in studies on social interaction. Robert Bales, for example, devised an efficient system for organizing and coding the the nonverbal behavior of individuals involved in group problem-solving activities. Bales's system, Interaction Process Analysis, or IPA, contains 12 kinds of distinctive behaviors that can be used for studying interaction (see Exhibit 9.1). Other social scientists, including scholars of political culture, have employed linguistic variables in studying leadership styles as well as political subcultures.

Extralinguistic Behavior

Words, in themselves, make up only a small portion of the linguistic content of behavior. The noncontent aspects of verbal behavior, such as the rate of speaking, loudness, the tendency to interrupt, and pronunciation peculiarities—characteristics generally referred to as **extralinguistic behavior** or **paralanguage**—constitute a fruitful source of data. The concept of "body language" refers to essentially the same phenomena.

Social scientists have documented the significance of paralanguage in numerous studies. For example, vocal characteristics such as pitch measure emotional states accurately.[11] The average duration of spontaneous speech increases as the size of the group increases.[12] The frequency with which one person interrupts another reflects differences in personal power. People express passive emotions such as sadness through slow, muted and lower-pitched speech; they communicate active emotions such as anger by fast, loud, and high-pitched speech. These examples can only hint at the range of topics that can be explored with this type of behavior.

TIMING AND RECORDING •

The second major set of issues influencing when to use observational methods concerns the timing and recording of the observations. Obviously, it is impossible to make an infinite number of observations; researchers must make decisions as to when to observe. One accepted approach to dealing with this problem is to follow a *time-sampling schedule.* **Time sampling** refers to the process of selecting *observation units,* specific points in

---

11. William F. Soskin and Paul E. Kauffman, "Judgment of Emotion in Word-Free Voice Samples," *Journal of Communication,* 11 (1961): 73–80.

12. William F. Soskin and John P. Vera, "The Study of Spontaneous Talk," in *The Stream of Human Behavior,* ed. Roger C. Baker (Norwalk, CT: Appleton & Lang, 1963).

Exhibit 9.1

IPA CODE OF CATEGORIES

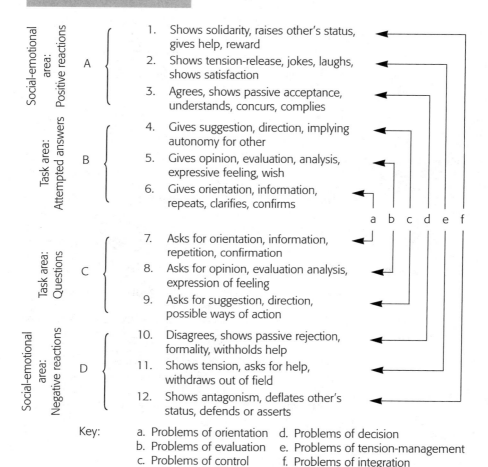

Key:
a. Problems of orientation   d. Problems of decision
b. Problems of evaluation   e. Problems of tension-management
c. Problems of control   f. Problems of integration

From Robert F. Bales, *Interaction Process Analysis*, by permission of the University of Chicago Press. Copyright © 1976 The University of Chicago Press.

time at which to make observations. This technique ensures the representativeness of the ongoing activities observed, otherwise known as the "defined population of behavior." For example, a researcher might make observations during a 15-minute period of each hour—the observation unit—selected randomly after stratifying the sample by day of the week and hour of the day. Another useful sampling procedure is *individual sampling*, also referred to as *specimen records*. In this case, the researcher selects one individual and records all the behavior and events experienced by that individual during a specified period of time. For example, when studying classroom aggression, the researcher might choose one child and record all instances of physical aggression between that child and other classmates for a period of 30 minutes. Every 30 minutes, a different child would be selected and observed. All the observations collected, the total data set, would then represent the behavior of the entire class.

The development of a time-sampling design also requires the development of a coding system for recording the observations. In order to transform the complexity of on-going events into data that can be quantified, one must first categorize and assign a code for each category. Such a coding system can be constructed by applying either a deductive approach or an inductive approach. When using a deductive approach, the researcher begins with a conceptual definition, specifies indicators of the behavior to be observed, and then standardizes and validates the resulting instrument. When implementing this approach during the course of the research, the observer assigns the observations to predefined categories at the time the observation is recorded. Conversely, the inductive approach requires the researcher to select indicators at the first stage of data collection and to postpone the construction of conceptual definitions until a pattern is identified. Each approach involves some risk. When using the deductive approach, it is difficult to foresee whether the conceptual definition is sufficiently precise. On the other hand, the inductive (or empirical) approach poses difficulties in interpreting the observations (see Chapter 14). The ideal way to reduce these risks is to combine the two approaches. Karl Weick suggests that

> in the ideal sequence, the researcher would start with the empirical approach, obtain extensive records of natural events, induce some concepts from the records, and then collect a second set of records which are more specific and pointed more directly at the induced concept.[13]

Regardless of whether researchers use a deductive or an inductive approach, the categories to which they assign observations must exhibit certain characteristics. The *category system* constructed must

> limit the observation to one segment or aspect of . . . behavior, and construct a finite set of categories into one and only one of which every unit observed can be classified.[14]

Put briefly, the categories must be explicit, exhaustive, and mutually exclusive. (For an in-depth discussion of categorization, see Chapter 14).

INFERENCE IN THE COURSE OF OBSERVATION   ●

The third major factor to be considered when structuring an observational study is the degree of inference required of the observer. Most observational data collection methods involve some degree of inference. When a researcher observes a certain act or behavior, he or she must process the information conveyed by the observation and infer whether the behavior indicates the variable being investigated. Some observations—straightforward acts such as "asks a question," "suggests a course of action," and "interrupts another group member"—demand a low degree of inference from the observer. Many acts, however, require a greater degree of inference. Suppose the researcher observes an adult striking a child. An inference has to be made as to whether this act represents "aggression," "frustration," "hostility," "violence," or some other variable. The

13. Weick, "Systematic Observational Methods," p. 102.

14. Donald M. Medley and Harold E. Mitzel, "Measuring Classroom Behavior by Systematic Observation," in *Handbook of Research on Teaching*, ed. Nathaniel L. Gage (Skokie, IL: Rand McNally, 1963), p. 298.

reliability of the inference depends to a large extent on the competence of the observer. Well-trained observers are likely to make more reliable inferences, other things being equal.

To increase observer competence and the reliability of the inferences made, training programs appropriate to various observational situations have been designed. Typically, a program begins with an exposition of the theory and the research hypotheses being studied, as well as an explanation of the categories and coding systems constructed to record the observations. After the trainees are given an opportunity to raise questions, they practice the application of the coding system in a real-life situation. Only after trainees have completed this trial run successfully do they begin the actual data collection.

TYPES OF OBSERVATION

Controlled and noncontrolled observational methods are differentiated by the extent to which decisions regarding behavior, timing, recording, and inference are systematically and rigorously implemented. **Controlled observational** methods are characterized by clear and explicit decisions made as to what, how, and when to observe; **noncontrolled observation** is considerably less systematic and allows for great flexibility. For example, in controlled observation, a time sample is usually drawn before making observations; in noncontrolled observation, sampling is rarely used. The choice between controlled and noncontrolled observation depends to a considerable extent on the research problem and research design; that is, social scientists use controlled observation most frequently with experimental research designs but seldom with preexperimental designs or qualitative studies. Controlled observation is discussed in this chapter; noncontrolled observation (qualitative research) is reviewed in Chapter 12.

Controlled Observation

Controlled observation can be carried out in the laboratory as well as in the field. In both settings, scientists wish to maximize control over extrinsic and intrinsic variables as a means to support the inference of causality. This control is exercised by employing one of a variety of experimental research designs and recording observations systematically.

LABORATORY EXPERIMENTATION

Laboratory experimentation is the most highly controlled method of data collection used in the social sciences. It involves the creation of a controlled environment, in the laboratory, where the situation's elements can be adjusted by the researcher according to a set plan. The laboratory setting permits simulation of certain features of a natural environment along with the manipulation of one or more elements, the independent variables, in order to observe the effects produced.

Solomon Asch's experiments on interpersonal influence are classic examples of laboratory experimentation. Asch's objective was to examine the social and personal factors that induce individuals to conform to or, alternatively, resist group pressures in situations where the group's perceived behavior appears to contradict the facts. Asch developed a procedure for arousing intense disagreement among peers and for measuring the effect of this relationship on the individual. In one such experiment, eight individuals were instructed to match the length of a given line with one of three unequal lines and to announce their judgments aloud. In the course of the experiment, one individual would suddenly be contradicted by the other seven members of the group, who were acting in accordance with Asch's instructions regarding when to respond with erroneous judgments. The errors of the majority were quite obvious, ranging between $\frac{1}{2}$ and $1\frac{3}{4}$ inches.

The eighth individual was therefore forced to confront a situation in which the group unanimously contradicted the evidence of his or her senses. The behavior of this individual, commonly referred to as the *critical subject,* was the true object of the investigation. Asch also employed a control group in which the errors made by the majority were not of the same order encountered under the experimental conditions. One of the interesting findings of these experiments was a marked movement made by the critical subject toward the positions taken by the majority within the experimental group:

> One third of all the estimates [of the critical subject] in the critical group were errors identical with or in the direction of the distorted estimates of the majority. The significance of this finding becomes clear in the light of the virtual absence of errors in the control group.[15]

Asch's experiments exemplify the two major advantages of laboratory experimentation: It allows rigorous control over extrinsic and intrinsic factors, and it provides unambiguous evidence about causation. Asch eliminated the effects of many variables that might have caused the critical subject to yield to or to resist group pressure. This increased the probability that the differences observed were due to changes that had been purposely introduced by the experimental treatment. Moreover, Asch could specify unambiguously what caused the movement of his critical subjects toward the majority opinion because he himself controlled and manipulated the independent variable—the seven members of the group and their responses. Furthermore, Asch modified the experimental treatment in a systematic way, thereby allowing precise specification of the relevant differences. Finally, Asch constructed the experiment in a way that enabled him to detect the effects of the experimental treatment clearly: The critical subjects had to state their judgments aloud. By openly expressing their judgments and taking a definite position vis-à-vis their peers, the critical subjects could not avoid the dilemma created within the experimental situation.

The ingenuity of Asch's experiments can only hint at the scope of experimental options available to the social scientist. Laboratory experiments do, in fact, vary in the complexity of their design, depending on the research problem and the ingenuity of the experimenter. In order for laboratory experiments to fulfill their potential, a set of procedures must be constructed that captures the meaning of the research problem as it is conceptualized by the researchers. These procedures must enable the testing of hypotheses. This requirement demands, in turn, the invention of measuring tools and a consideration of the influence the tools exert on the behavior of the participants in the experiment. In other words, the experimenter must construct a setting within which the manipulations of the independent variables make sense and the measurements are valid and reliable.

Experimental and Mundane Realism

Because the laboratory does not represent a real-world situation, questions may arise about how meaningful laboratory experimentation is for the participants. In the Asch

---

15. Solomon E. Asch, "Effects of Group Pressure upon the Modification Distortion of Judgments," in *Readings in Social Psychology*, ed. Eleanor Maccoby, Theodore Newcomb, and Eugene Hartley (New York: Holt, Rinehart and Winston, 1958), p. 177.

experiments, critical subjects were, after all, judging a very clear physical event (the length of lines) when they were contradicted by their peers. In everyday life, however, a situation where the obvious evidence of one's senses is contradicted by the unanimous judgments of one's peers is unlikely to occur.

This problem has led scientists to distinguish between two senses in which any given experiment can be said to be realistic.[16] In the first sense, an experiment is realistic if the situation is experienced as real by the research participants, that is, if it involves them and affects them. This kind of realism is generally termed **experimental realism.** In the Asch experiment, the critical subjects exhibited signs of tension and anxiety. This indicated that they were reacting to a situation that was as real for them as any of their experiences outside the laboratory.

The second sense of realism refers to the extent to which events taking place in the laboratory setting are likely to occur outside it, in the real world. This type of realism is called **mundane realism.** An experiment that is high on mundane realism and low on experimental realism does not necessarily yield more meaningful results than one that is high on experimental realism and low on mundane realism. Had Asch observed interpersonal behavior in the real world, he probably would not have found any situations so clearly structured that they would permit systematic observation of the effects of group pressure on individual members. Moreover, even if we assume that such a situation could have been found, because no control over the effects of intrinsic and extrinsic factors could have been exerted, the findings obtained would probably have been ambiguous and inconclusive. Therefore, by introducing both forms of realism into an experiment's design, one increases the internal validity of the experiment.

Sources of Bias in Laboratory Experiments

Notwithstanding the advantages of laboratory experiments, they do have certain inherent limitations. These can be classified as three potential types of bias: bias due to the demand characteristics of the experimental situation itself, bias due to the unintentional influence of the experimenters, and measurement artifacts.

DEMAND CHARACTERISTICS. Bias due to **demand characteristics** may occur when individuals who know that they are in an experimental situation, and who are aware that they are being observed, believe that certain responses are expected of them. Consequently, their responses to the experimental manipulation may not be straightforward. Instead, these may reflect the participants' interpretations of the behavior the manipulations are intended to elicit. Even if the experimenter states firmly that no responses are either right or wrong, the research participants may continue to believe that certain behaviors are being looked for and may thus try to comply with those expectations.[17] Research participants may also guess or find out what research hypothesis is being tested; as a result, they may respond in a manner they believe to be consistent with that hypothesis in an attempt to please the experimenter.

One device that experimenters commonly adopt in their attempts to counteract these sources of bias is to reduce the participants' awareness of being observed during

16. The following discussion is based on Elliot Aronson, Marilynn B. Brewer, and James Carlsmith, "Experimentation in Social Psychology," in *The Handbook of Social Psychology,* 3d ed., ed. Gardner Lindzey and Elliot Aronson (New York: Random House, 1985), pp. 481–483.

17. M. T. Orne, "Demand Characteristics and the Concept of Quasi-Controls," in *Artifacts in Behavioral Research,* ed. Robert Rosenthal and R. L. Rosnow (Orlando, FL: Academic Press, 1969).

the experimental situation. Another strategy is to limit their discussions of the project's objectives to general aims. The logic behind this approach is that if some individuals modify their behavior so as to support—or refute—what they erroneously believe to be the research hypothesis, the behavior relating to the true hypothesis may not be affected in a systematic way.[18]

EXPERIMENTER BIAS. Behavior on the part of the experimenter that is not intended to be part of the experimental manipulation but that nevertheless influences the participants is termed **experimenter bias** or the *experimental expectancy effect.* Experimenters may unintentionally communicate their expectations regarding the participants' behavior in various ways, such as showing tension or relief or by nodding when certain responses are made. Robert Rosenthal and his colleagues found that when 8 of 12 experimenters using the same methodology received biased data from their first two research participants (who were accomplices of Rosenthal and his colleagues), these early returns influenced the data they collected from the subsequent true research participants. The four experimenters who received hypothesis-confirming data from their first two research participants recorded the strongest positive data from the naïve participants who followed the planted research participants. The four experimenters who received contradictory data from their first two planted research participants recorded receiving the most contradictory data from their naïve participants. The comparison group of experimenters, who tested only naïve participants, obtained values ranging between those obtained by the other two groups of experimenters. Accordingly, the authors concluded that early returns bias the interpretation of subsequently obtained data.[19] Experimenter bias is thus the outcome of the observers'/experimenters' motivations.

By using tape recorders, television cameras, or other automated procedures to minimize interactions between experimenters and participants in experimental research, social scientists can minimize communication of expectations and thereby minimize unintentional experimenter bias. Such bias effects have also been mitigated by using a research staff composed of experimenters whose expectations of the outcome of the research differ from those of the social scientist who initiated and developed the

Three Sources of Bias in Experiments

+ *Demand characteristics:* When individuals know they are part of an experiment and try to respond in the way they think the experimenter wants them to.

+ *Experimenter bias:* When an experimenter unintentionally communicates his or her expectations about the behavior to be elicited to participants.

+ *Measurement artifacts:* When measurement procedures (e.g., cameras and test schedules) provide participants with hints about what is really going on in the experiment or otherwise influence their responses.

18. For a comprehensive discussion of bias-reducing methods, see Aronson et al., "Experimentation in Social Psychology."

19. Robert Rosenthal et al., "The Effects of Early Data Returns on Data Subsequently Obtained by Outcome-Biased Experimenters," *Sociometry,* 26 (1963): 487–493.

experimental design. In one study, expectations about the effects of the manipulated variables were included among the variables tested in the experimental design. In this case, the researchers attempted to assess whether their own differing expectations produced different outcomes.[20] Another proposed technique for reducing experimenter bias is the use of more than one observer or data gatherer. This technique modifies the effect of the individual researchers' personality traits, physical characteristics, and subtle differences in their treatment of participants.

MEASUREMENT ARTIFACTS.   Measurement is clearly a crucial element in the design of the experiment. In laboratory settings in particular, where the effects of an independent variable may be small, short, and sensitive—the reasons why the laboratory was chosen as the appropriate environment for studying the variable in the first place—precision is imperative. However, measurement procedures are not free of the problems that affect the research process as a whole. Like other aspects of the experiment, measurement procedures may introduce bias into the data by giving hints about the true purpose of the experiment. These hints may operate in a manner similar to experimenter bias or demand characteristics.

Most important, measuring instruments may be reactive in the sense that they may alter the phenomenon being measured. For instance, if researchers are using cameras to record responses, the individuals being studied may behave atypically just because they are aware of the cameras. Exposure to the measuring instrument in a pretest may familiarize individuals with its form and content, an experience that may influence their subsequent responses and scores. Even the timing of the measurement may produce misleading results: Measurement may be initiated before the independent variables have had sufficient time to affect the dependent variable or after those effects have waned, events that prevent the experimenter from capturing their influence. In a pioneering study, Carl Hovland and his associates provided a concrete illustration of this process. They found that discredited public figures were unable to persuade their listeners *immediately;* however, they sometimes did exert significant influence a month later, when the source of their statements was forgotten—unless the listeners were reminded of it.[21]

Recording Observations

The above discussion should sensitize us to the importance of how and when we record observations. In the laboratory, observations are recorded on the spot, during the experimental session. Mechanical devices such as video or movie cameras, tape recorders, and television are often used to obtain an overall view of what transpires. Next, the units of observation are assigned to a highly structured classificatory system such as the one reproduced in Exhibit 9.1. Categorization may take place during the experimental session if the system of recording has been prepared and pretested well in advance. With a well-prepared recording system and trained observers, the degree of inference required of the observers is minimal.

20. J. Merrill Carlsmith, Barry E. Collins, and Robert L. Helmreich, "Studies in Forced Compliance: I. The Effect of Pressure for Compliance on Attitude Change Produced by Face-to-Face Role Playing and Anonymous Essay Writing," *Journal of Personality and Social Psychology,* 4 (1966): 1–13.

21. Carl I. Hovland, Irving L. Janis, and Harold H. Kelley, *Communication and Persuasion* (New Haven, CT: Yale University Press, 1953).

FIELD EXPERIMENTS

As the terms imply, the major difference between laboratory experiments and field experiments is the setting in which the research is conducted. In the laboratory, social scientists introduce controlled conditions into the experimental environment that simulate certain features of a natural environment. In **field experiments,** because the research takes place in a natural environment, the investigator manipulates one or more independent variables under conditions that are as carefully controlled as the situation permits. In terms of research design, there is little difference between laboratory and field experiments (see Chapter 5). However, the difficulties involved in controlling intrinsic, and especially extrinsic, factors are considerably greater in field experiments.

An intriguing example of field experimentation is the often-cited Piliavin, Rodin, and Piliavin study on helping behavior—altruism.[22] The researchers conducted a field experiment to study the effects of several variables on helping behavior, using express trains on New York's Eighth Avenue subway line as laboratories on wheels. Four teams of students, each consisting of a victim, a model, and two observers, staged standardized events of a person collapsing in which the type of victim (ill or drunk), the race of the victim (African American or Caucasian), and the presence or absence of a model "helper" (the "altruist") were varied. Observations were recorded as to the number and race of bystanders, the inherent propensity to help (the latency of the helping response), the race of the helper, the number of helpers, the movement out of the "critical area" in which the event was staged, and spontaneous comments. Figure 9.1 illustrates the setting of this experiment.

The researchers found that (1) a person who appears to be ill is more likely to receive assistance than one who appears to be drunk; (2) the race of the victim has little effect on the race of the helper except when the victim appears to be drunk; (3) men are

Figure 9.1

Layout of the Altruism Field Experiment

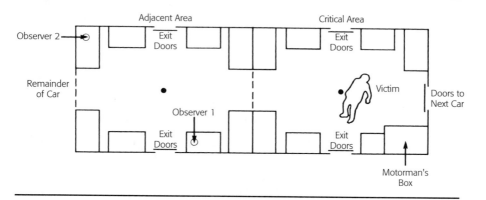

22. Irving M. Piliavin, Judith Rodin, and Jane Allyn Piliavin, "Good Samaritanism: An Underground Phenomenon?" *Journal of Personality and Social Psychology,* 13 (1969): 289–299.

considerably more likely to help than women; and (4) the longer the emergency continues without help being offered, the more likely it is that someone will simply leave the
area.

In this study, the experimenters relied primarily on systematic observation within a
natural setting. They did not control their setting fully; instead, they introduced a systematic variation—the type and behavior of accomplices—in order to study the helping behavior of bystanders in the largely uncontrolled context of a subway train. This example
illustrates that researchers conducting field experiments can construct different experimental situations as well as introduce experimental variations into natural environments.
In other types of field experiments, the researcher may chose not to manipulate the independent variables but to observe those variables (stimuli) that represent the theoretical concept of interest but that are already found within the natural setting.

As we pointed out earlier, the main appeal of field experiments is that they permit investigation of complex interactions, processes, and change in real-life, natural situations.
Their major weakness lies in the area of control: Researchers cannot control intrinsic and
extrinsic sources of validity as systematically in field experiments as they can in laboratory
experiments. For instance, research participant self-selection is a pervasive problem, and
randomization is often impossible. In order to estimate the effects of many of these non-
controllable elements on the research outcomes, a pilot study is often carried out. Pilot
studies, because they are test runs or pretests of the experiment, enable the investigator
to ascertain whether the research participants (or any other aspect of the research design) are likely to differ systematically on any relevant factor other than their responses to
the independent variable.[23]

Ethical issues are, of course, as major a concern in field experiments as they are in
laboratory experiments. Is it ethical to expose innocent bystanders to someone pretend-
ing to collapse and to be seriously ill? In laboratory experiments, the rights of the participants are protected by informed consent and by debriefing; they are also aware that
they are taking part in research. Even if the participants enter the experimental session
with no information about the experiment's objective, they know that they will receive
that information after the session is over. In contrast, the participants in field experiments
are often unaware that they are taking part in research. In such situations, the social scientist has to ensure that the privacy of the affected individuals is not violated and that
they are protected from undue embarrassment or distress. (Methods for ensuring privacy and confidentiality are discussed in Chapter 4.)

SUMMARY

1. To enhance the validity of their findings, social scientists employ triangulation, the
   use of two or more methods of observation and data collection when studying the
   same phenomenon.
2. Observation is the archetypal method of scientific research. If you want to understand, explain, and predict a phenomenon, you can simply observe it. However, if
   your findings are to be systematic and your conclusions valid, the observations
   must be carried out in accordance with the criteria associated with four crucial issues: what to observe, where and when to observe, how to record the data, and
   how much to infer when recording observations.

23. For other methods used to minimize validity problems, see Aronson et al., "Experimentation in Social
Psychology."

3. The research problem requires, first and foremost, designation of what type of behavior is to be observed—nonverbal, spatial, linguistic, or extralinguistic.
4. How to carry out your observations is the focus of the research design. If the objective is to test a hypothesis experimentally, the units of observation are defined explicitly, a setting is chosen—the laboratory or the field—a time sample is drawn, and the observations are recorded systematically. The observation and measurement procedures should involve as little inference on the part of the observer as possible.
5. It is helpful to distinguish between experimental realism—the extent to which an experimental situation is experienced as real by the research participants—and mundane realism—the relevance of an experimental situation to the real world.
6. Systematic bias may be introduced in experiments as a result of demand characteristics, experimenter bias, and measurement artifacts.
7. Laboratory experiments allow the social scientist to exercise the greatest amount of control over the intrinsic and extrinsic factors affecting the validity of the research design and its findings. On the other hand, field experiments present challenges to the social scientist because of the difficulties involved in controlling the setting (the natural environment), manipulating the independent variable, and preventing self-selection. Ethical issues are an even greater concern in field experiments because the observed individuals are unaware that they are involved in an experimental situation.

KEY TERMS FOR REVIEW ●

controlled observation (p. 196)
demand characteristics (p. 198)
experimental realism (p. 198)
experimenter bias (p. 199)
extralinguistic behavior (p. 193)
field experiments (p. 201)
linguistic behavior (p. 192)

mundane realism (p. 198)
noncontrolled observation (p. 196)
nonverbal behavior (p. 191)
paralanguage (p. 193)
spatial behavior (p. 192)
time sampling (p. 193)
triangulation (p. 189)

STUDY QUESTIONS ●

1. Why would a researcher choose to triangulate? Is triangulation more important in a laboratory or a field setting?
2. List a set of research goals and select the various methods of observation you think most appropriate to each goal. Explain your choice.
3. What is the difference between experimental and mundane realism? Discuss how each may influence your chosen method of observation for reaching the research goals listed in your response to Question 2.
4. Describe the major techniques for timing and recording observations.
5. Discuss the strengths and weaknesses of laboratory experiments versus field experiments as methods of observation.

ADDITIONAL READINGS ●

Bales, Robert F., Stephen P. Cohen, and Stephen A. Williamson. *SYMLOG: A Manual for the Multiple Case Study of Groups.* New York: Free Press, 1979.

Bonacich, Philip, and John Light. "Laboratory Experimentation in Sociology." *Annual Review of Sociology*, 4 (1978): 145–170.

Brewer, John, and Albert Hunter. *Multimethod Research: A Synthesis of Styles*. Thousand Oaks, CA: Sage, 1989.

Deacon, David, Alan Bryman, and Natalie Fenton. "Collision or Collusion: A Discussion and Case Study of the Unplanned Triangulation of Quantitative and Qualitative Research Methods." *International Journal of Social Research Methodology*, 1 (1998): 47–63.

Druckman, Daniel. *Nonverbal Communication*. Thousand Oaks, CA: Sage, 1982.

Emerson, Robert M. "Observational Field Work." *Annual Review of Sociology*, 7 (1981): 351–378.

Hertz, Rosanna, ed. *Reflexivity and Voice*. Thousand Oaks, CA: Sage, 1997.

Iyengar, Shanto, Mark D. Peters, and Donald R. Kinder. "Experimental Demonstrations of the 'Not-So-Minimal' Consequences of Television News Programs." *American Political Science Review*, 76 (1982): 848–888.

Maguire, Patricia. *Doing Participatory Research: A Feminist Approach*. Boston: University of Massachusetts, Center for International Education, 1987.

Ray, William J., and Richard Ravizza. *Methods Toward a Science of Behavior and Experience*, 5th ed. Pacific Grove, CA: Brooks Cole, 1996.

Rosenthal, Robert. *Meta-Analytical Procedures for Social Research*, rev. ed. Thousand Oaks, CA: Sage, 1991.

Rosnow, Ralph, and Robert Rosenthal. *Beginning Behavioral Research: A Conceptual Primer*, 2d ed. Paramus, NJ: Prentice-Hall, 1995.

Vargas, Marjorie F. *Louder Than Words: An Introduction to Nonverbal Communication*. Ames: Iowa State University Press, 1986.

Zelditch, Morris. *Some Methodological Problems of Field Studies*. Reprint. Irvington, NY: Irvington, 1993.

SURVEY RESEARCH

E-mail (electronic mail) is becoming an increasingly popular method of communication between parties with access to computers equipped with modems. Information and messages sent via e-mail reach their destination in minutes rather than days, as may be the case with conventional mail, and users can send fairly large files at a reasonable cost. Researchers looking for new methods of conducting surveys may soon find e-mail to be an alternative to traditional mail and telephone surveys. Professor Samuel Brown of Fordham University recently tested the viability of e-mail as a method of securing survey responses.[1] Using a different name and posing as a student needing information for a class project, he sent messages to 150 e-mail service subscribers living in Abilene, Texas. Although he had selected Abilene simply because it was at the top of an alphabetical list of cities, Brown described it as the "ideal" city and asked people for their views on the attributes of the city. Brown was somewhat surprised by the response to his message. Some of the potential respondents contacted their local newspaper to report that Abilene had been selected as an ideal city. When the newspaper checked the credentials of the researcher, they discovered that the student did not exist and uncovered Brown's deception. Nevertheless, Brown says he received about 30 responses to his survey and intends to have the members of his sociology class perform e-mail surveys.

In this chapter we discuss the advantages and disadvantages of more traditional survey methods. As you read the chapter, think about the possible advantages and disadvantages of e-mail as a data collection technique.

•| **SOCIAL SCIENCE RESEARCHERS** can choose from among three methods of gathering data with surveys: mail questionnaires, personal interviews, and telephone interviews. In this chapter, we explore the activities involved in conducting the three different types of surveys and discuss the advantages and disadvantages of each. We conclude the chapter by comparing the three methods.

Observational methods of data collection are suitable for investigating phenomena that researchers can observe directly. However, not all phenomena are accessible to the investigator's direct observation; very often, therefore, the researcher must collect data by asking people who have experienced certain phenomena to reconstruct their experiences. Keeping in mind budget restrictions and the availability of staff, the researcher must determine the survey method that will elicit the most complete responses from a sample of individuals presumed to have experienced the phenomenon of interest. The responses constitute the data on which the research hypotheses are examined. |

MAIL QUESTIONNAIRE •

The **mail questionnaire** is an impersonal survey method. Under certain conditions and for a number of research purposes, an impersonal method of data collection can be useful. As with any method, however, mail questionnaires have both advantages and disadvantages.

---

1. Richard Perez-Pena, "Professor's Plan Backfires: E-Mail Project Was Hoax," *The New York Times,* July 11, 1994, p. B2.

Advantages of the Mail Questionnaire

1. *Low cost.* Economy is one of the most obvious appeals of mail questionnaires. The mail questionnaire does not require a trained staff of interviewers; all it entails is the cost of planning, sampling, duplicating, mailing, and providing stamped, self-addressed envelopes for the returns. Processing and analysis are usually also simpler and cheaper than for other survey methods. The lower cost of administering a mail questionnaire is particularly evident when the population under study is spread over a large geographic area. Under such circumstances, the cost of interviewing could become prohibitive, and the mail questionnaire may be the only practicable instrument.

2. *Reduction in biasing error.* The use of a mail questionnaire reduces *biasing errors* that might result from the personal characteristics of interviewers and variability in their skills. Personal interview situations are fraught with possibilities for bias because of the nature of the interaction between the interviewer and the respondent. Investigators can avoid this pitfall by using a mail questionnaire.

3. *Greater anonymity.* The absence of an interviewer also provides greater anonymity for the respondent. The assurance of anonymity that a mail questionnaire provides is especially helpful when the survey deals with sensitive issues, such as sexual behavior or child abuse. People in the sample are more likely to respond to sensitive questions when they do not have to face an interviewer or speak to someone directly.

4. *Considered answers and consultations.* Mail questionnaires are also preferable when questions demand a considered (rather than an immediate) answer or if answers require respondents to consult personal documents or other people.

5. *Accessibility.* Finally, the mail questionnaire permits wide geographic contact at minimal cost. When a survey requires wide coverage and addresses a population that is dispersed geographically, interviewing would involve high travel costs and large investments of time.

Disadvantages of the Mail Questionnaire

1. *Requires simple questions.* Researchers can use the mail questionnaire as an instrument for data collection only when the questions are straightforward enough to be comprehended solely on the basis of printed instructions and definitions.

2. *No opportunity for probing.* The answers have to be accepted as final; researchers have no opportunity to probe beyond the given answer, to clarify ambiguous answers, or to appraise the nonverbal behavior of respondents.

3. *No control over who fills out the questionnaire.* With a mail questionnaire, researchers have no control over the respondent's environment; hence they cannot be sure that the appropriate person completes the questionnaire. An individual other than the intended respondent may complete it.

4. *Low response rate.* The final disadvantage of a mail questionnaire—and perhaps its most serious problem—is that it is often difficult to obtain an adequate response rate. The **response rate** is the percentage of respondents in the sample who return completed questionnaires. For many mail surveys, the reported response rates are much lower than for personal interviews. The typical response rate for a personal interview is about 95 percent, whereas the response rate for a mail survey without follow-up is between 20 and 40 percent. Researchers who use mail questionnaires

---

Advantages and Disadvantages of Mail Questionnaires ▲

ADVANTAGES

+ The cost is low compared to other methods.

+ Biasing error is reduced because respondents are not influenced by interviewer characteristics or techniques.

+ Questionnaires provide a high degree of anonymity for respondents. This is especially important when sensitive issues are involved.

+ Respondents have time to think about their answers and/or consult other sources.

+ Questionnaires provide wide access to geographically dispersed samples at low cost.

DISADVANTAGES

+ Questionnaires require simple, easily understood questions and instructions.

+ Questionnaires do not offer researchers the opportunity to probe for additional information or to clarify answers.

+ Researchers cannot control who fills out the questionnaire.

+ Response rates are low.

---

must almost always face the problem of how to estimate the effect the nonrespondents may have on their findings. (The response rate is of great significance when making generalizations; see Chapter 19). Nonrespondents are usually quite different from those who answer a questionnaire. Often they are the poorly educated who may have problems understanding the questions, the elderly who are unable to respond, or the more mobile who cannot be located. Consequently, the group of respondents is not likely to represent accurately the population originally defined by the investigators, and this will undoubtedly introduce bias into the study.

Factors Affecting the Response Rate of Mail Questionnaires

Researchers use various strategies to overcome the difficulty of securing an acceptable response rate to mail questionnaires and to increase the response rate.

SPONSORSHIP. The sponsorship of a questionnaire has a significant effect on respondents, often motivating them to fill it out and return it. Therefore, investigators must include information on sponsorship, usually in the cover letter accompanying the questionnaire. Sponsorship affects the response rate by convincing the respondent of the study's legitimacy and value as well as the perceived sanctions of a failure to reply. For example, the United States Bureau of the Census is successful in obtaining a response rate of nearly 95 percent on its National Health Interview Survey because it is government sponsored—which lends legitimacy and implies sanctions—and health is an important issue to the public. At the other extreme, only 5 percent of the sample responds in some mail surveys.[2] In general, government-sponsored questionnaires obtain high re-

---

2. Floyd Fowler, Jr., *Survey Research Methods* (Newbury Park, CA: Sage, 1989), p. 48.

sponse rates, while relatively little-known commercial organizations get low response rates.

INDUCEMENT TO RESPOND.   Researchers who use mail surveys must appeal to the respondents and persuade them that they should participate by filling out the questionnaires and mailing them back. Several methods can be used, which vary in their degree of effectiveness. One method is to appeal to the respondents' goodwill, telling them that the researchers need their help. For example, a student conducting a survey for a class project may mention that his or her grade may be affected by the response to the questionnaire.

Another widely used method is to offer the respondent a reward, such as a prize or money. In an effort to obtain cooperation, survey organizations are offering monetary incentives with increasing frequency, either at the outset of the survey or after the person has refused, in an attempt to convert the refusal.[3] The problem with offering a monetary incentive is that it may lead to expectations for such incentives in the future. Another concern is whether the offer of an incentive is likely to replace intrinsic motivation to participate with extrinsic motivation, with a resulting decline in the quality of responses.[4] However, most often respondents see the reward as a symbolic gesture, and they cooperate because they consider the study worthwhile.

Other inducements to respond include letters of support from professional associations and advertisements of the coming survey in publications of professional associations. Perhaps the most effective strategy, however, is to appeal to the respondents' altruistic sentiments and to convince them of the significance of the study. In the following example from a cover letter accompanying a questionnaire, the writer emphasizes the importance of the study and the respondents' potential contribution to its success:

> As you know, public service employment is a major part of the federal, state, and local strategy to overcome the employment and income problems of economically disadvantaged unemployed people. There is no question that the program is needed throughout the country. . . . You are probably also aware . . . that public service employment programs are quite controversial and their future may be in jeopardy. Part of the reason that these programs are so controversial is that no systematic evaluation of the benefits of these programs for the individuals employed and the communities served has been conducted.
>
> Because this specific evaluation has significant national implications, I strongly urge you to give this enclosed questionnaire your prompt attention and thank you for your cooperation in this evaluations.[5]

QUESTIONNAIRE FORMAT AND METHODS OF MAILING.   Designing a mail questionnaire involves several considerations: typography, color, and length and type of cover letter. A slightly larger investment in format and typography (e.g., high-quality paper and adequate spacing) will pay off in a higher response rate.

COVER LETTER.   Another factor to be considered in designing the questionnaire is the cover letter. The cover letter must succeed in convincing the respondents to fill out the

---

3. Eleanor Singer, John Van Hoewyk, and Mary P. Maher, "Does the Payment of Incentives Create Expectation Effects?" *Public Opinion Quarterly*, 62 (1998): 152–164.

4. Ibid., p. 154.

5. Mickey L. Burnim, *An Evaluation of the Public Service Employment Projects in Florida Created Under Title VI of the Comprehensive Employment and Training Act of 1973* (Tallahassee: Florida Department of Community Affairs, 1978), p. 164.

questionnaire and mail it back. It should therefore identify the sponsor of the study, explain its purpose, tell the respondents why it is important that they fill out the questionnaire, and assure them that the answers will be held in strict confidence. The investigator must choose between a formal or a semipersonal letter. Studies have shown that a semipersonal letter generates a slightly higher response rate than a formal form letter.

TYPE OF MAILING.   An important consideration is the type of mailing to be used. Questionnaires that are not accompanied by a postpaid return envelope obtain few responses. It is unreasonable to expect the respondent not only to fill out the questionnaire but also to find an envelope and then go to the post office to have it weighed and stamped. Hence it is a common practice to enclose a stamped, self-addressed envelope. (An official-looking business reply envelope tends to reduce the response rate.)

TIMING OF MAILING.   The timing of mailing has been shown to affect the response rate of mail questionnaires. For example, because summer and holidays produce the lowest response rate, it is not advisable to conduct the first wave of a mailing during those times.

THE TOTAL DESIGN METHOD (TDM).   In recent years, researchers have improved data collection with mail surveys considerably by applying the *total design method,* a standardized set of step-by-step procedures[6] that is divided into two parts: questionnaire construction and survey implementation.

The principles researchers follow in constructing TDM questionnaires include paying particular attention to details such as the outside of the envelope that contains the questionnaire, the front cover of the questionnaire, and the order of the questions. Researchers using TDM try to make sure that the questionnaire will be immediately differentiated from junk mail.

The TDM implementation procedures focus primarily on **follow-up.** The most common follow-up strategy is to send a reminder postcard to respondents who have not replied one week after the first mailing. The second follow-up consists of another reminder letter and a replacement questionnaire with a return envelope sent at the end of the third week. After seven weeks, another letter with a replacement questionnaire is sent, preferably by certified mail, to all of the individuals who have not responded.

Researchers tested the effectiveness of these follow-up methods on large statewide samples of the general population in four states. Table 10.1 shows the average and the cumulative response rates at the end of each step of the follow-up procedure. The results reveal the importance of a *multiwave follow-up.* Observe that each wave increases the response rate substantially in the most cost-effective manner. Postcards, the least expensive type of follow-up mailing, are sent to the greatest number of people. Certified mailings, the most expensive type of mailing, go out to the fewest people. Indeed, "with a mail methodology available which will consistently provide a high response, poor return rate can no more be excused than can inadequate theory or inappropriate statistics."[7] Recently, critics have suggested that the use of certified mail has some im-

6. Donald A. Dillman, "Mail and Other Self-Administered Questionnaires," in *Handbook of Survey Research,* ed. Peter H. Rossi, James D. Wright, and Andy B. Anderson (Orlando, FL: Academic Press, 1983), and Anton J. Nederhof, "Effects of a Final Telephone Reminder and Questionnaire Cover Design in Mail Surveys," *Social Science Research,* 17 (1988): 353–361.

7. Donald A. Dillman, James A. Christensen, Edward H. Carpenter, and Ralph M. Brooks, "Increasing Mail Questionnaire Response: A Four-State Comparison," *American Sociological Review,* 39 (1974): 755.

Table 10.1

Average and Cumulative Response Rates to Four Mailings

Mailing	Time	Average Response Rate	Cumulative Response Rate
1. First mailing	Week 1	23.8%	23.8%
2. Postcard follow-up	Week 2	18.2	42.0
3. First replacement questionnaire	Week 4	17.0	59.0
4. Second replacement sent by certified mail	Week 7	13.4	72.4

Adapted from Donald A. Dillman, James A. Christensen, Edward H. Carpenter, and Ralph M. Brooks, "Increasing Mail Questionnaire Response: A Four-State Comparison," *American Sociological Review,* 39 (1974): 755, and Donald A. Dillman and D. E. Moore, "Improving Response Rates to Mail Surveys: Results from Five Surveys," paper presented at the annual meeting of the American Association for Public Opinion Research, Hershey, PA, 1983.

portant drawbacks.[8] Respondents may feel coerced by the requirement of signing for receipt, and the cost in time and money may be even greater if the recipient has to go to the post office to retrieve the questionnaire. As an alternative, the final follow-up by certified mail may be replaced by a telephone reminder, which is as effective as certified mail in reducing nonresponse.

Although follow-up is clearly an important mechanism in raising the response rate, it creates several problems. First, because researchers send follow-up letters and questionnaires only to respondents who have not replied, it is necessary to identify all respondents; thus anonymity cannot be maintained. Researchers can get around this difficulty by assuring respondents that the replies will be held in strict confidence. Another limitation is that the quality of the responses declines with successive mailings. Individuals who do not respond the first time might be less likely to take the study seriously and thus may return incomplete questionnaires, or their answers may be unreliable. Researchers can examine bias due to this reason by comparing the responses of people who reply immediately with the responses of people who return the questionnaire after one or more follow-up steps are taken.[9]

SELECTION OF RESPONDENTS. The selection of respondents is determined largely by the nature of the study and the characteristics of the population. Thus, beyond the definition of the sampling population, there is very little a researcher can do during the selection process to increase the response rate. However, certain characteristics of potential respondents are associated with a high or low response rate. Recognizing this can help a researcher determine if a mail questionnaire should be used to begin with, or whether to use other strategies to increase the response rate. The most significant dimension a researcher needs to consider in selecting respondents is whether they consist of a heterogeneous or a homogeneous group. Heterogeneous groups consist of individuals who differ from one another in some way that might influence the phenomenon of interest. For

8. Nederhof, "Effects," p. 354.

9. Fowler, *Survey Research Methods,* p. 54.

example, a heterogeneous group could consist of individuals from various ethnic and racial backgrounds, with different levels of income, or from urban and rural locations. Homogeneous groups, by contrast, consist of individuals with similar characteristics. Heterogeneous groups are typically used in opinion polls, whereas in more specialized studies, questionnaires are sent to select groups, for example, to physicians, legislators, city managers, university professors, or members of the local chamber of commerce. The response rate for select groups is usually higher than it is for the general population because members of these groups are more likely to identify with the goals of the study and thus will be more motivated to respond. Beyond this distinction, certain background characteristics are associated with differences in response rates. Respondents who are more educated are more likely to fill out and return questionnaires. Interest in or familiarity with the topic under investigation is another important factor in determining the rate of return. Finally, in general, professionals tend to have the highest response rate among all occupations.

Table 10.2 ranks the various procedures discussed so far according to their relative effectiveness in increasing the rate of return of questionnaires. The ranks were deter-

Table 10.2

Techniques for Increasing Response Rate

Method	Rank (High to Low)	Optimal Conditions
Follow-up	1	More than one follow-up. Telephone could be used for follow-up.
Inducement	2	Questionnaires containing a token monetary reward produce better results than ones without. However, the population and the type of questionnaire have to be considered.
Sponsorship	3	People the respondent knows produce the best results.
Introductory letter	4	An altruistic appeal seems to produce the best results.
Method of return	—	A regular stamped envelope produces better results than a business reply envelope.
Format	—	Esthetically pleasing cover; a title that will arouse interest; an attractive page format.
Selection of respondents	—	• Nonreaders and nonwriters are excluded from participation.
		• Interest in or familiarity with the topic under investigation is a major factor in determining the rate of return.
		• The better educated are more likely to return the questionnaires.
		• Professionals are more likely to return questionnaires.

Adapted from Delbert C. Miller, *Handbook of Research Design and Social Measurement,* 5th ed. (Newbury Park, CA: Sage, 1991); Pamela L. Alreck and Robert B. Settle, *The Survey Research Handbook* (Homewood, IL: Irwin, 1985); and Francis J. Yammarino, Steven J. Skinner, and Terry L. Childers, "Understanding Mail Survey Response Behavior: A Meta-Analysis," *Public Opinion Quarterly,* 55 (1991): 613–639.

mined on the basis of various studies estimating the possible increase of total return for each procedure. Rank could not be determined for the last three procedures.

Evaluating the Response Rate

What is an acceptable response rate for a mail questionnaire? Most investigators attempt to maximize the response rate by using some or all of the strategies just discussed. Despite these efforts, however, many mail surveys achieve a response rate no greater than 50 percent. Nonresponse is a serious problem because nonrespondents differ considerably from respondents. Studies have shown that mail questionnaires addressed to the general population are likely to result in an upward bias in education: Better-educated people tend to respond more quickly to mail questionnaires.[10] Therefore, the bias resulting from nonresponse may limit the investigator's ability to make generalizations about the entire population.

The question of what constitutes an acceptable response rate cannot be answered easily because scientists do not agree on a standard for a minimum response rate. For example, surveys done under contract to the federal government are expected to yield a response rate higher than 75 percent. Academic survey organizations are usually able to achieve that level, but the response rates for surveys conducted by more obscure organizations are considerably lower.

Finally, there is some evidence that response rates to mail questionnaires have been improving with the increased standardization of follow-up techniques.[11]

Indeed, in recent years, survey research has become a widely used tool, not only of research and marketing organizations, but also of national and local government. Some citizens, though dedicated and loyal to the goals of research, may find themselves trying to decide which and how many of the questionnaires they receive each year deserve a response. The satirical questionnaire for questioners reprinted in Exhibit 10.1 is an attempt to sensitize the questioners to this problem.

PERSONAL INTERVIEW ●

The personal interview is a face-to-face, interpersonal role situation in which an interviewer asks respondents questions designed to elicit answers pertinent to the research hypotheses. The questions, their wording, and their sequence define the structure of the interview.

The Schedule-Structured Interview

The least flexible personal interview form is the **schedule-structured interview.** In scheduled interviews the number of questions and the wording of the questions are identical for all of the respondents. Thus interviewers should not reword questions or provide explanations of the questions if the respondent asks for clarification. In a structured interview the sequence in which the questions are asked is the same in every interview. The schedule-structured interview combines these two elements. Researchers use the schedule-structured interview to make sure that any variations among responses can be attributed to the actual differences among the respondents and not to variations in the interview. The researcher attempts to reduce the risk that changes in the way

10. Ibid., pp. 355–356.

11. Nederhof, "Effects," p. 356.

Exhibit 10.1

QUESTIONNAIRE FOR QUESTIONERS

Dear Questioner:

You are no doubt aware that the number of questionnaires circulated is rapidly increasing, whereas the length of the working day has, at best, remained constant. In order to resolve the problem presented by this trend, I find it necessary to restrict my replies to questionnaires to those questioners who first establish their *bona fide* by completing the following questionnaire:

1. How many questionnaires, per annum, do you distribute? _____

2. How many questionnaires, per annum, do you receive? _____

3. What fraction of the questionnaires you receive do you answer? _____

4. What fraction of the questionnaires you distribute are answered? _____

5. Do you think the ratio of the fraction 3:4 should be greater than 1, less than 1, any other value? (Please explain.) _____

6. What fraction of your time (or effort) do you devote to:

   a. Compiling questionnaires? _____

   b. Answering questionnaires? _____

   c. Examining the replies to your own questionnaires? _____

   d. Examining the replies to other people's questionnaires? _____

   e. Drawing conclusions from questionnaires? _____

   f. Other activities? _____

   $(a + b + c + d + e + f$ should add up to 100 percent. If not, please explain.)

7. Do you regard the ratio of $(a + b + c + d + e)/f$ as:

   a. Too small? _____

   b. Too large? _____

   c. Any other? _____ (check one only)

8. Do you ever distribute questionnaires exclusively to people whom you know distribute questionnaires?

9. Do you expect answers to questionnaires from people who themselves distribute questionnaires about questionnaires?

10. Do you consider it would be of value to distribute a questionnaire regarding answers to questionnaires to those individuals who receive questionnaires about the distribution of questionnaires?

   Yes _____

   No _____ (check one only)

   Any other answer? please explain.

Replies to this questionnaire must be signed. As you may surmise, they are not suitable, nor will they be used for statistical purposes.

From Samuel Devons, "A Questionnaire for Questioners," *Public Opinion Quarterly*, 39 (1975): 255–256.

questions are worded, for example, might elicit differences in responses. The schedule-structured interview is based on three crucial assumptions:

1. That for any research objective, "the respondents have a sufficiently common vocabulary so that it is possible to formulate questions which have the same meaning for each of them." [12]
2. That it is possible to phrase all questions in a form that is equally meaningful to each respondent.
3. That if the "meaning of each question is to be identical for each respondent, its context must be identical and, since all preceding questions constitute part of the contexts, the sequence of questions must be identical." [13]

The Focused Interview

The second basic personal interview form is the *non-schedule-structured* or **focused interview**. This form has four characteristics:[14]

1. It takes place with respondents known to have been involved in a particular experience.
2. It refers to situations that have been analyzed prior to the interview.
3. It proceeds on the basis of an interview guide specifying topics related to the research hypotheses.
4. It is focused on the subjects' experiences regarding the situations under study.

Although the encounter between the interviewer and respondents is structured and the major aspects of the study are explained, respondents are given considerable liberty in expressing their definition of a situation that is presented to them. For example, in her study of women's best friends and marriage, Stacey Oliker employed a focused interview that was "malleable enough to follow emergent leads and standardized enough to register strong patterns." [15] The focused interview permits the researcher to obtain details of personal reactions, specific emotions, and the like. The interviewer, having previously studied the situation, is alert and sensitive to inconsistencies and omissions of data that may be needed to clarify the problem.

The Nondirective Interview

The most flexible form of personal interviewing is the *nonstructured* or **nondirective interview**. Here the researcher does not employ a schedule to ask a prespecified set of questions, nor are the questions asked in a specified order. With little or no direction from the interviewer, respondents are encouraged to relate their experiences, to describe whatever events seem significant to them, to provide their own definitions of their situations, and to reveal their opinions and attitudes as they see fit. The interviewer has a great deal of freedom to probe various areas and to raise specific queries during the

---

12. Stephen Richardson, Barbara S. Dohrenwend, and David Klein, *Interviewing: Its Forms and Functions* (New York: Basic Books, 1965), p. 40.

13. Ibid., p. 43.

14. Robert K. Merton and Patricia L. Kendal, "The Focused Interview," *American Journal of Sociology*, 51 (1946): 541–557.

15. Stacey J. Oliker, *Best Friends and Marriage* (Berkeley: University of California Press, 1989), p. xvi.

Exhibit 10.2

THE SCHEDULE-STRUCTURED INTERVIEW

Interviewer's explanation to the respondent: We are interested in the kinds of problems teenagers have with their parents. We need to know how many teenagers have conflicts with their parents and what those conflicts are. We have a checklist here of some of the kinds of things that happen. Think about your own situation, and put a check mark to show which conflicts you have had and about how often they have happened. Be sure to put a check in every row. If you have never had such a conflict, put the check in the first column, where it says, "Never."

(Hand respondent the first card, dealing with conflicts over the use of the automobile, saying, "If you don't understand any of the things listed or have some other things you would like to mention about how you disagree with your parents over the automobile, let me know and we'll talk about it.")

Automobile	Never	Only Once	More Than Once	Many Times
1. Wanting to learn to drive				
2. Getting a driver's license				
3. Wanting to use the family car				
4. Using it too much				
5. Keeping the car clean				
6. Repairing the car				
7. Driving someone else's car				
8. Want to own a car				
9. The way you drive your own car				
10. Other				

(When the respondent finishes all rows, hand him or her card number 2, saying, "Here is a list of types of conflicts teenagers have with their parents over their friends of the same sex. Do the same with this as you did with the last list.")

Adapted from Raymond L. Gorden, *Interviewing: Strategy, Techniques, and Tactics*, 3d ed. (Homewood, IL: Dorsey, 1980), pp. 49–50.

course of the interview. Eleanor Miller's study of female street hustlers is based on such nondirective interviews:[16]

> Seventy women agreed to taped interviews with me during which they shared with me the details of their lives. Special attention was paid to the initiation of these women into street hustling and the development of a career line as a street hustler. Although the same broad

16. Eleanor M. Miller, *Street Women* (Philadelphia: Temple University Press, 1986).

topics were introduced during each interview, many of my questions changed over time. Initial taped interviews were played again and again after being recorded. Tentative hypotheses and emergent behavior categories arose out of these hours of listening. During subsequent interviews, . . . I would introduce questions to test these tentative hypotheses.[17]

Exhibits 10.2, 10.3, and 10.4 illustrate the differences in interviewing styles in the three types of interviews. All three are concerned with the same research problem. The purpose of the study is to discover the types of conflict between parents and teenagers and the relationship between these conflicts and juvenile crime. The interviews are conducted with two groups of children. One consists of teenagers who have committed no crimes, and the second consists of teenagers who have been known to commit several juvenile crimes.

An interview may be completely structured or nonstructured, as illustrated in the exhibits. Alternatively, an interview may combine structured and nonstructured elements, depending on the purpose of the study. For example, a researcher may use the schedule-structured interview for most questions but rely on the nondirective format for questions that are particularly sensitive.

Exhibit 10.3
THE FOCUSED INTERVIEW

Instructions to the interviewer: Your task is to discover as many specific kinds of conflicts and tensions between child and parent as possible. The more *concrete* and detailed the account of each type of conflict, the better. Although there are four areas of possible conflict that we want to explore (listed in question 3 below), you should not mention any area until after you have asked the first two questions in the order indicated. The first question takes an indirect approach, giving you time to build up rapport with the respondent.

1. What sorts of problems do teenagers have in getting along with their parents? (Possible probes: Do they always agree with their parents? Do any of your friends have "problem parents"?)

2. What sort of disagreements do you have with your parents? (Possible probes: Do they cause you any problems? In what way do they try to restrict you? Do they like the same things you do?)

3. Have you ever had any disagreement with either of your parents over:
   a. Using the family car?
   b. Friends of the same sex?
   c. Dating?
   d. Smoking?

Adapted from Raymond L. Gorden, *Interviewing: Strategy, Techniques, and Tactics,* 3d ed. (Homewood, IL: Dorsey, 1980), pp. 48–49.

17. Ibid., p. 26.

Exhibit 10.4

THE NONDIRECTIVE INTERVIEW

Instructions to the interviewer: Discover the kinds of conflicts that the teenager has had with the parents. Conflicts should include disagreements; tensions due to past, present, or potential disagreements; outright arguments; and physical conflicts. Be alert for as many categories and examples of conflicts and tensions as possible.

Adapted from Raymond L. Gorden, *Interviewing: Strategy, Techniques, and Tactics*, 3d ed. (Homewood, IL: Dorsey, 1980), p. 48.

PERSONAL INTERVIEW VERSUS MAIL QUESTIONNAIRE ●

Advantages of the Personal Interview

1. *Flexibility.* The interview allows great flexibility in the questioning process, and the greater the flexibility, the less structured the interview. Some interviews allow the interviewer to determine the wording of the questions, to clarify terms that are unclear, to control the order in which the questions are presented, and to probe for additional information and detail.

2. *Control of the interview situation.* One major advantage of the interview is that it gives the researcher greater control over the interviewing situation. An interviewer can ensure that the respondents answer the questions in the appropriate sequence or that they answer certain questions before they are asked subsequent questions. Moreover, in an interview situation, researchers can standardize the environment in order to ensure that the interview is conducted in private; thus, respondents do not have the opportunity to consult one another before giving their answers. It is also possible to record the exact time and place of the interview; this allows the researcher to interpret the answers more accurately, especially when an event occurring around the time of the interview could have influenced the respondent's answers.

3. *High response rate.* The personal interview results in a higher response rate than the mail questionnaire. Respondents who would not ordinarily take the time to reply to an impersonal mail questionnaire will often respond to a request for a personal interview. This is also true of people who have difficulties reading or writing or who do not understand the language well.

4. *Collection of supplementary information.* An interviewer can collect supplementary information about respondents. This may include background information about the respondents' personal characteristics and their environment that can aid the researcher in interpreting the results. Moreover, an interview situation often yields spontaneous reactions that the interviewer can record and that might be useful in the data analysis state.

Disadvantages of the Personal Interview

1. *Higher cost.* The cost of interview studies is significantly higher than that of mail surveys. Costs are involved in selecting, training, and supervising interviewers; in paying them; and in the travel and time required to conduct interviews. Furthermore, the cost of recording and processing the information obtained in nonstructured interviews is especially high.

2. *Interviewer bias.* The very flexibility that is the chief advantage of interviews leaves room for the interviewer's personal influence and bias. The lack of standardization in the data collection process also makes interviewing highly vulnerable to interviewer bias. Although interviewers are instructed to remain objective and to avoid communicating personal views, they nevertheless often give cues that may influence respondents' answers. Even when they avoid verbal cues, interviewers can fail to control nonverbal communication. Sometimes even the interviewer's race or gender can influence respondents, who may give socially admirable but potentially misleading answers because they are trying to please the interviewer.

3. *Lack of anonymity.* The interview lacks the anonymity of the mail questionnaire. Often the interviewer knows all or many of the potential respondents (or at least their names, addresses, and telephone numbers). Thus, respondents may feel threatened or intimidated by the interviewer, especially if a respondent is sensitive to the topic or some of the questions.

Advantages and Disadvantages of the Personal Interview

ADVANTAGES

+ *Flexibility in the questioning process.* Interviews can range from highly structured to nonstructured depending on the research problem under examination. In focused and nondirective interviews the interviewer can clarify questions and probe for additional information.

+ *Control of the interview situation.* Interviewers determine who answers questions, where the interview is conducted, and the order in which questions are answered.

+ *High response rate.*

+ *Fuller information.* Interviewers are able to collect supplementary information from respondents, including background information and spontaneous reactions.

DISADVANTAGES

+ *Higher cost.* Interviews can be expensive to implement, especially when respondents are widely dispersed geographically.

+ *Interviewer bias.* Innate characteristics of interviewers and differences in interviewer techniques may affect resopndents' answers.

+ *Lack of anonymity.* The presence of the interviewer may make the respondent feel threatened or intimidated.

PRINCIPLES OF INTERVIEWING ●

We now turn to a more detailed discussion of the principles and procedures of interviewing. The first step in the interviewing process is getting the respondent to cooperate and to provide the desired information. Three factors help in motivating the respondent to cooperate.[18]

1. *The respondents must feel that their interaction with the interviewer will be pleasant and satisfying.* It is up to interviewers to make respondents feel that they will be understanding and easy to talk to.

2. *The respondents need to see the study as being worthwhile.* The respondents should feel not only that the study may benefit them personally but also that it deals with a significant issue and that their cooperation is important. Interviewers should interest the respondents in the study by pointing out its significance and the contribution that the respondents can make by cooperating.

3. *Barriers to the interview in the respondents' minds need to be overcome.* Interviewers must correct misconceptions. Some respondents may be suspicious of the interviewers, seeing them as salespeople or as representatives of the government. The interviewers should explain, in a friendly manner, the purpose of the study, the method of selecting respondents, and the confidential nature of the interview.

The Survey Research Center of the University of Michigan's Institute for Social Research provides some useful pointers on how interviewers should introduce themselves to respondents.[19]

1. Tell the respondent who you are and whom you represent.

2. Tell the respondent what you are doing in a way that will stimulate his or her interest.

3. Tell the respondent how he or she was chosen.

4. Adapt your approach to the situation.

5. Try to create a relationship of confidence and understanding (rapport) between yourself and the respondent.

After the initial introduction, the interviewer is ready to begin the interview. There are specific techniques that the interviewer can use in this process:[20]

1. *The questionnaire should be followed, but it can be used informally.*

2. *The interview should be conducted in an informal and relaxed atmosphere, and the interviewer should avoid creating the impression that what is occurring is a cross-examination or a quiz.*

3. *The questions should be asked exactly as worded in the questionnaire.* This is particularly important, for even slight changes in the way the questions are presented may change the responses. Various studies have shown that even small omissions or changes in the phrasing of questions can distort the results.

18. Survey Research Center, *Interviewer's Manual* (Ann Arbor: Institute for Social Research, University of Michigan, 1976), p. 3-1.

19. Ibid. (edited slightly).

20. Survey Research Center, *Interviewer's Manual*, pp. 11–13 (edited slightly).

4. *Read each question slowly.* Studies have shown the ideal reading pace to be two words per second. A slow pace helps interviewers to enunciate more clearly and allows respondents time to understand the question and formulate an answer.

5. *Questions should be presented in the same order as in the questionnaire.* The researcher has planned the question sequence to provide continuity and to make sure that either the respondents' answers will not be influenced by their responses to previous questions or that each respondent is subject to the same influence.

6. *Ask every question specified in the questionnaire.* Sometimes respondents provide answers to questions before they are asked. When this occurs, the interviewer should still ask the question at the appropriate time while acknowledging the respondent's earlier answer. For example, "I know you answered this question earlier, but. . . . "

7. *Questions that are misinterpreted or misunderstood should be repeated and clarified.* In most cases, respondents will not have any problem interpreting or understanding a question. At most, some people will need more time before they respond to a particular question. Occasionally, however, respondents who have language or hearing problems will have difficulty understanding a question. The interviewer should then repeat the question. Only on rare occasions should the interviewer reword the question, and then only if convinced that otherwise the respondent would misinterpret it.

Probing

In the *Interviewer's Manual* of the University of Michigan Survey Research Center, **probing** is defined as

> the technique used by the interviewer to stimulate discussion and obtain more information. A question has been asked and an answer given. For any number of reasons, the answer may be inadequate and require the interviewer to seek more information to meet the survey objectives. Probing is the act of getting this additional information.[21]

Probes have two major functions: They motivate the respondent to elaborate or clarify an answer or to explain the reasons behind the answer, and they help focus the conversation on the specific topic of the interview.

In general, the less structured the interview, the more important probing becomes as an instrument for eliciting and encouraging further information.

The following exchange shows an interviewer probing to elicit additional information by "repeating the respondent's statements without including a direct question."[22]

RESPONDENT: The main reason I came to Antioch College was because of the combination of high academic standards and the work program. It appealed to me a lot.

INTERVIEWER: It appealed to you a lot?

RESPONDENT: That's right.

INTERVIEWER: Could you tell me a little more exactly why it had this appeal for you?

21. Survey Research Center, *Interviewer's Manual*, p. 5-1.

22. Raymond L. Gorden, *Interviewing: Strategy, Techniques, and Tactics*, 3d ed. (Homewood, IL: Dorsey, 1980), p. 436.

RESPONDENT: I don't know—it was just that the place sounded less stuffy and straightlaced than a lot of places with just as good an academic program.

INTERVIEWER: You don't like places that are stuffy and straightlaced?

RESPONDENT: You can say that again. A lot of places spend most of their time trying to work out a way of controlling the students, assuming that they are completely incapable of self-control. . . .

INTERVIEWER: Why do you suppose Antioch has less supervision by the administration?

RESPONDENT: Well, it is part of the educational philosophy. . . .

INTERVIEWER: Let me see if I have grasped the whole picture—you like a school with high academic standards, but one that is not too straightlaced and operates on the assumption that college students can exercise self-control. . . .

RESPONDENT: That hits it on the head.

TELEPHONE INTERVIEW •

The telephone interview, also called the *telephone survey,* can be characterized as a semipersonal method of collecting information. Not too long ago, social scientists viewed telephone surveys with skepticism or outright distrust. Some texts explicitly warned their readers to avoid them.[23] The primary reason for this reluctance to use telephone interviewing was the high likelihood of a serious sampling bias. When a substantial proportion of the population had no access to telephones, the sample tended to overrepresent those who were relatively well off and could afford a telephone. More recently, however, telephone surveys have gained general acceptance as a legitimate method of data collection in the social sciences.

The main rationale for employing telephone surveys more extensively today is that investigators are able to reach more than nine-tenths of the population. In 1958, only 72.5 percent of U.S. households had access to telephones; by the end of the 1980s, the figure was close to 98 percent. In addition, financial pressures have made the telephone survey more attractive. Increasing salaries and fuel costs make the personal interview extremely costly. In comparison, the telephone is convenient, and it produces a very significant cost saving. Moreover, the telephone interview results in a higher response rate than the personal interview. In some metropolitan areas, people are quite nervous about opening their doors to strangers. Finding respondents at home has also become increasingly difficult with the greater participation of married women in the labor force.

Technological changes and improvements in telephone equipment have also made telephone interviewing easier. It has become possible to draw a random sample of telephone numbers by a process called **random-digit dialing (RDD).** To use this method, the researcher first identifies all working telephone exchanges in the targeted geographic area. He or she then creates a potential telephone number by randomly selecting an exchange and then appending a random number between 0001 and 9999. Additional numbers are created by repeating these two steps. Nonresidential telephones and nonworking numbers are excluded during the interviewing process. Computers have made the process of random-digit dialing faster and easier because they can be programmed to select both the exchange and the final digits randomly, dial the number for the interviewer, and delete from future selections any numbers for which an interview has been completed or those that are nonresidential or nonworking.

---

23. William R. Klecka and Alfred J. Tuchfarber, "Random Digit Dialing: A Comparison to Personal Survey," *Public Opinion Quarterly,* 42 (1978): 105–114. Many details of our discussion derive from this source.

Advantages and Disadvantages of Telephone Interviews

ADVANTAGES

* *Moderate cost.*

* *Speed.* Telephone interviewers can reach a large number of respondents in a short time. Interviewers can code data directly into computers, which can later compile the data.

* *High response rate.* Telephone interviews provide access to people who might be unlikely to reply to a mail questionnaire or refuse a personal interview.

* *Quality.* High-quality data can be collected when interviewers are centrally located and supervisors can ensure that questions are being asked correctly and answers recorded properly.

DISADVANTAGES

* *Reluctance to discuss sensitive topics.* Respondents may be hesitant to discuss some issues over the phone.

* *The "broken-off" interview.* Respondents can terminate the interview before it is completed.

* *Less information.* Interviewers cannot provide supplemental information about the respondents' characteristics of environment.

Although the telephone survey provides the obvious advantages of low cost and speed, there remains the question of whether telephone surveys are an alternative to face-to-face interviewing. In the first major experiment designed to answer this question, William Klecka and Alfred Tuchfarber replicated a large, personal interviewing survey by means of a RDD telephone survey.[24] The personal interview survey on crime victimization had been conducted by the U.S. Bureau of the Census in 1974. Klecka and Tuchfarber compared the two samples on demographic-characteristic measures of crime victimization and attitudes toward crime and the police. The results were very similar, indicating that random-digit dialing is an accurate and cost-effective alternative to the personal interview. More recent studies that compared answers to the same questions in mail, telephone, and personal interviews found little difference in their validity.[25]

Aside from its relative accuracy, telephone interviewing tends to increase the quality of the data. In most cases, telephone interviewers are working from a central office, and supervisors can monitor their work constantly. This helps ensure that interviewers are asking the questions correctly and that researchers can identify and correct problems immediately.

One of the latest developments in telephone surveys is the use of computerized questionnaires. In **computer-assisted telephone interviewing (CATI),** the interviewer sits at a computer terminal and, as a question flashes on the screen, asks it over the telephone. The interviewer types and codes the respondents' answers directly onto a disk, and the next question then comes up on the screen. Among the advantages of CATI are

24. Ibid.

25. Seymour Sudman and Norman M. Bradburn, *Asking Questions* (San Francisco: Jossey-Bass, 1982).

its speed and the use of complex instructions, programmed in advance. For instance, in good CATI systems, coders are not allowed to input incorrect or out-of-range scores. The screen prompts them to put in a correct one. However, CATI is not suitable for open-ended questions.[26]

However, the weaknesses of telephone interviewing cannot be ignored. Telephone interviewing has created a new kind of nonresponse—the "broken-off" interview. In about 4 percent of the calls, respondents terminate the interview before it is completed—a rare occurrence in personal interviews.[27] Telephone interviews also produce less information; interviewers cannot describe the respondents' characteristics or their environment in detail. Moreover, proportionately more telephone respondents indicate that they feel uneasy about discussing some topics, especially financial status and political attitudes, over the telephone.

In summary, telephone interviewing should be used as an alternative to personal interviewing under certain circumstances—especially when the interview schedule is relatively simple. However, the question of whether personal and telephone interviews are interchangeable remains to be answered. In the future, most surveys may be conducted totally by telephone; others may combine telephone and personal interviews so that the two can complement each other to provide greater precision and increased response rate.

COMPARING THE THREE SURVEY METHODS ●

In deciding which survey method is best suited to your research, you have to determine which criteria are most significant to the research objective. For example, if you plan to conduct long interviews with a representative sample of the general population and wish to control for nonverbal behavior, and if sufficient funds are available, a form of a personal interview is preferable.[28] Conversely, if the interview can be simplified, and if funds and speed are concerns, the telephone survey can be used to collect the information. If you are using a rather lengthy questionnaire or one that includes threatening or sensitive questions,[29] and especially if the population to be investigated is relatively dispersed geographically or is a selective population, the mail questionnaire can be considered as an alternative.

Table 10.3 presents some of the comparative advantages and limitations of the three methods of survey research.

Survey Research and the Internet

As the proportion of people accessible through e-mail or the Internet continues to rise, these media provide a promising means for conducting surveys.[30] Nearly 50 percent of households now have computers, and for some groups access has reached almost 100 percent. The use of e-mail for surveying offers numerous advantages. First, it offers the

---

26. Ibid.

27. Institute for Social Research, University of Michigan, *Newsletter*, Autumn 1976, p. 4.

28. A sample is representative if the measurements made on its units produce results equivalent to those that would be obtained had the entire population been measured. See Chapter 8.

29. Floyd Jackson Fowler, Jr., Anthony M. Roman, and Zhu Xiao Di, "Mode Effects in a Survey of Medicare Prostate Surgery Patients," *Public Opinion Quarterly*, 62 (1998): 29–46.

30. David R. Schaffer and Don A. Dillman, "Development of a Standard E-Mail Methodology, *"Public Opinion Quarterly*, 62 (1998): 378–397.

Table 10.3

Evaluation of Three Survey Methods

Criterion	Personal Interview	Mail	Telephone
Cost	High	Low	Moderate
Response rate	High	Low	High
Control of interview situation	High	Low	Moderate
Applicability to geographically dispersed populations	Moderate	High	Moderate
Applicability to heterogeneous populations	High	Low	High
Collection of detailed information	High	Moderate	Moderate
Speed	Low	Low	High

possibility of very rapid surveying. E-mail surveys are faster to conduct than telephone surveys, especially for large samples. Second, this method is also cheaper, since it eliminates mailing or interviewer costs. Nonetheless, the use of e-mail surveys has been restricted by the tendency of researchers to apply it only to populations with nearly universal e-mail access.[31] The risk of a high nonresponse rate has prevented researchers from applying an e-mail methodology to other groups. However, recent studies have tested a mixed-mode design in which e-mail is used in conjunction with mail surveys for individuals who do not have an e-mail address. When such a procedure is employed, comparable response rates can be obtained for regular mail surveys and electronic mail surveys. Thus, researchers can take advantage of the capabilities and benefits of an e-mail methodology for populations without universal e-mail access.[32]

CONCLUSION ●

The survey method is one of the most important data collection methods in the social sciences, and as such it is used extensively to collect information on numerous subjects of research. In recent years, with public demands for government accountability, the emphasis on survey instruments has increased. Survey research is becoming a widely used tool of various government organizations. Studies of local governments indicate that 50 percent of cities with populations over 100,000 and counties with populations over 250,000 have used some form of survey. With the growth in the number of surveys conducted, the method has become the subject of increased criticism. Comments such as "Getting things right in social science research is not easy." "The sample of potential respondents was a hodgepodge of various procedures," and "I wouldn't trust any survey with a response rate like that" are typical. Although sometimes these remarks are justified, often they are not based on facts and simply pay "lip service" to the spirit of criticism. Yet there is no denying that we need a set of criteria that will help us evaluate the

31. Ibid., pp. 378–379.
32. Ibid., p. 390.

usefulness of surveys, detect and control errors in them, and compensate for these errors wherever possible.[33]

Half a century ago, Edward Deming wrote an article, now a classic, called "On Errors in Surveys."[34] In this article, Deming lists 13 potential errors researchers should consider when planning a survey and evaluating its results. The most important factors that might become potential errors in surveys were discussed in this chapter: interviewer bias, low response rate, and difficulty in asking sensitive questions. Reuben Cohen made the following remarks regarding these potential errors in a presidential address to the American Association for Public Opinion Research:

> Some 30 years ago, I was handed a reprint of W. Edward Deming's list of errors in surveys. The message was pretty obvious: Now that you know about them don't make them. With my relative inexperience, and my eternal optimism, I accepted the challenge. My first approach was to try to do the perfect survey. I am still trying, but I should know better. I quickly discovered Murphy's Law—if anything can go wrong, it probably will. But I also discovered something else. Even without the time and budget constraints that most of us complain about, there are no perfect surveys. Every survey has its imperfections. The world is not ideally suited to our work. The best we can do is think through the ideal approach to a survey design, or implementation, or analysis problem—what we would do if we had our druthers—then get as close to the ideal as we can within the constraints of time and budget which govern much of our work.[35]

And to readers who might be discouraged by these less than perfect goals, we offer the following advice:

> Practical work consists in good part of guessing what irregularities, where, and how much one can afford to tolerate. . . . The same is true for survey research. It should be done well. It can and should conform well, even if not perfectly, to an ideal approach.[36]

SUMMARY

1. In this chapter, we discussed the survey as a method of data collection. Three methods were described: the mail questionnaire, the face-to-face interview, and the telephone interview.

2. The mail questionnaire is an impersonal survey method. Its major advantages are low cost, relatively small biasing error, anonymity, and accessibility. Its disadvantages are a low response rate, no opportunity for probing, and lack of control over who fills out the questionnaire.

3. Because of the difficulty of securing an acceptable response rate to mail questionnaires, researchers use various strategies that are known to increase the response rate. Among those, the most effective are the use of follow-up mailings, information on sponsorship of the survey, and the appeal of the questionnaire. The format of the questionnaire and the methods of mailing an investigator uses will also affect the response rate.

---

33. Gregory Daneke and Patricia Klobus Edwards, "Survey Research for Public Administrators," *Public Administration Review*, 39 (1979): 421–426.

34. W. Edward Deming, *Some Theory of Sampling* (New York: Wiley, 1950).

35. Reuben Cohen, "Close Enough for All Practical Purposes," *Public Opinion Quarterly*, 43 (1979): 421–422.

36. Ibid., p. 424.

4. The personal interview is a face-to-face situation in which an interviewer asks respondents questions designed to obtain answers pertinent to the research hypotheses. The schedule-structured interview is the most structured form. The questions, their wording, and their sequence are fixed and identical for every respondent. The focused interview follows an interview guide specifying topics related to the research hypothesis. It gives respondents considerable liberty to express their views. Finally, nondirective interviews are the least structured, employing no prespecified set of questions. The interviewer has a great deal of freedom to probe various areas and to raise specific queries during the course of the interview.

5. Telephone interviewing has gained general acceptance as a substitute for personal interviewing. The telephone survey is convenient and cost effective. In addition, it sometimes results in a higher response rate than the personal interview. Technological changes and improvements in telephone equipment have also made telephone interviewing easier, especially when researchers use random-digit dialing and computer-assisted telephone interviewing.

KEY TERMS FOR REVIEW   ●

computer-assisted telephone interviewing (CATI) (p. 223)
focused interview (p. 215)
follow-up (p. 210)
mail questionnaire (p. 206)

nondirective interview (p. 215)
probing (p. 221)
random-digit dialing (RDD) (p. 222)
response rate (p. 207)
schedule-structured interview (p. 213)

STUDY QUESTIONS   ●

1. Describe the basic techniques of survey data collection.
2. Discuss the advantages and disadvantages of mail questionnaires, telephone interviews, and personal interviews.
3. List and describe the basic principles of interviewing.
4. What type of survey research would you use to study drug users? Defend the logic of your choice.
5. Suppose you are engaged in a research project to determine the attitudes in a small town toward welfare. You are planning to use a mailed questionnaire, and you have chosen a sample. Write the cover letter.

SPSS PROBLEMS   ●

1. How do church attendance and belief about the Bible affect attitudes toward abortion? The **gss96worth** file includes the following variables which can be used to examine this research question: "attend," "bible," "abany," "abdefect," "abhlth," "abnomore," "abpoor," "abrape," "absingle." Clicking on **Utilities** and **Variables** or on **File Info,** examine the survey questions for each of these variables.
   a. Assume that these questions are included in a questionnaire which will be mailed to a random sample of Americans 18 years or older. Compose a cover letter for this questionnaire. Remember that a cover letter must succeed in

convincing the respondents to fill out the questionnaire and mail it back (include *sponsorship, purpose,* and *inducement to respond*).

b. Now assume that you are administering the above questionnaire to undergraduate students in a college classroom. Write a brief introductory statement informing students about the purpose of the study and instructing them how to fill out the questionnaire.

2. How do income, sex, and race affect attitudes of liberalism? The **gss96worth** file includes the following variables which can be used to examine these research questions: "income," "sex," "race," "cappun," "homosex," "polviews," "racseg." Clicking on **Utilities** and **Variables** or on **File Info,** examine the survey questions for each of these variables. Discuss the advantages and disadvantages of examining this research question by the following methods: mail questionnaire, personal interview, and telephone interview.

ADDITIONAL READINGS ●

Czaja, Ronald, and Bob Blair. *Survey Research.* Newbury Park, CA: Pine Forge Press, 1995.

Davis, James A., and Tom W. Smith. *The NORC General Social Survey: A User's Guide.* Newbury Park, CA: Sage, 1992.

Dillman, Don A., Kristen K. West, and Jon R. Clark. "Influence of an Invitation to Answer by Telephone on Response to Census Questionnaires." *Public Opinion Quarterly,* 58 (1994): 557–569.

Fowler, Floyd J., Jr. *Improving Survey Questions: Design & Evolution.* Newbury Park, CA: Sage, 1995.

Gorden, Raymond L. *Basic Interviewing Skills.* Itasca, IL: Peacock, 1992.

Groves, Robert M. "Theories and Methods of Telephone Surveys." In *Annual Review of Sociology,* vol. 16, ed. W. Richard Scott and Judith Blake. Palo Alto, CA: Annual Reviews, 1990: 221–240.

Hyman, Herbert H., and Eleanor Singer. *Taking Society's Measure: A Personal History of Survey Research.* New York: Russell Sage Foundation, 1991.

Litwin, Mark S. *How to Measure Survey Reliability and Validity.* Thousand Oaks, CA: Sage, 1995.

Wentland, Ellen J., and Kent W. Smith. *Survey Responses: An Evaluation of Their Validity.* San Diego, CA: Academic Press, 1993.

Yammarino, Francis J., Steven J. Skinner, and Terry L. Childers. "Understanding Mail Survey Response Behavior: A Meta-Analysis." *Public Opinion Quarterly,* 55 (1991): 613–640.

Questionnaire Construction

How would you answer this question: "Does it seem possible or does it seem impossible to you that the Nazi extermination of the Jews never happened?" How many times did you have to read the question before you could answer it? Are you sure your answer really expresses your belief? If the question confused you, you are not alone. According to an article in *The New York Times,* the responses to this question led researchers at the Roper polling organization to conclude that one in five Americans thought the Holocaust never happened.[1] Was their conclusion correct? Probably not. According to Roper, their effort to provide an unbiased question resulted in such clumsy wording that it confused many respondents and caused them to answer inappropriately. The Gallup organization conducted an independent survey to test the validity of the Roper poll and found that when respondents were presented with a clearer question, less than 3 percent of Americans doubted the Holocaust happened. Roper has conducted a new poll using a more clearly worded question, and they have publicly apologized for their mistake.

Because the findings of surveys often influence policy decisions that have an impact on people's lives and may be the only source of information on an issue available to the public, survey questions must be carefully constructed and ordered to elicit accurate data. As you will see in this chapter, question construction is not as easy as it may seem.

•**IN THIS CHAPTER** we focus on the questionnaire as the main instrument in survey research. We start by discussing the foundation of all questionnaires—the question. We then look at the content of questions; differentiate between closed-ended, open-ended, and contingency-type questions; and analyze their format and sequencing. Next we explore possible biases in the wording of questions, as well as leading, double-barreled, and threatening questions. Finally, we give important pointers about the cover letter accompanying the questionnaire and the instructions included in it.

THE QUESTION •

The foundation of all questionnaires is the **question.** The questionnaire must translate the research objectives into specific questions; answers to such questions will provide the data for hypothesis testing. The question must also motivate the respondent to provide the information being sought. The major considerations involved in formulating questions are their content, structure, format, and sequence.

CONTENT OF QUESTIONS •

Survey questions may be concerned with facts, opinions, attitudes, respondents' motivation, and their level of familiarity with a certain subject. Most questions, however, can be classified in one of two general categories: factual questions and questions about subjective experiences.

---

1. John Kifner, "Pollster Finds Error on Holocaust Doubts," *The New York Times,* May 20, 1994, p. A12.

Factual Questions

Factual questions are designed to elicit objective information from the respondents regarding their backgrounds, environments, habits, and the like. The most common type of factual question is the background question, which is asked mainly to provide information that can be used to classify respondents. Background questions include such items as gender, age, marital status, education, or income. Such classifications may in turn aid in explaining differences in behaviors and attitudes. The following is an example of such a question:

What was the last grade you completed in school? (Please check one.)

_____   8th grade or lower

_____   9th or 10th grade

_____   11th or 12th grade: high school graduate? _____ Yes _____ No

_____   1 to 2 years of college

_____   3 to 4 years of college: college graduate? _____ Yes _____ No

_____   5 or more years of college

Other kinds of factual questions are intended to provide information about the respondent's social environment ("Would you please tell me, who are the people living in your household?"), means of transportation ("How do you generally get to work?"), or leisure activities ("How often do you go to the movies?").

People often think that factual questions are easier to design than other types of questions. However, even factual questions can present the researcher with problems. How accurately people report depends on what and how they are being asked. There are four reasons why respondents give less than accurate answers to factual questions:[2]

1. They do not know the information.
2. They cannot recall the information.
3. They do not understand the question.
4. They are reluctant to answer.

The researcher can take several steps to increase accuracy, including encouraging respondents to consult other members of the household, asking more than one question about the matter, repeating questions, and making respondents feel comfortable when asking about events that they may find embarrassing.

Questions About Subjective Experiences

Subjective experience involves the respondents' beliefs, attitudes, feelings, and opinions. Surveys conducted in the social sciences, particularly those designed to explore property–disposition relationships (see Chapter 6), often include questions about attitudes. **Attitudes** are general orientations that can incline a person to act or react in a certain manner when confronted with certain stimuli. Following is an example of a question about attitudes toward abortion. This question is included in the General Social Survey (GSS), a public opinion poll conducted yearly by the National Opinion Research Council.

2. Floyd J. Fowler, Jr., *Survey Research Methods* (Newbury Park, CA: Sage, 1989), p. 91.

Please tell me whether or not *you* think it should be possible for a pregnant woman to obtain a *legal* abortion if there is a strong chance of serious defects in the baby.

1. Yes
2. No
3. Don't know
4. No answer

Individuals express their attitudes through speech or behavior only when they perceive the object of the attitude. A person may have strong attitudes for or against abortion, but these are aroused and conveyed only when that person encounters some issue connected with abortion or is confronted with a stimulus such as a question in an interview.

Attitudes can be described by their content (what the attitude is about), their direction (positive, neutral, or negative feelings about the object or issue in question), and their intensity (an attitude may be held with greater or lesser vehemence). To one person, abortion may be of but passing interest; to another, it may be of great significance and lead that person to join a pro-choice or pro-life organization. The latter person would be expected to agree or disagree more strongly than the former on questions dealing with, say, whether the legislature should pass a constitutional amendment that would make abortion illegal.

In general, we are interested in measuring attitudes because they account for the respondent's general inclination. The study of opinion is of interest only insofar as the opinion is a symbol of an attitude. The main difference between asking for opinions and measuring attitudes is that researchers generally measure an **opinion** by estimating the proportion of the surveyed population that would say they agree with a single opinion statement. They measure attitudes using attitude scales consisting of five to two dozen or more attitude statements, with which the respondent is asked to agree or disagree. An essential requirement of attitude measurement is that such attitude statements be scaled, that is, that the researcher select the statements and put them together from a much larger number of attitude statements according to certain techniques. These techniques are discussed in Chapter 18.

The construction of survey questions about opinions and attitudes presents more problems than survey questions about facts. It is relatively simple to obtain accurate information on whether a person is married or single. The researcher may reasonably assume that the respondent knows if he or she is married. With opinions or attitudes, researchers cannot always make the assumption that respondents know what they think. Respondents may not have an attitude toward making abortions illegal, or if they do, it might be latent. Moreover, because many attitudes have numerous aspects or dimensions, the respondent may agree with one aspect and disagree with another. This is why attitudes cannot be measured by a single question. For example, if a person disagrees strongly with the statement "Abortions should be available to any woman who wants one," this does not imply a broad antiabortion attitude. This person's view may be different if the woman's life is in danger, if the pregnancy resulted from incest or rape, or if a doctor has determined that the baby will be severely deformed. By using several attitude statements, a researcher can ascertain more accurately both the strength of a respondent's attitude and the conditions under which his or her attitude might change.

Finally, answers to opinion and attitude questions are more sensitive to changes in wording, emphasis, and sequence than answers to factual questions. This reflects, in part, the multidimensionality of many attitudes. Questions presented in different ways sometimes reflect different aspects of the attitude and thus elicit different answers.

TYPES OF QUESTIONS   ●

The content of the questions is only one important aspect of constructing survey question-naires. The researcher must also consider the structure of the questions and the format of the response categories that accompany them. We will discuss three types of question structures: closed-ended questions, open-ended questions, and contingency questions.

Closed-Ended and Open-Ended Questions

Questions on a questionnaire can be either closed-ended or open-ended. In a **closed-ended question,** respondents are offered a set of answers and asked to choose the one that most closely represents their views. For example, to measure respondents' de-gree of satisfaction with family life, the General Social Survey used the following closed-ended question:

Tell me the number that shows how much satisfaction you get from your family life.

1. A very great deal
2. A great deal
3. Quite a bit
4. A fair amount
5. A little
6. Very little
7. None
8. Don't know
9. No answer

Answers to closed-ended questions can be more elaborate, such as the following question taken from a survey about racial attitudes.[3]

Some people feel that if Black people aren't getting fair treatment in jobs, the government in Washington ought to see to it that they do. Others feel that this is not the federal gov-ernment's business. How do you feel?

• The government in Washington should see to it that Black people get fair treatment in jobs.
• I have not had enough interest in this question to favor one side over the other.
• This is not the federal government's business.

Closed-ended questions are easy to ask and quick to answer, they require no writing by either respondent or interviewer, and their analysis is straightforward. Their major drawback is that they may introduce bias, either by forcing the respondent to choose from given alternatives or by offering the respondent alternatives that might not have otherwise come to mind.

Open-ended questions are not followed by any kind of specified choice, and the respondents' answers are recorded in full. For instance, the question "What do you per-sonally feel are the most important problems the government in Washington should try to take care of?" is an open-ended question used frequently in questionnaires designed to study public opinion. The virtue of the open-ended question is that it does not force the respondent to adapt to preconceived answers. Once respondents understand the in-tent of the question, they can express their thoughts freely, spontaneously, and in their own language. If the answers to open-ended questions are unclear, the interviewer may probe by asking the respondent to explain further or to give a rationale for something stated earlier. Open-ended questions enable the interviewer to clear up misunderstand-ings, and they encourage rapport. However, open-ended questions are difficult to answer

---

3. Maria Krysan, "Privacy and the Expression of White Racial Attitudes," *Public Opinion Quarterly,* 62 (1998): 506–544.

and still more difficult to analyze. The researcher has to design a coding frame in order to classify the various answers; in this process, the details of the information provided by the respondent might get lost (see Chapter 14).

The appropriateness of either closed-ended or open-ended questions depends on a number of factors. Some years ago, Paul Lazarsfeld suggested that researchers use the following considerations to determine appropriateness:[4]

1. *The objectives of the questionnaire.* Closed-ended questions are suitable when the researcher's objective is to lead the respondent to express agreement or disagreement with an explicit point of view. When the researcher wishes to learn how the respondent arrived at a particular point of view, an open-ended question is likely to be more appropriate.

2. *The respondent's level of information about the topic in question.* Open-ended questions provide opportunities for the interviewer to ascertain a lack of information on the part of the respondent, whereas closed-ended questions do not. Obviously, it is futile to raise questions that are beyond the experiences of respondents.

3. *The extent to which the topic has been thought through by the respondent.* The open-ended question is preferable in situations where respondents have not yet crystallized their opinions. Using a closed-ended question in such situations involves the risk that in accepting one of the alternatives offered, respondents may make a choice that is quite different from the opinion they would otherwise have expressed had they gone through the process of recalling and evaluating their past experiences.

4. *The ease with which respondents can communicate the content of the answer or the extent to which respondents are motivated to communicate on the topic.* The closed-ended question requires less motivation to communicate on the part of the respondent, and the response itself is usually less revealing (and hence less threatening) than in the case of the open-ended question. The researcher who uses closed-ended questions tends to encounter refusals to respond less frequently.

Sometimes there may be good reasons for asking the same question in both open-ended and closed-ended form. For example, an open-ended answer to the question "Who rules America?" will provide a clear idea of the respondent's perception of the political system and the significance that the person attaches to different power groups. Although this datum is most valuable, it might not allow the researcher to compare one group of respondents with another. Furthermore, the researcher cannot be sure that the respondent has mentioned all information of importance; factors such as the inability to articulate thoughts or a momentary lapse of memory may cause the respondent to omit significant points. Therefore, the researcher can ask the same question again, later in the interview, but this time in closed-ended form.

Contingency Questions

Frequently, questions that are relevant to some respondents may be irrelevant to others. For example, the question "Check the most important reasons why you will be going to college" obviously applies only to high school students who are planning to go to college. It is often necessary to include questions that might apply only to some respondents and not to others. Some questions may be relevant only to females and not to males, others will apply only to respondents who are self-employed, and so on.

---

4. Paul F. Lazarsfeld, "The Controversy over Detailed Interviews: An Offer for Negotiation," *Public Opinion Quarterly,* 8 (1944): 38–60.

A **contingency question**—a special-case closed-ended question—applies only to a subgroup of respondents. The investigator determines the relevance of the question to this subgroup by asking all respondents a preceding **filter question.** For example, in a news media survey, the filter question might read "Do you regularly follow the news in the papers?" The contingency question could be "What recent event do you remember reading about? (Give a brief description.)" The relevance of the second question to the respondent is contingent on his or her response to the filter question. Only respondents who answered "Yes" to the filter question will find the contingency question relevant. Therefore, the response categories of the filter questions will be "1. Yes (answer the following question); 2. No (skip to question 3)."

The formats for filter and contingency questions vary. One alternative is to write directions next to each response category of the filter question. Another common format is to use arrows to direct the respondent either to skip to another question or to answer the contingency question, as in the following example:

Is this the first full-time job you have held since you graduated from college?

1. Yes
2. No ————┐
What happened to the job you had before—were you promoted, laid off, or what? (Check one.)

1. Company folded
2. Laid off or fired
3. Job stopped; work was seasonal
4. Quit voluntarily
5. Promoted; relocated
6. Other

Another format is to box the contingency question and set it apart from the ordinary questions to be answered by everybody. An example of such a format appears in Exhibit 11.1. When the questionnaire is addressed to several subgroups and several contingency questions apply to each subgroup, it is useful to indicate by number which questions the respondent should answer. The instructions are written next to the appropriate response categories in the filter question. This is demonstrated in the following example:

Exhibit 11.1
CONTINGENCY QUESTION

ANSWER QUESTIONS BELOW IF YOU ARE A SENIOR PLANNING TO GO TO COLLEGE NEXT FALL. NONSENIORS SKIP TO QUESTION 144.

137. Did you take the College Entrance Board Exams?

_____ Yes

_____ No

138. Do you definitely know which college you will attend?

_____ Yes

_____ No

Three Types of Questions

+ *Closed-ended questions:* Respondents are given a set of responses and asked to choose the one that most closely describes their attribute or attitude.

+ *Open-ended questions:* Respondents are not given a specific set of responses. They are asked to describe their attributes or attitudes in their own words, and their answers are recorded in full either by the respondent or by an interviewer.

+ *Contingency questions:* A type of closed-ended question applicable to a subgroup of respondents. The subgroup may be identified by a filter question, which directs them to answer other relevant questions, or instructions may be provided that direct members of the subgroup to answer a question or set of questions and nonsubgroup members to skip to another question.

---

22. Are you looking for another job at this time?

_____ Yes
_____ No
_____ Don't know   } Go to question 25.
_____ Inappropriate

With computer-assisted telephone interviewing (CATI), the computer is preprogrammed to do the skipping automatically. If a respondent answered "no," "don't know," or "inappropriate" to the preceding question, question 25 would automatically appear on the screen.

QUESTION FORMAT

Researchers use several common techniques to structure the response categories of closed-ended questions. The general format is to present all possible answers and have the respondents choose the appropriate categories. The respondents can either circle or write the number of the answer or check a box or a blank, as shown here:

What is your marital status?

_____ Married	☐ Married		1. Married
_____ Single	or	☐ Single	or	2. Single
_____ Divorced		☐ Divorced		3. Divorced
_____ Widowed		☐ Widowed		4. Widowed

Of course, respondents need specific directions as to whether they are to circle a number or check a blank or a box. Among the three methods shown, the least recommended is the one with blanks because respondents may check between the blanks, making it difficult to tell which category was intended. Circling a code number is preferable because the code number can be easily transferred to a computerized storage device.

Rating

One of the most common formats for questions asked in social science surveys is the rating scale. Researchers use a **rating** scale whenever they ask respondents to make a judgment in terms of sets of ordered categories, such as "strongly agree," "favorable," or "very often"; for example:

Police should be allowed to conduct a full search of any motorist arrested for an offense such as speeding.

1. Agree strongly
2. Agree
3. Neither agree nor disagree
4. Disagree
5. Disagree strongly

The response categories of such questions are termed **quantifiers;** they reflect the *intensity* of the particular judgment involved. The following sets of response categories are quite common:

1. Strongly agree	1. Too little	1. More
2. Agree	2. About right	2. Same
3. Depends	3. Too much	3. Less
4. Disagree		
5. Strongly disagree		

The numerical codes that accompany these categories are usually interpreted to represent the intensity of the response categories, so that the higher the number, the more intense the response. Although we assume that the quantifiers involved are ordered by intensity, this ordering does not imply that the distance between the categories is equal. Indeed, rating scales such as these are most often measured on ordinal levels, which describe only whether one level is higher or lower than another level but do not indicate how much higher or lower, as discussed in Chapter 7.

Despite the difficulty in estimating intensities, we cannot typically ask respondents for exact responses because most of them would find this task very difficult. Although most respondents would find it relatively easy to report how many hours of television they had watched in the past week, they would find it much more difficult to give exact responses to questions dealing with issues that have low salience to them, such as attitudes about foreign policy.

Matrix Questions

The **matrix question** is a method of organizing a large set of rating questions that have the same response categories. The following is an example of such a device:

Indicate your reaction to each of the following statements.

	I strongly agree	I agree	It depends	I disagree	I strongly disagree
My vote gives me all the power I want in government affairs.	☐	☐	☐	☐	☐
If I complained to the people at a city agency, they would fix up whatever was wrong.	☐	☐	☐	☐	☐
I've sometimes wished that government officials paid more attention to what I thought.	☐	☐	☐	☐	☐

Ranking

Researchers use **ranking** in questionnaires whenever they want to obtain information regarding the degree of importance or the priorities that people give to a set of attitudes or objects. For instance, in a survey on the quality of life, respondents were asked to rank various dimensions they consider important.

"I would like you to tell me what you have found important in life. Please look at this card and tell me which of these is most important to *you* as a goal in *your* life, which comes next in importance, which is third, and which ranks fourth."

	Rank			
A prosperous life (having a good income and being able to afford the good things in life)	1	2	3	4
A family life (a life completely centered on my family)	1	2	3	4
An important life (a life of achievement that brings me respect and recognition)	1	2	3	4
A secure life (making certain that all basic needs and expenses are provided)	1	2	3	4

Ranking is a useful device because it provides some sense of relative order among objects or judgments. This is particularly important because many properties that social scientists measure (for example, "quality of life," "status") cannot be given any precise numerical value. However, with the use of ranking we can at least obtain information regarding their relative order. As with rating scales, however, ranking does not provide any information about the distance between the ranks. The difference between rank 1 and rank 2 may not be the same as the difference between rank 2 and rank 3.

SEQUENCE OF QUESTIONS

After the researcher has determined the question format, he or she must consider the order in which the questions are placed on the questionnaire. Researchers have found two general patterns of question sequence that are most appropriate for motivating respondents to cooperate: the *funnel sequence* and the *inverted funnel sequence*.

Funnel Sequence

In the funnel sequence, each successive question is related to the previous question and has a progressively narrower scope. For example, if you were interested in finding out how respondents' views of political, economic, and social problems are related to the newspapers they read, you might want to know what sorts of issues the respondents think of as problems, what the perceived relative significance of each problem is, how much information they have on the topic, what their sources of information are, and whether certain newspapers have influenced their thinking on the problem. The following questions form a funnel sequence:

1. What do you think are some of the most important problems facing the nation?
2. Of all the problems you have just mentioned, which do you think is the most important one?

3. Where have you obtained most of your information about this problem?
4. Do you read the *Washington Post?*

When the objective of the survey is to obtain detailed information and when the respondent is motivated to supply that information, the funnel approach helps the respondent recall details more efficiently. Furthermore, by asking the broadest questions first, the researcher can avoid imposing a frame of reference before obtaining the respondent's perspective. When the objective of the survey is to discover unanticipated responses, interviewers should pursue broader questions first.

Inverted Funnel Sequence

In the inverted funnel sequence, narrower questions are followed by broader ones. When the topic of the survey does not strongly motivate the respondents to communicate—either because the topic is not important to them or because their experiences are not recent enough to be vivid in their memories—it may be helpful to begin with the narrow questions, which are easier to answer, and reserve the broader (and more difficult) ones until later. If the purpose is to obtain a generalization in the form of a judgment regarding a concrete situation and if the researcher is unfamiliar with the facts but the respondent knows them, narrower questions aimed at establishing specific facts should precede questions requiring an overall judgment.

In the following example, the researcher is attempting to obtain the respondents' judgment regarding the effectiveness of rescue operations during a disaster. To help people make an unbiased judgment, the researcher felt that it was better to deal with the specifics first, asking for the generalization later.

1. How many people were killed in the tornado?
2. How many do you suppose were injured so seriously that they had to go to the hospital?
3. How long was it before most of the injured got to the hospital?
4. Did you see anyone administer first aid by giving artificial respiration or stopping bleeding? Who was it?
5. In general, how well do you think the first aid and rescue operations were carried out?

Studies have shown that the order in which the questions are presented affects the type of response given. For example, there is evidence that answers to attitude questions in surveys can vary markedly, depending on the preceding items in the questionnaire. For example, in an attitude survey about a number of social issues, respondents were asked about target issues such as abortion, defense spending, and welfare.[5] In one version of the questionnaire, target questions were preceded by related-context questions; in others, the target questions were preceded by neutral questions. For example, the abortion target question "Do you favor or oppose legalized abortion?" was preceded in the first version by a number of context questions about traditional values. Respondents were generally affected by related context questions, especially when they held conflicting beliefs about the target issue. There is also evidence that the position of an item in a list has a significant impact on its being chosen. Respondents most often choose items that appear first on the list. When they are asked to assign numerical values to a set of items (for example, according to their degree of importance), items appearing first tend to receive a higher rank.

5. Adapted from Roger Tourangeau, Kenneth A. Rasinski, Norman M. Bradburn, and Roy D'Andrade, "Carryover Effects in Attitude Surveys," *Public Opinion Quarterly,* 53 (1989): 495–524.

In the following question, respondents are more likely to assign the first rank to the first category than to the last one, simply because it is listed first.

Among the items below, what does it take to get to be important and looked up to by the other students here at school? (Rank from 1 to 6.)

_____ Coming from the right family

_____ Leader in activities

_____ Having a nice car

_____ High grades, honor roll

_____ Being an athletic star

_____ Being popular

This problem may arise especially in situations where the questions are subjective statements, such as attitudes, which are not central or salient to the respondent. In such situations, the item appearing first tends to form a point of reference for all items that follow. Researchers can overcome this problem by acquainting respondents with the list of items before respondents are asked to evaluate them. Alternatively, researchers can randomize the order of presentation so that the order effects will be randomized, too, and will not result in any systematic bias.

Finally, questions that are presented first in the questionnaire should put the respondent at ease; the initial questions in an interview should help create rapport between the interviewer and the respondent. Thus the opening question should be easy to answer, interesting, and noncontroversial. For example, questions about the respondent's drinking habits or sex life, if placed at the beginning, will in all likelihood increase the refusal rate. It is also recommended that open-ended questions be placed later, for they usually require more time and thought and thus may reduce the respondent's initial motivation to cooperate if they appear at the beginning.

AVOIDING BIAS: PITFALLS IN QUESTIONNAIRE CONSTRUCTION •

Wording

The question must be worded so that the respondent understands it. For example, the researcher's vocabulary might include a word such as *synthesize* that might not be understood by most other people. If the respondents come from all walks of life, the interviewer should use words that can be understood by the average sixth grader. Furthermore, researchers should either avoid or qualify words that are open to interpretation. For example, the question "Are you a liberal?" is too broad. You might be referring to the person's education, politics, profession, or sex life. But a question such as "Do you consider yourself liberal? Politically, I mean," instructs the respondent to use the political frame of reference in answering the question. Each question should be worded so that the respondent understands its meaning and so that the question has the same meaning to each respondent.

Response Set

A **response set** is the tendency to answer all questions in a specific direction regardless of their content. This problem may arise when a set of questions is presented together with the same response format, especially when the questions all refer to the same topic. For example, if a set of questions reflects a pro-choice attitude regarding abortion, respondents who are against abortion may check all the same response categories (for example, all "strongly disagree" or all "strongly agree") simply because they assume that these categories all express objection to abortion. Investigators can avoid creating a response set by changing the question format, either by varying the response categories for each question or by distributing questions on a topic throughout the questionnaire instead of placing them all together.

Leading Questions

A **leading question** is a question phrased in such a manner that it seems to the respondent that the researcher expects a certain answer. A question designed to elicit general attitudes toward legal abortions might read: "Do you favor or oppose legal abortions?" The same question phrased in leading form might read: "You wouldn't say that you were in favor of legal abortion, would you?" A more subtle form of leading question might be: "Would you say that you are not in favor of legal abortions?" This last question makes it easier for respondents to answer "yes" than "no," because most people feel more comfortable agreeing with the language of the question and not contradicting the interviewer.

Respondents also tend to agree with statements that support accepted norms or that are perceived as socially desirable. Respondents endorse statements that reflect socially undesirable behavior or attitudes less frequently than those high on the scale of social desirability. Similarly, the way that issues are labeled and enhanced can have a substantial effect on public support for some issues. Analyses of variations in question wording in the General Social Survey showed significant differences in responses when the same issue was labeled differently. For example, when a question on welfare spending read "Are we spending too much, too little, or about the right amount on welfare?" 23 percent said too little. But when the question was worded "Are we spending too much, too little, or about the right amount on assistance to the poor?" almost 63 percent said too little.[6]

A 1994 ABC/*Washington Post* poll contained the following question: "Is Clinton an old-style, tax-and-spend Democrat or a new-style Democrat who will be careful with the nation's money?" In a criticism of the national press, Jeff Faux points out that this question is both biased and leading.[7] Because the question labels liberals negatively and conservatives positively, it suggests that if the respondent is dissatisfied with Clinton's performance, it must be because he or she is an old-style liberal Democrat. A more value-free question, such as "Is Clinton a liberal Democrat or a conservative Democrat?" might elicit a different response.

Researchers who are looking for undistorted responses should avoid leading questions. Under certain circumstances, however, leading questions may serve the research objective. The question "Do you favor military intervention in Kosovo to prevent the massacre of Albanians?" could be used to determine the number of people who are so strongly opposed to military intervention in international conflicts abroad that they reject the idea even within the strong emotional context of "massacred Albanians."

Threatening Questions

Often it is necessary to include questions on topics that the respondent may find embarrassing and thus difficult to answer. **Threatening questions** usually deal with behaviors

---

6. Kenneth A. Rasinski, "The Effect of Question Wording on Public Support for Government Spending," *Public Opinion Quarterly,* 53 (1989): 388–394.

7. Jeff Faux, "Hey, Big Spender." *The Nation,* 31 (Oct. 1994): 480.

that are illegal, contra-normative, or private. Such questions may inquire about such subjects as drinking, drug use, or sexual practices.

There is considerable empirical evidence that threatening questions lead to **response bias**—respondents either deny the behavior in question or underreport it. In general, as the degree of threat in a question increases, respondents' tendency to report certain behaviors decreases. When they are presented with a threatening question, respondents are caught in a conflict between the role demands of the "cooperative respondent," who responds truthfully to all the questions, and the tendency for people to present themselves positively. Respondents usually resolve the conflict not by refusing to answer but by reporting that they did not engage in the particular activity when, in fact, they did.[8]

Because threatening questions may elicit biased responses, it is important for researchers first to determine whether certain questions are threatening. Norman Bradburn and Seymour Sudman suggest that the best method for determining the relative threat of questions is by asking respondents to rate question topics as to how uneasy they thought most people would feel in talking about them.[9] Interviewers can also ask respondents about their reactions to the questions or rate the degree of difficulty the topics caused in the interview.

Once researchers have identified threatening questions, what should they do about them? In a comprehensive study dealing with response effects to threatening questions in survey research, Bradburn and Sudman determined that the way questions are constructed makes a great deal of difference.[10] Perhaps their most significant finding was that the accuracy of the response is considerably increased by using a long introduction to the question rather than asking short questions, by employing an open-ended rather than a closed-ended format, and, to a lesser extent, by letting the respondents choose their own words when talking about sensitive topics. Bradburn and Sudman's questionnaire contained an item about the number of times in the past year the respondent had become intoxicated. In the short, closed form, the item read: "In the past year, how often did you become intoxicated while drinking any kind of beverage?" Respondents were asked to classify their response into one of the following categories: never, once a year or less, every few months, once a month, every few weeks, once a week, several times a week, and daily. In the open-ended, long form, the respondents were first asked to provide their own word for intoxication: "Sometimes people drink a little too much beer, wine, or whiskey so that they act different from usual. What word do you think we should use to describe people when they get that way, so that you will know what we mean and feel comfortable talking about it?" The intoxication item then read: "Occasionally people drink on an empty stomach or drink a little too much and become (respondent's word). In the past year, how often have you become (respondent's word) while drinking any kind of alcoholic beverage?" No response categories were provided for these questions.[11]

Double-Barreled Questions

Double-barreled questions combine two or more questions in one. Here is an example from an opinion poll about domestic violence:

8. Norman M. Bradburn, Seymour Sudman, Ed Blair, and Carol Stocking, "Question Threat and Response Bias," *Public Opinion Quarterly*, 42 (1978): 221–222.

9. Norman M. Bradburn and Seymour Sudman, *Improving Interview Method and Questionnaire Design* (San Francisco: Jossey-Bass, 1974), p. 165.

10. Ibid., pp. 14–25.

11. Ibid., p. 18.

Domestic violence and AIDS are the most serious problems facing America today.

_____ Agree   _____ Disagree
_____ Depends   _____ Strongly disagree

The problem with such a question is that it might confuse respondents who agree with one aspect of the question—say, domestic violence—but disagree with the other, AIDS. Many questions that contain *and* are very likely double-barreled. Questions with *and* can be used, however, if the dimensions separated by *and* are mutually exclusive and the respondent is asked to select one or to rank them according to some criterion, for instance:

> At the present time, the country is faced with two major problems: the environment and domestic violence. Which of these two problems would you say is the more important?
>
> _____ The environment
> _____ Domestic violence

COVER LETTER ●

After the researcher has constructed the questionnaire, the next step is to write an introductory statement (for a personal or telephone interview) or a cover letter (for a mail questionnaire) to explain the purpose of the survey to the respondents and to encourage a high response rate. The content of the cover letter is particularly important in mail questionnaires, where the difficulty of securing a high response rate, especially when the researcher needs to ask more than a few simple questions, is well documented (see Chapter 10).

A cover letter must succeed in overcoming any resistance or prejudice the respondent may have against the survey. It should (1) identify the sponsoring organization or the persons conducting the study, (2) explain the purpose of the study, (3) tell why it is important that the respondent answer the questionnaire, and (4) assure the respondent that the information provided will be held in strict confidence.

In general, the cover letter for a mail questionnaire needs to be more detailed than the introductory statement in a personal interview. In an interview, the interviewer is always there to explain or persuade the respondent should that become necessary. With a mail questionnaire, the cover letter is all there is, and thus its function is very significant.

Two examples of cover letters used in various mail surveys are presented here. The first, shown in Exhibit 11.2, was used with a mail questionnaire designed by the Institute of Social Research at Florida State University under the auspices of the State Department of Manpower Planning of Florida to evaluate the Public Service Employment and Training Act, Title VI (CETA).[12]

The second example, reprinted in Exhibit 11.3, is from a study on commitment to civil liberties conducted by investigators at the University of Wisconsin at Milwaukee.[13] The letter emphasizes the confidentiality of the study and explains in detail how the individual responses will be used.

Finally, researchers must carefully choose an appropriate style for the cover letter, that is, whether to make it a formal or a semipersonal letter. In the two examples, researchers sent out a form letter to all respondents included in the sample. As an alternative,

---

12. Mickey L. Burnim, *An Evaluation of the Public Service Employment Projects in Florida Created Under Title VI of the Comprehensive Employment and Training Act of 1973* (Tallahassee: Florida State University, 1978), p. 164.

13. Richard D. Bingham and James L. Gibson, "Conditions of Commitment to Civil Liberties," unpublished manuscript (Milwaukee: Department of Political Science, University of Wisconsin, 1979).

Exhibit 11.2

FLORIDA QUESTIONNAIRE COVER LETTER

To Program Operators:

The Office of Manpower Planning, Department of Community Affairs, in conjunction with the State Manpower Services Council, has funded a special evaluation of public service employment projects authorized under Title VI of the Comprehensive Employment and Training Act. This evaluation is being conducted by Dr. M. L. Burnim in the Institute for Social Research at Florida State University. The purpose of the evaluation is to determine the impact of public service employment projects on unemployed persons in Florida and to measure the benefit of these projects to the communities in which they are conducted.

As you know, public service employment is a major part of the federal, state, and local strategy to overcome the employment and income problems of economically disadvantaged, unemployed people. There is no question that the program is needed throughout the country to create jobs and training opportunities for the large numbers of people who remain unemployed. You are probably also aware, however, that public service employment programs are quite controversial and their future may be in jeopardy. Part of the reason that these programs are so controversial is that no systematic evaluation of the benefits of these programs for the individuals employed and the communities served has been conducted.

Because this specific evaluation has significant national policy implications, I strongly urge you to assist the research team in compiling the necessary data. It is very important that you complete the survey questionnaire transmitted to you as soon as possible.

Thank you for your cooperation.

Sincerely,

Edward A. Feaver, Director
Office of Manpower Planning

---

the researcher might choose to personalize the letter by inserting the respondent's name and address rather than addressing the letter to "Dear Friend" or "Dear Respondent." Most word processing programs can personalize letters automatically and inexpensively if the letter and the mailing list are both computerized, and it has been shown that a more personal letter generates a slightly higher response rate than a form letter.[14]

INSTRUCTIONS

Another element researchers must consider when constructing a questionnaire is the instructions that go with each question or with a set of questions. Instructions should be included with any questions that are not self-explanatory; the instructions may range

---

14. Michael T. Matteson, "Type of Transmittal Letter and Questionnaire Color as Two Variables Influencing Response Rates in a Mail Survey," *Journal of Applied Psychology,* 59 (1974): 532–536.

Exhibit 11.3

WISCONSIN QUESTIONNAIRE COVER LETTER

Dear Friend:

We are conducting a survey sponsored by the University of Wisconsin-Milwaukee and assisted by the American Civil Liberties Union (ACLU). Our purpose is to learn more about how people like yourself feel about certain aspects of civil liberties and how beliefs are related to behavior. You have been selected at random to participate in this survey—thus your opinions will represent the opinions of thousands of people much like yourself.

Enclosed find a copy of our questionnaire. While it is a bit lengthy and will require about 20 minutes to complete, we hope that you will take the time to complete it and return the questionnaire to us in the enclosed self-addressed envelope. The information you provide will contribute to an important study and may also be used to influence ACLU policy.

A bit about confidentiality. We promise you confidentiality under the academic ethics standards of the American Political Science Association. Your name will not be revealed or associated with your response nor will anyone outside of the project staff here at the University of Wisconsin-Milwaukee be allowed to see your response. Thus, while the ACLU may be interested in the policy implications of our study, they will not be furnished with any information which in any way identifies you as an individual. Please note the number in the upper right-hand corner of the questionnaire. This number allows us to temporarily identify you. By referring to this number we will know that you responded to the questionnaire and will not send you the follow-up mailing we will have to send to nonrespondents.

We appreciate your willingness to help us in our research effort. If you would like a copy of our completed study please indicate this on the last page of the questionnaire. We will make certain that you receive a copy of our results. We believe that you will find the questionnaire both interesting and provocative and look forward to receiving your reply.

Sincerely yours,

Richard D. Bingham   James L. Gibson
Assistant Professor   Associate Professor

Note: If by some chance you recently received and responded to this particular questionnaire, please return the blank questionnaire to us indicating "duplicate" on the first page.

from very simple ones such as "circle the appropriate category" to more complex guidelines that explain how to rank a set of priorities. When an interviewer administers a questionnaire, the instructions are usually written for him or her and thus are often short and concise, instructing the interviewer what to do when the respondent provides a certain answer, when to probe for a more detailed answer, or how to clarify a certain question.

The following is an example of instructions written for an interviewer:

Who was your employer on your last job?

(PROBE FOR CORRECT CATEGORY)

☐ Private   ☐ Self-employed
☐ City   ☐ Public, nonprofit
☐ County   ☐ Other _____ (specify)
☐ State   ☐ Doesn't know
☐ Federal

When a personal or telephone interview is used, the interviewer is available to answer any questions that the respondent may raise, but this is not the case with mail questionnaires, where any questions that are vague or unclear are likely to be answered incorrectly, if at all. Therefore, providing clear instructions is extremely important. They can vary from general instructions introducing the questionnaire or its subsections to specific details preceding individual questions.

The following is an example of general instructions given at the beginning of a questionnaire on attitudes toward civil liberties:[15]

INSTRUCTIONS: For each of the following questions please mark the answer that comes closest to the way you feel about the issue. There are no "right" or "wrong" answers — please answer the questions as honestly as possible. Answer each of the questions in the order in which it appears. If you wish to make additional comments on any of the specific questions or on the issues in general, use the space at the end of the questionnaire. Your opinions are extremely important for understanding these complex civil liberty issues — we greatly appreciate your cooperation!

The next example, taken from the General Social Survey, introduces a question presented in a ranking scale format:

INSTRUCTIONS: Some people think that the government in Washington ought to reduce the income differences between the rich and the poor, perhaps by raising the taxes of wealthy families or by giving income assistance to the poor. Others think that the government should not concern itself with reducing this income difference between the rich and poor.

Here is a card with a scale from 1 to 7. Think of a score of 1 as meaning that the government ought to reduce the income differences between rich and poor, and a score of 7 meaning that the government should not concern itself with reducing income differences. What score between 1 and 7 comes closest to the way you feel? (CIRCLE ONE):

```
┌─────────────┐
│   HAND      │
│ CARD OVER   │
└─────────────┘
```

GOVERNMENT SHOULD DO   GOVERNMENT SHOULD
SOMETHING TO REDUCE   NOT CONCERN ITSELF
INCOME DIFFERENCES   WITH INCOME
BETWEEN RICH AND POOR   DIFFERENCES

```
   |____|____|____|____|____|____|____|
   1    2    3    4    5    6    7
```

15. Bingham and Gibson, "Conditions of Commitment to Civil Liberties."

Finally, here is an example is of a specific instruction for replying to a single question.

About how many states have you lived in during your life? (Count only those states that you lived in for at least one year.)

CONSTRUCTING A QUESTIONNAIRE: A CASE STUDY ●

Many stages are involved in the construction of a questionnaire. The researcher begins with the research problem and goes through the process of formulating the questions and considering the format and the type of questions to be used. To illustrate these stages, we present in Exhibit 11.4 a questionnaire based on an actual study conducted by the Institute for Social Research at the University of Michigan.[16]

The objective of the study was to explore the attitudes and perceptions related to urban problems and race relations in 15 northern cities in the United States. The investigators sought to define the social and psychological characteristics as well as the aspirations of the black and white urban populations. Researchers selected a black sample and a white sample in each of the cities in the study. Approximately 175 black and 175 white respondents were interviewed in each city. In addition, 366 whites were interviewed in two suburban areas. Altogether, 2,809 black respondents and 2,950 white respondents were interviewed. Respondents were between the ages of 16 and 69 and lived in private households.

The researchers used two questionnaire forms, one for whites and one for blacks. The questions about background characteristics were almost identical in the two forms. The attitudinal questions were also identical in both interview forms, but a greater number of questions were addressed exclusively to one racial group or to the other. The questionnaires contained attitudinal questions probing the respondents' satisfaction with neighborhood services, their feelings about the effectiveness of the government in dealing with urban problems, their interracial relationships, their attitudes toward integration, and their perception of the hostility between the races. The questionnaire in Exhibit 11.4 is a shortened version of the original questionnaire addressed to blacks.

Notice that the questionnaire starts off with identification numbers for the person being interviewed as well as his or her location. There is also room for the interviewer to provide information on when the interview began. Question 1 is an example of an attitude question on degree of satisfaction with services provided by the city. The researcher used a matrix format for this question. Note also that instructions are provided both for the interviewer ("Code A below, and ask B through E") and the respondent.

Question 2 has a closed-ended and open-ended component (2A). Item 2A is also a contingency question. Questions 3, 5, 6, and 7 are likewise contingency questions. The first part is the filter question, and the second is the contingency question, which applies only to respondents who have checked specific categories in the first part. All questions use a numerical code, which is checked off by the interviewer.

The final section of the questionnaire demonstrates the relative advantage of an interview over other modes of filling out questionnaires (mail, telephone). The interviewer can provide detailed information on the general attitude of the respondents, which can help researchers interpret their response pattern.

---

16. Based on Angus Campbell and Howard Schuman, *Racial Attitudes in Fifteen American Cities* (Ann Arbor, MI: Social Science Archive, 1973).

Exhibit 11.4

URBAN PROBLEM STUDY QUESTIONNAIRE

| TIME INTERVIEW |
| BEGAN:_____A.M. |
| P.M. |

City
Number ☐☐ v.3

FOR OFFICE USE
ONLY

☐☐☐☐ v.2

Segment
Number ☐☐☐ v.9

DULS
Line
Number ☐☐☐☐ v.10

Person
Number ☐ v.19

1. First, I'd like to ask how satisfied you are with some of the main services the city is supposed to provide for your neighborhood. What about the quality of public schools in this neighborhood—are you generally satisfied, somewhat dissatisfied, or very dissatisfied?

(CODE A BELOW, AND
ASK B THROUGH E)

	Generally satisfied	Somewhat satisfied	Very dissatisfied	Don't know
A. Quality of public schools	1	2	3	8
B. Parks and playgrounds for children in this neighborhood	1	2	3	8
C. Sports and recreation centers for teenagers in this neighborhood	1	2	3	8
D. Police protection in this neighborhood	1	2	3	8
E. Garbage collection in this neighborhood	1	2	3	8

2. Thinking about city services like schools, parks, and garbage collection, do you think your neighborhood gets better, about the same, or worse services than most other parts of the city?

Better . . . . (ASK A) 1
About same 2
Worse . . . . (ASK A) 3
Don't know 8

A. IF BETTER OR WORSE: What is the reason this neighborhood gets (better/worse) services?

3. If you have a serious complaint about poor service by the city, do you think you can get city officials to do something about it if you call them?

RECODED
VALUES

Yes . . . . . . (ASK A) 1
No . . . . . . (ASK A) 5
Don't know . . (ASK A) . . 8

A. Have you ever called a city official with a complaint about poor service?

Yes   1
No   5

4. In general, do you think (CITY) city officials pay more, less, or the same attention to a request or complaint from a black as from a white person?

More 1	1
Less 2	3
Same 3	2
Don't know 8	8

Now let's talk about the problems of (CITY) as a whole.

5. Do you think the Mayor of (CITY) is trying as hard as he/she can to solve the main problems of the city, or that he/she is not doing all he/she could to solve these problems?

> Trying as hard as he/she can 1
> Not doing all he/she could (ASK A) X
> Don't know 8
> A. IF NOT DOING ALL HE/SHE COULD: Do you think he/she is try-
> ing fairly hard to solve these
> problems, or not hard at all?
> Fairly hard 2
> Not hard at all 3

6. How about the state government? Do you think they are trying as hard as they can to solve the main problems of cities like (CITY), or that they are not doing all they could to solve these problems?

> Trying as hard as they can 1
> Not doing all they could (ASK A) . . X
> Don't know 8
> A. IF NOT DOING ALL THEY COULD: Do you think they are trying
> fairly hard to solve these prob-
> lems, or not hard at all?
> Fairly hard 2
> Not hard at all 3

7. How about the federal government in Washington? Do you think they are trying as hard as they can to solve the main problems of cities like (CITY), or that they are not doing all they could to solve these problems?

> Trying as hard as they can 1
> Not doing all they could (ASK A) . . X
> Don't know 8
> A. IF NOT DOING ALL THEY COULD: Do you think they are trying
> fairly hard to solve these prob-
> lems, or not hard at all?
> Fairly hard 2
> Not hard at all 3

8. A black mayor has been elected in Cleveland and also in Gary, Indiana. What effect do you think this will have on solving city problems in Cleveland and Gary? Do you think it will make things better, worse, or won't there be much change?

> Better 1
> Worse 2
> Not much change 3
> Don't know . . . (ASK A) . . 8

Exhibit 11.4 *(continued)*

A. IF DON'T KNOW: What would you *guess* the effect would be—to make things better, worse, or won't there be much change?

Better 1
Worse 2
Not much change 3

Now I want to talk about some complaints people have made about the (CITY) police.

9. First, some people say the police don't come quickly when you call them for help. Do you think this happens to people in this neighborhood?

Yes . . . . . (ASK A) 1
No . . . . (GO TO Q. 10) . 5
Don't know . . . (ASK A) . . 8

A. IF YES OR DON'T KNOW: Has it ever happened to you?

Yes . . . . (ASK B & C) . . . 1
No . . . . . (ASK C) 5

B. IF YES TO A: How long ago was that (the last time)?

_____ years ago

C. IF YES OR NO TO A: Has it happened to anyone you know?

Yes 1
No 5

---

10. Some people say the police don't show respect for people or they use insulting language. Do you think this happens to people in this neighborhood?

Yes . . . . . (ASK A) 1
No . . . . (GO TO Q. 11) . 5
Don't know . . . (ASK A) . . 8

A. IF YES OR DON'T KNOW: Has it ever happened to you?

Yes . . . . (ASK B & C) . . . 1
No . . . . . (ASK C) 5

B. IF YES TO A: How long ago was that (the last time)?

_____ years ago

C. IF YES OR NO TO A: Has it happened to anyone you know?

Yes 1
No 5

---

11. Some people say the police frisk or search people without good reason. Do you think this happens often to people in this neighborhood?

RECODED
VALUES

Yes . . . . . (ASK A) 1
No . . . . (GO TO Q. 12) . 5
Don't know . . . (ASK A) . . 8

A. IF YES OR DON'T KNOW: Has it ever happened to you?

Yes . . . . (ASK B & C) . . . 1
No . . . . . (ASK C) 5

B. IF YES TO A: How long ago was that (the last time)?

_____ years ago

C. IF YES OR NO TO A: Has it happened to anyone you know?

Yes 1
No 5

12. Some people say the police rough up people unnecessarily when they are arresting them or afterwards. Do you think this happens to people in this neighborhood?

> Yes . . . . . (ASK A) 1
> No . . . . (GO TO Q. 13) . 5
> Don't know . . . (ASK A) . . 8

A. IF YES OR DON'T KNOW: Has it ever happened to you?

> Yes . . . . (ASK B & C) . . . 1
> No . . . . . (ASK C) 5

   B. IF YES TO A: How long ago was that (the last time)?

> _____ years ago

   C. IF YES OR NO TO A: Has it happened to anyone you know?

> Yes 1
> No 5

13. Do you think black citizens are generally given better treatment by black police officers, by white police officers, or that it doesn't make much difference?

> Black police officers (ASK A) . . . 1   1
> White police officers (ASK A) . . . 2   2
> Not much difference 3   2
> Don't know 8   8

A. IF BLACK OR WHITE POLICE OFFICERS: Why do you think this is?

14. In general, do you think judges in (CITY) are usually harder on blacks, harder on whites, or that there is not much difference?

> Harder on blacks 1   1
> Harder on whites 2   3
> Not much difference 3   2
> Don't know 8   8

15. Do you personally feel safer from crime now than you did two or three years ago, or is there no change, or do you feel less safe?

> Safer today 1
> No change 2
> Less safe 3

16. Here are some complaints you hear, sometimes about stores and merchants. Would you tell me if these things ever happen *to you* when you shop in stores in or near this neighborhood?

	Often	Sometimes	Rarely	Never	Don't shop in neighborhood
A. Do you think you are unfairly over-charged for goods often, sometimes, rarely, or never?	1	2	3	4	5 (GO TO D)
B. Do you think you are sold spoiled or inferior goods often, sometimes, rarely, or never?	1	2	3	4	

C. In such stores, are you treated disre-spectfully often, sometimes, rarely, or never?

1   2   3   4

D. IF NEVER SHOP IN NEIGHBORHOOD: Why don't you shop around here?

FILL IN ITEMS BELOW IMMEDIATELY AFTER LEAVING RESPONDENT

A. Total length of interview:

_____ Minutes

B. Cooperativeness of respondent:

Very cooperative 1
Somewhat cooperative . . . 2
Not cooperative 3

C. Interest of respondent in racial issues:

Great interest 1
Ordinary interest 2
Little interest 3

D. Respondent's understanding of questions:

Good understanding 1
Fair understanding 2
Poor understanding 3

E. What persons over 14 years of age were present during interview? CIRCLE *ALL* THAT APPLY.

v.63   None 0
Spouse 1
Parent 2
Child over 14 3
Other relative or friend . 4
Other (SPECIFY) 5

F. Neatness of home interior:

v.64   Very neat and clean . . . 1
Fairly neat and clean . . 2
Fairly messy 3
Very messy 4

G. Date of Interview: _____

v.69

H. Interviewer's Signature:

I. Please give here a brief description of the respondent, and of any special condi-tions that affected the interview.

---

1. The foundation of all questionnaires is the question. The questionnaire must trans-late the research objectives into specific questions. The answers to these ques-tions will provide the necessary data for hypothesis testing.

2. Most questions can be classified as either factual questions or questions about subjective experiences. Factual questions are designed to elicit objective informa-tion from the respondent. Subjective questions are concerned with inclinations,

preferences, prejudices, ideas, fears, and convictions. In general, subjective questions are much more complex and difficult to construct than questions about personal facts. Answers to subjective questions are more likely to change with changes in wording, emphasis, and sequence than are answers to factual questions.

3. Three types of question structure can be distinguished: closed-ended questions, open-ended questions, and contingency questions. In closed-ended questions, respondents are offered a set of response categories from which they must choose the one that most closely represents their view. Open-ended questions are not followed by any kind of choice, and the respondents' answers are recorded in full. A contingency question applies only to a subgroup of respondents. The relevance of the question to this subgroup is determined by the answers of all respondents to a preceding filter question.

4. One of the most common formats researchers use to ask questions in surveys is the rating scale, whereby the respondent makes judgments in terms of sets of ordered categories. There are several types of rating scales. The matrix question is a method of organizing a large set of rating questions that have the same response categories. Ranking is used in questionnaires when the objective is to obtain information regarding the degree of importance or the priorities that people apply to a set of attitudes or objects.

5. Questions must be worded so that all respondents can comprehend them. The way a *leading question* is phrased makes it appear to the respondent that the researcher expects a certain answer. *Threatening questions* raise the anxiety level of the respondents. Both types of questions may lead to response bias. Researchers should avoid leading questions and construct threatening questions with great sensitivity, using special techniques such as a long introduction to the question and an open-ended rather than a closed-ended format.

KEY TERMS FOR REVIEW ●

attitude (p. 231)
closed-ended question (p. 233)
contingency question (p. 235)
double-barreled question (p. 242)
factual question (p. 231)
filter question (p. 235)
leading question (p. 241)
matrix question (p. 237)
open-ended question (p. 233)

opinion (p. 232)
quantifiers (p. 237)
question (p. 230)
ranking (p. 238)
rating (p. 236)
response bias (p. 242)
response set (p. 240)
threatening question (p. 241)

STUDY QUESTIONS ●

1. Discuss the various ways in which questions can be used to get factual information, opinions, and attitudes from respondents.
2. Explain the uses of closed-ended, open-ended, and contingency questions.
3. List and describe the formats used to ask questions for various purposes.
4. Discuss the importance of question sequencing in a questionnaire.
5. List the various problems that may arise while constructing questionnaires.

SPSS PROBLEMS

1. Using the *Utilities* function, examine the variables in the **gss96worth** file. Identify three opinion questions and three factual questions. Print these questions.
2. Identify six rating scales in the **gss96worth** file. Identify the quantifiers in each question.
3. Using the *Utilities* function, examine the variables in the **gss96worth** file. Identify a set of questions where there is a risk of a response set. Explain.

ADDITIONAL READINGS

Abramson, Paul R., and Charles W. Ostrom. "Questions Wording and Partisanship: Change and Continuity in Party Loyalties During the 1992 Election Campaign." *Public Opinion Quarterly,* 58 (1994): 21–49.

Bishop, G. F., R. W. Oldendick, and Alfred J. Tuchfarber. "Effects of Filter Questions in Public Opinion Surveys," *Public Opinion Quarterly,* 47 (1983): 528–546.

Czaja, Ronald, and Bob Blair. *Survey Research.* Newbury Park, CA: Pine Forge Press, 1995.

Gaskell, George D., Colm A. O'Muircheartaigh, and Daniel B. Wright. "Survey Questions About Frequency of Vaguely Defined Events: The Effects of Response Alternatives." *Public Opinion Quarterly,* 58 (1994): 241–255.

Rasinski, Kenneth A., David Mingay, and Norman M. Bradburn. "Do Respondents Really 'Mark All That Apply' on Self-Administered Questions?" *Public Opinion Quarterly,* 58 (1994): 400–409.

Schuman, Howard, and Stanley Presser. *Questions and Answers in Attitude Surveys.* Orlando, FL: Academic Press, 1981.

Tourangeau, R. T., and K. Rasinski. *The Psychology of Survey Responding.* Cambridge, U. K.: Cambridge University Press, 1997.

QUALITATIVE RESEARCH

What goes on behind the scenes at a university rape crisis center, and how do you find out? Amy Fried was interested in how the beliefs volunteer counselors bring to their work shape and modify the goals of the organization and influence the counseling offered to victims of rape.[1] Fried chose to study a newly forming rape crisis center by becoming a volunteer counselor. Along with 15 other women and 4 men who served as the staff of the center, she attended training sessions and organizational meetings and observed the interaction among the other volunteer members, concentrating on how members defined rape and the language they used to describe victims. She found that two distinct subcultures emerged within the group. One subculture held what she called the political perspective. This faction consisted of feminists who believed rape was the result of the social power men hold over women. Their goal was to empower the victims of rape and ultimately effect social change. The other faction held a service perspective. They believed that both sex and power issues were involved in rape, but that the goal of the organization should be to help people—both women and the significant men in their lives—overcome the pain associated with being victimized by rape. Generalizing from her findings, Fried argues that the clash between these two subcultures weakens the ability of feminists to reform society and suggests that, perhaps, feminists need to form their own organizations to meet their mission. Fried employed qualitative methods to gather the data for her study. Her participant observer role allowed her to discover how meanings and beliefs enter into organizational goals.

●**IN THIS CHAPTER** we focus on the field research for qualitative study, concentrating on complete participant and participant-as-observer roles. We discuss how researchers select their topics, identify and gain access to their subjects, establish relationships, and record their observations. We also consider how field researchers develop grounded theory based on their data using the process of analytic induction. Finally, we consider the ethical and political dilemmas of field research.

So far we have discussed methods of data collection designed primarily for quantitative analyses. In this chapter, we describe the prototype of qualitative research—field research. Qualitative research, as a method of data collection and analysis, derives from the *Verstehen* tradition described in Chapter 1. Scientists must gain an empathic understanding of societal phenomena, and they must recognize both the historical dimension of human behavior and the subjective aspects of the human experience. In his study of asylums, Erving Goffman describes the process of actively participating in the daily life of the observed and the gaining of insights by introspection in the following way:

> My immediate object in doing field work at St. Elizabeth's was to try to learn about the social world of the hospital inmate, as this world is subjectively experienced by him. . . . It was then and still is my belief that any group of persons—prisoners, primitives, pilots, or patients—develop a life of their own that becomes meaningful, reasonable, and normal once you get close to it, and that a good way to learn about any of these worlds is to submit oneself in the company of the members to the daily round of petty contingencies to which they are subject.[2]

---

1. Amy Fried, "'It's Hard to Change What We Want to Change,'" *Gender & Society*, 8:4 (1994): 562–583.

2. Erving Goffman, *Asylums* (Garden City, NY: Doubleday, 1961), pp. ix–x.

Qualitative researchers attempt to understand behavior and institutions by getting to know the persons involved and their values, rituals, symbols, beliefs, and emotions. Applying such a perspective, researchers would, for example, study poverty by immersing themselves in the life of the poor rather than collecting data with a structured interview schedule. |

FIELD RESEARCH   ●

Field research is the most central strategy of data collection associated with qualitative methodology. In general terms, **field research** is defined as "the study of people acting in the natural courses of their daily lives. The fieldworker ventures into the worlds of others in order to learn firsthand about how they live, how they talk and behave, and what captivates and distresses them." [3] More explicitly, fieldwork is characterized by its location and by the manner in which it is conducted. [4] With respect to location, fieldwork is carried out in *natural* settings, for example, anthropologists living with remote tribes or sociologists sharing in and observing the daily life of a local community. Field research is also a way of empathizing with and understanding the subjective meanings of the people being studied. Typically, fieldworkers attempt to incorporate these two characteristics in their studies.

Contemporary sociological fieldwork has its origins in the social reform movement of the turn of the twentieth century. Reformers believed that descriptions of the conditions in which the poor lived would call attention to their plight and lead to social change and improvement in those conditions. The reform movement found its strongest academic expression in the Chicago School in the early 1920s. The Chicago School sociologists were intensely involved in the social reform movement centered outside the university. Robert Park, a leading figure in the Chicago School, saw in the city a critical area for sociological research and urged his students to observe life in its various enclaves firsthand:

> Go and sit in the lounges of the luxury hotels and on the doorsteps of the flophouses; sit on the Gold Coast settees and on the slum shake-downs; sit in Orchestra Hall and in the Star and Garter Burlesk. In short, gentlemen, go get the seat of your pants dirty in real research. [5]

At that time, the methodology of qualitative research was limited to assembling a variety of personal documents—autobiographies, life histories, letters, and diaries. Qualitative researchers had only a limited conception of how to participate in the lives of the people they were studying. During the following two decades, as fieldwork became more established in sociology, its methodology came to emphasize participation in the lives of those studied so that researchers could share, and consequently better understand, the subjective perspectives of the subjects.

PARTICIPANT OBSERVATION   ●

The method of data collection most closely associated with contemporary field research is **participant observation,** whereby the investigator attempts to attain some kind of membership in or close attachment to the group that he or she wishes to study. [6] In doing

---

3. Robert M. Emerson, ed., *Contemporary Field Research* (Boston: Little, Brown, 1983), p. 1.

4. Ibid.

5. John C. McKinney, *Constructive Typology and Social Theory* (Norwalk, CT: Appleton & Lang, 1966), p. 71.

6. Rosalie H. Wax, "Participant Observation," *International Encyclopedia of Social Sciences* (New York: Macmillan, 1968), p. 238.

so, the participant observer attempts to adopt the perspectives of the people in the situation being observed. The participant observer's role is that of "conscious and systematic sharing, insofar as circumstances permit, in the life activities, and on occasion, in the interests and effects of a group of persons." [7] Direct participation in the activities of the observed often entails learning the language, habits, work patterns, leisure activities, and other aspects of their daily lives. The researcher assumes either a complete participant role or a participant-as-observer role.

Complete Participant

In a **complete participant** role, the observer is wholly concealed; the research objectives are unknown to the observed, and the researcher attempts to become a member of the group under observation. The complete participant interacts with the observed "as naturally as possible in whatever areas of their living interest him and are accessible to him." [8]

For example, Festinger, Riecken, and Schachter studied a group of persons who predicted the destruction of the world. The nature of the group led the investigators to believe that if they presented themselves as researchers, they would not be allowed to observe the activities of the group. Consequently, they posed as individuals who shared the beliefs of the group and became full-fledged members trying to be "nondirective, sympathetic listeners, passive participants who were inquisitive and eager to learn whatever others might want to tell us." [9] Richard Mitchell, Jr., describes some of the difficulties he and his fellow researchers encountered in a field investigation of paramilitary survivalists. [10] In order to penetrate the secrecy surrounding the activities of most paramilitary survivalist groups, the researchers took advantage of the survivalist desire for new members by posing as potential recruits. Although they found themselves overdressed when they arrived for their first weekend among the survivalists, they were accepted and praised for their enthusiasm even though their costumes made it difficult to blend in. To gain membership in the group, the researchers had to participate in physical and social activities antithetical to their personal beliefs. Mitchell describes an occasion when he was required to tell a story proposing a solution to something the group considered to be a social problem.

> As I began a new man joined us. He listened to my idea and approved, introduced himself, then told me things not everyone knew, about plans being made, and actions soon to be taken. He said they could use men like me and told me to be ready to join. I took him seriously. Others did, too. He was on the FBI's "ten most wanted" list. [11]

Mitchell's story was good enough to gain him admittance to the inner circle of the group, but his success was not without cost. There was a possibility that his proposed solution, repulsive as it was to him, would be implemented by the survivalist. He tells how he felt about this.

7. Florence Kluckhohn, "The Participant-Observer Technique in Small Communities," *American Journal of Sociology*, 46 (1940): 331.

8. Raymond L. Gold, "Roles in Sociological Field Observation," *Social Forces*, 36 (1958): 219.

9. Leon Festinger, Henry Riecken, and Stanley Schachter, *When Prophecy Fails* (New York: Harper & Row, 1956), p. 234.

10. Richard Mitchell, Jr., "The Secrecy and Disclosure in Field Work," in *Experiencing Field Work: An Inside View of Qualitative Research*, eds. William B. Shaffir and Robert A. Stebbins (Newbury Park, CA: Sage, 1991), pp. 97–108.

11. Ibid., p. 107.

If there are researchers who can participate in such business without feeling, I am not one of them nor do I even hope to be. What I do hope is someday to forget, forget those unmistakable sounds, my own voice, my own words, telling that . . . story.[12]

Complete participation has been justified on the grounds that it makes possible the study of inaccessible groups or groups that do not reveal to outsiders certain aspects of their lives. Presumably, the fieldworker is treated as just another member of the group. Despite this research advantage, some researchers have severely criticized the complete participant role on methodological and ethical grounds. Kai Erikson, for example, rejects all field studies in which the researchers do not make their role and the intent of the study known beforehand. He maintains that such studies constitute an invasion of privacy and may harm the observed:

> The sheer act of entering a human transaction on the basis of deliberate fraud may be painful to the people who are thereby misled; and even if that were not the case, there are countless ways in which a stranger who pretends to be something else can disturb others by failing to understand the conditions of intimacy that prevail in the group he has tried to invade.[13]

Erikson points to the difficulties that may arise when a researcher takes on a complete participant role and uses as an illustration an incident reported in the Festinger et al. study, *When Prophecy Fails:*

> At one point in the study, two observers arrived at one of the group's meeting places under instructions to tell quite ordinary stories about their experience in Spiritualism in order to create as little commotion as possible. A few days afterwards, however, the leader of the group was overheard explaining that the two observers had appeared upset, excited, confused, and unsure of their errand at the time of their original visit, all of which helped confirm her suspicion that they had somehow been "sent" from another planet. In one sense, of course, this incident offered the observers an intriguing view of the belief structure of the cult, but in another sense, the leader's assessment of the situation was very shrewd: after all, the observers *had* been sent from another world, if not another planet, and she may have been quite right to sense that they were a bit confused and unsure of their errand during their early moments in the new job. "In both cases," the report informs us, the visits of the observers "were given as illustrations that 'strange things are happening. ' " Indeed, strange things *were* happening; yet we have no idea how strange they really were. It is almost impossible to evaluate the reaction of the group to the appearance of the pair of observers because we do not know whether they were seen as ordinary converts or as extraordinary beings. And it makes a difference, for in the first instance the investigators would be observing a response which fell within the normal range of the group's experience, while in the second instance they would be observing a response which would never have taken place had the life of the group been allowed to run its own course.[14]

The complete participant role poses several methodological problems. First, observers may become so self-conscious about revealing their true selves that they are handicapped when attempting to perform convincingly in the pretended role. Or they may "go native," that is, incorporate the pretended role into their self-conception and lose the research perspective.[15] Second, it is difficult for the researcher to decide what to observe because he or she cannot evoke responses or behavior and must be careful not to ask questions that might raise the suspicions of the persons observed. Third, recording

---

12. Ibid.

13. Kai T. Erikson, "A Comment on Disguised Observation in Sociology," *Social Problems,* 14 (1967): 368.

14. Ibid., pp. 371–372.

15. Gold, "Roles in Sociological Field Observation," p. 220.

Two Types of Field Research

+ *Complete participant:* Observers become participating members of the group of interest without revealing their identities or research goals to the group.

+ *Participant-as-observer:* Observers become participants in the activities of the group by revealing their identities and the goals of their research.

observations or taking notes is impossible on the spot; these have to be postponed until the observer is alone. However, time lags in recording observations introduce selective bias and distortions through memory.

Participant-as-Observer

In view of these limitations, contemporary fieldworkers most often assume the **participant-as-observer** role. When researchers adopt this type of role, they inform the group being studied that there is a research agenda. Researchers make long-term commitments to becoming active members of the group and attempt to establish close relationships with its members, who subsequently serve as both informants and respondents. John Van Maanen's research on police training illustrates the process of taking this role.

> While a graduate student at the University of California . . . , I began contacting police officials across the country seeking permission to conduct a one-man field study inside a large, metropolitan law-enforcement agency. . . . Although I encountered some initial difficulties in locating a department willing to tolerate my planned foray into its organizational spheres, eventually I managed to gain access to one police organization. . . . Throughout the study I worked in the fashion of a traditional ethnographer or participant observer, made no attempt to disguise my scholarly aim or identity, and met with little overt hostility from the men whose everyday affairs were the explicit subject of my investigation. In most respects I felt my mode of inquiry approximated both the substance and spirit of Evans-Pritchard's classic formulation of the ethnographic technique: "to get to know well the persons involved and to see and hear what they do and say." [16]

As this example demonstrates, the participant-as-observer role differs from complete participation in that the research goal is explicitly identified. Yet membership and participation in the observed group is still an important dimension in this form of research. With this method, the fieldworker gains a deeper appreciation of the group and its way of life and may also gain different levels of insight by actually participating rather than only observing. [17]

THE PRACTICE OF FIELD RESEARCH

Selecting a Research Topic

The first step in doing field research is to select a topic for investigation. Very often, the selection of a topic is influenced by personal interests or concerns. Such concerns may be related to the researcher's job, personal relationships, family history, social class, or

16. John Van Maanen, "The Moral Fix: On the Ethics of Fieldwork," in *Contemporary Field Research,* ed. Emerson, pp. 269–270.

17. Ibid., p. 270.

ethnic background. Lofland and Lofland, in their useful guide to doing qualitative re-search, describe this process as "starting where you are." [18] This practice originated in the 1920s with the Chicago School, where many well-known qualitative studies arose out of the unique experiences of students with little background in doing social research. Everett Hughes has described the beginning of this tradition in the following way:

> Most of these people didn't have any sociological background. . . . They didn't come in to become sociologists. They came in to learn something and Park picked up whatever it was in their experience which he could build on. . . . He took these people and he brought out of them whatever he could find there. . . . They might be Mennonites who were just a little unhappy . . . about wearing plain clothes . . . , girls who didn't like to wear long dresses and funny little caps; . . . or children of Orthodox Jews who really did-n't like to wear beards anymore. . . . And he got hold of people and emancipated them from something that was inherently interesting but which they regarded as a cramp. And he turned this "cramping orthodoxy" into something that was of basic and broad human interest. And that was the case for a lot of these people. He made their pasts interesting to them, much more interesting than they ever thought they could be. [19]

Field research requires that the investigators first determine what they care about in-dependent of scientific considerations. This emotional involvement in their work provides a meaningful link between the personal and emotional lives of the researchers and the rigorous requirement of the social scientific endeavor; not only does this emotional at-tachment make the involvement in social research more personally rewarding, it helps researchers to cope with problems that are inevitable in every research project. [20]

Choosing a Site and Gaining Access

Once a researcher has chosen a research topic, the next stage of field research is to se-lect and gain access to an appropriate research site. To a large extent, the choice of a topic determines the range of appropriate sites. For example, Festinger and his col-leagues were interested in how religious sects deal with prophetic failure. [21] This interest necessarily limited their choice to a contemporary research site where prophecies likely to fail had been made about events in the near future. They chose a religious sect that predicted a natural disaster on a given date. This allowed them to make observations *be-fore* the predicted disaster and *after* the date of the failed prophecy. In this case, sub-stantive and theoretical interest dictated the choice of setting.

Very often, geographic or other practical considerations will dictate the choice. More-over, it is tempting to choose a site that is easily accessible, where a researcher has an influential contact or is a member. However, in situations where would-be observers are close to the group and thus have easy access, they must find ways to distance them-selves emotionally when they engage in their analysis. Conversely, investigators who are outsiders to the research setting may have more difficulty gaining access and need to determine how much to reduce distance after entering the research site. When the re-searcher reduces the distance too much, he or she runs the risk of "going native." Re-searchers who "go native" internalize the lifestyle of the group being studied and lose their objectivity, which compromises the findings of the research project. Some

18. John Lofland and Lyn H. Lofland, *Analyzing Social Settings* (Belmont, CA: Wadsworth, 1984), p. 7.

19. Ibid., pp. 9–10.

20. Ibid.

21. Festinger et al., *When Prophecy Fails*.

researchers even abandon their research projects to protect their adopted group. If researchers maintain too much distance, however, they are unable to fully understand or empathize with the group being studied.

The ascriptive characteristics of the investigator are another important consideration in gaining access to a setting. For example, the gender, age, race, or ethnicity of the observers, if different from the observed, may create serious barriers in gaining access or in communication.[22] In the words of Rosalie Wax:

> Many tribal or folk societies not only maintain a strict division of labor between the sexes and ages, but the people who fall into these different categories do not converse freely or spontaneously with each other. . . .   I, as a middle aged woman, was never able to converse openly or informally with either the old or the young Indian men at Thrashing Buffalo. The older men, even when I knew them fairly well, would tend to deliver lectures to me; the younger men, as was proper, were always too bashful or formally respectful to say much. With the Indian matrons, on the other hand, I could talk for hours.[23]

On the basis of her experience in the field, Wax concluded that a biased view of "whole" cultures can be avoided by using research teams whose members have a variety of personal attributes similar to those of the group being studied.

The problems that confront young female fieldworkers in gaining access to male-dominated settings were discussed by Lois Easterday and her associates:

> One of us established rapport with the photographers of a special military photography programme by being a photographer and knowing their language. The relationship was sustained by insisting that the researcher not be photographed as a model, but rather that she be "one of the boys" on the other side of the lens. In an attempt to gain approval for the study from the programme's director, the researcher was denied full access with the statement, "It won't work. The men in the programme are a close bunch, and the talk is rough. They wouldn't be themselves if you are there." [24]

While these examples demonstrate that the status and gender of the researcher may be a handicap in field research, there are situations where differences have definite advantages. Blanche Geer wrote about women:

> The most handicapped observer is the one doing people and situations he/she is closest to. Hence, women are in luck in a male-run world. They can see how few clothes the emperor has on, question the accepted, what is taken for granted.[25]

In other words, being an outsider can sometimes seem less threatening to the observed, help a researcher gain access to the field, and contribute to the perceptiveness that the researcher brings to the field.

Establishing Relations with Members

The ease with which a researcher establishes relationships with members of a group depends to a large extent on the nature of the group and the skills of the researcher. Edward Evans-Pritchard gives an example:

---

22. Lofland and Lofland, *Analyzing Social Settings.*

23. Rosalie H. Wax, "The Ambiguities of Fieldwork," in *Contemporary Field Research*, ed. Emerson, pp. 194–195.

24. Lois Easterday, Diana Papedemas, Laura Schorr, and Catherine Valentine, "The Making of a Female Researcher: Role Problems in Fieldwork," in *Field Research: A Sourcebook and Field Manual*, ed. Robert G. Burgess (London: Allen & Unwin, 1982), pp. 63–64.

25. Ibid., p. 66.

Azande would not allow me to live as one of themselves; Nuer would not allow me to live otherwise. Among Azande I was compelled to live outside of the community; among Nuer I was compelled to be a member of it. Azande treated me as a superior; Nuer as an equal.[26]

Contemporary field researchers have emphasized that the phase of establishing social relations is perhaps the most central aspect of fieldwork: "Good fieldwork . . . depends crucially upon discovering the meaning of social relations, and not just those characterizing the natives' relations with each other. It depends equally upon discovering the meanings of anthropologists' relations with people they study." [27]

One basic requirement, significant especially when studying subcultures, is that the observer understand the jargon used by the particular group. Eleanor Miller, who studied "street women," describes her frustration in her initial encounter with the women she interviewed:

I remember very well my first visit to Horizon House. I had been invited to dinner after which I was to describe my study and recruit informants. Dinner was being served, so I sat down. There were, perhaps, eight others seated as well, mostly black women. . . . People talked and joked and occasionally sang along with the radio. I couldn't understand half of what was being said. With a sinking feeling I started to question whether or not I could ever be comfortable enough personally to do this study.[28]

The kinds of social relations that develop between the observer and the observed have several aspects. Rosalie Wax has noted that the identity that is chosen by the fieldworker and the role playing that takes place in the field are central to this social process. She suggests that in a well-balanced relationship, the fieldworker "strives to maintain a consciousness and respect for what he is and a consciousness and respect for what his hosts are." [29] The tendency to assume a "native" identity is one of the most serious errors that a fieldworker can commit. Ned Polsky, in his study of criminals, stresses the danger of "going native":

In doing field research on criminals you damned well better not pretend to be "one of them," because they will test this claim out and one of two things will happen: either you will . . . get sucked into participant observation of the sort you would rather not undertake, or you will be exposed, with still greater negative consequences. You must let the criminals know who you are; and if it is done properly it does not sabotage the research.[30]

There are no magic formulas for learning the ropes, and field researchers generally recommended that the researcher begin by participating in the daily life of the observed, a process described as "hanging around." [31] Learning the ropes and establishing relationships involve adopting a variety of roles. These roles are sometimes spontaneously invented and blend with the demands of the particular research setting. Rosalie Wax describes her experiences while conducting a fieldwork study of the Japanese relocation centers during World War II:

26. Edward E. Evans-Pritchard, *The Nuer* (Oxford: Clarendon, 1940), p. 15.

27. Ivan Karp and Martha B. Kendall, "Reflexivity in Field Work," in *Explaining Human Behavior: Consciousness, Human Action, and Social Structure*, ed. Paul F. Secord (Newbury Park, CA: Sage, 1982), p. 250.

28. Eleanor Miller, *Street Woman* (Philadelphia: Temple University Press, 1986), pp. 221–222.

29. Wax, "The Ambiguities of Fieldwork," p. 197.

30. Ned Polsky, *Hustlers, Beats, and Others* (Hawthorne, NY: Aldine, 1967), p. 124.

31. William B. Shaffir, Robert A. Stebbins, and Allan Turowetz, eds., *Fieldwork Experience: Qualitative Approaches to Social Research* (New York: St. Martin's Press, 1980), p. 113.

I would not have been able to do field work in Gila and Tule Lake if my respondents and I had not been able, jointly, to invent and maintain many of these relationships. Some Japanese Americans felt more comfortable if they could treat me like a sympathetic newspaper reporter. I knew very little about how a reporter behaved (indeed, I had never seen or spoken with one), but I responded and we were able to converse more easily. In Tule Lake the superpatriots and agitators found it easier to talk to me once they convinced themselves that I was German *Nisei,* "full of the courageous German spirit." I found this fantasy personally embarrassing, but I did not make a point of denying my German ancestry. Finally, I was not a geisha, even though a shrewd Issei once suggested that it was because I functioned as one that I was able to find out so much of what happened at Tule Lake. His explanation was that Japanese men—and especially Japanese politicians—do not discuss their plans or achievements with other men or with their wives, but they are culturally conditioned to speak of such matters with intelligent and witty women.[32]

As this example shows, learning the ropes and adopting the range of research roles is a flexible process that requires the researcher to exercise ingenuity and demonstrate sensitivity to the personalities and perceptions of the research participants.

Finding Resourceful and Reliable Informants

Once participant observers have established relationships with members of the group, they are regarded as provisional group members. They learn how to behave in the group and "teach" the observed how to act toward them. Next, observers are accepted as *categorical members* of the group. By this time, rapport will have been established, areas of observation will be agreed on, and **informants** will be providing information. William Whyte's experiences illustrate several phases in this process:

I began with a vague idea that I wanted to study a slum district. . . . I made my choice on very unscientific grounds: Cornerville best fitted my picture of what a slum district should look like. . . . I learned early in my Cornerville period the crucial importance of having the support of the key individuals in any groups or organizations I was studying. Instead of trying to explain myself to everyone, I found I was providing far more information about myself and my study to leaders such as Doc than I volunteered to the average corner boy. I always tried to give the impression that I was willing and eager to tell just as much about my study as anyone wished to know, but it was only with group leaders that I made a particular effort to provide really full information. . . . Since these leaders had the sort of position in the community that enabled them to observe much better than the followers what was going on and since they were in general more skillful observers than the followers, I found that I had much to learn from a more active collaboration with them.[33]

Intimate relationships with informants may, however, bias the researcher's reports, as Whyte himself has observed:

Doc found this experience of working with me interesting and enjoyable, and yet the relationship had its drawbacks. He once commented: "You've slowed me up plenty since you've been down here. Now, when I do something, I have to think what Bill Whyte would want to know about it and how I can explain it. Before, I used to do things by instinct.[34]

32. Wax, "The Ambiguities of Fieldwork," p. 200.

33. William F. Whyte, *Street Corner Society,* 2d ed. (Chicago: University of Chicago Press, 1955), pp. 279–358.

34. Ibid., p. 301.

Leaving the Field

The social complexity of field research is not limited to gaining access and establishing relationships. Leaving the field is no less problematic. This stage depends on the agreement the observer and the observed reached when the study began and on the kind of social relationships that developed during the research process. The research requirement of "getting involved" during the fieldwork itself presents a problem when it is time to leave, as Wax notes:

> Being by that time experienced fieldworkers, Murray and I had planned to stay six months in the field and spend six months writing our report. But rough as life was, I had become so attached to some of my Indian friends that I talked Murray into staying an extra month— even at temperatures of 30 below zero. I did not want to leave but I had to.[35]

Another problem in leaving the field is how it affects the subjects themselves. "As they see it, they stand to gain little, if anything, from our research findings and may even lose. A related reason for their reluctance is their impression that our work will add little to their own lives."[36]

Field exit processes range from the quick and sharply defined to the gradual and drawn out. Leaving can be a recurring phenomenon when research needs require the researcher to leave and come back numerous times. In the end, the procedure the researcher selects is a function of the commitment he or she made while conducting the research.[37]

Recording Observations

In field research, the primary sources of data are what people say and do. Researchers may record the behavior they observe by writing notes, tape recording, and on occasion photographing or videotaping. In some cases when the researcher's identity and purpose are known to the observed, recording can be done on the spot, during the event. In most cases, however, the researcher wants the members of the group to forget they are being observed so that their behavior and interaction remain natural. Recording in the presence of the group serves as a reminder of the researcher's agenda, which may influence the behavior of the group and also may limit the researcher's ability to participate in group activities. When the researcher's identity and purpose are unknown to the observed, it is usually impossible to document events as they occur.

When researchers cannot document observations overtly, they must use devices to help them remember events as they occurred so they can be fully documented at the earliest possible opportunity. Many researchers use moments of privacy—such as regular use of the rest room—to jot down key words that will help them to remember the sequence of events, relevant behaviors, and valuable quotations. When privacy is impossible, researchers may rely on mnemonic devices to help them remember. The key to mnemonic devices is the association of the things to be remembered with things that are familiar and easily recalled.

When researchers cannot fully document their observations immediately, the possibility of distortion and unintentional misrepresentation increases. The longer the researcher

35. David R. Maines, William B. Shaffir, and Allan Turowetz, "Leaving the Field in Ethnographic Research: Reflections on the Entrance Exit Hypothesis," in *Fieldwork Experience*, ed. Shaffir et al., p. 277.

36. Shaffir et al., *Fieldwork Experience*, p. 258.

37. Maines et al., "Leaving the Field," p. 273.

must wait to record observations, the greater is the possibility for flawed recall. It is helpful to employ certain notational conventions to minimize distortions. For example, a researcher could use quotation marks around recorded material to indicate exact recall; data with no quotation marks around it would be based on impressions or inferences. Such a recording practice is vulnerable because of observer inference, however. Lofland and Lofland suggest asking the following questions before the data is written up:[38]

1. Is the report firsthand?
2. What was the spatial location of the observer?
3. Did the research participant have any reason to give false or biased information?
4. Is the report internally consistent?
5. Can the report be validated by using other independent reports?

Although information gained from these questions does not guarantee that a report is true, it helps the researcher to assess the reliability of the data.

Analyzing Data

Data analysis in qualitative field research is an ongoing process. Observers formulate hypotheses and note important themes throughout their studies. As the research progresses, some hypotheses are discarded, others are refined, and still others are formulated. Bogdan and Taylor give an example of such a process:

> In the job training program study, the observer had an early hunch that men trainees clearly differentiated "women's factory work" from "men's factory work." The hunch came after one of the staff personnel had reported the following to the observer: "When the men saw women doing the work (soldering) on the assembly line, they didn't want any part of it." Since this sex differentiation would have important implications for the potential success of the program and for the meanings of work, the researcher presented his hunch on later visits to the setting. He found that, although men and women differed in the types of work they valued, men did not reject certain work as "women's work." For example, they expressed little pride in doing physical labor and openly avoided jobs that were dangerous or "too hard." The observer dropped his earlier hypothesis and turned to the pursuit of others.[39]

An important aspect of data analysis during the period of data collection is establishing files and coding field notes (see Chapter 14 for more information on inductive coding). Essentially, this is a process of dissecting field notes. In the early stages of fieldwork, a researcher may develop simple categories based on the characteristics of the people being observed and the events that occur. For example, a researcher might classify members of the group as leaders, followers, and renegades. Field notes pertaining to the actions of each type of group member are filed or coded under the appropriate classification. Interactions between different types of group members are filed under both classifications. As the fieldwork progresses, researchers use what they have learned to refine and, sometimes, redefine their categories. After each refinement the researcher must review and refile all relevant field notes. It is during the process of categorization that researchers develop tentative hypotheses.

Researchers can create files by actually cutting apart a copy of their field notes and filing the pieces of paper into file folders, or they can use a word processing program to

---

38. Lofland and Lofland, *Analyzing Social Settings*, p. 51.

39. Robert Bogdan and Steven J. Taylor, *Introduction to Qualitative Research Methods* (New York: Wiley, 1975), pp. 80–81.

excerpt portions of the field notes into separate data files. The labels on the file folders or data files reflect the categories the researcher has developed.

Becker and Geer, in their study of a medical school, found it useful to prepare data for analysis by making a running summary of their field notes. They coded the data into separate incidents, summarizing for each incident their observation of a student's action. First, they tentatively identified the major areas or categories during the fieldwork process. Then, when going through a summarized incident, they marked it with a number standing for each area into which it could be classified. The following examples from their field notes and their subsequent analysis illustrates this process:

> "Mann says that now that he and the other students have found out what Dr. Prince, the staff physician, is like, they learn the things they know he's going to try to catch them on and keep him stumped that way." This incident contains some references to student–faculty relations and would accordingly be coded under that category. It also refers indirectly to the phenomenon of student cooperation on school activities and would be coded under that category as well. The next stage in the analysis would be to inspect the various items coded under one area, and formulate a more detailed statement of the content of this area or perspective citing examples of actions and statements that characterize it.[40]

Once researchers have identified actions and statements that support their emerging hypotheses, their next step is to look for **negative cases**—instances that refute the hypotheses. Researchers must compare positive and negative cases to determine whether the hypothesis can be modified to better fit all of the data or if the hypothesis must be rejected entirely. In addition, the range of the perspective is checked, that is, how widely the items of data were distributed through a number of different situations.

When analyzing qualitative data, it is useful to look for certain regularities or patterns that emerge from the numerous observations made during the fieldwork stage. A researcher can perform this task by posing a number of questions:[41]

1. What type of behavior is it?
2. What is its structure?
3. How frequent is it?
4. What are its causes?
5. What are its processes?
6. What are its consequences?
7. What are people's strategies?

The written report is the culmination of the field research study. The final report describes the background for the study, the theoretical framework guiding it, and the design and methodology of the study. It provides a detailed analysis and interpretation of the data and also explores what the findings imply in terms of further analysis or public policy decisions.

Using Computers

Data analysis can be enhanced by using computers. Software programs designed for the analysis of qualitative data can speed up analysis and facilitate the coding process and

---

40. Howard S. Becker and Blanche Geer, "Participant Observation: The Analysis of Qualitative Field Data" in *Field Research*, ed. Burgess, p. 245.

41. Lofland and Lofland, *Analyzing Social Settings*, p. 94.

the generating and testing of theories. Computer programs can also simplify the preparation of the final research report.[42] QSR NUD*IST is one of the most popular software programs for qualitative analysis. NUD*IST assists researchers in handling *N*onnumeric *U*nstructured *D*ata by *I*ndexing, *S*earching, and *T*heorizing.

A QSR NUD*IST project has two parts. The first part is a document system manager that holds all your data, including interview transcripts, field notes, memos, and possibly photos and videos. The data can be imported as text files from a word processing program and is managed in a Document Explorer window. In this window you can edit, annotate, and code the material. The second part of the NUD*IST program is the index system, which is accessed through the Node Explorer window. In this window, researchers create nodes as storage devices for ideas, coding, and the results of searches. This highly flexible system allows the creation and exploration of theories by coding, merging, and progressively enhancing existing categories as well as building new ones. For more information on how to use NUD*IST, you can check the Web site, http://www.qsr.com.au.

THE THEORY OF FIELD RESEARCH   ●

When researchers engage in quantitative research, their goal is to either falsify, modify, or provide support for existing theory. They accomplish this goal deductively by deriving hypotheses from theory and using the data they collect to statistically test the hypotheses. Qualitative field research moves in the opposite direction, using a process call **analytic induction.** Researchers collect data, formulate hypotheses based on the data, test their hypotheses using the data, and attempt to develop theory. The theory they develop is called **grounded theory** because it arises out of and is directly relevant to the particular setting under study:

> While in the field, the researcher continually asks questions as to fit, relevance, and workability about the emerging categories and relationships between them. By raising questions at this point in time the researcher checks those issues while he still has access to the data. As a result, he continually fits his analysis to the data by checking as he proceeds.[43]

Researchers must approach the field with an open mind to ensure that their ultimate theory is grounded. Because field research is based on observation, preconceived ideas and rigid hypotheses may influence the observations a researcher chooses to record for analysis, which can compromise the resultant theory. Since most researchers do not spend all of their time in the field, they may, however, use very loosely defined hypotheses to decide when and how to make their initial observations. Subsequently, researchers will use observations to refine, reject, and reformulate hypotheses throughout the research process. Blanche Geer exemplifies this method in the following excerpt:

> My use of hypotheses falls roughly into three sequential types. The first operation consisted of testing a crude yes-or-no proposition. By asking informants or thinking back over volunteered information in the data . . . I stated a working hypothesis in the comments and began the second operation in the sequence: Looking for negative cases or setting out deliberately to accumulate positive ones. . . . Working with negatively expressed hypotheses gave me a specific goal. One instance that contradicts what I say is enough to force modification of the hypothesis. . . . The third state of operating with hypotheses in

42. Lyn Richards, "How to Use QSR NUD*IST for Qualitative Analysis," in *Investigating the Social World*, ed. Russell K. Schutt (Thousand Oaks, CA: Pine Forge Press, 1999), pp. 568–579.

43. Barney G. Glaser, *Theoretical Sensitivity* (Mill Valley, CA: Sociology Press, 1978), p. 39.

the field involves two-step formulations and eventually rough models. Hypotheses take the form of predictions about future events which may take place under specific conditions or changes in information over time in conjunction with events.[44]

Theory building in analytic induction consists of finding and delineating relationships between categories of observations. Often, researchers attempt to distinguish a core category and explain how various subcategories influence the core category. The researcher's goal in developing grounded theory is to produce a set of propositions that explains the totality of the phenomenon. Qualitative researchers use examples of their observations and quotations from members of the group under study to support their theories. In some cases, researchers can use grounded theory to develop empirically testable hypotheses amenable to statistical analysis.

A classic instance of field research using analytic induction is Donald Cressey's study of embezzlement.[45] Cressey defined embezzlement as the phenomenon of accepting a position of trust in good faith and then violating this trust by committing a crime. He initially formulated a hypothesis that these violations of trust occurred when embezzlers conceived of the thefts as "technical violations" but rejected this hypothesis after finding embezzlers who said they knew their behavior had been wrong and illegal. Cressey next hypothesized that violators defined the illegal use of funds as an emergency that could not be met by legal means. But he revised this hypothesis again when he observed violators who did not report an emergency or who noted an even greater emergency in the past. Next Cressey noted that violators were individuals who felt they needed to use "secret means." But again, he had to reformulate this hypothesis when he discovered deviant cases. The final hypothesis, according to Cressey, is the one that accounts for all cases observed:

> Trusted persons became trust violators when they conceive of themselves as having a financial problem which is non-shareable, are aware that this problem can be secretly resolved by violation of the position of financial trust, and are able to apply to their own conduct in that situation verbalizations which enable them to adjust their conceptions of themselves as trusted persons with their conceptions of themselves as users of the entrusted funds or property.[46]

BLUE-COLLAR COMMUNITY: AN EXAMPLE OF FIELD RESEARCH   ●

Before concluding our discussion of field research, it is useful to illustrate the various stages with one inclusive study, *Blue-Collar Community,* conducted by William Kornblum in South Chicago.[47] Kornblum used a variety of methods to gather data, including discussions with community residents, archival records, census data, interviewing, and attending community meetings. However, the study leans primarily on Kornblum's firsthand involvement and participation in the life of the community. As such, it is a good example of a field study employing participant observation as the main method of analysis.

---

44. Blanche Geer, "The First Days in the Field," in *Sociologists at Work,* ed. Phillip Hammond (Garden City, NY: Doubleday, 1967), pp. 389–390.

45. Donald R. Cressey, *Other People's Money: A Study in the Social Psychology of Embezzlement* (New York: Free Press, 1953).

46. Ibid., p. 273.

47. William Kornblum, *Blue-Collar Community* (Chicago: University of Chicago Press, 1974).

Choosing the Research Topic and the Research Site

The general topic was suggested to Kornblum by his professors in graduate school, who were interested in sponsoring a study of Chicago's south Slavic ethnic groups. Kornblum conducted some research on local community organizations in Yugoslavian communities and was interested in the general question of how Yugoslav immigrants adapted in the United States. He decided to focus on the south Slavic settlement in South Chicago and on the Pulaski–Milwaukee section on the Northwest side and started interviewing Croatian and Serbian immigrants. He also visited the immigrant coffee shops, soccer clubs, and taverns and was gradually drawn toward the steel mill neighborhoods of South Chicago. Kornblum describes his choice of the community in the following way:

> South Chicago fascinated me. I had never seen such heavy industry at close range, and I was awed by the immensity of the steel mills and the complexity of the water and rail arteries which crisscrossed the area's neighborhoods. In the people's faces and in their neighborhoods I saw more of the spectrum of cultural groups which had settled and built the community. Thus, I was beginning to see that my study would have to concern itself as much with the larger community as it would with the cultural and social adaptations of Serbian and Croatian settlers.[48]

Kornblum found a Serbian immigrant restaurant where he was introduced to some of the regular patrons. The majority of them were Serbian immigrant men in their mid-thirties to early forties, most of whom were steelworkers. Although it was a congenial spot, the restaurant was socially peripheral because its patrons were mostly recent immigrants. At this point, Kornblum wanted to make contacts with American-born Serbian and Croatian residents, so he began looking for a place to settle in the community.

Gaining Access

Soon after moving into the community, Kornblum started attending public meetings to identify local leaders and to arrange an introductory meeting with them. He identified himself as a researcher only to a few; to most residents he said he was teaching at the nearby Indiana University while his wife was a student at the University of Illinois in the central city and that the neighborhood was a halfway point for both of them.

Gradually, Kornblum became friendly with a larger number of political activists and leaders, in particular with a group of steelworkers who ran the local union at one of the mills. He began to feel that it was necessary to make more of a commitment to South Chicago's lifestyle:

> I felt like a knowledgeable outsider who was missing some of the most important experiences of life in the community. . . . A friend whose opinion I highly valued, the Serbian president of a local steel union, confronted me with a serious challenge, "How can you really understand what goes on here . . . if you've never spent any time inside a steel mill?"[49]

Subsequently, Kornblum was hired as a subforeman in the steel mill that became the focus of his study.

Establishing Relations with Members

Kornblum's job as a subforeman proved to be an ideal position from a research perspective. As subforeman he had to understand how the work at his end of the mill fit with

---

48. Ibid., p. 232.
49. Ibid., pp. 235–236.

the overall division of labor in the entire plant. As a manager he could walk freely throughout the mill and converse informally with workers. This made him sensitive to the interactions that took place in the mill, especially to the meaning of unionism. He began to understand how steel production creates an occupational community inside the mill.

Kornblum was particularly interested in understanding the community's political leaders, especially unionist politicians. At that time, the community was involved in choosing the leaders of its central institutions. Therefore, many of his friends and informants were actively involved in politics and were sometimes members of opposing factions. This created a problem that is quite typical of field research. Kornblum notes:

> I began to feel that I could not remain aloof from political commitment when all the people I care for had so much more at stake than I did. Aside from the personal aspect of this decision, there are very real limitations to what one can learn about political processes through informants. If one wishes actually to watch decisions being made in a competitive political system, it is often necessary to become part of the decision-making body itself. I did this by taking highly partisan although "behind the scenes" roles in most of the political campaigns reported in this study. The liabilities of this strategy are numerous and deserve some attention. First, it is obvious that the more committed one is to a particular faction, the less one can learn, at first hand, about others. . . . In consequence of this, whenever I committed myself to a given faction I attempted to function as much as possible in capacities which would require little public exposure. In order to keep up with events in opposing factions I attempted to explain my affiliations as frankly as possible to friends on opposite sides, in much the same terms as any other resident of the community would. In this way it was possible to act as a partisan and still communicate with friends in opposing factions who acted as my informants. . . . Another problem in taking on partisan roles as a researcher is that it almost inevitably causes bias in favor of those to whom one is committed. In my case, again, the answer to this problem was to maintain close informants on opposing sides, and to try, in the analysis of events, to be on guard against my own partialities so that I might correct them or use them knowingly.[50]

Leaving the Field

Kornblum and his family moved from South Chicago to Seattle, where the study was written. Periodically, he returned to South Chicago to continue his involvement in local political life.

ETHICAL AND POLITICAL ISSUES OF FIELDWORK   ●

Because fieldwork is characterized by long-term and intimate participation in the daily life of the people being studied, it is associated with a number of ethical, legal, and political dilemmas. Two ethical issues are associated with fieldwork: the problem of potential deception and the impact the fieldwork may have on the lives of those studied.[51]

Earlier in this chapter, we saw that fieldworkers sometimes conduct their study under a false identity in order to gain access to the field and that this kind of fieldwork has generated considerable controversy and criticism. However, some field researchers defend the use of disguised observation; they claim that it is the only way to gain access to important research sites. Furthermore, they argue that covert methods have never directly harmed the people studied in any significant way.

50. Ibid., pp. 240–241.

51. Emerson, *Contemporary Field Research*, p. 255.

Obviously, this is a serious controversy that cannot be easily resolved. We must stress, however, that anyone planning to use disguised identity in a field study should be aware of the serious ethical implications of doing so. If at all possible, the researcher should examine alternative ways of gaining access to the research site.

Another important ethical issue is the unanticipated effect that any kind of fieldwork may have on the people being studied. Very often the fieldworkers have more power than their hosts. Subjects may perceive fieldworkers as sources of material resources, political connections, and social prestige. For example, in a study conducted in New Guinea, the Papuan settlers (mistakenly) credited the fieldworkers with getting the government to change certain land policies.[52] Obviously, such a perception could be very harmful to the relations between the researcher and the study population, especially if the fieldworker fails to perform in ways that the people expect.

The research community has become more concerned with the political issues associated with field research as governments and other political groups have become increasingly interested in who gets studied and in what ways.[53] This concern has particular relevance in cases where the results of research dealing with disadvantaged groups may have political and social implications. In addition, many of these groups are now claiming the right to review both research proposals and prepublication drafts of research reports.

In spite of these ethical and political concerns, qualitative field research can yield rich descriptions of cultures that cannot be attained through quantitative research. When we have little or no information about a group or subculture, field research can serve as an exploratory tool in the development of quantitative measures. Researchers who engage in field research must act responsibly to ensure that social scientists do not lose the opportunity to use this valuable tool.

SUMMARY

1. Field research is the most central strategy of data collection associated with the qualitative method. Scientists conduct field research in natural settings in an effort to understand subjectively the people being studied.

2. The method of data collection most closely associated with field research is participant observation, the process through which the investigator attempts to obtain membership in or a close attachment to the group he or she wishes to study. The researcher can assume either a complete participant role or a participant-as-observer role. Complete participants conceal their identities and do not make their research objectives known, whereas participants-as-observers make their presence known to the group being studied.

3. The practice of field research can be divided into the following distinct stages: selecting a research topic, choosing an appropriate research site and obtaining access, establishing relations with members of the group and finding reliable informants, and leaving the field and analyzing the data.

4. The goal of field research is to develop grounded theory using the method of analytic induction. The researcher constructs analytic categories from the data and develops hypotheses based on the relationships between categories. Both the ana-

---

52. Ibid.

53. Ibid., p. 266.

lytic categories and the hypotheses are revised and refined as the research progresses by comparing positive and negative cases.

5. Fieldwork is associated with a number of ethical and political dilemmas. The first problem is the potential for deception, which is especially likely in studies in which the observer disguises his or her identity. The unanticipated consequences of the research are a second important ethical issue. Subjects may perceive researchers as sources of material resources, political connections, and social prestige, resources that are unrelated to the research process or its objectives.

KEY TERMS FOR REVIEW ●

analytic induction (p. 268)
complete participant (p. 258)
field research (p. 257)
grounded theory (p. 268)

informant (p. 264)
negative case (p. 267)
participant-as-observer (p. 260)
participant observation (p. 257)

STUDY QUESTIONS ●

1. Discuss the main differences between qualitative and quantitative research.
2. Compare and contrast the *complete participant* and *participant-as-observer* roles.
3. Describe the difficulties associated with gaining access to a research site.
4. What is analytic induction?
5. What are the major ethical and political issues of fieldwork?

ADDITIONAL READINGS ●

Agar, Michael H. *Speaking of Ethnography*. Newbury Park, CA: Sage, 1986.

Bailey, Carol A. *A Guide to Field Research*. Newbury Park, CA: Pine Forge Press, 1996.

Berg, Bruce L. *Qualitative Research Methods*. Boston: Allyn & Bacon, 1998.

Denzin, N. K., and Y. S. Lincoln, eds. *Handbook of Qualitative Research*. Beverly Hills, CA: Sage, 1994.

Lofland, John, and Lynn H. Lofland. *Analyzing Social Setting*. Belmont, CA: Wadsworth, 1984.

Patton, Michael Quinn. *Qualitative Evaluation and Research Methods*, 2d ed. Newbury Park, CA: Sage, 1990.

Shaffir, William B., and Robert A. Stebbins, eds. *Experiencing Fieldwork: An Inside View of Qualitative Research*. Newbury Park, CA: Sage, 1991.

Strauss, Anslem, and Juliet Corbin. *Basics of Qualitative Research: Grounded Theory, Procedures, and Techniques*. Newbury Park, CA: Sage, 1990.

Secondary Data Analysis and Sources

Art can sometimes follow science, as in the case of Umberto Eco's novel, *Foucault's Pendulum*.[1] In the novel, Jacopo Belbo, an eccentric but intriguing editor, is running for his life and has asked his good friend Casaubon for help. In order to solve the personal and intellectual mysteries surrounding Belbo's plight, Eco, the distinguished Italian linguist, provides his characters with tools that combine fantasy with the important empirical methodology of content analysis. He sends Casaubon on a chase for clues through volumes of ancient texts, including biographies, as well as through computer files whose entry codes must first be cracked. Casaubon searches for recurring phrases, for shared themes, and for references to specific events. As would any good social scientist, he checks the validity of these sources against the empirical facts of history and his hypotheses concerning motivation in order to solve the puzzle and assist his friend. In the following chapter, although we confine ourselves to empirical reality, we present guidelines for the systematic use of secondary data in the social sciences.

• **IN THIS CHAPTER,** we first discuss the reasons for the increased use of secondary data; we then point out the advantages and inherent limitations of secondary data analysis. Next, we examine the major sources of secondary data, including the census, special surveys, simple observation, archival data, and the Internet, and describe how they are used. Finally, we present content analysis as one of the major methods for systematically analyzing data obtained from archival records, documents, and newspapers.

The data collection methods that we have discussed so far generate *primary* data. Data collection of this sort takes place in either an artificial (laboratory) or natural setting (e.g., field research), where the research participants may or may not be aware that they are being studied. In these instances, data are collected firsthand; that is, the researcher either collects the data personally or has trained observers or interviewers do so. Increasingly, however, social scientists are making use of data collected by *other* investigators, usually for purposes that *differ* from the original research objectives. *Secondary data analysis* thus refers to methods for studying research problems based on data collected by others. For example, social scientists use census data collected by governments for administrative and policy purposes to investigate a range of research topics: demographic trends, household structure, income distribution and redistribution, immigration and migration patterns, characteristics of racial and ethnic groups, environmental changes, occupational structures, social mobility, and attributes of rural, urban, and metropolitan areas, among others. Or data collected by Gallup and other national survey research organizations on current issues can be used to study political attitudes, voting patterns and their determinants, and political changes in public opinion over time.

WHY SECONDARY DATA ANALYSIS?   •

Secondary data analysis in the social sciences has a rich tradition. The French sociologist Emile Durkheim (1858–1917) examined government statistics on suicide rates in different countries and found that the suicide rates in predominantly Protestant countries

---

1. Umberto Eco, *Foucault's Pendulum* (London: Pan Books, 1990).

were higher than those in Catholic countries.[2] Karl Marx used official economic statistics to substantiate his "class struggle" theory and argue for economic determinism.[3] In his rebuttal to Marx, Max Weber analyzed historical documents, such as the official ideological proclamations made by early Protestant church leaders, to support his own argument that religion determined sociopolitical behavior.[4]

Social scientists are increasingly using the masses of data collected by others in their research. Referring specifically to survey research, Norval Glenn has observed that

> . . . an almost revolutionary change in survey research would seem to be occurring. Until recently, survey data were analyzed primarily by the persons who designed the surveys, but there seems to be a rather strong trend toward separation of survey design from data analysis. One can almost envision a time when some survey researchers will specialize in survey design and others will specialize in data analysis.[5]

Three basic factors are encouraging the increasing use of secondary data: conceptual-substantive reasons, methodological reasons, and cost.

Conceptual-Substantive Factors

From a conceptual-substantive point of view, secondary data may be the only data available for the study of certain research problems. Social and political historians, for example, must rely almost exclusively on secondary data because of the nature of their research topics. In research on more contemporary issues, as Herbert Hyman points out, incorporating secondary data enables one to search through a wider range of materials covering larger areas and longer periods of time than would be possible using only primary data.[6] With the aid of such secondary sources, we can better understand the historical context; by analyzing data collected in different times on similar issues, we can also describe patterns of change and attempt to explain their determinants. For these reasons, the Inter-university Consortium for Political and Social Research (ICPSR) at the University of Michigan maintains systematic survey data on all the U.S. national elections held since 1952.[7] Relatively easy access to this data set has enabled social scientists to identify and interpret, for example, trends in political attitudes, trust in government institutions, patterns of party identification, and voting behavior.

Secondary data can also be used for purposes of comparison. Comparisons within and between nations or social groups may expand the scope of generalizations and provide additional insights into events and processes. The ICPSR, therefore, has obtained data sets gathered from election studies conducted in European democracies. Inasmuch as these studies measure many variables similar to those examined in U.S. studies, this databank makes it possible to compare variables such as political participation and the

2. Emile Durkheim, *Suicide* (New York: Free Press, 1966). Originally published 1897.

3. Karl Marx, *Capital* (New York: International Publishers, 1967). Originally published 1867.

4. Max Weber, *The Protestant Ethic and the Spirit of Capitalism*, trans. Talcott Parsons (New York: Scribner, 1977). Originally published 1905.

5. Norval D. Glenn, "The General Social Surveys: Editorial Introduction to a Symposium." *Contemporary Sociology*, 7 (1978): 532.

6. Herbert H. Hyman, *Secondary Analysis of Sample Surveys* (Middletown, CT: Wesleyan University Press, 1987), chap. 1.

7. Warren E. Miller, Arthur H. Miller, and Edward J. Schneider, *American National Elections Studies Data Sourcebook, 1952–1978* (Cambridge, MA: Harvard University Press, 1980).

structures of conflict (or consensus), both nationally and internationally. As Hyman suggests (particularly with respect to survey research):

> Secondary analysis of a series of comparable surveys from different points in time provides one of the rare avenues for the empirical description of long-term changes and for examining the way phenomena vary under the contrasted conditions operative in one [or several] society[ies] at several points.[8]

Methodological Factors

There are several methodological advantages to secondary analysis. First, secondary data, if reliable and accurate, provide opportunities for replication: Remember, the credibility of research findings increases if similar findings are reported in a number of independent studies. By comparing data collected by others to his or her own, a researcher avoids the need to replicate studies personally. Second, the availability of data collected at different points in time enables the researcher to employ longitudinal research designs. One can employ measurements made in studies conducted decades ago as a baseline; similar data, gathered more recently, is then incorporated into the present research. Indeed, when social scientists compare their own primary data with data collected in earlier studies, they are essentially conducting a follow-up study of the original research. Third, secondary analysis may improve the validity of measurement by expanding the scope of the independent variables employed when operationalizing major concepts. In Hyman's words, the secondary analyst

> . . . must examine a diverse array of concrete indicators, assorted specific manifestations of behavior or attitude. . . . He is likely to be more exhaustive in his definition of a concept, to think about it not only in his accustomed ways, but in all sorts of odd ways.[9]

This expansiveness enables the researcher to understand and empirically explore the research problem in great depth. Fourth, by using secondary data we can increase the sample size, its representativeness, and the number of observations—factors that contribute to more encompassing generalizations. Finally, secondary data can be used for triangulation (the use of different kinds of data to test the same hypothesis), thereby increasing the validity of the findings obtained from primary data.

Cost Factors

Primary research is a costly undertaking. A survey of a national representative sample of 1,500 to 2,000 individuals can cost as much as $300,000 or more. This is a prohibitive sum for university professors, independent researchers, and graduate students, especially in light of increasing cutbacks in research support and funding opportunities. It is infinitely less expensive to use existing data than to collect new data.

PUBLIC OPINION AND PUBLIC POLICY: AN EXAMPLE   •

What effect, if any, does public opinion have on government policy? To study this important question, Benjamin Page and Robert Shapiro examined several hundred surveys based on national samples of American voters conducted between 1935 and

---

8. Hyman, *Secondary Analysis*, p. 17.

9. Ibid., p. 24.

1979 by Gallup, the National Opinion Research Center, and the Center for Political Studies' Survey Center at the University of Michigan.[10] They created a file of all the 3,319 questionnaire items referring to policy preferences; they then isolated the 600 of these items that were asked in identical form at two or more points in time. The authors then identified every instance in which there was a significant change in opinion from one survey to the next (6 percent or more). They found 357 such instances of change in Americans' policy preferences, covering a wide range of foreign and domestic issues such as taxation, government spending, regulation, trade, and military action.

For each instance of opinion change, Page and Shapiro measured indicators of policy outputs beginning two years before the initial opinion survey was conducted and ending four years after the final survey. Using these two sets of data, the authors coded agreements and disagreements between the instances of opinion change and the policy indicators. Upon analyzing the data, they found a great deal of congruence between changes in public opinion and changes in policy during the half-century they studied. Furthermore, congruence was considerably greater when the policy makers had time to react to changes in public opinion. The authors concluded that "public opinion, whatever its sources and quality, is a factor that genuinely affects government policies in the United States."[11]

LIMITATIONS OF SECONDARY DATA ANALYSIS ●

Like other data collection methods, secondary data analysis has certain inherent limitations. Perhaps the most serious problem in using secondary data is that the data often only approximate the kinds of data that the investigator would like to employ for testing hypotheses. There is an inevitable gap between the primary data the investigator collects personally with specific research purposes in mind and the data collected by others for different purposes. Differences are likely to appear in sample size and design, question wording and sequence, the interview schedule and method, and the structure of laboratory experiments.

A second problem in using secondary data is access. Although thousands of studies are available in data archives, it may be difficult to find the ones that contain the variables of interest. Sometimes the relevant data may be inaccessible because the original investigator will not release them: Researchers are not, after all, required to make their data available to others. This problem often prods researchers into a creative use of their skills in locating sources of relevant data and measuring the variables.

A third problem associated with secondary data analysis may arise if the researcher has insufficient information about how the data were collected. This information is important for determining potential sources of bias, errors, or problems with internal or external validity. The ICPSR, for example, has resolved this problem by assigning data to four classes according to the amount of information, documentation, and effort devoted by the original investigators as well as ICPSR staff in standardizing and inspecting the data (see Exhibit 13.1).

---

10. Benjamin I. Page and Robert Y. Shapiro, "Effects of Public Opinion on Policy," *American Political Science Review,* 77 (1983): 175–190.

11. Ibid., p. 189.

Exhibit 13.1

ICPSR DATA CLASSES

The ICPSR currently employs two systems to describe the extent of processing data collections have undergone. The first, repeated below, categorizes the collections according to the extent of processing performed by the ICPSR on the original data. The second system, implemented in 1992, replaces the data class system with codes describing the discrete processing steps performed on the data by the ICPSR, the principal investigators, or the data producers.

All ICPSR collections undergo a basic inspection to determine that the data and documentation correspond and that confidential or sensitive information, such as names or dates, have been recoded to protect anonymity. A codebook containing bibliographic citations and introductory materials describing the data collection is also supplied.

Class I

Class I data sets have been inspected, corrected if necessary, and formatted to ICPSR specifications. The data may also have been recoded and reorganized in consultation with the investigator to maximize their utilization and accessibility. A computer-readable codebook is available. This codebook fully documents the data and may include descriptive statistics such as frequencies or means. Class I studies are often available in multiple technical formats, and SAS and SPSS data definition statements have been prepared for many Class I collections (see Appendix A, which includes a discussion of the General Social Survey, or GSS).

Class II

Class II studies have been inspected and formatted to ICPSR specifications. Most nonnumeric codes have been removed. Many studies in this class are available in multiple technical formats, often with corresponding SAS and SPSS data definition statements. Any peculiarities in the data are indicated in the documentation.

Class III

Class III studies have been inspected by the ICPSR staff for the appropriate number of records per case and accurate data locations as specified by the investigator's codebook. Known data discrepancies and other problems, if any, are communicated to the user at the time the data are requested.

Class IV

The Class IV studies are distributed in the form received by the ICPSR from the original investigator. The documentation for Class IV studies is reproduced from the material originally received.

From Inter-university Consortium for Political and Social Research, *Guide to Resources and Services, 1994–1995* (Ann Arbor: University of Michigan, Institute for Social Research, Center for Political Studies, 1994), p. xxiii.

THE CENSUS   ●

A *census,* or population enumeration, is defined as the collection and recording of the demographic data that describe a population in a strictly defined territory, carried out by a government at a specific time and at regular intervals. A census should, in principle, be universal; that is, it should include every person living in the designated area.[12]

There are some indications that censuses were conducted as early as 3800 B.C.E. in Babylon, about 3800 B.C.E. in China, and 2500 B.C.E. in Egypt. Reports have also been cited of censuses made in ancient Greece, Rome, and Incan Peru. Modern censuses, however, were first undertaken in Canada in 1666 and in the United States in 1790. A decennial (every 10 years) census has been taken in both countries ever since.[13]

The primary reason for undertaking a census in any period is to collect data that can facilitate the government in performing those activities associated with implementing domestic policies such as taxation, induction into the military, appropriation of government aid, and apportionment of elected bodies. The scope of the contemporary census has been enlarged; the data collected now provides information for much of the research conducted by government, industry, and the academic community.[14]

The U.S. Census

The first U.S. census was conducted in 1790 by U.S. marshals under the supervision of Thomas Jefferson. Later, in 1902, Congress established a permanent census office, the Bureau of the Census, which currently is responsible for enumerating the population every 10 years. In addition, the Bureau of the Census conducts numerous ongoing focused surveys of the population; housing and construction; business and industry; federal, state, and local governments; and foreign trade.

The Bureau of the Census has introduced or participated in devising a number of statistical and technological innovations. Among the most important are the method of population sampling, which increased the scope of the census; development of the first computer program designed for mass data processing; and, more recently, the development of the Topologically Integrated Geographic Encoding and Referencing (TIGER) system. TIGER is an automated geographic database that provides coordinate-based digital map information, including political and statistical area boundaries and codes, for the entire United States. Users can obtain census and other statistical data separately and add them to the TIGER database with appropriate software designed to assist them in such tasks as drawing new political, administrative, and service-area boundaries; delineating high-crime areas; and plotting projected population growth in specific jurisdictions.[15]

The census of population and housing taken every 10 years is called a **complete count census;** its aim is to reach every household in the country. The decennial census uses two questionnaires: a short form that requests basic demographic information on each member of the household plus a few questions about the housing unit; and a long form, or sample questionnaire, which contains additional questions on socioeconomic status and housing. The complete count census is conducted by using the short form alone.

---

12. William Peterson, *Population* (New York: Macmillan, 1975).

13. Mortimer Spiegelman, *Introduction to Demography* (Cambridge, MA: Harvard University Press, 1968).

14. Ibid.

15. For further discussion, see *TIGER: The Coast-to-Coast Digital Map Data Base* (Washington, DC: U.S. Department of Commerce, Bureau of the Census, November 1990).

In addition, a population sample, consisting of 17 percent of all households surveyed, completes the longer questionnaire. In April 1990, the date of the most recent complete count census, a long form was sent to 17.7 million of an estimated 106 million housing units.

A complete count census of the population is necessary because census statistics determine the number of seats apportioned to each state in the U.S. House of Representatives. Moreover, federal funds to state and local governments are distributed on the basis of decennial census data. In addition, only a complete count census can provide information on small geographic areas such as a small town or a **census block**—the smallest geographic area for which census data are gathered. However, the prohibitive cost and administrative complexity of a complete count census limit its use to collecting only the most basic types of information. Population sampling (questions to be asked of only a portion of the surveyed population) is then employed because it has a number of advantages over a complete count census: It is more economical, more efficient, and faster to complete; therefore, it reduces the time lag between collection of the data and publication of initial results. Moreover, the use of population sampling allows the Bureau of the Census to expand the scope and detail of the data gathered regarding an individual's housing conditions and employment status. Some population sample surveys conducted by the Census Bureau are designed to collect information regarding attitudes toward a wide variety of issues that may not be purely demographic in nature.

Census data are generally provided for two types of geographic clusters: political units such as states, counties, or congressional districts; and statistical areas, which are regions defined for statistical purposes on the basis of primarily geographic criteria. Among the most common statistical areas used in research are **Metropolitan Statistical Areas (MSA), Census Designated Places (CDP),** and **census tracts.** An MSA is defined as one or more counties having a large population nucleus and surrounding communities that display a high degree of interaction.[16] The CDPs are designated as densely settled population centers lacking legally defined corporate limits or powers.[17] Census tracts are small, locally defined statistical areas, having an average population of 4,000, and found within metropolitan areas and some counties.[18]

Errors in Census Statistics

The modern census constitutes an important source of reliable statistical information. However, errors do occur, and users of population enumerations need to be aware of the methodological limitations of the data.

Census data are prone to two types of errors: errors in coverage and errors in content. *Errors in coverage* mean that a person or a group is either not counted at all or is counted twice. Duplicate counts are less serious than undercounts. The phenomenon of undercounting has long been of concern to elected officials, researchers, and the public because uncounted individuals and groups (especially groups such as the homeless and migrant workers) often lose their ability to be represented in national, state, and local governments.

One rather significant category of undercounted individuals consists of persons who cannot be located due to their lack of a permanent address. Another is made up of peo-

---

16. From *Census 1990 Basics* (Washington, DC: U.S. Department of Commerce, Bureau of the Census, December 1985), p. 5.

17. Ibid.

18. Ibid.

ple who deliberately avoid identification, such as illegal residents. In this case, it is difficult for the Bureau of the Census to estimate error because illegal residents are not likely to appear in other official records, such as those kept by the Social Security Administration, which can be used to verify census statistics.

Errors in content occur whenever information is incorrectly reported or tabulated. Apart from errors due to carelessness, errors in content often occur because the persons surveyed may deliberately give inaccurate responses to questions measuring the variables, especially social status. For example, individuals have been misclassified into higher or lower income, occupation, or education categories as a result of their misleading responses. Such errors can have serious consequences for the validity of research findings pertaining to domestic policies if they are based solely on those data.

Census Products

Census products, the collected and/or tabulated data, are available from the Bureau of the Census in various formats: printed reports, computer tapes, microfiche, and CD-ROM laser disks. Printed statistical reports are convenient and readily available. Data in printed reports are presented in the form of tables showing designated sets of data for a specified geographic area. These reports are released in series. Some series provide information for all the levels—the nation as a whole, the states, MSAs, urban areas, cities, and counties. The *Small Area* series presents block and census tract statistics. The subject series summarizes data on selected subjects at the national level.

Subject reports focus primarily on housing and on population issues, but each publication centers on a particular aspect within these general areas. For example, one report, entitled *Journey to Work: Metropolitan Community Flows,* contains statistics on local and national commuting patterns for each of the MSAs in the United States as well as information about where the employed live and work. Another report, *Living Arrangements of Children and Adults,* which is useful for studies of the transitions undergone by the American household, contains national-level statistics. It provides information on children in various age groups according to their relationship to the householder and the marital status of the parents. For researchers who need census statistics in greater detail or for smaller geographic and statistical units than those available in the various printed reports, the Bureau of the Census provides census data on computer tapes in two forms—Summary Tape Files (STFs), which contain detailed summary tables, and Public-Use Microdata Sample files (PUMS), which consist of a small sample of unidentified households and contain all the census data collected about each person in the household. PUMS files enable users to prepare specialized tabulations and cross-tabulations of specific items on the census questionnaire. These are of great value to academic researchers interested in a more intensive study of some characteristics.[19]

Microfiche containing statistics for a subset of census blocks is available from the 1980 census. The microfiche reproduce a subset of the tabulations for blocks found in the Summary Tape Files. In 1990, the entire nation was "blocked" for the first time. This has increased the number of blocks for which the Bureau of the Census provides data for areas containing populations from 2.5 million (in 1980) to about 7 million (in 1990). The cost and storage of block data of this magnitude would be prohibitive if they were published in printed reports.[20]

19. Ibid., p. 13.
20. Ibid., p. 16.

CD-ROM (compact disk—read-only memory), is the most common technology used for data storage and retrieval. One $4\frac{3}{4}$-inch CD-ROM can hold the contents of approximately 1,500 flexible diskettes, or three to four high-density tapes.[21] Special peripherals enable CD-ROMs to be read by personal computers. Because of its enormous capacity and ease of use, more and more census data are being made available in this form.

Other Data Collected by the Bureau of the Census

Although the decennial census of population and housing is the main source of information about U.S. residents, it cannot cover every subject of interest. In any case, the census information may become outdated for many purposes after a few years. Hence, the Bureau of the Census conducts a number of ongoing special censuses and sample surveys. Here we describe several that may be of particular interest to social scientists.

CURRENT POPULATION SURVEY (CPS).   The *Current Population Survey* is a monthly sample survey of the civilian population (it excludes soldiers, prisoners, and long-term hospital patients) of the United States. Its primary aim is to generate statistics on unemployment and provide current information on the personal characteristics (e.g., age, sex, race, marital and family status, and educational background) of the labor force. The survey also provides information on other subjects that are added periodically to its list of fundamental items. The Bureau of the Census publishes a number of reports based on these data under the title *Current Population Reports.*

AMERICAN HOUSING SURVEY (AHS).   Every two years, the Bureau of the Census interviews respondents in a representative sample of all housing units in the United States. The *American Housing Survey* includes extensive household-level data on housing quality, reasons for housing choices, and evaluations of public services and the general quality of life in the neighborhood. This survey contributes to the measurement of changes in the nation's housing stock resulting from losses, new construction, mobile home placement, and demographic characteristics of the occupants.[22]

CONSUMER EXPENDITURE SURVEY.   Consumer expenditure surveys are designed to monitor changes in prices. Data from these surveys are essential for measuring the rate of inflation and its impact on the cost of living in the United States. Data from this survey are also used by the Bureau of Labor Statistics to update its monthly Consumer Price Index (CPI). Consumer expenditure surveys take three forms: *The Quarterly Interview Survey, The Diary Survey,* and the *Point of Purchase Survey.*

The *Quarterly Interview Survey* is conducted monthly by means of household interviews and provides data on living expenses incurred during the three months prior to the interview.[23]

The *Diary Survey,* also conducted monthly, collects data on the daily living expenses of individuals living in households over two consecutive one-week periods.[24] The information is recorded on special "diary" forms, hence the name of the survey.

---

21. Ibid.

22. From *Census Surveys: Measuring America* (Washington, DC: U.S. Department of Commerce, Bureau of the Census, December 1985), p. 6.

23. Ibid., p. 12.

24. Ibid.

The annual *Point of Purchase Survey* is conducted to identify the kinds of stores and businesses frequented by consumers as they purchase a variety of goods and services. It is particularly useful for the analysis of economic trends and the planning of commercial activities.

The Bureau of the Census also publishes several useful guides: the *1990 Census User's Guide* is the basic guide for using 1990 census data; the *Census and You* is the Bureau's monthly newsletter directed at data users; the *Census Catalog and Guide* provides a comprehensive list of all new publications, computer tape files, special tabulations, and other products available from the Bureau.

In addition to its main headquarters in Washington, DC, the Bureau operates 12 regional offices that are staffed by information services specialists who answer questions by telephone, in person, or through correspondence. Databanks can be purchased by universities, major city libraries, and other large organizations dealing with research.

SEARCHING FOR SECONDARY DATA ●

With the plethora of studies available in this country and abroad, how do you locate the precise data you need? William Trochim offers these guidelines to expedite the search:[25]

1. *Specify your needs:* Examine subject indexes of archive holdings and identify relevant keywords.

2. *Familiarize yourself with the material:* Search the guides, catalogs, and data archives or organizations' listings that may have the desired data.

3. *Make initial contacts:* First contact people familiar with the archive and obtain information on using the data.

4. *Make secondary contacts:* Use professional staff to verify information and learn how to formally request the data.

5. *Check accessibility:* Obtain information on possible problems from people who have used the data.

6. *Conduct initial and supplemental analyses:* Obtain additional data if needed after conducting your initial analysis.

The main resources available to secondary data analysts searching for data are catalogs, guides, directories of archives, and organizations established to assist researchers. Useful catalogs of archives include the *Government Research Centers Directory,* 11th ed., ed. A. M. Palmer (Detroit: Gale Research Co., 1997). Major guides to government databases include the *Directory of Federal Libraries and Information Centers,* published by the U.S. Government Printing Office, Washington, DC.

The ICPSR at the University of Michigan and the Roper Center at the University of Connecticut are the largest archives of secondary data in the United States. The ICPSR publishes a *Documentation Listing* that lists information for each of the data collections it has released. The listing is also available on the Internet. Other major organizations include the Bureau of Applied Social Research, Columbia University; the Laboratory for Political Research, Social Science Data Archive, University of Iowa; the National Opinion

25. William M. K. Trochim, "Resources for Locating Public and Private Data," in *Reanalyzing Program Evaluations,* ed. Robert F. Boruch (San Francisco: Jossey-Bass, 1981), pp. 57–67.

Research Center (NORC), University of Chicago; and the European Association of Scientific Information Dissemination Centers.

This selection can only hint at the wealth of databanks and published information sources. Their steady growth in number and quality requires that students and researchers be in constant touch with the information services attached to universities, government offices, and other organizations.[26]

THE INTERNET   ●

By the end of the 1990s, the "Internet revolution" had penetrated many aspects of contemporary life. We will therefore concentrate on what the Internet has contributed to the process of research and leave its history and technical description to others.

What the Internet has done, quite simply, is to expand accessibility to sources of information. In many respects, computers and their peripherals have replaced much of the equipment used to do research: card catalogs in libraries, means of transportation to archives, and just plain walking. With the expanding capability for converting paper and ink into electronic modes of transmission, information is becoming handier. Governments and international agencies, such as the World Bank, are steadily making more of their official internal documents, publications, and collected data available through the Internet. The same applies for university libraries, research institutions, databanks, and any number of private interests, ranging from newspapers to department stores to individuals who are replacing ham radios with computers. If you add e-mail and audio possibilities— for those who have the state-of-the-art software and hardware—your technical repertoire can make communicating a very dynamic process. The Internet has, in many respects, severed the direct link between the resources required for research (time and money) and the sources of information, whose magnitude is growing geometrically. It's all there, at the click of a keyboard button—if you know how to work the system.

But what, exactly, is the Internet? Technically, the Internet is, at heart, a *web* of computers linked together by means of telephone lines. A *Web site* is, therefore, the electronic address of one of those computers. A *server*, a special program in your personal computer that administers the web site electronically, enables you to enter the system. The search and subsequent connection to web site addresses is handled by a *browser*, another special program that requests documents from the server and then displays them. The documents themselves are listed in *directories*, according to subject areas (the general directory of firms listed, travel, people, transport, etc.). Specialized items (e.g., youth hostels in Bangkok, authors of science fiction, international shipping figures) are identified by keywords that, when clicked, provide you with the address of the related web site or connect you to the pertinent documents.

Because the Internet is a public system, it is available to all, free of charge. However, connecting to the Internet requires use of on-line services, which are private. On-line services, such as AOL (America On Line) and MSN (Microsoft Network), provide the electronic feeder lines that connect one computer (user) to a repository of other computers (users). Because these access lines are private, they must be paid for, or you cannot connect to the sites covered by them. (The profits to be made by charging for access and the ensuing transactions have given birth to a new branch of economics, Internet economics.) Once access to the Internet is obtained, reaching the computers on the web is open to virtually everyone (although some organizations may charge special fees

---

26. See also the references listed in the section "The Internet," later.

for obtaining access to portions of their databanks). Importantly, just about anyone can join the system by creating a web site. The information included on the web site, other than the address, which is determined by a communications protocol, is unlimited. Hence, if you have done research on pollution and want to make your findings (including good sources of information on the topic) available to the general public, you can do so by creating your own web site. The Internet, as a phenomenon penetrating many arenas of life, is presenting many challenges to social scientists. It provides access to secondary sources of data at the same time that it provides primary sources, the raw data of trends, a situation that few anticipated in the 1980s.

The unanticipated growth of the Internet and the unlimited opportunities it provides to transmit information of all sorts have raised some important questions about its regulation. Because the Internet is an international system, it is difficult to regulate. Thus, the opportunities it offers to expand the avenues of self-expression have resurrected some crucial issues involving the positive and negative aspects of free speech: Besides recipes, weather conditions, courses in advanced algebra, and voting statistics, web sites provide free access to political propaganda, pornography, and instructions on how to build home-made bombs. Attempts to legislate restrictions on computer media in the United States have not been successful (specifically, the Computer Decency Act was judged unconstitutional by a federal court in Philadelphia). A private means for contending with the problem is to acquire a program that blocks access to specific sites.

With the spread of the Internet, the number of books and articles describing or analyzing the system is growing at a commensurate pace. We can only provide a smattering of sources to help the novice researcher cope with the possibilities available. General sourcebooks include *Public Records on Internet,* edited by David Vine (Princeton, NJ: David Vine Associates, 1998); *The Prentice Hall Directory of On-Line Social Studies Resources: 1,000 of the Most Valuable Social Studies Web Sites, Electronic Mailing Lists, and News Groups,* edited by Ronald L. Partin (Paramus, NJ: Prentice-Hall, 1997); and *The American Government Internet Guide,* 3d ed. (Belmont, CA: Wadsworth, 1999). The *Worldwide Government Directory* 14th ed., edited by Ken Gause (Detroit: Gale, 1998) provides access to sources of information and data for those interested in doing comparative research. For those interested in collecting statistical information, *Statistics Sources,* 23rd ed. (Detroit: Gale, 1997) tells you which web site contains the data required. The U.S. Government Printing Office also has a web site—as do the majority of government agencies—that lists all its publications, including purchasing instructions and costs. One book that might prove interesting for those wanting to understand the effects of the Internet on daily life is Don Tapscott's *Growing Up Digital: The Rise of the Net Generation* (Maidenhead, Berkshire, UK: McGraw-Hill, 1997).

UNOBTRUSIVE MEASURES ●

Among the most prevalent methods for obtaining data in the social sciences are those known as unobtrusive measures. An **unobtrusive measure** (also known as a *nonreactive measure*) is any method of data collection that removes the researcher from any direct contact with the interactions, events, or behavior being investigated. For example, the examination of documents in public archives is an unobtrusive measure because the researcher has no influence on the conditions under which the data are collected. Unobtrusive measures avoid data contamination, a problem that often arises when investigators and research participants interact in data collection situations (see the discussion on sources of bias in laboratory experiments, p. 198). With unobtrusive measures, the individual "is not aware of being tested, and there is little danger that the act of measurement will itself serve as a force for change in behavior or elicit role-playing that confounds the data." [27] These measures range from consulting private and public archives to simply observing people working or participating in leisure activities, from physical trace analysis to contrived observations. For example, the physical evidence (traces) left behind by a society or social group are generated without the producers' knowledge of the future use researchers will make of that evidence.

Eugene Webb and his colleagues distinguish between two broad classes of physical evidence: erosion measures and accretion measures.[28] **Erosion measures** are the signs left after use of an object. For example, the wear on library books is an index of their popularity, and the number of miles accumulated by police officers in their patrol cars is a measure of their daily activity. Thus, a researcher can confirm the verbal reports of daily activities made by police officers by checking the number of miles accumulated in their patrol cars.

Accretion measures constitute the evidence deposited by a group in the course of their activities. In this case, the researcher examines remnants that are suggestive of some type of behavior. For example, the amount of dust on machines has been taken as an indicator of the frequency of their use; similarly, the popularity of different radio stations can be estimated by noting the settings found on radios when cars are brought in for servicing.

Both the time needed for its collection and the dubious quality of the data make physical trace analysis problematic. Even more important, in many instances the researcher lacks sufficient information on the population producing the evidence to enable him or her to draw valid generalizations from these measures.

Simple Observation

Simple observation is another fundamental unobtrusive measure. It is used in situations "in which the observer has no control over the behavior or sign in question, and plays an unobserved, passive and unobtrusive role in the research situation." [29] Although researchers making simple observations employ the methodology of other observational methods in all other respects, simple observation is a distinct method because the researcher does not intervene in the production of the data (as compared with the experimental observation methodologies described in Chapter 8). There are four basic types of simple observation: observation of exterior body and physical signs, analysis of expressive movement, physical location analysis, and observation of language behavior.

OBSERVATION OF THE EXTERIOR BODY AND OTHER PHYSICAL SIGNS.   In this type of simple observation, researchers observe the exterior body and its physical aspects as if they were indicators or signs of behavior patterns and attitudes. Examples of such measures are tattoos, hairstyles, clothing, ornamental items such as jewelry, and other objects. The signs posted in public places are included in this category. For example, a change in the language of store signs serves as a measure of social change because it indicates that new immigrant groups have settled in the neighborhood.

---

27. Eugene J. Webb, Donald T. Campbell, Richard D. Schwartz, Lee Sechrest, and Janet Belew Grove, *Nonreactive Measures in the Social Sciences* (Boston: Houghton Mifflin, 1981), p. 175.

28. Ibid., pp. 35–52.

29. Ibid., p. 112.

ANALYSIS OF EXPRESSIVE MOVEMENT. A second type of simple observation involves the **analysis of expressive movement.** Observers focus on the self-expressive features of the body and how these movements indicate social interactions. People communicate many feelings as well as social norms through body language—how close together people stand, how much they look at each other, and how often they touch.

When researchers investigate facial expressions and bodily gestures, they confront a major problem: determining what a particular gesture conveys. For instance, a smile may mean the person is embarrassed or happy. The observer's role is to determine the meaning of that gesture for the person making it as well as for the object (the recipient) of the gesture within the context being observed. The same movement may, after all, convey different emotions in different situations and in different cultures.

PHYSICAL LOCATION ANALYSIS. The main purpose of **physical location analysis** is to investigate the ways in which individuals use their bodies in a naturally occurring social space. For example, before the demise of the Soviet empire, observers of Soviet internal politics always took note of who stood next to whom on the dais as the leadership observed the annual May Day parade in Red Square. Their positions served as clues of stability or change in the makeup of the political elite. Another example is protocol—its rules essentially institutionalize the physical representation of status. The researcher should therefore be sensitive to variations in protocol when studying political or social change.

OBSERVATION OF LANGUAGE BEHAVIOR. This fourth form of simple observation focuses on **language behavior,** that is, conversations and the interrelationship of speech patterns to locale, social categories, and time of day. The analysis combines the study of physical location with that of expressive movements. In her popular books, Dr. Deborah Tannen makes effective use of language behavior in analyzing how relationships between people are structured and maintained. For example, after closely observing conversations, she notes that men are more sensitive to "messages," the explicit meaning of what is said; women are more sensitive to "metamessages," the implicit meaning of what is said that conveys attitudes about the conversation and about the people talking or listening.[30]

The Pros and Cons of Simple Observation

The main advantage of simple observation is that the researcher has no responsibility for structuring the observation situation and remains unobserved throughout. This eliminates the bias that might otherwise be introduced (see Chapters 5 and 9). The other major benefit of simple observation lies in the fact that it provides the researcher with the means for observing real-life behavior in its most natural setting—how it actually occurs. This aspect is particularly important when either the situation (e.g., crowds, legislative sessions) or the research participants (e.g., children) cannot or should not be manipulated. These decisions and constraints are guided by the research hypothesis and purposes.

Simple observation, however, does have its limitations. First, the recorded observations may not represent a wide enough population, thus limiting the scope of generalizations based on them. Second, bias may be introduced as a result of unintended, uncontrolled

---

30. Deborah Tannen, *You Just Don't Understand: Women and Men in Conversation* (New York: Ballantine Books, 1990), p. 32.

changes in the way the observation is carried out. If the observer becomes more or less attentive, adept, or involved over the period the observation is carried out, bias in how the observations are made or recorded might creep in. Third, in order to ensure that the observer remains unnoticed, settings must be chosen that "hide" the observer. The settings most amenable to simple observation are, then, public, which narrows the scope of observable behaviors because the observer is limited in the scope of behaviors he or she can observe at any one time. Fourth, much of the data collected by simple observation do not automatically invite clear-cut explanations: "The data . . . don't offer the 'why,' but simply establish a relationship." [31] This ambiguity limits the applicability of simple observation as a data collection method and, as a result, the validity of the findings based on the data. These drawbacks are important despite the method's advantage, replication.

ARCHIVAL RECORDS ●

Archival records provide important opportunities for unobtrusive data collection, partially because they are quite diverse in character. Archival records include public records—actuarial records, electoral and judicial records, government documents, the mass media—as well as private records—autobiographies, diaries, and letters. Some of these records have been compiled for general use, whereas others have been prepared specifically for purposes of research.

Public Records

Four basic kinds of public records may be distinguished. First, there are actuarial records describing the rudimentary individual demographic characteristics of the population served by the record-keeping agency—births and deaths, marriages and divorces, and so on. Second are legislative and other official records, including judicial papers concerning court decisions, legislative activities, public votes, and budget decisions. Third are governmental and quasi-governmental documents containing information on diverse topics, such as crimes committed, social welfare programs, length of stay in hospitals, and the weather. Fourth are the reports, news items, editorials, and other information produced or transmitted by the mass media. All of these four types of public records have been used for numerous and varied research purposes.

ACTUARIAL RECORDS.   Most societies maintain records of births, deaths, marriages, and divorces. Researchers use such **actuarial records** for both descriptive and explanatory purposes. For example, Russell Middleton examined fertility levels with two sets of data: fertility values expressed in magazine fiction and actuarial fertility levels for three different time periods: 1916, 1936, and 1956. Middleton first estimated fertility values by observing the size of fictional families in eight American magazines. When he compared these values with population data for the same years, the results showed that shifts in the size of fictional families closely paralleled shifts in the actual fertility level of the United States.[32]

Lloyd Warner used a number of official records in his original study on the meaning of death and its social expression in an American city. Warner investigated official ceme-

---

31. Webb et al., *Nonreactive Measures*, p. 127.

32. Russell Middleton, "Fertility Values in American Magazine Fiction, 1916–1956," *Public Opinion Quarterly*, 24 (1960): 139–143.

tery documents to establish a social history of the dead. He indeed found that the social structure of the city was mirrored in its cemetery. For example, the father was most often buried in the center of the family plot, and headstones of males were larger than those of females. Moreover, a family that had raised its social status moved the graves of its relatives from less prestigious cemeteries to more prestigious ones.[33]

LEGISLATIVE AND OTHER OFFICIAL RECORDS. Political scientists in particular make extensive use of legislative and other official records (such as judicial decisions) to study phenomena such as socioeconomic behavior and shifts in political ideologies. To cite one example, Hood, Kidd and Morris[34] used roll-call votes as one indicator to measure trends toward "liberalization" of voting patterns in the American South.

Numerous published volumes provide statistics of voting behavior and other expressions of a nation's political culture. Collections such as *A Review of Elections of the World,* issued biennially by the Institute of Electoral Research in London, and the series *America at the Polls: A Handbook of American Presidential Election Statistics* (e.g., Volume II, covering 1960–1996, edited by Alice V. McGillivray and Richard M. Scammon [Washington DC: Congressional Quarterly, 1998]) provide useful historical data on voting. Another good source is *America at the Polls, 1996,* edited by Everett K. Ladd (Storrs, CT: Roper Center for Public Opinion Research, 1997). *The Congressional Quarterly Almanac* contains information on the U.S. Congress, including data on the backgrounds of members of Congress, information on major items of legislation, tabulations of roll-call votes, and a survey of political developments. In the *World Handbook of Political and Social Indicators* (New Haven, CT: Yale University Press, 1983; reprint now available from Books on Demand), Charles L. Taylor and David Jodice report comparative data on 148 political and social measures, such as electoral participation, riots by country per year, numbers of irregular government changes, and inequalities in income distribution. Harold W. Stanley and Richard G. Niemi, in *Vital Statistics on American Politics,* 6th ed. (Washington, DC: Congressional Quarterly, 1998), present useful data on political institutions, public opinion, and government policies.

The *Congressional Record* contains information that can be used to study the behavior not only of members of Congress but also of the people who deal with legislators in some way. For example, it is a common practice for members of Congress to insert in the *Record* newspaper columns that reflect their personal points of view. In an early study of political columnists, Eugene Webb employed these data to estimate the prevalence of conservative and liberal beliefs among Washington's press corps. Webb assigned a score on a liberal–conservative continuum to individual members of Congress by evaluating their voting records as published by two opposing groups—the conservative Americans for Constitutional Action and the liberal Committee on Political Action of the AFL-CIO. He then ranked columnists vis-à-vis the mean score of the members of Congress who had placed their articles in the *Record.*[35]

GOVERNMENTAL DOCUMENTS. Just as birth and death records can be fruitful resources, other public and quasi-public documents may likewise serve as sources of data.

---

33. Lloyd W. Warner, *The Living and the Dead: A Study of the Symbolic Life of Americans* (New Haven, CT: Yale University Press, 1965).

34. M.V. Hood III, Quentin Kidd, and Irwin L. Morris, "Of Byrd[s] and Bumpers: Using Democratic Senators to Analyze Political Change in the South, 1960–1995," *American Journal of Political Science,* 43(2), (1999): 465–487.

35. Eugene J. Webb, "How to Tell a Columnist," *Columbia Journalism Review,* 2 (1963): 20.

Cesare Lombroso, for instance, was interested in discovering what, other than economic or social resources, might contribute to scientific creativity. He used governmental documents to study the effect of weather and time of year on scientific creativity. After drawing a sample of 52 discoveries in physics, chemistry, and mathematics, he noted the season in which they occurred. His evidence showed that 22 of the major discoveries were made in the spring, 15 in the autumn, 10 in the summer, and 5 in winter.[36]

City budgets are especially fertile sources for much of the research in the social sciences. Robert Angell used such data in his unique study on the moral integration of American cities. He constructed a "welfare effort index" by computing local per-capita expenditures for welfare; he combined this with a "crime index," based on FBI data, to arrive at an "integration index." [37] Budgets have also been used as indicators of policy commitments. The expenditure side of the budget shows "who gets what" from public funds, whereas the revenue side tells "who pays the price." Budgets are so useful because the budgetary process provides a systematic framework for reviewing government programs, assessing their cost, relating them to financial sources and alternative expenditures, and determining the financial commitment that governments are willing to make for these programs. In their classic study on this process, Davis, Dempster, and Wildavsky examined the federal budget in consecutive periods and identified two variables that explain the level of agency appropriations of the greatest proportion of budgetary requests presented in a given year:

1. The agency's annual budget request is comprised of a fixed percentage of the congressional appropriation in the previous year plus a random component for the current year.

2. The congressional appropriation for an agency in any year is a fixed percentage of the agency's request in that year plus a component representing some deviation from the usual relationship between Congress and the agency for the previous year.[38]

THE MASS MEDIA. The mass media constitute the most easily available source of data for social science research. The mass media record people's communications; these can be used to study a variety of research topics. The development of content analysis, to be discussed later in this chapter, enabled researchers to expand their use of the mass media as a primary source of data. Accordingly, research using data obtained from the mass media is voluminous.[39] We will cite only one example. Gina Daddario studied TV sportscasters' descriptions of and commentaries on women's events during the 1992 Winter Olympics. Her data indicate that the style of the commentaries and the language used attempt to present the female athlete as an adolescent ideal rather than a serious role model despite the on-screen depiction of physically challenging events, activities that contradict stereotypical images of femininity. Daddario concludes that the masculine imagery sportscasters use maintains the marginalization of female sports.[40]

36. Webb et al., *Nonreactive Measures*, p. 72.

37. Robert C. Angell, "The Moral Integration of American Cities," *American Journal of Sociology*, 57 (1951): 1–140.

38. Otto A. Davis, M. A. H. Dempster, and Aaron Wildavsky, "A Theory of the Budgetary Process," *American Political Science Review*, 60 (1966): 529–547.

39. For studies using the mass media as a source of unobtrusive data, see Webb et al., *Nonreactive Measures*.

40. Gina Daddario, "Chilly Scenes of the 1992 Winter Games: The Mass Media and the Marginalization of Female Athletes," *Sociology of Sports Journal*, 11 (1994): 275–288.

Private Records

The difficulty of obtaining private records may in some ways relate to their value for re-searchers wishing to gain insights into events. Private records transmit individuals' own definitions of situations or events in which they either participated directly or which they observed. These documents include autobiographies, diaries, letters, essays, and the like. *Autobiographies* are the most frequently used private record: They reflect the author's (sometimes official) interpretation of his or her personal experiences. The *diary* is a more spontaneous account, as its author tends to be unconstrained by the sense of mis-sion that often motivates the writing of autobiographies. *The Diary of Anne Frank* is per-haps the best example of such a document that we can cite. Both autobiographies and diaries are initially directed to a single audience—the author. *Letters,* in contrast, have a dual audience—the writer and the recipient—from the very outset, and often reflect the interaction between them.[41] Because these three types of private records focus on the author's personal experiences and express his or her personal reflections, they are usu-ally produced at the author's own initiative.

One of the major issues researchers face in using private records is their **authentic-ity.** There are two kinds of inauthentic records: records that have been produced by de-liberate deceit and records that have been unconsciously misrepresented. Records may be falsified or forged for various purposes, a primary one being prestige or material re-wards. For example, writers who claim to have an intimate knowledge of the subject's life can more easily sell an alleged biography to a publishing company. An infamous case was the bogus biography of the eccentric billionaire Howard Hughes, sold in 1972 to a reputable publisher.

As a means of ensuring authenticity, several procedures can be employed. First, the researcher needs to examine authorship critically. Second, he or she must estab-lish the date of the document and verify the accuracy of the dates of the events men-tioned. For instance, if the author refers to a particular event—say, an earthquake—the date of this event can be verified through another source, such as contemporary newspaper accounts. If the writer refers to an event whose timing cannot be corrobo-rated by other documents, the accuracy of the original record should be taken as suspect.

The second kind of inauthenticity is much more difficult to detect. Although docu-ments may not be false, they may nevertheless misrepresent the truth for the following reasons: The authors of letters, diaries, or autobiographies may not clearly remember the facts; they may be trying to please or amuse their readers by exaggerating; or, perhaps, they may be constrained by social norms and conventions and thus compelled to pre-sent a somewhat distorted picture. Stuart Chapin has suggested that a researcher should answer the following central questions before accepting a document as an authentic record:[42]

1. What did the author mean by a particular statement? Is its underlying meaning different from its literal meaning?

2. Was the statement made in good faith? Was the author influenced by sympathy or antipathy? By vanity? By public opinion?

---

41. Norman K. Denzin, *The Research Act: A Theoretical Introduction to Sociological Methods,* 3d ed. (Engle-wood Cliffs, NJ: Prentice-Hall, 1989), chap. 8.

42. Stuart F. Chapin, *Field Work and Social Research* (New York: Ayer, 1979), p. 37. Originally published 1920.

3. Was the statement accurate? Was the author a poor observer because of a mental defect or abnormality? Was the author badly situated in time and place to observe the event objectively?

When the researcher has obtained answers to these questions, he or she is in a better position to evaluate the record.

AUTOBIOGRAPHIES.   The uniqueness of the autobiography is that it provides a view of a person's life and experiences uncontaminated by another person's analysis of the events. Autobiographies thus allow researchers to gain access to a person's life in its natural setting, in a form that is presumably communicated directly and free of intervening influences.

Gordon Allport distinguishes three major types of autobiographies, each of which may serve different research objectives.[43] The first is the *comprehensive autobiography,* which covers the full cycle of the person's life starting from his or her earliest memory and integrating a large number of experiences. Helen Keller's accounts of her life as a blind deaf-mute exemplifies this category. The second type of autobiography is the *topical autobiography,* which focuses on a limited aspect of the person's life. For example, Edwin Sutherland's study of a professional thief was based on an individual's personal account, written and dictated, of one phase of his life:

> The principal part of this book is a description of the profession of theft by a person who had been engaged almost continuously for more than twenty years in this profession. This description was secured in two ways: first, the thief wrote approximately two-thirds of it on topics and questions prepared by me; second, he and I discussed for about seven hours a week for twelve weeks what he had written, and immediately after each conference I wrote in verbatim form . . . all that he had said in the discussion.[44]

The third type is the *edited autobiography,* which is an abridged version of the person's account: The researcher selects only those experiences that are relevant to the research purpose. Through editing, the material is clarified and organized so that it illuminates the research hypotheses.

DIARIES.   A diary provides a firsthand account of the writer's life and thoughts. Written close to the time the events occurred, it conveys immediate experiences, undistorted by memory. People who write diaries are not inhibited by the fear of public exposure; therefore, they reveal the details that they consider significant at the time the event occurred.

Diaries have been classified into three types. The *intimate journal* is a continuous record of a person's subjective perception of his or her experiences over a long period of time. The second type, the *memoir,* is rather impersonal and resembles a more objective record of the individual's affairs. The third type, the *log,* is also impersonal; it contains a record of events, meetings, visits, and other activities engaged in by the individual during a limited period of time. It usually lacks the individual's interpretations or details of the context in which the events occurred.

Some researchers find the intimate journal especially useful because it contains authentic expressions of a person's perceptions of events over a prolonged period of time. For example, as a means for further enlightening the reader about the character of his

---

43. Gordon W. Allport, *The Use of Personal Documents in Psychological Research* (New York: Social Science Research Council, 1942).

44. Edwin H. Sutherland, *The Professional Thief* (Chicago: University of Chicago Press, 1988), p. v.

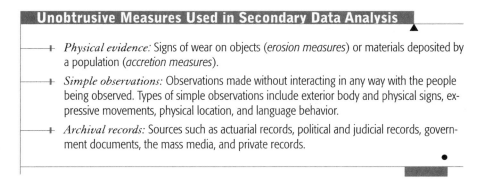

Unobtrusive Measures Used in Secondary Data Analysis

Physical evidence: Signs of wear on objects (*erosion measures*) or materials deposited by a population (*accretion measures*).

Simple observations: Observations made without interacting in any way with the people being observed. Types of simple observations include exterior body and physical signs, expressive movements, physical location, and language behavior.

Archival records: Sources such as actuarial records, political and judicial records, government documents, the mass media, and private records.

subject, one biography of the poet Dylan Thomas contains portions of his personal diary, notes he kept on poems he was writing, reflections on his financial state, and comments on his relations with the world of art.[45] By chronicling a person's subjective perceptions over an extended period, the intimate journal allows the researcher to compare various stages in a person's life and to identify major shifts in its course.

LETTERS.   Historians and literary critics have made extensive use of letters when attempting to reconstruct the lives of historical and literary figures. One of the earliest attempts to employ letters as a source of data in scientific social research was made by William Thomas and Florian Znaniecki in their study of Polish peasants who immigrated to the United States. Thomas and Znaniecki collected letters sent between Poland and the United States during the period 1901–1914 as a major source of information on the problems arising when ethnic communities immigrate. The letters permitted the investigators to examine, among other things, the writers' personalities and the kinds of interactions carried on with their correspondents in the old country.[46]

CONTENT ANALYSIS

Content analysis provides social scientists with a systematic methodology for analyzing the data obtained from archival records, documents, and the mass media. Letters, diaries, newspaper articles, minutes of meetings, live reportage (as in the example from the 1992 Winter Olympics cited on p. 292), films, TV and radio shows can all be analyzed by content analysis, which can be employed as a method of observation as well. Instead of observing people's behavior directly or asking them questions about that behavior, the researcher obtains copies of the communications produced (when available) and asks questions about these records. The content of the communication serves as the basis for making inferences. In *Megatrends,* John Naisbitt analyzed the economic, social, and political currents in the United States as a basis for his forecasts of new trends.[47] The methodology he employed in his study involved the content analysis of

---

45. Bill Read, *The Days of Dylan Thomas* (New York: McGraw-Hill, 1964).

46. William I. Thomas and Florian Znaniecki, *The Polish Peasant in Europe and America* (Champaign: University of Illinois Press, 1984).

47. John Naisbitt, *Megatrends: Ten New Directions Transforming Our Lives* (New York: Warner Books, 1984).

more than 2 million articles about local events published over a 12-year period in local newspapers throughout the country. This method of analysis revealed, among other things, that five states (California, Florida, Washington, Colorado, and Connecticut) are the homes of the greatest number of social innovations.

Broadly defined, **content analysis** is "any technique for making inferences by systematically and objectively identifying specified characteristics of messages."[48] Researchers attempt to guarantee objectivity by carrying out their analyses according to explicit rules that enable different investigators to obtain the same results from the same messages or documents (i.e., under conditions that permit replication). When conducting systematic content analysis, the "inclusion or exclusion of content is done according to consistently applied criteria of selection; this requirement eliminates analyses in which only materials supporting the investigator's hypotheses are examined."[49]

Applications of Content Analysis

Although content analysis is always performed on a message, researchers may also utilize this method to explore other elements of communication. It was Harold Lasswell who formulated the basic question to be raised by researchers employing content analysis: "Who says what, to whom, how, and with what effect?"[50] More explicitly, a researcher may analyze messages to test hypotheses about characteristics of the text, what inspired the message, or the effects brought on by communicating that message. These three aspects may differ according to the questions researchers ask about the data, the type of communication they analyze, and the research design they employ.

Content analysis is most frequently applied in describing the attributes of messages. For example, early research on revolutions and the development of international relations involved a survey of political symbols found in the texts of various documents. The researchers constructed several research designs that enabled them to test hypotheses on "world revolution" by identifying trends in the use of symbols representing the major goals and values of modern states. In one study, researchers analyzed editorials from 10 prestigious newspapers in the United States, England, France, Germany, and Russia/the Soviet Union for the period 1890–1949. Editorials appearing on the first and the fifteenth day of each month were coded for the presence of 416 key symbols. These symbols included 206 geographic terms, such as names of countries and international organizations, and 210 ideological references, such as equality, democracy, and communism. When a symbol appeared, the coders scored it as present and recorded the attitudes expressed toward that symbol in one of three categories: approval, disapproval, or neutrality. The researchers used the data collected from the content analysis of 19,553 editorials to trace changing attitudes and foci of public attention.[51]

Content analysis need not, however, be used only with respect to verbal data. Philip White and James Gillett analyzed 916 advertisements in *Flex*, a popular American bodybuilding magazine, in a study designed to decode the basic themes communicated by

48. Ole R. Holsti, "Content Analysis," in *The Handbook of Social Psychology*, ed. Gardner Lindzey and Elliot Aronson (Reading, MA: Addison-Wesley, 1968), p. 601. The following discussion is based on this work.

49. Ibid., p. 598.

50. Harold D. Lasswell, "Detection: Propaganda Detection and the Courts," in *The Language of Politics: Studies in Quantitative Semantics*, ed. Harold D. Lasswell and Nathan Leites (Cambridge, MA: MIT Press, 1965), p. 12.

51. Ithiel de Sola Pool, *Symbols of Democracy* (Westport, CT: Greenwood Press, 1981). Originally published 1952.

the pictures and text. The themes White and Gillett discerned were: positioning the reader as inferior (43 percent of the content), promises of transformation (64.5 percent), and the muscular body as a sign of hegemonic masculinity (70.6 percent). They then applied cultural and ideological conceptual frameworks to explain the results. They concluded that these advertisements legitimate substituting the body for reality and emotions, and that for readers of the magazine, male muscularity served as a symbol of male superiority and a compensatory mechanism for diminished privileges in other areas of life. These processes support, in turn, a gender ideology in which biological attributes provide the foundations for gender differences in the sociocultural and economic realms.[52]

The second application of content analysis—who says what and why to whom—occurs when a text is analyzed in order to make inferences about the sender of the message and about its causes or antecedents. A well-known attempt to determine the sender's identity is the Frederick Mosteller and David Wallace study of the authorship of the *Federalist Papers,* Nos. 49–58, 62, and 63. The authors started with four sets of papers: those known to have been written by Madison, those thought to have been written by Madison or by Hamilton, and those thought to have been written by both. After examining the texts of the acknowledged set of papers for stylistic elements, the investigators were able to select words that were used selectively by each author. For example, Hamilton tended to use the word *enough,* whereas Madison did not. Mosteller and Wallace then used such keywords in combination with other terms to attribute the authorship of the disputed papers. The data strongly supported the claim that Madison wrote the disputed documents.[53] This finding helped to resolve certain historical questions about the intellectual foundations of the Constitution.

Content analysis has also been used to infer elements of culture and cultural change. David McClelland tested his "need for achievement" (i.e., n-Achievement) theory by analyzing the content of literature written in different cultures. In McClelland's view, an individual with high n-Achievement is someone who wants to succeed, who is nonconforming, and who enjoys tasks that involve elements of risk. An n-Achievement score is thus "a sum of the number of instances of achievement 'ideas' or images" appearing in a culture's literary production. McClelland's hypothesis was that "a society with a relatively high percentage of individuals with high n-Achievement should contain a strong entrepreneurial class which will tend to be active and successful particularly in business enterprises so that the society will grow in power and influence." He tested this hypothesis by scoring samples of literature from different periods of Greek civilization.[54]

In the third major application of content analysis, researchers make inferences about the effects of messages on recipients. The researcher determines the effects of, say, A's messages on B, by analyzing the content of B's responses. An additional avenue of research would be to study the effects of the communication by examining other aspects of the recipient's behavior. In summary, content analysis helps to isolate the relevant factors that can explain the recipient's behavior within the process of communication.

52. Philip G. White and James Gillett, "Reading the Muscular Body, A Critical Decoding of Advertisements in *Flex* Magazine," *Sociology of Sport Journal,* 11(1994): 18–39.

53. Frederick Mosteller and David L. Wallace, *Inference and Disputed Authorship: The Federalist Papers* (Reading, MA: Addison-Wesley, 1964).

54. David C. McClelland, "The Use of Measures of Human Motivation in the Study of Society," in *Motives in Fantasy, Action and Society,* ed. John W. Atkinson (New York: Van Nostrand, 1966), p. 518.

Units and Categories

Content analysis involves the interaction of two processes: *specification* of the characteristics of the content measured and *application of rules* for identifying and recording the characteristics appearing in the texts analyzed. The categories into which content is coded vary with the nature of the data and the research purpose.

Before discussing general procedures for constructing categories, we should define some basic terms—recording units and context units—and distinguish between them. The **recording unit** is the smallest body of content (or text) in which a *reference* appears and is noted (a reference is a single occurrence of the content element). The **context unit** is the largest body of content (or text) that must be examined when characterizing a recording unit. For example, the recording unit may be a single term, but in order to decide whether the term is treated favorably, the researcher has to consider the entire sentence in which the term appears (the context unit). Thus the whole sentence is taken into account when the researcher records (and subsequently codes) the term.

Five major recording units have been used in content analysis research: *words* or *terms, themes, characters, paragraphs,* and *items.* The word is the smallest unit generally applied in research. When the recording unit is a word, the analysis yields a list reporting the frequencies with which these words or terms appear. For many research purposes, the theme is a useful recording unit, particularly in the study of propaganda, attitudes, images, and values. In its simplest form, a theme is a simple sentence, that is, a subject and a predicate. Because themes can be found in clauses, paragraphs, and illustrations, researchers specify which of these the coder will search when using the theme as a recording unit. For example, a coder may consider only the primary theme in each paragraph or count every theme in the text.

In some studies, a character is employed as the recording unit. In these cases, the researcher counts the number of persons appearing in the text rather than the number of words or themes. This choice permits examination of the personality traits of the individuals appearing in various texts.

Because of its complexity, the paragraph is used infrequently as a recording unit. Coders have difficulty classifying and coding the numerous different elements found in a single paragraph.

The *item* is the whole unit the producer of a message employs. The item may be an entire book, an article, a speech, or the like. Analysis by the entire item is appropriate whenever the variations within the item are small and insignificant. For example, news stories can often be classified by subject matter, such as crime, labor, or sports.

Eventually, recording units are combined and coded into *categories.* Category construction, as Bernard Berelson points out, is the most crucial aspect of content analysis:

> Content analysis stands or falls by its categories. Particular studies have been productive to the extent that the categories were clearly formulated and well adapted to the problem and to the content. Content analysis studies done on a hit or miss basis, without clearly formulated problems for investigation and with vaguely drawn or poorly articulated

categories, are almost certain to be of indifferent or low quality as research productions. . . . Since the categories contain the substance of the investigation, a content analysis can be no better than its system of categories.[55]

Among the types of categories frequently employed in content analysis research are the following:[56]

"What Is Said" Categories

SUBJECT MATTER.   What is the communication about?

DIRECTION.   How is the subject matter treated (for example, favorably or unfavorably)?

STANDARD.   What is the basis on which the classification is made?

VALUES.   What values, goals, or desires are revealed?

METHODS.   What methods are used to achieve goals?

TRAITS.   What are the characteristics used in describing people?

ACTOR.   Who is presented as undertaking certain acts?

AUTHORITY.   In whose name are statements made?

ORIGIN.   Where does the communication originate?

LOCATION.   Where does the action take place?

CONFLICT.   What are the sources and levels of conflict?

ENDINGS.   Are conflicts resolved happily, ambiguously, or tragically?

TIME.   When does the action take place?

"How It Is Said" Categories

FORM OR TYPE OF COMMUNICATION.   What is the medium of communication (radio, newspaper, speech, television, etc.)?

FORM OF STATEMENT.   What is the grammatical or syntactical form of the communication?

DEVICE.   What is the rhetorical or propagandistic method used?

The analytic categories must relate to the research purpose; they must be exhaustive and mutually exclusive. *Exhaustiveness* ensures that every recording unit relevant to the study can be classified. *Mutual exclusivity* guarantees that no recording unit will be included in more than one category within the system (see Chapter 14). The researcher also has to specify explicit criteria for deciding which recording units fall into each category. This step enables replication of the study, as essential for objective and systematic content analysis as it is for all scientific research.

Most content analysis is quantitative in one form or another. In order to perform quantification, researchers employ one of the following four systems of enumeration:

1. A *time-space system* based on measures of space (e.g., column inches) or units of time (e.g., minutes devoted to a news item on the radio) to describe the relative emphases of different categories in the analyzed material.

2. An *appearance system* in which coders search the material for the appearance of certain attributes. The size of the context unit determines the frequency with which repeated recording units occurring in close proximity to each other are counted separately.

3. A *frequency system* in which every occurrence of a given attribute is recorded.

---

55. Bernard Berelson, *Content Analysis in Communication Research* (New York: Hafner, 1971), p. 147.

56. Holsti, "Content Analysis."

4. An *intensity system,* generally employed in studies dealing with attitudes and values.

Whereas the first three systems are fairly clear-cut and direct, methods of quantifying *intensity* are based on the prior construction of scales (see Chapter 18). For instance, in order to decide which of two recording units indicates greater intensity of an attitude, an attitude scale based on the paired-comparison technique developed by Thurstone can be used. With the help of this scale, categories are constructed into which the raters enter the individual recording units.[57]

SUMMARY

1. Secondary data analysis is performed on data collected by others. Secondary data may be the only source available to study certain research problems. It may also be used for comparative purposes. There are several methodological advantages to using secondary analysis: It provides an opportunity for replication; it permits longitudinal research; and it may improve the measurement of certain variables by enabling us to increase the sample size. Finally, secondary data are considerably less expensive to obtain than are primary data.
2. A widely used source of secondary data is the census data collected by governments for administrative and public policy purposes. Census data are used to investigate, among other things, changes in population, the structure of households, neighborhood and housing characteristics, and trends in family composition. The Bureau of the Census makes available printed statistical reports, as well as computer tapes for users needing census data in greater detail or for smaller geographic and statistical units than are available in the printed reports. The Bureau also makes such data available on CD-ROMs.
3. The Internet is rapidly becoming a major source of secondary data. This electronic "library" provides easy access to public and private records at low to no cost. Given that, the accuracy and authenticity of the information available on web sites cannot be taken for granted. For these reasons, issues of regulation and freedom of speech have arisen once more.
4. Unobtrusive measures are an important source of data that removes the investigator from the population being researched. With unobtrusive measures, individuals are not aware they are being researched, and there is little chance that the act of measurement itself will influence the behavior or elicit the role playing that might bias the data. The three basic types of unobtrusive measures are: physical traces, simple observation, and archival records.
5. Individuals leave physical traces without any awareness that they will be used by researchers. The two broad classes of physical traces are erosion measures and accretion measures.
6. Simple observation occurs in situations in which the observer has no control over the behavior in question and remains unobserved during the research. There are four types of simple observation: observation of exterior body and physical signs, analysis of expressive movement, physical location analysis, and observation of language behavior.

57. The most recent development in content analysis is the programming of computers to process the various operations involved in textual analysis. It is beyond the scope of this book to survey these developments, but a good start would be Robert P. Weber, *Basic Content Analysis* (Thousand Oaks, CA: Sage, 1990).

7. Another unobtrusive measure is the analysis of public and private archival records. These data are collected from diverse sources, such as actuarial records, legislative and other official records, governmental documents, the mass media, and private records, including autobiographies, diaries, and letters. A major problem with private records is establishing their authenticity.

8. Content analysis permits researchers to systematically analyze data obtained from written or spoken texts. Instead of observing people's behavior directly, the investigator uses the communications that people have produced (whether public or private records) and asks questions about the messages transmitted. Content analysis involves the interaction of two processes: Researchers specify the content characteristics to be analyzed and apply rules for identifying and recording these characteristics when they appear in the texts analyzed. The categories into which content is coded vary with the nature of the research problem and the type of data.

KEY TERMS FOR REVIEW

accretion measures (p. 288)
actuarial records (p. 290)
analysis of expressive movement
   (p. 289)
archival records (p. 290)
authenticity (p. 293)
census block (p. 282)
Census Designated Places (CDPs)
   (p. 282)
census tract (p. 282)
complete count census (p. 281)

content analysis (p. 296)
context unit (p. 298)
erosion measures (p. 288)
language behavior (p. 289)
Metropolitan Statistical Areas (MSAs)
   (p. 282)
physical location analysis (p. 289)
recording unit (p. 298)
simple observation (p. 288)
unobtrusive measures (p. 287)

STUDY QUESTIONS

1. What are the advantages of secondary data analysis? What are its limitations?
2. Propose a research problem and specify how to obtain the relevant secondary data.
3. Define the main types of census data and indicate the research purposes most appropriate for their use.
4. Explain how simple observation differs from experimental observation.
5. Discuss the major methodological issues in content analysis and how you would go about resolving them.

ADDITIONAL READINGS

Balderhahn, Edward I., R. Mothat, and M. Schader. *Classification: Data Analysis and Data Highways.* New York: Springer-Verlag, 1998.

Bertaux, Daniel, and Paul Thompson. *International Handbook of Oral History and Life Stories,* Vol. 2. New York: Oxford University Press, 1993.

Bloch, Marc. *The Historian's Craft.* New York: McGraw-Hill, 1992. Originally published 1964.

Bouchard, J. T. "Unobtrusive Measures: An Inventory of Uses," *Sociological Methods and Research,* 4 (1976): 267–300.

Davis, James A., and Tom W. Smith. *General Social Surveys: Cumulative Codebook.* Chicago: National Opinion Research Center, 1996.

Denzin, Norman K. *Interpretive Ethnography.* London: Sage, 1996.

Felson, M. "Unobtrusive Indicators of Cultural Change: Neckties, Girdles, Marijuana, Garbage, Magazines, and Urban Sprawl," *American Behavioral Scientist,* 26 (1983): 534–542.

Hakim, Catherine. *Research Design: Strategies and Choices in the Design of Social Research.* New York: Routledge, Chapman & Hall, 1987.

Jacob, Herbert. *Using Published Data: Errors and Remedies.* Thousand Oaks, CA: Sage, 1984.

Krippendorff, Klaus. *Content Analysis: An Introduction to Its Methodology.* Thousand Oaks, CA: Sage, 1980.

Krippendorff, Klaus. *Information Theory: Structural Models for Qualitative Data.* London: Sage, 1986.

Muller, Nathan J. *Desktop Encyclopedia of the Internet: Internet Technology.* Norwood, MA: Artech House, 1998.

Stewart, David W., and Michael A. Kamins. *Secondary Research: Information Sources and Methods,* 2d ed. Thousand Oaks, CA: Sage, 1993.

Toulouse, Chris, and Timothy W. Luke. *The Politics of Cyberspace.* New York: Routledge, 1998.

Weber, Robert P. *Basic Content Analysis.* Thousand Oaks, CA: Sage, 1990.

Data Preparation and Analysis

It took the U.S. Census Bureau almost seven years to hand tally and tabulate the data collected for the 10th census, the census of 1880. By the time this work was completed 10 years later, the information was almost too obsolete to be used for apportioning taxes and political representation. It was obvious that the Census Bureau had to develop new techniques to allow for a more timely counting of the American population. Herman Hollerith, an employee of the Bureau, invented an electric tabulating machine that, in 1890—the 11th decennial census—permitted the data to be tabulated in two and a half years. Hollerith's machine "tallied items by causing an electrical current to trigger simple clock-like counting devices. When an electrical current flowed through a hole punched into non-conducting paper strips, a counter was activated by an electromagnet." [1]

As the Census Bureau prepared for the 22nd census conducted in the year 2000, Hollerith's electric tabulating machine seemed like a relic from the ancient past. For instance, Hollerith's machine processed 10,000 to 20,000 data cards per day during the 1890 census; the Census Bureau's mainframe computers currently can tabulate 1 million data items per minute. As this story illustrates, methods of data preparation and analysis have improved substantially since the days of the 1890 census.

•| **IN THIS CHAPTER** we examine common contemporary methods of preparing and coding data. We discuss deductive coding—in which researchers derive codes from theory—as well as inductive coding—in which researchers identify categories from data—and provide rules for coding and codebook construction. We address the issue of coding reliability and discuss methods researchers can use to increase reliability. Finally, we describe various coding devices and the use of computers in storing, processing, accessing, and analyzing data sets.

Today, data collected for analysis is almost always coded, stored, retrieved, and analyzed using computerized systems. Whether you are comfortable using a personal computer, minicomputer, or mainframe, the logic of the data handling and management is similar. The purpose of this chapter is to acquaint students with common methods of preparing data for coding and codebook construction. When researchers assign numeric codes to their data, they increase their ability to use computers to retrieve and analyze data.|

CODING SCHEMES   •

As you learned in Chapter 6, measurement consists of devising a system for assigning numbers to observations. These assignments may be purely arbitrary (as they are for nominal-level variables), or they may reflect the ranking of ordinal or interval variables. The number assigned to an observation is called a **code**. This code should be consistent across cases or units of analysis when the same condition exists. For example, if a code of 1 means "female," the variable associated with gender should be coded as 1 for each female. Information on what a code means should be listed in a codebook that accompanies the data set. This section describes the process by which researchers assign codes to observations.

---

1. George E. Biles, Alfred A. Bolton, and Bernadette DiRe, "Herman Hollerith: Inventor, Manager, Entrepreneur—A Centennial Remembrance," *The Journal of Management*, 15 (1989): 603–615.

Researchers can also use codes to group various classifications of a concept. Suppose that an investigator has gathered information on the occupations of several hundred individuals. The following are examples of the occupations listed:

Lawyer	*Practical nurse*
Barber	*Migrant farm laborer*
Carpenter	*Executive*
Broker	*Engineer*
Elevator operator	*Electrician*
Veterinarian	*Advertising agent*

Before these data can be analyzed, the researcher needs to organize the occupations into categories. The following is one acceptable way to classify occupations into categories:

1. *Professional and managerial:* lawyer, veterinarian, executive, engineer
2. *Technical and sales:* advertising agent, broker
3. *Service and skilled labor:* barber, elevator operator, practical nurse, electrician, carpenter
4. *Unskilled labor:* migrant farm worker

This system categorizes occupations according to the level of income, prestige, and education that they have in common, and permits the researcher to use four well-defined categories in his or her analysis rather than several dozen specific occupations. Systems of categories such as this one, used to classify responses or acts that relate to a single item or variable, are referred to as **coding schemes.** The principles involved in constructing such schemes are discussed in the following sections.

Rules of Coding

Since coding is the process by which responses are classified into meaningful categories, the initial rule of coding is that the numbers assigned must make intuitive sense. For example, higher scores on a variable should be assigned higher codes than lower scores. This is most easily demonstrated with interval-level variables. A person who is older than another should receive a higher code on age. Intuitively, a 28-year-old person would receive an age code of 28. A person who is 46 years old should receive a code higher than the one for the 28-year-old—probably 46 if coded in years. Even if age categories are grouped ordinally, a higher age should be associated with a higher grouping code. That makes intuitive sense.

However, for some variables (nominal ones), by definition there is no intuitively pleasing rationale for assigning numbers. Someone with a gender of 2 ("female") does not have more gender than one with 1 ("male"). Moreover, it would not make any difference whether you assigned the numbers 6 and 4, respectively, or even 4 and 6. However, in order to maintain the reliability of your coding, you would probably want to confine coding numbers to those starting with 0 or 1 and increasing by 1 over each category. Sequentially numbering the categories starting at 0 or 1 helps to minimize the risk of miscoding (see "Editing and Cleaning the Data" later on).

THEORY AND DEDUCTIVE CODING. A researcher's intuition is one of several factors involved in coding decisions; theory, mutual exclusively, exhaustiveness, and detail must also be considered. Researchers who engage in quantitative analysis generally test hypotheses derived from theory, and the coding system they use should be linked to the theory they hope to support or falsify. An examination of the theory will provide the researchers with an idea of the types of responses they may expect from respondents. Many issues are multidimensional and require a separate category for each dimension. For example, a researcher interested in examining "liberalism" would learn from theory that this concept is multidimensional. A person who is a social liberal (e.g., one who believes in a woman's right to birth choice) may not be a fiscal liberal (e.g., the same person does not believe that the government should fund contraception). In this case, a high score on social liberalism does not correlate with a high score on fiscal liberalism. The researcher would have to provide categories for both social and fiscal liberalism.

The actual categories the researcher develops must be mutually exclusive and exhaustive. That is, each response should clearly fall into only one category (mutually exclusive), and every response must fall into a category (exhaustive). Researchers must also ensure that the categories they choose are not so broad that important differences are obscured (detail).

MUTUAL EXCLUSIVITY.   Under the rule of **mutual exclusivity,** the coding categories for each variable must be designed so that each case or unit of analysis can be coded into one and only one category of the variable. For example, consider the following categories designed to determine the living arrangements of students:

1. Live in dormitory
2. Live with parent(s)
3. Live off campus
4. Live with spouse

These categories are not mutually exclusive because students who live with their parent(s) most likely also live off campus, and students who live with a spouse might live either in a dormitory or off campus. Respondents could not be sure which category they should mark, and people with the same living arrangement might choose different categories. The purpose of the research and the theory from which the research question is derived can clarify the categories we choose. If we are interested in learning whether students in supervised, semisupervised, and unsupervised living arrangements differ in academic performance, we might use these categories:

1. Live with parent(s) (supervised)
2. Live in dormitory (semisupervised)
3. Live off campus either alone, with friends, or with spouse (unsupervised)

EXHAUSTIVENESS.   The rule of **exhaustiveness** dictates that the enumeration of categories is sufficient to exhaust all the relevant categories expected of respondents—each and every response or behavior can be classified without a substantial number being classified as "other." Theory and knowledge about the expected sample can help the researcher to determine exhaustiveness. An example of a lack of exhaustiveness is the common classification of marital status into four categories only: "married," "single," "divorced," and "widowed." Since respondents who are "living together" but not legally married would not fit into the coding scheme, the requirement of exhaustiveness is violated. If the sample included only junior high school students, not only would the original coding scheme be exhaustive, it would also be irrelevant (the variable would be a constant), since virtually all junior high school students are unmarried.

DETAIL. The **detail** of categories in a coding scheme depends on the research question, but some general guidelines exist. First, when in doubt, add another category. You can always collapse categories to generalize responses (see Appendix A for examples of how to do this with the statistical computer package SPSS); you cannot, however, disaggregate responses coded to a more general level. Second, the theory and your knowledge of the subject matter and sample should all guide the level of detail of the categories. It would make no sense to ask medical doctors to report their incomes in the categories under $5,000, $5,000 to $10,000, $10,000 to $15,000, $15,000 to $20,000, and $20,000 and above, whereas those distinctions would be appropriate when surveying people living in poverty.

  Deductive coding allows researchers to use theory to construct response categories before they administer the instrument to respondents. Researchers using deductive coding often pretest the instrument on a small sample of the population of interest so they can modify the categories suggested by theory to fit the specific population. Closed-ended questions are an example of precoding in which responses are classified directly into categories.

INDUCTIVE CODING. When a study is exploratory or when there is little theory informing the researcher about the kind of responses to expect, **inductive coding** may be appropriate. In inductive coding, the researcher designs the coding scheme on the basis of a representative sample of responses to questions (particularly open-ended questions), data from documents, or data collected through participant observation (see Chapter 12). Once the researcher has identified a coding scheme, it is applied to the remainder of the data set. Consider the responses to the following question, designed to determine women's reactions to being abused by a husband or a live-in partner.[2]

> In general, if a man physically abuses his wife or live-in partner, what do you think the woman should do?
>
> **1.** She should stay and try to work out the problem.
> **2.** She should leave the house or apartment.
> **3.** She should call a social service agency for advice.
> **4.** She should call the police.
> **5.** She should obtain a temporary restraining order against the abuser.
> **6.** She should call a friend or relative for help.
> **7.** Other (specify) _____
> **8.** Don't know/refused to answer.
> **9.** Missing.

  In an inductive coding scheme, the responses mentioned most frequently are included in the coding scheme used to analyze the data. In the preceding example, values 1 through 6 were mentioned frequently enough to merit their own categories. Values 7 through 9 were added once the inductive approach generated the first categories. In the final coding scheme, the researcher will use the "other" category for less frequently mentioned responses.

  Categories are not always easily identified, and a comprehensive coding scheme can take a long time to construct. The researchers' time is spent switching back and forth between the raw data and the evolving scheme until the categories are applicable to and tied in with the general purpose of the study. Paul Lazarsfeld and Alan Barton, examining

---

2. Adapted from *Spouse Abuse in Texas: A Study of Women's Attitudes and Experiences* (Huntsville, TX: Criminal Justice Center, 1983).

Table 14.1

How Norms Bear on Individual Behavior in Combat

Underlying Source of Norms	Channels
	Direct
	(a) Formal sanctions
	(b) Internal sanctions
Norms of formal authorities	*Via group norms:*
	(c) Informal group sanctions
	(d) Internal sanctions
Norms of informal groups	(e) Formal group sanctions
	(f) Internal sanctions
Individual norms	(g) Internal sanctions

From Paul F. Lazarsfeld and Alan Barton, "Qualitative Measurements in the Social Sciences: Classification, Typologies, and Indices," in *The Policy Sciences,* ed. Daniel Lerner and Harold D. Lasswell (Stanford, CA: Stanford University Press, 1951), p. 161. Reprinted with permission.

some general principles of coding, illustrate this process by using some of the coding schemes constructed in the classic study *The American Soldier.*[3] In an attempt to determine which factors offset combat stress, the researchers who were investigating the American soldier drew up a preliminary list of categories on the basis of many responses:

1. Coercive formal authority
2. Leadership practices (e.g., encouragement)
3. Informal group:
   a. Affectional support
   b. Code of behavior
   c. Provision of realistic security and power
4. Convictions about the war and the enemy
5. Desire to complete the job by winning war, to go home
6. Prayer and personal philosophies

These preliminary coding schemes enabled the investigators in this study to classify the raw data and substantially reduce the number of responses to be analyzed. The investigators introduced a further modification after they noted that formal sanctions are often more effective when channeled through informal group sanctions and internal sanctions. Conversely, the norms of the informal groups are influenced by formal sanctions as well as by individual conscience. On this basis, the researchers reanalyzed the responses and obtained additional information to produce a modified coding scheme (Table 14.1).

3. Paul F. Lazarsfeld and Alan Barton, "Qualitative Measurement in the Social Sciences: Classification, Typologies, and Indices," in *The Policy Sciences,* ed. Daniel Lerner and Harold D. Lasswell (Stanford, CA: Stanford University Press, 1951), p. 160, and Samuel A. Stouffer, *The American Soldier* (New York: Wiley, 1965).

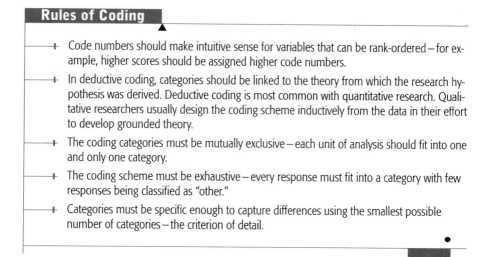

Rules of Coding

- Code numbers should make intuitive sense for variables that can be rank-ordered – for example, higher scores should be assigned higher code numbers.

- In deductive coding, categories should be linked to the theory from which the research hypothesis was derived. Deductive coding is most common with quantitative research. Qualitative researchers usually design the coding scheme inductively from the data in their effort to develop grounded theory.

- The coding categories must be mutually exclusive – each unit of analysis should fit into one and only one category.

- The coding scheme must be exhaustive – every response must fit into a category with few responses being classified as "other."

- Categories must be specific enough to capture differences using the smallest possible number of categories – the criterion of detail.

The following responses conform to the modified categories found in Table 14.1:

(a) I fight because I'll be punished if I quit.

(b) I fight because it's my duty to my country, the army, the government; it would be wrong for me to quit.

(c) I fight because I'll lose the respect of my buddies if I quit.

(d) I fight because it would be wrong to let my buddies down.

(e) You have to look out for your buddies even if it means violating orders, or they won't look out for you.

(f) You have to look out for your buddies even if it means violating orders because it would be wrong to leave them behind.

(g) I am fighting because I believe in democracy and hate fascism.

The chief advantages of the inductive approach are its flexibility and its richness, which enable the researcher to generate explanations from the findings. Moreover, it allows researchers to apply a variety of coding schemes to the same observation, and it often suggests new categories as well. The shortcoming of this method is that researchers may be bogged down by the mass of details as they try to explain the data. Sometimes too little context is preserved for the coder to determine which details are trivial and can therefore be eliminated.

CODEBOOK CONSTRUCTION ●

Once you have developed a coding scheme for each of the variables in a research project, you should compile this information in a **codebook.** Codebooks vary in their detail; however, all good codebooks contain information regarding each variable's name or number, the coding scheme, and codes for missing data. The codebook serves as a guide for the coders who will translate the raw data onto an input device for later use in computerized statistical analysis. It is also a reference for the principal researcher and any

EXHIBIT 14.1

A CODEBOOK FORMAT: THE GENERAL SOCIAL SURVEY

Variable Name	Question Content	Column Numbers
ABANY	Abortion if woman wants it for any reason	4
	1 Yes	
	2 No	
	8 Don't know	
	9 No answer	
	0 Not applicable	
ATTEND	How often R attends religious services	5
	0 Never	
	1 Less than once a year	
	2 About once or twice a year	
	3 Several times a year	
	4 About once a month	
	5 2–3 times a month	
	6 Nearly every week	
	7 Every week	
	8 Several times a week	
	9 Don't know, no answer	
DEGREE	Respondent's degree	6
	0 Less than high school	
	1 High school	
	2 Associate/junior college	
	3 Bachelor's	
	4 Graduate	
	8 Don't know	
	9 No answer	
FEWORK	Should women work	7
	1 Approve	
	2 Disapprove	
	8 Don't know	
	9 No answer	
	0 Not applicable	

Adapted from the General Social Survey, 1996.

other researchers who wish to use the data set. For research involving the use of surveys, the actual survey question is often included in the codebook. A subset of a codebook used in the 1996 General Social Survey is reproduced in Exhibit 14.1.

Note that each variable in Exhibit 14.1 is identified by its name (e.g., ABANY), brief question content, the coding scheme employed (values), column numbers, which values stand for a missing value, and any other special coding rules employed on a variable-by-variable basis. Statistical computer programs arrange data in spreadsheet form. The variables are arrayed in the columns and the cases in the rows. Each column number in Exhibit 14.1 tells any researcher interested in using the data set which columns contain the values for specific variables. From the information contained in the code-book, any researcher should be able to reconstruct the data set.

Coding Reliability and Data Entry Devices

Once the researcher has constructed the codebook, the data need to be "coded" or transferred to a form from which someone can enter them into a statistical computer program for storage and analysis. For instance, someone must translate a circled number on a questionnaire to the proper column or "field" represented by the variable (and de-fined in the codebook). The coder may be the researcher himself or herself or may be a hired or student research assistant. Raw data can be coded in a number of ways to facili-tate efficient computer entry.

Coding Reliability

Studies with a well-constructed codebook, precoded and closed-ended questions, and proper coder training are prone to fewer problems with coder reliability than other stud-ies, all things being equal, because coders do not have to exercise their own judgment in deciding what code to give a response. One of the biggest problems in these studies is making sure that the coders place the code in the correct column. It is standard practice to recheck or verify a sample of each coder's work to ensure that he or she has not been lax. The coding devices we will discuss demonstrate the trade-offs for coder relia-bility based on choice of device.

Coders are required to exercise more judgment in classifying responses when they are coding open-ended questions or other nonstructured material. When the rules for classifying responses do not clearly apply to a specific response, different coders may classify the same response differently. In such instances, the coding process becomes unreliable, a problem that is just as serious as the unreliability of interviewers or ob-servers. Indeed, very often the coding phase of data analysis contributes the largest com-ponent of error. To increase coding reliability, researchers need to keep the schemes as simple as possible and train coders thoroughly. The simplest solution is to compare the codings of two or more coders and resolve all differences by letting them decide on problematic items.

Discrepancies can occur in the way coders and respondents interpret the meaning of a given response. This problem is discussed in the literature much less frequently, but was addressed by Kenneth Kammeyer and Julius Roth in a study that attempted to as-sess whether respondent and coder would agree on the meaning of a response.[4]

In other words, how would the research participants themselves code their answers within the set of categories provided by the researcher? If the research participants who provide the responses could also serve as coders, would their code differ from that of other coders, or would the research participants code their own responses as they are coded by others? Kammeyer and Roth asked 64 college students to complete a ques-tionnaire that included fixed-alternative questions as well as open-ended ones. Later, every research participant independently coded the questionnaires of several other par-ticipants as well as his or her own. The researchers then compared each participant's coding of his or her own response with the way that response was coded by others. The comparison revealed that coders often interpreted responses differently than research

4. Kenneth C. W. Kammeyer and Julius A. Roth, "Coding Response to Open-ended Questions," in *Sociological Methodology*, ed. Herbert L. Costner (San Francisco: Jossey-Bass, 1971).

participants, which resulted in a misrepresentation of the research participants' actual attitudes. The direction of the deviation was determined by the content of the item. The less structured the item, the larger was the discrepancy between a respondent's interpretation and that of a coder. These findings raise some serious doubts regarding the process of coding nonstructured material. It is clear that such bias might distort the findings about the relationships between the variables the researcher is investigating.

Coding Devices

TRANSFER SHEETS. Years ago, all data were keypunched onto computer cards and read into the computer. Coders used *transfer sheets,* which were paper representations of the keypunch card, to record data in the columns specified by the codebook, and keypunchers then transferred the data to the cards. Although such cards are no longer used, researchers may still use a version of the transfer sheet when dealing with complex questionnaires or when gathering data from a number of sources. Coders can use spreadsheet forms to organize cases in the rows and values of the variables across the columns. Most statistical programs require that data be arranged in this manner, and data entry personnel can quickly key in each line from the spreadsheet. However, the use of any kind of transfer sheet requires multiple handling of the data, which increases the possibility of miscodings and threatens reliability.

EDGE CODING. The use of **edge coding** is one way researchers have eliminated the need for transfer sheets. In this method, coders transfer questionnaire information directly onto spaces at the outside edge of the instrument. Note that in Figure 14.1 the column numbers associated with each variable are indicated on the right edge of the form. When the instrument has been edge-coded, a data entry worker can key the information from the edge directly to the data storage device. Reliability is enhanced because the coders' eyes do not have to leave the instrument, and they do not have to keep close track of column positions, as is the case with transfer sheets.

DIRECT DATA ENTRY. Perhaps the most important innovations in coding have come from **direct data entry.** There are two forms of direct data coding: coding from a questionnaire and coding by telephone interview. Both forms are based on computer programs that display each questionnaire item on a screen and prompt the coder or interviewer to key in the response to the question displayed.

Material coded from questionnaires must be edited to ensure that missing responses have a designated code for the input. The coder then keys in the response. When a case is completed, the computer program adds the information directly into the raw data file. Again, this method reduces the number of data handlers, which enhances reliability.

Computer-assisted telephone interviewing (CATI) is a highly sophisticated system that greatly reduces miscoding. Interviewers read questionnaire items directly to respondents from the computer screen and input responses as they are given. If the coder keys in an inappropriate code (a value that is not designated for the particular variable), the coder is prompted to give a "real" value. CATI also automatically skips questions or jumps to others as a result of filter questions, and interviewers do not have to flip through screens to access the appropriate next item. Therefore, not only does the program increase coder reliability, it also ensures that respondents do not answer inappropriate questions. Because improvements in CATI technology have resulted in high response rates, ease of implementation and use, and increased reliability of data collection and coding, CATI has sharply reduced the use of mail surveys.

Figure 14.1

An Edge-Coded Questionnaire

FOR PROJECT USE ONLY

THE UNIVERSITY OF WISCONSIN—MILWAUKEE
College of Letters and Science
Department of Political Science

№ 2183

Civil Libertarian Project

INSTRUCTIONS: For each of the following questions please mark the answer that comes closest to the way you feel about the issue. There are no "right" or "wrong" answers — please answer the questions as honestly as possible. Answer each of the questions in the order in which it appears. If you wish to make additional comments on any of the specific questions or on the issues in general, use the space at the end of the questionnaire. Your opinions are extremely important for understanding these complex civil liberty issues — we greatly appreciate your cooperation!

We would like to begin with a few questions about your relationship with the American Civil Liberties Union (ACLU).

6 __1__

1a. About how many years have you been a member of ACLU? _____ years.

7 __ 8 __

1b. Why did you join the ACLU? That is, was there any particular cause that the ACLU was supporting or defending that prompted you to join the organization?
- ☐ Specific cause(s) — – → Which cause(s) _____
- ☐ No specific cause
- ☐ Don't remember

9 ___

1c. Have you been very active in the affairs of the ACLU? For instance, have you done any of the following in the last five years?

	Yes	No	Don't Remember	
a. made financial contributions (beyond membership dues)	☐	☐	☐	10 ___
b. written letters to ACLU leaders	☐	☐	☐	11 ___
c. served in a leadership role	☐	☐	☐	12 ___
d. attended local meetings of ACLU	☐	☐	☐	13 ___
e. read ACLU newsletters and literature	☐	☐	☐	14 ___
f. written letters to public officials at the urging of ACLU	☐	☐	☐	15 ___
g. attended an ACLU party or benefit	☐	☐	☐	16 ___
h. done volunteer work for ACLU (e.g., office assistance, phone calling, etc.)	☐	☐	☐	17 ___
i. participated in a court case or public hearing at the urging of ACLU	☐	☐	☐	18 ___

1d. The ACLU publishes a number of specialized newsletters and magazines that not all of the members receive. We would like to know if you have received any of these publications and, if so, how frequently you found the time to read them. For each of the following please check the most appropriate box.

	I have not received this publication	I received the publica- tion and usually read it	I received the publica- tion but rarely had time to read it	Don't Know	
a. Civil Liberties Review	☐	☐	☐	☐	19 ___
b. Children's Rights Report	☐	☐	☐	☐	20 ___
c. First Principles	☐	☐	☐	☐	21 ___
d. Notes from the Women's Rights Project	☐	☐	☐	☐	22 ___
e. Civil Liberties Alert	☐	☐	☐	☐	23 ___
f. The Privacy Report	☐	☐	☐	☐	24 ___
g. Civil Liberties	☐	☐	☐	☐	25 ___

1e. Over the course of your membership, how satisfied have you been, in general, with the positions ACLU has taken on major issues?
- ☐ always in agreement   ☐ usually in disagreement   ☐ don't know
- ☐ usually in agreement   ☐ always in disagreement

26 ___

2a. There are always some people whose ideas are considered bad or dangerous by other people. For instance, somebody who is against all churches and religion.

	Yes	No	No Opinion	
a. If such a person wanted to make a speech in your community against churches and religion, should he/she be allowed to speak or not?	☐	☐	☐	27 ___
b. Should such a person be allowed to organize a march against churches and religion in your community?	☐	☐	☐	28 ___
c. Should such a person be allowed to teach in a college or university, or not?	☐	☐	☐	29 ___
d. If some people in your community suggested that a book he/she wrote against churches and religion should be taken out of your public library, would you favor removing the book, or not?	☐	☐	☐	30 ___

Source: Reprinted by permission of Greenwood Publishing Group, Inc., Westport, CT, from *Civil Liberties and the Nazis* by James L. Gibson and Richard D. Bingham. Copyright © 1985, Praeger Publishers, New York, NY.

Editing and Cleaning the Data

Editing and cleaning the data are important steps in data processing that should always precede analysis of the collected information. **Data editing** occurs both during and after the coding phase. Coders perform some editing by checking for errors and omissions and by making sure that all interview schedules have been completed as required. Most of the editing, however, especially in large-scale surveys, is performed by a supervisor who reviews each completed questionnaire to evaluate the interviews' reliability and check for inconsistencies in responses. For example, the National Opinion Research Center, which conducts the General Social Survey, instructs supervisors to check that all filter (contingency) questions have been marked correctly so that the data will fit into the correct skip (or "go to") pattern. If more than one response is given to the filter question or if the filter question was left blank, the supervisor will determine what the code should be.

Data cleaning is the proofreading of the data to catch and correct errors and inconsistent codes. Computers perform most of the data cleaning for large-scale efforts using software designed to test for logical consistency in the coding specification.[5] Though many questions are answered and coded independently, others are interconnected and must be internally consistent. For example, if a respondent has no children, all questions relating to children must be coded NA ("no answer") or left blank. Similarly, an error is indicated if a respondent reporting her age as five years old also responds that she has two children.

Another function of data cleaning is checking for wild codes. For example, the question "Do you believe there is a life after death?" may have legitimate codes of 1 for "yes," 2 for "no," 8 for "undecided," and 9 for "no answer." Any code other than these four would be considered illegitimate. The simplest procedure to check for wild codes is to generate a frequency distribution (discussed in Chapter 15) for each variable. This method of data cleaning is also outlined in Appendix A.

USING COMPUTERS IN SOCIAL SCIENCE RESEARCH   ●

By now everyone is affected by and familiar with the use of computers in many facets of life, and computers have been used in social science research for decades. Computer technology has changed drastically over time, but the rationale for the use of computers in research has remained the same across the years. Computers are simply tools that help us to store, process, access, and analyze data sets more quickly and easily. Once we understand the research methods and statistics discussed in this book, we can let a computer calculate the statistics and provide printouts of the results. However, it is up to the researcher to supply correct and reliable data, choose statistics that are appropriate for the level of data, and interpret the results properly.

Types of Computers

Researchers use two basic kinds of computers to analyze social science data: mainframes and personal computers (PCs). Mainframe computers are large central-site computers that handle the computing needs of many users simultaneously. Users tend to "time-share" the capacity of the central processing unit so that the greatest number of users can access the computer at any given time. Mainframe sites also tend to have the capacity for reading magnetic data tapes sent by data repositories to members or clients. The Inter-

---

5. For example, Winona Ailkins, *EDIT: The NORC Cleaning Program: A Program to Develop Sequential Files* (Chicago: National Opinion Research Center, 1975).

university Consortium for Political and Social Research at the University of Michigan is the largest repository for social science data. Besides storing academic research, it holds the data sets from national opinion firms such as Roper, Harris, and the National Opinion Research Center (NORC), which form the basis for many research projects. Because mainframes also support the major statistical packages used to analyze social science data, individual researchers and students do not have to purchase multiple software packages.

In response to the increasing affordability and use of personal computers, the major statistical software manufacturers have developed PC versions of the mainframe software researchers have used for years. For example, the Statistical Package for the Social Sciences (SPSS) (described in Appendix A) has a PC version. Manufacturers have also developed and marketed statistical packages designed specifically for use on personal computers. Since data can be transferred between most of the statistical packages, researchers using PCs can choose to purchase the package with which they are most familiar or that they can best afford.

SUMMARY

1. Data processing is a link between data collection and data analysis whereby observations are transformed into codes that are amenable to analysis. At the first stage of data processing, researchers classify numerous individual observations into a smaller number of categories to simplify the description and analysis of the data. Such systems are referred to as coding schemes.

2. Coding schemes must be linked to theory and the problem under study, which dictates the categories to be included. Other requirements of a coding scheme are that it be both exhaustive and mutually exclusive so that all observations can be classified and each observation falls into only one category. Researchers use coding schemes to translate data into a format that allows computer processing. The translation is usually guided by a codebook, which presents the schemes with their assigned values together with coding instructions.

3. A variety of coding devices may be used to organize the raw data. These include edge coding and direct data entry. The choice of method depends on the format of the research and the technology available to the researcher. Each method has implications for coding reliability. In general, the fewer times the data are transferred, the greater the reliability. Computer-assisted telephone interviewing (CATI) provides high reliability because responses are recorded directly into the computer as the questions are asked.

4. Social scientists have been using computers to organize the research process for many years. Technology is rapidly changing in this area, and now students are able to use personal computers to analyze data.

KEY TERMS FOR REVIEW

code (p. 304)
codebook (p. 309)
coding scheme (p. 305)
data cleaning (p. 314)
data editing (p. 314)
deductive coding (p. 307)

detail (p. 307)
direct data entry (p. 312)
edge coding (p. 312)
exhaustiveness (p. 306)
inductive coding (p. 307)
mutual exclusivity (p. 306)

STUDY QUESTIONS

1. Discuss the differences between inductive and deductive coding schemes.
2. What are the main criteria of coding schemes?
3. Describe the steps involved in determining coding reliability.
4. What are the different types of data processing?

SPSS PROBLEMS

1. The data reported below show the "ID Number," "percentage of children in extreme poverty," and "juvenile arrest rates for 25 states." Use the SPSS data editor to input these data. Assign numerical codes for "State." Use the **Define Variables** procedure to name your variables and provide value labels as needed. Run **Frequencies** on all variables and clean the data set, checking for coding errors. Save your data set.

ID NUMBER	STATE	% of CHILDREN IN POVERTY	JUVENILE ARREST RATE (per 100,000)
001	AL	10.1	209
002	AK	3.7	250
003	AZ	9.6	522
004	AR	11.8	274
005	CA	6.2	634
006	CO	7.3	518
007	DE	5.9	430
008	DC	21.7	1,487
009	GA	11.8	345
010	HI	3.6	241
011	IL	11.3	376
012	IA	4.7	186
013	KS	5.2	346
014	LA	20.5	552
015	ME	6.9	108
016	MA	5.5	559
017	MN	6.7	250
018	MO	9.2	539
019	NE	6.5	129
020	NH	4.7	102
021	NM	10.9	358
022	NY	10.7	1,025
023	ND	7.4	64
024	VT	4.0	49

Source: "Kids Count Data Book," The Annie E. Casey Foundation, 1992.

ADDITIONAL READINGS

Bryman, Alan, and Duncan Cramer. *Quantitative Data Analysis for Social Scientists*. New York: Routledge, 1994.

Dey, Ian. *Qualitative Data Analysis: A User Friendly Guide for Social Scientists*. New York: Routledge, 1993.

Shermis, Mark D. *Using Microcomputers in Social Science Research*. Boston: Allyn & Bacon, 1991.

The Univariate Distribution

How does economic change in a society shape women's lives? Following World War II, as the result of a joint effort between the governments of Puerto Rico and the United States, Puerto Rico was industrialized. The transformation from an agricultural to a low-wage service and manufacturing economy increased the demand for women's labor while decreasing the demand for men. Recently, researchers Barbara Zsembik and Chuck Peek examined possible reasons why married Puerto Rican women increasingly return to the paid workforce within 12 months of the birth of their first child.[1] They noted that since 1950, Puerto Rican women have increased their investment in formal education and training, which has resulted in higher costs for women who leave the workforce to raise children.

To determine whether the investments in the form of education differ between men and women, the researchers compared the average educational level of men and women by computing the mean years of formal education for each. They found that, on the average, women completed 11.74 years of formal schooling, and men completed 11.84 years of school; thus Puerto Rican men and women appear to invest equally in education. To determine whether these nearly equal means were the result of similar distributions, the researchers computed the standard deviations—which show how widely scores are dispersed from the mean—for the distributions. The standard deviation was 3.69 for women and 3.71 for men, showing that the distributions were also similar.

•| **IN THIS CHAPTER** we explain the main characteristics of single-variable, or univariate, distributions. First we define and describe frequency distributions, which researchers use to organize their data for statistical analysis. Then we focus on measures of central tendency and measures of dispersion, which can be used to describe distributions. Finally, we deal with the general form of distributions, emphasizing the normal curve.

Since the 1950s, all social science disciplines have experienced a rapid increase in the use of statistics, and they have become essential to the field. Without statistics, we could not see the patterns and regularities in the phenomena we study. We need statistical methods to organize data, to display information in a meaningful manner, and to describe and interpret the observations in terms that will help us evaluate our hypotheses.

The word *statistics* has a dual meaning. Although it is used to refer to numbers—per-capita income, batting averages, and the like—it is also a field of study. We refer to the latter usage in our discussion, which will cover some of the basic applications of statistics in the social sciences. |

THE ROLE OF STATISTICS •

The field of statistics involves methods for describing and analyzing data and for making decisions or inferences about phenomena represented by the data. Methods in the first category are referred to as *descriptive statistics;* methods in the second category are called *inferential statistics.*

---

1. Barbara A. Zsembik and Chuck W. Peek, "The Effect of Economic Restructuring on Puerto Rican Women's Labor Force Participation in the Formal Sector," *Gender & Society,* 8(4) (1994): 525–540.

Descriptive statistics enable researchers to summarize and organize data in an effective and meaningful way. They provide tools for describing collections of statistical observations and reducing information to an understandable form.

Inferential statistics allow researchers to make decisions or inferences by interpreting data patterns. Researchers use inferential statistics to determine whether an expected pattern designated by the theory and hypotheses is actually found in the observations. We might hypothesize, for example, that blue-collar workers are politically more conservative than professionals. To decide whether this hypothesis is true, we might survey blue-collar workers and professionals, asking them about their political views. We would then use descriptive statistics to make comparisons between these groups, and we would employ inferential statistics to determine whether the differences between the groups support our expectations.

Both descriptive and inferential statistics help social scientists develop explanations for complex social phenomena that deal with relationships between variables. Statistics provides the tools to analyze, represent, and interpret those relationships.

FREQUENCY DISTRIBUTIONS ●

After data have been coded and prepared for processing, they are ready for analysis. The researcher's first task is to construct frequency distributions to examine the pattern of response to each of the independent and dependent variables under investigation. (In the following discussion, *responses, answers, observations, cases, acts,* and *behavior* are used interchangeably.) A frequency distribution of a single variable, known as a *univariate frequency distribution,* is a table that shows the frequency of observations in each category of a variable. For example, to examine the pattern of response to the variable "religious affiliation," a researcher would describe the number of respondents who claimed they were Protestants, Catholics, Jews, Muslims, and so on.

To construct a **frequency distribution,** the researcher simply lists the categories of the variable and counts the number of observations in each. Table 15.1 shows the frequency distribution of the variable "feelings about the Bible" included in the 1996 General Social Survey (GSS). The table has five rows, the first four listing the categories of the variable "feelings about the Bible" in the left-hand column. The right-hand column shows the number of observations in each category. This number is called a *frequency,* and is usually denoted by the letter *f*. The last row (marked *Total*) is the total of all the frequencies appearing in the table. Table 15.1 shows that in 1996, the majority (500) of a rep-

▌ Table 15.1

Feelings About the Bible

The Bible Is	Frequency (*f*)
Word of God	291
Inspired word	500
Book of fables	159
Other	4
Total (*N*)	954

Source: General Social Survey, 1996.

Table 15.2

Should Government Assist Low-Income Students?

Should Government Assist Low-Income Students?	Frequency (f)
Definitely should	145
Probably should	219
Probably should not	44
Definitely should not	14
Total (N)	422

Source: General Social Survey, 1996.

resentative national sample of 954 reported that they believed the Bible was "inspired word," 291 said it was the "word of God," and only 159 respondents believed the Bible was a "book of fables." The final category, "other," includes 4 respondents who marked "other" as their feelings about the Bible.

The order in which the researcher lists the categories of the variable in the frequency distribution is determined by the level at which the data were measured. As we discussed in Chapter 7, there are four levels of data measurement—nominal, ordinal, interval, and ratio. At all levels the categories must be both exhaustive and mutually exclusive. At the nominal level the categories are simply names, which do not imply any kind of ranking. Gender, ethnicity, and religious preference are examples of nominal variables. The categories of ordinal-level variables may be ranked from highest to lowest or vice versa, but the categories do not reflect how much greater or smaller one level is in comparison to another. At the interval and ratio levels, the categories of the variable reflect both the rank of the categories and the magnitude of the difference between categories. The only difference between interval- and ratio-level variables is that ratio variables have a true zero point, which allows researchers to say, for example, that one category is twice as great as another.

With nominal variables, the researcher may list the categories in any order. Thus, for the variable "gender," either category—"male" or "female"—may be listed first. Similarly, "feelings about the Bible" in Table 15.1 is a nominal variable and thus its three categories do not have to be listed in any particular order. In contrast, because the categories of ordinal variables represent different rankings, they must be arranged in increasing or decreasing order. Consider the frequency distribution in Table 15.2, showing the responses of Americans to the question, "Should government assist low-income college students?" The responses to this question are ranked-ordered from "definitely should" to "definitely should not" and thus constitute an ordinal variable. Therefore the categories should be arranged in ascending or descending order.

Frequency Distributions with Interval or Ratio Variables

When a researcher is summarizing interval or ratio variables in frequency distributions, he or she must first decide on the number of categories to use and the cutting points between them. Because interval variables are ordinarily continuous, the classification into distinct categories may be quite arbitrary. For example, age may be classified into one-year, two-year, or five-year groups. Similarly, income can be classified in a number of ways.

Table 15.3

Age, by Decades

Age Category	Frequency (f)
18–19	13
20–29	199
30–39	226
40–49	218
50–59	139
60–69	87
70–79	62
80–89	33
Total (N)	977

Source: General Social Survey, 1996.

The intervals are usually of equal width, but the width depends on both the number of observations to be classified and the research purpose. The larger the number of observations, the wider the intervals become. However, wider categories also result in greater loss of detailed information. A general guideline to follow is that an interval should not be so wide that two measurements included in it have a difference between them that is considered important. For example, Table 15.3 is a grouped distribution of age arranged in decades for Americans who were surveyed by the National Opinion Research Center (NORC) in 1996.

Percentage Distributions

Summarizing the data by constructing frequency distributions of single variables is only the first step in data analysis. Next the researcher must convert the frequencies into measures that can be interpreted meaningfully. An absolute frequency is meaningless in itself; it must be compared with other frequencies. For instance, an investigator can assess the significance of 2,000 registered Democrats in one community only in relation to the number of all registered voters, to the number of registered Republicans, or to the number of registered Democrats in other communities.

To facilitate comparisons, researchers convert frequencies to *proportions* or *percentages*. You obtain a proportion by dividing the frequency of a category by the total number of responses in the distribution. When multiplied by 100, a proportion becomes a percentage. Proportions are usually expressed as f/N and percentages as $f/N \times 100$. Both proportions and percentages reflect the relative frequency of a specific category in the distribution. For example, the relative frequency of the response "the Bible is the word of God" in Table 15.1 is expressed by the proportion $291/954 = .305$ or by the percentage $(291/954)100 = 30.5$ percent. These figures indicate that about one of every three respondents interviewed in 1996 believed the Bible is the "word of God." Table 15.4 displays both the frequency and percentage distributions of the variable "feelings about the Bible."

Proportions and percentages permit the researcher to compare two or more frequency distributions. Note, for instance, that the social-class distributions of black and white

Table 15.4

Feelings About the Bible
(in Frequencies and Percentages)

The Bible Is	Frequency (f)	Percentage
Word of God	291	30.5
Inspired word	500	52.4
Book of fables	159	16.7
Other	4	0.4
Total (N)	954	100.0

Source: General Social Survey, 1996.

respondents in the 1996 General Social Survey. These distributions are displayed in Tables 15.5 and 15.6.

Although there are more working-class white respondents than black respondents (327 versus 90), a straightforward comparison of the absolute frequencies is misleading because the total number of responses (N) is different in each population. To assess the relative weight of the categories within each distribution, we need to convert the frequencies to percentages. The percentages reveal that the impression gained from the absolute frequencies was indeed misleading. The working class constitutes 62.1 percent of the black, compared with only 42.5 percent of the white, group. The new figures make it easier to compare the two frequency distributions.

USING GRAPHS TO DESCRIBE DISTRIBUTIONS   ●

Frequency distributions provide researchers with a way to communicate information about their data to other social scientists and, in some cases, to the public. However, some people find it difficult to read and understand numerical tables. Graphs provide researchers with an alternative method of displaying the information organized in frequency distributions. By using graphs to create a visual impression of the data, re-

Table 15.5

Social Class: Black Respondents

Social Class	Frequency (f)	Percentage
Lower class	12	8.3
Working class	90	62.1
Middle class	39	26.9
Upper class	4	2.8
Total (N)	145	100.0

Source: General Social Survey, 1996.

Table 15.6

Social Class: White Respondents

Social Class	Frequency (*f*)	Percentage
Lower class	25	3.2
Working class	327	42.5
Middle class	385	50.0
Upper class	33	4.3
Total (*N*)	770	100.0

Source: General Social Survey, 1996.

searchers can often communicate information more effectively. Three of the graphs researchers most commonly use are the pie chart, the bar chart, and the histogram. Both the pie chart and the bar chart can be used to present data measured at the nominal and ordinal levels. Researchers use the histogram to display data measured at interval or ratio levels.

The Pie Chart

The **pie chart** shows differences in frequencies or percentages among categories of nominal or ordinal variables by displaying the categories as segments of a circle. The segments are either differently shaded or differently patterned to differentiate among them, and they sum to either 100 percent or the total frequencies. While one pie chart can be used to represent a single distribution, researchers often use two or more pies to compare distributions. When you want to highlight some aspect of the data, you can move or "cut" one or more segments from the others to call attention to that aspect.

Table 15.7 displays percentage distributions of opinions of government spending on law enforcement and on education. The data in Table 15.7 show that people are more willing to support government spending on education (26.8 percent favor much more

Table 15.7

Opinion About Government Spending on Law Enforcement and Education

Government Should Spend:	On Law Enforcement (%)	On Education (%)
Much more	10.9	26.8
More	47.6	49.5
No change	32.7	18.5
Less	7.3	3.4
Much less	1.6	1.8
Total (*N*)	100 (441)	100 (444)

Source: General Social Survey, 1996.

Government Spending on Education

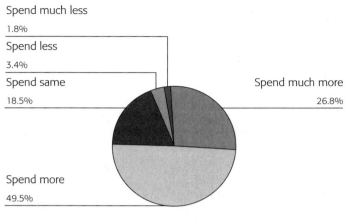

Spend much less
1.8%

Spend less
3.4%

Spend same
18.5%

Spend much more
26.8%

Spend more
49.5%

Source: General Social Survey, 1996.

spending and 49.5 percent favor more spending) than on law enforcement (10.9 percent favor much more spending and 47.6 percent favor more spending).

The pie charts shown in Figures 15.1 and 15.2 display the same information presented in Table 15.7. The pie charts allow you to see immediately the differences in levels of support, without going through the process of analyzing the percentage distribution.

Government Spending on Law Enforcement

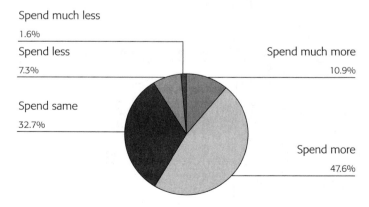

Spend much less
1.6%

Spend less
7.3%

Spend same
32.7%

Spend much more
10.9%

Spend more
47.6%

Source: General Social Survey, 1996.

Table 15.8

Preference in Hiring Blacks by Race of Respondent

Preference in Hiring Blacks	White (%)	Minority (%)
Strong support	4.8	31.8
Support	6.4	11.2
Oppose	27.6	23.5
Strongly oppose	61.2	33.5
Total (*N*)	100 (729)	100 (179)

Source: General Social Survey, 1996.

The Bar Chart

Like the pie chart, the **bar chart** provides researchers with a tool for displaying nominal or ordinal data. Unlike the pie chart, two or more distributions may be presented on a single bar chart. Bar charts are constructed by labeling the categories of the variable along the horizontal axis and drawing rectangles of equal width for each category. The height of each rectangle is proportional to the frequency or percentage of the category. Bar charts may be displayed either horizontally or vertically.

Table 15.8 shows the percentage distributions of attitudes toward preference in hiring blacks for white and minority respondents. The table shows that whites and minorities are divided in their opinion regarding preference in hiring blacks. Only 4.8 percent of whites strongly support preference in hiring, compared with 31.8 percent of minority respondents. In contrast, an overwhelming majority of whites (61.2 percent), compared with only about a third of minorities, strongly oppose preference in hiring blacks.

The bar chart presented in Figure 15.3 shows these opposing trends of whites and minorities toward preference in hiring blacks. The contiguous pairs of rectangles

Figure 15.3

Black and White Preferences in Hiring Blacks (%)

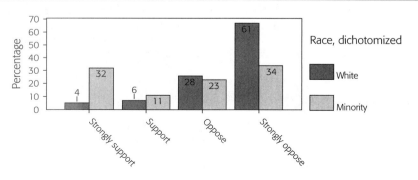

Source: General Social Survey, 1996.

Figure 15.4

Age by Decades, 1996

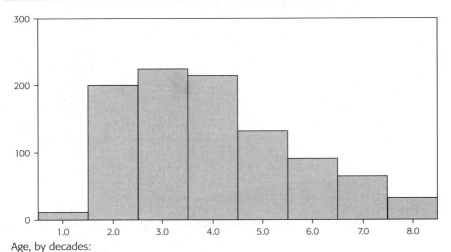

Age, by decades:
1 = 18–19; 2 = 20–29; 3 = 30–39; 4 = 40–49; 5 = 50–59; 6 = 60–69;
7 = 70–79; 8 = 80–89

Source: General Social Survey, 1996.

represent the two groups, whites and minorities. Notice that the rectangles representing each group are shaded differently to facilitate comparisons, and each category of the variable "preference in hiring blacks" contains a pair of rectangles.

The Histogram

Researchers use the **histogram** to display frequency distributions of interval- or ratio-level data. The histogram looks like a bar graph with no spaces between the rectangles. The rectangles are constructed contiguously to show that the variable is continuous, and intervals, rather than discrete categories, are displayed across the horizontal axis. The heights of the rectangles in the histogram reflect the percent or frequency of the interval. Unlike the bar chart, the histogram cannot be used to display information for more than one variable. Table 15.3 and Figure 15.4 show the distribution of age by decades for the 1996 General Social Survey.

MEASURES OF CENTRAL TENDENCY

When only a short summary of the data is required, the entire distribution need not be presented. While you could use a frequency distribution to describe the educational level of Americans, your table could be rather cumbersome. Instead, you could point out that most Americans are high school graduates or that the average level of education in the United States is 12 years.

In most distributions, the observations tend to cluster around a central value. For instance, an income distribution can be characterized by the most common income or an average income. Similarly, attitude distributions cluster around a certain range. This property allows researchers to represent a distribution using a single value rather than a large table and makes it easier for them to compare different distributions. For example, you could compare the average income in the United States with the average income in England or contrast the average intelligence scores of Russian students with those of American students.

Statistical measures that reflect a "typical" or an "average" characteristic of a frequency distribution are referred to as *measures of central tendency.* The three measures social scientists most commonly use are the mode, the median, and the arithmetic mean.

Mode

The **mode** is the category or observation that appears most frequently in the distribution. It is used as a measure of central tendency mostly with distributions of nominal variables. You identify the mode by singling out the category containing the largest number of responses. For example, consider the distribution of prayer frequency for a random sample of American adults who were surveyed in 1996. The frequency distribution displayed in Table 15.9 includes six categories ranging from "several times a day" to "never." The second category, "once a day," is the most frequent ($f = 142$). This category is thus the mode of the distribution.

Most distributions are unimodal; that is, they include only one category in which the most cases are concentrated. At times, however, the distribution is bimodal: It has two such maximum points. Such a pattern usually exists in distributions that combine two populations. For instance, the distribution of the heights of adults is bimodal; It comprises both men and women, and each gender is characterized by a different typical height.

The advantage of the mode is that it is easy to identify by inspecting the frequency distribution, and therefore it can be used as a first and quick indicator of the central tendency in a distribution. Although it is easy to determine, the mode is a sensitive indicator. Its position can shift if the researcher changes the way the distribution is divided into categories. Therefore, it is not a very stable measure of central tendency.

Table 15.9

Distribution of Prayer Frequency

Prayer Frequency	Frequency (f)
Several times a day	125
Once a day	142
Several times a week	78
Once a week	35
Less than once a week	90
Never	9
Total (*N*)	479

Source: General Social Survey, 1996.

Median

The **median** is a positional measure that divides the distribution into two equal parts. It is defined as the observation that is located halfway between the smallest and the largest observations in the distribution. For example, in the series 1, 3, 4, 6, 7, the median is 4. The median can only be calculated for observations that are ranked according to size, and thus it is suitable for use with variables measured at or above the ordinal level.

A researcher can obtain the median of ungrouped data by identifying the middle observation. For an odd number of cases, it is the observation $(N + 1)/2$, where N is the total number of cases. Consider the following set of nine observations:

$$6, \quad 9, \quad 11, \quad 12, \quad 16, \quad 18, \quad 21, \quad 24, \quad 30$$
$$\uparrow$$
$$\text{Median}$$

The fifth observation $[(9 + 1)/2]$ divides the distribution in half; the median is therefore the value of the fifth observation, 16. With an even number of observations, the median is located halfway between the two middle observations and is calculated as an average of the observations $N/2$ and $N/2 + 1$. For example, in the following set of observations,

$$1, \quad 3, \quad 4, \quad 5, \quad 6, \quad 7, \quad 8, \quad 9$$
$$\uparrow$$
$$\text{Median}$$

the median is the average of the fourth $(8/2)$ and the fifth $(8/2 + 1)$ observations: $(5 + 6)/2 = 5.5$.

For data arranged in frequency distribution, the procedure for locating the median is a bit more involved. For example, the frequency distribution displayed in Table 15.10 shows the level of support for cuts in government spending for GSS respondents in 1996.

To determine the median, we must locate the category containing the cumulative percentage of 50 percent. The category "strongly in favor" has a cumulative percentage of 41.4 percent, and the category "in favor" has a cumulative percentage of 81.8 per-

Table 15.10

Support for Cuts in Government Spending

Cuts in Government Spending	Frequency (f)	Percentage	Cumulative Percentage
Strongly in favor	184	41.4	41.4
In favor	179	40.3	81.8
Neither	59	13.3	95.0
Against	16	3.6	98.6
Strongly against	6	1.4	100.0
Total (N)	444	100.0	

Source: General Social Survey, 1996.

Table 15.11

Median Family Income of GSS
Respondents by Gender and Race

	Black	White
Male	$33,375	$48,858
Female	$23,441	$38,065

Source: General Social Survey, 1996.

cent; thus the category "in favor" must contain the 50 percent cumulative percentage. The median for this distribution is therefore "in favor."

Table 15.11, which displays the median family income of 1996 GSS respondents by gender and race, provides an example of the application of the median. The median allows us to compare the 1996 family income of black and white men and women. Since the family income of white males is the highest in comparison with all other groups, it is useful to look at each group's median income relative to the income of white males. For example, in 1996, white women's family income was just 78 cents for every $1 earned by white men ($38,065/$48,858 = 0.78). For men and women of color, the gap was greater. In 1996, black men's family income was 68 cents ($33,375/$48,858 = 0.68) and for black women it was 48 cents ($23,441/$48,858) for every $1 earned by white men.

Other Measures of Location

At times it is useful to identify values that divide the distribution into not just two but three, four, or ten groups. For example, the admissions office of a university that has decided to accept one-fourth of its applicants will be interested in finding the 25 percent with the highest scores on the entrance examinations. The median, then, is a special case of a more general set of measures of location called percentiles. The nth percentile is a number such that n percent of the scores fall below it and $(100 - n)$ percent fall above it. The median is the 50th percentile; that is, it is a number that is larger than 50 percent of the measurements and smaller than the other 50 percent.

To locate positional measures such as the seventy-fifth percentile (also called the upper quartile, or Q_3) or the twenty-fifth percentile (also called the lower quartile, or Q_1), we adapt the same procedure used to locate the median in a frequency distribution. For example, Table 15.12 presents the income distribution for the GSS in 1996. To identify the lower quartile (Q_1), we locate the income associated with the respondent with the cumulative percentage of 25 percent. Since this percentage is located in the first category, Q_1 is $17,500 or less. Similarly, Q_3 is $35,000–$59,000, since it corresponds to the cumulative percentage of 75 percent.

Arithmetic Mean

The **arithmetic mean** is the most frequently used measure of central tendency. Although the mode and the median are both considered to be averages, the mean is what most people commonly consider to be the average. When we talk about such things as the average score on a test or the average height of a professional basketball player, we

Table 15.12

Family Income — GSS 1996

Income	Frequency (f)	Percentage	Cumulative Percentage
< $17,500	223	25.6	25.6
$17,500 – $34,999	243	27.9	53.5
$35,000 – $59,999	219	25.1	78.6
$60,000+	186	21.4	100.0
Total	871	100.0	

Source: General Social Survey, 1996.

are usually talking about the mean. The mean is suitable for representing distributions measured on an interval or ratio level and lends itself to mathematical calculations; it also serves as a basis for other statistical measures. The arithmetic mean is defined as the sum total of all observations divided by their number.

In symbolic notation, the mean is defined as

$$\bar{X} = \frac{\Sigma X}{N} \tag{15.1}$$

where $\bar{X}$ = the arithmetic mean

ΣX = the sum of total observations

N = the number of observations

According to this equation, the mean $(\bar{X})$ of the series 6, 7, 12, 11, 10, 3, 4, 1 is 54/8 = 6.75.

When you are computing the mean from a frequency distribution, it is not necessary to add up all the individual observations. Instead, you can give each category its proper weight by multiplying it by its frequency, and the following equation can be used:

$$\bar{X} = \frac{\Sigma fX}{N} \tag{15.2}$$

where ΣfX = the sum total of all categories multiplied by their respective frequencies.

Table 15.13 presents data on the amount of schooling received by 34 individuals. The mean education of this group can be calculated by using Equation (15.2). To calculate the value of ΣfX (column 3), we have multiplied each category (column 1) by its frequency (column 2), and added up the products. The mean number of years of schooling is therefore

$$\bar{X} = \frac{278}{34} = 8.18$$

Unlike the mode and the median, the arithmetic mean takes into account all the values in the distribution, making it especially sensitive to extreme values. For example, if

Table 15.13

Distribution of Years of Study

(1) Years of Study	(2) f	(3) fX
2	3	6
3	2	6
6	5	30
8	10	80
10	8	80
12	4	48
14	2	28
Total	(N) = 34	ΣfX = 278

one person in a group of 10 earns $60,000 annually and each of the others earns $5,000, the mean income of the group is $10,500, which is not a good representation of the distribution. The mean will thus be a misleading measure of central tendency whenever there are some observations with extremely high or low values.

Exhibit 15.1 illustrates the procedure for finding the three measures of central tendency.

Comparison of the Mode, the Median, and the Mean

All three measures of central tendency can be used to represent univariate distributions. However, each has its own characteristics, which both prescribe and limit its use. The mode indicates the point in the distribution with the highest density, the median is the distribution's midpoint, and the arithmetic mean is an average of all the values in the distribution. Accordingly, these measures cannot be applied mechanically. How, then, does a researcher know when it is appropriate to use a certain measure? There is no simple answer to the question; it depends on the objective of the study. For example, if the

The Three Measures of Central Tendency

▲

+ *Mode:* The category or observation that appears most frequently in the distribution. Researchers find the mode by locating the category with the largest number of responses.

+ *Median:* The observation, category, or interval that divides the distribution into two equal parts. To find the median for ungrouped data with an uneven number of scores, the researcher lists the observations in increasing order and locates the middle score. If the number of scores is even, the median is located between the middle two scores.

+ *Arithmetic mean:* The mean is equal to the sum of all of the observations divided by the total number of observations. The formula for finding the mean of ungrouped data can be found in Equation (15.1), and the formula for finding the mean of grouped data can be found in Equation (15.2).

●

Exhibit 15.1

FINDING THE THREE AVERAGES

Mode = the most frequent category = 9

Each * represents one observation
Total cases = 39

```
                        9
                8       *
                *       *
            6   *       *
            *   *       *   5
        4   *   *   *   *
        *   *   *   *   *   3
    2   *   *   *   *   *   *
    *   *   *   *   *   *   *   1   1
    *   *   *   *   *   *   *   *   *
─────────────────────────────────────────
    5   6   7   8   9   10  11  12  13
```
Value of the Variable

Median = the midpoint = $(N + 1) \div 2$
$= (39 + 1) \div 2 = 20$

5 5 6 6 6 6 7 7 7 7 7 7 8 8 8 8 8 8 8 8 9 9 9 9 9 9 9 9 9 10 10 10 10 10 11 11 11 12 13
↑
Midpoint = the 20th case = 8

Mean = the arithmetic average =

$$
\begin{aligned}
5 \times 2 &= 10 \\
6 \times 4 &= 24 \\
7 \times 6 &= 42 \\
8 \times 8 &= 64 \\
9 \times 9 &= 81 \\
10 \times 5 &= 50 \\
11 \times 3 &= 33 \\
12 \times 1 &= 12 \\
13 \times 1 &= \underline{13} \\
329 &\div 39 = 8.44
\end{aligned}
$$
(total)   (cases)   (mean)

researcher is investigating the average level of income of a group in order to establish how much each person would receive if all incomes were distributed equally, the mean would be most pertinent, as it reflects the highest as well as the lowest income. If, by contrast, an administrator needs the information to estimate the eligibility of the group to receive financial aid, the mode would be appropriate, for it shows the most typical income and is unaffected by extreme values.

A researcher must also consider the level of measurement of the variable being analyzed when deciding which measure of central tendency to apply. The mode can be used at any level of measurement, but it is the only appropriate measure of central tendency for nominal variables such as party affiliation. The median can be applied to ordinal-level variables such as political attitudes, but it may also be used to describe variables measured at a higher level. The arithmetic mean may be used with interval or ratio variables such as income and age.

BASIC MEASURES OF DISPERSION ●

Measures of central tendency identify the most representative value of the distribution and provide researchers with a way to summarize their data; however, they do not always tell researchers all they need to know about the distribution. For example, consider the following two distributions:

(1)   8, 8, 9, 9, 9, 10, 10, 10, 10, 10, 11, 11, 11, 12, 12

(2)   4, 5, 6, 7, 8, 9, 10, 10, 10, 11, 12, 13, 14, 15, 16

In both groups the mean, median, and mode are 10, and we can summarize the distributions using one of these central values. However, this single summarizing measure may give the impression that the two distributions are the same when they clearly are not. In the first distribution, the numbers tend to cluster around the central value; in the second distribution, they are more widely dispersed. A complete description of any distribution requires that we measure the extent of dispersion about the central value. (In the following discussion, the terms *dispersion, scatter,* and *variation* are used interchangeably.) The actual observations are distributed among many values, and the extent of their spread varies from one distribution to another. For example, two classes may have the same average grade; however, one class may include some excellent students as well as some very poor ones, whereas all the students in the other class may be of average ability. Similarly, income distributions with an identical mean may present different patterns of dispersion. In some distributions, most incomes are clustered around the mean; in others, the incomes are widely dispersed. Researchers obtain a description of the extent of dispersions about the central value by using measures designated as measures of dispersion. We shall discuss the measure of qualitative variation, the range, the mean deviation, the variance, the standard deviation, and the coefficient of variation.

Measure of Qualitative Variation

Researchers can assess the extent of dispersion in nominal distributions by means of an index of heterogeneity designated as the **measure of qualitative variation.** This index reflects the number of differences among the categories of the distribution and is based on the number of categories and their respective frequencies. In general, the larger the number of categories and the greater the overall differences among them, the greater the degree of variation. Likewise, the smaller the number of categories and their differences, the smaller the variation within the distribution. Consider the racial/ethnic composition of two states—New Mexico and Vermont. The population in Vermont is composed mainly, although not exclusively, of whites. In New Mexico, only about half of the population is white. The remainder of the population is composed largely of Hispanics and, to a lesser degree, Native Americans, but other racial/ethnic groups are also represented. The amount of variation depends on the racial/ethnic composition of the state. When most people belong to a single racial/ethnic group, the number of racial differences among the members of the state will be relatively small. Conversely, when most members are divided among several racial/ethnic groups, the number of differences will be large. Variation is small in Vermont, and in New Mexico it is large. The measure of qualitative variation is based on the ratio of the total number of differences in the distribution to the maximum number of possible differences within the same distribution.

CALCULATING THE TOTAL NUMBER OF DIFFERENCES. To find the total number of differences in the distribution, a researcher would count and sum the differences between each category and every other category. For instance, in a group of 50 whites and 50 blacks, there would be 50 × 50 = 2,500 racial differences. Similarly, with 70 whites and 30 blacks, you would count 70 × 30 = 2,100 differences, and with 100 whites and no blacks, there would be 0 × 100 = 0 racial differences.

The procedure for calculating the total number of differences can be expressed in the following equation:

$$\text{Total observed differences} = \Sigma f_i f_j, \quad i \neq j \tag{15.3}$$

where f_i = frequency of category i

f_j = frequency of category j

For example, in a group of 20 Catholics, 30 Jews, and 10 Muslims, there would be (20 × 30) + (20 × 10) + (30 × 10) = 1,100 religious differences.

CALCULATING THE MAXIMUM POSSIBLE DIFFERENCES. Because each distribution has a different number of categories and frequencies, the total of observed differences is meaningful only in relation to the maximum possible number of differences. By relating the observed differences to the maximum possible differences, the researcher can control for these factors. The maximum number of differences occurs when each category in the distribution has an identical frequency. Thus the maximum number of frequencies is computed by finding the number of differences that would be observed if all frequencies were equal. Symbolically,

$$\text{Maximum possible differences} = \frac{n(n-1)}{2}\left(\frac{F}{n}\right)^2 \tag{15.4}$$

where n = the number of categories in the distribution

F = total frequency

For the sample with 20 Catholics, 30 Jews, and 10 Muslims, the maximum possible differences are

$$\left(\frac{3 \times 2}{2}\right)\left(\frac{60}{3}\right)^2 = 1,200$$

The measure of qualitative variation is the ratio between the total observed differences and the maximum possible differences. In other words,

$$\text{Measure of qualitative variation} = \frac{\text{total observed differences}}{\text{maximum possible differences}}$$

Symbolically, the measure is expressed in the following equation:

$$\text{Measure of qualitative variation} = \frac{\Sigma f_i f_j}{\frac{n(n-1)}{2}\left(\frac{F}{n}\right)^2} \tag{15.5}$$

The measure of variation for our example is thus

$$\text{Measure of qualitative variation} = \frac{1,100}{1,200} = .92$$

The measure of qualitative variation varies between zero and one. Zero indicates the absence of any variation, and one reflects maximum variation. The measure will be zero whenever the total observed differences are zero. It will take the value of one when the number of observed differences is equal to the maximum possible differences.

At the beginning of this section we asked you to consider the racial/ethnic composition of two states—New Mexico and Vermont—and stated that the amount of racial/ethnic variation was large in New Mexico and small in Vermont. We can use the index of qualitative variation to compare the amount of diversity in the two states. Table 15.14 shows the population by race and ethnicity and the measure of qualitative variation (IQV) for 17 states. The table is arranged in order of decreasing diversity. You can see that there is wide variation in racial/ethnic diversity in the United States. New Mexico, with an IQV of .70, is the most diverse state; Vermont, with an IQV of only .04, is the most homogeneous state.

Range and Interquartile Range

The **range** measures the distance between the highest and lowest values of the distribution. For example, in the following set of observations,

4, 6, 8, 9, 17

the range is the difference between 17 and 4; that is, 13 ($17 - 4 = 13$). To calculate the range, the observations must be ranked according to size; thus the range can be applied in cases where the distribution is at least on an ordinal level of measurement. The range has a special significance when a dearth of information produces a distorted picture of reality. For instance, suppose that two factories with annual average wages of $15,000 have different pay ranges: One has a range of $2,000, and the other has a range of $9,000. Without the additional information supplied by the range, a comparison of the averages would give you the impression that the wage scales in both factories were identical. Although the range is a useful device for gaining a quick impression of the data, it is a crude measure of dispersion because it takes into account only the two extreme values of the distribution. Thus it is sensitive to changes in a single score.

An alternative to the range is the **interquartile range,** which is the difference between the lower and upper quartiles (Q_1 and Q_3). Because it measures the spread of the middle half of the distribution, it is less affected by extreme observations. The lower and upper quartiles will vary less from distribution to distribution than the most extreme observations. The range can also be calculated for other measures of location. For example, you can calculate the range between the tenth and ninetieth percentiles to measure the dispersion of the middle 80 percent of the observations.

LIMITATIONS.   The major drawback of the range and the interquartile range is that because they are based on only two values, they reflect only the dispersion in some defined section of the distribution. In order to get a more accurate picture of the distribution, some measure must be devised that will reflect the aggregate dispersion in the distribution. However, to measure aggregate dispersion it is necessary to establish the deviation of all the values in the distribution from some criterion. In other words, the

Table 15.14

Population by Race and Ethnicity and IQVs for 17 States

State	White	Black	Native American Eskimo, or Aleut	Asian or Pacific Islander	Other	Hispanic	IQV
New Mexico	764,164	27,642	128,068	12,587	3,384	579,224	0.70
Texas	10,291,680	1,976,360	52,803	303,825	21,937	4,339,905	0.66
Mississippi	1,624,198	911,891	8,316	12,543	337	15,931	0.57
Florida	9,475,326	1,701,103	32,910	146,159	8,285	1,574,143	0.52
New Jersey	5,718,966	984,845	12,490	264,341	9,685	739,861	0.51
Alaska	406,722	21,799	84,594	18,730	395	17,803	0.48
Delaware	528,092	111,011	1,938	8,854	453	15,820	0.43
Colorado	2,658,945	128,057	22,068	56,773	4,249	424,302	0.39
Arkansas	1,933,082	372,762	12,393	12,144	468	19,876	0.35
Missouri	4,448,465	545,527	18,873	40,087	2,419	61,702	0.28
Pennsylvania	10,422,058	1,072,459	13,505	134,056	7,303	232,262	0.26
Rhode Island	896,109	34,283	3,629	17,584	6,107	45,752	0.23
Kentucky	3,378,022	261,360	5,518	17,201	1,211	21,984	0.19
Utah	1,571,254	10,868	22,748	32,490	893	84,597	0.18
Minnesota	4,101,266	93,040	48,251	76,229	2,429	53,884	0.14
West Virginia	1,718,896	55,986	2,363	7,252	491	8,489	0.10
Vermont	552,184	1,868	1,651	3,159	235	3,661	0.04

Source: 1990 Census of the Population: General Population Characteristics. Distributed by the U.S. Department of Commerce Economic and Statistics Administration, Bureau of the Census, CP-1-1 through CP-1-512.

researcher must decide on some norm that will permit him or her to determine which value is higher or lower than expected. For example, the evaluation of income as "high" or "low" is meaningful only in relation to some fixed criterion. Income evaluated as high in India would be considered low in the United States.

A researcher can choose any of the measures of central tendency as a norm. It is possible to measure deviations from the mode, the median, or the arithmetic mean; however, the mean is the most widely employed.

MEASURES OF DISPERSION BASED ON THE MEAN   ●

The simplest way to obtain a measure of deviation is to calculate the average deviation from the arithmetic mean:

$$\text{Average deviation} = \frac{\Sigma(X - \bar{X})}{N}$$

where X = each individual observation

$\bar{X}$ = the arithmetic mean

N = the total number of observations

However, the sum of the deviations from the mean is always equal to zero;[2] thus the average deviation will be zero, for its numerator will always be zero. To compensate for this property of the mean, we square each deviation to calculate standard deviation — the measure of dispersion most commonly applied to interval-level data.

Variance and Standard Deviation

Whenever possible, researchers will choose to use variance and standard deviation as measures of dispersion because they can be used in more advanced statistical calculations. Variance and standard deviation are calculated by squaring and summing the deviations, then dividing the sum by the total number of observations. The definitional formula for the **variance** is[3]

$$s^2 = \frac{\Sigma(X - \bar{X})^2}{N} \tag{15.6}$$

where s^2 = variance. In other words, the arithmetic mean is subtracted from each score; the differences are then squared, summed, and divided by the total number of observations. The numerical example in Table 15.15 illustrates the various steps involved in the computation of the variance. Applying Equation (15.6) to the data, we get

$$s^2 = \frac{200}{5} = 40$$

2. For example, the mean of the numbers 2, 4, 6, and 8 is 5. If we subtract 5 from each of these numbers we get -3, -1, 1, and 3. The total of these differences $-(-3) + (-1) + 1 + 3-$ is equal to zero.

3. The formulas for standard deviation and variance in this chapter are population formulas. When researchers calculate standard deviation and variance for samples of the population, they use $(N - 2)$ in the denominator rather than N.

To calculate variance, researchers use a computational formula instead of the definitional formula. In the computational formula of the variance, the squared mean is subtracted from the squared sum of all scores divided by the number of observations; that is,

$$s^2 = \frac{\Sigma X^2}{N} - (\bar{X})^2 \tag{15.7}$$

When we apply Equation (15.7) to the same data in Table 15.15, we get the following result:

$$s^2 = \frac{605}{5} - (9)^2 = 121 - 81 = 40$$

The variance expresses the average dispersion in the distribution not in the original units of measurement but in squared units. We can bypass this problem, however, by taking the square root of the variance, thereby transforming the variance into the standard deviation. The **standard deviation** is a measure expressing dispersion in the original units of measurement. Symbolically, the standard deviation is expressed in Equations (15.8) and (15.9), which correspond to Equations (15.6) and (15.7), respectively:

$$s = \sqrt{\frac{\Sigma(X - \bar{X})^2}{N}} \tag{15.8}$$

$$s = \sqrt{\frac{\Sigma X^2}{N} - (\bar{X})^2} \tag{15.9}$$

where s = standard deviation. For our earlier example, the value of the standard deviation, using Equation (15.8), is

$$s = \sqrt{\frac{200}{5}} = \sqrt{40} = 6.3$$

The data in Table 15.15 are displayed in an ungrouped frequency distribution with a single frequency for each value of X. When data are arranged in a frequency distribution, we can use the following modified formula to calculate variance:

$$s^2 = \frac{\Sigma fY^2}{N} - \left(\frac{\Sigma fY}{N}\right)^2$$

Table 15.15

Computation of the Variance

X	X − X̄	(X − X̄)²	X²
3	−6	36	9
4	−5	25	16
6	−3	9	36
12	3	9	144
20	11	121	400
Total		200	605

$\bar{X} = 9$

Table 15.16

Mean and Standard Deviation on an Index of Life Satisfaction in Four Western Nations (Hypothetical Data)

	England	Germany	Italy	United States
Mean	6.7	6.7	6.6	6.5
Standard deviation	1.0	1.2	3.2	1.3

Standard Deviation: Advantages and Applications

The standard deviation has various advantages over other measures of dispersion. First, it is more stable from sample to sample (on sampling, see Chapter 8). Second, it has some important mathematical properties that enable the researcher to obtain the standard deviation for two or more groups combined. Furthermore, its mathematical properties make it a useful measure in more advanced statistical work, especially in the area of statistical inferences (discussed in Chapters 8 and 19).

The application of standard deviation as a research device is illustrated in the following example. Table 15.16 compares differences in feelings of life satisfaction among people who live in several countries, using the mean and standard deviation of the variable "life satisfaction" in each country. The mean scores are almost identical, implying that satisfaction with life is similar in the four countries. However, there are differences in the standard deviations of each country. The relatively low standard deviations in England, Germany, and the United States indicate that these countries are homogeneous as far as satisfaction is concerned; that is, people have a satisfaction score that is close to their group's mean score. In Italy, however, the dispersion is greater, suggesting that the degree of satisfaction reflected by the mean is not common to all the Italians in the group studied.

Coefficient of Variation

In instances where the distributions the researcher is comparing have very different means, he or she cannot compare the absolute magnitudes of the standard deviations. A standard deviation of 2, for instance, would convey a different meaning in relation to a mean of 6 than to a mean of 60. Therefore, the researcher needs to calculate the degree of dispersion relative to the mean of the distribution. This principle is reflected in the **coefficient of variation,** which reflects relative variation. Symbolically, the coefficient of variation is defined as follows:

$$V = \frac{s}{\bar{X}}$$

(15.10)

where V = the coefficient of variation

s = the standard deviation

$\bar{X}$ = the arithmetic mean

Table 15.17 on attitudes toward federal support for abortion presents the means and standard deviations of the distributions in four states. In absolute magnitudes, there are

Table 15.17

Attitudes Toward Federal Support for Abortion in Four States (Hypothetical Data)

	Wisconsin	Illinois	Alabama	Massachusetts
Mean	5.48	4.82	3.67	5.82
Standard deviation	2.9	2.9	2.8	2.7

no significant differences among the standard deviations in the four states. However, there are substantial differences between the means, indicating varying degrees of support for abortion in each state. In Alabama, for example, the mean is much lower than in the other states, but the degree of dispersion is almost identical. Assuming that we have measured attitudes on a scale from 1 to 10, with 1 indicating strong opposition to federal support for abortion and 10 indicating strong support, it seems, intuitively, that a deviation of 2.8 has a greater significance in relation to a mean of 3.67 than to a mean of 4.82 or 5.48 because a mean of 3.67 is more extreme than a mean of either 4.82 or 5.48. To correct for these discrepancies, the standard deviations were converted into coefficients of variation. The results are displayed in Table 15.18. Note that, indeed, the relative deviation from the mean is higher in Alabama than in other states, reflecting the lower degree of homogeneity of attitudes toward abortion.

Measures of Dispersion

+ *Measure of qualitative variation:* An index that indicates the heterogeneity or homogeneity of a population. It is determined by comparing the total observed differences in a distribution to the maximum possible number of differences and is calculated using Equations (15.3), (15.4), and (15.5).

+ *Range:* The distance between the highest and the lowest values of the distribution. The range can provide misleading information to researchers because it takes into account only the two extreme scores in a distribution.

+ *Interquartile range:* The difference between the lower quartile (25th percentile) and the upper quartile (75th percentile). Because it measures the spread of the middle half of the distribution, the interquartile range is not affected by extreme scores.

+ *Variance:* Variance is the average of the squared deviations from the mean. It can be calculated using either the definitional formula or the simpler computational formula. These formulas have several variations. Equations (15.6) and (15.7) show formulas for the variance.

+ *Standard deviation:* Standard deviation is equal to the square root of the variance. Unlike variance, the standard deviation expresses dispersion in the original units of measurement. Standard deviation can be calculated using Equations (15.8) and (15.9), or can be determined by taking the square root of the variance.

Table 15.18

Means of Attitudes Toward Federal Support for Abortion and Coefficient of Variation in Four States (Hypothetical Data)

	Wisconsin	Illinois	Alabama	Massachusetts
Mean	5.48	4.82	3.67	5.82
Coefficient of variation	0.53	0.60	0.76	0.46

TYPES OF FREQUENCY DISTRIBUTIONS   ●

Our discussion of univariate distributions has so far been limited to measures that allow researchers to describe their data in terms of central tendencies and dispersion. The next step in describing a distribution is to identify its general form. Distributions may have distinctive forms with few low scores and many high scores, with many scores concentrated in the middle of the distribution, or with many low scores and few high scores. The simplest way to describe a distribution is by a visual representation. Examples of different forms are presented in Figure 15.5.

The values of the variable are represented along the baseline, and the area under the curve represents the frequencies. For example, in the distribution in Figure 15.5a, the frequency of the interval 25–35 is represented by the area under the curve in that interval. The distribution in Figure 15.5a is symmetrical; that is, the frequencies at the right and left tails of the distribution are identical, so if the distribution is divided into two halves, each will be the mirror image of the other. This usually means that most of the observations are concentrated at the middle of the distribution and that there are few observations with very high or very low scores. Male height is an example of a symmetrical distribution. Few men are very short or very tall; most are of medium height. Many other variables tend to be distributed symmetrically, and this form of distribution plays an important role in the field of statistical inference.

In nonsymmetrical or **skewed distributions,** there are more extreme cases in one direction of the distribution than in the other. A nonsymmetrical distribution in which there are more extremely low scores is referred to as a *negatively skewed distribution*

Figure 15.5

Types of Frequency Distributions

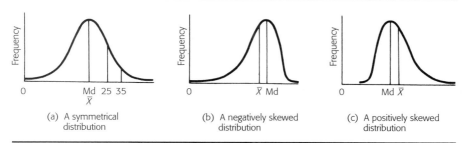

(a) A symmetrical distribution

(b) A negatively skewed distribution

(c) A positively skewed distribution

(Figure 15.5b). When there are more extremely high scores, the distribution is *positively skewed* (Figure 15.5c). Most income distributions are positively skewed, with few families having extremely high incomes.

Skewness can also be identified according to the positions of the measures of central tendency. In symmetrical distributions, the mean will coincide with the median and the mode; in skewed distributions, there will be discrepancies between these measures. In a negatively skewed distribution, the mean will be pulled in the direction of the lower scores; in a positively skewed distribution, it will be located closer to the higher scores. This property of skewed distributions makes the choice of a measure of central tendency a critical issue. Since the mean is pulled in the direction of the extreme scores, it loses its typicality and hence its usefulness as a representative measure. In such instances, it might be advisable to employ the median or the mode instead.

Normal Curve

One type of symmetrical distribution, called the **normal curve,** has great significance in the field of statistics. A normal curve is shown in Figure 15.6. Its principal properties are as follows:

1. It is symmetrical and bell-shaped.
2. The mode, the median, and the mean coincide at the center of the distribution.
3. The curve is based on an infinite number of observations.
4. A single mathematical formula describes how frequencies are related to the values of the variable.

The fifth property of the normal curve is its most distinct characteristic: *In any normal distribution, a fixed proportion of the observations lies between the mean and fixed units of standard deviations.* The proportions can be seen in Figure 15.6. The mean of the distribution divides it exactly in half; 34.13 percent of the observations fall between the mean and one standard deviation to the right of the mean; the same proportion fall between the mean and one standard deviation to the left of the mean. The plus signs indicate standard deviations above the mean; the minus signs, standard deviations below the mean. Thus 68.26 percent of all observations fall between $\bar{X} \pm 1s$; 95.46 of all

Figure 15.6

Proportions Under the Normal Curve

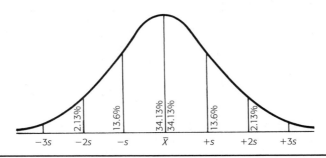

| | 2.13% | 13.6% | 34.13% | 34.13% | 13.6% | 2.13% | |
| $-3s$ | $-2s$ | $-s$ | $\bar{X}$ | $+s$ | $+2s$ | $+3s$ |

the observations fall between $\bar{X} \pm 2s$; and 99.73 percent of all the observations fall between $\bar{X} \pm 3s$.

In any univariate distribution that is normally distributed, the proportion of observations included within fixed distances of the mean can be determined. For example, in a distribution of intelligence quotients with a mean of 110 and a standard deviation of 10, 68.26 percent of all subjects will have an IQ of $110 \pm 1s$—that is, between 100 and 120—and 95.46 percent will have a score that is not below 90 and does not exceed 130.

Standard Scores

Researchers can use the normal curve to evaluate the proportion of observations included within a desired interval, but the raw scores must be converted to standard deviation units to use the table, which reports areas under the normal curve. When raw scores have been converted to standard scores, a single table can be used to evaluate any distribution regardless of the scale on which the data were measured, and distributions measured on different scales can be directly compared. If, for instance, we want to find the proportion of cases that have an IQ between 110 and 130, we must determine how many standard deviations away from the mean the score of 130 is located. Observations are converted into standard deviation units by means of Equation (15.11):

$$Z = \frac{X - \bar{X}}{s} \tag{15.11}$$

where Z = number of standard deviation units

X = any observation

$\bar{X}$ = the arithmetic mean

s = the standard deviation

Z, sometimes referred to as a **standard score,** expresses the distance between a specific observation (X) and the mean in terms of standard deviation units. A Z of 2 means that the distance between the mean of the distribution and X is two standard deviations. For example, in a distribution with a mean of 40 and a standard deviation of 5, the score of 50 is expressed as follows:

$$Z = \frac{50 - 40}{5} = \frac{10}{5} = 2$$

The score of 50 lies two standard deviations above the mean. Similarly, 30 is two standard deviations below the mean:

$$Z = \frac{30 - 40}{5} = \frac{-10}{5} = -2$$

Special tables have been constructed for the standard form of the normal curve. These tables enable you to determine the proportion of observations that lie between the mean and any observation in the distribution. (See Appendix E for an example of such a table.) The table shows proportions for various Z values. The first two digits of Z are listed in the left-hand column; the third digit is shown across the top. Thus, for example, the proportion included between the mean and a Z of 1 is .3413, or 34.13 percent;

Figure 15.7

Proportion of Population Earning Between $11,000 and $15,000

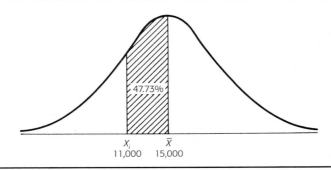

the value of a Z of 1.65 is .4505. The table shows only half of the curve's proportions because the curve is symmetrical. Thus the distance between the mean and a Z of -1.0 is identical to the area between the mean and a Z of 1.0. To use the table, find the appropriate Z score for any particular observation by applying Equation (15.11), and then consult Appendix E.

To illustrate the use of the standard normal table, suppose that the distribution of income in a particular community is normal, its mean income is $15,000, and the standard deviation is $2,000. We want to determine what proportion of the people in this community have an income between $11,000 and $15,000. First, we convert $11,000 into standard deviation units:

$$Z = \frac{\$11,000 - \$15,000}{\$2,000} = -2$$

Figure 15.8

Proportion of Population Earning Between $16,000 and $20,000

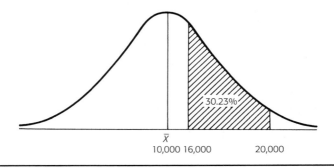

Next, we consult Appendix E to determine that .4773 of all observations are included between the mean and a Z of 2. In other words, 47.73 percent of all people in the community earn between $11,000 and $15,000 a year. This is shown in Figure 15.7.

What proportion of the community earns between $16,000 and $20,000? We determine this by converting both figures into standard scores:

$$Z_1 = \frac{\$16,000 - \$15,000}{\$2,000} = 0.5$$

$$Z_2 = \frac{\$20,000 - \$15,000}{\$2,000} = 2.5$$

Appendix E indicates that .4938 as included between the mean and 2.5 standard deviation units and .1915 between the mean and 0.5 units. Therefore, the area included between $16,000 and $20,000 is .4938 − .1915 = .3023 (30.23 percent). This is shown in Figure 15.8.

SUMMARY ●

1. During the preliminary stage of analysis, researchers use quite ordinary methods designed to provide a straightforward description of the data. Once coded, each item is summarized in some tabular form, and measures such as averages and percentages are calculated to describe its main characteristics. Researchers usually begin the analysis by showing how the respondents are distributed on all the items of the investigation. A distribution might show, for instance, that 20 of the 80 respondents included in a sample are males and the rest are females; that 46 are Democrats, 20 are Republicans, and 14 do not identify with either party. Such listings of the number of observations that fall into each of several categories are termed *frequency distributions.* Frequencies are often converted into proportions or percentages; these are helpful in assessing the weight of a single category in relation to other categories of the distribution or in relation to other distributions.

2. Often it is useful to obtain some average value that is representative of the distribution. For example, a researcher may need to answer such questions as "What is the most typical political orientation of this group of respondents?" or "What is their average income?" These questions can be answered by using measures of central tendency. The three most commonly used statistical measures of central tendency are the mode, the median, and the arithmetic mean.

3. Measures of central tendency can be misleading if they are not accompanied by measures that describe the amount of dispersion in the distribution. Whereas the measures of central tendency reflect the most typical or average characteristics of the group, the measures of dispersion indicate how many members of the group deviate from it and the extent of the deviation. A small deviation denotes that most responses are clustered around the measure of central tendency; a large deviation indicates that the measure of central tendency is a poor representation of the distribution.

4. One of the important steps in examining a distribution is to identify its general form. Certain forms are characteristic of different empirical phenomena. For instance, many income distributions have few extremely high incomes; most incomes are concentrated in the middle or lower ranges. Such distributions are skewed toward the higher values. In contrast, intelligence distributions are typically

symmetrical; most scores are concentrated in the middle range, with very few extremely high or extremely low scores.

KEY TERMS FOR REVIEW

arithmetic mean (p. 331)
bar chart (p. 327)
coefficient of variation (p. 341)
descriptive statistics (p. 321)
frequency distribution (p. 321)
histogram (p. 328)
inferential statistics (p. 321)
interquartile range (p. 337)
measure of qualitative variation (p. 335)

median (p. 330)
mode (p. 329)
normal curve (p. 344)
pie chart (p. 325)
range (p. 337)
skewed distribution (p. 343)
standard deviation (p. 340)
standard score (p. 345)
variance (p. 339)

STUDY QUESTIONS

1. The following table describes the employment status of women in two communities. What conclusions can be drawn from the absolute numbers? From the percentages?

	Community A		Community B	
In labor force:				
Professional	20,000	4%	20,000	10%
Skilled	45,000	9%	24,000	12%
Semiskilled	70,000	14%	28,000	14%
Unskilled	170,000	34%	28,000	14%
Not in labor force:	195,000	39%	100,000	50%
Total	500,000	100%	200,000	100%

2. Give two examples of problems in which (a) the mean is the best measure of central tendency; (b) the mode is the best measure of central tendency; (c) the median is the best measure of central tendency.

3. Give the mean, median, and mode of the following distribution:

22, 41, 43, 56, 33, 22, 20, 37

4. The following is the income distribution of a group of workers:

Income	Frequency
$18,000	6
22,000	3
27,500	3
30,000	2
75,000	1
	$N = 15$

    a. Which measure of central tendency would you use to represent the income of this group?

    b. Compute the measure of central tendency you would use.

5. On the curve shown here, what would be the approximate position of the mean? The median? The mode? Define the curve with respect to skewness.

6. Suppose that you obtain a set of scores of attitudes toward legal abortion from a group of respondents and that the standard deviation of this set of scores is zero. What does this imply about the group?

7. Attitudes toward authority often can be treated as an interval variable. Suppose that this variable is normally distributed with a mean score of 60 and a standard deviation of 10.

    a. What proportion of cases have scores between 60 and 63?

    b. What proportion have scores of less than 48?

    c. What proportion score between 72 and 83? Between 52 and 55?

SPSS PROBLEMS

1. Imagine that you are conducting a study on religiosity. You might want to begin by describing the strength of religious affiliations of Americans. Use the **Frequencies** procedure to produce a frequency table for the variable "reliten" (strength of religious affiliation). Using the frequency table, answer the following questions.

    a. What percentage of the sample has no religion?

    b. What percentage feels strong affiliation?

    c. How many respondents indicated that their religious affiliation is not very strong?

2. Suppose that an organization in your state is lobbying to make X-rated movies and pornography illegal because they believe that they lead to a breakdown in morals. You have been hired by this organization to make a presentation on how Americans feel about these issues, using the 1996 General Social Survey (**gss96worth**). Variables appropriate for your report include "pornlaw" and "xmovie".

    a. Using the **Graph** procedure, construct pie charts for these variables.

    b. Now construct bar charts for the same variables.

    c. Describe the attitudes of Americans toward these issues, using either the pie or the bar charts.

3. Using the **Frequencies** procedure, produce a frequency table and the mode, median, and mean (*Hint:* Use **Statistics**) for the variables "marital" and "attend." Which measure of central tendency is most appropriate to represent central tendency of "marital"? Of "attend"? Explain why.

4. Use the Frequencies procedure to compare the variability in the the number of hours "hrs1" that males and females work each week. Choose the appropriate measure of variability for this variable (*Hint:* Consider the level of measurement of this variable). Is there a difference in the variability of men's and women's hours worked? Explain the difference.

ADDITIONAL READINGS

Elifson, Kirk, Richard P. Runyon, and Audrey Haber. *Fundamantals of Social Statistics.* New York.: McGraw-Hill, 1998.

Healey, Joseph F. *Statistics: A Tool for Social Research.* Belmont, CA: Wadsworth, 1999.

Knoke, David, and George W. Bohrnstedt. *Statistics for Social Data Analysis.* Itasca, IL: Peacock, 1994.

Witte, Robert S., and John S. Witte. *Statistics.* Orlando, FL: Harcourt Brace, 1997.

BIVARIATE ANALYSIS

Fantasies about sex are as old as humankind, but the facts about what Americans do in bed, with whom, and how often have been studied systematically only during the last half-century. In 1992, a team of researchers from the University of Chicago released the results of a comprehensive survey of nearly 3,500 Americans, ages 18 to 59. Their findings, published in a book titled *Sex in America: A Definitive Survey,* include, among others, the observation that the majority of Americans are largely monogamous; 71 percent have one sexual partner a year and have had an average of three sexual partners since age 18. The study also confirms that teenagers do have sex earlier now; about half of all adolescents have their first sexual experience by the time they are 17 years old.[1]

The study *Sex in America* is significant not only because it describes patterns of sexual behavior in America, but also because it focuses on how sexual behavior varies by gender, race, or religion. For example, the study confirms that men think about sex more than women and that men and women have different views about what constitutes consent. Sexual practice also varies by religious affiliation; Roman Catholics are the most likely to be virgins, and Jews have the most sexual partners.

The examination of differences in sexual behavior between men and women, or between Roman Catholics and Jews, is what social scientists call bivariate analysis. Bivariate analysis allows us to examine the relationship between two variables. For example, the researchers of *Sex in America* analyzed the bivariate relation between gender and sexual practice by comparing the sexual practices of men and women. They also analyzed the relationship between religious affiliation and sexual practice by comparing the differences in the sexual practices of Roman Catholics and Jews (as well as other religious groups).

● **IN THIS CHAPTER** we explore the concept of relationships between two variables and examine different methods for measuring bivariate relationships. In the first section we discuss the concept of bivariate relationship; the second section describes nominal measures of relationship; the third section deals with ordinal measures of relationship; and the last section presents interval measures of relationship.

THE CONCEPT OF RELATIONSHIP ●

Each of us knows what relationships are. We know that in the world around us, things go together. We observe that as children grow, their weight increases; that cities tend to be more polluted than rural areas; and that women earn less money than men. Each of these observations is a statement of a relationship: between age and weight, between degree of urbanization and pollution, and between gender and earnings.

To say that cities tend to be more polluted than rural areas is to describe a relationship between urbanization and pollution. This statement can be made only if we can show that the level of pollution in the more urbanized cities is higher than the level of pollution in the less urbanized rural areas. In other words, to state a relationship between *X* and *Y* is to say that certain categories of the variable *X* go with certain categories of the variable *Y*. This principle of *covariation* is basic to the notion of association and relation.

---

1. Robert T. Michael, John H. Gagnon, Edward O. Laumann, and Gina Kolata, *Sex in America: A Definitive Survey* (New York: Little, Brown, 1994).

As a first step in examining a relationship between two variables, researchers usually construct a bivariate table.

How to Construct a Bivariate Table

In a bivariate table, two variables are cross-classified. Such a table consists of rows and columns; the categories of one variable are labels for the rows, and the categories of the second variable are labels for the columns. Usually, the independent variables is the column variable (listed across the top) and the dependent variable is the row variable (listed at the left side of the table). Exhibit 16.1 is an illustration of how a bivariate table is constructed. Sixteen individuals are first listed by their gender and their job satisfaction

Exhibit 16.1

CONSTRUCTING A BIVARIATE TABLE

ID Number	Gender Male = M Female = F	Job Satisfaction High = H Medium = M Low = L
1	M	H
2	M	H
3	F	H
4	M	M
5	F	L
6	F	L
7	F	L
8	M	M
9	M	H
10	F	M
11	M	H
12	M	H
13	M	L
14	F	M
15	F	L
16	F	H

Table 16.1

Job Satisfaction by Gender

Job Satisfaction	Gender		Row Totals
	Male	Female	
High	5	2	7
Medium	2	2	4
Low	1	4	5
Column totals	8	8	16

● *Part IV   Data Processing and Analysis*

scores. Then these observations are tallied and classified by their joint position on gender and job satisfaction into the appropriate cells in Table 16.1. The table is a 3 × 2 table because it has three rows and two columns, each representing a category of either the variable "gender" or the variable "job satisfaction." The fourth row represents the column totals; the third column, the row totals.

Principle of Covariation: An Example

The principle of covariation is demonstrated in Tables 16.2, 16.3, and 16.4. These tables summarize hypothetical information on two variables: religious denomination and social class. Table 16.2 illustrates a pattern of perfect covariation of the variables: All the Catholics are classified into the low-social-class category, all Jews belong to the middle class, and the Protestants occupy the high-social-class category. The two variables covary because specific categories of the variable "religious denomination" go with specific categories of the variable "social class."

The same pattern recurs in Table 16.3, but to a lesser extent because not all members of a given religious denomination belong to the same class. Yet it can still be said that most members of a particular religion belong to a particular social stratum.

When variables are not related, we say that they are independent of each other; that is, they do not "go together." Table 16.4 illustrates this situation. There is no clear pattern

Table 16.2

Social Class by Religious Denomination (Perfect Covariation)

Social Class	Religious Denomination			Total
	Catholic	Jewish	Protestant	
Upper	0	0	8	8
Middle	0	8	0	8
Lower	8	0	0	8
Total	8	8	8	24

Table 16.3

Social Class by Religious Denomination (Moderate Covariation)

Social Class	Religious Denomination			Total
	Catholic	Jewish	Protestant	
Upper	0	2	6	8
Middle	1	6	1	8
Lower	7	0	1	8
Total	8	8	8	24

Table 16.4

Social Class by Religious Denomination (Near-Zero Covariation)

	Religious Denomination			
Social Class	Catholic	Jewish	Protestant	Total
Upper	2	3	3	8
Middle	3	2	3	8
Lower	3	3	2	8
Total	8	8	8	24

for any of the religious groups in the table. Catholics can be in the upper, middle, and lower classes; the same goes for Jews and Protestants. In other words, you cannot say anything about a person's socioeconomic status on the basis of the person's religion.

Tables 16.2, 16.3, and 16.4 are examples of bivariate distributions arranged in tabular form. The bivariate distribution consists of the categories of two variables and their joint frequencies. Its components are displayed in the bivariate tables of our example. Each table has two dimensions, one per variable. The variables are divided into a number of categories; for example, the variable "social class" has been divided into the categories "upper," "middle," and "lower," and the variable "religious denomination" into "Catholic," "Jewish," and "Protestant." The cells of the table constitute an intersection between two categories, each of one variable. The frequencies in each cell are of observations that have two traits in common. For example, Table 16.4 shows two Catholics from the upper class, three from the middle class, and three from the lower class. The Jews have three members of the upper class, two members in the middle class, and three in the lower class; finally, there are three Protestants in the upper class, three in the middle class, and two in the lower class.

The bivariate table can also be visualized as a series of univariate distributions.[2] By splitting each table down its columns and taking each column separately, we will have divided each bivariate distribution into three univariate distributions, representing the class standing of Protestants, Catholics, and Jews. When we compare the three univariate distributions derived from, say, Table 16.3, we can see that each distribution differs from the others in its pattern of dispersion. In the Protestant distribution, most of the respondents tend to cluster at the upper extremity of the distribution, the Jews are clustered in the center, and the Catholics tend toward the lower section. This tendency is even more pronounced in Table 16.2; it becomes absolute (that is, all Protestants are upper class, and so on). In Table 16.4, by contrast, there is practically no difference among the three distributions, the dispersion being identical in each. Thus a researcher can determine the amount of covariation in a bivariate table by comparing the univariate distributions that constitute the table. The larger the difference, the higher the degree of covariation of the two variables.

2. Theodore R. Anderson and Morris Zelditch, Jr., *A Basic Course in Statistics* (Fort Worth, TX: Holt, Rinehart & Winston, 1968), chap. 6.

Percentaging Bivariate Tables

A useful way of summarizing a bivariate table and comparing its univariate distributions to assess relationship is by expressing its frequencies as percentages. Percentaging tables is appropriate whenever the variables are nominal, ordinal, or when an interval variable is grouped into a limited number of categories. In Table 16.5, church attendance and attitudes toward abortion have been cross-tabulated to examine the hypothesis that opinions about a woman's right to abortion for any reason are associated with frequency of church attendance. The table has been set up in the conventional way: "Church attendance" (the independent variable) is at the top of the table, and "abortion attitudes" (the dependent variable) is on the left-hand side. Each church attendance group can be visualized as a univariate distribution, and its frequencies can be transformed into percentages by using the total number of cases in each distribution as a base for percentaging (that is, 472 respondents who attend church less than once a month and 434 who attend church at least once a month each represent 100 percent). The percentages are presented in Table 16.6. Our next step is to compare the univariate distributions to determine the extent of association between church attendance and abortion attitudes. Whereas we compute percentage within each column, we compare them across the columns. The percentage of respondents who attend church less than once a month and support (those who said "yes") abortion for any reason is compared with the per-

Table 16.5

Distribution of Abortion Attitudes by Church Attendance

| Abortion for Any Reason | How Often R Attends Religious Services | | Total |
	Less Than Once a Month	At Least Once a Month	
Yes	267	147	414
No	205	287	492
Total	472	434	906

Source: General Social Survey, 1996.

Table 16.6

Distribution of Abortion Attitudes by Church Attendance (in percentages)

| Abortion for Any Reason | How Often R Attends Religious Services | | Total |
	Less Than Once a Month	At Least Once a Month	
Yes	56.6	33.9	45.7
No	43.4	66.1	54.35
Total	100 (N = 472)	100 (N = 434)	100 (N = 906)

Source: General Social Survey, 1996.

Figure 16.1

Abortion for Any Reason, by Church Attendance

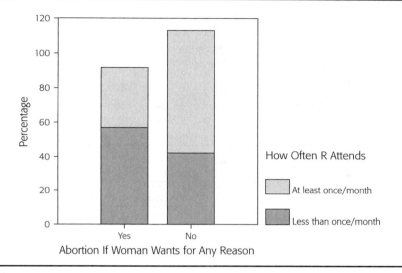

How Often R Attends

At least once/month

Less than once/month

centage of supporters who attend church at least once a month (56.6 percent and 33.9 percent, respectively). Table 16.6 displays a clear pattern of association: Church attendance is associated with abortion attitudes. The two univariate distributions differ in their pattern of distribution: Frequent church goers are less likely to support abortion for any reason. This relation is also depicted in Figure 16.1.

Whenever one variable is considered the independent variable and the other the dependent one, the percentages should be computed in the direction of the independent variable. If church attendance were considered a dependent variable and abortion for any reason the independent variable, percentages would be computed across the rows instead of along the columns.

For further details on reading tables, see Exhibit 16.2 and Appendix A.

Median and Mean as Covariation Measures

When the variables of a bivariate distribution are ordinal, we can compare the medians to determine if the two variables are associated. In Table 16.10 on page 361, 479 General Social Survey (GSS) respondents were classified according to their age and how often they pray. The dependent variable "frequency of praying" is on the left-hand side, and each age group ("under 40" and "40 and over") is assumed to be a univariate distribution. The variable "frequency of praying"—an ordinal variable—is ranked from "several times a day" to "never." The appropriate summary measure for ordinal data is the median, which can be used to summarize each of the two age distributions. By examining the cumulative percentages for each distribution and identifying the category associated with the cumulative percentage closest to 50 percent, we can see that, for those who are "under 40," the median is "several times a week," whereas among respondents who are "40 and over," the median is "once a day." Thus the data from the General Social Survey indicate that prayer frequency increases with age. *(Text continues on p. 361.)*

Exhibit 16.2

THE PRINCIPLES OF TABLE READING

Social scientists use statistical tables extensively as a way of presenting research results. The following discussion is a quick guide to reading tables.

1. *Look for the title.* The title describes the information that is contained in the table. In Table 16.7, the title tells about differences in abortion attitudes between men and women.

2. *Examine the source.* As in Table 16.7, the source of the data is usually written at the bottom of the table. Identifying the source will help you to assess the reliability of the information as well as to find the original data in case you need further information.

Table 16.7

Abortion Attitudes for Men and Women
(compiled from the General Social Survey, 1988–1991)

Abortion Attitudes	Gender		Totals
	Men	Women	
Pro-life	41%	37%	39%
Situationalist	53	54	53
Pro-choice	6	9	8
Totals	100%	100%	100%
	(N = 1,300)	(N = 1,600)	(N = 2,900)

Source: Adapted from Elizabeth Addel Cook, Ted G. Jelen, and Clyde Wilcox, "The Social Bases of Abortion Attitudes," chap. 2 in *Between Two Absolutes: Public Opinions and the Politics of Abortion* (Boulder, CO: Westview Press, 1992).

3. *Determine in which direction the percentages have been computed.* This step is crucial and should be done carefully. It is important to examine whether the percentages have been computed down the columns, across the rows, or on the basis of the whole table. Or is the table an abbreviated one, in which the percentages, as presented, do not add up to 100 percent? Determine the direction by examining where "100%" or the figure for total cases has been inserted. In Table 16.7, the percentages have been computed down the column. By contrast, in Table 16.8, the percentages have been computed in the opposite direction, across the rows. Figures 16.2a and 16.2b are simple bar charts illustrating the two methods of calculating percentages as depicted in Tables 16.7 and 16.8.

4. *Make comparisons.* Comparing the differences among the percentages in the table is a quick method for assessing the extent of a relationship between the variables. You should always make comparisons in the direction opposite to the one in which the percentages have been computed. If the percentages have been computed down the column, as in Table 16.7, then we compare percentages across the rows. The percentage of men who are pro-life is compared to the percentage of women who are pro-life (41 percent to 37 percent). We can also compare the percentage of men and women who are situationalist (53 percent and 54 percent) or pro-choice (6 percent with 9 percent). By making these comparisons, we determine that there are virtually no gender differences in abortion attitudes. Both men and women are equally likely to support or oppose abortions.

Exhibit 16.2 (continued**)**

Figure 16.2

Bar Charts Comparing Column and Row Percentage Shown in Tables 16.7 and 16.8

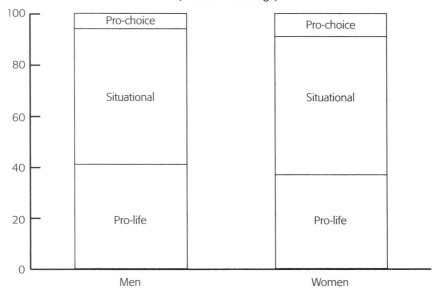

(a)   Attitudes Toward Abortion by Gender
(Column Percentage)

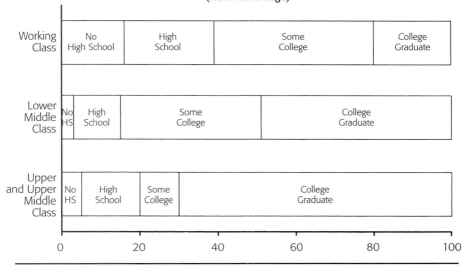

(b)   Education in Relation to Social Class
(Row Percentage)

Exhibit 16.2 (*continued*)

Table 16.8

Level of Education in Relation to Social Class

Social Class	Did Not Finish High School	Graduated from High School but Did Not Enter College	Entered College but Did Not Finish	Completed a Four-Year College Program	Total
Upper and upper middle	5%	15%	10%	70%	100% (N = 600)
Lower middle	3%	12%	36%	49%	100% (N = 420)
Working	16%	23%	41%	20%	100% (N = 510)

In Table 16.8, because the percentages have been calculated across the rows, we compare up or down the columns. For instance, we can compare the percentage of working-class, lower-middle-class, and upper-middle-class respondents who completed a four-year college (20 percent, 49 percent, and 70 percent). Similar comparisons can be made for other levels of education. Based on these comparisons, we can say that level of education is associated with social class.

Table 16.9

Gender and the Percentage of People Who Report Some Same-Sex Desires or Experiences

Gender	Percentage of Each Group Who Reported Same-Sex Desires
Men	10.1 (N = 1,700)
Women	8.6 (N = 1,650)

Source: Adapted from *The New York Times,* "So, Now We Know What Americans Do in Bed. So?" October 9, 1994, p. 3.

Often, for the sake of simplicity, a researcher will present only part of the table. Table 16.9 is an example. It is based on the survey *Sex in America* reported earlier. The table compares the same-sex experiences of men and women. It is important to observe that the two percentages in this table do not add up to 100 percent and that they are to be compared directly. They represent the different proportion of individuals in the two categories of the independent variable (gender) who belong to one response category of the dependent variable (having same-sex experience or desire).

Based on Roberta G. Simmons, "Basic Principles of Table Reading," in *The Logic of Survey Analysis*, Morris Rosenberg, ed. (New York: Basic Books, 1968), pp. 251–258.

Table 16.10

Frequency of Praying by Age

	Age			
	Under 40		40 and Over	
How Often Does R Pray	Percentage	Cumulative Percentage	Percentage	Cumulative Percentage
Several times a day	17.4	17.4	33.1	33.1
Once a day	25.4	42.8	33.1	66.2
Several times a week	21.1	63.9	12.4	78.6
Once a week	8.0	71.9	6.8	85.4
Less than once a week	24.9	96.8	13.9	99.3
Never	3.3	100.1	0.8	100.1
Total	100.1 (N = 213)		100.1 (N = 266)	

Source: General Social Survey, 1996.

With interval variables, we can use the arithmetic mean as a comparative measure. Table 16.11 presents the mean family income by race and gender for the 1996 GSS sample. The average income can be compared across racial and gender groups. Note that income varies both by race and gender. White respondents enjoy the highest average income; however, within each racial group the average income for women is lower than for men.

Table 16.11

Mean Family Income by Race and Gender

Black		White	
Male	Female	Male	Female
$33,375	$23,441	$48,858	$38,065

Source: General Social Survey, 1996.

MEASUREMENT OF RELATIONSHIP ●

So far, we have assessed the extent of covariation of two variables by comparing the univariate distributions that constitute the bivariate table. However, there are various statistical techniques that allow the researcher to assess the extent to which two variables are associated by a single summarizing measure. Such measures of relationship, often referred to as **correlation coefficients,** reflect the strength and the direction of association between the variables and the degree to which one variable can be predicted from the other.

The notion of prediction is inherent in the concept of covariation. When two variables covary, it is possible to use one to predict the other; when they do not, information about one will not enable us to predict the other. Consider Tables 16.2, 16.3, and 16.4 again; assume that no information is available about the religious denomination of the 24 persons and that we are forced to guess the social status of each one. Generally, our best guess would be the most frequent category. However, since in all three tables the frequencies of all the categories are identical, we could arbitrarily select any category. Suppose that we choose the middle class as the best guess for each person. Since only eight cases in each table do in fact belong to the middle class, we will make 16 errors out of 24 guesses in each of the three tables.

Religious denomination can be used to predict social class only if it is likely to reduce the number of errors in prediction. Suppose we predict that all Protestants are upper class, all Jews are middle class, and all Catholics are lower class. In Table 16.2, this prediction is accurate in each of the 24 cases; in Table 16.3, there are 5 errors; in Table 16.4, there are 16 errors.

As Exhibit 16.3 demonstrates, we can calculate the advantage of employing religious denomination to predict social class by subtracting the new number of errors from the previous total. In Table 16.2 the advantage is absolute, because the reduction in the number of errors is the greatest ($16 - 0 = 16$). In Table 16.3 we gain a considerable advantage as well, since the number of errors is reduced by 11 ($16 - 5 = 11$). In Table 16.4 there is no change in the number of errors, despite the employment of religious denomination ($16 - 16 = 0$). The number of errors in this case is the same as if we had predicted that each person is middle class.

Proportional Reduction of Error

We can assess the strength of the association between social class and religious denomination by calculating the proportional reduction in prediction error when using one variable to predict another. The **proportional reduction of error** is defined as follows:[3]

$$\frac{b - a}{b} \tag{16.1}$$

where b = the original number of errors (before employing the independent variable as a predictor)

a = the new number of errors (after employing the independent variable as a predictor)

The proportion varies between 0 and 1 and is expressed as a percentage, with 0 indicating that there is no reduction in prediction error (0 percent) and 1, that there is a 100 percent reduction in prediction error.

3. John Henry Mueller, Karl F. Schuessler, and Herbert L. Costner, *Statistical Reasoning in Sociology* (Boston: Houghton Mifflin, 1970), p. 248.

Exhibit 16.3

COVARIATION AND PREDICTION

Number of errors if we predict that each person is middle class: 16.

For Table 16.2: *Perfect Covariation*

	Prediction	
Upper Class P P P P P P P P	All Protestants are upper class Number of errors:	0
Middle Class J J J J J J J J	All Jews are middle class Number of errors:	0
Lower Class C C C C C C C C	All Catholics are lower class Number of errors:	0
Total number of errors:		0

For Table 16.3: *Moderate Covariation*

	Prediction	
Upper Class J J P P P P P P	All Protestants are upper class Number of errors:	2
Middle Class C J J J J J J P	All Jews are middle class Number of errors:	2
Lower Class C C C C C C C P	All Catholics are lower class Number of errors:	1
Total number of errors:		5

For Table 16.4: *Near-Zero Covariation*

	Prediction	
Upper Class C C J J J P P P	All Protestants are upper class Number of errors:	5
Middle Class C C C J J P P P	All Jews are middle class Number of errors:	6
Lower Class C C C J J J P P	All Catholics are lower class Number of errors:	5
Total number of errors:		16

Using Equation (16.1), you can calculate the proportional reduction in errors of prediction from Tables 16.2, 16.3, and 16.4.

For Table 16.2: $\dfrac{16 - 0}{16} = \dfrac{16}{16} = 1$

For Table 16.3: $\dfrac{16 - 5}{16} = \dfrac{11}{16} = .69$

For Table 16.4: $\dfrac{16 - 16}{16} = \dfrac{0}{16} = 0$

The proportional reduction of error is absolute in Table 16.2, as reflected in the magnitude of the coefficient of 1 (100 percent reduction of error), expressing a perfect relationship between the variables "religious denomination" and "social status." In Table 16.3, the number of errors has been reduced by almost 70 percent by employing religious denomination as a predictor. This is expressed by the coefficient of .69. In Table 16.4, however, there is no advantage in using religious denomination. The coefficient of 0 expresses the absence of any association between the two variables.

Any measure of association can be developed using similar logic, provided that it is based on two kinds of rules:

1. A rule that allows the researcher to predict the dependent variable (e.g., social class) on the basis of an independent variable (e.g., religious denomination).

2. A rule that allows the prediction of the dependent variable independently of an independent variable.[4]

On this basis, any measure of association can be defined as in Equation (16.2):

$$\frac{\text{Error by rule 2} - \text{error by rule 1}}{\text{error by rule 2}} \qquad (16.2)$$

We will analyze most of the measures of relationship introduced in this chapter according to this definition. We shall discuss lambda, which measures the relation between nominal variables; gamma and Kendall's tau-*b*, which are ordinal coefficients; and Pearson's *r*, an interval measure of relation.

NOMINAL MEASURES OF RELATIONSHIP ●

Lambda, the Guttman Coefficient of Predictability

The correlation **lambda** (λ), also known as the **Guttman coefficient of predictability,** is suitable for calculating relationships between nominal variables.[5] Suppose that we are interested in predicting the party identification of nonsouthern whites in a local election in 1996. One possibility is to use party identification during 1996, thereby making use of prediction rule 2. The univariate distribution of party identification is presented in Table 16.12.

---

4. Herbert L. Costner, "Criteria for Measures of Association," *American Sociological Review,* 30 (1965): 344.

5. Louis Guttman, "An Outline of the Statistical Theory of Prediction," in *The Prediction of Personal Adjustment,* ed. Paul Horst (New York: Social Science Research Council, 1941).

▌ Table 16.12

1996 Party Identification Among Nonsouthern Whites
(Hypothetical Data)

Party Identification	f
Democrat	126
Independent	78
Republican	96
Total	300

The most effective way of guessing the party identification of each of these 300 voters on the basis of the distribution from 1996 is to use a measure of central tendency that will yield the smallest number of errors in prediction. Because party identification is a nominal variable, the mode is the most appropriate measure to use. Since Democrats are in the most frequent category ($f = 126$), the best guess is that each voter is identified with the Democratic party, for the number of errors will not exceed 174 (78 independents and 96 Republicans). Any other guess would magnify the number of errors. When guessing voters' party identification on the basis of the dependent variable alone, you should choose the most frequent category. According to this prediction (rule 2), the number of errors is 174 out of 300 guesses, that is, 58 percent.

The percentage of error might be reduced if another variable, "1992 party identification," is used as a predictor. Information is available on each of the 300 voters regarding their party identification in 1992. On this basis, we can construct a bivariate table (Table 16.13) in which all voters are classified according to two variables: their party identification in 1992 and in 1996. With this additional information, we can predict the party identification of nonsouthern whites prior to the elections of 1996 on the basis of their 1992 party identification. First, take those who declared themselves Democratic in 1992; there were 108 respondents, 93 of whom gave the same identification in 1996. As this is the most frequent category, we assume that anyone who identified with the Democratic party in 1992 did so again in 1996. By making this assumption, however, we make 15 errors of prediction because 15 of the 108 identified themselves otherwise in 1996.

▌ Table 16.13

1992 and 1996 Party Identification Among Nonsouthern Whites
(Hypothetical Data)

Party Identification, 1996	Party Identification, 1992			
	Democrat	Independent	Republican	Total
Democrat	93	27	6	126
Independent	15	48	15	78
Republican	—	15	81	96
Total	108	90	102	300

Ninety voters identified themselves as independents in 1992; 48 of them did so again in 1996. We can therefore assume that whoever identified themselves as independents in 1992 did so in 1996 as well. With this assumption, the number of errors is $27 + 15 = 42$, the number who did not identify themselves as independents. Finally, for the 102 who identified with the Republicans in 1992, if it is assumed that their preference patterns did not change in 1996, $15 + 6 = 21$ errors are made.

The total number of errors made by using rule 1 is $15 + 42 + 21 = 78$ errors out of 300 predictions, or 26 percent. Using an independent variable as a predictor leads to a decrease in the error of prediction, as expressed in the magnitude of the correlation, which can now be calculated:

Error stemming from rule 2 = 174

Error stemming from rule 1 = 78

$$\lambda = \frac{174 - 78}{174} = .55$$

Thus we eliminate 55 percent of the errors of prediction concerning party identification in 1996 by using the identification pattern during the 1992 elections.

Lambda is an asymmetrical coefficient, in that it reflects relationships between variables in one direction only. In practice, it is often represented as λ_a, a indicating that it is asymmetrical. The coefficient .55 expresses the relationship between party identification in 1992 and 1996, with that of 1992 serving as an independent variable. The correlation coefficient can also be calculated in the opposite direction, with 1996 serving as the independent variable and 1992 as the dependent variable. The method of calculation is identical: We compute the number of errors made when estimating 1992 identification patterns without reference to 1996 data and then calculate the advantage obtained by gauging the 1992 data from those of 1996. Thus, when switching the order of the variables, lambda would be

$$\lambda = \frac{193 - 78}{193} = .60$$

Notice that lambda calculated in the opposite way results in a different answer. By using 1996 data to predict 1992 party identification, we have reduced 60 percent of the errors of prediction.

ALTERNATIVE PROCEDURE FOR COMPUTING LAMBDA. Lambda can also be computed by a slightly simpler procedure using Equation (16.3)[6]

$$\lambda_a = \frac{\Sigma f_i - F_d}{N - F_d} \qquad (16.3)$$

where f_i = the modal frequency within each category of the independent variable

F_d = the modal frequency in the marginal totals of the dependent variable

N = the total number of cases

6. Linton C. Freeman, *Elementary Applied Statistics* (New York: Wiley, 1965), p. 74.

We can now repeat our calculation of the correlation between the data from 1992 and those from 1996, with the 1992 party identification serving as an independent variable.

$$\Sigma f_i = 93 + 48 + 81 = 222 \qquad N = 300$$

$$F_d = 126 \qquad\qquad \lambda_a = \frac{222 - 126}{300 - 126} = \frac{96}{174} = .55$$

To summarize, the magnitude of lambda expresses the proportional reduction in error of estimate when switching from rule 2 to rule 1. The strength of the association between the two variables reflects the improvement in prediction we can attain with the aid of a second variable. Lambda may range from zero to one; zero indicates that there is nothing to be gained by shifting from one prediction rule to another, whereas one reflects a situation where by using an independent variable we can predict the dependent variable without any error at all.

LIMITATIONS OF LAMBDA.   Lambda has a limitation in situations where the modal frequencies of the independent variable are all concentrated in one category of the dependent variable. In such a case, lambda will always be zero, even in instances where the two variables are in fact related. For example, in the bivariate distribution presented in Table 16.14, we can see that place of residence is associated with self-esteem. More residents of rural areas (75 percent) have high self-esteem than residents of cities (66 percent). However, because the sum of all modal frequencies of the variable "place of residence" ($\Sigma f_i = 300 + 200$) is equal to the modal frequency of the marginal totals of the variable "self-esteem" ($F_d = 500$), lambda will take on the value of zero. Such a pattern of distribution is likely to occur when the marginal totals of the dependent variable are extremely uneven. Lambda would then be inappropriate.

ORDINAL MEASURES OF RELATIONSHIP ●

When both variables of a bivariate distribution are ordinal, the construction of a measure of relationship is based on the principal property of the ordinal scale. Researchers use the ordinal scale to rank observations in relation to the variables being measured. With a single variable, researchers are generally interested in evaluating the relative position of the observations on the variable. For example, professions can be ranked according to the amount of prestige they command, and students can be ranked according to their relative degree of political tolerance. The same principle can be applied with two variables. Here the researcher is interested in examining whether the ranking of observations on each of the vari-

Table 16.14

Place of Residence and Self-Esteem

	Place of Residence		
Self-Esteem	Rural Areas	Urban Areas	Total
High	300	200	500
Low	100	100	200
Total	400	300	700

ables is identical, similar, or different. The investigator compares every two observations and notes whether one that is ranked higher on one variable is also ranked higher with regard to the other variable. For instance, we can examine whether the ranking of professions by their prestige in the 1950s resembles their ranking in the 1990s or whether persons with a conservative orientation on foreign affairs show a similar tendency on domestic issues.

When observations display the same order on both variables, the relationship is said to be positive; when the order is inverse, so that the observation ranking highest on one variable is the lowest on the second variable, the relationship is negative. When there is no clear pattern in the relative position of the observations on both variables, the variables are said to be independent. Consider the following example. If all military personnel with high rank are also more liberal on political issues than lower-ranking officers, one may say that military rank and political liberalism are positively related. If, however, the high-ranking officers are less liberal, the association is negative. If some high officers are liberal and others are not, rank and liberalism are independent of each other.

The Pair Concept

Most ordinal measures of relationship are based on the *pair* as a unit of analysis and the relative ranking of the two parts of the pair on both variables.

Suppose that six officers are classified according to their military rank and degree of liberalism. The observations are presented in Table 16.15.

For the purpose of illustration we have assigned names to each of the officers in Table 16.15. Their names are presented in Table 16.16.

In Table 16.17 we pair these six people and describe their rank order on the variables military rank and liberalism.[7] The first column lists the name of each member of a pair; the second column designates their cell number; and the third and fourth columns, their rank and degree of liberalism. The last column describes the relative position of the pair on the two variables.

For instance, John from cell 11, and Susan from cell 12, are designated as tied on *Y* (liberalism). They have different rank but share the same political views. Pairs tied on *Y* are officers of different ranks sharing the same political views; pairs tied on *X* (for instance, John and Alice) are officers of the same rank but of different political views; pairs designated as "same" are officers who have the same relative position on both variables, so the officer with the higher rank would be the more liberal as well. Pairs designated as "inverse" have a different relative position on both variables, so the officer with the higher rank would be the less liberal of the pair.

Types of Pairs

From Table 16.17 on page 370, the following groups of pairs can be distinguished:

1. Pairs that display the same order on both *X* and *Y*; they will be denoted as *Ns*.
2. Pairs that display an inverse order on *X* and *Y*; they will be denoted as *Nd*.
3. Pairs tied on *X*, denoted as *Tx*.
4. Pairs tied on *Y*, denoted as *Ty*.

---

7. We have not listed the pairs that can be created within each cell (e.g., John and Ruth) because such pairs share the same rank on both variables and are therefore not relevant to the discussion of the ordinal measures presented in this chapter.

Table 16.15

Liberalism by Military Rank (Hypothetical Data)

		Military Rank (X)		
	Liberalism (Y)	Column 1 Low	Column 2 High	Total
Row 1	Low	$2_{(11)}$	$1_{(12)}$	3
Row 2	High	$1_{(21)}$	$2_{(22)}$	3
Total		3	3	6

The numbers in parentheses designate the cell numbers, with row numbers designated first and column numbers second. For example, (11) indicates cell 11 corresponding to the frequency with column 1 (low rank) and row 1 (low liberalism).

Table 16.16

Liberalism by Military Rank for Six Officers

	Military Rank (X)		
Liberalism (Y)	Low	High	Total
Low	John, Ruth$_{(11)}$	Susan$_{(12)}$	3
High	Alice$_{(21)}$	Jim, Glenn$_{(22)}$	3
Total	3	3	6

1. To find Ns in the general bivariate table, multiply the frequency in every cell by the total of all the frequencies in the cells below it and to its right, and add up the products. In Table 16.15, the number of pairs displaying the same ranking on both variables is $2 \times 2 = 4$.

2. To calculate Nd in the general bivariate table, multiply the frequency in each cell by the total of all the frequencies in the cells below it and to its left, and add up the products. In Table 16.15, the number of pairs displaying different rankings on the two variables is $1 \times 1 = 1$.

3. To find the number of pairs tied on X (Tx), multiply the frequency in every cell by the total of all the frequencies in the cells in that column, and add up the products. The number of pairs tied on X is $(2 \times 1) + (1 \times 2) = 4$.

4. To find the number of pairs tied on Y (Ty), multiply the frequency in each cell by the sum of the frequencies in the cells in that row, and add up the products. The number of pairs tied on Y in Table 16.15 is $(2 \times 1) + (1 \times 2) = 4$.

Table 16.17

Relative Position of Officers in Military Rank and Liberalism

Person	From Cell	Military Rank of Officer (X)	Degree of Liberalism (Y)	Order
John	11	L	L	Tie on Y
Susan	12	H	L	
Ruth	11	L	L	Tie on Y
Susan	12	H	L	
John	11	L	L	Tie on X
Alice	21	L	H	
Ruth	11	L	L	Tie on X
Alice	21	L	H	
John	11	L	L	Same
Jim	22	H	H	
Ruth	11	L	L	Same
Jim	22	H	H	
John	11	L	L	Same
Glenn	22	H	H	
Ruth	11	L	L	Same
Glenn	22	H	H	
Susan	12	H	L	Inverse
Alice	21	L	H	
Susan	12	H	L	Tie on X
Jim	22	H	H	
Susan	12	H	L	Tie on X
Glenn	22	H	H	
Alice	21	L	H	Tie on Y
Jim	22	H	H	
Alice	21	L	H	Tie on Y
Glenn	22	H	H	

Gamma

Gamma (γ or **G**), a coefficient used for measuring the association between ordinal variables, was developed by Leo Goodman and William Kruskal.[8] It is a symmetrical statistic, based on the number of same-order pairs (Ns) and the number of different-order pairs (Nd). Tied pairs play no part in the definition of gamma.

The coefficient is defined by Equation (16.4):[9]

$$\gamma = \frac{0.5(Ns + Nd) - \text{minimum } (Ns, Nd)}{0.5(Ns + Nd)} \tag{16.4}$$

8. Leo A. Goodman and William H. Kruskal, "Measure of Association for Cross Classification," *Journal of the American Statistical Association*, 49 (1954): 732–764.

9. Mueller et al., *Statistical Reasoning in Sociology*, p. 282.

Table 16.18

Political Tolerance of College Students by Class Standing

	Class Standing						
	Fresh-man	Sopho-more	Junior	Senior	Graduate Student (Full-Time)	Graduate Student (Part-Time)	Total
Less tolerant	30	30	34	33	40	15	182
Somewhat tolerant	66	75	79	79	120	45	464
More tolerant	28	51	59	63	151	34	386
Total	124	156	172	175	311	94	1,032

To illustrate the calculation of gamma, consider the data presented in Table 16.18 on class standing and political tolerance of students. The researchers collected data to examine the hypothesis that students tend to become politically more liberal as their class standing increases. They assumed that if these two variables are associated, it will be possible to predict students' political tolerance on the basis of their class standing with a minimum of error.

First, we need to count the number of pairs that can be constructed from 1,032 observations. With tied pairs excluded, the overall number of pairs that can be constructed from a bivariate table is $Ns + Nd$. Ns and Nd are calculated according to the definitions presented on page 368.

$$Ns = 30(75 + 51 + 79 + 59 + 79 + 63 + 120 + 151 + 45 + 34)$$
$$+ 66(51 + 59 + 63 + 151 + 34)$$
$$+ 30(79 + 59 + 79 + 63 + 120 + 151 + 45 + 34)$$
$$+ 75(59 + 63 + 151 + 34)$$
$$+ 34(79 + 63 + 120 + 151 + 45 + 34)$$
$$+ 79(63 + 151 + 34) + 33(120 + 151 + 45 + 34)$$
$$+ 79(151 + 34) + 40(45 + 34) + 120(34)$$
$$= 157,958$$

$$Nd = 15(120 + 151 + 79 + 63 + 79 + 59 + 75 + 51 + 66 + 28)$$
$$+ 45(151 + 63 + 59 + 51 + 28)$$
$$+ 40(79 + 63 + 79 + 59 + 75 + 51 + 66 + 28)$$
$$+ 120(63 + 59 + 51 + 28)$$
$$+ 33(79 + 59 + 75 + 51 + 66 + 28)$$
$$+ 79(59 + 51 + 28) + 34(75 + 51 + 66 + 28) + 79(51 + 28)$$
$$+ 30(66 + 28) + 75(28)$$
$$= 112,882$$

The total number of pairs (tied pairs excluded) is $Ns + Nd = 157,958 + 112,882 = 270,840$.

Next we determine the relative political tolerance of the students on the basis of the dependent variable alone—rule 2. To find the relative position of each of the 270,840 pairs, we use a random system. For example, we can label members of each pair as heads or tails and by flipping a coin decide which member is more tolerant. If this process is repeated for each pair, we can expect that in the long run, 50 percent of the guesses about the relative position of the students will be accurate, whereas the other 50 percent will be erroneous. Hence prediction rule 2 will produce $(Ns + Nd)/2 = 135{,}420$ errors.

Prediction rule 1 states that if more pairs display the same order (Ns), this order will be predicted for all other pairs as well. In that case, the number of errors will be Nd, that is, the number of pairs whose ranking is different on the two variables. In the same way, should the number of inverted pairs (Nd) be greater, this order would be predicted for all remaining pairs, and the number of errors will equal Ns.

The calculations based on the information in Table 16.18 indicate that the number of pairs with the same ranking is greater than the number whose ranking is inverted ($Ns > Nd$). Hence we predict the relative position of political tolerance for each pair on the basis of its members' class standing, meaning that the student with the greater seniority exhibits greater tolerance. If Mary is a sophomore and John is a freshman, Mary will be more tolerant than John. As not all pairs display the same order, the number of errors made by such a prediction rule is $Nd = 112{,}882$.

We can now formulate the relationship between class standing and political tolerance, using the general formula for measures of association:

$$\frac{b - a}{b}$$

where $b = (Ns + Nd)/2$ and $a = (Ns, Nd)_{\text{min}}$. Accordingly,

$$\gamma = \frac{\dfrac{(Ns + Nd)}{2} - Nd}{\dfrac{(Ns + Nd)}{2}} = \frac{135{,}420 - 112{,}882}{135{,}420} = \frac{22{,}538}{135{,}420} = .17$$

A value of .17 for γ reflects the advantage we gain by using the variable "class standing" in predicting political tolerance. By using this variable, we eliminate 17 percent of the total number of errors.

ANOTHER FORMULA FOR GAMMA. Gamma can also be calculated by using Equation (16.5):

$$\gamma = \frac{Ns - Nd}{Ns + Nd} \tag{16.5}$$

This formula reflects the relative predominance of same-order or different-order pairs. When same-order pairs predominate, the coefficient is positive; when different-order pairs predominate, it is negative. Gamma can vary from 0 to ± 1. When all the pairs are same-order pairs ($Nd = 0$), gamma equals 1.0.

$$\gamma = \frac{Ns - 0}{Ns + 0} = \frac{Ns}{Ns} = 1.0$$

When all the pairs are different-order pairs ($Ns = 0$), gamma equals -1.

$$\gamma = \frac{0 - Nd}{0 + Nd} = \frac{-Nd}{Nd} = -1.0$$

A coefficient of ± 1.0 indicates that the dependent variable can be predicted on the basis of the independent variable without any error.

When the number of different-order pairs is equal to the number of same-order pairs, gamma is zero:

$$\gamma = \frac{Ns - Nd}{Ns + Nd} = \frac{0}{Ns + Nd} = 0$$

A gamma of zero reflects that there is nothing to be gained by using the independent variable to predict the dependent variable.

LIMITATIONS OF GAMMA. The main weakness of gamma as a measure of ordinal association is the exclusion of tied pairs from its computation. Hence it will reach a value of ± 1 even under conditions of less than perfect association. For example, a perfect relationship was described early in the chapter as in the following table:

50	0
0	50

$$\gamma = 1$$

However, because gamma is based on untied pairs only, it becomes 1 under the following conditions as well:

50	50
0	50

$$\gamma = 1$$

In general, when a large proportion of the observations are concentrated in only few categories, there will be many tied pairs, and gamma will be based on the smaller proportion of untied pairs.

Kendall's Tau-b

When there are many tied pairs, researchers use a different measure that handles the problem of ties. It is **Kendall's tau-b**, defined as follows:

$$\tau b = \frac{Ns - Nd}{\sqrt{(Ns + Nd + Ty)(Ns + Nd + Tx)}} \tag{16.6}$$

Tau-b varies from -1 to $+1$ and is a symmetrical coefficient. It has the same numerator as gamma but has a correction factor for ties in its denominator (Ty and Tx). For example, for the following bivariate distribution,

X

	30	70	100
Y	30	20	50
	60	90	150

we get

$$Ns = 600 \qquad Ty = 2,700$$
$$Nd = 2,100 \qquad Tx = 2,300$$

Therefore,

$$\tau b = \frac{600 - 2,100}{\sqrt{(600 + 2,100 + 2,700)(600 + 2,100 + 2,300)}} = \frac{-1,500}{5,196} = -.29$$

Note that under the same conditions, gamma gives a considerably higher figure than tau-*b*:

$$\gamma = \frac{600 - 2,100}{600 + 2,100} = \frac{-1,500}{2,700} = -.56$$

Gamma will always exceed tau-*b* when there are tied pairs. With no ties, its value will be identical with tau-*b*.

INTERVAL MEASURES OF RELATIONSHIP •

At lower levels of measurement, a researcher's ability to make predictions is restricted, even when the variables he or she is considering are associated. At most, researchers can point out an interdependence of certain categories or properties, such as the fact that Catholics tend to vote Democratic, or they can expect the same relative position of observations on two variables, for instance, that military rank is associated with liberalism. However, predictions of this type are imprecise, and there is frequently a need for more accurate predictive statements, as, for example, when an investigator wishes to predict individuals' future income on the basis of their level of education or a country's gross national product per capita from its level of industrialization.

Prediction Rules

When the variables they are analyzing are at least interval, researchers can be more precise in describing the nature and the form of the relationship.

Most relationships between interval variables can be formulated in terms of a linear function rule. A function is said to be linear when pairs of (X, Y) values fall exactly into a function that can be plotted as a straight line. All such functions have rules of the form $Y = a + bX$, where a and b are constant numbers.

For example, there is a perfect linear relationship between the distance and the time that a car travels at a fixed speed (Table 16.19). If its speed is 60 miles per hour, it will

Table 16.19

Distance by Time

X (miles)	Y (time in minutes)
1	1
3	3
5	5
10	10
15	15

go 60 miles in one hour, or X miles in Y time. The linear function expresses the relationship between the time and the distance that the car travels. Such a function takes the form of $Y = 1X$, reflecting the fact that a change of one unit of distance (miles) will bring about a change of one unit of time (minutes). The constant 1 preceding X in the formula is b, called the slope, and expresses the number of units of change in Y accompanying one unit of change in X.

Linear Regression

The method of specifying the nature of a relationship between two interval variables using a linear function is referred to as *regression analysis.* Scientists use regression to find some algebraic expression by which to represent the functional relationship between the variables. The equation $Y = a + bX$ is a linear regression equation, meaning that the function describing the relation between X and Y is that of a straight line. Ordinarily, researchers display the observations of X and Y—and the **regression line** connecting them—in the form of a graph. The variables X and Y are represented by two intersecting axes. Each observation is entered as a dot at the point where the X and Y scores intersect. In Figure 16.3 we have entered the observations from Table 16.19 to illustrate the graphical presentation of bivariate observations and the functional form that describes their interrelationship. The independent variable, X, is placed on the horizontal axis; Y, the dependent variable, is placed on the vertical axis; and each observation is plotted at the intersection of the two axes. For example, the last observation of Table 16.19 is plotted at the intersection of the two axes on the score 15, to represent its score of 15 on the two variables.

The regression line does not always pass through the intersection of the X and Y axes. When a straight line intersects the Y axis, another constant needs to be introduced into the linear regression equation. This constant is symbolized by the letter a and is called the Y intercept. The intercept reflects the value of Y when X is zero. Each of the three regression lines in Figure 16.4 has different values for a and b. The three different values of a (6, 1, 2) are reflected in the three different intersections of the lines. The different values of b (−3, 0.5, 3) reflect the steepness of the slopes. The higher the value of b, the steeper the slope. Finally, the sign of b expresses the direction of the relationship between X and Y: When b is positive, an increase in X is accompanied by an increase in Y (Figures 16.4b and 16.4c); when b is negative, Y decreases as X increases (Figure 16.4a).

Most relationships in the social sciences can be fairly well expressed by the linear function. For example, the equation $Y = 5,000 + 1,000X$ could express the relation

Figure 16.3

Regression of *Y* on *X*

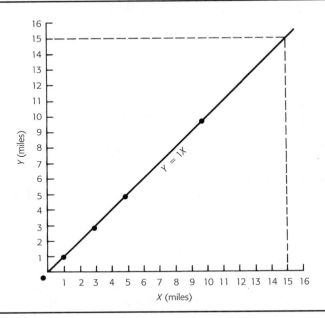

between income and education; *a* would stand for the initial yearly salary ($5,000) for individuals who had no education at all and *b* for an increment of $1,000 for each additional year of education. Using this prediction rule, we could expect individuals having 10 years of schooling to make $15,000 [*Y* = $5,000 + $1,000(10)].

Figure 16.4

Regression Lines

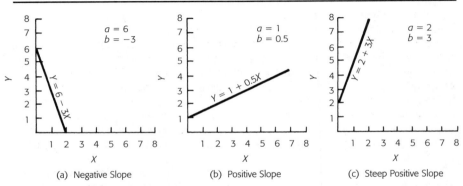

(a) Negative Slope   (b) Positive Slope   (c) Steep Positive Slope

Criterion of Least Squares

The regression equation, however, is only a prediction rule; thus there are discrepancies between actual observations and the ones predicted. The goal is to construct an equation in which the deviations, or **error of prediction,** will be at a minimum. If the researcher adopts a specific criterion in determining a and b of the linear equation, it is possible to create a function that will minimize the variance around the regression line. This is the **criterion of least squares,** which minimizes the sum of the squared differences between the observed Y's and the Y's predicted with the regression equation. This prediction equation is

$$\hat{Y} = a + bX \tag{16.7}$$

where $\hat{Y}$ denotes predicted scores of the variable Y.

According to the least-squares criterion, a and b can be calculated by the following formulas:

$$b = \frac{\Sigma(X - \bar{X})(Y - \bar{Y})}{\Sigma(X - \bar{X})^2} \tag{16.8}$$

$$a = \frac{\Sigma Y - b \Sigma X}{N} = \bar{Y} - b\bar{X} \tag{16.9}$$

A more convenient formula for computing b is

$$b = \frac{N\Sigma XY - (\Sigma X)(\Sigma Y)}{N\Sigma X^2 - (\Sigma X)^2} \tag{16.10}$$

AN ILLUSTRATION.   As an illustration of how to construct a precise prediction rule for interval variables, consider the series of observations in Table 16.20 on the number of robberies (per 100,000 population) and the percentage of the urban population living in metropolitan areas. These observations on 10 states are presented in order to explore the relationship between the degree of urbanization and the crime rate. The variable to be predicted (the dependent variable) is "robberies per 100,000 population," and the independent variable is "percentage of urban population."

To predict the number of robberies in any state without any additional information, we will choose a value that will produce the smallest possible number of errors as an estimate for each state in the distribution. The arithmetic mean is the best guess for each interval distribution because the mean of its squared distribution is lower than for any other value. The average robbery rate for 100,000 population, according to the data, is

$$\bar{Y} = \frac{\Sigma Y}{N} = \frac{1,531}{10} = 153.1$$

To assess the prediction error, we subtract each observation from the mean (to calculate the deviations), and square the deviations. We then select the sum of the squared deviations, referred to as total variation about $\bar{Y}$, as an estimate of error of prediction—rule 2—because it produces the minimum amount of errors. The total variation about $\bar{Y}$ is defined as in Equation (16.11):

Total variation: $\Sigma(Y - \bar{Y})^2$ \tag{16.11}

Table 16.20

Robbery Rate in 1995 and Percentage of Urban Population in 1990

State	Percentage of Urban Population (1990) (X)	Robberies per 100,000 Population (1995) (Y)	XY	X²	Y²
MA	84.3	150	12,645	7,106.49	22,500
WI	65.7	105	6,898.5	4,316.49	11,025
SD	50	26	1,300	2,500	676
VA	69.4	132	9,160.8	4,816.36	17,424
SC	54.6	176	9,609.6	2,981.16	30,976
TX	80.3	180	14,454	6,448.09	32,400
AZ	87.5	174	15,225	7,656.25	30,276
CA	92.6	331	30,650.6	8,574.76	109,561
AR	53.5	126	6,741	2,862.25	15,876
HI	89	131	11,659	7,921	17,161
Totals	726.9	1,531	118,343.5	55,182.85	287,875

Source: U.S. Bureau of the Census, *Statistical Abstracts of the United States: 1997.*

Our next step is to reduce the errors of prediction of number of robberies by employing a second variable, "percentage of urban," as a predictor. We accomplish this by constructing a prediction rule in the form of a regression equation that will best describe the relationship between these two variables and that will allow us to predict the number of robberies in any state on the basis of percentage of urban population with a minimum of error.

The observations in Table 16.20 can be displayed in a scatter diagram, which is a graphic device providing a first approximation of the relationship between the two variables (Figure 16.5). Each pair of letters (representing the abbreviation for each state) represents an observation that has a fixed X and Y characteristic. For example, point WI represents Wisconsin, with 105 robberies per 100,000 population and 65.7 percent of its population in metropolitan areas. After we have plotted all points, we draw a line that best approximates the trend displayed by the points. Obviously, we could draw several such lines among the points, but only one—the line of least squares—comes as close as possible to all the individual observations. Before drawing this line, we need to calculate the constants a and b:

$$b = \frac{10(118,343.5) - (726.9)(1,531)}{10(55,182.85) - (726.9)^2} = 3.01$$

$$a = 153.1 - 3.01(72.69) = -65.70$$

The resulting linear equation is therefore

$$\hat{Y} = -65.7 + 3.01$$

Figure 16.5

Robberies per 100,000 Population and Percentage of Urban Population

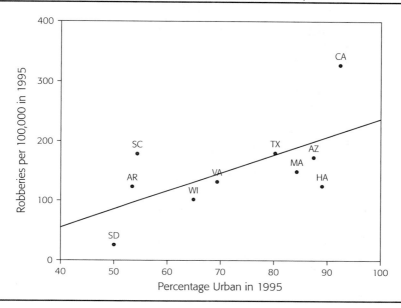

We can now draw the estimated regression line and apply it to predict the robbery rate for every level of urban population. For example, if 50 percent of a state's population were in metropolitan areas, its predicted robbery rate per 100,000 population would be

$$\hat{Y} = -65.7 + 3.01(50) = 84.8$$

Errors of Prediction

As you can see from Figure 16.5, most of the observations are spread around the regression line. These deviations of the actual observations from the predicted ones represent the errors produced when we use the prediction rule specified for predicting the robbery rate based on the percentage of urban population (rule 1).

We can estimate the error involved in predicting robberies based on the percentage of urban population by measuring the deviations of the actual observations from the regression line. First we subtract the predicted robbery rate for each state from the actual observations recorded in Table 16.20. In Texas, for example, the predicted robbery rate per 100,000 population according to the prediction rule is

$$\hat{Y} = -65.7 + 3.01(80.3) = 176$$

The actual robbery rate for Texas is 180; the error of prediction, therefore, is 180 − 176 = 4.

The sum of the squared errors of prediction is the variation unexplained by the independent variable. It is defined in Equation (16.12):

$$\text{Unexplained variation} = \Sigma\,(Y_i - \hat{Y})^2 \tag{16.12}$$

where Y_i = actual observations and $\hat{Y}$ = predicted observations.

Another measure of error that is widely used is the *standard error of estimate* (*Sy.x*). It is based on the *unexplained variation* around the regression line and is defined as follows:

$$Sy.x = \sqrt{\frac{\Sigma\,(Y_i - \hat{Y})^2}{N}} \tag{16.13}$$

The standard error of estimate closely parallels the standard deviation, discussed in Chapter 15.

Pearson's Product–Moment Correlation Coefficient (r)

There are two measures of variability for Y. The first, the total variation about $\bar{Y}$, is the error obtained when we predict Y with no prior knowledge of X—rule 2. (Rule 2 is the total variation about $\bar{Y}$.) The second, the unexplained variation, as defined by Equation (16.12), is the error obtained when using linear regression as the prediction rule—rule 1. These two estimates of error permit us to construct an interval measure of association that reflects a proportional reduction in error when one shifts from rule 2, the mean, to rule 1, the linear regression equation, to evaluate Y. This measure, r^2, is defined in Equation (16.14):

$$r^2 = \frac{\text{total variation} - \text{unexplained variation}}{\text{total variation}} \tag{16.14}$$

The unexplained variation is subtracted from the original error of prediction to evaluate the proportional reduction in error. The proportional reduction in error is reflected by r^2 when X is used to predict Y.

An unexplained variation of zero means that the regression equation eliminated all errors in predicting Y, and r^2 then equals one, meaning that any variation in Y can be explained by X. Conversely, when the unexplained variation is identical to the total variation, r^2 is zero, indicating complete independence between X and Y.

Conventionally, the square root of r^2, or r, designated *Pearson's product–moment correlation coefficient* or **Pearson's r**, rather than r^2, is used as a coefficient of correlation. Pearson's r ranges from -1.0 to $+1.0$, where a negative coefficient indicates an inverse relation between the variables. A simple formula for computing r is

$$r = \frac{N\,\Sigma\,XY - (\Sigma\,X)(\Sigma\,Y)}{\sqrt{[N\,\Sigma\,X^2 - (\Sigma\,X)^2][N\,\Sigma\,Y^2 - (\Sigma\,Y)^2]}} \tag{16.15}$$

For our example the correlation coefficient will be

$$r = \frac{10(118,343.5) - (726.9)(1,531)}{\sqrt{[10(55,182.85) - (726.9)^2][10(287,875) - (1,531)^2]}} = .63$$

Thus r^2 is $.63^2 = .397$, which indicates a proportional reduction of error of 39.7 percent when percentage of urban population is used to predict robberies per 100,000 popula-

Measures of Relationships

Measures of relationships indicate the proportional reduction in error of estimate when the dependent variable is predicted on the basis of the independent variable (rule 1) instead of independently of the independent variable (rule 2).

- *Lambda* (λ): Lambda is used for nominal variables and is calculated using Equation (16.2) or (16.3).
- *Gamma* (γ): Gamma is used for measuring the association between ordinal variables, and is calculated using Equation (16.4) or (16.5).
- *Kendall's tau-b:* Tau-b is used for measuring the association between ordinal variables when there are many tied pairs. It is calculated using Equation (16.6).
- *Linear regression:* A method of specifying a relationship between two interval variables using a linear function of the form $\hat{Y} = a + bx$.
- *Pearson's r:* Pearson's r is used for measuring the association between interval variables, which can be plotted on a graph. It is calculated using Equation (16.15).
- *Criterion of least squares:* A method of selecting a regression equation that minimizes the sum of the square differences between the observed and the predicted Y's. ●

tion. Another way to express this is to say that 39.7 percent of the variance in robbery rate is accounted for by the percentage of urban population.

The size of r^2 or r is determined by the spread of the actual observations around the regression line. Thus if all the observations are on the line, r will be 1.0; if they are randomly scattered, r will approximate zero. Figure 16.6 illustrates a hypothetical strong positive relationship, a weak positive relationship, and no relationship. However, when r or r^2 approximates or equals zero, you should not rush to the conclusion that the variables are not related. The relationship may be curvilinear—that is, it may not be described by a

Figure 16.6

Recognizing Trends from Scatter Diagrams

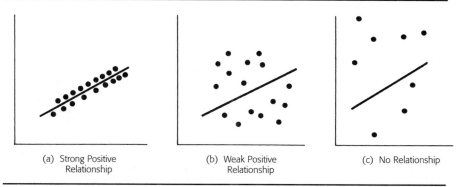

| (a) Strong Positive Relationship | (b) Weak Positive Relationship | (c) No Relationship |

straight line—so that a coefficient based on the linear model would not give a correct picture of the statistical relationship. In general, careful scrutiny of the scatter diagram will indicate the extent to which the observations display a linear or a curvilinear trend or none at all.[10]

SUMMARY

1. This chapter focused on the nature of relationships between two variables and on the construction of measures of relationship. Variables that are related vary together: Specific categories of one variable "go together" with specific categories of the second, or there is some correspondence in the relative position of the two variables.
2. Researchers can assess a relationship between two variables by comparing the univariate distributions that constitute the bivariate table, using summary measures such as the median or the mean. Alternatively, they can describe associations by special measures of relationships that reflect the relative utility of using one variable to predict another.
3. Measures of relationship usually correspond to the variables' level of measurement. Nominal relations can be assessed by lambda. Either gamma or Kendall's tau-*b* is used to calculate relations between ordinal variables.
4. It is sometimes possible to describe the relationship between interval variables by employing specific functions that permit exact predictions. The linear regression equation is such a function. Pearson's *r* is an interval measure of relationship that reflects the proportional reduction of error when one shifts from the mean as a prediction rule to the linear regression equation.

KEY TERMS FOR REVIEW

correlation coefficient (p. 361)
criterion of least squares (p. 377)
error of prediction (p. 377)
gamma (γ) (p. 370)
Kendall's tau-*b* (p. 373)

lambda (λ) (Guttman coefficient of predictability) (p. 364)
Pearson's *r* (p. 380)
proportional reduction of error (p. 362)
regression line (p. 375)

STUDY QUESTIONS

1. Discuss the concept of relationship between variables in terms of the proportional reduction of error.
2. Give an example of a bivariate nominal distribution for which lambda is not suitable as a measure of relationship. What measure would you use instead?
3. The following is a bivariate distribution of alienation by social status. By making a percentage comparison, assess the following hypothesis: As status increases, the degree of alienation decreases. What other measures of relationships can you use to test this hypothesis?

---

10. It is beyond the scope of this text to discuss curvilinear relations. For further discussion, see George W. Bohrnstedt and David Knoke, *Statistics for Social Data Analysis* (Itasca, IL: Peacock, 1988).

	Social Status			
Alienation	Low	Medium	High	Total
High	93	41	10	144
Medium	77	78	46	201
Low	68	128	140	336
Total	238	247	196	681

4. Construct a 2 × 2 table based on 200 respondents, of whom 69 percent are Democrats and 58 percent are for legalizing marijuana. Of the Democrats, 56 percent are for legalizing marijuana. With attitudes toward the legalization of marijuana as the dependent variable, compute lambda. Discuss the relationship between the two variables.

5. Suppose that the correlation $r = .28$ exists between social class and college intentions. Analyze the meaning of this correlation.

6. Social scientists have been attempting to identify social variables that may be associated with economic variables. Use the following data to investigate the relationship between unemployment rates and other variables. Discuss the relationship between each of the independent variables and unemployment. Base your discussion on the following measures: b, r, r^2.

Country	Unemployment Rate	Political Stability	Level of Economic Development	Rate of Urbanization
United States	4.2	8.0	2.34	1.8
New Zealand	4.0	8.6	1.71	.8
Norway	3.1	8.6	1.41	1.2
Finland	3.6	8.1	.83	.7
Uruguay	6.2	3.2	.46	.9
Israel	4.8	8.1	.40	.9
Taiwan	5.8	7.2	.80	.6
Ghana	8.1	5.0	.02	.2
England	8.2	2.6	1.46	1.1
Greece	8.8	2.1	.09	.9

SPSS PROBLEMS

1. The 1996 GSS data contain responses to questions about respondents' church attendance ("attend") and their opinion about the Bible ("bible"). Before you consider the question of whether church attendance affects opinions about the Bible, you may want to recode "attend" into two categories so that everyone who

attends religious services less than once a month is put into one group, and everyone who attends at least once a month is put into a second group. Analyze the relationship between these two variables (*Hint:* Use the recoded "attend" as the independent variable), requesting the appropriate cell percentages. Is there a relationship between church attendance and opinions about the Bible? Describe the relationship using the appropriate percentages. (You should save the "new" recoded "attend," since you may need to use it for other problems.)

2. Use SPSS to construct a table showing the relationship between opinions about the Bible ("bible") and attitudes toward women working ("fefam"). Use "bible" as the independent variable.
   a. What percentage of respondents who believe that the Bible is the word of God agree that it is better for a man to work and for a woman to tend the home?
   b. What percentage of respondents who believe that the Bible is a book of fables agree that it is better for a man to work and for a woman to tend the home?
   c. Is there a relationship between attitudes toward women working and opinions about the Bible? Describe the relationship using the appropriate percentages.

3. Calculate the appropriate measure of association for the relationship examined in Problem 2. Interpret the measure using **PRE.**

4. Use the **gss96worth** file to study the relationship between education ("educ") and total family income ("income91").
   a. Construct a scatterplot of these two variables. Describe the relationship between education and income.
   b. Using the **Regression** procedure, calculate the bivariate regression equation predicting income with education. Write out the regression equation. What are the intercept and the slope? What is the predicted income for someone with only a high school education? With a college education?

ADDITIONAL READINGS

Elifson, Kirk, Richard P. Runyon, and Audrey Haber. *Fundamantals of Social Statistics.* New York: McGraw-Hill, 1998.

Fox, John. *Applied Regression Analysis, Linear Models, and Related Methods.* Thousand Oaks, CA: Sage, 1997.

Healey, Joseph F. *Statistics: A Tool for Social Research.* Belmont, CA: Wadsworth, 1999.

Rawlings, John, Sastry G. Pantula, and David A. Dickey. *Applied Regression Analysis: A Research Tool.* New York: Springer, 1998

Von Eye, Alexander, and Christof Schuster. *Regression Analysis for Social Sciences.* San Diego, CA: Academic Press, 1998.

Witte, Robert S., and John S. Witte, *Statistics.* Orlando, FL: Harcourt Brace, 1997.

CONTROL, ELABORATION, AND MULTIVARIATE ANALYSIS

Does social class standing affect men's participation in household tasks in dual-earner families in the United States? Guided by Marxian theory, Wright et al. hypothesized that this was the case.[1] Using bivariate techniques, they found that class had a marginal effect on the division of labor in dual-earner homes. The researchers then questioned whether other variables might affect men's household work. Using multivariate techniques, they examined the relative effects of eight variables: class, wife's educational level, wife's hours of paid work, wife's contribution to total family income, total family income, respondent's gender ideology (what he or she perceived to be proper roles for men and women), age, and whether there were children under age 16 in the household. When the researchers controlled for these other variables, they found that the original small class effects disappeared. Only the number of hours the wife spent on paid work and the respondent's age had strong effects on how much of the household work was performed by husbands; gender ideology had a weak effect.

If the researchers in this study had used only bivariate techniques to examine the relationship between class and men's work in the home, they might have erroneously concluded that class has at least some effect. Multivariate techniques allowed them to control for the effects of other variables, and they avoided coming to an erroneous conclusion.

•| **IN THIS CHAPTER** we focus on the methods researchers use to analyze more than two variables. The analysis of more than two variables serves three major functions in empirical research: control, elaboration, and prediction. The first function substitutes for the mechanism of experimental control when it is lacking. The second function clarifies bivariate relationships by introducing intervening or conditional variables. The third function is served by analyzing two or more independent variables to account for the variation in the dependent variable. This chapter discusses ways in which a third variable may enter into empirical research. First, we consider the strategy of controlling for a third variable through elaboration. Then we examine multivariate counterparts to the bivariate measures of relations. Finally, we examine the techniques of causal modeling and path analysis.

The examination of a bivariate relationship is but the first step in data analysis. In the next step, researchers evaluate the substantive implications of their findings and draw causal inferences. In other words, after researchers establish covariation and its direction using a bivariate measure, they interpret the findings and assess the causal priorities of the investigated variables by introducing other variables into the analysis. Suppose that you find a relationship between parents' age and child-rearing practices, that is, that older parents tend to be more restrictive than younger parents with their children. What interpretation can you give to this finding? You may claim that the variables are causally related and that increasing age of parents is associated with a shift from permissive toward restrictive attitudes. However, it is possible that a difference in child-rearing practices is due not to a difference in age but rather to a difference in orientation: Older parents were exposed to an orientation stressing restriction, whereas younger parents behave according to a more liberal orientation advocating more permissive practices. In other

---

1. Erik Olin Wright, Karen Shire, Shu-Ling Hwang, Maureen Dolan, and Janeen Baxter, "The Non-Effects of Class on the Gender Division of Labor in the Home: A Comparative Study of Sweden and the United States," *Gender & Society*, 8(4) (1992): 252–282.

words, the relationship between parents' age and child-rearing practices may be due to the fact that the variables "age" and "child-rearing practices" are both associated with a third variable, "orientation."

An observed correlation between two or more variables does not, of itself, permit the investigator to make causal interpretations. A bivariate relationship may be the product of chance, or it may exist because the variables are related to a third, unrevealed variable. Furthermore, the phenomenon under investigation can often be explained by more than a single independent variable. In any case, the introduction of additional variables serves the purpose of clarifying and elaborating the original relationship. |

CONTROL ●

An association between two variables is not a sufficient basis for an inference that the two are causally related. Other variables must be ruled out as alternative explanations. For example, a relationship between height and income can probably be accounted for by the variable "age." Age is related to both income and height, and this joint relationship produces a statistical relationship that has no causal significance. The original relation between height and income is said to be a **spurious relation.** Spuriousness is a concept that applies to situations where an extraneous variable produces a "fake" relation between the independent and dependent variables. It is essential that an investigation uncover the extraneous factors contaminating the data in this way. Thus, in validating bivariate associations, an important step is to rule out the largest possible number of variables that might conceivably explain the original association. Researchers rule out variables through the process of *control,* a basic principle in all research designs.

In experimental designs, control is accomplished by randomly assigning research participants to experimental and control groups. The logic of controlled experimentation assures the researcher that all extraneous variables have been controlled for and that the two groups differ only with regard to their exposure to the independent variable. However, as we have seen in earlier chapters, social scientists find it difficult to manipulate social groups and to apply experimental treatment prior to observations. Consequently, they lack control over numerous factors that throw doubt on any association between independent and dependent variables employed in the investigation.

In quasi-experimental designs, statistical techniques substitute for the experimental method of control. Researchers employ these techniques during data analysis rather than at the data collection stage. There are three methods of statistical control. The first entails subgroup comparisons using the technique of cross-tabulation. The second technique, partial correlation, employs mathematical procedures to readjust the value of a bivariate correlation coefficient. The third method is multiple regression, which enables us to estimate the effect of an independent variable on the dependent variable while controlling for the effect of other variables.

METHODS OF CONTROL ●

Cross-Tabulation as a Control Operation

We can compare the **cross-tabulation** method of control to the procedure of matching employed in experiments. In both techniques, the investigator attempts to equate the groups examined with respect to variables that may bias the results. In experiments, researchers equate research participants prior to their exposure to the independent variable by identifying pairs of participants that are identical with respect to the controlled factors and physically allocating one member of each pair to the experimental group and one member to the control group. With cross-tabulation, investigators allocate research participants to the respective groups only during the analysis stage. Whereas matching is a physical control mechanism, cross-tabulation is a statistical operation.

Cross-tabulation involves the division of the sample into subgroups according to the categories of the controlled variable (called the **control variable**). The researcher then reassesses the original bivariate relation within each subgroup. By dividing the sample into subgroups, the researcher removes the biasing inequality by computing a measure of relationship for groups that are internally homogeneous with respect to the biasing factor.

Generally, only variables that are associated with both the independent variable and the dependent variable can potentially bias the results. Thus the researcher selects as

Table 17.1

Political Liberalism by Urban–Rural Location

Political Liberalism	Urban Area	Rural Area
High	50%	28%
	(200)	(140)
Low	50%	72%
	(200)	(360)
Total	100%	100%
	(400)	(500)

Figure 17.1

Liberalism by Urban–Rural Location

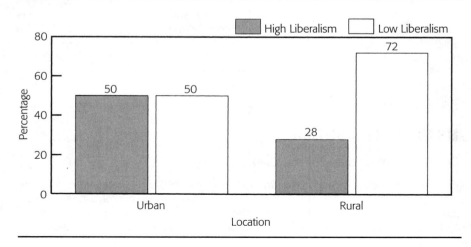

Table 17.2

Education by Urban–Rural Location

Education	Urban Area	Rural Area
High	75%	20%
	(300)	(100)
Low	25%	80%
	(100)	(400)
Total	100%	100%
	(400)	(500)

Table 17.3

Political Liberalism by Education

Political Liberalism	Education	
	High	Low
High	65%	20%
	(240)	(100)
Low	40%	80%
	(160)	(400)
Total	100%	100%
	(400)	(500)

control variables only variables that show an association with the independent and dependent variables under investigation.

AN ILLUSTRATION. The following example illustrates the steps involved in controlling for a third variable through cross-tabulation. Suppose we select a sample of 900 respondents to test the hypothesis that people from urban areas are politically more liberal than rural dwellers. The data obtained are presented in Table 17.1 and illustrated in Figure 17.1. We observe that 50 percent of urban residents are liberal, compared to only 28 percent of the respondents from rural areas. Thus we may conclude that political liberalism is associated with place of residence. The question is whether this association is direct (in which case the hypothesis may be supported) or is based on a spurious relation with another variable. One such additional variable might be education, which is associated with both place of residence and political liberalism, as reflected in the hypothetical bivariate distributions of Tables 17.2 and 17.3, which are illustrated in Figure 17.2.

Partial Tables

To control for education, we divide the 900 persons into two groups according to level of education (high, low). Within each group, urban–rural location is cross-tabulated with

Figure 17.2

The Relationship Between Liberalism, Urban–Rural Location, and Education

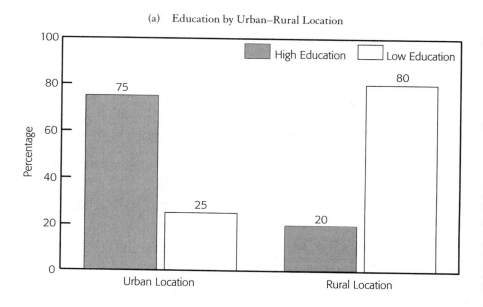

(a)   Education by Urban–Rural Location

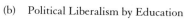

(b)   Political Liberalism by Education

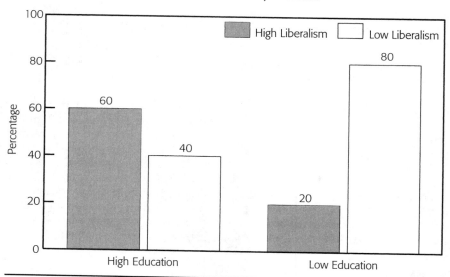

Table 17.4

Political Liberalism by Urban–Rural Location, Controlling for Education
(Spurious Relationship)

Political Liberalism	High Education		Low Education	
	Urban Area	Rural Area	Urban Area	Rural Area
High	60%	60%	20%	20%
	(180)	(60)	(20)	(80)
Low	40%	40%	80%	80%
	(120)	(40)	(80)	(320)
Total	100%	100%	100%	100%
	(300)	(100)	(100)	(400)

political liberalism. We then estimate the original bivariate association in each of the sub-groups. The controlled data are summarized in Table 17.4 and illustrated in Figure 17.3.

The resulting two bivariate tables of Table 17.4 are referred to as **partial tables** because each reflects only part of the total association. Each pair of parallel cells in the two partial tables adds up to the corresponding cell in the original table (Table 17.1). For example, the 180 highly educated respondents who come from urban areas and are liberals plus the 20 respondents who are urban liberals with a low level of education together constitute the 200 urban, liberal respondents in the original bivariate table.

Figure 17.3

Political Liberalism by Location, Controlling for Education (Spurious Relationship)

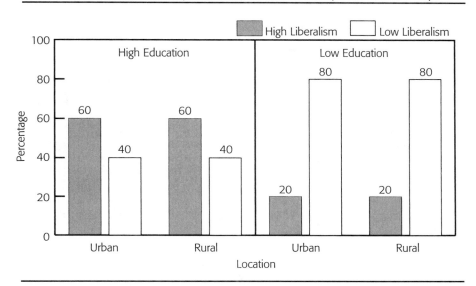

To assess the partial association, we compute a measure of relationship for each of the control groups and compare it with the original results, selecting appropriate measures in the same way as for regular bivariate distributions. We can use difference of percentages, gamma, or Pearson's *r*, depending on the level of measurement.

The value of the partial association can be either identical or almost identical to the original association, it can vanish, or it can change. For the examination of spurious relationships, only the first two possibilities are relevant. When the partial association is identical or almost identical to the original association, we can conclude that the control variable does not account for the original relation and that the relation is direct. If it vanishes, the original association is said to be spurious. (A third variable may intervene between the dependent and independent variables, in which case the partial association will also vanish or approximate zero. We will consider an example of this situation shortly.)

If the partial association does not vanish but is different from the original association or if it is different in each of the partial tables, the independent and dependent variables are said to *interact.* We will return to interaction later.

SPURIOUS ORIGINAL ASSOCIATION.   In the example of Table 17.4, a percentage comparison shows that education completely accounts for the relation between residence and liberalism, for there is no difference between rural and urban residents in their degree of liberalism within either of the two education groups. Sixty percent of the highly educated rural residents, like 60 percent of the highly educated urban residents, are politically liberal. Within the low-education group, 20 percent are liberal wherever they reside. The overall association between the independent and dependent variables is completely accounted for by the association of each with education, as is illustrated in the bar graph shown in Figure 17.3. This pattern can also be represented by the drawing shown in Figure 17.4.

Education determines both political liberalism and place of residence. That is, people who are educated tend to live in cities and are generally politically liberal. There is no inherent link between political liberalism and place of residence, and the association between them is spurious.

DIRECT ORIGINAL ASSOCIATION.   The control of a third variable may lead to entirely different results, however. In the hypothetical example of Table 17.5, the original bivariate association remains unchanged by educational level. In the total sample, as well as in each educational group, a percentage comparison shows that 50 percent of urban residents are liberal, compared with 28 percent of rural residents. The bar graph presented in Figure 17.5 clearly shows that the overall relationship between the two original vari-

Figure 17.4

Overall Association of Variables in Table 17.4

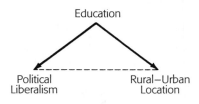

Table 17.5

Political Liberalism by Urban–Rural Location, Controlling for Education
(Nonspurious Relationship)

Political Liberalism	High Education		Low Education	
	Urban Area	Rural Area	Urban Area	Rural Area
High	50%	28%	50%	28%
	(50)	(35)	(150)	(105)
Low	50%	72%	50%	72%
	(50)	(90)	(150)	(270)
Total	100%	100%	100%	100%
	(100)	(125)	(300)	(375)

ables is not accounted for by the control variable. The investigator can be confident that education is an irrelevant factor with respect to this particular association and that the association between the two original variables is direct.

In practice, the results are not as clear-cut as presented here. It is very rare for associations either to vanish or to remain identical with the original results. Often the partial tables show a clear decrease in the size of the original relationship; at times the reduction is slight. This is because of the numerous factors that can account for a bivariate association.

Figure 17.5

Political Liberalism by Location, Controlling for Education (Nonspurious Relationship)

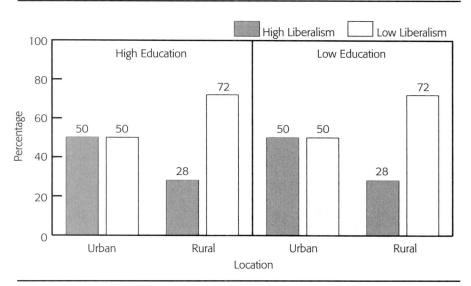

In our example, other variables, such as income, party identification, or religious affiliation, might conceivably explain the relationship between urban–rural location and political liberalism. Statisticians refer to this characteristic of variables as "block-booking,"[2] a term that reflects the multidimensionality of human beings and of their social interaction. When researchers compare people in terms of social class, they consider only one dimension of human experience. People may differ thoroughly from each other in a great many things, and all these other factors may enter into the phenomenon to be explained. The block-booked factors become our control variables; but when we control for only one or some of them, the rest may still explain the remaining residual in the dependent variable.

The procedure, then, is to hold constant all other variables that may be relevant to the subject of investigation. The selection of these variables is a logical and theoretical operation, the only statistical guideline being the requirement that the potential control factor be related to both the independent and dependent variables. Of course, a researcher can never be completely sure that he or she has introduced all relevant variables into the analysis. However, the greater the number of relevant factors controlled for, the greater is the confidence that the relationship is not spurious.

ELABORATION ●

The mechanism of control is designed to uncover factors that might invalidate the original bivariate association. In that case, the investigators are likely to turn to other factors that they can employ as independent variables and then repeat the process of validating the relationship. However, if the relationship observed is nonspurious, researchers can proceed to a more advanced stage of analysis and elaborate the bivariate association. **Elaboration** usually involves the introduction of other variables to determine the links between the independent and dependent variables or to specify the conditions under which the association takes place.

Some concrete examples will help us illustrate the meaning of elaboration. In the past decade, social scientists have paid close attention to the effect of early childbearing on the life chances of adolescent parents. Investigators have discovered that early childbearers are more likely to experience economic hardship and family disruption in later life than later childbearers.[3] Early childbearing appears to be linked to dropping out of school, particularly for adolescent mothers. Low educational attainment in turn makes it more difficult for teenage mothers to find stable and remunerative employment. We can represent these relationships schematically as follows:

Early childbearing ⟶ low educational attainment ⟶ economic disadvantage

In this scheme, low educational attainment provides a link between early childbearing and economic disadvantage. It is an **intervening variable** between the independent variable (early childbearing) and the dependent variable (economic disadvantage).

Although low educational attainment accounts for the economic disadvantage of many teenage mothers, the life chances of these women vary enormously. For instance, a recent study found that one-fourth of early childbearers were on welfare while another fourth were relatively comfortable economically, with a family income of more than

---

2. Morris Rosenberg, *The Logic of Survey Analysis* (New York: Basic Books, 1968), pp. 26–28.

3. Frank F. Furstenberg, Jr., J. Brooks-Gunn, and S. Philip Morgan, *Adolescent Mothers in Later Life* (Cambridge: Cambridge University Press, 1987).

$25,000 a year.[4] To account for these differences, researchers controlled for a number of variables. One of these variables was race. They discovered that white mothers were more likely to attain a higher economic level than black mothers. In this example, the original bivariate association between early childbearing and economic disadvantage is pronounced only among one subgroup, black mothers. The control variable, race, is thus said to be a **conditional variable,** and the pattern is called **interaction.** Schematically, this pattern may be represented as follows:

Early childbearing ⟨ → black ⟶ economic disadvantage
                     → white ⟶ no economic disadvantage

We shall examine empirical examples of both intervening variables and interaction.

Intervening Variables

Let us return to the first case, in which the controlled variable is said to intervene between the independent and dependent variables. Table 17.6 shows the relationship between childbearing and economic status. The data demonstrate that these two variables are associated: Early childbearers are more likely to have low economic status. The investigators hypothesized that these differences could be explained by the variable "educational attainment." That is, early childbearing affects economic status indirectly through educational attainment, because young mothers are more likely to drop out of school than nonmothers.

As a means of testing this hypothesis, the investigators held educational attainment constant and reexamined the original relationship. If, as suggested, childbearing has only an indirect influence on economic status, then when the intermediate link is controlled for, the association between childbearing and economic status should disappear. The results in Table 17.7 confirm the hypothesis: There are no differences in economic status between mothers and nonmothers when the level of educational attainment is the same. The original relationship vanishes when educational attainment is controlled for.

In order to infer that a control variable links the independent and dependent variables, the researcher must demonstrate that the control variable is associated with both

▌ Table 17.6

Childbearing and Economic Status (Hypothetical Data)

Economic Status	Early Childbearing		Total
	Yes	No	
Low	54%	33%	
	(869)	(653)	(1,522)
High	46%	67%	
	(731)	(1,347)	(2,078)
Total	100%	100%	
	(1,600)	(2,000)	(3,600)

4. Ibid., p. 48.

Table 17.7

Childbearing and Economic Status by Educational Attainment (Hypothetical Data)

Economic Status	High Educational Attainment Early Childbearing		Low Educational Attainment Early Childbearing		Total
	Yes	No	Yes	No	
Low	18%	18%	64%	65%	
	(90)	(216)	(704)	(512)	(1,522)
High	82%	82%	36%	36%	
	(410)	(984)	(396)	(288)	(2,078)
Total	100%	100%	100%	100%	
	(500)	(1,200)	(1,100)	(800)	(3,600)

the independent and dependent variables and that when it is controlled for, the original relationship vanishes (or diminishes considerably) in all categories of the control variable. You may be exclaiming that these were the identical conditions required for declaring the relationship spurious, and we can confirm that this is indeed true. The statistical tests in both cases are identical, but the interpretation is significantly different. With a spurious interpretation, the statistical results invalidate a hypothesis about the relationship between the independent and dependent variables; an intervening interpretation, by contrast, clarifies and explains such a relationship. How, then, can we distinguish between the two?

Morris Rosenberg maintains that the difference is a theoretical issue rather than a statistical one and that it lies in the assumed causal relationship among the variables.[5] With a spurious interpretation, it is assumed that there is no causal relation between the independent and dependent variables; in the case of an intervening variable, the two are indirectly related through an intermediate link, the control variable.

Interaction

For the second type of elaboration, interaction, the researcher specifies the conditions or contingencies necessary for the relationship to occur. We will illustrate the meaning of interaction using the example of childbearing, economic status, and race. The bivariate association between childbearing and economic status already presented in Table 17.6 demonstrated that these two variables are associated. To gain further insight, a researcher might control for race. The results are presented in Table 17.8.

The results clearly demonstrate an interactive relationship, since the relationship between childbearing and economic status is different for white and black women: For black women, early childbearing has a considerable impact on economic status (66 percent of the early childbearers have a low economic status, compared to only 31 percent of women who are not early childbearers); whereas among white women, there is no relationship between these two variables. For white women, a little over one-third in both groups (36 percent and 38 percent) are in the low-status group. Based on these

5. Rosenberg, *The Logic of Survey Analysis*, pp. 54–66.

Table 17.8

Childbearing and Economic Status by Race (Hypothetical Data)

Economic Status	Black Early Childbearing		White Early Childbearing		Total
	Yes	No	Yes	No	
Low	66%	31%	36%	38%	
	(594)	(372)	(252)	(304)	(1,522)
High	34%	69%	64%	62%	
	(306)	(828)	(448)	(496)	(2,078)
Total	100%	100%	100%	100%	
	(900)	(1,200)	(700)	(800)	(3,600)

results, it may be concluded that early childbearing and race interact in their effect on economic status; that is, the relationship between the independent and dependent variables is conditioned by race. One possible interpretation is that early childbearing has economic consequences only for women who are already disadvantaged.

Conditional relationships such as this one are quite common in social science research and can be inferred whenever the relative size or direction of the original bivariate relationship is more pronounced in one category of the control variable than in another. The presence of such differences between subgroups reflects the nature of social reality, in which each variable can be broken down into various components. Indeed, many conditional factors are associated with almost any two-variable relationships. This social complexity makes the analysis of interaction one of the most important aspects of statistical analysis.

INTEREST AND CONCERN AS A CONDITION. Herbert Hyman analyzed the various factors that are generally considered conditions for most bivariate association and classified them into three major groups.[6] The first class consists of variables that specify relationships in terms of interest and concern. In many situations, interest and concern specify the conditions under which the effectiveness of an independent variable is more or less pronounced. People tend to differ in their interests, which in turn affect their attitudes and behavior patterns. Thus social stimuli are likely to have differential effects on them, and the identification of these differing patterns may prove to be essential to the social scientist. For instance, consider Morris Rosenberg's finding that self-esteem is associated with intensity of political discussion.[7] Adolescents with low self-esteem, who are more self-conscious, tend to avoid expressing their political views. Taking into account the level of political interest, Rosenberg observed that the relationship holds only among those who are interested in politics. Those who are not interested in politics also do not discuss politics, even though they might have a high degree of self-esteem. Thus the use of the conditional factor helps to clarify the original findings.

6. Herbert H. Hyman, *Survey Design and Analysis* (New York: Free Press, 1955), pp. 295–311.

7. Morris Rosenberg, "Self-Esteem and Concern with Public Affairs," *Public Opinion Quarterly*, 26 (1962): 201–211.

Types of Elaboration

+ *Intervening variables:* Variables that link the independent and dependent variables and explain the relationship between them. In order to conclude that a variable links the independent and dependent variables, the researcher must show that the control variable is associated with both the independent and dependent variables and that when it is controlled for, the original relationship decreases significantly, or disappears, in all categories of the control variable.

+ *Interaction:* To demonstrate interaction, the researcher must determine the conditions or contingencies necessary for the relationship to occur. Researchers can infer conditional relationships whenever the relative size or direction of the original bivariate relationship is more pronounced in one category of the control variable than in another.

TIME AND PLACE AS A CONDITION. The second class of factors specifies associations in terms of time and place. A relationship between two variables can vary according to the time and place at which it is studied. In studies in comparative politics, researchers typically introduce "place" as a control variable. The effect of class, gender, and race on voting, for example, differs from one country to another.

Specification by time is meaningful too. Often a relationship that holds at one time will be dismissed or changed at another time. For example, a growing body of research has documented a gender difference in support of women in politics, with women more likely than men to reject stereotypical notions that "politics is for men."[8] In a number of studies comparing the effect of gender on attitudes toward women in politics over time, researchers have hypothesized that time will reduce gender differences because of the presence of more female political role models. Research into the general process of development and socialization offers another example. The family is known to affect various behavioral patterns in children. This effect is pronounced, especially at the early stages, when the child is more exposed and more vulnerable to his or her family. At later stages, however, other aspects of socialization play an important role, and the family's influence diminishes. Thus a relationship between family characteristics and behavioral orientations would not stay constant if a researcher examined them at different times.

BACKGROUND CHARACTERISTICS AS A CONDITION. Background characteristics of the units of analysis are the last class of factors. Often associations are likely to differ for persons or groups that do not share the same characteristics. Thus the relation between class position and voting behavior is different for men and for women, and the effect of teachers' encouragement on self-esteem is not identical for black and white children. Background characteristics are perhaps the most common among the types of conditions employed in the social sciences. In fact, some researchers employ such control variables as "social class," "level of education," "gender," and "age" almost automatically, reexamining all relationships obtained.

---

8. Diane Gillespie and Cassie Spohn, "Adolescents Attitudes Toward Women in Politics: A Follow-up Study," *Women and Politics*, 10 (1990): 1–16.

Partial Correlation as a Control Operation

The cross-tabulation control operation is quite popular in empirical research, and it is applied to all levels of measurement. However, it has a drawback that limits its use when the number of cases is relatively small. In order to use the cross-tabulation method of control, the researcher must subdivide the sample into progressively smaller subgroups, according to the number of categories of the controlled factor. Subdividing the sample reduces the number of cases that serve as a basis for computing the coefficient, and a small sample size calls into question the validity and reliability of the findings. This problem is particularly acute when several variables are controlled simultaneously.

A second method of control, which is not limited by the number of cases, is the **partial correlation.** This method, a mathematical adjustment of the bivariate correlation, is designed to cancel out the effect of the control variable on the independent and dependent variables. The logic underlying the calculation of this measure of association is similar to that of cross-tabulation. The original association between the independent and dependent variables is reassessed to determine whether it reflects a direct association, independent of the variables' association to a third extraneous factor.

The formula for calculating partial correlation coefficients employs certain notational conventions with which you must be familiar. The independent variable is designated as X_1, the dependent variable as X_2, and the control variable as X_3. Additional control variables are designated as X_4, X_5, X_6, and so forth. The symbol r is a shorthand notation for the correlation coefficient, and researchers use the X subscripts to show which correlation they are describing. For example, r_{12} denotes the correlation between the independent variable (X_1) and the dependent variable (X_2). The correlations between the control variable (X_3) and the independent and dependent variables are shown as r_{31} and r_{32}, respectively.

Suppose that a correlation of $r_{12} = .60$ is found between self-esteem (X_1) and educational expectation (X_2). To test the nature of this association, the researcher can introduce an additional variable such as social class (X_3), which is related to both self-esteem ($r_{31} = .30$) and educational expectation ($r_{32} = .40$). The researcher can use partial correlation to obtain a measure of association with the effect of social class removed. The formula for calculating the partial correlation coefficient is

$$r_{12.3} = \frac{r_{12} - (r_{31})(r_{32})}{\sqrt{1 - (r_{31})^2}\sqrt{1 - (r_{32})^2}} \tag{17.1}$$

where X_1 = independent variable (in our example self-esteem)

X_2 = dependent variable (educational expectation)

X_3 = control variable (social class)

The symbol to the right of the dot indicates the variable to be controlled. Thus $r_{12.3}$ is the correlation between variables X_1 and X_2 controlling for variable X_3. Similarly, a partial coefficient between variables X_1 and X_3 controlling for X_2 would be denoted $r_{13.2}$. A partial with one control is referred to as a *first-order partial* to distinguish it from a bivariate correlation, often denoted as a *zero-order correlation.* A partial with two controls is referred to as a *second-order partial,* and so on. When more than one variable is controlled for simultaneously, their numbers are added to the right of the dot. Thus, controlling for variables X_3 and X_4 would be expressed as $r_{12.34}$.

We can now calculate the partial correlation for self-esteem and educational expectation:

$$r_{12.3} = \frac{.60 - (.30)(.40)}{\sqrt{1 - (.30)^2}\,\sqrt{1 - (.40)^2}} = \frac{.48}{\sqrt{.7644}} = \frac{.48}{.87} = .55$$

When the partial correlation is squared, the result reflects the proportion of variation left unexplained by the control variable and explained by the independent variable. Thus about 30 percent $[(.55)^2 \times 100]$ of the variation in educational expectation was explained by self-esteem after removing the effect of social class.

In contrast to the cross-tabulation method of control, the partial correlation yields a single summarizing measure that reflects the degree of correlation between two variables while controlling for a third. Thus the partial correlation does not reflect variation in the partial associations in different categories of the controlled variable because it averages out the different partials. This property of the measure is its main disadvantage, as it might obscure otherwise essential information. In cases where the investigator suspects that there are significant differences between the partials of the various subgroups, it is advisable to use the cross-tabulation technique instead.

Multiple Regression as a Control Operation

Another method that allows us to assess the relationship between two variables while controlling for the effect of others is **multiple regression.** Multiple regression is a simple extension of bivariate regression, which was discussed in Chapter 16. A multiple regression equation, shown in Equation (17.2), describes the extent of linear relationships between the dependent variable and a number of other independent (or control) variables:

$$\hat{Y} = a + b_1X_1 + b_2X_2 \tag{17.2}$$

where $\hat{Y}$ is the dependent variable and X_1 and X_2 are the independent variables. Designated as partial regression coefficients, b_1 and b_2 are the slope of the regression line for each independent variable, controlling for the other. Thus b_1 reflects the amount of change in Y associated with a given change in X_1, holding X_2 constant; b_2 is the amount of change in Y associated with a given change in X_2, holding X_1 constant; and a is the intercept point on the Y axis for both X_1 and X_2.

As with bivariate regression, the constants of the multiple linear regression equation are estimated so as to minimize the average squared error in prediction. This is accomplished by using the least-squares criterion to obtain the best fit to the data. The least-squares estimates of a, b_1, and b_2 are shown in Equations (17.3), (17.4), and (17.5):

$$b_1 = \left(\frac{s_Y}{s_1}\right)\frac{r_{y1} - r_{y2}r_{12}}{1 - (r_{12})^2} \tag{17.3}$$

$$b_2 = \left(\frac{s_Y}{s_2}\right)\frac{r_{y2} - r_{y2}r_{12}}{1 - (r_{12})^2} \tag{17.4}$$

$$a = \bar{Y} - b_1\bar{X}_1 - b_2\bar{X}_2 \tag{17.5}$$

We will illustrate the computation of the multiple regression constants using Equations (17.3), (17.4), and (17.5) by attempting to estimate the effects of self-esteem and education on political liberalism.

We have designated liberalism as Y, education as X_1, and self-esteem as X_2. Liberalism has been measured on a scale from 1 to 10 and self-esteem has been measured on a scale from 1 to 9, with higher numbers indicating higher levels of each of these variables. Education is measured in years of school. The following are the hypothetical means, standard deviations, and bivariate correlation coefficients for these variables:

$$\bar{Y} = 6.5 \qquad s_Y = 3 \qquad r_{y1} = .86 \text{ (liberalism by education)}$$

$$\bar{X}_1 = 8.9 \qquad s_1 = 4.1 \qquad r_{y2} = .70 \text{ (liberalism by self-esteem)}$$

$$\bar{X}_2 = 5.8 \qquad s_2 = 2.2 \qquad r_{12} = .75 \text{ (education by self-esteem)}$$

For this problem, b_1 stands for the effect of education on liberalism controlling for self-esteem and b_2 for the effect of self-esteem on liberalism controlling for education.

Substituting the data into the formulas for b_1 and b_2, we have

$$b_1 = \left(\frac{3}{4.1}\right) \frac{.86 - (.70)(.75)}{1 - (.75)^2} = .56$$

$$b_2 = \left(\frac{3}{2.2}\right) \frac{.70 - (.86)(.75)}{1 - (.75)^2} = .17$$

The intercept for the multiple regression equation is

$$a = 6.5 - (.56)(8.9) - (.17)(5.8) = .53$$

With the obtained values of b_1, b_2, and a, the complete multiple regression equation for predicting liberalism on the basis of education and self-esteem is therefore

$$\hat{Y} = .53 + 56X_1 + .17X_2$$

It indicates the extent of political liberalism that would be expected, on the average, with a given level of education and a given level of self-esteem. For example, for a person with 10 years of schooling and a self-esteem score of 8, the expected level of liberalism would be

$$\hat{Y} = .53 + (.56)(10) + (.17)(8) = 7.49$$

As the b coefficients reflect the net effect of each variable, we can compare them in order to denote the relative importance of the independent variables. However, since each variable is measured on a different scale in different units, b *must be standardized to be comparable.* The standardized equivalent of the b coefficient is called the *beta weight* or *beta coefficient;* it is symbolized as β. We obtain the beta weights by multiplying b by the ratio of the standard deviation of the independent variable to the standard deviation of the dependent variable. Thus β_1 and β_2 would be expressed as follows:

$$\beta_1 = \left(\frac{s_1}{s_Y}\right) b_1$$

$$\beta_2 = \left(\frac{s_2}{s_Y}\right) b_2$$

For our example, we get

$$\beta_1 = \left(\frac{4.1}{3}\right)(.56) = .765$$

$$\beta_2 = \left(\frac{2.2}{3}\right)(.17) = .125$$

The intercept for a standardized regression equation is zero. Therefore, we have

$$\hat{Y}_z = X_{1z} + X_{2z}$$

The subscript z indicates that the variables have been standardized.

The standardized regression equation shows that for every increase of one standard deviation in education, political liberalism increases by .765 standard deviations, and with an increase of one standard deviation in self-esteem, liberalism increases by .125 standard deviations. One main advantage to using the standardized regression equation is that it translates the variables to a uniform scale that lets us easily compare the relative strength of education and self-esteem in their effect on liberalism. It is evident that education contributes more to liberalism (.765) than does self-esteem (.125).

Three Methods of Statistical Control

▲

+ *Cross-tabulation:* When researchers use cross-tabulation as a method of control, they divide the original sample into subgroups according to the categories of the control variable and reassess the original bivariate relation within each subgroup. The researcher must select as control variables only those associated with the independent and dependent variables under investigation. The resulting partial tables are analyzed to determine whether the relation is spurious, direct, caused by an intervening variable, or the result of an interaction. Cross-tabulation allows researchers to clarify relationships between variables measured at nominal and ordinal levels and can also be used with interval-level data.

+ *Partial correlation:* Partial correlation can only be used with interval-level data. Researchers use partial correlation to adjust the bivariate correlation mathematically to cancel out the effect of the control variable on the independent and dependent variables, and the result reflects only the direct association between the independent and dependent variables. A partial with one control is called a first-order partial, one with two controls is called a second-order partial, and so forth. The squared partial correlation reflects the proportion of variation left unexplained by the control variable and explained by the independent variable. The partial correlation is calculated using Equation (17.1).

+ *Multiple regression:* A multiple regression equation describes the extent of linear relationships between the dependent variable and a number of independent or control variables. Researchers use Equations (17.2), (17.3), (17.4), and (17.5) to determine the extent of these relationships. Before we can compare the relative importance of independent variables measured on different scales and/or in different units, the effects of the variables, or b coefficients, must be standardized. To do this researchers calculate what is called the beta weight or beta coefficient — symbolized as β.

●

Just as the partial correlation coefficient measures the effect of one independent variable on the dependent variable while controlling for another, the multiple regression coefficient measures the amount of change in the dependent variable with one unit change in the independent variable while controlling for all other variables in the equation.

In fact, beta weights and partial correlation coefficients are directly comparable, are usually similar in size, and always have the same sign indicating the direction of the relationship.

MULTIVARIATE ANALYSIS: MULTIPLE RELATIONSHIPS ●

Up to this point, we have considered only situations in which one independent variable is said to determine the dependent variable being studied. However, in the social world, we rarely find that only one variable is relevant to what is to be explained. Often numerous variables are associated directly with the dependent variable. Population change, for example, is explained by four variables: "birth rate," "death rate," "immigration rate," and "emigration rate." Similarly, differences in support for legal abortion are often explained by differences in "religion," "gender," and "age." Thus there are often several independent variables, each of which may contribute to our ability to predict the dependent variable.

In a typical research problem, say, in which a researcher is attempting to explain differences in voting behavior, he or she would use a number of independent variables, for example, "social class," "religion," "gender," and "political attitudes." The researcher would attempt to look at the effects of each independent variable while controlling for the effects of others, as well as at the combined effect of all the independent variables on voting.

The technique of multiple regression introduced earlier in this chapter is most appropriate for problems involving two or more independent variables. We have seen that the standardized regression coefficient—the beta weights—allows us to assess the independent effect of each variable in the regression equation on the dependent variable.

To examine the *combined* effect of all the independent variables, we compute a measure called the *coefficient of determination,* denoted R^2.

Just as with simple bivariate regression, in multiple regression we need to estimate how well the regression rule fits the actual data. In simple regression, the fit (or the relative reduction of error) was measured using r^2, which is defined as the ratio of the variation explained to the total variation in the dependent variable. Similarly, when the prediction is based on several variables, an estimate of the relative reduction of error is based on the ratio of the variation explained with several variables simultaneously to the total variation. This measure, R^2, designates the percentage of the variation explained by all the independent variables in the multiple regression equation. The square root of R^2 indicates the correlation between all independent variables taken together with the dependent variable; it is thus the *coefficient of multiple correlation.*

For the three-variable case, the two formulas for R^2 are as follows:

$$R_{y.12}^2 = \frac{r_{y1}^2 + r_{y2}^2 - 2r_{y1}r_{y2}r_{12}}{1 - (r_{12})^2} \tag{17.6}$$

or

$$R_{y.12}^2 = \beta_1 r_{y1} + \beta_2 r_{y2} \tag{17.7}$$

As an example, let us calculate the percentage of variation in political liberalism (Y) using education (X_1) and self-esteem (X_2) as predictors. We will use the data we presented in our discussion of multiple regression on pages 400–403 and Equation (17.7) to calculate R^2.

$$r_{y.12}^2 = (.765)(.86) + (.125)(.70) = .745$$

This means that almost 75 percent of the variation in political liberalism is accounted for by the combined effects of education and self-esteem.

CAUSAL MODELS AND PATH ANALYSIS •

So far our discussion has focused on methods of control that provide an interpretation of the relation between two variables. We indicated that a direct relationship is one that does not prove to be spurious. This is determined by the time sequence of the variables and the relative size of the partial associations.

Paul Lazarsfeld suggested that these two elements—the size of the partials relative to the original bivariate associations and the assumed time order between the variables—are the kind of evidence required for inferring causation:

> We can suggest a clear-cut definition of the causal relation between two attributes. If we have a relationship between X and Y, and if for any antecedent test factor c the partial relationship between X and Y does not disappear, then the original relationship should be called a causal one.[9]

Although we can never demonstrate causality directly from correlational data, it is possible for us to make causal inferences concerning the adequacy of specific causal models.

Statistical methods that enable us to draw causal inferences involve a finite set of explicitly defined variables, assumptions about how these variables are interrelated causally, and assumptions about the effect of outside variables on the variables included in the model.[10]

Some Examples of Causal Diagrams

Hypothetically, there could be six causal connections between three variables X_1, X_2, and X_3, as follows:

$$X_1 \Longleftrightarrow X_2$$
$$\diagdown \diagup$$
$$X_3$$

In the diagram, the causal order between two variables is represented by a single-headed arrow, with the head pointing to the effect and the tail to the cause. A simplifying assumption[11] rules out two-way causation either directly in the form $X_1 \Longleftrightarrow X_2$

---

9. Paul F. Lazarsfeld, "The Algebra of Dichotomous Systems," in *Studies in Items Analysis and Prediction*, ed. Herbert Solomon (Stanford, CA: Stanford University Press, 1959), p. 146.

10. Herbert A. Simon, *Models of Man: Social and Rational* (New York: Wiley, 1957).

11. Hubert M. Blalock, Jr., *Causal Inference in Nonexperimental Research* (Chapel Hill: University of North Carolina Press, 1964).

or indirectly as in

$$X_1 \longrightarrow X_2$$
$$\nwarrow \quad \swarrow$$
$$X_3$$

Furthermore, under this assumption a dependent variable cannot cause any of the variables preceding it in the causal sequence. Thus, in a causal system where X_1 is the independent variable, X_2 the intervening variable, and X_3 the dependent variable, X_2 cannot cause X_1, and X_3 cannot cause X_2 or X_1.

With these assumptions, we can construct some possible models explaining relations between X_1, X_2, and X_3; some examples are presented in Figure 17.6.

These diagrams display direct relations, indirect relations, and no effect between the variables. Diagram (a) shows a direct effect of X_1 on X_2, a direct effect of X_2 on X_3, and an indirect effect of X_1 on X_3 through X_2. Similarly, in diagram (b), X_1 and X_2 affect X_3 directly and X_1 has no effect on X_2.

To illustrate how some of these ideas are applied, let us look at the following example of research on voting behavior and its determinants. It is hypothesized that voting behavior (X_4) is determined directly by party identification (X_1), candidate evaluation (X_2), and perception of campaign issues (X_3), and that candidate evaluation and campaign issues are determined directly by party identification. Furthermore, party identification influences voting behavior indirectly, through candidate evaluation and campaign issues. These ideas are presented in Figure 17.7.

The variables U, V, and W are called *residual variables;* the arrows between them and each of the dependent variables in the model express the fact that variation in the dependent variables is not solely accounted for by variables in the model. Thus W, for

Figure 17.6

Models for Three Variables

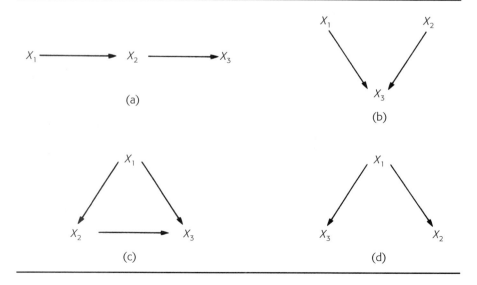

Figure 17.7

A Path Diagram of Voting Behavior

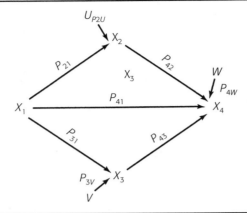

example, would represent variation in voting behavior not accounted for by party identification, candidate evaluation, or perceptions of campaign issues.

Path Analysis

Path analysis is a technique that uses both bivariate and multiple linear regression techniques to test the causal relations among the variables specified in the model. It involves three major steps:

1. The researcher draws a path diagram based on a theory or a set of hypotheses.
2. The researcher then calculates path coefficients (direct effects) using regression techniques.
3. Finally, the researcher determines indirect effects.

Our illustration on voting behavior on pages 405–406 provides an example of the first step of path analysis. Therefore, we will start with a discussion of step 2. You will notice that Figure 17.7 includes a set of coefficients identified as P_{ij}, i being the dependent variable and j the independent variable. These values are called **path coefficients.** For example, P_{31} is the path coefficient connecting X_1 with X_3, with X_3 being determined by X_1. Similarly, P_{4w} is the path coefficient linking X_4 with the residual variable W.

To estimate the path coefficients, we first write a set of regression equations that represent the structure of the model. We should have as many equations as we have dependent variables. Thus to represent the model of Figure 17.7, we have

$$X_2 = P_{21}X_1 + P_{2u}U$$

$$X_3 = P_{31}X_1 + P_{3v}V$$

$$X_4 = P_{41}X_1 + P_{42}X_2 + P_{43}X_3 + P_{4w}W$$

You will notice that each equation includes as many terms as there are arrows leading to the dependent variable. Thus X_4 has four arrows, each representing a determining factor: X_1, X_2, X_3, and W.

To obtain estimates of the path coefficients, we simply regress each dependent variable on the independent variables in the equation. To estimate P_{21}, we regress X_2 on X_1. For P_{31}, we regress X_3 on X_1, and for P_{41}, P_{42}, and P_{43}, we regress X_4 on X_1, X_2, and X_3. The path coefficients are simply the beta weights for each equation; that is,

$$P_{21} = \beta_{21} \qquad P_{42} = \beta_{42}$$
$$P_{31} = \beta_{31} \qquad P_{43} = \beta_{43}$$
$$P_{41} = \beta_{41}$$

The residual path coefficient (P_{2u}, P_{3v}, P_{4w}) is the square root of the unexplained variation in the dependent variable under analysis. For the model presented in Figure 17.7, the residual paths are

$$P_{2u} = \sqrt{1 - R^2_{2.1}}$$
$$P_{3v} = \sqrt{1 - R^2_{3.1}}$$
$$P_{4w} = \sqrt{1 - R^2_{4.123}}$$

By estimating the path coefficient, we obtain an assessment of the direct effects on all variables in the model. Thus P_{21} expresses the direct effect of X_1 on X_2; P_{31}, the direct effect of X_1 on X_3; P_{41}, the direct effect of X_1 on X_4; and so on. However, as can be observed in Figure 17.7, X_1 affects X_4 indirectly as well, through X_2 and X_3.

To estimate the **indirect effects,** we multiply the path coefficients of paths connecting two variables via intervening variables. Thus for Figure 17.7, the indirect effect of X_1 on X_4 via X_2 would be expressed by $P_{21} P_{42}$, and the indirect effect of X_1 on X_4 via X_3 would be $P_{31} P_{43}$.

One interesting application of path analysis is a study by Robert R. Kaufman and Leo Zuckerman, who attempted to shed light on public opinion toward economic reform in Mexico.[12] This study examined public opinion about economic reform in Mexico, drawing on data from national opinion surveys conducted between 1992 and 1995. Their analysis focused primarily on the extent to which opinions about reform are influenced by orientations toward the president and the ruling party, which for almost seven decades have been the core institutions of the Mexican political regime.

Drawing on the theoretical literature, Kaufman and Zuckerman constructed a path model that includes seven variables: personal income (INCOME), region (MEXCITY), perception of the country's economic situation (ECON), approval of president (PRES), party sympathies (PRI), personal expectation about the future (EXPECT), and preference about economic reform (POLICY INDEX). The researchers hypothesized that region (MEXCITY) influences preference about reform (POLICY INDEX) through its effect on political orientation (PRI), whereas income (INCOME) affects policy preferences (POLICY INDEX) through a different path: Wealthier individuals may be expected to have more positive views of the economy (ECON) and more positive expectations about the

---

12. Robert R. Kaufman and Leo Zuckerman, "Attitudes Toward Economic Reform in Mexico: The Role of Political Orientation, *American Political Science Review,* 92 (2) (1998): 359–375.

Figure 17.8

Causal Model for Policy Index, 1994

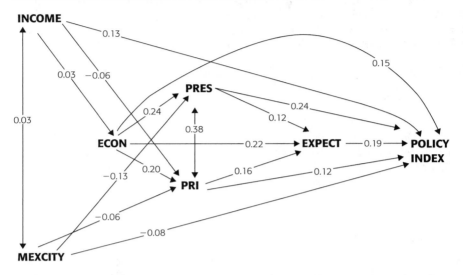

Adapted from Robert R. Kaufman and Leo Zuckerman, "Attitudes Toward Economic Reform in Mexico: The Role of Political Orientation," *American Political Science Review,* 92 (2) (1998): 370.

future (EXPECT), which in turn would encourage positive views of reform (POLICY INDEX).

Figure 17.8 shows the path coefficients obtained in the analysis. Both region (MEX-CITY) and income (INCOME) have a direct effect on POLICY INDEX (0.13; −0.80); however, this effect is relatively weak. The strongest direct influence on POLICY INDEX comes from four variables: perception of the country's economic situation (ECON; .15), approval of the president (PRES; .24), party sympathies (PRI; .12), and personal expectations about future improvements (EXPECT; 0.19). Judgment about the economy (ECON) also affects POLICY INDEX indirectly through its effect on EXPECT (0.22 × 0.19 = 0.042), PRES (0.2 × 0.24 = 0.058), and PRI (0.20 × 0.12 = 0.024). Similarly, POLICY INDEX is affected indirectly through EXPECT by both PRES (0.12 × 0.19 = 0.023) and PRI (0.16 × 0.19 = 0.03).

1. Multivariate analysis has three basic functions: control, interpretation, and prediction. Statistical control is a substitute for experimental control and is accomplished through cross-tabulation, partial correlation, or multiple regression. With cross-tabulation, the researcher attempts to equate groups exposed to the independent variable with those not exposed in all relevant matters. The selection of relevant con-

trol variables is based on theoretical as well as statistical considerations. The control variable must be associated with both the independent and dependent variables. When they use the partial correlation method, researchers adjust the bivariate correlation statistically to cancel out the effect of the control variable on the independent and dependent variables. Multiple regression estimates the effect of one variable on another while controlling for the effect of others.

2. When the mechanism of control is applied to a bivariate association, it can either cancel out the original relationship or have no effect on it. In the first case the association is either spurious or is mediated by the control variable; in the second case the association is considered direct and is subject to further analysis. Whereas an interpretation of spuriousness invalidates a bivariate association, an intervening interpretation clarifies it and explains how the independent and dependent variables are related. A second class of interpretation specifies the conditions under which the association holds. These conditions can be interest and concern, time and place, and specific qualifications or characteristics.

3. Multiple regression and correlation comprise a technique for assessing the simultaneous effect of several independent variables on the dependent variable under study. In multiple regression, the researcher estimates a prediction rule that evaluates the extent of change produced in the dependent variable by an independent variable, holding other relevant independent variables constant. The multiple correlation estimates the degree of fit of the prediction equation with the empirical data. R^2, the multiple correlation coefficient, measures the amount of variance in the dependent variable explained by the independent variables employed.

4. Path analysis is a multivariate technique based on linear regression analysis that makes it possible for researchers to test causal relations among a set of variables. Researchers employing path analysis draw diagrams founded in theory and then determine direct and indirect effects of variables.

KEY TERMS FOR REVIEW ●

conditional variable (p. 395)
control variable (p. 388)
cross-tabulation (p. 387)
elaboration (p. 394)
indirect effect (p. 407)
interaction (p. 395)
intervening variable (p. 394)

multiple regression (p. 400)
partial correlation (p. 399)
partial tables (p. 391)
path analysis (p. 406)
path coefficient (p. 406)
spurious relation (p. 387)

STUDY QUESTIONS ●

1. The first table below shows the relationship between religion and life satisfaction. The second table shows the relationship between religion and life satisfaction when a third variable is held constant.
    a. Examine the relationship between the independent and dependent variables in the two tables by making a percentage comparison.
    b. Define the control variable. How does it affect the original relationship?

Life Satisfaction by Religion

	Religion	
	Protestant	Catholic
Satisfied	256	126
Not satisfied	258	139
Total	514	265

Life Satisfaction by Religion Controlling for a Third Variable

	Education					
	High		Medium		Low	
	Prot-estant	Cath-olic	Prot-estant	Cath-olic	Prot-estant	Cath-olic
Satisfied	89	13	116	35	51	78
Not satisfied	104	20	124	59	30	60
Total	193	33	240	94	81	138

2. The accompanying table shows the relationship between voting and social class, controlling for gender.
   a. Examine and describe (by making a percentage comparison) the relationship between the independent and dependent variables in the partial tables.
   b. Reconstruct the bivariate table showing the relationship between gender and social class.
   c. Reconstruct the bivariate table showing the relationship between gender and voting.
   d. Reconstruct the bivariate table showing the relationship between voting and social class.

Voting by Social Class Controlling for Sex

	Male			Female		
	Upper Class	Lower Class	Total	Upper Class	Lower Class	Total
Democratic	55	45	100	115	285	400
Republican	545	355	900	285	615	900
Total	600	400	1,000	400	900	1,300

3. Using the data from Question 6 in Chapter 16:
   a. Obtain the partial correlation between unemployment and political stability controlling for economic development.
   b. Obtain the partial correlation between unemployment and economic development controlling for political stability.

c. Obtain the multiple regression equation using political stability and level of economic development as independent variables and unemployment rate as the dependent variable. Evaluate the relative effect of each independent variable on unemployment by comparing the beta weights.
d. What percentage of the variance in unemployment is explained by the two independent variables taken together?

SPSS PROBLEMS ●

1. In Chapter 16, SPSS Problem 2, you used SPSS to analyze the relationship between opinions about the Bible ("bible") and attitudes toward women working ("fefam"), using "bible" as the independent variable. (If you did not keep the output for this problem, do it again.) Next, examine the relationship between "bible" and "fefam" separately for men and women (*Hint:* Control for "sex"). Does the relationship differ by gender? Describe the relationship between "bible" and "fefam" separately for men and women using the appropriate percentages. What might account for the difference?
2. In this problem you will consider the question of whether church attendance ("attend") affects attitudes about women having access to abortion when the pregnancy is the result of rape ("abrape"). Before you consider this question you should recode "attend" (you may already have done that for previous problems) into two categories so that everyone who attends religious services less than once a month is put into one group, and everyone who attends at least once a month is put into a second group. Use SPSS to construct a table showing the relationship between church attendance (recorded "attend") and "abrape." (*Hint:* Use "abrape" as the dependent variable.) Next, use SPSS to construct tables showing the same relationship controlling for "sex." Describe the relationship between "attend" (the recoded variable) and "abrape" using the appropriate percentage. Then examine the same relationship separately for men and women. Is the relationship different for men and women? What might account for the difference?
3. How safe do men and women feel about walking at night in their neighborhoods? Examine this question by constructing a table showing the relationship between "fear" and "sex." (Use "fear" as the dependent variable.) Describe the relationship using the appropriate percentages. Next use SPSS to construct tables showing the same relationship controlling for "race." Compare the relationship between "fear" and "sex" among blacks and whites. Does race make a difference? Support your answer with the appropriate percentages.

ADDITIONAL READINGS ●

Allison, Paul. *Multiple Regression: A Primer.* Thousand Oaks, CA: Pine Forge Press, 1999.

Fox, John. *Applied Regression Analysis, Linear Models, and Related Methods.* Thousand Oaks, CA: Sage, 1997.

Healey, Joseph F. *Statistics: A Tool for Social Research.* Belmont, CA: Wadsworth, 1999.

McClendon, McKee J. *Multiple Regression and Causal Analysis.* Itasca, IL: Peacock, 1994.

Rawlings, John, Sastry G. Pantula, and David A. Dickey. *Applied Regression Analysis: A Research Tool.* New York: Springer, 1998.

Von Eye, Alexander, and Christof Schuster. *Regression Analysis for Social Sciences.* San Diego, CA: Academic Press, 1998.

Witte, Robert S., and John S. Witte. *Statistics.* Orlando, FL: Harcourt Brace, 1997.

INDEX CONSTRUCTION AND SCALING METHODS

"How's the nation (. . . or the city) doing?" Candidates for public office, voters, and social scientists have asked this question in any number of situations, not just during elections. The answers they seek are often found in special "thermometers" designed for that purpose: the Consumer Price Index, which measures the ups and downs of inflation; the FBI Uniform Crime Report, which serves as a measure of social order; and the World Bank's Social Indicators of Development, which provides data indicating how the world's nations have progressed and how they compare to each other on a number of dimensions. One group of concerned social scientists, centered at the Fordham Institute for Innovation in Social Policy in Tarrytown, New York, has developed an index, described in its report "The Index of Social Health," that measures the progress made toward solving social problems. The institute's researchers keep track of changes in 16 socioeconomic indicators, including teenage suicide, high school dropout rates, and out-of-pocket health costs for the elderly. They then calculate a single, summary figure, ranging from 0 to 100. The higher the figure, the healthier the nation is. In their 1992 report, 9 of the 16 indicators either stayed the same or declined; the rise in the other 7 was sufficient to raise the total index—a sign that total social health is improving. Dr. Marc L. Miringoff, the institute's director and author of this report, notes that the index often rises during presidential election years, a response, he believes, to the increase in funding typical of those periods.[1]

How social scientists construct such indexes, and why they do so, are the major topics discussed in this chapter.

•| **IN THIS CHAPTER,** we introduce more sophisticated data measurement techniques by introducing index construction and scaling methods. In Chapter 7 we defined measurement as a procedure in which the researcher assigns symbols or numbers to empirical properties according to predetermined rules. We also discussed the structure of measurement, the idea of isomorphism, the four levels of measurement, and techniques for assessing validity and reliability. Using these skills and ideas we can construct indexes and scales that can assess human behavior.

We first discuss the logic of index construction and present several techniques for doing so. Next, we discuss Likert scaling, a technique that measures attitudes on the ordinal and the interval levels of measurement. Then we describe, with an illustrated example, Guttman scaling or scalogram analysis. The Guttman technique can be applied to nominal and ordinal levels of analysis.

Indexes and scales are measuring instruments designed to represent the complexities inherent in human behavior in a more reliable way. Social scientists require the use of these instruments when they try to measure concepts such as power, bureaucracy, gender relations, freedom, and intelligence that are composite variables, that is, phenomena having several empirical properties. This makes them extremely difficult to measure. Hence, indexes and scales tend to be composite measures, constructed by combining two or more variables that are employed as indicators. These variables are referred to as **items.** For example, socioeconomic status is a common index constructed by combining three indicators: income, education, and occupation.

---

1. "Social Health Is Improving, a Study Says," *The New York Times*, October 24, 1994, p. A15.

There are several reasons why social scientists employ scales and indexes, some of which are quite practical. First, indexes and scales enable researchers to represent several variables by a single score, a quality that reduces the difficulties of dealing with complex data. Second, the quantitative measurements obtained with scales and indexes are amenable to more precise statistical analysis. Finally, using indexes and scales increases the reliability of measurement itself. This last feature is based on the fact that a score on a scale or an index is based on responses to more than a single question or item. To clarify this issues, let's consider one of the more pedestrian scales used regularly—exams and their grades (or scores). Few students would like to have an exam grade determined solely by their answer to a single multiple-choice or true-false question. In the first place, it is unlikely that the total universe of course material can be covered by a single question and answer. Second, if a student misinterprets or makes a mistake on a one-question exam, that one error could mislead the professor in his or her judgment of how much knowledge the student has absorbed. If there are several questions, the grade will be more accurate because the student will have additional opportunities to demonstrate how much was learned.

Another illustration is the measurement of sexual harassment. How can we predict the effect of harassment on a person's health—or calculate the amount of compensation due if a case goes to court—if we cannot gauge the severity of the behavior considered to be harassing? Therefore, some instrument has to be devised to differentiate between, say, an offensive remark made by a superior and that superior's preventing an employee's promotion if sex is denied.

Following this line of argument, it becomes obvious that researchers use multiple-item scales and indexes to increase the reliability and precision of their measurements. The reasons for doing so are theoretical, methodological, and practical.

Scales differ from indexes by their greater rigor. Whereas researchers in all the sciences construct indexes by simply accumulating scores, when social scientists are constructing scales, they pay special attention to tests of validity and reliability. These tests can be applied because most scales incorporate the principle of **unidimensionality** in their construction. According to this principle, the items comprising a scale reflect a single dimension and can be placed on a continuum presumed to apply to one and only one concept..

A scale's unidimensionality does, however, permit its use for a variety of purposes and in conjunction with numerous techniques. Some scales are employed to identify questions or items that do not belong to the set of items in which they were originally placed. Other scaling techniques permit us to rank items by their level of difficulty or intensity. In addition, some scaling methods produce interval-level scales and thereby avoid the limitations imposed by nominal or ordinal data.

Before constructing a new scale, the literature should be surveyed to ascertain whether an appropriate scale is already available. The additional readings at the end of this chapter represent a comprehensive list of sources of information on the scales currently available in the social sciences.

INDEX CONSTRUCTION ●

If you combine two or more items or indicators to create a composite measure, you are constructing an **index.** The familiar Consumer Price Index (CPI) is a composite measure because it presents the changes taking place in the retail prices of eight major product categories—food, housing, apparel, transportation, medical care, personal care, reading and recreation, and other goods and services—as a group, together. The approximately

400 commodities and services included in the CPI were selected because researchers consider the changes in the prices of these items to be representative of the price trends displayed by related items. These items include the cost of commodities ranging from the price of hamburgers, gasoline, and men's work gloves to home computers, and services such as haircuts, legal advice, and interest on mortgages. The U.S. Department of Labor collects the data in 50 urban areas. These areas have been selected on the basis of their representativeness in terms of urban characteristics—size, climate, population density, income level, and so forth—that affect the way in which families spend their money. Within each city, prices are recorded as they appear in the shops where families typically purchase goods and services. For each item, the prices reported by the various sources are combined and weighted to ascertain average price changes for the area. The Department of Labor prepares an index of these figures monthly for the country as a whole and for each of five major cities, and quarterly for other cities.[2]

Four major issues influence the construction of indexes: the purpose for which the index is being compiled, the sources of the data, the base of comparison, and methods for aggregating and weighting the data.

The Purpose of the Index

Two essential questions must be answered before the process of index construction can begin: "What are we attempting to measure?" and "How are we going to use the measure?" Logically, if *A* is an index (or indicator) of *X*, *A* may still be only one of several indexes of *X*. Thus, some kind of supporting evidence is needed to make the case that the values of *A* correspond to the values of *X* in a more precise and valid way than other indexes do. Most often, *X* is a broad concept, such as public welfare or technological change or political participation. Such concepts consist of a complex combination of phenomena, some of which may be subject to differing interpretations. Accordingly, no single indicator will be capable of covering all the dimensions involved, and a number of indicators will have to be selected. Each possible indicator will serve a specific purpose, set forth and explained prior to construction of the index.

The Sources of the Data

Social scientists can employ either obtrusive or unobtrusive (or both) methods of data collection when constructing indexes. What source of data should be used depends on the purpose of the index and on the research design employed. In all cases, the investigator must ascertain whether the data relate strictly to the phenomenon being measured. This decision involves application of the validity and reliability standards discussed in Chapter 7.

The Base of Comparison

Indexes are expressed in the form of a proportion, a percentage, or a ratio in order to simplify comparison of the data. Each of these measures can be calculated either in terms of the actual data collected or reported, or in terms of another year's data, which is used as a numerical base for adjusting nonequivalent figures in order to enable their comparison. A *proportion* is defined as the frequency of observations in any given cate-

2. The following discussion is based on U.S. Bureau of Labor Statistics, *The Consumer Price Index: A Short Description of the Index as Revised* (Washington, DC: U.S. Government Printing Office, 1964), and William H. Wallace, *Measuring Price Changes: A Study of Price Indexes* (Richmond, VA: Federal Reserve Bank of Richmond, 1970).

Table 18.1

Selected Offenses and Source of Information

Selected Offenses	CNJ			MCD		
	f	Proportion	%	f	Proportion	%
Armed robbery	23	.04	4.0	0	.00	0.0
Robbery	17	.03	3.0	5	.01	1.0
Atrocious assault	13	.02	2.0	2	.007	0.7
Simple assault	223	.40	40.0	250	.89	89.0
Break and entry	206	.37	37.0	1	.003	0.3
Larceny	78	.14	14.0	24	.09	9.0
Total	560	1.00	100.0	282	1.00	100.0

gory (f_i) divided by the total number of observations (N), or f_i/N. A proportion may range from zero to one. A proportion becomes a *percentage* when multiplied by 100 $[(f_i/N) \times 100]$; a percentage, by definition, may range from zero to 100. A *ratio* is a fraction that expresses the relative magnitude of any two sets of frequencies. To find the ratio between two frequencies, divide the first frequency by the second. For example, if a group consists of 500 females and 250 males, the ratio of females to males is found by dividing 500 by 250, or 2/1.

Table 18.1 illustrates the use of these measures. It shows the frequencies, proportions, and percentages of selected criminal offenses in a New Jersey city reported by the sources of the official data.[3] The data represented in the first three columns, representing the frequency, proportion, and percentage of crimes in New Jersey (CNJ), is compiled annually by the office of the state attorney general. The data for the other three columns, representing the frequency, proportion, and percentage of crimes in the city, were compiled from municipal court dockets (MCD).

An examination of the table reveals serious ambiguities in the crime data. First, there are differences in the amounts of officially reported crimes: The state's attorney general reports more offenses than court dockets do. This is consistent with the fact that the jurisdiction providing the information reported in the MCD columns is different from the jurisdiction providing the information reported in the CNJ columns: CNJ offenses are those known to police and hence to the attorney general, whereas court dockets report only those cases in which offenders have been identified, arrested, and booked in response to official complaints. Given that many offenders are not apprehended, we would expect the attrition of cases reported as we move up through the legal system. Second, the data for the "simple assault" category are highly problematic because the official records indicate that municipal courts heard more cases than were known to the police in a city where the courts and the police share the same jurisdiction. Because such a situation is quite improbable, an index based on these data will be misleading.

3. The frequencies are reported in W. Boyd Littrell, "The Problem of Jurisdiction and Official Statistics of Crime," in *Current Issues of Social Policy,* ed. W. Boyd Littrell and Gideon Sjoberg (Thousand Oaks, CA: Sage, 1976), p. 236.

Table 18.2

Changing the Base of an Index Number

Year	Values Based on Old Index (1995 = 100)	Values Based on New Index (1990 = 100)
1990	70	100.0
1991	80	114.3
1992	60	85.7
1993	95	135.7
1994	100	142.9
1995	115	164.3
1996	120	171.4
1997	118	168.6
1998	105	150.0

SHIFTING THE BASE. In order to make meaningful comparisons of different indexes, or of the same index during different years or between regions, we are often required to "shift the base" of the index. When we *shift a base,* we are converting or standardizing the data in such a way as to make them comparable. This procedure is often methodologically necessary because only by converting the data to a uniform base can social scientists analyze trends or changes in the phenomena studied. For example, we might shift the base of an index number series from one year to another. Uniformity would be achieved by setting the values for that year at 100. As we shall see, the Cost of Living Index employs such a procedure. It uses the prices for a selected year as the base for comparing prices for the next 5 or 10 years.

In the following example (see Table 18.2), we will be converting the values of the index of, let's say, small business start-ups based on 1995 data into a new index, one based on 1990 data. We do so because we have hypothesized that interest rates for small-business loans in an earlier year, 1990, may have had a greater long-term impact on start-ups than did interest rates in the later year, 1995. To obtain the new index (values based on 1990 data) for 1995, we divide the original figure (based on the 1995 index) for 1990 by 70 (the number of indexed start-ups for 1990) and then multiply by 100. This results in $(70/70) \times 100 = 100$. The new value for 1991 equals $(80/70) \times 100 = 114.3$, and so forth, until all the original figures have been converted into the new series.

Methods of Aggregation and Weighting

A common method for constructing indexes is the computing of aggregate values. The aggregates can be either simple or weighted, depending on the purpose of the index.

SIMPLE AGGREGATES. Table 18.3 illustrates the construction of a **simple aggregate** price index. The prices of each commodity (C_i) in any given year are added to give the index for that year. As noted earlier, it is convenient to designate some year as a base, which is set equal to 100. In this example, all the indexes are expressed in the last row as a percentage of the 1995 figure, obtained by dividing each of the numbers by the aggregate value in the base year ($20.13) and multiplying by 100. Symbolically,

Table 18.3

Construction of Simple Aggregative Index Numbers
(Hypothetical Unit Prices)

Commodities	1995	1996	1997	1998	1999
C_1	$3.21	$4.14	$4.90	$5.80	$6.10
C_2	5.40	5.60	5.10	6.40	7.18
C_3	6.62	8.10	9.00	8.35	7.90
C_4	4.90	5.40	5.10	7.25	6.80
Aggregate value	$20.13	$23.24	$24.10	$27.80	$27.98
Index	100.00	115.45	119.72	138.10	139.00

$$PI = \Sigma P_n / \Sigma P_o \times 100 \tag{18.1}$$

where PI = price index

p = the price of an individual commodity

o = the base period according to which the price changes are measured

n = the period being compared with the base

The formula for a particular year (for instance 1999, with 1995 being the base) is

$$PI_{95,99} = \Sigma p_{99} / \Sigma p_{95} \times 100 \tag{18.2}$$

Thus,

$$PI_{95,99} = \frac{6.10 + 7.18 + 7.90 + 6.80}{3.21 + 5.40 + 6.62 + 4.90} \times 100$$

$$= \frac{27.98}{20.13} \times 100 = 139.00$$

WEIGHTED AGGREGATES. Simple aggregates may conceal the relative influence exerted by each indicator used in the index. To prevent such misrepresentation, **weighted aggregates** are often used. To construct a weighted aggregative price index for the data displayed in Table 18.3, list the quantities of the specific commodities (i.e., consumption) and determine the aggregate value of those goods, that is, how much the total is worth in each year's current prices. This means that each unit price is multiplied by the number of units of the commodity marketed, produced, or consumed, with the resulting values summed for each period. Symbolically,

$$PI = \Sigma p_n q / \Sigma p o q \times 100 \tag{18.3}$$

where q represents the quantity of the commodity marketed, produced, or consumed during the base year, that is, the quantity weight or multiplier. The procedure, using the quantities in 1995 as multipliers, is illustrated in Table 18.4. Because the total value changes while the components of the aggregate do not, these changes must be due to

Table 18.4

Construction of Aggregative Index Weighted by Consumption in 1995

Commodity	Consumption	Value of 1995 Quantity at Price of Specified Year				
		1995	1996	1997	1998	1999
C_1	800	$ 2,568	$ 3,312	$ 3,920	$ 4,640	$ 4,880
C_2	300	1,620	1,680	1,530	1,920	2,154
C_3	450	2,979	3,645	4,050	3,758	3,555
C_4	600	2,940	3,240	3,060	4,350	4,080
Aggregate value		$10,107	$11,877	$12,560	$14,668	$14,669
Index		100.0	117.5	124.3	145.1	145.1

price changes. Thus, the aggregative price index measures the changing value of a fixed aggregate of goods.

Index Construction: Examples

Let us look first at a simple index developed to evaluate the statistics textbooks used in the social sciences according to students' instructional needs.[4] The index, the Statistics Textbook Anxiety Rating Test (START), uses seven factors keyed to the students' needs. These factors are related to possible deficiencies in the students' math backgrounds and the corresponding anxieties they arouse:

1. Reviews basic algebraic operations
2. Contains a section on notations
3. Includes exercise answers
4. Explains exercise answers
5. Does not use definitional formulas
6. Uses relevant examples
7. Addresses student statistics or math anxiety explicitly

The index works as follows: Textbooks are given a score on each factor—1 if the book meets the criterion, 0 if it does not. Summing all the scores yields a composite score ranging from 0 to 7. When the index was used to evaluate 12 popular textbooks, the scores ranged from 0 to 4.

Another well-known example is the Sellin and Wolfgang Index of Delinquency. In order to evaluate crime control policies, policy makers require at least three major types of information: data on the incidence of crimes, data on the response of the criminal justice system, and data on the offenders' sociodemographic characteristics. With respect to the incidence of crimes, a major problem is that offenses vary in nature and magnitude. Some result in death, others inflict losses of property, and still others merely cause inconvenience. One common way of comparing, say, one year's incidence of crime with

4. Steven P. Schacht, "Statistics Textbooks: Pedagogical Tools or Impediments to Learning?" *Teaching Sociology*, 18 (1990): 390–396.

another's has been simply to count offenses, disregarding the differences in their character. Given the range of crimes and the varying degrees of their seriousness, such unweighted indexes are misleading. A police report showing an overall decrease or increase in the total number of offenses committed says little if significant changes have occurred in the types of offenses committed. For example, a 10 percent decrease in auto theft but a 30 percent increase in rape could lead to a decline in an unweighted crime index because reported auto thefts are usually much greater in absolute numbers than are reported rapes.

In a pioneering attempt to tackle this problem with respect to delinquency, Thorsten Sellin and Marvin Wolfgang developed a weighting system by distributing 141 carefully prepared accounts of different crimes to three samples of "evaluators": police officers, juvenile court judges, and college students.[5] The accounts included combinations of circumstances, such as death or hospitalization of the victim, type of weapon, and value of property stolen, damaged, or destroyed—for example, "The offender robs a person at gunpoint," "The victim struggles and is shot to death," "The offender forces open a cash register in a department store and steals five dollars," "The offender smokes marijuana." The evaluators were asked to rate each of these accounts on a "category scale" and a "magnitude estimating scale." Sellin and Wolfgang used these ratings to construct the weighting system. For example, a crime with the following "attributes" would be given the following number of points:

A house is forcibly entered	1
A person is murdered	26
The spouse receives a minor injury	1
Between $251 and $2,000 is taken	2
Total score	30

With such an index, policy makers and social scientists can make meaningful comparisons over time and between different communities because the seriousness of the crimes committed are taken into account in addition to their frequencies.

Attitude Indexes

To construct an *attitude index,* researchers prepare a set of questions, selected a priori. Numerical values (e.g., 0 to 4 or 1 to 5) are assigned arbitrarily to the item or question responses. The values assigned by the respondents are added to obtain total scores. The scores are then interpreted as indicators of the respondents' attitudes. Consider the following five statements designed to measure alienation:

1. Sometimes I have the feeling that other people are using me.
   ☐ Strongly agree   ☐ Disagree
   ☐ Agree   ☐ Strongly disagree
   ☐ Neither agree nor disagree
2. We are just so many cogs in the machinery of life.
   ☐ Strongly agree   ☐ Disagree
   ☐ Agree   ☐ Strongly disagree
   ☐ Neither agree nor disagree

5. Thorsten Sellin and Marvin E. Wolfgang, *The Measurement of Delinquency* (New York: Wiley, 1964).

3. The future looks very dismal.
   ☐ Strongly agree   ☐ Disagree
   ☐ Agree   ☐ Strongly disagree
   ☐ Neither agree nor disagree
4. More and more, I feel helpless in the face of what's happening in the world today.
   ☐ Strongly agree   ☐ Disagree
   ☐ Agree   ☐ Strongly disagree
   ☐ Neither agree nor disagree
5. People like me have no influence in society.
   ☐ Strongly agree   ☐ Disagree
   ☐ Agree   ☐ Strongly disagree
   ☐ Neither agree nor disagree

Suppose that we arbitrarily assign response scores in the following way: Strongly agree = 4; Agree = 3; Neither = 2; Disagree = 1; and Strongly disagree = 0. A respondent who answers "Strongly agree" to all five statements will have a total score of 20, indicating a high degree of alienation; a respondent who answers "Strongly disagree" to all five statements will have a total score of 0, indicating that that person is not alienated at all. In reality, most respondents will obtain scores between these two extremes. The researcher will then work out a system that classifies respondents according to their degree of alienation on the basis of their total scores—for example, respondents who score 0 to 6 are not alienated, respondents who score from 7 to 13 are somewhat alienated, and those who score between 14 and 20 are most alienated.

This type of index is sometimes termed an *arbitrary scale* because nothing about the procedure guarantees that any one statement or item taps the same attitude as the other items. Do items 3 and 5 tap the same aspect of alienation? Does item 4 correspond to the aspects of alienation not covered by items 3 and 5? Will another researcher who uses the index obtain the same findings? That is, is the index reliable? We will address these important questions next, in our discussion of scaling methods.

SCALING METHODS   •

Likert Scales

Likert scaling is a method designed to measure attitudes. To construct a **Likert scale,** researchers usually follow six steps: They (1) compile a list of possible scale items, (2) administer these items to a random sample of respondents, (3) compute a total score for each respondent, (4) determine the *discriminative power* of the items, (5) select the scale items, and (6) test the scale's reliability.

COMPILING POSSIBLE SCALE ITEMS.   In the first step, a series of items is compiled that expresses a wide range of attitudes, from extremely positive to extremely negative. The respondent is then requested to check one of five offered fixed-alternative expressions, such as "strongly agree," "agree," "neither agree nor disagree," "disagree," and "strongly disagree," which comprise a continuum of responses. (Occasionally, three, four, six, or seven fixed-alternative expressions are used. Optional expressions include "almost always," "frequently," "occasionally," "rarely," and "almost never.") In this five-point continuum, values of 1, 2, 3, 4, 5 or 5, 4, 3, 2, 1 are assigned. These values express the relative weights and direction of the responses, determined by the favorableness or unfavorableness of the item.

In a classic use of the Likert method, Wayne Kirchner developed a 24-item scale to measure attitudes toward employment of senior citizens. The following four items illustrate his scoring technique.[6]

1. Most companies are unfair to older employees.
   ☐ Strongly agree   ☐ Disagree
   ☐ Agree   ☐ Strongly disagree
   ☐ Uncertain

2. I think that older employees make better employees.
   ☐ Strongly agree   ☐ Disagree
   ☐ Agree   ☐ Strongly disagree
   ☐ Uncertain

3. In a case where two people can do a job about equally well, I'd pick the older person for the job.
   ☐ Strongly agree   ☐ Disagree
   ☐ Agree   ☐ Strongly disagree
   ☐ Uncertain

4. I think older employees have as much ability to learn new methods as other employees.
   ☐ Strongly agree   ☐ Disagree
   ☐ Agree   ☐ Strongly disagree
   ☐ Uncertain

Kirchner scored this scale by assigning higher weights to responses to positive items (acceptance of the idea of hiring older persons) as follows: Strongly agree, 5; Agree, 4; Uncertain, 3; Disagree, 2; Strongly disagree, 1. If he had included negative items (items indicating rejection of the idea of hiring older persons) in the scale, their weights would have been reversed.

ADMINISTERING ALL THE ITEMS. In the second step, a large number of respondents, selected randomly, are asked to indicate their attitudes on the list containing all of the proposed items.

COMPUTING A TOTAL SCORE. In this step, the researcher calculates a total score for each respondent by summing the value of all items checked. Suppose that a respondent checked "Strongly agree" in item 1 (score 5), "Uncertain" in item 2 (score 3), "Agree" in item 3 (score 4), and "Disagree" in item 4 (score 2). This person's total score would be $5 + 3 + 4 + 2 = 14$.

DETERMINING THE DISCRIMINATIVE POWER. In the fourth step, the researcher has to determine a basis for the selection of items for the final scale. Regardless of the scaling method employed, the objective is to find items that consistently distinguish respondents who are high on the attitude continuum from those who are low. This can be done by applying either the *internal consistency method*—that is, by correlating each item with the total score and retaining those with the highest correlations—or with *item analysis*. Both methods yield an internally consistent scale. With item analysis, the researcher subjects each item to a measurement of its ability to differentiate the highs

6. Wayne K. Kirchner, "The Attitudes of Special Groups Toward the Employment of Older Persons," *Journal of Gerontology*, 12 (1957): 216–220.

Table 18.5

Table for Computing the *DP* for One Item

Group	Number in Group	1	2	3	4	5	Weighted Total*	Weighted Mean†	DP $(Q_1 - Q_3)$
High (top 25%)	9	0	1	2	3	3	35	3.89	
									2.00
Low (bottom 25%)	9	1	8	0	0	0	17	1.89	

*Weighted total = score × number who check that score

†Weighted mean = $\dfrac{\text{weighted total}}{\text{number in group}}$

(clearly positive attitudes) from the lows (clearly negative attitudes). This measure is called the **discriminative power (DP)** of the item. In calculating the *DP,* we add the scored items for each respondent and place the scores in an array, usually from lowest to highest. Next we compare the range above the upper quartile (Q_1) with that below the lower quartile (Q_3), and calculate the *DP* as the difference between the weighted means of the scores above Q_1 and of those that fall below Q_3, as illustrated in Table 18.5.

SELECTING THE SCALE ITEMS.   The *DP* value is computed for each of the possible scale items; those items with the highest *DP* values are selected. These are the items that best discriminate among the individuals expressing differing attitudes toward the attitude being measured.

TESTING RELIABILITY.   The reliability of the scale can be tested in much the same manner as we would test other measuring procedures. For example, we can select enough items for two scales (at least 100) and divide them into two sets, constituting two scales. We can then employ the split-half reliability test (see Chapter 7).

Other Composite Measures

Social scientists have developed various scaling procedures that incorporate a number of features taken from Likert scaling techniques. These procedures almost always include the steps described above, such as initial compilation of possible scale items, administration of items to a large number of respondents, and some methods for selecting the set of items to be included in the final scale. The most common format for the items is a rating scale on which respondents are asked to make a judgment in terms of sets of ordered categories.

Most statistical computer programs today include procedures and statistics that make it easier to select items for your own scales and to evaluate how well the various items measure the underlying phenomena.

One of the simplest statistics used to examine items is the bivariate correlation coefficient (Pearson's *r*), which indicates how closely linked each item is with other items or the entire scale. In general, items that are strongly associated with other items will show higher overall correlations with the total scale. Examining the bivariate correlation helps researchers to decide which items to include in the scale and which items to discard:

Items that correlate strongly with one another should be selected, and vice versa. Another helpful statistic is *Cronbach's alpha,* which estimates the average of all possible split-half reliability coefficients. (For a discussion of reliability, see Chapter 7.) The alpha measures the extent to which the individual items comprising the scale "hang together." [7] A high alpha (.70 is an acceptable level) indicates that the items in the scale are "tightly connected."

Guttman Scaling

The **Guttman scale,** first developed by Louis Guttman in the early 1940s, was designed to empirically test the unidimensionality of a set of items when constructing scales. Guttman suggested that if the items comprising the scale tap the same dimension underlying an attitude, they can be arranged along a continuum that indicates the strength of that dimension. More explicitly, Guttman scales are unidimensional and cumulative. The cumulative characteristic implies that a researcher can order the items by degree of difficulty (or intensity or specificity) and that respondents who reply positively to a difficult item will also respond positively to less difficult items when presented in the appropriate order. Similarly, a respondent who (dis)agrees with a statement expressing a strong attitude will also (dis)agree with a statement expressing a milder version of that attitude. If we take an example from the physical world, we know that if an object is 4 feet long, it is longer than 1 foot and also longer than 2 or 3 feet. In the social world, we know that if an executive director of a corporation would approve of his daughter marrying an electrician, he would also approve of an electrician belonging to his country club. Similarly, if he did not object to an electrician being a member of his club, he would not mind having an electrician for a neighbor.

Table 18.6 illustrates the scale that would result from administering these three items to a group of respondents. This scale is unidimensional as well as cumulative—the items can be ranked on a single underlying dimension, social acceptability in this case; the scale is cumulative because none of the respondents gave totally mixed responses to the questions in the order in which they were presented to them. Thus information on

| ____ Table 18.6

A Hypothetical Perfect Guttman Scale

Respondent	Items in the Scale			
	Item 1: Admit to close kinship by marriage	Item 2: Admit to the same social club	Item 3: Admit as a neighbor	Total Score
A	+	+	+	3
B	−	+	+	2
C	−	−	+	1
D	−	−	−	0

+ indicates agreement with the statement; − indicates disagreement.

7. See William Sims Bainbridge, *Survey Research: A Computer-Assisted Introduction* (Belmont, CA: Wadsworth, 1989).

the position of any respondent's last positive response allows the researcher to predict all of the responses to the scale items following the selected item.

In practice, a perfect Guttman scale is rarely obtained. In most cases, inconsistencies appear. Consequently, a criterion is set for the purpose of evaluating how unidimensional and cumulative the scale really is. The **coefficient of reproducibility (CR)**, developed by Guttman, does just that: It measures the degree of conformity of the scale to what would be a perfectly unidimensional and cumulative scale. The greater the conformity of the scale being constructed to a perfectly arranged scale, the greater is the validity of the scale. The *CR* is discussed further later in the chapter.

SELECTING SCALE ITEMS. Raymond L. Gorden lists three conditions, in their order of importance, that must be met in the process of discovering and selecting items for a Guttman scale:[8]

1. An attitude toward the object (class of objects, events, or ideas) must actually exist in the minds of the population to be sampled and tested.
2. Statements about the object can be constructed that have meaning to the members of the sample and elicit responses that are valid indicators of that attitude.
3. The items in the set of statements or questions must represent different degrees along a single dimension.

Attitude scale items can be selected by a variety of methods and from any available source: newspapers, books, scholarly articles, personal knowledge of the phenomenon. Experts in interviewing as well as a small group of respondents, chosen from the population to be studied, can also contribute good items. (It should be clear by now that the process of securing the items for scales is very similar to that involved in index construction.) After a large set of potential items is compiled, the researcher selects a preliminary set of items. These items should relate clearly to the attitude being measured and should cover the total continuum from strongly favorable to strongly unfavorable. Two to seven response categories may be constructed for each statement expressing the item. The most common formats are Likert-type items with five-point scales, as in the following example:

Please indicate how much you agree or disagree with the following statement:

Nowadays a person has to live pretty much for today and let tomorrow take care of itself.
- ☐ Strongly agree   ☐ Disagree
- ☐ Agree   ☐ Strongly disagree
- ☐ Neither agree nor disagree

The selected items are then included in a questionnaire (the pretest) that the researcher administers to a sample of the target population. Before the answers to the questionnaire are scored, items are arranged so that higher values will consistently stand for either the most positive or most negative feelings or beliefs. Items that do not correspond to this pattern should be rearranged.

CALCULATING THE COEFFICIENT OF REPRODUCIBILITY. The coefficient of reproducibility is defined as the extent to which the total response pattern on a set of items can be reproduced even if the total score alone is known. This reproducibility depends

---

8. Raymond L. Gorden, *Unidimensional Scaling of Social Variables* (New York: Macmillan, 1977), p. 46.

on the extent to which the pattern of responses attained conforms to a perfectly scalable pattern, demonstrated in Table 18.6. When the obtained coefficient of reproducibility is below the required .90 criterion, the scale needs to be refined until the coefficient of reproducibility reaches the desired level. The *CR* is calculated as follows:

$$CR = 1 - \frac{\Sigma_e}{Nr} \qquad (18.4)$$

where *CR* = the coefficient of reproducibility

Σ_e = the total number of inconsistencies

Nr = the total number of responses (number of cases × number of items)

A *CR* of .90 is the minimum standard for accepting a scale as unidimensional and cumulative.

Guttman Scale Application: An Example

After the researcher has developed and refined a Guttman scale, the results can be used to describe the distribution of the variable measured as well as to relate the scale to other variables in the study. Jules J. Wanderer's study on the severity of riots in American cities is a particularly interesting application of the Guttman scaling technique because it is based on behavioral indicators rather than on attitudes.[9] Wanderer analyzed 75 reports of riots and criminal disorders that took place during the summer of 1967. The information Wanderer used in the construction of the scale was provided by municipalities at the request of a U.S. Senate subcommittee. The scale includes the following items of riot severity: killing, calling up of the National Guard, calling up of the state police, sniping, looting, interference with firefighters, and vandalism. These items are ordered from most to least severe and by the frequency with which they are reported. The coefficient of reproducibility of this Guttman scale of riot severity is .92. Cities are then organized into eight scale types according to the degree of severity of the riots reported, with 8 indicating the least severe and 1 the most severe riot activity. Table 18.7 presents the scale and the distribution of the cities along the scale.

At the second stage of the analysis, Wanderer treated riot severity, as measured by the Guttman scale, as a dependent variable. He then examined a set of independent variables in terms of their relationship to riot severity. For example, he found a relationship between the percentage of nonwhites participating in a riot and the degree of riot severity as measured by the scale: Once a riot has begun, the higher the percentage of nonwhites participating, the greater is the severity of the riot.

The Guttman scale of riot severity developed in this study suggests that the events that constitute riots and civil criminal disorders are neither erratic nor randomly occurring. On the contrary, by employing a Guttman scale, the researcher could predict the sequence of events that will take place at each level of riot severity.

Factor Analysis

Factor analysis is a statistical technique for classifying a large number of interrelated variables into a limited number of dimensions or factors. It is a useful method for

---

9. Jules J. Wanderer, "An Index of Riot Severity and Some Correlates," *American Journal of Sociology,* 74 (1969): 503.

Table 18.7

A Guttman Scale of Riot Severity

Scale Type	Percentage of Cities ($n = 75$)	Items Reported
8	4	No scale items
7	19	"Vandalism"
6	13	All of the above and "interference with firefighters"
5	16	All of the above and "looting"
4	13	All of the above and "sniping"
3	7	All of the above and "called state police"
2	17	All of the above and "called National Guard"
1	11	All of the above and "law officer or civilian killed"
Total	100	

Based on Jules J. Wanderer, "An Index of Riot Severity and Some Correlates," *American Journal of Sociology*, 74 (1969): 503.

constructing multiple-item scales, where each scale represents a dimension of a highly abstract concept. Factor analysis, by helping to identify the most powerful indicators of a concept, contributes to increasing the efficiency as well as validity of the research. Consider, for example, community satisfaction. Many statements or items can be used to describe community satisfaction: satisfaction with public schools, shopping facilities, personal safety, cultural amenities, the friendliness of the neighborhood, and so forth. However, the measurement of community satisfaction can be simplified by identifying the underlying dimensions of community satisfaction.

Some studies dealing with community satisfaction have indeed adopted this approach. Researchers divided community or neighborhood satisfaction into the following subconcepts (factors): (1) satisfaction with service delivery, (2) satisfaction with community organization, (3) satisfaction with neighborhood quality, and (4) satisfaction with cultural amenities. The relationship between the subconcepts and community satisfaction could then be expressed as follows:

$$\text{Community satisfaction} = S(\text{service delivery}) + S(\text{community organization})$$
$$+ S(\text{neighborhood quality}) + S(\text{cultural amenities})$$

where S = satisfaction.

In this formulation, community satisfaction is a construct represented by four basic factors. In factor analysis, the factors are not observed directly; rather, they are defined by a group of variables or items that are components of the abstract factors. The research actually begins by selecting a large number of items (employed as indicators) that may define each of the factors. These items are presented to respondents in the form of questionnaire statements.

In the first stage of factor analysis, the bivariate correlations (Pearson's r) between all the items are computed. The researcher then arranges the correlations in a matrix. The correlation matrix becomes input to the factor analysis procedure. The construction of factors is based on the identification of strong relations between a set of items. The method assumes that variables or items representing a single factor will be highly correlated with that factor.

The correlation between an item and a factor is represented by a **factor loading**. A factor loading is similar to a correlation coefficient; its values range between 0 and 1.0, and it can be interpreted in the same way. Table 18.8 presents the factor loadings of 14 items expressing community satisfaction on their four underlying factors. The items with the highest loading on each factor are underlined; these items are taken as the best indicators for these factors. Among the 14 items, only 3 have a high loading on factor 1. These items all refer to satisfaction with services; thus we can identify factor 1 as representing the dimension of *service delivery*. Similarly, factor 2 represents satisfaction with *community organization;* factor 3, *quality of life;* and factor 4, *cultural amenities*. Loadings of .30 or below are generally considered too weak to represent a factor. Examination of the results reveals that although all items display loadings on each of the factors, most item loadings are too weak to be considered as good indicators of the dimensions investigated.

Let us consider another example, sexual harassment. If we want to understand just what makes such behavior so threatening, it may not be sufficient merely to scale the severity of different acts. In attempting to devise an instrument that could measure the influence of the components underlying harassment, Maureen Murdoch and Paul McGovern conducted a factor analysis of the items on their Sexual Harassment Inventory. They calculated the factor loadings and alpha coefficients of each item with

Table 18.8

Factor Loadings of Community Satisfaction Items

	Item Description	Factor 1	Factor 2	Factor 3	Factor 4
1.	Neighborliness	.12361	.03216	.76182	.32101
2.	Parks and playgrounds	.62375	.33610	.32101	.02120
3.	Public schools	.74519	.34510	.12102	.01320
4.	Shopping facilities	.32100	.06121	.68123	.12356
5.	Police protection	.90987	.12618	.21361	.01320
6.	Local churches	.21032	.75847	.21362	.11620
7.	Church groups and organizations in the community	.01362	.83210	.01231	.11632
8.	Community entertainment and recreational opportunities	.25617	.01320	.12341	.75642
9.	Cultural activities	.16320	.12310	.32134	.82316
10.	Quality of air	.02313	.11621	.83612	.32131
11.	Noise level	.26154	.21320	.78672	.21368
12.	Overcrowding	.24321	.02151	.91638	0.2016
13.	Racial problems	.08091	.11320	.82316	.16342
14.	Neighborhood pride	.18642	.11218	.71321	.18321
	Percentage of variance	18.2	5.6	40.1	2.4

Table 18.9

Standardized Factor Score Coefficients

Item	Coefficient
1	.6812
10	.7234
11	.6916
12	.8162
13	.8110
14	.6910

respect to three underlying variables: hostile environment, quid pro quo behavior, and criminal sexual misconduct (the last being the most serious cases of harassment, i.e., rape and attempted rape). Taken together, the three factors accounted for 57 percent of the variance in the model. The authors intend to use these findings to predict the influence of different types of sexual harassment on the health of the victims, as well as the relationship between hypothesized risk factors and harassment.[10]

The extent to which each factor is expressed by the item's loadings is reflected in the percentage of explained variance. Generally, factors with the highest percentage of explained variance provide the clearest representation of the items. That is, this factor can be employed fairly exclusively to represent the dimension studied. Table 18.8, which indicates the results of the loadings received by each factor in the community satisfaction study, reveals that the factor most clearly representing community satisfaction is quality of life (40.1 percent); the most ambiguous factor is cultural amenities (2.4 percent). Practically speaking, this means that items related to cultural activities (e.g., number of movie houses, frequency of public concerts) can be eliminated from the questionnaire without significantly reducing the quality of the research.

In the final step of factor analysis, the researcher develops a composite scale for each factor. For each observation or item, a *factor score* (scale score) is calculated. A factor score is an item's score on a factor. It is obtained by using yet another type of coefficient, a **factor score coefficient.** To construct an item factor score, we multiply the factor score coefficients for each item by the standardized values of the variable obtained for that item. For example, Table 18.9 represents the factor score coefficients for the items that load on factor 3. We may construct an item's factor score f_3, a composite scale representing factor 3, as follows:

$$f_3 = .6812Z_1 + .7234Z_{10} + .6916Z_{11} + .8162Z_{12} + .8110Z_{13} + .6910Z_{14}$$

Z_1 through Z_{14} represent the standardized values of items 1 through 14 for that case.

In conclusion, factor analysis is an efficient method for reorganizing the items a researcher is investigating into conceptually more precise groups of variables.

10. Maureen Murdoch and Paul G. McGovern, "Measuring Sexual Harassment: Development and Validation of the Sexual Harassment Inventory," *Violence and Victims*, 13(3) (1998): 203–215.

SUMMARY ●

1. An index is a composite measure of two or more variables or items. Four major issues are involved in constructing indexes: the purpose for which the index is being compiled, the sources of the data, the base of comparison, and methods of aggregation and weighting. The Consumer Price Index (CPI), which is a composite measure of changes in retail prices, is one of the best-known and most frequently used indexes.

2. Scaling is a method of measuring the amount of a property possessed by a class of objects or events. It is most often associated with the measurement of attitudes. Attitude scales consist of statements expressing different attitudes, with which the respondent is asked to agree or disagree. Scaling techniques are applied to order the statements along some continuum. That is, they transform qualitative variables into a series of quantitative variables. The scales discussed in this chapter are either unidimensional or can be tested for unidimensionality. This means that the items comprising the scale can be arranged on a continuum presumed to reflect one and only one concept.

3. One technique for scale construction is Likert scaling. Likert scaling requires the researcher to compile a list of possible scale items, administer them to a random sample of respondents, compute a total score for each respondent, determine the discriminative power of each item, and only then select the final scale items.

4. Another method of scaling is the Guttman scaling technique. This method was designed to incorporate an empirical test of the unidimensionality of a set of items within the scale construction process. Guttman scale items are unidimensional—ranked on a single underlying dimension—as well as cumulative, in that information on any respondent's last positive response allows the researcher to predict all of that person's responses to the other items in the series. To measure the degree of conformity of a proposed scale to a perfectly scalable pattern, Guttman developed the coefficient of reproducibility (*CR*). A coefficient of reproducibility of .90 is the criterion used to decide whether a scale is indeed unidimensional.

5. Factor analysis is a statistical technique for classifying a large number of interrelated variables into a smaller number of factors. These factors represent a more complex dimension of a more abstract phenomenon. Factor analysis is a useful method for constructing multiple-item scales, where each scale represents a specific factor.

KEY TERMS FOR REVIEW ●

coefficient of reproducibility (*CR*) (p. 426)
discriminative power (*DP*) (p. 424)
factor analysis (p. 427)
factor loading (p. 429)
factor score coefficient (p. 430)
Guttman scale (p. 425)

index (p. 415)
item (p. 414)
Likert scale (p. 422)
simple aggregate (p. 418)
unidimensionality (p. 415)
weighted aggregate (p. 419)

STUDY QUESTIONS ●

1. What is the difference between a scale and an index? Can you identify commonly used examples of each?

2. Why do social scientists use scales and indexes in their research?
3. Develop an index to measure "popularity" among college students. Interview at least 10 persons (fellow students, teachers) to obtain the data for your scale. Use a method of aggregation with items of the type "How many times . . . ?" "How often . . . ?" "How many . . . ?" Incorporate weighting procedures when appropriate. Discuss the problems of validity and reliability as they apply to your index. On the basis of your results, submit a revised index of popularity.
4. Based on the results to Question 3, suggest how the index can be converted into a scale.
5. When would factor analysis be preferable to scaling? State your methodological as well as theoretical reasons for choosing between them.

SPSS PROBLEMS

1. Construct a scale measuring abortion attitudes. Include the following variables in your scale: "abany," "abdefect," "abhlth," "abnomore," "abpoor," "absingle." Generate **Frequencies** of your scale and determine the percentage of respondents who have the highest score on your scale. Describe their overall attitude toward abortion. How about those with the lowest score? Next, use SPSS to evaluate the reliability of your scale. What is the alpha coefficient for your scale?
2. Examine the relationship between church attendance ("attend") and the abortion scale constructed in Problem 1. Note that your new scale is an interval variable. Use the **Bivariate Correlations** procedure to analyze the relationship. What do you conclude?
3. Construct a scale measuring tolerance. Include the following variables in your scale: "colmil," "colhomo," "colrac." What is the alpha coefficient for your scale? Can you improve the alpha coefficient for the scale? How?

ADDITIONAL READINGS

Beere, Carole A. *Gender Roles: A Handbook of Tests and Measures.* Westport, CT: Greenwood Press, 1990.

Brodsky, Stanley L., and H. O'Neal Smitherman. *Handbook of Scales for Research in Crime and Delinquency.* New York: Plenum Press, 1983.

Cox, T. *Multidimensional Scaling.* New York: Routledge, Chapman & Hall, 1994.

Dawes, R. H., and T. W. Smith. "Attitude and Opinion Measurement." In *The Handbook of Social Psychology,* 3d ed., ed. Gardner Lindzey and Elliot Aronson. Hillsdale, NJ: Erlbaum, 1985, pp. 507–566.

Kim, Jae-On, and Charles W. Mueller. *Introduction to Factor Analysis: Statistical Methods and Practical Issues.* Thousand Oaks, CA: Sage, 1978.

Kirelsuk, Thomas, Aaron Smith, and Joseph Cardillo. *Goal Attainment Scaling: Applications, Theory and Measurement.* Mahwah, NJ: Erlbaum, 1994.

Lodge, Milton. *Magnitude Scaling.* Thousand Oaks, CA: Sage, 1981.

Lodge, Milton, and Kathleen M. McGraw, eds. *Political Judgment: Structure and Process.* Ann Arbor: University of Michigan Press, 1995.

Long, J. Scott. *Confirmatory Factor Analysis.* Thousand Oaks, CA: Sage, 1983.

Long, J. Scott. *Common Problems—Proper Solutions: Avoiding Error in Quantitative Research.* Thousand Oaks, CA: Sage, 1988.

Miller, Delbert C. *Handbook of Research Design and Social Measurement*, 5th ed. Thousand Oaks, CA: Sage, 1991.

Robinson, John P. *Measures of Political Attitudes*. San Diego, CA: Academic Press, 1998.

Robinson, John P., Philip R. Shaver, and Lawrence S. Wrightsman, eds. *Measuring Social Psychological Attitudes*. San Diego, CA: Academic Press, 1990.

Sullivan, John L., and Stanley Feldman. *Multiple Indicators: An Introduction*. Newbury Park, CA: Sage, 1979.

Touliatos, John, Barry F. Perlmutter, and Murray A. Straus. *Handbook of Family Measurement Techniques*. Thousand Oaks, CA: Sage, 1989.

INFERENCES

Throughout the history of the United States, white men have enjoyed higher occupational prestige than women and members of racial or ethnic minorities. Researchers in numerous studies have examined the individual effects of race or ethnicity and gender on occupational prestige, but few have investigated the interactive effects of these variables. Two researchers, however, *have* studied these effects. Wu Xu and Ann Leffler drew a sample of occupations from 1980 census data, which they used to assess the relative effects of race or ethnicity and gender on occupational prestige.[1] They compared prestige across four racial or ethnic groups (white, black, Asian American, and Hispanic), between genders, and between genders within each racial or ethnic group. They found that race has a stronger effect than gender on occupational prestige, but gender affects prestige differently in different racial groups. Their study showed that whites and Asian Americans of both genders enjoy higher occupational prestige than blacks and Hispanics. Within groups they found that white and Asian American women enjoy less occupational prestige than their male counterparts, but gender has a much stronger effect among Asian Americans than among whites. They found that black and Hispanic women have more occupational prestige than black and Hispanic men; however, the gender difference among Hispanics is very small. In the four groups, gender most affects the occupational prestige of Asian Americans and least affects Hispanics.

The researchers in this study used hypothesis testing to support their theory that both race and gender influence occupational prestige. Using statistical techniques, they were able to make inferences about the entire population of the United States from their findings about a sample of the population.

● **IN THIS CHAPTER** we describe the strategy of hypothesis testing by focusing on concepts such as the sampling distribution, Type I and Type II errors, and the level of significance. We then consider several methods of testing hypotheses about the relationship between two variables: difference between means, Pearson's *r*, and the chi-square test.

In Chapter 8 we introduced the general idea of inferential statistics, which deal with the problem of evaluating population characteristics when only the sample evidence is given. We demonstrated that sample statistics may give good estimates of particular population parameters but that virtually any estimate will deviate from the true value because of sampling fluctuations. The process of statistical inference enables investigators to evaluate the accuracy of their estimates.

Researchers also use inferential statistics to assess the probability of specific sample results under assumed population conditions. This type of inferential statistics is called *hypothesis testing* and will occupy us throughout this chapter. With estimation, a researcher selects a sample to evaluate the population parameter; when a researcher tests hypotheses, by contrast, he or she makes assumptions about the population parameter in advance, and the sample then provides the test of these assumptions. With estimation, the sample provides information about single population parameters such as the mean income or the variance of education; with hypothesis testing, a researcher is usually making an inference about relationships among variables—for example, the relationship between education and income or between occupation and particular political attitudes.

---

1. Wu Xu and Ann Leffler, "Gender and Race Effects on Occupational Prestige, Segregation, and Earnings," *Gender & Society,* 6 (3) (1992): 376–391.

THE STRATEGY OF TESTING HYPOTHESES   ●

The first step in testing a hypothesis is to formulate it in statistical terms. We have already discussed how to draw a hypothesis from a theory or how to formulate a research problem as a hypothesis. However, in order to test the hypothesis, a researcher must formulate it in terms that can be analyzed with statistical tools. For example, if the purpose of the investigation is to establish that educated individuals have higher incomes than noneducated individuals, the statistical hypothesis might be that there is a positive correlation between education and income or that the mean income of a highly educated group will be greater than the mean income of a group with a lower level of education. In both cases, the researcher formulates the statistical hypothesis in terms of descriptive statistics (such as a correlation or a mean) and specifies a set of conditions about these statistics (such as a positive correlation or a difference between the means).

The statistical hypothesis always applies to the population of interest. If the researcher could test the population directly, no inferences would be necessary, and any difference between the means (or a positive correlation of any size) would support the hypothesis. However, sample results are subject to sampling fluctuations, which could also account for the difference between the means or the positive coefficient. Thus a result that supports the hypothesis may imply either that the hypothesis is true or that it is false, with the results being due to chance factors. Conversely, if the sample results deviate from the expected population value, the deviation could mean either that the hypothesis is false or that it is true, with the difference between the expected and obtained values being due to chance. Table 19.1 illustrates these four possibilities.

Whether a sample result matches or deviates from expectation, either case can imply that the hypothesis is either *true or false*. Therefore, sample results cannot be interpreted directly; researchers need a decision rule to enable them to reject or retain a hypothesis about the population on the basis of sample results. The procedure of statistical inference enables the researcher to determine whether a particular sample result falls within a range that can occur by an acceptable level of chance. This procedure involves the following steps, which we will discuss in some detail.

1. Formulate a null hypothesis and a research hypothesis.
2. Choose a sampling distribution and a statistical test according to the null hypothesis.
3. Specify a significance level (α), and define the region of rejection.
4. Compute the statistical test, and reject or retain the null hypothesis accordingly.

Table 19.1

Alternative Interpretations of Sample Results

	Sample Results	
Hypothesis Status	According to Expectation	Deviation from Expectation
True	Results validate hypothesis	Results due to sampling fluctuation
False	Results due to sampling fluctuation	Results validate hypothesis

NULL AND RESEARCH HYPOTHESES

Two statistical hypotheses are involved in hypothesis testing. The first is the **research hypothesis**, which is usually symbolized by H_1. The second, symbolized by H_0, is the **null hypothesis**; H_0 is determined by H_1, which is really what you want to know; H_0 is the antithesis of H_1.

Suppose that the research hypothesis states that Catholics have larger families than Protestants. With the mean score for the size of family in the Catholic population designated as μ_1 and in the Protestant population as μ_2, the research hypothesis is

$$H_1: \mu_1 > \mu_2$$

The null hypothesis is

$$H_0: \mu_1 = \mu_2$$

The null hypothesis can be expressed in several ways. However, it is usually an expression of no difference or no relationship between the variables. Researchers express both the null hypothesis and the research hypothesis in terms of the population parameters, not in terms of the sample statistics. The null hypothesis is the one that the researcher tests directly; the research hypothesis is supported when the null hypothesis is rejected as being unlikely.

The need for two hypotheses arises out of a logical necessity: The null hypothesis is based on negative inference in order to avoid the *fallacy of affirming the consequent*— that is, researchers must eliminate false hypotheses rather than accept true ones. For instance, suppose that theory A implies empirical observation B. When B is false, one knows that A must also be false. But when B is true, A cannot be accepted as true, because B can be an empirical implication of several other theories that are not necessarily A. Therefore, if a researcher accepts A as true, he or she is committing the fallacy of affirming the consequent.

Emile Durkheim's theory of suicide may serve as an illustration. One of its propositions (A) is that people in individualistic situations are more likely to commit suicide. The empirical observation (B) derived from this proposition is that the suicide rate will be higher among single than among married individuals. If B proves to be false (if there is no difference in the suicide rates of married and single persons), theory A is false. But what if B is true? A cannot be accepted as true; there are many other explanations for B that are not necessarily A. For instance, the higher suicide rate of single persons might be explained not by individualism but rather by excessive drinking, which may lead to depression and to suicide. Thus observation B might imply that A_1, another theory, is true.

Usually, many alternative theories might explain the same observations; the researcher has to select the most credible one. The credibility of a theory can be established only by the elimination of all alternative theories.

SAMPLING DISTRIBUTION

Having formulated a specific null hypothesis, the investigator proceeds to test it against the sample results. For instance, if the hypothesis states that there is no difference between the means of two populations ($\mu_1 = \mu_2$), the procedure would be to draw a random sample from each population, compare the two sample means ($\bar{X}_1$ and $\bar{X}_2$), and make an inference from the samples to the populations. However, the sample result is subject to sampling error; therefore, it does not always reflect the true population value. If samples of the same size are drawn from the population, each sample will usually produce a different result.

To determine the accuracy of the sample statistic, the researcher has to compare it to a statistical model that gives the probability of observing such a result. Such a statistical model is called a **sampling distribution.** A sampling distribution of a statistic is obtained by drawing a large number of random samples of the same size from the defined population, computing the statistic for each sample, and plotting the frequency distribution of the statistic. In Chapter 8 we saw an example of such a distribution: the sampling distribution of the mean. It is possible to construct a sampling distribution of any other statistic, for example, of the variance (s^2), of the standard deviation (s), of the difference between means ($\bar{X}_1$ and $\bar{X}_2$), or of proportions (p).

As an illustration, let us go back to Durkheim's theory of suicide. The hypothesis to be tested is that single people have a relatively higher suicide rate than the general population. One way of evaluating the proportion of suicide among single people is to compare the number of suicides in this group to the average proportion in the population at large. Suppose that the records of health centers indicate that the national suicide rate in the adult population is 20 out of every 100, or .20. The research hypothesis would then imply that the rate of suicide among single people is higher than .20. Thus

H_1 : The proportion of suicides among single people > .20

The null hypothesis would state that the proportion of suicides among single people is the same as the national average:

H_0 : The proportion of suicides among singles = .20

Suppose we draw a sample of 100 from the health centers' records for single people, and we find that the rate of suicide is .30. Is this result sufficiently larger than .20 to justify the rejection of the null hypothesis? To assess the likelihood of obtaining a rate of .30 under the assumption of the null hypothesis, we compare the rate to a distribution of suicide rates of the entire adult population. Let us assume that 1,000 random samples of 100 each are drawn from the health centers' records for all adults and that the suicide rate is computed for each sample. Table 19.2 presents the obtained hypothetical sampling distribution.[2] This sampling distribution may serve as a statistical model for assessing the likelihood of observing a suicide rate of .30 among single people if their rate were equivalent to that of the adult population. The probability of observing any particular result can be determined by dividing its frequency in the distribution by the total number of samples.

The probabilities we would obtain are displayed in the third column of Table 19.2. For example, the suicide rate of .38–.39 occurred five times; therefore, the probability that any sample of size $n = 100$ will have this suicide rate is 5/1,000, or .005; that is, we would expect to obtain such a result in approximately .5 percent of the samples of 100 drawn from the population. Similarly, the probability of obtaining a rate of .30–.31 is .015, or 1.5 percent. The probability of obtaining a rate of .30 or more is equal to the sum of the probabilities of .30–.31, .32–.33, .34–.35, 36–.37, .38–.39, and .40 or more; that is, .015 + .010 + .010 + .010 + .005 + .000 = .050. Thus we would

---

2. Such a distribution is often called an *experimental sampling distribution* because it is obtained from observed data.

Table 19.2

Hypothetical Sampling Distribution of Suicide Rates for
All Adults for 1,000 Random Samples ($n = 100$)

Suicide Rate	Number of Samples (f)	Proportion of Samples ($p = f/n$)
.40 or more	0	.000
.38–.39	5	.005
.36–.37	10	.010
.34–.35	10	.010
.32–.33	10	.010
.30–.31	15	.015
.28–.29	50	.050
.26–.27	50	.050
.24–.25	50	.050
.22–.23	150	.150
.20–.21	200	.200
.18–.19	150	.150
.16–.17	100	.100
.14–.15	100	.100
.12–.13	50	.050
.10–.11	15	.015
.08–.09	10	.010
.06–.07	10	.010
.04–.05	10	.010
.02–.03	5	.005
.01 or less	0	.000
Total	1,000	1.000

expect 5 percent of all samples of 100 drawn from this population to have a suicide rate of .30 or more.

LEVEL OF SIGNIFICANCE AND REGION OF REJECTION ●

After we have constructed the sampling distribution, we can evaluate the likelihood of the result of .30 (given the assumption of the null hypothesis). The decision as to what result is sufficiently unlikely to justify the rejection of the null hypothesis is quite arbitrary. We can select any set of extreme results as a basis for rejecting the null hypothesis. The range of these results is designated as the **region of rejection.** The sum of the probabilities of the results included in the region of rejection is denoted as the **level of significance,** or α. It is customary to set the level of significance at .05 or .01, which means that the null hypothesis is to be rejected if the sample outcome is among the results that would have occurred by chance no more than 5 percent or 1 percent of the time.

Figure 19.1 presents the sampling distribution of Table 19.2 and the region of rejection with $\alpha = .05$ graphically. The region of rejection includes all the suicide rates of .30

Figure 19.1

Sampling Distribution of Suicide Rates for 1,000 Samples ($n = 100$)

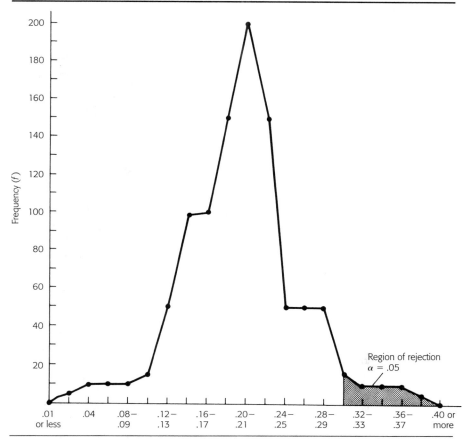

and above. As we have seen, the sum of the probabilities of these results is equal to the level of significance, .05.

The sample result of .30 that we obtained falls within the region of rejection; thus the null hypothesis can be rejected at the .05 level of significance. The rejection of the null hypothesis lends support to the research hypothesis that the suicide rate of single people is higher than the rate in the general adult population.

One-Tailed and Two-Tailed Tests

In the preceding example we selected the set of extreme results from the right tail of the sampling distribution. However, extreme sample outcomes are also located at the left-hand tail. In Table 19.2 the probability of a suicide rate of .11 and below is equal to the probability of obtaining a rate of .30 and above; in both cases it is .05.

Figure 19.2

Right-Tailed and Left-Tailed Tests

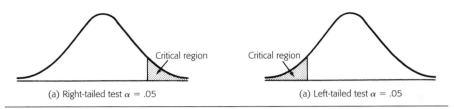

(a) Right-tailed test $\alpha = .05$ (a) Left-tailed test $\alpha = .05$

A statistical test may be *one-tailed* or *two-tailed.* In a **two-tailed test,** the region of rejection is located at both the left and right tails. In a **one-tailed test,** extreme results leading to rejection of the null hypothesis can be located at either tail.

The decision to locate the region of rejection in one or two tails will depend on whether H_1 implies a specific direction to the predicted results and whether it specifies large or small values. When H_1 predicts larger values, the region of rejection will be located at the right tail of the sampling distribution (as in the example of suicide). When H_1 implies lower values, the left tail is selected as the region of rejection. For instance, suppose that the research hypothesis had implied that single people have a lower suicide rate than the general adult population; that is,

H_1: The proportion of suicide in single population $< .20$

The results considered unlikely under this hypothesis are at the left tail of the distribution. At the .05 level of significance, the critical region will consist of the following rates: .10−.11, .08−.09, .06−.07, .04−.05, .02−.03, .01 or less. The sum of the probabilities of these results is .015 + .010 + .010 + .010 + .005 + .000 = .050. Figure 19.2 presents the right-tailed and left-tailed alternatives.

There are occasions when we cannot predict the direction of the research hypothesis accurately. For example, suppose we suspect that single persons have a different suicide rate but are unable to specify the direction of the difference. We would express the research hypothesis as

H_1: The proportion of single persons' suicide $\neq 20$

When we cannot specify the direction of H_1 accurately, we reject H_0 whenever we obtain extreme values in either direction. In such a case, the statistical test is designated as a two-tailed test, and the level of significance is divided in two. Thus a .05 level of significance would mean that H_0 will be rejected if the sample outcome falls among the lowest 2.5 percent or the highest 2.5 percent of the sampling distribution. This alternative is diagrammed in Figure 19.3.

Let us select the .05 level of significance and make use of a two-tailed test in the suicide example. The critical region will consist of the alternatives .34−.35, .36−.37, .38−.39, .40 or more (.010 + .010 + .005 + .000 = .025) and .06−.07, .04−.05, .02−.03, .01 or less (.010 + .010 + .005 + .000 = .025). With a two-tailed test, a sample result of .30 is not in the region of rejection; thus the null hypothesis would not be rejected in this case.

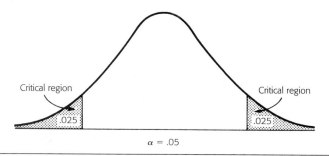

Figure 19.3

A Two-Tailed Test

Critical region   .025

Critical region   .025

$\alpha = .05$

Type I and Type II Errors

Because the entire population is not measured directly in statistical hypothesis testing, the statistical test can never prove if the null hypothesis is true or false. The only evidence it provides is whether the sample result is sufficiently likely or unlikely to justify the decision to retain or to reject the null hypothesis.

The null hypothesis can be either true or false, and in both cases it can be rejected or retained. If it is true and is rejected nonetheless, the decision is in error. The error is the *rejection of a true hypothesis*—a **Type I error.** If the null hypothesis is false but is retained, the error committed is the *acceptance of a false hypothesis;* this error is designated as a **Type 11 error.** These four alternatives are presented schematically in Table 19.3.

The probability of rejecting a true hypothesis—a Type I error—is defined as the *level of significance.* Thus, in the long run, an investigator employing the .05 level of significance will falsely reject 5 percent of the true hypotheses tested. Naturally, researchers are interested in minimizing the error of rejecting a true hypothesis, which they can do by making the level of significance as low as possible. However, Type I errors and Type II errors are inversely related: A decrease in the probability of rejecting a true hypothesis leads to an increase in the probability of retaining a false one. Under these conditions, the selection of α is determined by (1) the type of problem one is investigating and (2) the consequences of rejecting a true hypothesis or retaining a false one. If, for example, the researcher is investigating the effect of an experimental teaching method on the achievement of disadvantaged children and the results of the study will determine whether the teaching method is implemented throughout the school system, he or she

Table 19.3

Alternative Decisions in Hypothesis Testing

Decision	Null Hypothesis Is True	Null Hypothesis Is False
Reject hypothesis	Type I error	No error
Accept hypothesis	No error	Type II error

should carefully consider the consequences of making a mistake. Suppose that the null hypothesis states that the new teaching method has negative effects. If the researcher rejected the null hypothesis when it was actually true, the consequences could be very severe; hundreds of thousands of disadvantaged children would be harmed. If, conversely, it is not rejected when it is actually false, the school system could postpone implementation of the new method until further evidence became available. Therefore, in this case it would be preferable to minimize α because the implications of rejecting a true hypothesis are more severe than those of retaining a false one.

When a study does not have practical implications, the selection of α will be arbitrary, but the choice will usually be governed by accepted conventions. The significance levels commonly used in social science research are .001, .01, and .05.

PARAMETRIC AND NONPARAMETRIC TESTS OF SIGNIFICANCE •

The tests of significance that are most common in social science research are divided into two major groups: parametric tests and nonparametric tests. A **parametric test** is a statistical test based on several assumptions about the parameters of the population from which the sample was drawn. Among the most important ones are the assumptions that (1) the observations must be drawn from a normally distributed population and (2) the variables are measured on at least an interval scale. The results of a parametric test are meaningful only insofar as these assumptions are valid.

A **nonparametric test** neither specifies the normality condition nor requires an interval level of measurement. Certain assumptions are associated with most nonparametric tests; however, they are weaker and fewer than those associated with parametric tests.

In practice, researchers do not need to go through the laborious procedure of constructing a sampling distribution. In many instances, sampling distributions have been constructed by previous researchers and are known in advance. Moreover, distributions exist that can be used as approximations of certain sampling distributions. For example, the sampling distribution of the mean closely approximates the normal curve distribution; therefore, researchers can use the normal curve distribution in testing hypotheses about means.

In the discussion of specific tests that follows, we will refer to existing sampling distributions that have been constructed in advance or that approximate the desired distribution. The sampling distributions employed in this section are provided in Appendixes E through I.

Selected Parametric Tests

DIFFERENCE BETWEEN MEANS.   Many hypotheses in empirical research involve a comparison between populations. For example, to assess the relationship between social class and voting, a researcher could compare different social classes with respect to their voting patterns. Similarly, in comparing Asian Americans and Hispanic Americans with respect to achievement, a researcher is relating ethnicity to achievement.

When the dependent variable we are investigating is measured on an interval scale, we can compare means in order to reflect the amount of relationship between two variables (see Chapter 16). To assess the significance of a difference between means, we use the **difference-between-means test.**

To illustrate the testing of hypotheses about the difference between means, data are presented in Table 19.4 that show scores on attitudes on gender issues for two samples:

Table 19.4

Mean Scores of Attitudes on Gender
Issues for Evangelical Women and Others
(Hypothetical Data)

	Evangelicals	Others
n	126	101
$\overline{X}$	3.60	6.10
s	3.04	4.52

evangelical and nonevangelical women. A higher mean score indicates a more feminist attitude on gender issues. According to the literature, evangelicals are less likely to take feminist positions than nonevangelicals.[3] This would lead to the following research hypothesis: $H_1: \mu_1 > \mu_2$ where μ_1 is the mean score of the population of nonevangelical women and μ_2 is the mean score of evangelical women. The null hypothesis could state that there is no difference in the mean score of the two populations; that is, $H_0: \mu_1 = \mu_2$.

The data reveal a difference between the two sample means of 2.50 (6.10 − 3.60). Although this difference is in the expected direction, we need to determine its probability of occurrence under the assumption of the null hypothesis. If such a difference is unlikely to occur, assuming that the population means are identical, we must reject the null hypothesis.

The sampling distribution we select for testing the difference between means depends on the sample size. When each sample is larger than 30 ($n > 30$), the sampling distribution of the difference between means approaches normality, and thus we can use the normal curve (Appendix E) as the statistical model. The procedure is similar to the one employed in estimating population means (see Chapter 8). We can translate the difference between the means to standard Z scores and then determine its probability of occurrence according to the normal curve distribution. For a two-tailed test, using the .05 level of significance, the critical region expressed in Z scores includes all the positive scores of 1.96 and above or all the negative scores of −1.96 and below, whose likelihood of occurrence is .025. For a one-tailed test, the critical region contains all scores of 1.65 and above or −1.65 and below. Similarly, for the .01 level of significance, Z is ±2.58 and ±2.33, respectively.

To test the null hypothesis on difference in attitudes on gender issues, we can select a right-tailed test because H_1 is a directional hypothesis implying larger values. The level of significance selected will be .01; any value larger than 2.33 will lead to rejection of the null hypothesis.

To determine the significance of the difference between the means using the normal curve, we must first convert the difference to standard scores. This conversion can be accomplished using a test statistic denoted as t, which is defined in Formula (19.1):

$$t = \frac{(\overline{X}_1 - \overline{X}_2) - (\mu_1 - \mu_2)}{\hat{\sigma}_{\overline{x}1 - \overline{x}2}} \tag{19.1}$$

3. Clyde Wilcox and Elizabeth Adell Cook, "Evangelical Women and Feminism: Some Additional Evidence," *Women and Politics*, 9 (1989): 27−49.

where $\bar{X}_1 - \bar{X}_2$ = the difference between the sample means

$\mu_1 - \mu_2$ = the means of the sampling distribution of the difference between means

$\hat{\sigma}_{\bar{x}1 - \bar{x}2}$ = estimate of the standard error[4] of the sampling distribution of the difference between the means

Like Z, t measures deviations from the means in terms of standard deviation units; $\bar{X}_1 - \bar{X}_2$ replaces X, $\mu_1 - \mu_2$ replaces $\bar{X}$, and $\hat{\sigma}$ replaces s. We cannot calculate Z, however, when the variances of the two populations (σ_1^2 and σ_2^2) are unknown. That is, t substitutes for Z whenever sample variances (s_1^2 and s_2^2) are used as estimates of the populations' parameters. Because the populations' variances are almost never available, for all practical purposes, the t statistic is used to transform mean differences to standard scores. The t is normally distributed when $n > 30$; thus the normal distribution can be employed whenever each sample size is greater than 30. However, when $n \leq 30$, the normal approximation is not appropriate, and the sampling distribution of t must be used.

We can obtain the estimate of the standard error ($\hat{\sigma}_{\bar{x}1 - \bar{x}2}$) by two methods. The first assumes that the two population variances are equal—for instance, $\sigma_1^2 = \sigma_2^2$—and thus the variances of the two samples are combined into a single estimate of σ_1^2 or σ_2^2. The standard error under these conditions is

$$\hat{\sigma}_{\bar{x}1 - \bar{x}2} = \sqrt{\frac{n_1 s_1^2 + n_2 s_2^2}{n_1 + n_2 - 2}} \sqrt{\frac{n_1 + n_2}{n_1 n_2}} \qquad (19.2)$$

where n_1 and n_2 are the sample sizes of sample 1 and sample 2, respectively, and s_1^2 and s_2^2 are the variances of sample 1 and sample 2.

When there is no basis for assuming that the population variances are identical, it is not possible to pool the sample variance. In this instance, we estimate the two variances separately, and the formula obtained for the standard error is

$$\hat{\sigma}_{\bar{x}1 - \bar{x}2} = \sqrt{\frac{s_1^2}{n_1 - 1} + \frac{s_2^2}{n_2 - 1}} \qquad (19.3)$$

To calculate t for the data summarized in Table 19.4, we assume that $\sigma_1^2 = \sigma_2^2$ and calculate the pooled estimate of the standard error:

$$\hat{\sigma}_{\bar{x}1 - \bar{x}2} = \sqrt{\frac{(101)(4.52)^2 + 126(3.04)^2}{101 + 126 - 2}} \sqrt{\frac{101 + 126}{(101)(126)}} = .50$$

Because under the null hypothesis it has been assumed that $\mu_1 = \mu_2$, the definition of t reduces to

$$t = \frac{\bar{X}_1 - \bar{X}_2}{\hat{\sigma}_{\bar{x}1 - \bar{x}2}} \qquad (19.4)$$

---

4. The standard error is the standard deviation of the sampling distribution; see Chapter 8 for a discussion of this concept.

We obtain the following result for our example:

$$t = \frac{6.1 - 3.6}{.50} = \frac{2.5}{.50} = 5$$

Referring to the normal curve table (Appendix E), we observe that the value of t is in fact greater than the value needed for rejection (2.33) at the .01 level of significance. In other words, the difference between the sample mean of evangelical women and that of nonevangelical women students is not likely to be due to sampling error. Accordingly, we reject H_0 and conclude that the difference between the samples reflects different attitudes toward gender issues.

THE t DISTRIBUTION. When either or both of the sample sizes is less than 30, the normal curve does not approximate the sampling distribution of the difference between means. As a result, using the normal curve to determine the probability of H_0 will yield inaccurate conclusions, and the sampling distribution of t has to be used instead. The t is actually a family of curves, each determined by the sample size. Thus, for a sample size of 7, t has a different distribution from that for a sample size of 10. The sampling distribution of t is reproduced in Appendix F. The values in this table are given in terms of the significance level (one tail and two tails) and the degrees of freedom.

DEGREES OF FREEDOM. The concept of **degrees of freedom (df)** is a basic one that researchers use in several statistical tests, including the t **test,** which can be used when the normal curve does not apply. When we use the normal curve, our calculations are based on the total sample size (N) and the shape of the curve is always the same. When we use other distributions to test hypotheses, we must adjust the sample size to reflect restrictions placed on our choice of cases to be included in the sample because the shape of the distribution changes depending on how many cases can be freely chosen to be in the sample. *Degrees of freedom* refers to the number of free choices you can make in repeated random samples that constitute a sampling distribution and reflects the adjustment to the sample size. To determine degrees of freedom, you must know the sample size and whether there are any restrictions that limit your choice of observations to be included in the sample, because we calculate degrees of freedom by subtracting the number of restrictions on our choices from the total sample size.

For example, suppose you are asked to choose any two numbers from a group of numbers ranging from 0 to 10. The sample size in this case is 2, there are no restrictions on the numbers you can choose, and the degrees of freedom is 2 (2 cases $-$ 0 restrictions $=$ 2 df). Now suppose that you are asked to choose two numbers from the same group that sum to 10. We have now placed a restriction on the number of free choices you can make. You can choose one number freely, but you have no choice about the value of the second number. If you choose 10 as the first number, the second number must be 0, and the degrees of freedom is 1 (2 cases $-$ 1 restriction $=$ 1 df). The number of degrees of freedom of the t distribution is limited by the fact that for each sample, the population variance has to be estimated, so only $n - 1$ quantities are free to vary in each sample (one restriction has been applied to each sample). When we use the t distribution to test a hypothesis about a difference between two samples, we determine the total number of degrees of freedom by summing the number of degrees of freedom for the two samples; thus df is equivalent to $(n_1 - 1) + (n_2 - 1) = n_1 + n_2 - 2$.

To illustrate the use of the t table, we shall test the hypothesis that students' achievement is associated with their assignment to tracks in a secondary school. The data are

Table 19.5

Mean Achievement of Students in College
Preparatory and Noncollege Tracks

	College Preparatory Track	Noncollege Track
n	13	6
$\bar{X}$	48.3	20.5
s	23.6	12.2

summarized in Table 19.5. The investigators hypothesized that achievement and track assignment were related, so that a college preparatory track had more students who were high achievers than a noncollege track. The null hypothesis to be tested is that the means of the two populations are identical, whereas the research hypothesis states that the mean achievement of the college preparatory track (μ_1) is higher than that of the noncollege track (μ_2):

$$H_0: \mu_1 = \mu_2$$

$$H_1: \mu_1 > \mu_2$$

We can follow the same procedure in calculating the standard error and the t ratio, using Equations (19.2) and (19.4):

$$\hat{\sigma}_{\bar{x}1 - \bar{x}2} = \sqrt{\frac{13(23.6)^2 + 6(12.2)^2}{13 + 6 - 2}} \sqrt{\frac{13 + 6}{(13)(6)}} = 10.8$$

$$t = \frac{48.3 - 20.5}{10.8} = \frac{27.8}{10.8} = 2.574$$

The obtained t can now be compared with the appropriate value in the sampling distribution of t. The number of degrees of freedom for sample sizes of 13 and 6 is 17 ($13 + 6 - 2$). At the .01 level of significance with a one-tailed test (right tail), the t for which H_0 will be rejected is 2.567. A t larger than 2.567 is unlikely to occur if H_0 is true. As 2.574 is larger than 2.567, the null hypothesis is rejected, and the investigator can conclude that the difference in achievement between the two tracks is statistically significant.

A SIGNIFICANCE TEST FOR PEARSON'S r. The correlation coefficient Pearson's r—like $\bar{X}$, Md, or b—is a statistic obtained from sample data; as such, it is just an estimate of a population parameter. Pearson's r corresponds to the population correlation denoted as ρ or rho. As with other sample statistics, r is subject to sampling fluctuations; the test of its statistical significance is an assessment of the likelihood that the obtained correlation is due to sampling error. For example, a researcher may test the hypothesis that liberalism is correlated with income and draw a random sample of 24, obtaining an r of .30. It is probable that in the population these two variables are not correlated at all and that the coefficient obtained is a result of chance factors. In other words, is an r of .30 large enough to make the hypothesis of no relation unlikely?

The strategy of testing such a hypothesis is similar to that used in the difference-of-means test; the null hypothesis states that the correlation in the population is zero, and the research hypothesis, that it is different from zero:

$$H_0: \rho = 0$$
$$H_1: \rho \neq 0$$

TESTING THE SIGNIFICANCE OF r WHEN ρ IS ZERO. When ρ is assumed to be zero under the null hypothesis, the researcher can test the statistical significance of r by converting r to a standard score using the t test statistic with $n - 2$ degrees of freedom. Thus t is defined as

$$t = \frac{r\sqrt{n - 2}}{\sqrt{1 - r^2}} \tag{19.5}$$

To illustrate the use of t in testing the significance of Pearson's r, let us suppose that we have obtained a correlation of .30 between income and years of schooling from a sample of $n = 24$ ($df = 22$). The t is equal to

$$t = \frac{.30\sqrt{22}}{\sqrt{1 - .30^2}} = 1.475$$

From the distribution of t in Appendix F, we see that at the .05 level of significance for a two-tailed test and with 22 df, the value of t required to reject the null hypothesis is 2.074. As the obtained t is smaller than this value, the null hypothesis cannot be rejected, and the relationship between income and years of schooling is said to be not significant.

Researchers can also test the significance of r by using a test statistic called F. The F statistic is based on the ratio of the explained (r^2) to the unexplained ($1 - r^2$) variance. It is defined in Equation (19.6), where $n - 2$ stands for the degrees of freedom:

$$F = \frac{r^2}{1 - r^2} (n - 2) \tag{19.6}$$

Using the data from our example on income and years of schooling, we have

$$F = \frac{.30^2}{1 - .30^2} (24 - 2) = 2.17$$

To evaluate the F statistic, we use the F distribution given in Appendix G. F values are given for $\alpha = .05$ (light numbers) and $\alpha = .01$ (bold numbers). The number of degrees of freedom for the explained variance (across the top of the table) is equal to the number of groups we are comparing minus 1 (in our example we are comparing two groups, thus the number of degrees of freedom is $2 - 1 = 1$) and the number of degrees of freedom for the unexplained variance is equal to $n - 2$ (left-hand column); $24 - 2 = 22$ in our example. H_0 is rejected when F is larger than or equal to the F value appearing in the table. Thus, to find the significance of $F = 2.17$, we locate the F value corresponding to 1 (across the top) and 22 (left-hand column). There are two F values, $F = 4.30$, corresponding to $\alpha = .05$; and $F = 7.94$, corresponding to $\alpha = .01$. In either case, the obtained value of $F = 2.17$ is smaller than the F required to reject H_0, and we must conclude that the relationship between income and years of schooling is not significant.

Parametric Tests of Significance

Assumptions basic to parametric tests: The observations must be drawn randomly from a normally distributed population and the variables are measured on at least an interval scale.

+ *Difference between means:* Researchers use the *t* test to assess the significance of differences between the means of samples drawn from different populations. The probability of the difference between the sample means occurring by chance if the null hypothesis is true is calculated using Equation (19.1). If we can assume that the population variances are equal, we calculate the standard error using Equation (19.2). When there is no reason to assume the population variances are the same, we must use Equation (19.3), the equation for standard error. When both sample sizes are at least 30, we use the normal curve table to evaluate *t*. If either sample size is less than 30, we use the *t* table to evaluate *t*.

+ *Significance tests for Pearson's r:* Researchers can use two tests to test the significance of a correlation coefficient. When the null hypothesis assumes that the correlation in the population is zero ($\rho = 0$), the *t* distribution can be used to determine the significance of the correlation and is calculated with Equation (19.5). Researchers can also use the *F* distribution to assess the significance of a correlation. The *F* statistic is based on the ratio of the explained to the unexplained variance, using Equation (19.6).

Nonparametric Test

CHI-SQUARE (χ^2).   Chi-square is a general test designed to evaluate whether the difference between observed frequencies and expected frequencies under a set of theoretical assumptions is statistically significant. Researchers most often apply the **chi-square test** to problems in which two nominal variables are cross-classified in a bivariate table. The data summarized in Table 19.6 are an example of a research problem to which the chi-square test is applicable. Table 19.6 is a bivariate table of mens' attitudes toward traditional gender roles during the 1970s and the 1980s. When the frequencies are converted to percentages (in parentheses), it is observed that in the 1970s, 69 percent of

Table 19.6

Percentage of Men Supporting and Opposing Traditional Male Provider Role in the 1970s and 1980s

Better if man achieves outside and woman takes care of home and family	Year		
	1970s	1980s	Total
Yes	36 (69%)	80 (47%)	116
No	16 (31%)	90 (53%)	106
Total	52	170	222

Adapted from Jane Riblett Wilkie, "Changes in U.S. Men's Attitudes Toward the Family Provider Role, 1972–1989," *Gender and Society,* 7(2) (1993): 261–279.

the men believed it was better if men worked outside the home and women cared for the home and family; in the 1980s, only 47 percent of the men held this belief. We want to examine whether such differences are statistically significant. Under the null hypothesis, we assume that there are no differences in beliefs between men surveyed in the 1970s and those surveyed in the 1980s. We then compute the frequencies, given this assumption, and compare them with the observed frequencies. If the differences between the observed and expected frequencies are so large as to occur only rarely (5 percent or 1 percent of the time), the null hypothesis is rejected.

The statistic used to evaluate these differences is chi-square (χ^2), which is defined as

$$\chi^2 = \Sigma \frac{(f_o - f_e)^2}{f_e} \tag{19.7}$$

where f_o = observed frequencies and f_e = expected frequencies.

To compute the expected frequencies for any cell, use the following formula:

$$f_e = \frac{(\text{row total})(\text{column total})}{n} \tag{19.8}$$

For Table 19.6, the expected frequency for men who responded "yes" in the 1970s (row 1, column 1) is

$$f_e = \frac{(116)(52)}{222} = 27$$

Table 19.7 is the reconstructed table containing frequencies we would expect if men's attitudes toward traditional gender roles had not changed from the 1970s to the 1980s.

CALCULATING CHI-SQUARE (χ^2). To compute χ^2, we subtract the expected frequencies of each cell from the observed frequencies, square them, divide by the expected frequency of the cell, and then sum for all cells. These calculations are summarized in Table 19.8. Note that χ^2 will be zero if the observed frequencies are identical to the expected frequencies. That is, the larger the difference between what is observed and what is expected were the hypothesis of no relations true, the larger will be the value of χ^2.

To evaluate the χ^2 statistic, we need to compare it to the sampling distribution of χ^2 and observe whether the value of 8.1 is large enough and thus unlikely if the null

| **Table 19.7**

Percentage of Men Supporting and Opposing Traditional Male Provider Role in the 1970s and 1980s: Expected Frequencies

Better if man achieves outside and woman takes care of home and family	Year		Total
	1970s	1980s	
Yes	27	89	116
No	25	81	106
Total	52	170	222

Table 19.8

Calculation of χ^2 for the Data of Tables 19.6 and 19.7

f_o	f_e	$f_o - f_e$	$(f_o - f_e)^2$	$(f_o - f_e)^2/f_e$
36	27	9	81	3.0
16	25	−9	81	3.2
80	89	−9	81	.9
90	81	9	81	1.0
				$\chi^2 = 8.1$

hypothesis is true. The sampling distribution of χ^2 is reproduced in Appendix I. Two factors determine the distribution: the level of significance (α) and the number of degrees of freedom. Thus χ^2 is really a family of distributions, each determined by different parameters. We shall select for this problem a level of significance of .01, which means that only if we obtain a χ^2 larger than what we would expect to find in no more than 1 out of 100 of our samples will the null hypothesis be rejected.

The number of degrees of freedom of the χ^2 sampling distribution is set by the number of cells for which expected frequencies can be selected freely. For any bivariate table, the cells that can be determined arbitrarily are limited by the marginal total of both variables. Thus, in a 2 × 2 table, for instance, only one cell is free to vary; the three others are predetermined by the marginal totals. Generally, we can compute the number of degrees of freedom using the following formula:

$$df = (r - 1)(c - 1) \tag{19.9}$$

where r = the number of rows and c = the number of columns. Thus

In a 2 × 2 table: $df = (2 - 1)(2 - 1) = 1$

In a 3 × 3 table: $df = (3 - 1)(3 - 1) = 4$

In a 4 × 3 table: $df = (4 - 1)(3 - 1) = 6$

The probabilities under H_0 are given at the top of each column in Appendix I, and the row entries indicate the number of degrees of freedom.

The sampling distribution of χ^2 is positively skewed, with higher values in the upper tail of the distribution (to the right). Therefore, with the χ^2 test, the critical region is located at the upper tail of the sampling distribution.

For our example, with 1 df and a .01 level of significance, the entry is 6.635, indicating that a value of 6.635 will occur in only 1 percent of the samples. Our obtained sample result of 8.1 is larger than 6.635 and is unlikely under the null hypothesis. However, at higher levels of significance—of .001, for example ($\chi^2 = 10.827$)—we would not reject the null hypothesis. Researchers generally choose the level of significance before calculating statistics by considering the consequences of Type I and Type II errors. Most researchers in the social sciences set their significance levels at .05 or .01. Using this as a rule of thumb, we would reject the null hypothesis that men's attitudes toward traditional gender roles did not change from the 1970s to the 1980s.

A Nonparametric Test of Significance

The chi-square test: The chi-square test may be used with nominal variables cross-classified in a bivariate table to determine whether the difference between the observed and expected frequencies is statistically significant. Chi-square is obtained using Equations (19.7) and (19.8). Using the chi-square distribution, we locate the appropriate minimum value needed to reject the null hypothesis in the table in Appendix I. We determine the minimum value by locating the row containing the appropriate degrees of freedom and the column containing the desired level of significance. The chi-square value obtained can then be compared to the minimum value. If the value obtained is larger, we can reject the null hypothesis.

●

SUMMARY

1. Statistical inference refers to a procedure that allows the investigator to decide between two hypotheses about a population parameter on the basis of a sample result.

2. The first step in testing a hypothesis is to formulate it in statistical terms. The statistical hypothesis always applies to the population of interest. Two statistical hypotheses are involved in hypothesis testing. The first is the research hypothesis, symbolized by H_1. The second, symbolized by H_0, is the null hypothesis, which is set up for logical purposes. The null hypothesis is the one that is tested directly. When the null hypothesis is rejected as being unlikely, the research hypothesis is supported.

3. The need for two hypotheses arises out of a logical necessity. The null hypothesis is based on negative inference in order to avoid the fallacy of affirming the consequent; that is, the researcher must eliminate false hypotheses rather than accept true ones.

4. After formulating a specific null hypothesis, the investigator proceeds to test it against the sample result. The researcher does this test by comparing the sample result to a statistical model that gives the probability of observing such a result. Such a statistical model is called a sampling distribution. A sampling distribution of a statistic is obtained by drawing a large number of random samples of the same size from the defined population, computing the statistic for each sample, and plotting the frequency distribution of the statistic.

5. The sampling distribution allows us to estimate the probability of obtaining the sample result. This probability is called the level of significance, or α, which is also the probability of rejecting a true hypothesis (Type I error). When the likelihood of obtaining the sample result is very small under the assumptions of the null hypothesis, H_0 is rejected, and the rejection adds to our confidence in the research hypothesis.

6. Statistical tests are divided into two major groups: parametric tests and nonparametric tests. A parametric test is a statistical test based on several assumptions about the parameters of the population from which the sample was drawn. One of the most important assumptions is that the observations have been drawn

from a normally distributed population and that the variables were measured on at least an interval scale. A nonparametric statistical test is one whose model does not specify that the population be normally distributed nor does it require an interval-level measurement. The difference-between-means test and a significance test for Pearson's *r* are parametric tests. The chi-square test is a nonparametric test of significance.

KEY TERMS FOR REVIEW ●

chi-square test (χ^2) (p. 450)
degrees of freedom (*df*) (p. 447)
difference-between-
   means test (p. 444)
level of significance (p. 440)
nonparametric test (p. 444)
null hypothesis (p. 438)
one-tailed test (p. 442)

parametric test (p. 444)
region of rejection (p. 440)
research hypothesis (p. 438)
sampling distribution (p. 439)
t test (p. 447)
two-tailed test (p. 442)
Type I error (p. 443)
Type II error (p. 443)

STUDY QUESTIONS ●

1. Discuss the role of the null hypothesis and the research hypothesis in the logic of hypothesis testing.
2. What is the difference between using a level of significance of .50 and using one of .05?
3. What is the difference between one-tailed and two-tailed tests?
4. Show in a diagram the difference between Type I and Type II errors.
5. Distinguish between parametric and nonparametric tests of significance.

SPSS PROBLEMS ●

1. In SPSS Problem 1 in Chapter 16, we examined the relationship between church attendance ("attend") and opinions about the Bible ("bible").
   a. Reexamine the relationship using the **Crosstabs** procedure, requesting the chi-square statistic.
   b. Is the relationship between "attend" and "bible" statistically significant? Explain.
   c. At what level of significance can you reject the null hypothesis?
2. Using SPSS, construct a table showing the relationship between opinions about the Bible ("bible") and attitudes toward women working ("fefam"). Use "bible" as the independent variable. Request the chi-square statistic and test the null hypothesis that "bible" and "fefam" are statistically independent. What are the results of the test? Explain.
3. Is there a statistically significant relationship between race ("race") and education ("educ")? Examine this question using the difference-between-means test (*t*-test) procedure.
   a. What is the null hypothesis?
   b. What is the research hypothesis?

   c. What is the value of the obtained t?
   d. Can you reject the null hypothesis?
   e. At what level of significance?

ADDITIONAL READINGS ●

Cuzzort, R. P., and James S. Vrettos. *The Elementary Forms of Statistical Reason.* New York: St. Martin's Press, 1996.

Frankfort-Nachmias, Chava. *Social Statistics for a Diverse Society.* Thousand Oaks, CA: Pine Forge Press, 1999.

Healey, Joseph F. *Statistics: A Tool for Social Research.* Belmont, CA: Wadsworth, 1999.

Introduction to SPSS

Chava Frankfort-Nachmias

The Statistical Package for the Social Sciences (SPSS), Release 9, is one of the most widely used and popular software packages for data analysis. SPSS was designed especially for the analysis of social science data and includes most of the procedures that social scientists employ. In fact, all the statistical procedures described in this text can be executed using SPSS. The program also enables users to transform data by recoding variables and computing new ones as well as deal with missing information. In addition, with SPSS you can sample, weight, and select subgroups or cases from a data set.

In this appendix we supply the tools necessary to set up an SPSS file, to open an existing file, and to execute basic data analyses. The appendix is not by any means an exhaustive display of either the variety of subprograms available or the intricacies of the more high-powered types of analyses possible with SPSS. Rather, the examples we use parallel the work covered in this text.

The diskette that comes with the textbook includes the data file (**gss96worth** and **gss96student**) for the end-of-chapter exercises and the examples discussed in this appendix. These files are from the 1996 General Social Survey (GSS). The GSS, which has been conducted nearly every year since 1972 by the National Opinion Research Center in Chicago, is designed to provide social science researchers with a readily accessible database of socially relevant attitudes, behaviors, and attributes of a cross section of the U.S. adult population.

The GSS surveys a sample of people from across the United States every year. The data, obtained through a sampling design known as a multistage probability sample, are representative of Americans 18 years and older. This means that the GSS data set allows us to estimate the characteristics, opinions, and behaviors of all noninstitutionalized, English-speaking, American adults in a given year.

Using SPSS, you can read the data files directly from the diskette, but this will be slower than first copying them to the hard drive of your computer. You can copy them just as you would any file, using the Explorer program in Windows.

GETTING ACQUAINTED WITH SPSS FOR WINDOWS •

SPSS for Windows, Version 9, is a well-integrated Windows program that adheres to many typical Windows conventions and commands. The Windows version of SPSS is very easy to use and allows even the inexperienced to perform complex tasks through the use of the graphical interface. If you are new to the Windows environment you may want to familiarize yourself with the basics of Windows, which includes the use of *drop-down menus, toolbars,* and *dialog boxes.* Like other Windows-based programs, all operations in SPSS involve the use of one or more of these elements. In the following section we will introduce the drop-down menus, toolbars, and dialog boxes in SPSS.

HOW TO START SPSS ●

You can start SPSS either by double-clicking on the **SPSS** icon (if you see it on your Desktop) or by clicking on the **Start** button, then on **Programs,** and finally on **SPSS.** The first window you will see is the SPSS Data Editor, which is called the **data window** (Figure A.1). Notice that the blue strip along the top left of the window says **Untitled-SPSS for Windows Data Editor.**

If you are using SPSS Version 8 or 9 you will also see a dialog box superimposed on this screen (Figure A.2). This is the **What would you like to do?** dialog box. Like other dialog boxes you will encounter while using SPSS, this dialog box presents you with a number of options to choose from. We will get to dialog boxes later on in this section. For now, click on the x button in the upper right corner to close this window. Another way to get this window out of the way is to click on **Cancel** in the bottom right corner of the screen.

As you can see, the data window is now empty. We will need to get some data before we can use it. However, before we do that, let's talk about drop-down menus, toolbars, and dialog boxes.

DROP-DOWN MENUS, TOOLBARS, AND DIALOG BOXES ●

Drop-down menus appear at the top of each SPSS screen. The drop-down menu gives you a set of options, such as **File, Edit,** etc. If you want to work with a data file, click on **File** and then choose an appropriate option such as **Open** (open a new file) or **Save**

Figure A.1

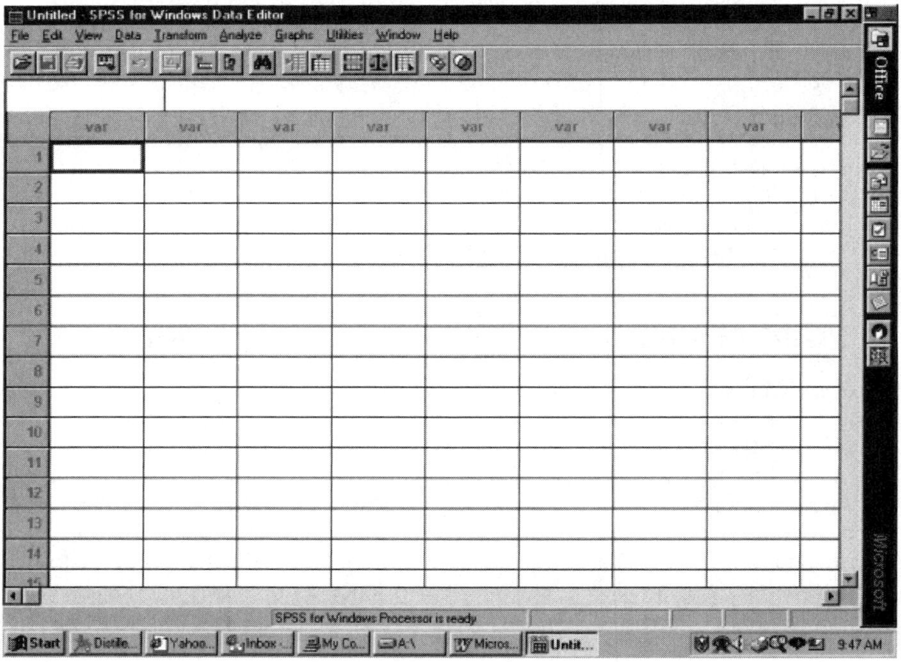

Figure A.2

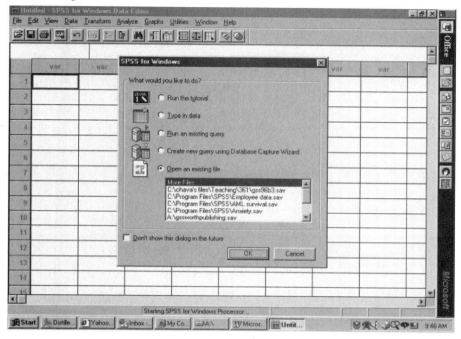

(save a file). Similarly, if you want to edit your file, click on **Edit** and choose one of the available options, such as **Cut** or **Paste**.

Another way to run SPSS procedures is to use the toolbar. The toolbar includes many of the options available through the drop-down menu and is sometimes quicker and easier to use. To identify the procedure associated with each of the symbols, simply point your mouse and wait for a second or so; the name of the procedure will appear (shaded in yellow).

Finally, dialog boxes are another way to communicate with SPSS. Dialog boxes are activated through either a drop-down menu or a toolbar. For example, the **Open File** dia-

Figure A.3

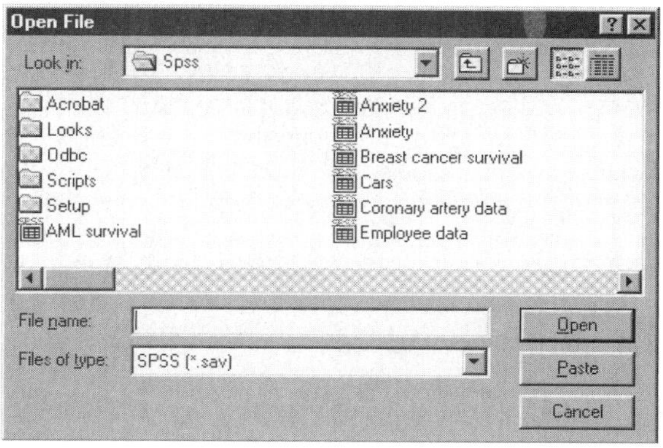

log box in Figure A.3 was activated when I clicked on **Open File** in the toolbar. This dialog box lists all the SPSS files stored on my hard drive. To activate any of these files I would highlight the name of the file and then click on **Open.**

WORKING WITH A DATA SET ●

Earlier we got acquainted with the SPSS data editor. However, to work with the data editor we need first to get some data. There are two basic methods of obtaining data in SPSS: creating your own data set or working with a set of data that already exists. In this section we discuss briefly how to enter your own data and how to access the data set that comes with this text.

Entering Your Own Data Set

Entering data in the **Data Editor** window is very similar to entering data in any Windows spreadsheet program. You enter data one cell at a time into the current active cell. The active cell is always the immediate target cell for data entry or editing, and it is clearly identifiable by the thicker border surrounding it. Any cell can be made the active cell simply by clicking on it; however, the default active starting cell is always at row 1, column 1. Figure A.1 shows the **Data Editor** window with the active cell at row 1, column 1.

In SPSS for Windows, a column contains all of a single variable's values and a row contains all of a single case's values. You begin by entering a value for the first case on the first variable. To do so, with the active cell in the position of row 1/column 1, you only need to type the appropriate numerical value and then hit **Enter.** For example, let's consider an example in which we have collected data on the abortion attitudes of four individuals. Each person has a value on (1) gender, coded 1 for males and 2 for females and (2) abortion attitudes, coded 1 for pro-choice and 2 for anti-choice. The data are given below:

Gender	Abortion Attitude
1	2
2	1
2	2
1	1

To enter the first person's gender, type a 1 and press the **Enter** key on your keyboard. You will notice that as you type, the value appears near the top of the screen where the cursor is blinking. Upon hitting **Enter** the first time, two things happen: (1) The value you typed enters into the first cell, and (2) the column label above the cell in column 1 is now labeled as "var00001." Next click on the cell to the right and enter 2 to represent the first person's abortion attitude. Now click on the first cell in the second row and enter the gender of the second person. Continue this process until all data have been entered. The **Data Editor** window should now look like Figure A.4.

Labeling the Variables

After you enter the data values for your variables, you will want to assign names to the variables and value labels for each of the numerical codes. To label your first variable

Figure A.4

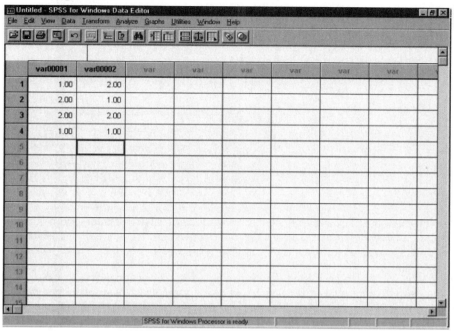

(var00001), click anywhere in the first column and then call up the **Define Variable** dialog box by clicking

Data → **Define Variable**

The **Define Variable** dialog box is shown in Figure A.5. The rectangular box labeled **Variable Name** is where you type the new variable name—gender—for var00001. Simply

Figure A.5

| Define Variable | ✕ |

Variable Name: var00001

Variable Description
Type:　　　　Numeric8.2
Variable Label:
Missing Values:　None
Alignment:　　Right

Change Settings

Type...　　Missing Values...

Labels..　　Column Format...

Measurement

⊙ Scale　　◯ Ordinal　　◯ Nominal

OK　　Cancel　　Help

Figure A.6

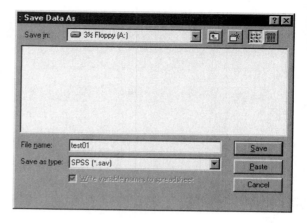

hit the Backspace key and type "gender." Now click on **OK** (or hit **Enter**). Notice that the word "gender" now replaces var00001 at the top of column 1 in the data editor (not shown). Now choose a label for var0002 (how about "abortion"?) and repeat the process.

When you have completed entering your data (and/or naming your variables) or if you need to stop at this point, you would normally save your data set so that you can use it again later. To save your data set, click on

F̲ile → S̲ave

This calls up the **Save Data As** dialog box shown in Figure A.6. Note that we have de-cided to save our data to a 3½ floppy (drive A) (if you want to save your data to an-other drive, just switch to the appropriate drive), and that we have named our data set "test01." Finally, click on S̲ave to complete this step.

Loading a Data Set

Most of the time you will be using SPSS with an existing data file. This book includes two data sets comprising 119 and 44 variables respectively. Both data sets are from the 1996 General Social Survey. The data are stored on a diskette and are included in the files gss96worth and gss96student. We use these data files in all the demonstrations of SPSS included in this appendix as well as in the end-of-chapter exercises. To load the gss96worth data file, click on

F̲ile → O̲pen

This will bring up the **Open File** dialog box. To access the data set, insert your diskette in the disk drive and then select the drive by clicking on the Down Arrow until you get to the proper drive (usually drive A). The **Open File** dialog box in Figure A.7 shows the file gss96worth or gss96student located on drive A. Select gss95worth or gss96student by clicking on it and then click on the O̲pen button. After a few seconds SPSS will retrieve your data file and display it in the data window, which will look something like Figure A.8.

The gss96worth data file we have selected contains 995 cases and 119 variables. Thus it will have 995 rows and 119 columns. You can easily scroll up and down or across the data window by clicking on the appropriate arrows at the top, bottom right, or left side of the Data Editor window or by using the arrow keys on your keyboard.

Figure A.7

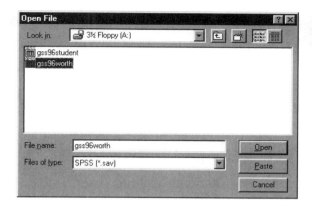

Figure A.8

	id	hrs1	marital	childs	age	educ	sex	race	income	rincome	income91	rincom91
1	1	.	1	0	79	12	1	1	13	.	22	
2	4	20	1	4	50	6	2	1	12	8	18	
3	5	.	4	4	56	8	2	3	8	.	8	
4	7	40	4	3	48	12	1	2	12	12	18	1
5	9	35	4	0	40	13	2	2	11	11	13	1
6	10	.	4	4	46	13	2	2	8	.	8	
7	11	55	5	0	37	19	2	1	12	12	19	1
8	12	40	3	0	43	16	2	1	12	12	20	2
9	14	10	3	0	44	13	1	1	1	.	1	
10	18	55	5	0	32	19	1	1	12	12	16	1
11	20	.	5	2	24	12	2	2	10	.	11	
12	21	.	3	4	53	12	1	2	10	10	11	1
13	23	35	5	1	41	15	1	2	12	12	15	1
14	24	39	1	0	24	12	2	2	12	12	17	1
15	27	40	1	1	38	20	2	1	12	12	21	1

Looking at the Data

After you have loaded the data set, you may want to examine it. Notice that the variable names ("sex," "race," "income") appear at the top of each column. Each variable name refers to a specific question in the 1996 GSS survey. To see the full label for each variable, simply place the cursor on the variable name. For example, the full label for the variable "income" is "total family income." Notice that the first respondent (first row) has an income score of 13, while the second respondent's income is coded as 12. To find

Figure A.9

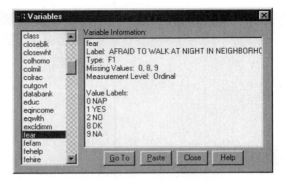

out what these codes stand for we need to locate the value labels, which are descriptive labels for the numeric codes used for each of the variables.

The simplest way to examine the value labels in SPSS is by clicking on the toolbar button that looks like a price tag (it is located on the right-hand side of the toolbar). Click on it and you will see the value labels replace the numerical codes. Note that the first respondent's code for income (13) is replaced by the label "refused," and that the second respondent's code of 12 is equivalent to an income of $25,000.

Another way to look up the value labels is by using the **Variables** dialog box, which you can get to by clicking

Utilities → Variables

The **Variables** dialog box (Figure A.9) has two parts. On the left side are the variable names arranged alphabetically. When you move the cursor over a variable name, the window on the right displays information about this variable. For example, we highlighted the variable "fear." The information on the right side includes the complete label for the variable (AFRAID TO WALK AT NIGHT IN THE NEIGHBORHOOD), the classification of the level of measurement of the variable (Ordinal), and the specific value label for each of the different numerical codes.

SETTING OPTIONS IN SPSS ●

Before continuing, you should check the options that SPSS uses to display information on your computer monitor or to display the output. To activate the **Options** dialog box, click on

Edit → Options

The Options dialog box, shown in Figure A.10, has a series of tabs at the top of the screen. The **General** tab should be clicked; if not, click on it. Check the **Variable Lists** options, where the **Display names** and **alphabetical** buttons should be checked. (If they are not, check them.) These settings tell SPSS to display the short names of the variables and arrange them in alphabetical order. The next settings you want to examine are for the output produced by SPSS. Click on the **Output Labels** tab and look at the settings under **Outline Labeling.** The rectangle marked **Variable in item labels shown as** should say **Names.** If it does not, click on the Down Arrow and then on the **Names** option displayed.

Figure A.10

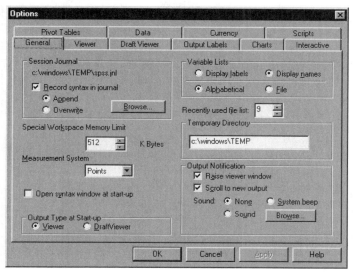

The rectangle marked **Variable values in item labels shown as:** should say **Values and Labels.** Choosing this options tells SPSS that you want to see both the codes (numbers) for your variables as well as the labels assigned to these codes in all your output.

UNIVARIATE DISTRIBUTIONS (Chapter 15) •

Producing Frequency Distributions

One of the first steps in data analysis is the examination of frequency distributions. The **Frequencies** dialog box in SPSS is activated by clicking on

Analyze → Descriptive Statistics → Frequencies

The **Frequencies** dialog box shown in Figure A.11 allows you to request a frequency distribution for a single variable or for several variables at once. Simply click on the variable

Figure A.11

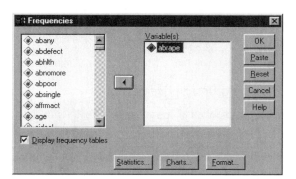

Figure A.12

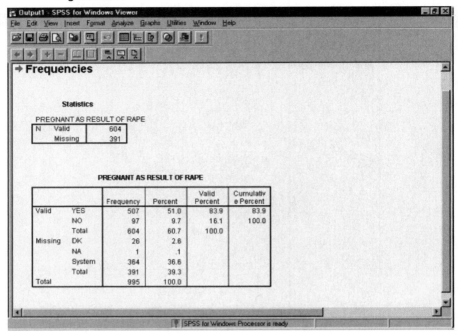

name(s) and transfer to the **Variable(s)** box. We have already placed the variable "abrape" in this box. When you have placed the desired variables in the **Variable(s)** box, click **OK**.

The frequency tables for the variable "abrape"(ABORTION IF A WOMAN IS PREG-NANT AS A RESULT OF RAPE) are displayed in the **Output** window shown in Figure A.12. There are two tables in the window. The first, the **Statistics** table, lists the number of valid and missing cases for this variable. Missing cases includes those respondents who did not answer the question. There are 391 such cases and 604 valid cases for the variable "abrape." The second table shows the frequencies associated with each category of the variables. Note that there are four columns of frequencies. The first column ("Frequency") shows the raw frequencies for this variable, including the categories of "don't know" (DK) and "not applicable" (NA). The second column—the "Percent" column—calculates the percentages for the entire sample, including DK and NA. Usually, the third column ("Valid Percent") is more useful, since it removes all the missing cases and recalculates the percentages. You can see that 83.9 percent of those who responded to this question support abortion when a woman is pregnant as a result of rape. The last column, "Cumulative Percent," calculates cumulative percentages.

Producing Descriptive Statistics

SPSS can produce all measures of central tendency and dispersion discussed in Chapter 15 except for IQV. The frequencies procedure we have just discussed calculates these measures. Thus you should begin with the **Frequencies** dialog box, select the variables for which you want descriptive statistics, and click **Statistics**. This activates the **Statistics** dialog box shown in Figure A.13.

Figure A.13

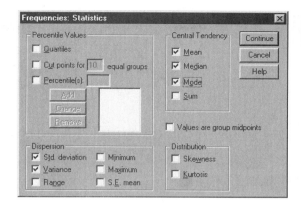

The measures of central tendency and dispersion are listed in separate boxes. We will calculate various statistics for the variable "chldidel," "ideal number of children." Because this is an interval-ratio variable, we can calculate the mean, mode, and median as well as the variance and standard deviation. These statistics are presented in the output window shown in Figure A.14. The mode is 2, which means that the highest number of respondents consider 2 to be the ideal number of children. Two children is also the median response to this question. Notice, however, that the mean is higher—2.45. Because the mean is greater than both the mode and the median, we can conclude that the distribution of "chldidel" is positively skewed. Finally, both the variance and the standard deviation are shown in the table. The standard deviation of .88 indicates that there is a moderate amount of variation in the desired number of children. The variance, .77, is the square of the standard deviation.

Figure A.14

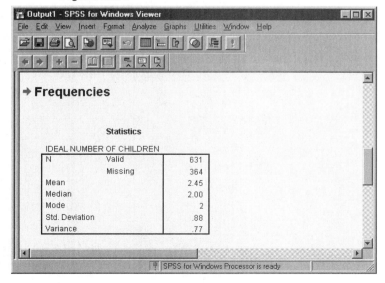

Figure A.15

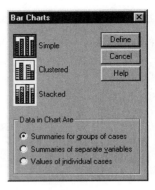

Producing Charts

SPSS makes pie charts, bar charts, and histograms of univariate distributions. To activate the graphics program, click on **Graphs** and then select the type of chart you want. In this section we will illustrate how to construct the most common graph for nominal or ordinal variables—the bar chart. The dialog box in Figure A.15 was activated after we clicked on **Graphs** and **Bar.**

The **Bar Charts** dialog box allows you to choose from three types of bar charts. We have selected the simple bar charts to display the distribution of the variable "race." After clicking on **Simple** and then on **Define,** the main dialog box for bar charts is displayed as shown in Figure A.16.

Place the variable "race" in the box labeled **Category Axis** and click on the **"% of cases"** button, which tells SPSS to calculate the percentage distribution for the variable. Finally, click on **Options** to generate the **Options** dialog box (not shown here). SPSS automatically includes missing values in many graphs. To delete missing values, click on the box labeled **Display groups defined by missing values** to turn off this option. Then click **Continue** and **OK.** The bar chart for "race" (Figure A.17) displays the race distribu-

Figure A.16

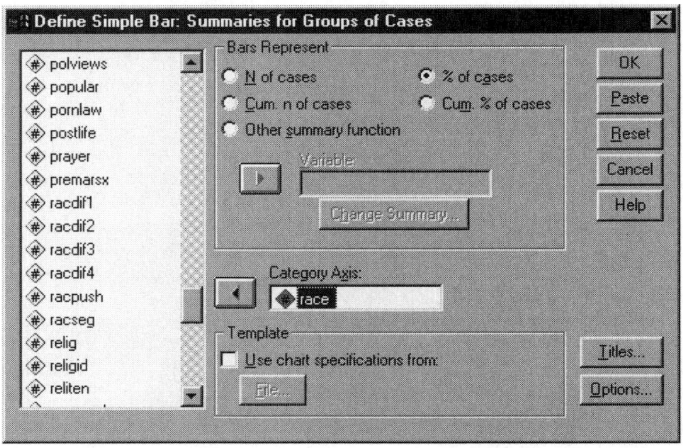

Figure A.17

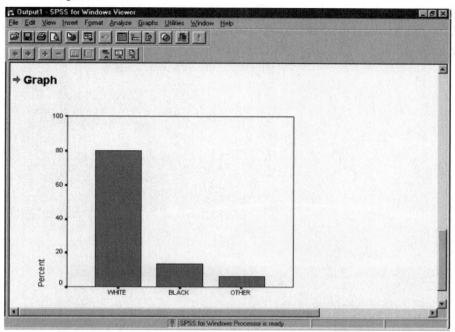

tion for the GSS sample. It is possible to edit this chart by double-clicking on it. This opens the Chart Editor window, which displays various editing tools.

BIVARIATE DISTRIBUTIONS (Chapter 16)

Producing Bivariate Tables and Statistics

Now that we have learned how to describe univariate distributions, let's move on to examine relationships between two variables. One of the most basic methods for analyzing relationship is the bivariate table. Let's examine the relationship between the variables "bible" (FEELINGS ABOUT THE BIBLE) and "abany" (ABORTION FOR ANY REASON) with "bible" as the independent variable. Click on the following sequence in the menus:

Analyze → Descriptive statistics → Crosstabs

In the **Crosstabs** dialog box (Figure A.18), put the dependent variable "abany" in the box marked **Row(s)** and the independent variable "bible" in the box marked **Column(s)**. Then click on **Cells** and choose **Column percentages** in the **Crosstabs: Cell Display** dialog box (not shown). Click **Continue** and then finally click **OK** in the **Crosstabs** dialog box.

The bivariate table displayed in the **Output** window (Figure A.19) shows a strong relationship between feeling about the Bible and attitude toward abortion. Almost 74 percent of respondents who believe that the Bible is the word of God oppose abortions for any reason. In contrast, only 28.6 percent of those who feel that the Bible is a book of fables oppose abortion for any reason.

Figure A.18

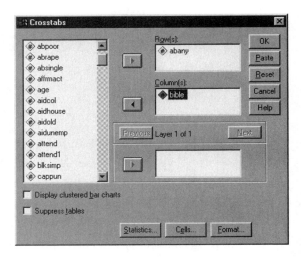

Figure A.19

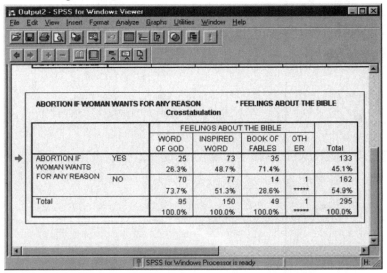

Bivariate Statistics

The **Crosstabs** procedure can also produce measures of association for nominal and ordinal data. To request the desired statistics, click on **Statistics** in the **Crosstabs** dialog box to generate the **Crosstabs: Statistics** dialog box (Figure A.20). This dialog box has about a dozen statistics listed in separate boxes for "Nominal" and "Ordinal" variables. You can also obtain the chi-square statistics through this procedure. The chi-square statistics are discussed in depth in Chapter 19. We have selected lambda for the association between "bible" and "abany" because both are nominal variables. Now click on **Continue** and **OK** to produce the table, as shown in Figure A.21.

Figure A.20

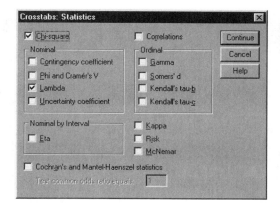

Notice that the output window includes two tables. The first, titled "Chi-Square Tests," includes the Pearson chi-square which we discussed in Chapter 16. Its value is 28.850, with 3 degrees of freedom. The significance of this chi-square is reported as .000, which means that $p < .000005$. Based on these results, we can conclude that "feelings about the Bible" and "abortion attitude" are related in the population.

The second table, titled "Directional Measures," includes a lot of information that is beyond the scope of this book. You need concern yourself only with the first column of the table ("Value") in the box marked "Lambda." Notice that SPSS calculates several

Figure A.21

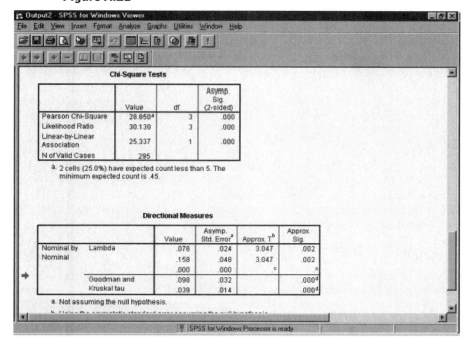

Figure A.22

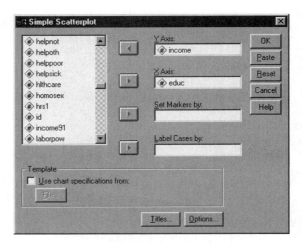

lambdas depending on which variable is considered the dependent variable. Since we have selected "bible" as the dependent variable, the relevant coefficient for lambda is .158, which indicates weak to moderate strength. SPSS always provides the Goodman and Kruskal tau statistics whenever lambda is requested. Goodman and Kruskal tau is another nominal statistic that is beyond the scope of this book.

Scatter Diagrams

One of the first steps in analyzing a relationship between interval and ratio variables is by a visual assessment using the scatter diagram. We will look at the relationship between education ("educ") and "income." SPSS will plot the relationship between these variables after you select **Graphs** and **Scatter** from the main menu and then click on **Simple** and **Define.** In the **Simple Scatterplot** dialog box (Figure A.22), specify the **Y Axis** and **X Axis** variables and click **OK.**

As a result of this action SPSS displays the scatter diagram in the **Output** window (Figure A.23). The scatter diagram seems to suggest that the relationship between education and income is positive.

Bivariate Regression

The procedure **Regression** can be used to calculate the best-fitting regression line as well as the coefficient of determination (R^2) and a number of statistical tests. We will employ this procedure to analyze the relationship between years of education ("educ"), the independent variable, and number of children ("childs"), the dependent variable. To get to the **Regression** dialog box, click on

<u>A</u>nalyze → Regression → Linear

In the **Linear Regression** dialog box (Figure A.24), enter your dependent and independent variables in the appropriate boxes and click on **OK.** SPSS calculates a number of statistics organized in separate tables (see Figure A.25). The first table, labeled "Model Summary," shows the value of R Square (R^2), which is .082, indicating that education explains 8.2% (.082*100) of the variation in the number of children. The ANOVA table

Figure A.23

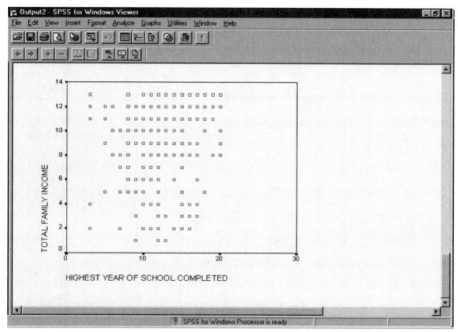

includes the results of the ANOVA procedure, which is not discussed in this text. However, the table includes the F statistic (87.552) and its significance level (.000), both of which are discussed in some detail in Chapter 19. Note that F is highly significant, with $p < .000005$. The regression equation results are presented in the table labeled "Coefficients" (Figure A.26). The regression equation coefficients are listed in column "B." The b

Figure A.24

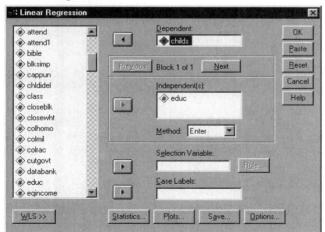

Figure A.25

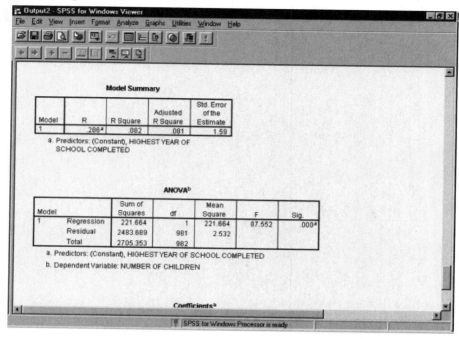

Figure A.26

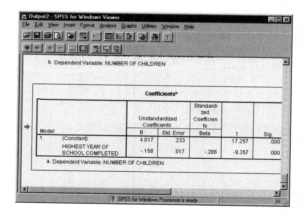

coefficient for "educ" is − .158; the intercept *a* is 4.017. This means that every year of education decreases the number of children by − .158. Based on these coefficients, we would predict that a person with 12 years of education would have, on average, 4.017 − 12(.158) children, or about 2.121.

Pearson Product — Moment Correlation

To activate the **Bivariate Correlations** dialog box, click on

   Analyze → Correlate → Bivariate

Figure A.27

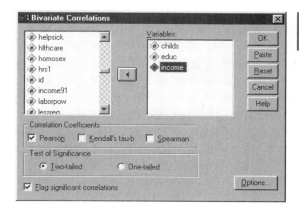

In the dialog box (Figure A.27), enter the variables you want to correlate. We are asking to obtain the bivariate correlations between education ("educ"), income ("income"), and number of children ("childs"). After clicking **OK** we obtain the output organized in a table labeled "Correlations" (Figure A.28). The table includes the Pearson product–moment correlation coefficient (Pearson's *r*) and tests of significance using a two-tailed *t* test. The Pearson's *r* product–moment correlation between "educ" and "childs" is −.286; between "educ" and "income" it is .275, and finally, .008 is the correlation between "income" and "childs." Note that the correlations are starred according to their significance level. Thus, for example, the correlation between "educ" and "income" is significant at the .01 (*) level, whereas the correlation between "childs" and "income" is not significant.

Figure A.28

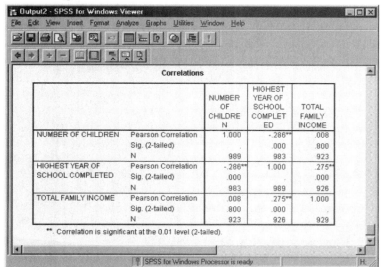

MULTIVARIATE ANALYSIS (Chapter 17)

The three major functions of multivariate analysis, as we learned in Chapter 17, are control, interpretation, and prediction. Mechanically, the first two functions are covered by using control variables in the equations; the procedures **Crosstabs** and **Partial Corr** can provide for these controls. Prediction is enhanced by **Multiple Regression.**

Multivariate Crosstabs

We have already presented the basic format of the **Crosstabs** procedure. In Multivariate Crosstabs a third variable—a control variable—is added in the layer section of the main dialog box. (The **Crosstabs** procedure allows you to control for more than one variable, but we will limit out discussion to one control variable). For this illustration we will examine the bivariate relation between "sex" and "cappun" (FAVOR OR OPPOSE THE DEATH PENALTY FOR MURDER), and control for the variable "race." In the **Crosstabs** dialog box, put the dependent variable "cappun" in the box marked **Row(s)** and the independent variable "sex" in the box marked **Column(s).** Then put the variable "race" in the box marked **Layer 1 of 1.** After selecting **Column percentages,** click **Continue** and then finally click **OK** in the **Crosstabs** dialog box.

SPSS produces a bivariate table (Figure A.29) showing the relationship between "sex" and "cappun" separately for whites and blacks. In the first table (for whites), we see that males and females differ in their level of support for the death penalty. About 83.3 percent of males favor the death penalty, compared with 75.6 percent of females.

Figure A.29

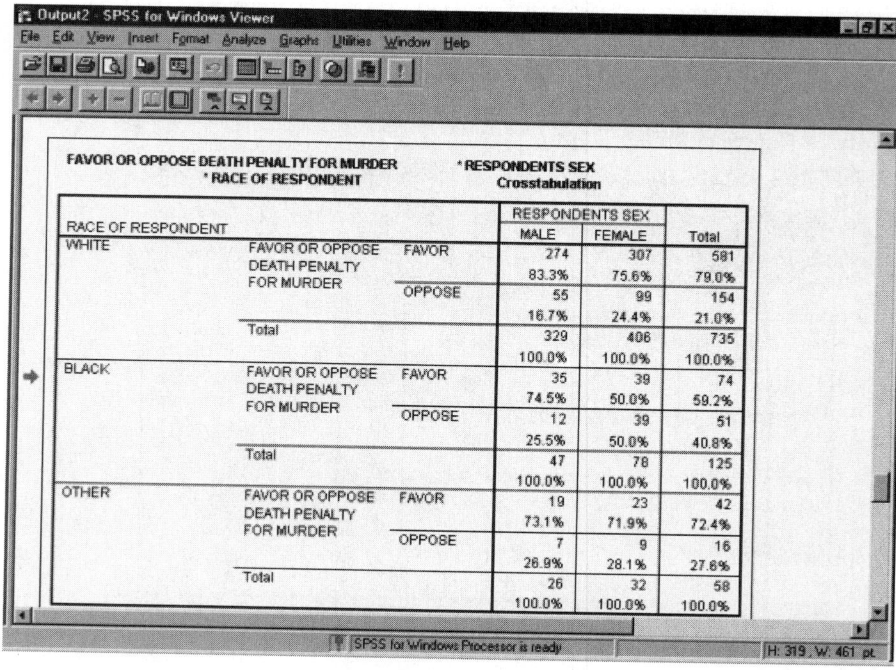

FAVOR OR OPPOSE DEATH PENALTY FOR MURDER * RESPONDENTS SEX * RACE OF RESPONDENT Crosstabulation

RACE OF RESPONDENT			RESPONDENTS SEX MALE	FEMALE	Total
WHITE	FAVOR OR OPPOSE DEATH PENALTY FOR MURDER	FAVOR	274	307	581
			83.3%	75.6%	79.0%
		OPPOSE	55	99	154
			16.7%	24.4%	21.0%
	Total		329	406	735
			100.0%	100.0%	100.0%
BLACK	FAVOR OR OPPOSE DEATH PENALTY FOR MURDER	FAVOR	35	39	74
			74.5%	50.0%	59.2%
		OPPOSE	12	39	51
			25.5%	50.0%	40.8%
	Total		47	78	125
			100.0%	100.0%	100.0%
OTHER	FAVOR OR OPPOSE DEATH PENALTY FOR MURDER	FAVOR	19	23	42
			73.1%	71.9%	72.4%
		OPPOSE	7	9	16
			26.9%	28.1%	27.6%
	Total		26	32	58
			100.0%	100.0%	100.0%

In the second table (for blacks), the differences between males and females are sharper. Whereas about 3 out of 4 black males (74.5 percent) favor the death penalty for murder, only half of black females favor the death penalty. This tables indicate that the relation between "sex" and "cappun" is conditioned by "race."

Partial Correlations

Partial correlations are conceptually similar to Multivariate Crosstabs in that the effects of other variables are controlled when analyzing the relationship between the original variables. Whereas **Crosstabs** physically removes the effects by portioning the cases based on the value of the control, **Partial Corr** removes the effects statistically. This difference can be very important when you are controlling for more than one variable because separating the cases reduces the cell frequencies. Thus, when the analysis involves interval- or ratio-level variables, you should use **Partial Corr.** To activate the **Partial Corr** procedure, click on

> Analyze → Correlate → Partial

This will activate the **Partial Correlations** dialog box (not shown). In the **Variables** box, insert the variables you want to correlate and then select your control variable(s) in the box labeled **Controlling for.** Click on **OK** and SPSS will calculate the partial correlations for the selected variables. We asked to correlate "educ" and "income" controlling for "childs." The output is presented in Figure A.30.

Figure A.30

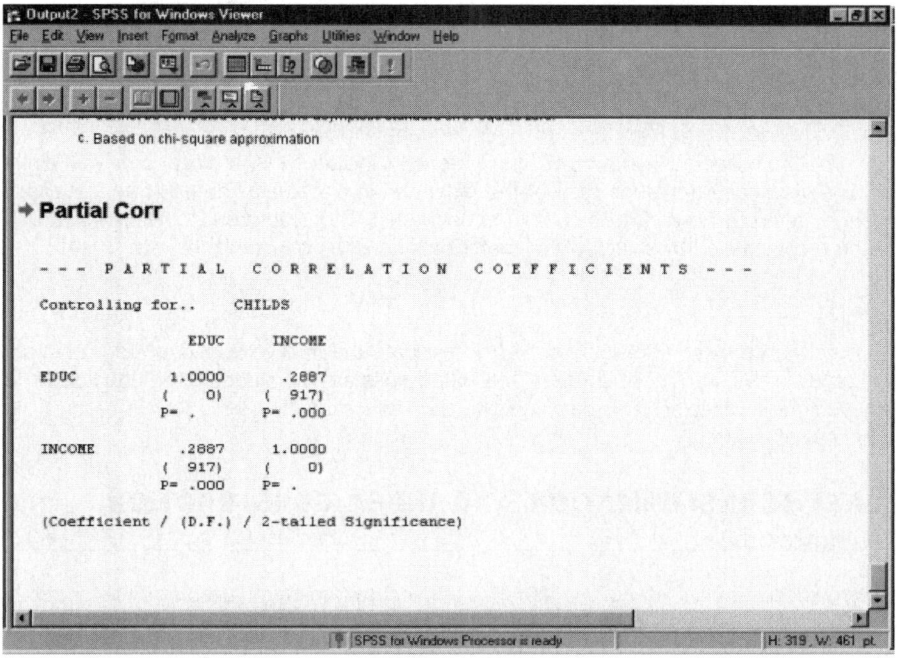

Figure A.31

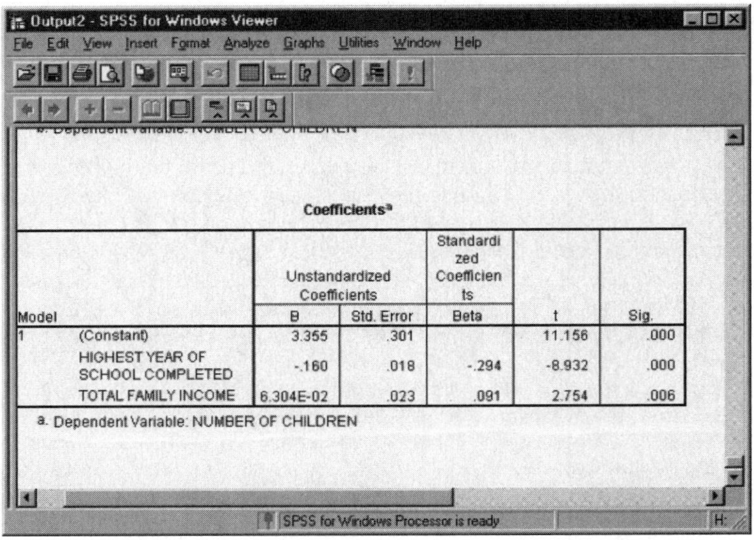

Coefficients[a]

Model		Unstandardized Coefficients B	Unstandardized Coefficients Std. Error	Standardized Coefficients Beta	t	Sig.
1	(Constant)	3.355	.301		11.156	.000
	HIGHEST YEAR OF SCHOOL COMPLETED	-.160	.018	-.294	-8.932	.000
	TOTAL FAMILY INCOME	6.304E-02	.023	.091	2.754	.006

a. Dependent Variable: NUMBER OF CHILDREN

Multiple Regression

The multiple regression procedure in SPSS is a simple extension of bivariate regression. You activate the **Linear Regression** dialog box and enter the dependent variable in the box marked **Dependent** and the independent variables in the box marked **Independent(s).** We are going to look at the effects of education ("educ") and income ("income") on the number of children ("childs"). You have an option in choosing the method of entering the independent variables into the equation. We have selected the method **Enter,** which introduces the independent variables all at once.

The table labeled "Coefficients" in Figure A.31 includes the intercept *a* as well as the *b* and *Beta* coefficients for each of the independent variables. The *t* test and its significance are also shown for each of the coefficients. The prediction equation for "childs" can be constructed by selecting the coefficients from the column labeled B:

"childs" = 3.355 − .160 ("educ") + .006304 ("income")

The column headed "Beta" allows you to evaluate the relative impact of education and income on the number of children. The Beta values are the standardized coefficients for the different variables. The data indicate that education has the most impact on the number of children.

DATA TRANSFORMATION AND INDEX CONSTRUCTION (Chapter 18)

Often social science researchers find it convenient to transform variables by recoding the original categories using the **Recode** command or by creating new variables using the **Compute** command. The **Compute** command can be used for scale and index construction.

Recoding Variables

The **Recode** procedure is usually used to reduce the number of categories of a variable. Consider, for example, the variable "attend" (HOW OFTEN RESPONDENT ATTENDS RELIGIOUS SERVICES). Originally it is coded into nine categories from 0 ("Never") to 8 ("More than once a week"). Let's say we want to recode it into two categories so that everyone who attends religious services less than once a month is put in a single group, and everyone who attends at least once a month is put into a second group. To accomplish this task we are going to create a new variable, "attend1." Click

<u>T</u>ransform → Recode → Into Different Variables

In the **Recode into Different Variables** dialog box (Figure A.32), put the variable "attend" in the **Numeric Variable → Output Variable** box; type the new variable name in the **<u>N</u>ame** box and the new label in the **<u>L</u>abel** box. Finally, click on **<u>C</u>hange** and then on **<u>O</u>ld and New Values . . . ,** which will take you to the next dialog box: **Old and New Values** (Figure A.33). In this dialog box you tell SPSS how the old values are to be recoded. We want everyone in categories 0−3 (from "Never" to "Several times a year") to be in group 1 and everyone in categories 5−8 (from "2−3× a month" to "More than once a week") to be in group 2. On the left side of the dialog box we enter 0−3 in the

Figure A.32

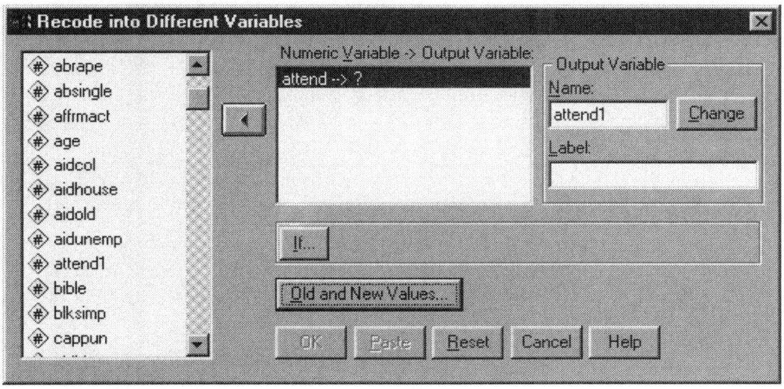

Figure A.33

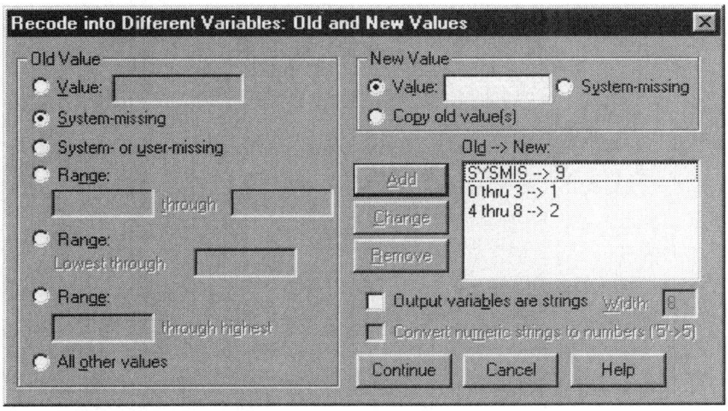

box labeled **Range** and then on the right side of the dialog box we tell SPSS to collapse these values into a single value: 1. We then click on **Add** and continue with the second set of scores (4–8), which we recode into 2. Finally, we click on **Continue** and then **OK.**

As a final step, we should create labels for our new numeric codes. To create new labels we activate the **Define Variable** dialog box by clicking on the new variable "attend1" in the data window and then on **Data** → **Define Variable** from the menu. In the **Define Variable** dialog box (Figure A.34), click on **Labels,** which will activate the **Define Labels** dialog box (Figure A.35). In this box put the value you want to label in the **Value** box and the label you want to give the value in the **Value Label** box. Click **Add** and continue with the remaining values. When you are done, click **Continue.** Remember to tell SPSS what values are defined as missing values. This can be accomplished by clicking on **Missing Values** in the **Define Variable** dialog box, which will activate a **Missing Values** dialog box where missing values should be specified.

Now let's review the results of the recoding process by looking at the frequency distribution of the new variable (Figure A.36). If we are satisfied with the result, we can save the file with the new variable.

Figure A.34

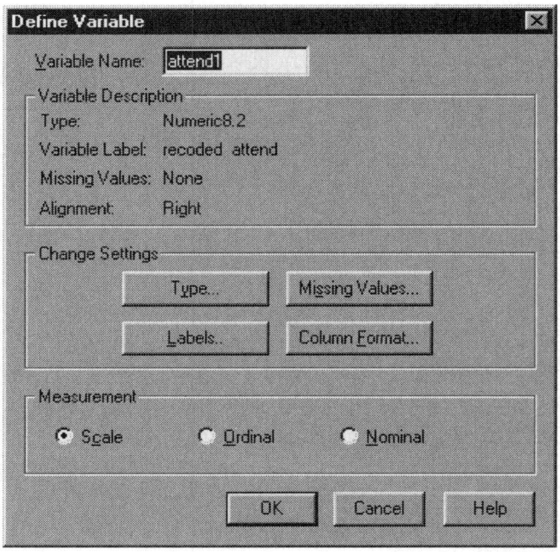

Define Variable

Variable Name: attend1

Variable Description
Type: Numeric8.2
Variable Label: recoded attend
Missing Values: None
Alignment: Right

Change Settings
Type...   Missing Values...
Labels...   Column Format...

Measurement
○ Scale   ○ Ordinal   ○ Nominal

OK   Cancel   Help

Figure A.35

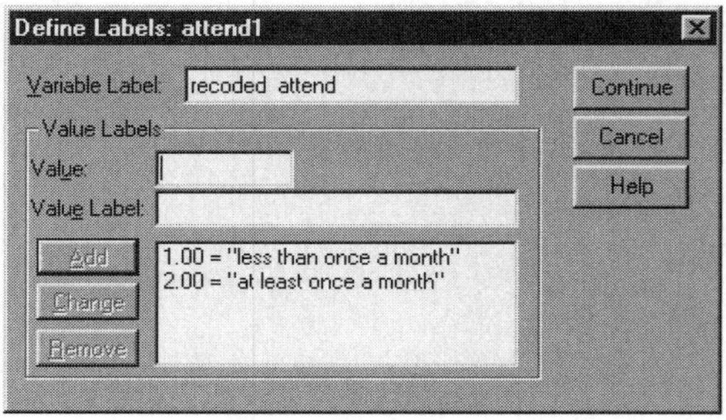

Define Labels: attend1

Variable Label: recoded attend   Continue

Value Labels
Value: Cancel
Value Label: Help

Add
Change
Remove

1.00 = "less than once a month"
2.00 = "at least once a month"

Figure A.36

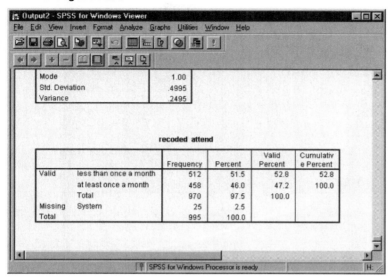

recoded attend

		Frequency	Percent	Valid Percent	Cumulativ e Percent
Valid	less than once a month	512	51.5	52.8	52.8
	at least once a month	458	46.0	47.2	100.0
	Total	970	97.5	100.0	
Missing	System	25	2.5		
Total		995	100.0		

Constructing an Index

Let's look at another procedure to modify data. Social scientists are often interested in creating an index, or a scale composed from a number of variables. For example, consider the variables "aidcol" (GOVERNMENT SHOULD ASSIST LOW-INCOME COLLEGE STUDENTS), "aidold" (IT IS THE GOVERNMENT'S RESPONSIBILITY TO PROVIDE FOR THE ELDERLY), "aidhouse" (GOVERNMENT SHOULD PROVIDE HOUSING TO POOR), and "aidunemp" (IT IS THE GOVERNMENT'S RESPONSIBILITY TO PROVIDE FOR THE UNEMPLOYED). All four variables measure how people feel about the responsibility of government in creating a safety net for those in need. These variables were coded as follows:

1. Definitely should
2. Probably should be
3. Probably should not be
4. Definitely should not be

(For all four questions, 0, 8, and 9 were defined as missing values.)

We can create a new variable—an index—which will be the sum of the reponses to the four questions. For example, a person who answered "Definitely should" to all questions would have a score of 4 ($1 + 1 + 1 + 1 = 4$). Someone who answered "Definitely should not be" to all four questions would have score of 16 ($4 + 4 + 4 + 4 = 16$). A low score on on the new variable would reflect a high level of support for government responsibility, whereas a high score would indicate a low level of support.

To activate the **Compute Variable** dialog box, click **Transform** → **Compute.** In the **Target Variable** box (see Figure A.37), type a name for your new variable and then create the mathematical expression to compute the index in the box labeled **Numeric Expression.** When you are done, click **OK.** SPSS will follow the equation you created and

Figure A.37

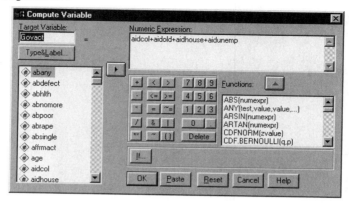

will compute a new variable, "govact," based on responses to "aidcol," "aidold," "aid-house," and "aidunemp."

Reliability Analysis

To assess the internal consistency (reliability) of our new scale, "govact," we will calculate the alpha coefficient. The value of alpha can range from 0 (no internal consistency) to 1 (complete internal consistency). An acceptable level of internal consistency would be reflected in an alpha value of no less than .70. To calculate alpha, click on <u>A</u>nalyze → **Scale** → **Reliability Analysis.** In the **Reliability Analysis** dialog box (Figure A.38), enter the variables included in the scale—"aidcol," "aidold," "aidhouse," and "aidunemp." Click on **Statistics** to get to the **Reliability Analysis: Statistics** dialog box (not shown here) and check **Item, Scale,** and **Scale if item deleted** in the box marked **Descriptives for.** Now click on **Continue** and **OK** to obtain the output (Figure A.39).

As you can see, the coefficient alpha is .8275, which meets the minimum reliability criterion. The section "Item-total Statistics" shows you (see last column, entitled "Alpha if Item Deleted") how the value of alpha will change by deleting specific elements of the scale. For example, alpha will be .7633 if "aidcol" is deleted from the scale.

Figure A.38

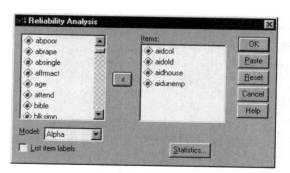

Figure A.39

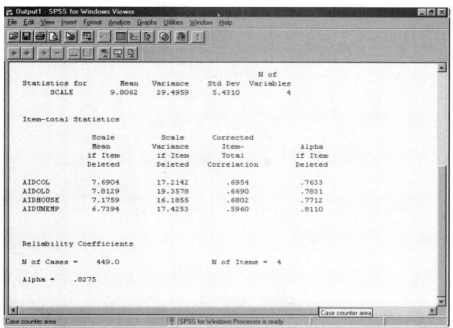

```
                                                  N of
  Statistics for        Mean     Variance    Std Dev  Variables
       SCALE           9.8062    29.4959     5.4310       4


  Item-total Statistics

                    Scale          Scale       Corrected
                    Mean         Variance        Item-              Alpha
                   if Item        if Item        Total            if Item
                   Deleted        Deleted      Correlation        Deleted

  AIDCOL           7.6904         17.2142        .6954             .7633
  AIDOLD           7.8129         19.3578        .6690             .7831
  AIDHOUSE         7.1759         16.1855        .6802             .7712
  AIDUNEMP         6.7394         17.4253        .5960             .8110


  Reliability Coefficients

  N of Cases =      449.0                   N of Items =   4

  Alpha =      .8275
```

INFERENCES (Chapter 19) ●

SPSS includes statistical tests among its procedure. Thus we have seen how to calculate the chi-square test in conjunction with the **Crosstabs** procedure and the *F* test in connection with the **Regression** procedure. Another test discussed in Chapter 19 is the difference-between-means test—the *t* test. This test can be used when the dependent variable is measured on an interval scale. The two-sample *t*-test procedure can be found under the **Analyze** → **Compare Means** → **Independent-Samples T test** menu choices. In the **Independent Samples T Test** dialog box (not shown), place the dependent variable(s) in the **Test Variable(s)** box and the independent variable in the **Grouping Variable** box. We will perform a *t* test to test the null hypothesis that men and women work the same number of hours each week. We placed the variable "hrs1" in the **Test Variable(s)** box and the variable "sex" in the **Grouping Variable** box. Notice that a question mark appears next to "sex," indicating that the two groups defined by "sex" need to be defined. Click on **Define Groups** and put "1" in the first box and "2" in the second box. Finally, click on **Continue** and **OK.** The output for the difference-between-means test contains two *t* statistics. The first assumes equal variances, and the second assumes unequal variances. We will assume that the variances are equal and thus will choose the first one. The actual *t* value is thus 4.437, with 657 degrees of freedom (see Figure A.40). The two-tailed test reports a significance level of .000, which means that $p < .0005$. Based on these results, we can reject the null hypothesis and conclude that there is a mean difference in hours worked between men and women.

Figure A.40

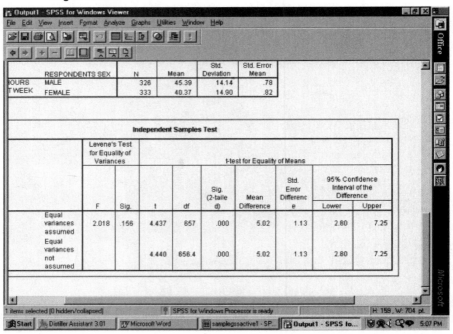

RESPONDENTS SEX		N	Mean	Std. Deviation	Std. Error Mean
IOURS	MALE	326	45.39	14.14	.78
T WEEK	FEMALE	333	40.37	14.90	.82

Independent Samples Test

		Levene's Test for Equality of Variances		t-test for Equality of Means						
		F	Sig.	t	df	Sig. (2-taile d)	Mean Difference	Std. Error Differenc e	95% Confidence Interval of the Difference	
									Lower	Upper
	Equal variances assumed	2.018	.156	4.437	657	.000	5.02	1.13	2.80	7.25
	Equal variances not assumed			4.440	656.4	.000	5.02	1.13	2.80	7.25

1 items selected (0 hidden/collapsed)   SPSS for Windows Processor is ready   H: 159 , W: 704 pt.

Start | Distiller Assistant 3.01 | Microsoft Word | samplegssactive1 - SP... | Output1 - SPSS fo... | 5:07 PM

CONCLUSION   •

After following this SPSS manual you will find that computerized data analysis is less complicated than you thought. We hope that this appendix will encourage you to choose SPSS procedures that lend themselves to your data analysis needs and methodological expertise. As you work with this statistical package to answer the end-of-chapter computer exercises or to analyze data for a research project, you will learn more about its many capabilities and potentials. We hope that this process will prove to be an interesting and a productive learning experience.

Writing Research Reports

Nina Reshef

Research report writing is a specialized skill, but one that can easily be learned. Although academic disciplines vary somewhat in the details of the formats considered acceptable, the basic elements are quite consistent for the full range of reports, from take-home tests to doctoral dissertations and scholarly journal articles. The goal of this appendix is to provide guidelines that will simplify the writing of your own research reports.

The purpose of a research report dictates its structure: Form follows function. The function of research reports, as differentiated from other reports, is not only to relay findings but to link those findings to a theoretical model and, in many cases, to one or more empirically testable hypotheses. The structure of research reports has become standardized into models that shape the presentation into a consistent, logical framework. This makes reporting and writing easier.

WHY WRITE A RESEARCH REPORT?

The basic question preceding any activity is: "Why do it?" In scholarly research, the answer is the desire to expand the horizons of human knowledge, to enhance methodologies, and to increase the incisiveness of analysis. These lofty aims are, however, insufficient to guarantee a well-written report; nor are they always a student's primary motivation.

If we consider what makes a successful report, two themes become apparent. The first is how much the writer is involved with the subject or excited about the process and product of research. The second is how well the subject is defined and presented. If the topic is interesting to the author, it may very well be interesting to the reader, at first a course instructor and then, perhaps, a wider audience. In addition, readers will be more readily convinced of the value of the report if the organization of the ideas, the presentation of findings, and the quality of the writing are professional. Our purpose is to provide a blueprint for effectively communicating the results of your research effort to another person.

MATCHING YOUR FORMAT TO YOUR AUDIENCE

In effective report writing, the character of the reading audience is just as important to the writer as the character of the listening audience is to the speaker. The more general the audience, the more general the content will be and the looser the format. Reports geared toward professional audiences should be technical and specialized. That is, with the audience in mind, the writer can choose the appropriate format, the degree of detail, and the right vocabulary. Keeping the audience in mind also helps the writer determine whether the assumptions underlying the report will be recognized and understood. In short, the writer's strategy—as expressed by the report's internal structure—should be geared toward a specific target audience, never left to chance.

TYPES OF REPORTS •

Social science research is generally divided into two main types: qualitative and quantitative. Qualitative research may include quantitative elements such as diagrams and flow charts, and quantitative research may move beyond numbers to analyze the link between the measurement of a variable and a causal theory. Therefore, it is important not to confuse the devices used to present findings with the character of the report. Nonetheless, despite the difference in their focus and content, the principles dictating the structure of both qualitative and quantitative reports are basically the same.

Qualitative Reports

Qualitative research, an outgrowth of the *Verstehen* tradition of empathic understanding of social phenomena, is inductive in nature. Qualitative researchers use field research methods, primarily case studies and participant observation, within natural settings (see Chapter 12). The researcher interferes as little as humanly possible in the course of the events. Consequently, the report will present much descriptive material. The report should also show how the observations prompted the researcher to analyze and isolate variables (induction) and how these variables may contribute to the development of a theory. Two important points should be remembered when writing a report based on qualitative research. The first is to stick to the main theoretical themes or concepts; the second is to avoid excessive description. Too many details taken from the field research can distract the reader and interfere with a clean presentation of your argument.

Quantitative Reports

Because quantitative research is deductive, researchers deal directly with operationalization, the manipulation of empirical variables, prediction, and testing. Quantitative research therefore places great emphasis on methodology, on procedure, and on statistical measures of validity. Consequently, quantitative research reports should be organized to show a clear progression from theory to operationalization of concepts, from choice of methodology and procedures to the data collected, from statistical tests to findings and conclusions.

If the report entails hypothesis testing, each hypothesis should be clearly labeled (e.g., 1, 2, and so on; or A, B, and so on) and even set off by using a different typeface or by underlining. This method makes it easier for the reader to identify the question asked and its relation to the research findings. Highlighting the question helps you to organize your thoughts as well as hold the reader's attention. This is important because much of the text of quantitative research reports deals with the verbal elaboration of the data presented in the tables and charts. Clearly marking the research questions helps the reader keep track of the exposition as well as the conclusion, in which the findings are evaluated within both methodological and theoretical contexts.

Oral Reports

Oral reports in the classroom have become accepted tools for introducing the student not only to report writing but to the give and take of academic peer judgment. When you give a short oral report on your research, you need to organize your material not only in terms of content but also in terms of tone and audience. In short, oral presentations may be perceived as abstracts, or prologues, of the final written paper. Therefore, everything we have said about the organization of written reports applies, but with a change in emphasis. In an oral presentation, you need to pay more attention to the main point of your report and to your pace and tone—you do not want your audience to fall asleep or to be aroused to excessive criticism. Practicing your report helps you learn to control the amount of material you present in the time available; it also helps you develop techniques for maintaining good rapport with your audience.

Oral presentations made during conferences for professional audiences follow the same basic rules but on a more sophisticated level. Therefore, you should think of classroom reports as opportunities to hone your speaking and presentation skills.

CHOOSING THE TOPIC

Choosing a topic for research is the most important and perhaps the most difficult stage in the research process. Current events, life experiences, or intellectual puzzles stimulate curiosity and yield original research topics. Avoid topics that have been extensively researched by other students or by scholars, no matter how enticing they appear at first glance. When in doubt, consult your instructor. In any case, even overworked topics, such as alcoholism, can be interesting if approached with ingenuity.

You can test both your understanding of the topic and its appropriateness by attempting to convert the purpose of your paper into one of these questions: What are you trying to learn, to explore, to promote? Can the topic be stated as a "who," "what," or "when" question? Can it be answered in a linear, analytical manner or as a historical narrative? Can it be stated as a hypothesis, with measurable variables that can be tested with strict experimental methods? Avoid topics that cannot be translated into a clear and precise research question—such topics are either muddled, too broad, or not amenable to study using the method you have chosen.

For the student, the two most important criteria for choosing to research a topic are its relevance to the course and the empirical data to be collected. A quick review of the available literature will acquaint the student with the scope of the topic and stimulate ideas. This review will also help the student ascertain if the research question, as originally conceived, is manageable or if it has to be redefined or limited. A great deal of precious time and effort can be saved by doing such background reading before plunging into the research.

Manageability

The term *manageability* is often mentioned as a criterion for selecting a topic, but what does it actually mean? Basically, manageability in research refers to the theoretical complexity of the event or concept to be explained, to the amount and availability of the pertinent data, and to the time it takes to collect and analyze the data before writing can begin. For the student, manageability may be translated into the number of books and journal articles that should be read as part of the literature review; for the academic scholar, manageability may mean the number of trips abroad needed to review documents stored in government archives, or the number and complexity of the theoretical models needed to explain the phenomenon.

Every researcher must ask just how manageable the topic is, given the confines of the report and the resources available. It is always preferable to limit a topic and investigate it thoroughly as opposed to expanding its scope to the point where you have neither the time nor the space to present a reasoned argument and supporting data adequately. Consider this hypothetical example: For a researcher at the University of Chicago, an analysis of the proceeds from property tax collection in the state of Illinois from 1919 to 1929 may be a more manageable topic than the system of property tax collection in pre—World War II Chicago. In this case, if the Illinois data are better organized within existing files, the greater accessibility may simplify the analytic and statistical procedures the researcher needs to employ, even if it might take him or her more time to collect all the data.

THE DIRECT AIM OF THE REPORT •

After choosing a research topic, the writer has to decide the direct aim of the report, which is more limited than the general reason for writing the report at all. If the report's aim is kept precise and focused, organizing the material and writing the report will be much easier.

Research reports aim at answering five basic questions: "who," "what," "where," "when," and "how." Underlying these is a sixth question: "why." That is, the purpose of a research report is to relay findings that are empirically and logically related to some conception of causation, to a theory. The writer is free to emphasize only one of these questions in any particular piece. The choice of aims should be dictated by personal interests (even though, in some cases, the topic may be assigned by the instructor) and, of course, the data available.

The purpose of the majority of research reports can also be conceptualized according to three general categories: *description* of an incident or a research technique; *exploration* of a new idea or unusual event; and *explanation* of causal relationships. A fourth category, one that encompasses both your findings and your opinions, is *submission of proposals* for solving social problems.[1]

Your goals and assumptions should be clearly communicated in the introduction to the report. For example, exploratory reports present tentative findings about what occurred and set the stage for further research. The content and legitimacy of the proposals you may present for changing—let us say, the penalties for speeding violations or dumping industrial wastes—may be based on assumptions and values that are unacceptable to your audience. By clearly stating your goals and assumptions, you will ensure that the report is placed in its proper context. Readers can therefore judge your report in a more balanced way.

ORGANIZING THE REPORT •

Research reports are organized according to fairly consistent formats in order to facilitate communication. Nothing is more frustrating than trying to read a muddled report about an interesting idea or finding. Therefore, although every author has a degree of freedom in his or her style and choice of devices for conveying information (e.g., tables, figures), all writers should follow this outline when reporting their research.

Introduction

The introduction should clearly and concisely state your purpose in writing the report. It should relate the type of report (e.g., exploratory) and the specific research question asked as well as your conclusions. (An abstract is an even more concise introduction and generally precedes the text in published articles.) The introduction, therefore, presents an overview of the content and, most important, the study's contribution to your discipline. Although the latter may seem to be beyond the scope of a report submitted by a student, it relates directly to the scientific value of the question or issue explored.

Use your imagination in writing your opening sentence, the main attention-getting device after the title.[2] Your skills as a stylist should be freely displayed here. Many strate-

1. Earl Babbie, *The Practice of Social Research* (New York: Wadsworth, 1995), app. B, p. A-10.

2. Michael Meyer, *The Little, Brown Guide to Writing Research Papers* (New York: Harper Collins, 1991), pp. 113–114.

gies are available to you: Cite a dramatic event in the news, quote a pointed but relevant comment, state the paradox your study resolves, or make a particularly forceful statement of your purpose. You should then state the purpose of your report succinctly if it has not been used as the opening sentence. Avoid lengthy explanations of your purpose until you reach the discussion section of the text. You should also state the methodological or theoretical limitations of your report, but in a way that does not minimize your contribution. For the student, if your instructor thinks the study was worth doing, that should be enough.

Many beginning writers feel that because the introduction opens the report, it should be written first. This is not true. For many writers, the first words of a document are major stumbling blocks and can delay the whole process of writing. If you have organized your work properly and outlined the text, and if you are fairly sure of what you are going to say (although there may be interesting surprises in store—writing always involves thinking, and thinking can lead you anywhere), try waiting until you have drafted the rest of the report before writing the introduction.

Literature Review

Because of the systematic and cumulative nature of science, scholarly research rests on the findings and insights of others. In other words, research is never conducted in a vacuum, no matter how innovative the topic or the procedure. Therefore, a literature review is necessary to set the stage for your report.

Literature reviews summarize past research and can be presented in several ways. Although the strategy you adopt can vary, it should be logically connected to the purpose of the report. For example, if you are exploring the validity of a particular statistical test, you will want to review when the test was used to measure variables and test hypotheses similar to those of interest to you. After clearly and briefly reviewing the test's successes and failures, and the methodological issues waiting to be resolved, you should state cogently how your study fits into the debate surrounding the test's validity. This type of review, whose focus is on the methodological aspects of the inquiry, is termed an *integrative research review.*[3]

Another type of review is the *theoretical review.*[4] It can be organized according to schools of thought, such as Freudian, Jungian, and Skinnerian in psychology; or according to analytical approaches, for example, the rational approach to decision making. Theoretical reviews are meant to summarize the ideas scholars have adopted to explain the phenomenon in terms of breadth, internal consistency, and type of predictions. The review should also mention any significant experiments or inquiries conducted on the basis of these theories. Alternatively, your review may be by subject area—the 1990 Gulf War, for instance. Such a review might encompass a wide range of works in the social sciences, history, and the arts. Literature reviews that combine all these aspects are the most comprehensive and appear most commonly. Whatever the strategy, the review should be selective and include only those sources that are most relevant—conceptually and empirically—to your report: the problem, its operationalization, the research methodology, and the conclusions you hope to reach.

It is important to bear in mind that not all sources can be legitimately used in writing literature reviews. Always use scholarly texts, those that directly involve theories or that

---

3. Harris M. Cooper, *Integrative Research: A Guide for Literature Reviews* (Thousand Oaks, CA: Sage, 1989), p. 13.

4. Ibid.

test hypotheses. It is inappropriate, therefore, to include newsmagazine articles in this section.[5] Their place is in the section that reports data and their collection, precisely because the purpose of such articles is to relay the details of events, not to interpret them. Therefore, they can be used as sources only until other, more methodologically rigorous sources are available.

Obviously, how you go about searching for and writing your literature review depends on your research objectives. The search process is quite complex. The wealth of hard-copy and computerized indexes should not fool you—preparing a literature review is a time-consuming and exacting process. Its salience within the report dictates the effort to be expended in determining which items will be included. For now, it will suffice to say that all social scientists, including novice researchers, are responsible for employing two basic standards in selecting the literature incorporated in their reviews: objectivity and open-mindedness. Objectivity means being critical in terms of the quality and relevance of the studies and theoretical works chosen; open-mindedness means being sensitive to new sources, news ideas, and new angles for developing your own ideas. More will be said later about how to construct the literature review.

Methodology and Findings

The section on methodology and findings is devoted to transmitting the details of your procedure, its methodological foundations, the reasoning behind your choice of case or procedure, and the findings. It is not necessary to repeat your research purposes unless it helps the reader to follow the methodology. The more empirical and quantitative the research, the more this section will be devoted to the orderly presentation of hypotheses, the equations employed to test the findings, and tables containing the statistical results of the tests of the data (see p. 496 for a discussion of tables). As we have noted earlier, numbering the hypotheses makes it easier to organize the material. Because tables should be inserted in the order in which the findings are discussed, you only need to refer to the table number (e.g., "see Table 31") when integrating the relevant data into the text.

Qualitative research findings can be organized according to their historical development or the concepts explored, depending on the type of methodology employed.

Discussion

The discussion section of the report contains the bulk of your analysis—your interpretations of the findings, their integration with the research question(s), their relationship to previous research (supportive and nonsupportive alike), and their implications for further research. In this section you can employ all your analytic skills and imagination to draw conclusions and criticize your method or your findings. Therefore, begin with a brief restatement of your purpose and then indicate whether or not your findings support your original hypothesis or validate your methodology. You should also evaluate your contribution without placing undue emphasis on negative results or problems. In short, your presentation should be to the point—clear, concise, and balanced.

Conclusion

The purpose of the conclusion is to close the circle of research, moving from past research to the place of your report in the cumulative stock of scientific knowledge. This requires you to link your theoretical or methodological conclusions with the current state of research. However, the conclusion also presents an opportunity to suggest new avenues of research—ideas on how to conduct follow-up research based on what you have discovered. Although these recommendations may appear to be a heavy burden for the beginner, they present an opportunity to use your investigative imagination; they help place your findings within the continuing flow of research; and they indicate humility, the admission that the report's contribution represents only one addition to the expanding reservoir of knowledge. This section may be only a paragraph in length, but without it your work will lack closure. If your conclusion is very short, it can be integrated into the discussion section.

WRITING THE REPORT ●

Drafting the Report

After all the effort you put into the research, writing the report may still present the greatest obstacle. Writing is a challenge because it forces you to think and to be self-critical. In this section, we will not emphasize writing style, other than to state that simple, short sentences are better, especially when you are trying to communicate complex ideas or procedures.

One good way to begin writing your report is to start early. Write descriptions of your procedures and what you have discovered more or less as you go along. Besides providing summaries and keeping the material fresh in your mind, this strategy gives you the opportunity to begin checking your original ideas as well as developing new ones. These summaries become, in fact, preliminary drafts of the final report.

After you have completed your first draft, the next step is to review it several times, revising as necessary. During at least one review of your draft, take the position of the reader, not the writer. If, as a reader, you cannot follow the line of argument, then you should look for flaws in your thinking as well as in your style. This review may lead you to reassess your argument and perhaps improve it. It may also inspire new ideas that you can mention and develop in another paper. Therefore, write as many drafts as you see fit and have time for.

Constructing a Literature Review

To review quickly, a literature review is included in any research report for a number of reasons. First, it places the report you are writing within the history of social science research. This does not require that you, as a novice researcher, contribute something revolutionary to the accumulated body of knowledge. It does mean that you are responsible for showing your awareness of how your predecessors have dealt conceptually and empirically with the same or similar research problems. Second, the process of constructing a review does more than inform: It also helps you as a social scientist to clarify the concepts and constructs you have used in thinking about the problem, the exactness with which you have operationalized these concepts and constructs, and the methods you have chosen to conduct the study.

Perhaps the most concise way to explain the principles involved in constructing a literature review is by demonstrating how to prepare a *research review coding sheet*.[6] A research review coding sheet is a device that helps you organize the information found in the articles and books you intend to include in your review. The categories in the coding

---

6. Cooper, *Integrative Research*, pp. 30–34.

sheet are determined by your research problem. They pertain to the type and level of detail found in the studies. Coding sheets are often revised, based on how well the categories and codes fit the studies reviewed and your research needs. Any information that is even remotely related to the study should be entered: It is easier to eliminate an item than it is to search for it again at a later date. After coding the items, you can decide just how relevant the material is, how many sources are required, and whether your current conceptualizations of the problem and methods need to be refined. Following is a list of the categories that should be included in every research review coding sheet. Items 1–8 refer directly to empirical studies; items 1 and 9–12 refer to theoretical works.

1. *Identifying characteristics:* Authors, source (book, professional journal, conversation with researcher, etc.), year of publication, how the study was found (e.g., review of the *Social Science Citation Index,* random Internet search)

2. *Research design:* One-group pretest–posttest, correlational, nonequivalent control group, nonequivalent control group with matching or statistical control, random assignment to treatments, time series

3. *Details regarding manipulation of the variable:* How the independent variable was measured, intensity and duration of treatment, etc.

4. *Characteristics of the control or comparison group:* Use of alternative treatments, differences between studies that might influence study outcomes, etc.

5. *Measuring techniques:* Measuring instrument, scales used, test reliability, dependent variables, etc.

6. *Characteristics of participants:* Number of participants in each stage of the study, their demographic characteristics, location of the study, restrictions imposed, etc.

7. *Quantitative/qualitative outcomes:* Direction of outcomes (positive or negative), outcomes of statistical tests (e.g., standard deviation, level of association between the variables), value of inference test statistic, sample size, etc.

8. *Impact on participants:* Responses of participants to the experience of participation (usually inferred by the reviewer), etc.

9. *Level of analysis:* Micro (individual) to macro (e.g., country), level of inference, etc.

10. *Discipline/subdiscipline:* Sociology, anthropology, political science, communications, social psychology (particularly important when interdisciplinary research is being conducted), etc.

11. *Causal model applied:* Dialectic materialism, behaviorism, deconstructionism, rationalism, etc.

12. *Context:* Issue addressed, whether research was inspired by major historical events, sources of data, etc.

Completing such an inventory supports your decisions about the adequacy of your literature review. There is no fixed answer to how many sources should be included, nor to the scope of the material covered. Time and other resources always limit the scope of the review. However, the validity of the review rests, in essence, on the quality of the sources (to be discussed below), and the number and specificity of the operational definitions used in your own research. If the various operational definitions found in the search result in the same conclusions, the likelihood of rival explanations of the phenomenon studied can be more readily ruled out. However, the number of operational definitions bears no relation to their specificity. Narrow definitions reduce the level of generality or robustness of the results you will obtain. In the process of filling out the code sheet, you may find alternative definitions that may cause you to reconceptualize your own. You may also find information that places your decisions about how to test your hypothesis in a new light. A review's adequacy is, then, dependent on how directly it relates to the subject of your inquiry, the operational definitions you have chosen, and the methodology you plan to employ.

Validating Sources

Regardless of how long your review is or how disparate the sources are, the sources' validity says a great deal about how well you understand the research problem and how good the material is. A poor literature review may predict a poor report.

Just what are we referring to when we question the validity of a source and the consequent literature review? Validity refers to (1) how the studies differ from each other in their input (or how much each source contributes something new to our understanding of the topic and your approach to the problem), and (2) how the elements included in the studies differ from those elements excluded (or how well your sources cover the population you are interested in studying). The second element is more difficult for the apprentice researcher to contend with for it requires exercising critical judgment about the scope of the phenomenon and the populations affected. Whether or not a study or theoretical paper is included in your review depends on whether the target population of that source matches the target population of your own inquiry. If these populations do not overlap, you must identify who is eliminated and how this elimination affects the relevance of the source to your own project. This aspect is just part of a greater issue, to be discussed next: how to make judgments about the scientific quality of the sources you wish to include in your literature review.

Judging Quality

The quality of an empirical research report (we will concentrate on this type of source) is determined, first and foremost, by whether it is primary research (the direct item) or a research review itself. It often appears easier to use the literature review previously constructed by a more experienced researcher. The standards of the scientific method and the peer evaluation process "disinfect" many of the biases found in the original study. However, scholars have their own personal inclinations for the type of research they read and how the studies are read; personal biases always enter into that choice. How critical they may be cannot be determined in advance. When a literature review is based entirely on primary sources, the biases tend to be that of the writer of the study and yourself, rather than someone else's.

As to the quality of the research itself, several criteria are employed. Of course, a published article has usually been reviewed by experts in the field, which somewhat reduces the burden placed on the student but does not eliminate it entirely. Publication is neither an automatic nor a uniform criterion of quality; students who include inferior studies in their literature review may threaten the quality of their own research. This problem is particularly acute if the student has access to informal channels for retrieval of information, if studies contain preliminary results, or if they are in draft form.

Two of the basic tests of the quality of studies that report the results of empirical research are their internal validity and external validity, as discussed in Chapter 5. *Internal validity* relates to the degree of correspondence between the experimental treatment and the experimental result. The more closely they are related, the more confident we can be that the dependent variable was indeed influenced by the independent variable. The methodology used relates to how stable the results are, whether the experiment is replicable, and other criteria discussed previously. *External validity* relates to the generalizability of the results, to the size and type of population for which the results may be true. That is, external validity refers to how representative the participants, setting, and findings are of the population found outside the experimental setting. The latter is much harder to determine than the former.

The quality of the research and of the consequent report can be assessed by applying all the criteria for good research listed in this volume: levels of statistical significance, sampling, interviewing techniques, and, of course, the logical consistency of the theory or model presented and the hypotheses researched.

Other Sources

Literature reviews are composed primarily of published reports, but these are not the only possible channels for information retrieval. When available, original databanks may be incorporated. Unpublished reports, summaries of research in progress that are obtained informally, and conversations with experts in the field all supplement journals and books. In Chapter 13, the major sources of secondary data were listed; these are also the major sources of items to be surveyed in your review. Here, we add a few of the major indexes, many of which are now in computer-readable form: *Sources of Information in the Social Sciences, Psychological Abstracts,* the *Thesaurus of ERIC* [Educational Resources Information Center] *Descriptors, Dissertation Abstracts International,* the *Social Sciences Citation Index,* and PsychINFO. The Internet has a wealth of information but requires a good deal of time, patience, and a sharply critical reading of the documents, which do not need to meet academic standards to be listed.

Editing

A research report must be written according to the structure we have described, but it must also be edited or rewritten. Editing means making sure that only the details that are most relevant to your method and your argument appear. Editing likewise makes sure that you have expressed yourself clearly and logically. However, be aware that there is a point of no return, where you have read the text so often you cannot see the problems. This is the point at which to stop.

Editing should take place with your audience in mind. For example, suppose you are reporting a study using survey research methods to investigate attitudes toward flexible working hours. If your report is geared to survey researchers and statisticians, you will probably include many more methodological details and more mathematical logic than you would if your audience was composed of personnel managers. For the latter, you might include more information about the populations surveyed and the types of questions asked.

Finally, once you are satisfied with your complete draft, you should review it for style and for errors in grammar and spelling. Personal computers make these tasks simpler by providing programs for correcting spelling and style and by making it easier to alter the order of the paragraphs. Nevertheless, despite technology, the process still requires a good deal of time and concentration. If you do not have a printer readily available and must do at least some of your corrections by hand, remember that too many handwritten corrections on the final draft, even if they are only of typing errors, make the text look unprofessional and hint at a lack of concern on your part. If you have more than two corrections on a page, you should reprint or retype it.

Tone and Sexist Language

Two stylistic factors should be considered when writing your report: tone and sexist language. Keep your audience in mind when you decide how formal or informal your style should be. Formality assumes a more rigid sentence structure and internal organization. Neither formal nor informal style precludes humor, but both demand consistency. Whichever you choose, make sure you are comfortable in your choice. Being sure of your own attitude will guarantee coherence in style and purpose.

Sexist language, on the other hand, is something to be avoided throughout your report, whether you are using a formal or informal style. Take advantage of the many style manuals that offer alternatives to traditional male-oriented phrasing.

Length

Two factors control the length of a research report: its aim and its topic. The aims of a report are varied and, for the student, may include the improvement of personal research skills. Another factor bearing on length may be the influence of the paper on the final grade. An instructor may require only 3 pages for an exercise but up to 30 pages for a paper that serves as the sole basis for a grade. Master's and doctoral theses are, of course, much longer. Journal articles may be limited by the editors to 40 manuscript pages, and monographs to perhaps 50 typewritten pages. Papers in the field of statistics may be shorter because so much information is summarized in equations. If you have a length limitation, use shortcuts for presenting material, such as flow charts to illustrate causal models.

Plagiarism[7]

Why should a text in social science research methodology include a section on plagiarism? Isn't it taken for granted that using another person's ideas and phrases without giving direct credit is immoral and illegal? Unfortunately, plagiarism continues to crop up in academia and elsewhere. Because of the pressure to publish or to pass a course, people are often tempted to "borrow" from others, on the assumption that no one will catch on. However, as stated above, the development of knowledge is based on the work of our forerunners. It tends to be incremental, progressing piece by piece; hence it really is difficult to "get away" with plagiarism for any length of time. In addition, an instructor is likely to be sufficiently familiar with the level of work expected from students, as well as the material on an approved research topic, to spot any attempts to plagiarize. Plagiarism is wrong, and it is a risky strategy to adopt.

For most students, plagiarism may be unintentional. It is not always absolutely clear when quotation marks should be used or when a page number must be cited together with the text's author and title. Therefore, we offer the following basic rules for avoiding plagiarism to assist those who are baffled and to discourage those who are tempted.

1. Always use quotation marks and cite the author, text, and page number when incorporating another author's exact words into your text. In general, U.S. copyright laws are infringed whenever a string of at least eight words is used without citing the source. The following examples, taken from item 69 in Exhibit 4.1 of this text, can be used as guides.

Plagiarism: When relating research findings, the procedures should be described fully and accurately in reports, including all evidence regardless of whether it supports the research hypotheses.

Correct: In reporting findings, "[research] procedures should be described fully and accurately in reports, including all evidence regardless of the support it provides for the research hypotheses . . . " (Reynolds, 1979, pp. 447–448).

---

7. This section incorporates many ideas and examples from Babbie, *The Practice of Social Research,* pp. A11–A12, and Meyer, *The Little, Brown Guide to Writing Research Papers,* pp. 109–114.

2. When paraphrasing an author, cite the author's name and the source, according to the citation style required.

Plagiarism: Whether or not the evidence supports the hypothesis investigated, the procedures should be accurately and completely described in the concluding report.

Correct: Whether or not the evidence supports the hypothesis investigated, the procedures should be accurately and completely described in the concluding report (see Reynolds, 1979, pp. 447–448).

3. Another author's ideas, even if rephrased, should never be presented as your own; you should state that you accept them and cite the original source. If you have independently reached the same conclusions found in the literature, state so clearly and cite the supporting author.

Plagiarism: I would conclude that all the procedures used in collecting evidence, whether or not they support the original hypothesis, should be reported.

Correct: Following the normative principles of scientific methodology presented in Frankfort-Nachmias and Nachmias (1995), I would conclude that all the procedures used in collecting evidence, whether or not they support the original hypothesis, should be reported. In fact, this concept has been stated as an ethical principle by Paul Davison Reynolds (1979, pp. 447–448).

4. Common knowledge does not have to be attributed as long as you are confident that the information is in fact commonly known. For example, the fact that Washington, DC, the nation's capital, has no representation in the Senate may be common knowledge for students of American history or politics, but the reasons behind that status may not be. Therefore, a source should be cited when giving these reasons.

Perhaps the best way to avoid plagiarism is simply to be honest. When in doubt, cite your sources. Remember that you demonstrate your research skills by knowing when and where to give credit.

TABLES ●

Tables and figures are really very compact summaries of your findings. They are used in all quantitative research but may also be used in qualitative research to simplify the presentation of a theoretical argument—see, for example, Figures 1.1 and 2.1 of this text. These figures use only words—concepts—to summarize the ideas and information discussed in the text.

Following are some basic technical guidelines for constructing tables.[8]

1. Tables should be self-explanatory—that is, understandable without reference to the text. Therefore, they must be clear, logically planned in terms of the relationships examined, and accurate. Summary columns should appear last.

2. Each table or graph should be given its own number (e.g., Table 1, Figure 2), placed at the top and, for most academic reports, centered. Titles are also centered.

3. The title should clearly and succinctly refer to the table's contents (what, where, when). Underneath the title, indicate the type of entries expressed in the figures (e.g., percentages, frequencies, currency base). If not indicated under the title, then each type of entry should be designated in the appropriate column. Foot-

---

8. Adapted in part from guidelines prepared by David G. Wegge, St. Norbert College.

notes can be used for this purpose if no room is available within the column. The table title and related information should be centered.

4. Text references to table entries should refer to the headings in the table.

5. Column headings should refer to independent variables, row headings to dependent variables. Column and row headings should be clearly distinguishable from each other and may be numbered for clarity.

6. Columns of figures should be centered, aligned on decimal points, and aligned with the row headings.

7. The only abbreviations that are generally permitted are "n.a." (not available) and *N* (frequency). The *N*, if small, may appear in parentheses directly below the numerical findings but should always appear as part of the column summary figures (see Table 16.6 as an example).

8. Asterisks or other symbols may be used as indicators of explanatory footnotes or of unique data sources. Keep these to a minimum to avoid clutter and confusion on the part of the reader (see Table 18.5 as an illustration.)

9. Explanatory footnotes appear directly under the table, in full citation form. Sources of data, also in full citation form, appear underneath the footnotes.

The point to remember is that a table is used to assist the reader; therefore, the number of tables, figures, or other visual devices used is a direct consequence of your argument as well as of the amount of data collected. Use your judgment and do not overburden the text by introducing tables that contribute little to your presentation.

DOCUMENTATION ●

Many disciplines have their own format for documenting sources. The basic manuals are available in your college bookstore and library. The following books provide guidelines for the three common documentation styles.

American Psychological Association. *Publication Manual of the American Psychological Association,* 4th ed. Washington, DC: APA, 1994.

The Chicago Manual of Style, 14th ed. Chicago: University of Chicago Press, 1993.

Gibaldi, Joseph. *MLA Handbook for Writers of Research Papers,* 5th ed. New York: Modern Language Association of America, 1999.

In addition, many journals have developed their own style for documentation. Your references should be typed in the format demanded by the journal to which you are sending the manuscript. The instructor is usually the authority for the format required in his or her own course. As always, the rule of thumb is consistency.

ADDITIONAL READINGS ●

Cooper, Harris M. *Integrative Research: A Guide for Literature Reviews.* Thousand Oaks, CA: Sage, 1989.

Meyer, Michael. *The Little, Brown Guide to Writing Research Papers.* New York: Harper Collins, 1991.

The Sociology Writing Group. *A Guide to Writing Sociology Papers,* 3d ed. New York: St. Martin's Press, 1994.

APPENDIX C

Σ: The Summation Sign

In statistics, it is frequently necessary to make use of formulas involving sums of numerous quantities. As a shorthand substitute for writing out each of these sums at length, the Greek letter Σ (capital sigma), which means to summate or add, is used. As a rule, whenever Σ appears, it means that *all* quantities appearing to the right of it should be summed.

If you want to add ten scores, we can always write

$$X_1 + X_2 + X_3 + X_4 + X_5 + X_6 + X_7 + X_8 + X_9 + X_{10}$$

or the same expression can be shortened to

$$X_1 + X_2 + \cdots + X_{10}$$

which means the same thing. The three dots ($\cdots$) mean "and so on." This same instruction may be put in still another way:

$$\sum_{i=1}^{10} X_i$$

Σ instructs us to add up everything that follows (X_i), starting with the case specified below the symbol ($i = 1$) and ending with the case specified above (10). This example may be read as follows: add up (Σ) all the observations (X_i) ranging from the first ($i = 1$) through the tenth (10). If we want only to sum the observations 4 and 5 ($X_4 + X_5$), we can write

$$\sum_{i=4}^{5} X_i$$

and if we wish to indicate that all of some unspecified number of cases should be added together, we can use N to symbolize the unspecified number of cases and write

$$\sum_{i=1}^{N} X_i$$

This says to sum all the observations from the first to the Nth; it is a general instruction for the addition of all cases regardless of their number. When this general instruction is intended, and when the range of values to be summed is obvious, it is customary to omit the notation of limits and write

$$\Sigma X_i$$

or even

$$\Sigma X$$

This indicates that the summation is to extend over all cases under consideration.

Rules for the Use of Σ

There are a number of rules for the use of Σ. For example,

$$\sum_{i=1}^{N} (X_i + Y_i) = \sum_{i=1}^{N} X_i + \sum_{i=1}^{N} Y_i$$

which says that the summation of the sum of the two variables (X and Y) is equal to the sum of their summations. It makes no difference whether one adds each X_i to each Y_i and then sums their total from 1 to N or sums all X_i and then all Y_i and adds their sums; the result is the same.

Another rule is expressed in the following equation:

$$\sum_{i=1}^{N} kX_i = k \sum_{i=1}^{N} X_i$$

A constant k may be moved across the summation sign. That is to say, if we are instructed to multiply each of a series of numbers by a constant

$$kX_1 + kX_2 + \cdots + kX_N$$

we can simply sum our numbers and multiply that sum by the constant; the result is the same.

A third rule is the following:

$$\sum_{i=1}^{N} k = kN$$

The summation of a constant is equal to the product of that constant and the number of times it is summed.

Another rule states that

$$\left(\sum_{i=1}^{N} X_i \right)^2 = (X_1 + X_2 + \cdots + X_N)^2$$

$$= X_1^2 + X_2^2 + \cdots + X_N^2 + 2X_1X_2$$

$$+ 2X_1X_3 + \cdots + 2X_{N-1}X_N$$

$$\neq X_1^2 + X_2^2 + \cdots + X_N^2$$

That is, we must distinguish between

$$\sum_{i=1}^{N} X_1^2$$

and

$$\left(\sum_{i=1}^{N} X_i \right)^2$$

Random Digits

Line/Col.	(1)	(2)	(3)	(4)	(5)	(6)	(7)	(8)	(9)	(10)	(11)	(12)	(13)	(14)
1	10480	15011	01536	02011	81647	91646	69179	14194	62590	36207	20969	99570	91291	90700
2	22368	46573	25595	85393	30995	89198	27982	53402	93965	34095	52666	19174	39615	99505
3	24130	48360	22527	97265	76393	64809	15179	24830	49340	32081	30680	19655	63348	58629
4	42167	93093	06243	61680	07856	16376	39440	53537	71341	57004	00849	74917	97758	16379
5	37570	39975	81837	16656	06121	91782	60468	81305	49684	60672	14110	06927	01263	54613
6	77921	06907	11008	42751	27756	53498	18602	70659	90655	15053	21916	81825	44394	42880
7	99562	72905	56420	69994	98872	31016	71194	18738	44013	48840	63213	21069	10634	12952
8	96301	91977	05463	07972	18876	20922	94595	56869	69014	60045	18425	84903	42508	32307
9	89579	14342	63661	10281	17453	18103	57740	84378	25331	12566	58678	44947	05585	56941
10	85475	36857	53342	53988	53060	59533	38867	62300	08158	17983	16439	11458	18593	64952
11	28918	69578	88231	33276	70997	79936	56865	05859	90106	31595	01547	85590	91610	78188
12	63553	40961	48235	03427	49626	69445	18663	72695	52180	20847	12234	90511	33703	90322
13	09429	93969	52636	92737	88974	33488	36320	17617	30015	08272	84115	27156	30613	74952
14	10365	61129	87529	85689	48237	52267	67689	93394	01511	26358	85104	20285	29975	89868
15	07119	97336	71048	08178	77233	13916	47564	81056	97735	85977	29372	74461	28551	90707
16	51085	12765	51821	51259	77452	16308	60756	92144	49442	53900	70960	63990	75601	40719
17	02368	21382	52404	60268	89368	19885	55322	44819	01188	65255	64835	44919	05944	55157
18	01011	54092	33362	94904	31273	04146	18594	29852	71585	85030	51132	01915	92747	64951
19	52162	53916	46369	58586	23216	14513	83149	98736	23495	64350	94738	17752	35156	35749
20	07056	97628	33787	09998	42698	06691	76988	13602	51851	46104	88916	19509	25625	58104
21	48663	91245	85828	14346	09172	30168	90229	04734	59193	22178	30421	61666	99904	32812
22	54164	58492	22421	74103	47070	25306	76468	26384	58151	06646	21524	15227	96909	44592
23	32639	32363	05597	24200	13363	38005	94342	28728	35806	06912	17012	64161	18296	22851
24	29334	27001	87637	87308	58731	00256	45834	15398	46557	41135	10367	07684	36188	18510
25	02488	33062	28834	07351	19731	92420	60952	61280	50001	67658	32586	86679	50720	94953

26	95725	79666	87074	13300	14780	76797	14778	66566	82651	24878	96423	04839	72295	81525
27	25280	80428	57102	92259	12659	86645	81536	89768	20849	46901	26432	68086	20591	29676
28	98253	96096	64584	64760	96067	98947	61362	32832	40027	84673	66432	39064	57392	00742
29	90449	34693	66520	75470	66134	45766	63904	37937	44048	44407	26422	25669	04213	05366
30	69618	07844	42416	91402	64568	71500	22209	39972	25940	26766	94305	64117	26418	91921
31	76630	62028	76655	43808	42607	81817	99547	74087	35126	42206	77341	87917	04711	00582
32	88006	77919	65855	76038	93161	84637	36086	76222	88072	86324	56170	62797	69884	00725
33	48501	12777	80150	29841	59920	40801	08625	26575	27354	18088	55293	95876	65795	69011
34	03547	85963	54262	33611	69774	65424	82271	18912	48708	67917	88604	29888	57948	25976
35	88050	38917	37888	34952	41688	05998	35797	28290	18317	30883	12908	73577	83473	09763
36	73211	79656	09250	29080	84855	55536	99730	29880	86385	04024	30134	27958	42595	91567
37	42791	36103	83517	73708	02008	18059	20542	06115	59931	20044	49127	90999	56349	17955
38	87338	20562	53389	56942	15475	28168	58727	20655	51038	02304	49618	18845	18584	46503
39	20468	35509	21246	25555	48413	44137	25417	09922	82834	84610	78171	94824	89634	92157
40	18062	77490	20103	89656	49518	61607	56307	56873	47358	39667	81263	35605	62765	14577
41	45709	46880	04102	46565	45585	04880	98420	66969	92477	01638	64270	33362	07523	98427
42	69348	77775	88803	70663	70002	32427	40836	87589	17032	34476	82765	88720	63976	34914
43	66794	00102	72828	19661	94884	69975	25832	94970	53416	23219	46473	39475	28277	70060
44	97809	06541	46634	47363	88267	80287	42878	11398	82948	68350	67245	06990	54914	53976
45	59583	60697	14222	41151	96189	39911	80059	22987	25774	58745	07391	40980	29515	76072
46	41546	56228	57375	31720	14361	55657	83765	50490	38857	65831	29992	83974	52210	90725
47	51900	23726	04110	35931	89286	97473	92351	59744	24413	14883	31926	33339	67412	64364
48	81788	78547	45578	48373	69352	56891	35648	81249	34072	61642	25388	31662	00358	08962
49	92277	62730	14777	28865	17247	02349	54328	76463	04542	10592	70765	93526	68379	95012
50	85653	32261	22923	46751	48223	27195	81652	59516	21999	91132	38391	20492	10493	15664

Appendix D (*continued*)

Line/Col.	(1)	(2)	(3)	(4)	(5)	(6)	(7)	(8)	(9)	(10)	(11)	(12)	(13)	(14)
51	16408	81899	04153	53381	79401	21438	83035	92350	36693	31238	59649	91754	72772	02338
52	18629	81953	05520	91962	04739	13092	97662	24822	94730	06496	35090	04822	86774	98289
53	73115	35101	47498	87637	99016	71060	88824	71013	18735	20286	23153	72924	35165	43040
54	57491	16703	23167	49323	45021	33132	12544	41035	80780	45393	44812	12515	98931	91202
55	30405	83946	23792	14422	15059	45799	22716	19792	09983	74353	68668	30429	70735	25499
56	16631	35006	85900	98275	32388	52390	16815	69298	82732	38480	73817	32523	41961	44437
57	96773	20206	42559	78985	05300	22164	24369	54224	35083	19687	11052	91491	60383	19746
58	38935	64202	14349	82674	66523	44133	00697	55552	35970	19124	63318	29686	03387	59846
59	31624	76384	17403	53363	44167	64486	64758	75366	76554	31601	12614	33072	60332	92325
60	78919	19474	23632	27889	47914	02584	37680	20801	72152	39339	34806	08930	85001	87820
61	03931	33309	57047	74211	63445	17361	62825	39908	05607	91284	68833	25570	38818	46920
62	74426	33278	43972	10119	89917	15665	52872	73823	73144	88662	88970	74492	51805	99378
63	09066	00903	20795	95452	92648	45454	09552	88815	16553	51125	79375	97596	16296	66092
64	42238	12426	87025	14267	20979	04508	64535	31355	86064	29472	47689	05974	52468	16834
65	16153	08002	26504	41744	81959	65642	74240	56302	00033	67107	77510	70625	28725	34191
66	21457	40742	29820	96783	29400	21840	15035	34537	33310	06116	95240	15957	16572	06004
67	21581	57802	02050	89728	17937	37621	47075	42080	97403	48626	68995	43805	33386	21597
68	55612	78095	83197	33732	05810	24813	86902	60397	16489	03264	88525	42786	05269	92532
69	44657	66999	99324	51281	84463	60563	79312	93454	68876	25471	93911	25650	12682	73572
70	91340	84979	46949	81973	37949	61023	43997	15263	80644	43942	89203	71795	99533	50501
71	91227	21199	31935	27022	84067	05462	35216	14436	29891	68607	41867	14951	91696	85065
72	50001	38140	66321	19924	72163	09538	12151	06878	91903	18749	34405	56087	82790	70925
73	65390	05224	72958	28609	81406	39147	25549	48542	42627	45233	57202	94617	23772	07896
74	27504	96131	83944	41575	10573	08619	64482	73923	36152	05184	94142	25299	84387	34925
75	37169	94851	39117	89632	00959	16487	65536	49071	39782	17095	02330	74301	00275	48280

76	11508	70225	51111	38351	19444	66499	71945	05422	13442	78675	84081	66938	93654	59894
77	37449	30362	06694	54690	04052	53115	62757	95348	78662	11163	81651	50245	34971	52924
78	46515	70331	85922	38329	57015	15765	97161	17869	45349	61796	66345	81073	49106	79860
79	30986	81223	42416	58353	21532	30502	32305	86482	05174	07901	54339	58861	74818	46942
80	63798	64995	46583	09785	44160	78128	83991	42865	92520	83531	80377	35909	81250	54238
81	82486	84846	99254	67632	43218	50076	21361	64816	51202	88124	41870	52689	51275	83556
82	21885	32906	92431	09060	64297	51674	64126	62570	26123	05155	59194	52799	28225	85762
83	60336	98782	07408	53458	13564	59089	26445	29789	85205	41001	12535	12133	14645	23541
84	43937	46891	24010	25560	86355	33941	25786	54990	71899	15475	95434	98227	21824	19585
85	97656	63175	89303	16275	07100	92063	21942	18611	47348	20203	18534	03862	78095	50136
86	03299	01221	05418	38982	55758	92237	26759	86367	21216	98442	08303	56613	91511	75928
87	79626	06486	03574	17668	07785	76020	79924	25651	83325	88428	85076	72811	22717	50585
88	85636	68335	47539	03129	65651	11977	02510	26113	99447	68645	34327	15152	55230	93448
89	18039	14367	61337	06177	12143	46609	32989	74014	64708	00533	35398	58408	13261	47908
90	08362	15656	60627	36478	65648	16764	53412	09013	07832	41574	17639	82163	60859	75567
91	79556	29068	04142	16268	15387	12856	66227	38358	22478	73373	88732	09443	82558	05250
92	92608	82674	27072	32534	17075	27698	98204	63863	11951	34648	88022	56148	34925	57031
93	23982	25835	40055	67006	12293	02753	14827	23235	35071	99704	37543	11601	35503	85171
94	09915	96306	05908	97901	28395	14186	00821	80703	70426	75647	76310	88717	37890	40129
95	59037	33300	26695	62247	69927	76123	50842	43834	86654	70959	79725	93872	28117	19233
96	42488	78077	69882	61657	34136	79180	97526	43092	04098	73571	80799	76536	71255	64239
97	46764	86273	63003	93017	31204	36692	40202	35275	57306	55543	53203	18098	47625	88684
98	03237	45430	55417	63282	90816	17349	88298	90183	36600	78406	06216	95787	42579	90730
99	86591	81482	52667	61582	14972	90053	89534	76036	49199	43716	97548	04379	46370	28672
100	38534	01715	94964	87288	65680	43772	39560	12918	86537	62738	19636	51132	25739	56947

Areas Under the Normal Curve

Fractional parts of the total area (10,000) under the normal curve, corresponding to distances between the mean and ordinates that are Z standard deviation units from the mean.

Z	.00	.01	.02	.03	.04	.05	.06	.07	.08	.09
0.0	0000	0040	0080	0120	0159	0199	0239	0279	0319	0359
0.1	0398	0438	0478	0517	0557	0596	0636	0675	0714	0753
0.2	0793	0832	0871	0910	0948	0987	1026	1064	1103	1141
0.3	1179	1217	1255	1293	1331	1368	1406	1443	1480	1517
0.4	1554	1591	1628	1664	1700	1736	1772	1808	1844	1879
0.5	1915	1950	1985	2019	2054	2088	2123	2157	2190	2224
0.6	2257	2291	2324	2357	2389	2422	2454	2486	2518	2549
0.7	2580	2612	2642	2673	2704	2734	2764	2794	2823	2852
0.8	2881	2910	2939	2967	2995	3023	3051	3078	3106	3133
0.9	3159	3186	3212	3238	3264	3289	3315	3340	3365	3389
1.0	3413	3438	3461	3485	3508	3531	3554	3577	3599	3621
1.1	3643	3665	3686	3718	3729	3749	3770	3790	3810	3830
1.2	3849	3869	3888	3907	3925	3944	3962	3980	3997	4015
1.3	4032	4049	4066	4083	4099	4115	4131	4147	4162	4177
1.4	4192	4207	4222	4236	4251	4265	4279	4292	4306	4319
1.5	4332	4345	4357	4370	4382	4394	4406	4418	4430	4441
1.6	4452	4463	4474	4485	4495	4505	4515	4525	4535	4545
1.7	4554	4564	4573	4582	4591	4599	4608	4616	4625	4633
1.8	4641	4649	4656	4664	4671	4678	4686	4693	4699	4706
1.9	4713	4719	4726	4732	4738	4744	4750	4758	4762	4767
2.0	4773	4778	4783	4788	4793	4798	4803	4808	4812	4817
2.1	4821	4826	4830	4834	4838	4842	4846	4850	4854	4857
2.2	4861	4865	4868	4871	4875	4878	4881	4884	4887	4890
2.3	4893	4896	4898	4901	4904	4906	4909	4911	4913	4916
2.4	4918	4920	4922	4925	4927	4929	4931	4932	4934	4936
2.5	4938	4940	4941	4943	4945	4946	4948	4949	4951	4952
2.6	4953	4955	4956	4957	4959	4960	4961	4962	4963	4964
2.7	4965	4966	4967	4968	4969	4970	4971	4972	4973	4974
2.8	4974	4975	4976	4977	4977	4978	4979	4980	4980	4981
2.9	4981	4982	4983	4984	4984	4984	4984	4985	4985	4986
3.0	4986.5	4987	4987	4988	4988	4988	4989	4989	4989	4990
3.1	4990.0	4991	1991	4991	4992	4992	4992	4992	4993	4994
3.2	4993.129									
3.3	4995.166									
3.4	4996.631									
3.5	4997.674									
3.6	4998.409									
3.7	4998.922									
3.8	4999.277									
3.9	4999.519									
4.0	4999.683									
4.5	499.966									
5.0	4999.997133									

From Harold O. Rugg, *Statistical Methods Applied to Education* (Boston: Houghton Mifflin, 1917), pp 389–390. Reprinted by permission of the publisher.

Distribution of *t*

df	Level of significance for one-tailed test					
	.10	.05	.025	.01	.005	.0005
	Level of significance for two-tailed test					
	.20	.10	.05	.02	.01	.001
1	3.078	6.314	12.706	31.821	63.657	636.619
2	1.886	2.920	4.303	6.965	9.925	31.598
3	1.638	2.353	3.182	4.541	5.841	12.941
4	1.533	2.132	2.776	3.747	4.604	8.610
5	1.476	2.015	2.571	3.365	4.032	6.859
6	1.440	1.943	2.447	3.143	3.707	5.959
7	1.415	1.895	2.365	2.998	3.499	5.405
8	1.397	1.860	2.306	2.896	3.355	5.041
9	1.383	1.833	2.262	2.821	3.250	4.781
10	1.372	1.812	2.228	2.764	3.169	4.587
11	1.363	1.796	2.201	2.718	3.106	4.437
12	1.356	1.782	2.179	2.681	3.055	4.318
13	1.350	1.771	2.160	2.650	3.012	4.221
14	1.345	1.761	2.145	2.624	2.977	4.140
15	1.341	1.753	2.131	2.602	2.947	4.073
16	1.337	1.746	2.120	2.583	2.921	4.015
17	1.333	1.740	2.110	2.567	2.898	3.965
18	1.330	1.734	2.101	2.552	2.878	3.922
19	1.328	1.729	2.093	2.539	2.861	3.883
20	1.325	1.725	2.086	2.528	2.845	3.850
21	1.323	1.721	2.080	2.518	2.831	3.819
22	1.321	1.717	2.074	2.508	2.819	3.792
23	1.319	1.714	2.069	2.500	2.807	3.767
24	1.318	1.711	2.064	2.492	2.797	3.745
25	1.316	1.708	2.060	2.485	2.787	3.725
26	1.315	1.706	2.056	2.479	2.779	3.707
27	1.314	1.703	2.052	2.473	2.771	3.690
28	1.313	1.701	2.048	2.467	2.763	3.674
29	1.311	1.699	2.045	2.462	2.756	3.659
30	1.310	1.697	2.042	2.457	2.750	3.646
40	1.303	1.684	2.021	2.423	2.704	3.551
60	1.296	1.671	2.000	2.390	2.660	3.460
120	1.289	1.658	1.980	2.358	2.617	3.373
∞	1.282	1.645	1.960	2.326	2.576	3.291

Abridged from R. A. Fisher and F. Yates, *Statistical Tables for Biological, Agricultural and Medical Research*, 6th ed. (London: Longman, 1974), tab. III. Used by permission of the authors and Longman Group Ltd.

Critical Values of F

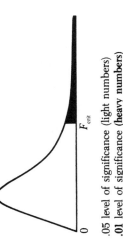

.05 level of significance (light numbers)
.01 level of significance (**heavy numbers**)

Degrees of Freedom in Numerator

Degrees of Freedom in Denominator	1	2	3	4	5	6	7	8	9	10	11	12	14	16	20	24	30	40	50	75	100	200	500	∞
1	161	200	216	225	230	234	237	239	241	242	243	244	245	246	248	249	250	251	252	253	253	254	254	254
	4,052	**4,999**	**5,403**	**5,625**	**5,764**	**5,859**	**5,928**	**5,981**	**6,022**	**6,056**	**6,082**	**6,106**	**6,142**	**6,169**	**6,208**	**6,234**	**6,258**	**6,286**	**6,302**	**6,323**	**6,334**	**6,352**	**6,361**	**6,366**
2	18.51	19.00	19.16	19.25	19.30	19.33	19.36	19.37	19.38	19.39	19.40	19.41	19.42	19.43	19.44	19.45	19.46	19.47	19.47	19.48	19.49	19.49	19.50	19.50
	98.49	**99.00**	**99.17**	**99.25**	**99.30**	**99.33**	**99.34**	**99.36**	**99.38**	**99.40**	**99.41**	**99.42**	**99.43**	**99.44**	**99.45**	**99.46**	**99.47**	**99.48**	**99.48**	**99.49**	**99.49**	**99.49**	**99.50**	**99.50**
3	10.13	9.55	9.28	9.12	9.01	8.94	8.88	8.84	8.81	8.78	8.76	8.74	8.71	8.69	8.66	8.64	8.62	8.60	8.58	8.57	8.56	8.54	8.54	8.53
	34.12	**30.82**	**29.46**	**28.71**	**28.24**	**27.91**	**27.67**	**27.49**	**27.34**	**27.23**	**27.13**	**27.05**	**26.92**	**26.83**	**26.69**	**26.60**	**26.50**	**26.41**	**26.35**	**26.27**	**26.23**	**26.18**	**26.14**	**26.12**
4	7.71	6.94	6.59	6.39	6.26	6.16	6.09	6.04	6.00	5.96	5.93	5.91	5.87	5.84	5.80	5.77	5.74	5.71	5.70	5.68	5.66	5.65	5.64	5.63
	21.20	**18.00**	**16.69**	**15.98**	**15.52**	**15.21**	**14.98**	**14.80**	**14.66**	**14.54**	**14.45**	**14.37**	**14.24**	**14.15**	**14.02**	**13.93**	**13.83**	**13.74**	**13.69**	**13.61**	**13.57**	**13.52**	**13.48**	**13.46**
5	6.61	5.79	5.41	5.19	5.05	4.95	4.88	4.82	4.78	4.74	4.70	4.68	4.64	4.60	4.56	4.53	4.50	4.46	4.44	4.42	4.40	4.38	4.37	4.36
	16.26	**13.27**	**12.06**	**11.39**	**10.97**	**10.67**	**10.45**	**10.27**	**10.15**	**10.05**	**9.96**	**9.89**	**9.77**	**9.68**	**9.55**	**9.47**	**9.38**	**9.29**	**9.24**	**9.17**	**9.13**	**9.07**	**9.04**	**9.02**
6	5.99	5.14	4.76	4.53	4.39	4.28	4.21	4.15	4.10	4.06	4.03	4.00	3.96	3.92	3.87	3.84	3.81	3.77	3.75	3.72	3.71	3.69	3.68	3.67
	13.74	**10.92**	**9.78**	**9.15**	**8.75**	**8.47**	**8.26**	**8.10**	**7.98**	**7.87**	**7.79**	**7.72**	**7.60**	**7.52**	**7.39**	**7.31**	**7.23**	**7.14**	**7.09**	**7.02**	**6.99**	**6.94**	**6.90**	**6.88**
7	5.59	4.47	4.35	4.12	3.97	3.87	3.79	3.73	3.68	3.63	3.60	3.57	3.52	3.49	3.44	3.41	3.38	3.34	3.32	3.29	3.28	3.25	3.24	3.23
	12.25	**9.55**	**8.45**	**7.85**	**7.46**	**7.19**	**7.00**	**6.84**	**6.71**	**6.62**	**6.54**	**6.47**	**6.35**	**6.27**	**6.15**	**6.07**	**5.98**	**5.90**	**5.85**	**5.78**	**5.75**	**5.70**	**5.67**	**5.65**

8	5.32	4.46	4.07	3.84	3.69	3.58	3.50	3.44	3.39	3.34	3.31	3.28	3.23	3.20	3.15	3.12	3.08	3.05	3.03	3.00	2.98	2.96	2.94	2.93
	11.26	8.65	7.59	7.01	6.63	6.37	6.19	6.03	5.91	5.82	5.74	5.67	5.56	5.48	5.36	5.28	5.20	5.11	5.06	5.00	4.96	4.91	4.88	4.86
9	5.12	4.26	3.86	3.63	3.48	3.37	3.29	3.23	3.18	3.13	3.10	3.07	3.02	2.98	2.93	2.90	2.86	2.82	2.80	2.77	2.76	2.73	2.72	2.71
	10.56	8.02	6.99	6.42	6.06	5.80	5.62	5.47	5.35	5.26	5.18	5.11	5.00	4.92	4.80	4.73	4.64	4.56	4.51	4.45	4.41	4.36	4.33	4.31
10	4.96	4.10	3.71	3.48	3.33	3.22	3.14	3.07	3.02	2.97	2.94	2.91	2.86	2.82	2.77	2.74	2.70	2.67	2.64	2.61	2.59	2.56	2.55	2.54
	10.04	7.56	6.55	5.99	5.64	5.39	5.21	5.06	4.95	4.85	4.78	4.71	4.60	4.52	4.41	4.33	4.25	4.17	4.12	4.05	4.01	3.96	3.93	3.91
11	4.84	3.98	3.59	3.36	3.20	3.09	3.01	2.95	2.90	2.86	2.82	2.79	2.74	2.70	2.65	2.61	2.57	2.53	2.50	2.47	2.45	2.42	2.41	2.40
	9.65	7.20	6.22	5.67	5.32	5.07	4.88	4.74	4.63	4.54	4.46	4.40	4.29	4.21	4.10	4.02	3.94	3.86	3.80	3.74	3.70	3.66	3.62	3.60
12	4.75	3.88	3.49	3.26	3.11	3.00	2.92	2.85	2.80	2.76	2.72	2.69	2.64	2.60	2.54	2.50	2.46	2.42	2.40	2.36	2.35	2.32	2.31	2.30
	9.33	6.93	5.95	5.41	5.06	4.82	4.65	4.50	4.39	4.30	4.22	4.16	4.05	3.98	3.86	3.78	3.70	3.61	3.56	3.49	3.46	3.41	3.38	3.36
13	4.67	3.80	3.41	3.18	3.02	2.92	2.84	2.77	2.72	2.67	2.63	2.60	2.55	2.51	2.46	2.42	2.38	2.34	2.32	2.28	2.26	2.24	2.22	2.21
	9.07	6.70	5.74	5.20	4.86	4.62	4.44	4.30	4.19	4.10	4.02	3.96	3.85	3.78	3.67	3.59	3.51	3.42	3.37	3.30	3.27	3.21	3.18	3.16
14	4.60	3.74	3.34	3.11	2.96	2.85	2.77	2.70	2.65	2.60	2.56	2.53	2.48	2.44	2.39	2.35	2.31	2.27	2.24	2.21	2.19	2.16	2.14	2.13
	8.86	6.51	5.56	5.03	4.69	4.46	4.28	4.14	4.03	3.94	3.86	3.80	3.70	3.62	3.51	3.43	3.34	3.26	3.21	3.14	3.11	3.06	3.02	3.00
15	4.54	3.68	3.29	3.06	2.90	2.79	2.70	2.64	2.59	2.55	2.51	2.48	2.43	2.39	2.33	2.29	2.25	2.21	2.18	2.15	2.12	2.10	2.08	2.07
	8.68	6.36	5.42	4.89	4.56	4.32	4.14	4.00	3.89	3.80	3.73	3.67	3.56	3.48	3.36	3.29	3.20	3.12	3.07	3.00	2.97	2.92	2.89	2.87
16	4.49	3.63	3.24	3.01	2.85	2.74	2.66	2.59	2.54	2.49	2.45	2.42	2.37	2.33	2.28	2.24	2.20	2.16	2.13	2.09	2.07	2.04	2.02	2.01
	8.53	6.23	5.29	4.77	4.44	4.20	4.03	3.89	3.78	3.69	3.61	3.55	3.45	3.37	3.25	3.18	3.10	3.01	2.96	2.89	2.86	2.80	2.77	2.75
17	4.45	3.59	3.20	2.96	2.81	2.70	2.62	2.55	2.50	2.45	2.41	2.38	2.33	2.29	2.23	2.19	2.15	2.11	2.08	2.04	2.02	1.99	1.97	1.96
	8.40	6.11	5.18	4.67	4.34	4.10	3.93	3.79	3.68	3.59	3.52	3.45	3.35	3.27	3.16	3.08	3.00	2.92	2.86	2.79	2.76	2.70	2.67	2.65
18	4.41	3.55	3.16	2.93	2.77	2.66	2.58	2.51	2.46	2.41	2.37	2.34	2.29	2.25	2.19	2.15	2.11	2.07	2.04	2.00	1.98	1.95	1.93	1.92
	8.28	6.01	5.09	4.58	4.25	4.01	3.85	3.71	3.60	3.51	3.44	3.37	3.27	3.19	3.07	3.00	2.91	2.83	2.78	2.71	2.68	2.62	2.59	2.57

Degrees of Freedom in Numerator

Degrees of Freedom in Denominator	1	2	3	4	5	6	7	8	9	10	11	12	14	16	20	24	30	40	50	75	100	200	500	∞
19	4.38 / 8.18	3.52 / 5.93	3.13 / 5.01	2.90 / 4.50	2.74 / 4.17	2.63 / 3.94	2.55 / 3.77	2.48 / 3.63	2.43 / 3.52	2.38 / 3.43	2.34 / 3.36	2.31 / 3.30	2.26 / 3.19	2.21 / 3.12	2.15 / 3.00	2.11 / 2.92	2.07 / 2.84	2.02 / 2.76	2.00 / 2.70	1.96 / 2.63	1.94 / 2.60	1.91 / 2.54	1.90 / 2.51	1.88 / 2.49
20	4.35 / 8.10	3.49 / 5.85	3.10 / 4.94	2.87 / 4.43	2.71 / 4.10	2.60 / 3.87	2.52 / 3.71	2.45 / 3.56	2.40 / 3.45	2.35 / 3.37	2.31 / 3.30	2.28 / 3.23	2.23 / 3.13	2.18 / 3.05	2.12 / 2.94	2.08 / 2.86	2.04 / 2.77	1.99 / 2.69	1.96 / 2.63	1.92 / 2.56	1.90 / 2.53	1.87 / 2.47	1.85 / 2.44	1.84 / 2.42
21	4.32 / 8.02	3.47 / 5.78	3.07 / 4.87	2.84 / 4.37	2.68 / 4.04	2.57 / 3.81	2.49 / 3.65	2.42 / 3.51	2.37 / 3.40	2.32 / 3.31	2.28 / 3.24	2.25 / 3.17	2.20 / 3.07	2.15 / 2.99	2.09 / 2.88	2.05 / 2.80	2.00 / 2.72	1.96 / 2.63	1.93 / 2.58	1.89 / 2.51	1.87 / 2.47	1.84 / 2.42	1.82 / 2.38	1.81 / 2.36
22	4.30 / 7.94	3.44 / 5.72	3.05 / 4.82	2.82 / 4.31	2.66 / 3.99	2.55 / 3.76	2.47 / 3.59	2.40 / 3.45	2.35 / 3.35	2.30 / 3.26	2.26 / 3.18	2.23 / 3.12	2.18 / 3.02	2.13 / 2.94	2.07 / 2.83	2.03 / 2.75	1.98 / 2.67	1.93 / 2.58	1.91 / 2.53	1.87 / 2.46	1.84 / 2.42	1.81 / 2.37	1.80 / 2.33	1.78 / 2.31
23	4.28 / 7.88	3.42 / 5.66	3.03 / 4.76	2.80 / 4.26	2.64 / 3.94	2.53 / 3.71	2.45 / 3.54	2.38 / 3.41	2.32 / 3.30	2.28 / 3.21	2.24 / 3.14	2.20 / 3.07	2.14 / 2.97	2.10 / 2.89	2.04 / 2.78	2.00 / 2.70	1.96 / 2.62	1.91 / 2.53	1.88 / 2.48	1.84 / 2.41	1.82 / 2.37	1.79 / 2.32	1.77 / 2.28	1.76 / 2.26
24	4.26 / 7.82	3.40 / 5.61	3.01 / 4.72	2.78 / 4.22	2.62 / 3.90	2.51 / 3.67	2.43 / 3.50	2.36 / 3.36	2.30 / 3.25	2.26 / 3.17	2.22 / 3.09	2.18 / 3.03	2.13 / 2.93	2.09 / 2.85	2.02 / 2.74	1.98 / 2.66	1.94 / 2.58	1.89 / 2.49	1.86 / 2.44	1.82 / 2.36	1.80 / 2.33	1.76 / 2.27	1.74 / 2.23	1.73 / 2.21
25	4.24 / 7.77	3.38 / 5.57	2.99 / 4.68	2.76 / 4.18	2.60 / 3.86	2.49 / 3.63	2.41 / 3.46	2.34 / 3.32	2.28 / 3.21	2.24 / 3.13	2.20 / 3.05	2.16 / 2.99	2.11 / 2.89	2.06 / 2.81	2.00 / 2.70	1.96 / 2.62	1.92 / 2.54	1.87 / 2.45	1.84 / 2.40	1.80 / 2.32	1.77 / 2.29	1.74 / 2.23	1.72 / 2.19	1.71 / 2.17
26	4.22 / 7.72	3.37 / 5.53	2.98 / 4.64	2.74 / 4.14	2.59 / 3.82	2.47 / 3.59	2.39 / 3.42	2.32 / 3.29	2.27 / 3.17	2.22 / 3.09	2.18 / 3.02	2.15 / 2.96	2.10 / 2.86	2.05 / 2.77	1.99 / 2.66	1.95 / 2.58	1.90 / 2.50	1.85 / 2.41	1.82 / 2.36	1.78 / 2.28	1.76 / 2.25	1.72 / 2.19	1.70 / 2.15	1.69 / 2.13
27	4.21 / 7.68	3.35 / 5.49	2.96 / 4.60	2.73 / 4.11	2.57 / 3.79	2.46 / 3.56	2.37 / 3.39	2.30 / 3.26	2.25 / 3.14	2.20 / 3.06	2.16 / 2.98	2.13 / 2.93	2.08 / 2.83	2.03 / 2.74	1.97 / 2.63	1.93 / 2.55	1.88 / 2.47	1.84 / 2.38	1.80 / 2.33	1.76 / 2.25	1.74 / 2.21	1.71 / 2.16	1.68 / 2.12	1.67 / 2.10
28	4.20 / 7.64	3.34 / 5.45	2.95 / 4.57	2.71 / 4.07	2.56 / 3.76	2.44 / 3.53	2.36 / 3.36	2.29 / 3.23	2.24 / 3.11	2.19 / 3.03	2.15 / 2.95	2.12 / 2.90	2.06 / 2.80	2.02 / 2.71	1.96 / 2.60	1.91 / 2.52	1.87 / 2.44	1.81 / 2.35	1.78 / 2.30	1.75 / 2.22	1.72 / 2.18	1.69 / 2.13	1.67 / 2.09	1.65 / 2.06
29	4.18 / 7.60	3.33 / 5.42	2.93 / 4.54	2.70 / 4.04	2.54 / 3.73	2.43 / 3.50	2.35 / 3.33	2.28 / 3.20	2.22 / 3.08	2.18 / 3.00	2.14 / 2.92	2.10 / 2.87	2.05 / 2.77	2.00 / 2.68	1.94 / 2.57	1.90 / 2.49	1.85 / 2.41	1.80 / 2.32	1.77 / 2.27	1.73 / 2.19	1.71 / 2.15	1.68 / 2.10	1.65 / 2.06	1.64 / 2.03

30	4.17	3.32	2.92	2.69	2.53	2.42	2.34	2.27	2.21	2.16	2.12	2.09	2.04	1.99	1.93	1.89	1.84	1.79	1.76	1.72	1.69	1.66	1.64	1.62
	7.56	5.39	4.51	4.02	3.70	3.47	3.30	3.17	3.06	2.98	2.90	2.84	2.74	2.66	2.55	2.47	2.38	2.29	2.24	2.16	2.13	2.07	2.03	2.01
32	4.15	3.30	2.90	2.67	2.51	2.40	2.32	2.25	2.19	2.14	2.10	2.07	2.02	1.97	1.91	1.86	1.82	1.76	1.74	1.69	1.67	1.64	1.61	1.59
	7.50	5.34	4.46	3.97	3.66	3.42	3.25	3.12	3.01	2.94	2.86	2.80	2.70	2.62	2.51	2.42	2.34	2.25	2.20	2.12	2.08	2.02	1.98	1.96
34	4.13	3.28	2.88	2.65	2.49	2.38	2.30	2.23	2.17	2.12	2.08	2.05	2.00	1.95	1.89	1.84	1.80	1.74	1.71	1.67	1.64	1.61	1.59	1.57
	7.44	5.29	4.42	3.93	3.61	3.38	3.21	3.08	2.97	2.89	2.82	2.76	2.66	2.58	2.47	2.38	2.30	2.21	2.15	2.08	2.04	1.98	1.94	1.91
36	4.11	3.26	2.86	2.63	2.48	2.36	2.28	2.21	2.15	2.10	2.06	2.03	1.98	1.93	1.87	1.82	1.78	1.72	1.69	1.65	1.62	1.59	1.56	1.55
	7.39	5.25	4.38	3.89	3.58	3.35	3.18	3.04	2.94	2.86	2.78	2.72	2.62	2.54	2.43	2.35	2.26	2.17	2.12	2.04	2.00	1.94	1.90	1.87
38	4.10	3.25	2.85	2.62	2.46	2.35	2.26	2.19	2.14	2.09	2.05	2.02	1.96	1.92	1.85	1.80	1.76	1.71	1.67	1.63	1.60	1.57	1.54	1.53
	7.35	5.21	4.34	3.86	3.54	3.32	3.15	3.02	2.91	2.82	2.75	2.69	2.59	2.51	2.40	2.32	2.22	2.14	2.08	2.00	1.97	1.90	1.86	1.84
40	4.08	3.23	2.84	2.61	2.45	2.34	2.25	2.18	2.12	2.07	2.04	2.00	1.95	1.90	1.84	1.79	1.74	1.69	1.66	1.61	1.59	1.55	1.53	1.51
	7.31	5.18	4.31	3.83	3.51	3.29	3.12	2.99	2.88	2.80	2.73	2.66	2.56	2.49	2.37	2.29	2.20	2.11	2.05	1.97	1.94	1.88	1.84	1.81
42	4.07	3.22	2.83	2.59	2.44	2.32	2.24	2.17	2.11	2.06	2.02	1.99	1.94	1.89	1.82	1.78	1.73	1.68	1.64	1.60	1.57	1.54	1.51	1.49
	7.27	5.15	4.29	3.80	3.49	3.26	3.10	2.96	2.86	2.77	2.70	2.64	2.54	2.46	2.35	2.26	2.17	2.08	2.02	1.94	1.91	1.85	1.80	1.78
44	4.06	3.21	2.82	2.58	2.43	2.31	2.23	2.16	2.10	2.05	2.01	1.98	1.92	1.88	1.81	1.76	1.72	1.66	1.63	1.58	1.56	1.52	1.50	1.48
	7.24	5.12	4.26	3.78	3.46	3.24	3.07	2.94	2.84	2.75	2.68	2.62	2.52	2.44	2.32	2.24	2.15	2.06	2.00	1.92	1.88	1.82	1.78	1.75
46	4.05	3.20	2.81	2.57	2.42	2.30	2.22	2.14	2.09	2.04	2.00	1.97	1.91	1.87	1.80	1.75	1.71	1.65	1.62	1.57	1.54	1.51	1.48	1.46
	7.21	5.10	4.24	3.76	3.44	3.22	3.05	2.92	2.82	2.73	2.66	2.60	2.50	2.42	2.30	2.22	2.13	2.04	1.98	1.90	1.86	1.80	1.76	1.72
48	4.04	3.19	2.80	2.56	2.41	2.30	2.21	2.14	2.08	2.03	1.99	1.96	1.90	1.86	1.79	1.74	1.70	1.64	1.61	1.56	1.53	1.50	1.47	1.45
	7.19	5.08	4.22	3.74	3.42	3.20	3.04	2.90	2.80	2.71	2.64	2.58	2.48	2.40	2.28	2.20	2.11	2.02	1.96	1.88	1.84	1.78	1.73	1.70
50	4.03	3.18	2.79	2.56	2.40	2.29	2.20	2.13	2.07	2.02	1.98	1.95	1.90	1.85	1.78	1.74	1.69	1.63	1.60	1.55	1.52	1.48	1.46	1.44
	7.17	5.06	4.20	3.72	3.41	3.18	3.02	2.88	2.78	2.70	2.62	2.56	2.46	2.39	2.26	2.18	2.10	2.00	1.94	1.86	1.82	1.76	1.71	1.68
55	4.02	3.17	2.78	2.54	2.38	2.27	2.18	2.11	2.05	2.00	1.97	1.93	1.88	1.83	1.76	1.72	1.67	1.61	1.58	1.52	1.50	1.46	1.43	1.41
	7.12	5.01	4.16	3.68	3.37	3.15	2.98	2.85	2.75	2.66	2.59	2.53	2.43	2.35	2.23	2.15	2.06	1.96	1.90	1.82	1.78	1.71	1.66	1.64
60	4.00	3.15	2.76	2.52	2.37	2.25	2.17	2.10	2.04	1.99	1.95	1.92	1.86	1.81	1.75	1.70	1.65	1.59	1.56	1.50	1.48	1.44	1.41	1.39
	7.08	4.98	4.13	3.65	3.34	3.12	2.95	2.82	2.72	2.63	2.56	2.50	2.40	2.32	2.20	2.12	2.03	1.93	1.87	1.79	1.74	1.68	1.63	1.60

Appendix G (continued)

Degrees of Freedom in Numerator

Degrees of Freedom in Denominator	1	2	3	4	5	6	7	8	9	10	11	12	14	16	20	24	30	40	50	75	100	200	500	∞
65	3.99	3.14	2.75	2.51	2.36	2.24	2.15	2.08	2.02	1.98	1.94	1.90	1.85	1.80	1.73	1.68	1.63	1.57	1.54	1.49	1.46	1.42	1.39	1.37
	7.04	4.95	4.10	3.62	3.31	3.09	2.93	2.79	2.70	2.61	2.54	2.47	2.37	2.30	2.18	2.09	2.00	1.90	1.84	1.76	1.71	1.64	1.60	1.56
70	3.98	3.13	2.74	2.50	2.35	2.23	2.14	2.07	2.01	1.97	1.93	1.89	1.84	1.79	1.72	1.67	1.62	1.56	1.53	1.47	1.45	1.40	1.37	1.35
	7.01	4.92	4.08	3.60	3.29	3.07	2.91	2.77	2.67	2.59	2.51	2.45	2.35	2.28	2.15	2.07	1.98	1.88	1.82	1.74	1.69	1.62	1.56	1.53
80	3.96	3.11	2.72	2.48	2.33	2.21	2.12	2.05	1.99	1.95	1.91	1.88	1.82	1.77	1.70	1.65	1.60	1.54	1.51	1.45	1.42	1.38	1.35	1.32
	6.96	4.88	4.04	3.56	3.25	3.04	2.87	2.74	2.64	2.55	2.48	2.41	2.32	2.24	2.11	2.03	1.94	1.84	1.78	1.70	1.65	1.57	1.52	1.49
100	3.94	3.09	2.70	2.46	2.30	2.19	2.10	2.03	1.97	1.92	1.88	1.85	1.79	1.75	1.68	1.63	1.57	1.51	1.48	1.42	1.39	1.34	1.30	1.28
	6.90	4.82	3.98	3.51	3.20	2.99	2.82	2.69	2.59	2.51	2.43	2.36	2.26	2.19	2.06	1.98	1.89	1.79	1.73	1.64	1.59	1.51	1.46	1.43
125	3.92	3.07	2.68	2.44	2.29	2.17	2.08	2.01	1.95	1.90	1.86	1.83	1.77	1.72	1.65	1.60	1.55	1.49	1.45	1.39	1.36	1.31	1.27	1.25
	6.84	4.78	3.94	3.47	3.17	2.95	2.79	2.65	2.56	2.47	2.40	2.33	2.23	2.15	2.03	1.94	1.85	1.75	1.68	1.59	1.54	1.46	1.40	1.37
150	3.91	3.06	2.67	2.43	2.27	2.16	2.07	2.00	1.94	1.89	1.85	1.82	1.76	1.71	1.64	1.59	1.54	1.47	1.44	1.37	1.34	1.29	1.25	1.22
	6.81	4.75	3.91	3.44	3.14	2.92	2.76	2.62	2.53	2.44	2.37	2.30	2.20	2.12	2.00	1.91	1.83	1.72	1.66	1.56	1.51	1.43	1.37	1.33
200	3.89	3.04	2.65	2.41	2.26	2.14	2.05	1.98	1.92	1.87	1.83	1.80	1.74	1.69	1.62	1.57	1.52	1.45	1.42	1.35	1.32	1.26	1.22	1.19
	6.76	4.71	3.88	3.41	3.11	2.90	2.73	2.60	2.50	2.41	2.34	2.28	2.17	2.09	1.97	1.88	1.79	1.69	1.62	1.53	1.48	1.39	1.33	1.28
400	3.86	3.02	2.62	2.39	2.23	2.12	2.03	1.96	1.90	1.85	1.81	1.78	1.72	1.67	1.60	1.54	1.49	1.42	1.38	1.32	1.28	1.22	1.16	1.13
	6.70	4.66	3.83	3.36	3.06	2.85	2.69	2.55	2.46	2.37	2.29	2.23	2.12	2.04	1.92	1.84	1.74	1.64	1.57	1.47	1.42	1.32	1.24	1.19
1000	3.85	3.00	2.61	2.38	2.22	2.10	2.02	1.95	1.89	1.84	1.80	1.76	1.70	1.65	1.58	1.53	1.47	1.41	1.36	1.30	1.26	1.19	1.13	1.08
	6.66	4.62	3.80	3.34	3.04	2.82	2.66	2.53	2.43	2.34	2.26	2.20	2.09	2.01	1.89	1.81	1.71	1.61	1.54	1.44	1.38	1.28	1.19	1.11
∞	3.84	2.99	2.60	2.37	2.21	2.09	2.01	1.94	1.88	1.83	1.79	1.75	1.69	1.64	1.57	1.52	1.46	1.40	1.35	1.28	1.24	1.17	1.11	1.00
	6.64	4.60	3.78	3.32	3.02	2.80	2.64	2.51	2.41	2.32	2.24	2.18	2.07	1.99	1.87	1.79	1.69	1.59	1.52	1.41	1.36	1.25	1.15	1.00

From George W. Snedecor and William G. Cochran, *Statistical Methods*, 7th ed. © 1980 by the Iowa State University Press, 2121 South State Avenue, Ames, Iowa 50010.

Distribution of χ^2

df	.99	.98	.95	.90	.80	.70	.50	.30	.20	.10	.05	.02	.01	.001
							Probability							
1	$.0^3157$	$.0^3628$	.00393	.0158	.0642	.148	.455	1.074	1.642	2.706	3.841	5.412	6.635	10.827
2	.0201	.0404	.103	.211	.446	.713	1.386	2.408	3.219	4.605	5.991	7.824	9.210	13.815
3	.115	.185	.352	.584	1.005	1.424	2.366	3.665	4.642	6.251	7.815	9.837	11.341	16.268
4	.297	.429	.711	1.064	1.649	2.195	3.357	4.878	5.989	7.779	9.488	11.668	13.277	18.465
5	.554	.752	1.145	1.610	2.343	3.000	4.351	6.064	7.289	9.236	11.070	13.388	15.086	20.617
6	.872	1.134	1.635	2.204	3.070	3.828	5.348	7.231	8.558	10.645	12.592	15.033	16.812	22.457
7	1.239	1.564	2.167	2.833	3.822	4.671	6.346	8.383	9.803	12.017	14.067	16.622	18.475	24.322
8	1.646	2.032	2.733	3.490	4.594	5.527	7.344	9.524	11.030	13.362	15.507	18.168	20.090	26.125
9	2.088	2.532	3.325	4.168	5.380	6.393	8.343	10.656	12.242	14.684	16.919	19.679	21.666	27.877
10	2.558	3.059	3.940	4.865	6.179	7.267	9.342	11.781	13.442	15.987	18.307	21.161	23.209	29.588
11	3.053	3.609	4.575	5.578	6.989	8.148	10.341	12.899	14.631	17.275	19.675	22.618	24.725	31.264
12	3.571	4.178	5.226	6.304	7.807	9.034	11.340	14.011	15.812	18.549	21.026	24.054	26.217	32.909
13	4.107	4.765	5.892	7.042	8.634	9.926	12.340	15.119	16.985	19.812	22.362	25.472	27.688	34.528
14	4.660	5.368	6.571	7.790	9.467	10.821	13.339	16.222	18.151	21.064	23.685	26.873	29.141	36.123
15	5.229	5.985	7.261	8.547	10.307	11.721	14.339	17.322	19.311	22.307	24.996	28.259	30.578	37.697
16	5.812	6.614	7.962	9.312	11.152	12.624	15.338	18.418	20.465	23.542	26.296	29.633	32.000	39.252

Appendix H (*continued*)

df	.99	.98	.95	.90	.80	.70	.50	.30	.20	.10	.05	.02	.01	.001
17	6.408	7.255	8.672	10.085	12.002	13.531	16.338	19.511	21.615	24.769	27.587	30.995	33.409	40.790
18	7.015	7.906	9.390	10.865	12.857	14.440	17.338	20.601	22.760	25.989	28.869	32.346	34.805	42.312
19	7.633	8.567	10.117	11.651	13.716	15.352	18.338	21.689	23.900	27.204	30.144	33.687	36.191	43.820
20	8.260	9.237	10.851	12.443	14.578	16.266	19.337	22.775	25.038	28.412	31.410	35.020	37.566	45.315
21	8.897	9.915	11.591	13.240	15.445	17.182	20.337	23.858	26.171	29.615	32.671	36.343	38.932	46.797
22	9.542	10.600	12.338	14.041	16.314	18.101	21.337	24.939	27.301	30.813	33.924	37.659	40.289	48.268
23	10.196	11.293	13.091	14.848	17.187	19.021	22.337	26.018	28.429	32.007	35.172	38.968	41.638	49.728
24	10.856	11.992	13.848	15.659	18.062	19.943	23.337	27.096	29.553	33.196	36.415	40.270	42.980	51.179
25	11.524	12.697	14.611	16.473	18.940	20.867	24.337	28.172	30.675	34.382	37.652	41.566	44.314	52.620
26	12.198	13.409	15.379	17.292	19.820	21.792	25.336	29.246	31.795	35.563	38.885	42.856	45.642	54.052
27	12.879	14.125	16.151	18.114	20.703	22.719	26.336	30.319	32.912	36.741	40.113	44.140	46.963	55.476
28	13.565	14.847	16.928	18.939	21.588	23.647	27.336	31.391	34.027	37.916	41.337	45.419	48.278	56.893
29	14.256	15.574	17.708	19.768	22.475	24.577	28.336	32.461	35.139	39.087	42.557	46.693	49.588	58.302
30	14.953	16.306	18.493	20.599	23.364	25.508	29.336	33.530	36.250	40.256	43.773	47.962	50.892	59.703

For larger values of df, the expression $\sqrt{2x^2} - \sqrt{2df} - 1$ may be used as a normal deviate with unit variance, remembering that the probability for χ^2 corresponds to that of a single tail of the normal curve.

Reprinted from R. A. Fisher and F. Yates, *Statistical Tables for Biological, Agricultural and Medical Research*, 6th ed. (London: Longman, 1974), tab. IV. Used by permission of the authors and Longman Group Ltd.

GLOSSARY

Glossary terms are cross-referenced to text discussions, indicated by the boldface text page number following each term.

accretion measures   Unobtrusive measures that use the physical evidence left by a group in the course of its activities **(288)**

actuarial records   Public records containing information on the demographic characteristics of the population served by the recordkeeping agency **(290)**

ad-hoc classificatory system   Arbitrary categories constructed to organize and summarize empirical observations; the lowest level of theory **(34)**

analysis of expressive movement   The observation of the self-expressive features of the body and how these movements indicate social interactions **(289)**

analytic induction   A theoretical approach to field research where a researcher begins with a tentative hypothesis explaining the phenomenon observed and then attempts to verify the hypothesis by observing a small number of cases. If the hypothesis does not fit these cases, it is either rejected or reformulated so that the cases account for it **(268)**

anonymity   Protection of research participants' identities, carried out by separating indicators of their identities from the information they have provided **(78)**

archival records   These include both public records—actuarial records, electoral and judicial records, government documents, and the mass media—and private records—autobiographies, diaries and letters—and provide important opportunities for unobtrusive data collection **(290)**

arithmetic mean   The sum total of all observations divided by their number **(331)**

assumptions of science   The fundamental premises, unproven and unprovable; the prerequisites for conducting a scientific discourse **(5)**

attitude   All of a person's inclinations, prejudices, ideas, fears, and convictions about any specific topic **(231)**

attitude index   A measure that comprises a series of questions, selected a priori, whose cumulative score indicates the respondent's attitudes **(421)**

authenticity   The genuineness of private records **(293)**

axiomatic theory   A theoretical system containing (a) a set of concepts and operational definitions, (b) a set of statements describing the situation in which the theory applies, (c) a set of relational statements (axioms and theorems), and (d) a system of logic relating all the concepts within the statements, used to deduce theorems **(37)**

bar chart   A graphic device used for displaying nominal or ordinal data. Researchers construct bar charts by labeling the categories of the variable along the horizontal axis and drawing rectangles of equal width for each category. The rectangles are separated by spaces, and the height of each rectangle is proportional to the frequency percentage of the category **(327)**

census block   The smallest geographic area for which census data is collected **(282)**

Census Designated Places (CDP)   Densely populated areas lacking legally defined corporate limits or powers **(282)**

census tract   A small, locally defined statistical area found in metropolitan areas and counties, having an average of population of 4,000 **(282)**

chi-square test (χ^2)   A test statistic that allows one to decide whether observed frequencies are essentially equal to or significantly different from frequencies predicted by a theoretical model. The outcome of the test allows decisions as to whether or not frequencies are distributed equally among categories, whether or not a distribution is normal, or whether or not two variables are independent **(450)**

classic experimental design   An experimental design format, usually associated with research in the biological and social sciences, that consists of two comparable groups: an experimental group and a control group. These two groups are equivalent except that the experimental group is exposed to the independent variable and the control group is not **(90)**

closed-ended question   A question that offers respondents a set of answers from which they are asked to choose the one that most closely reflects their views **(233)**

cluster sample   A type of probability sample that involves (1) selecting groupings (clusters) of units and then (2) selecting sampling units from those clusters; frequently used in large-scale studies because it is the least expensive sampling design **(173)**

code   The number assigned to an observation. A code should be consistent across cases or units of analysis when the same condition exists **(304)**

codes of ethics   The guides to ethical research practices developed by major professional societies, meant to respond to the problems and issues encountered while carrying out research in specific professional spheres **(80)**

codebook   A book compiled by the researcher identifying a specific item of observation and the code number assigned to describe each category included in that item **(309)**

coding   Assigning codes in the form of numerals (or other symbols) for each category of each variable in a study **(305)**

coding reliability   The extent of agreement between different coders when classifying their individual responses according to the coding scheme **(311)**

coding scheme   A system of categories used to classify responses or behaviors that relate to a single item or variable **(305)**

coefficient of multiple correlation   The correlation between a number of independent variables with a dependent variable **(400)**

coefficient of reproducibility (CR)   A measure that indicates how precisely a score on a Guttman scale can be used to reproduce the total response pattern on the items that compose the scale **(426)**

coefficient of variation   A measure of variation based on the standard deviation and the mean and reflects relative variation. It is defined as the ratio of the standard deviation to the mean of the distribution **(341)**

combined designs   The merging of two or more research designs into a single study to increase the inferential powers of that study **(129)**

comparison   The operational process required to demonstrate that two variables are correlated **(94)**

competence   The assumption that the decision to participate in research is made by a responsible, mature individual who has been given the relevant information **(73)**

complete count census   The census of population and housing, taken every ten years, that attempts to reach every household in the country; it includes only basic demographic information on each member of the household plus a few questions about the housing unit **(281)**

complete participant   A role taken by the observer where the observer is wholly concealed; the research objectives are unknown to the observed, and the researcher attempts to become a member of the group under observation **(258)**

comprehension   An important element of informed consent, it refers to the research participant's understanding of the nature of the research and the risks involved **(76)**

computer-assisted telephone interviewing (CATI)   Type of telephone survey where the interviewer sits at a computer terminal and, as a question flashes on the screen, asks it over the telephone. Respondents' answers are typed and coded directly on a disk, and the next question comes up on the screen **(223)**

concept   An abstraction representing an object, a property of an object, or a phenomenon that scientists use to describe the empirical world **(24)**

conceptual definition A definition of one concept that uses other concepts—primitive and derived terms—as their building blocks **(26)**

conceptual framework The third level of theory, that is, a broad systematic structure of explicit propositions that define the relationships between the empirical properties of the phenomena belonging to the descriptive categories employed **(35)**

conditional variable A contingency necessary for the occurrence of the relationship between the independent and dependent variable **(395)**

confidence interval A range, measured in units of standard error (*z*-scores) or percentages (confidence levels), that identifies the probability with which the value of a sample mean is identical to the value of the mean of the population parameter **(179)**

confidentiality Protection of sensitive information provided by research participants **(71)**

congruence The agreement between the conceptual and operational definitions of a phenomenon **(30)**

construct validity The state where a measuring instrument reflects the concepts and theoretical assumptions of a general theoretical framework **(152)**

constructive criticism In scientific methodology, the questioning of claims of knowledge by investigating the logic of the explanation, the accuracy of the observations, the validity of the testing procedure, and so on **(13)**

content analysis The systematic analysis of the messages transmitted in written or spoken form, used to make inferences about the data **(296)**

content validity The concept that the measurement instrument covers all the attributes of the concept you are trying to measure: nothing relevant to the phenomenon under investigation is left out **(149)**

context of discovery Activities that lead to making scientific discoveries; at this initial stage of exploration, no formalized rules or logic need be followed **(17)**

context of justification Activities that help scientists verify, logically and empirically, any claim for knowledge **(17)**

context unit The largest body of content (or text) that must be examined when characterizing a recording unit **(298)**

contingency question A question that applies only to a subgroup of respondents because it is relevant only to certain people **(235)**

continuous variable A variable that does not have a minimum-size unit although specific units can be accurately measured **(52)**

contrasted groups Comparison of groups that are known to differ in some important attributes **(119)**

control A procedure designed to eliminate alternative sources of variation that may distort the research results. Methods of control include holding variables constant under experimental conditions or during statistical analysis **(95)**

control group The group in an experimental research design that is not exposed to the independent variable **(90)**

control-series design A quasi-experimental design that attempts to control the aspects of history, maturation, and test-retest effects shared by the experimental and comparison groups **(128)**

control variable A variable used to test whether the observed relations between the independent and dependent variables are real or spurious **(50, 388)**

controlled observation A method characterized by clear, explicit, and systematic decisions as to what, how, and when to observe behavior **(196)**

correlation coefficient A measure of linear association between two interval variables. Pearson's product-moment correlation coefficient (*r*) estimates the direction and magnitude of the association **(361)**

correlational design The most predominant research design employed in the social sciences, most often identified with survey research, where data are used to examine relationships between properties and dispositions, establish causal relations between these properties and dispositions, or to simply describe the pattern of relation before any attempt at causal inference is made **(116)**

covariation Occurs when two or more variables consistently vary together, either positively or negatively **(53, 93)**

cover letter The letter that accompanies a mail questionnaire **(243)**

criterion of least squares The criterion that minimizes the sum of the squared vertical distances between the regression line and actual observations **(377)**

cross-sectional design A research design most predominant in survey research and used to examine relations between properties and dispositions. A cross-sectional design can approximate the posttest-only control group design by using statistical data analysis techniques **(116)**

cross-tabulation A table showing the relationship between two or more variables by presenting all combinations of categories of variables **(387)**

data cleaning A process that precedes analysis of collected information whereby data is proofread to catch and correct errors and inconsistent codes. Most data cleaning is performed by special computer programs that are designed to test for logical consistency set up in the coding specifications **(314)**

data editing Process performed by coders both during and after the data coding phase of data processing that involves checking for errors and omissions and making sure that all interview schedules have been completed as required **(314)**

deception In social science research, participants' rights to self-determination and dignity need to be balanced against the sometimes necessary use of deception, which is utilized to elicit scientifically valid results. This conflict is the essence of the ethical dilemma in social science research **(71)**

deductive coding Requires that data be recorded to some preconceived scheme that is constructed before the measurement instrument is administered **(307)**

deductive explanation The most powerful form of reasoning, in which all cases of a phenomenon are logically deduced (derived) from a (set of) universal generalization(s) **(8)**

degrees of freedom (df) A characteristic of the sample statistics that determines the appropriate sampling distribution **(447)**

demand characteristics Responses to an experimental manipulation that reflect what the research participants think is expected of them rather than their true responses. This situation introduces bias into the experimental results **(198)**

dependent variable The variable that the researcher is trying to explain **(49)**

derived term A term, used in conceptual definitions, that can be defined by other terms **(27)**

descriptive statistics Statistical procedures used for describing and analyzing data that enable the researcher to summarize and organize data in an effective and meaningful way. These procedures provide tools for describing collections of statistical observations and reducing information to an understandable form **(321)**

detail The rule of detail in a coding scheme lets one add categories as necessary, with the knowledge that categories can always be collapsed to generalize responses; in addition, the rule of detail dictates that one uses commonsense categories appropriate to the research question **(307)**

difference-between-means test A test used to assess the significance of a difference between means to reflect the amount of relationship between two variables **(444)**

discrete variable A variable having a minimum-size unit; hence, it can be measured and mathematically manipulated with the greatest degree of precision **(52)**

discriminative power (*DP*) A measure of the ability of scale items to consistently distinguish between the highest and lowest values of responses concerning an attitude **(424)**

double-barreled question   A question combining two or more questions, thus confusing respondents who might agree with one aspect of the question but disagree with the other **(242)**

ecological fallacy   Inferences about individuals inappropriately drawn from data gathered about groups, societies, or nations **(48)**

elaboration   A method of introducing other variables to the analysis in order to determine the links between the independent and dependent variables **(394)**

empirical knowledge (empiricism)   Knowledge that relies only on experience, perceptions, and behavior; empiricism represents the fundamental tenet of the scientific approach **(6)**

empirical validity   If a measuring instrument is valid, scientists assume that the results produced by applying the instrument should be quite similar to the relationships existing among the variables measured in the real world **(150)**

epistemology   The study of the foundations of knowledge **(5)**

erosion measures   Unobtrusive measures employed to examine the physical signs left after an object's use **(288)**

error of prediction   The deviation of the actual observations from the ones predicted by the regression line **(377)**

ethical dilemma   The conflict that arises when deciding whether the possible contribution of the research warrants the denial of a participant's rights during the conduct of the research **(72)**

exhaustiveness   The rule of exhaustiveness dictates that the enumeration of categories is sufficient to exhaust all the relevant categories expected of respondents **(306)**

experimental group   The group exposed to the independent variable in an experimental research design **(90)**

experimental mortality   Refers to the dropout problems that prevent the researcher from obtaining complete information on all cases. When individuals drop out selectively from the experimental or control group, the final sample on which complete information is available may be biased **(96)**

experimental realism   The extent to which an experimental situation is experienced as real by the research participants **(198)**

experimenter bias   The bias introduced when a research participant's response reflects the experimenter's expectations, which have been unintentionally communicated **(199)**

explanation (scientific explanation)   A systematic and empirical analysis of the antecedent factors that caused the event or behavior **(7)**

explanatory variable   The variable the researcher assumes is the cause of the observed changes in the values of the dependent variable; also called the "independent variable" **(49)**

extended time-series design   A research design that presents the data as part of a broadened time series and therefore controls for maturation **(125)**

external validity   The extent to which the research findings can be generalized to larger populations and applied to different settings **(101)**

extralinguistic behavior   The noncontent aspects of behavior, such as the rate of speaking, the tendency to interrupt, and the physical proximity maintained between people; often referred to as paralanguage or body language **(193)**

extrinsic factors   Biases resulting from the differential recruitment of research participants to the experimental and control groups **(95)**

face validity   The investigators' subjective evaluation of the validity (appropriateness) of a measuring instrument **(150)**

factor analysis   A statistical technique for classifying a large number of interrelated variables into a limited number of dimensions or factors **(427)**

factor loading   The correlation coefficient calculated between the values of a variable and a factor **(429)**

factor score coefficients   The coefficients used to obtain factor scores **(430)**

factor scores   An item's score on a factor, obtained by multiplying the factor score coefficients for each item by the standardized variable values obtained for that item **(430)**

factorial design   A research design that allows one to examine simultaneously the effects of two or more independent variables on the dependent variable and also to detect interaction between the variables **(108)**

factual question   A question designed to elicit objective information from respondents regarding their background, environment, and habits **(231)**

fallacy of reification   The error of treating abstractions as if they were real rather than the products of thought **(25)**

field experimentation (research)   Research that takes place in a natural setting, in which the investigator can manipulate one or more independent variables under conditions that are as carefully controlled as the situation permits **(201, 257)**

filter question   In questionnaire design, the question that precedes a contingency question: the relevance of the contingency question is contingent on the response to the filter question **(235)**

focused interview   Type of personal interview (following an interview guide) that specifies topics related to the research hypothesis and gives considerable liberty to the respondents to express their views. The interview focuses on the subject's experiences regarding the situation under study **(215)**

follow-up   In mail questionnaires, a strategy used to secure an acceptable response rate (e.g., sending a series of reminder postcards and/or a replacement questionnaire) **(210)**

frequency distribution   The number of observations of each value of a variable **(321)**

funnel sequence   A technique of questionnaire construction in which the questionnaire begins with general queries and then "funnels down" to more specific items **(238)**

gamma (γ)   A coefficient of association indicating the magnitude and direction of the relationship between ordinal variables **(370)**

generalizability   The extent to which the research findings can be generalized to larger populations and applied to different settings **(157)**

grounded theory   In field research, the development of a theory that is closely and directly relevant to the particular setting under study whereby the researcher first develops conceptual categories from data and then makes new observations to clarify and elaborate these categories. Concepts and tentative hypotheses are then developed directly from data **(268)**

Guttman scale   A method designed to test empirically the unidimensional and cumulative character of the items used in an attitude scale **(425)**

histogram   A graphic device used to display frequency distributions of interval or ratio level data. The histogram looks like a bar chart with no spaces between the rectangles. The rectangles are constructed contiguously and their heights reflect the percent or frequency of the interval **(328)**

history   All events occurring during the time of the research study that might affect the individuals studied and provide a rival explanation for the change in the dependent variable **(96)**

hypothesis   A tentative answer to a research question or problem, expressed in the form of a relationship between independent and dependent variables **(56)**

independent variable   The explanatory variable, that is, the hypothesized or presumed cause of the changes in the values of the dependent variable **(49)**

index   A measuring instrument (composite measure) constructed by combining indicators of two or more variables **(415)**

indicator   A concept's empirical, observable referent **(142)**

indirect effect   When the effect of one variable on another is mediated through a third intervening variable **(407)**

individualist fallacy   Inferences about groups, societies, or nations inappropriately drawn from data gathered about individuals **(48)**

inductive coding   When the coding scheme is designed on the basis of a representative sample, responses, or other kinds of data, and is then applied to the remainder of the data **(307)**

inference   A claim for knowledge or a conclusion logically derived (inferred) from either prior assumptions or empirical evidence **(12)**

inferential statistics   Allows the researcher to make decisions or inferences about characteristics of a population based on observations from a sample taken from the population **(321)**

informant   In field research, participants who provide information to the researcher **(264)**

informed consent   The agreement of an individual to participate in a study after being fully informed about the study's procedures and possible risks **(72)**

instrumentation   A process that designates changes in the measuring instrument between the pretest and the posttest. To associate the difference between posttest and pretest scores with the independent variable, one must show that repeated measurements with the same measurement instrument under unchanged conditions will yield the same result **(97)**

interaction   A difference in the relationship between two variables within different categories of a control variable **(395)**

interaction process analysis (IPA)   A set of 12 categories, devised by Robert Bales, used to code linguistic interaction in groups **(193)**

internal validity   The requirement that the research be constructed so as to rule out the possibility that factors other than those being investigated are responsible for the changes in the dependent variable's values **(95)**

interpretive approach   An approach based on the belief that the phenomena studied by social scientists are different from those studied by natural scientists; this implies that the findings and explanatory principles of the social sciences may be more difficult to substantiate according to the strict criteria of scientific methodology **(11)**

interquartile range   The difference between the lower and upper quartiles (Q_1 and Q_3). It measures the spread in the middle half of the distribution and is less affected by extreme observations **(337)**

intersubjectivity   The ability of scientists to share knowledge, that is, to understand and evaluate the methods used by others; a necessary condition for replicating research **(14)**

interval level   The level of measurement at which the distances between observations are exact and can be precisely measured in constant units **(146)**

intervening variable   A variable mediating between an independent and a dependent variable **(394)**

intrinsic factors   Changes in units under study that occur during the study period, changes in the measuring instrument, and the reactive effect of the observation itself **(96)**

isomorphism   Similarity or identity in structure between the properties of a variable and the properties of the instrument used to measure it **(141)**

items   Variables that are used to construct indexes and scales **(414)**

Kendall's tau-*b*   A coefficient of association between ordinal variables incorporating ties **(373)**

known-groups technique   The administration of a measuring instrument to groups of subjects having known attributes, employed for the purpose of predicting the direction of the differences to be found among groups with respect to a specified variable **(153)**

lambda (Guttman coefficient of predictability)   A measure of association indicating the magnitude and direction of the relationship between nominal variables **(364)**

leading question   A question phrased in such a manner that the respondent believes that the researcher expects a certain answer **(241)**

level of measurement   The different ways of measuring a variable; the higher the level of measurement, the more precise the measurement and the greater the number of statistical manipulations that can be applied **(143)**

level of significance   The probability of rejecting a true null hypothesis; that is, the possibility of making a Type I error **(440)**

Likert scale   A scale designed to measure the strength of attitudes on the ordinal and internal level **(422)**

linear relation   A relation between two variables X and Y of the form $Y = a + bX$, where a and b are constant values; the graph of a linear relation is a straight line **(374)**

linguistic (language) behavior   The content and structural characteristics of speech **(192, 289)**

log   A record of the events, meetings, visits, and other activities undertaken by an individual over a given period of time **(294)**

logic   A system of reasoning comprising statements that are universally valid, certain, and independent of the empirical world **(13)**

logical empiricists   Researchers who take the position that objective knowledge can be attained when studying the social as well as the natural world by means of scientific methodology **(11)**

magnitude of a relation   The extent to which variables covary positively or negatively **(55)**

mail questionnaire   An impersonal survey method in which questionnaires are mailed to respondents, whose responses constitute the data on which research hypotheses are tested **(206)**

manipulation   A procedure that allows the researcher in experimental settings to have some form of control over the introduction of the independent variable. This procedure allows for the determination that the independent variable preceded the dependent variable **(95)**

matching   A method of control that involves equating the experimental and control groups on extrinsic variables that are presumed to relate to the research hypothesis **(96)**

matrix question   A method of organizing a large set of rating questions that have the same response categories **(237)**

maturation   Biological, psychological, or social processes that produce changes in the individuals or units studied with the passage of time. These changes could possibly influence the dependent variable and lead to erroneous inferences **(96)**

mean deviation   Computed by taking the differences between each observation and the mean, summing the absolute value of these deviations, and dividing the sum by the total number of observations **(339)**

measure of qualitative variation   An index of heterogeneity based on the ratio of the total number of differences in the distribution to the maximum number of possible differences within the same distribution **(335)**

measurement   The assignment of numerals—numbers or other symbols—to empirical properties according to a prescribed set of rules **(138)**

measurement artifacts   The biased results that occur when measurement procedures or instruments, such as cameras or test schedules, influence research participants' responses by providing hints about the true purpose of the experiment **(200)**

measurement errors   Differences in measurement scores that are due to some factor other than the real differences among the variables measured **(149)**

measures of central tendency   Statistical measures that reflect a typical or an average characteristic of a frequency distribution **(329)**

measures of dispersion   Statistical measures that reflect the degree of spread or variation in a distribution **(335)**

median   A measure of central tendency defined as the point above and below which 50 percent of the observations fall **(330)**

methodology   A system of explicit rules and procedures on which research is based and against which claims for knowledge are evaluated **(12)**

Metropolitan Statistical Area (MSA)   A geographic area containing one or more counties characterized by a large population nucleus that displays a high degree of interaction with its nearby communities **(282)**

mode   A measure of central tendency defined as the most frequently occurring observation category in the data **(329)**

model   A likeness of reality, consisting of symbols and/or concepts, that represents the characteristics of the phenomenon **(39)**

multiple regression   A statistical technique that allows us to assess the relationship between an interval variable and two or more interval, ordinal, or nominal variables **(400)**

mundane realism   The degree to which an experimental situation is experienced as real or likely to occur in the real world **(198)**

mutual exclusivity   Under the rule of mutual exclusivity, the coding categories for each variable must be designed so that each case or unit of analysis can be coded into one and only one category of the variable **(306)**

negative case   Actions and statements that refute a field researcher's hypothesis. Researchers compare positive and negative cases to determine whether the hypothesis can be modified to better fit all of the data or must be rejected entirely **(267)**

negative relation   An association between variables exhibiting the following property: as the value of one variable increases, the value of the other decreases, i.e., the values change in opposite directions **(54)**

nominal level   The level of measurement at which the properties of objects in any given category are identical and mutually exclusive for all its cases; represents the lowest level of measurement **(143)**

noncontrolled observation   A set of rather flexible observational methods, such as field research and participant observation, used in qualitative research **(196)**

nondirective interview   The least structured form of interviewing; no prespecified set of questions is employed, nor is an interview schedule used. The interviewer has a great deal of freedom to probe various areas and to raise specific queries during the course of the interview **(215)**

nonparametric test   A statistical test that requires either no assumptions or very few assumptions about the population distribution **(444)**

nonprobability sample   A sampling method in which there is no way of specifying the probability of a unit's inclusion in the sample **(167)**

nonresponse error   The most pervasive error in survey research, it occurs when the selected sampling units refuse to respond or are absent or their responses are lost **(182)**

nonverbal behavior   Bodily movements, such as facial expressions, that convey a wide range of emotions; they can be used as valid indicators of social, political, and psychological processes **(191)**

normal curve   A theoretical distribution of great significance in the field of statistics. Some of its major properties are (1) it is symmetrical and bell-shaped; (2) the mode, the median, and the mean coincide at the center of the distribution; (3) the curve is based on an infinite number of observations; (4) a single mathematical formula describes how frequencies are related to the values of the variable; and (5) in any normal distribution, a fixed proportion of the observations lie between the mean and fixed units of standard deviations **(344)**

normal distribution   A type of symmetrical distribution of great significance in the field of statistics. It is a mathematically defined curve. Under certain circumstances, it is permissible to treat frequency distributions of variables as close approximations of the normal distribution **(344)**

normal science   The routine verification of an era's dominant paradigm as conducted by scientists **(15)**

null hypothesis   A statement of no relationship between variables; the null hypothesis is rejected when an observed statistic appears unlikely under the null hypothesis **(438)**

one-tailed test   A statistical test where extreme results leading to rejection of the null hypothesis can be located at either tail **(442)**

one-shot case study   An observation of a single group or event at a single point in time, usually subsequent to some phenomenon that allegedly produced change **(131)**

open-ended question   A question that is not followed by any kind of specified choice; the respondents' answers are recorded in full **(233)**

operational definition   A set of procedures that bridges the conceptual–theoretical and empirical–observational levels by describing the activities required to observe and measure a phenomenon **(28)**

opinion   The verbal expression of an attitude **(232)**

ordinal level   the level of measurement at which all sets of observations generate a complete ranking of objects (e.g., from the "most" to the "least"), although the distances between the ranks cannot be precisely measured **(144)**

panel   A design in survey research that offers a close approximation of the before-and-after condition of experimental designs by interviewing the same group at two or more points in time **(123)**

paradigm   The explanatory or descriptive theory that dominates scientific activity in any historical period **(15)**

paralanguage   The noncontent aspects of behavior; see *extralinguistic behavior* **(193)**

parallel-forms technique   A technique used to overcome the limitations of the test-retest method by administering two parallel versions of a measuring instrument to the same group of research participants **(156)**

parameter   An attribute found in the population that is capable of being measured **(163)**

parametric test   A hypothesis test based on assumptions about the parameter values of the population **(444)**

partial correlation   A statistical control that involves a mathematical adjustment of the bivariate correlation, designed to cancel out the effect of other variables on the independent and dependent variables **(399)**

partial tables   Tables that reflect only part of the total association between the independent and dependent variables **(391)**

participant-as-observer   Role most often assumed by contemporary fieldworkers, where the researcher's presence is made known to the group being studied, and the researcher becomes an active member and a participant in the group being observed **(260)**

participant observation   A method of data collection most closely associated with contemporary field research whereby the investigator attempts to attain some kind of membership in or close attachment to the group that he or she wishes to study **(257)**

path analysis   Technique that uses both bivariate and multiple linear regression techniques to test the causal relations among the variable specified in the model. It involves three steps: drawing of a path diagram based on theory or a set of hypotheses, the calculation of path coefficients (direct effects) using regression techniques, and the determination of indirect effects **(406)**

path coefficient   A standardized regression coefficient that reflects the causal relationship between two variables in path analysis **(406)**

Pearson's *r*   The Pearson product-moment correlation coefficient, a statistic that specifies the magnitude and direction of relation between two interval-level variables, is the most commonly used statistic in correlational analysis **(380)**

personal interview   A face-to-face situation in which an interviewer asks respondents questions designed to obtain answers pertinent to the research hypotheses **(213)**

physical location analysis   The investigation of how individuals use their bodies in naturally occurring social spaces **(289)**

pie chart   A graphic device used to show differences in frequencies or percentages among categories of nominal or ordinal variables. The frequencies or percentages of different categories are shown as segments of a circle **(325)**

planned variation   A research design that exposes individuals to stimuli (the independent variables) that have been systematically varied in order to assess their causal effects **(122)**

population   The complete set of relevant units of analysis **(163)**

positive relation   An association between variables exhibiting the following property: as the value of one variables increases (decreases), the value of another variable also increases (decreases), i.e., the values change in the same direction **(53)**

posttest   The measurement taken after exposure to the independent variable **(90)**

prediction   The process of forecasting an event on the basis of generalizations or of experience **(9)**

predictive validity   The assessment of a measuring instrument conducted by comparing the outcomes of one measuring instrument against another with respect to an external criterion **(151)**

pretest   The measurement taken prior to the introduction of the independent variable **(90)**

pretest-posttest design   A preexperimental design that compares the measures of the dependent variable before and after exposure to the independent variable **(90)**

primitive term   A concept so basic that it cannot be defined by another concept **(27)**

probabilistic (inductive) explanation   Explanations based on generalizations that express either an arithmetic ratio (n percent of $X = Y$) or tendencies (X tends to cause Y) displayed by the phenomenon in the past **(8)**

probability sample   A sample, used in representative sampling, for which we can specify the probability of drawing each of the sampling units; this design ensures that a variable's values, found in the different samples drawn from a given population, will not differ from the values of the population parameter by more than a specified amount **(167)**

probing   The technique used by an interviewer to stimulate discussion and obtain more information **(221)**

property–disposition relationship   The relationship between some characteristic or quality of a person (property) and a corresponding attitude or inclination (disposition) **(115)**

proportional reduction of error   A method used to measure the magnitude of the relations between two variables wherein one variable is used to predict the values of another **(362)**

quantifiers   The responses categories of the rating scale that reflect the intensity of the particular judgement involved **(237)**

question   The foundation of all questionnaires. The questionnaire must translate the research objectives into specific questions; answers to such questions will provide the data for hypothesis testing **(230)**

quota sample   A sample whose characteristics closely replicate those of the population; used in nonprobability sampling **(168)**

random-digit dialing (RDD)   Drawing a random sample of telephone numbers by selecting an exchange and then appending random numbers between 0001 and 9999 **(222)**

randomization   A method of control that helps to offset the confounding effects of known as well as unforseen factors by randomly assigning cases to the experimental and control groups **(100)**

range   Measure of the distance between the highest and lowest values of a distribution **(337)**

ranking   In questionnaire research, when researchers obtain information regarding the degree of importance of the priorities that people have given to a set of attitudes or objects. This procedure is a useful device in providing some sense of relative order among objects or judgments **(238)**

rating   A judgment made by the respondent in terms of sets of ordered categories such as "strongly agree," "favorable," or "very often" **(236)**

ratio level   The level of measurement appropriate for variables having a natural zero point; allows for use of the most precise measuring instruments **(147)**

rationalism   A school of philosophy claiming that all knowledge can be acquired by strict adherence to the forms and use of logic **(4)**

reasonably informed consent   The consent given by research participants after being given a limited amount of information about the research; occurs in situations where fully informed consent would make it impossible to conduct the research. Six basic elements of information must be communicated for consent to be reasonably informed **(75)**

recording unit   The smallest body of content or text in which a reference (a single occurrence of the content element or phenomenon studied) appears and is noted **(298)**

region of rejection   The area under the sampling distribution specified by the null hypothesis that covers the values of the observed statistic that led to the rejection of the null hypothesis. In a one-tailed test, there is one region of rejection; in a two-tailed test, there are two regions of rejection **(440)**

regression artifact   An error that occurs when individuals have been assigned to the experimental group on the basis of their extreme scores on the dependent variable. When this happens, and measures are unreliable, individuals who scored below average on the pretest will appear to have improved upon retesting. Conversely, individuals who scored above average on the pretest would appear to have done less well upon retesting **(97)**

regression line   A line based on the least-squares criterion that is the best fit to the points in a scatterplot **(375)**

relation   The existence of something shared by two or more variables that causes them to covary **(53)**

reliability   The consistency of a measuring instrument, that is, the extent to which a measuring instrument exhibits variable error **(154)**

reliability measure   A statistical measure used to test the reliability of a measuring instrument **(155)**

replication   The repetition of an experiment for the purpose of confirming the research results **(13)**

representative sample   A set of sampling units whose values for the variables studied closely approximate the values of the population parameters being measured **(167)**

research design   The program that guides the investigator in the process of collecting, analyzing, and interpreting observations **(89)**

research hypothesis   Used in statistical hypothesis testing, the research hypothesis states what the researcher is attempting to show in the study. The research hypothesis is not directly tested, but it is supported when the null hypothesis is rejected **(438)**

research problem   A question or problem that stimulates a response in the form of a structured scientific inquiry **(46)**

research process   The overall scheme of activities engaged in by scientists for the purpose of producing knowledge **(18)**

research-then-theory strategy   A research plan that begins with empirical observation, description of attributes, measurement, and analysis of the resulting data, prior to constructing a generalization or theory **(42)**

response bias   The phenomenon that respondents to questionnaires will either deny the behavior in question or underreport it in reply to threatening questions **(242)**

response rate   The percentage of individuals who respond to a given questionnaire **(207)**

response set   The tendency to answer all questions, regardless of their content, in a specific direction; it especially tends to happen if the questions are all in the same format **(240)**

revolutionary science   The abrupt appearance of a rival paradigm (theory) to the paradigm currently dominant in the scientific community **(16)**

right to privacy An individual's freedom to choose the time, circumstances, and extent to which his or her beliefs and behavior are to be shared or withheld from others **(76)**

sample Any subset of a population **(163)**

sampling distribution A theoretical distribution that can be specified for any statistic that can be computed for samples from a population **(439)**

sampling frame The list of all the units from which the chosen units will be selected **(165)**

sampling unit A single unit of a sample population or, as in cluster sampling, a collection of sampling units **(164)**

sampling validity The degree to which the measuring instrument adequately captures the property being measured; alternatively, the degree to which a given population is adequately sampled by the measuring instrument **(150)**

schedule-structured interview An interview in which the questions (their wording and their sequence) are fixed and identical for every respondent **(213)**

science The methodology for acquiring knowledge that is empirically valid **(2)**

sensitivity of information The degree to which information collected by the researcher is either private or potentially threatening to the respondent **(77)**

simple aggregate Groups of data, used in indexes, in which the relative weight of each item making up the group is counted equally, regardless of its actual influence on the aggregate data **(418)**

simple observation A form of measurement in which the observer plays an unnoticed, passive, and unobtrusive role **(288)**

simple random sample A probability sampling design that assigns an equal probability of being selected to each of the sampling units of the population; it is the basic type of probability sample **(169)**

skewed distribution A distribution in which more observations fall to one side of the mean than the other **(343)**

spatial behavior The attempts people make to structure the space around them **(192)**

split-half method A method of assessing the reliability of an instrument by dividing items into two equivalent parts and correlating the scores obtained from one part with the scores obtained from the other **(156)**

spurious relation A relation between the independent and dependent variables that appears to be valid but is actually explained by variables other than those stated in the hypothesis **(50, 387)**

standard deviation A commonly used measure of variability whose size indicates the dispersion of a distribution **(340)**

standard error A statistical measure indicating how closely sample results reflect (or deviate from) a parameter's values; it is calculated from the distribution of all the sample means about the mean of the total of those samples **(177)**

standard score An individual observation that belongs to a distribution with a mean of zero and a standard deviation of one **(345)**

statistic The value of a variable obtained from a sample rather than from the population exhibiting the characteristic **(163)**

stimulus–response relationship A relationship characterized by an independent variable that can be manipulated by the researcher **(115)**

stratified sample A probability sampling design in which the population is first divided into homogeneous strata, followed by sampling conducted within each strata **(172)**

subset Any combination of sampling units that does not include the entire set of sampled units **(177)**

systematic sample A sample in which every Kth case is selected, usually from a random starting point, with the value K kept constant throughout **(171)**

***t* test** A hypothesis test that uses the *t* statistic and the *t* distribution to determine whether to reject or retain the null hypothesis **(447)**

tautology A statement that is true by virtue of its logical form even though the statements within it may say nothing about reality (i.e., they may be empty) **(5)**

taxonomy A level of theory that consists of a system of categories constructed to fit the empirical observations in a way that allows relationships among the categories to be constructed **(34)**

test–retest method A method of assessing the reliability of an instrument by administering it twice to the same group of participants and then correlating the scores obtained **(155)**

theoretical import The meaning concepts acquire in the context of the theory in which they appear **(32)**

theoretical system A systematic combination of taxonomies, conceptual frameworks, descriptions, explanations, and predictions that provides an encompassing explanation of an empirical phenomenon **(36)**

theory-then-research strategy A research plan beginning with the development of ideas and followed by the attempt to confirm or refute those ideas through empirical research **(41)**

threatening question A question that respondents may find embarrassing or sensitive **(241)**

time sampling The process of selecting observation units at different points in time in order to ensure the representativeness of the sampling events or units with respect to the variable investigated **(193)**

time-series design A quasi-experimental design in which pretest and posttest measures are available on a number of occasions before and after exposure to an independent variable **(125)**

topical autobiography The type of autobiography (private record) that focuses on a limited aspect of a person's life **(294)**

triangulation Use of more than one form of data collection method to test the same hypothesis within a unified research plan **(188)**

two-tailed test A statistical test where extreme results leading to the rejection of the null hypothesis will be located at both left and right tails **(442)**

Type I error The rejection of a true null hypothesis **(443)**

Type II error The acceptance of a false null hypothesis **(443)**

unidimensionality The principle underlying the construction of a scale; it implies that the scale's items reflect a single dimension and belong on a continuum that reflects one and only one theoretical concept **(415)**

unit of analysis (level of analysis) The most elementary part of the phenomenon to be studied; its character influences research design, data collection, and data analysis decisions **(47)**

unobtrusive measures Observation method that removes the researcher from any direct contact with the interactions, events, or behavior being investigated. This implies that (a) the subjects are unaware that they are being observed, and (b) there is little danger that the act of measurement might bias the data **(287)**

validity The degree to which an instrument measures what it is supposed to measure **(149)**

variable An empirical property that can take on two or more values **(49)**

variance A measure of quantitative variation reflecting the average dispersion in the distribution; the square of the standard deviation **(339)**

Verstehen Empathic understanding of human behavior **(10)**

voluntarism The participant's freedom to choose whether or not to take part in a research project; guarantees that exposure to known risks is undertaken voluntarily **(74)**

weighted aggregate Groups of data, used in indexes, that indicate the relative influence of each indicator or item analyzed **(419)**

Acknowledgments

Grateful acknowledgment is made for kind permission to reprint the following. This constitutes an extension of the copyright page.

Exhibit 4.1 from Paul Davidson Reynolds, *Ethical Dilemmas and Social Science Research* (San Francisco: Jossey-Bass, 1979), pp. 443–448. Copyright © 1979 by Jossey-Bass, Inc., Publishers. Reprinted with the permission of the publishers.

Table 5.3 adapted from Michael J. Robinson, "Public Affairs Television and the Growth of Political Malaise: The Case of 'The Selling of the Pentagon,'" *American Political Science Review*, 70 (1976): 412. Copyright © 1976 by the American Political Science Association. Reprinted with the permission of the publishers.

Table 6.1 from Robert R. Kaufman and Leo Zuckerman, "Attitudes Toward Economic Reform in Mexico: The Role of Political Orientations," *American Political Science Review*, 92 (1998): 359–371. Copyright © 1998 by the American Political Science Association. Reprinted with the permission of the publishers.

Figure 6.9 from Donald T. Campbell, "Reforms as Experiments," *American Psychologist*, 24 (1969): 419. Copyright © 1969 by the American Psychological Association, Inc. Reprinted with the permission of the publishers.

Box (p. 175) "Description of Four Probability Samples" based on Russell Ackoff, *The Design of Social Research* (Chicago: University of Chicago Press, 1953). Reprinted with the permission of The University of Chicago Press.

Figure 8.1 from Survey Research Center, *Interviewer's Manual, Revised Edition* (Ann Arbor: Institute for Social Research, 1976). Reprinted with the permission of the Institute for Social Research, University of Michigan.

Exhibit 9.1 from Robert F. Bales, *Interaction Process Analysis* (Chicago: University of Chicago Press, 1976). Copyright © 1976 by The University of Chicago. Reprinted with the permission of The University of Chicago Press.

Table 10.1 adapted from Don A. Dillman, James A. Christensen, Edward H. Carpenter, and Ralph M. Brooks, "Increasing Mail Questionnaire Response: A Four-State Comparison," *American Sociological Review*, 39 (1974): 755, and Don A. Dillman and Dan E. Moore, "Improving Response Rates to Mail Surveys: Results from Five Surveys," unpublished paper presented at the annual meeting of the American Association for Public Opinion Research, Hershey, Pa., 1983. Reprinted with the permission of the American Sociological Association and Don A. Dillman.

Exhibit 10.1 from Samuel Devons, "A Questionnaire for Questioners," *Public Opinion Quarterly*, 39 (1975): 255–256. Reprinted with the permission of The University of Chicago Press.

Exhibits 10.2, 10.3 and 10.4 adapted from Raymond L. Gorden, *Interviewing: Strategy, Techniques, and Tactics, Third Edition* (Homewood, Ill.: Dorsey Press, 1980), pp. 48–50. Copyright © 1975 by Raymond L. Gorden. Reprinted with the permission of the author.

Exhibit 11.4 based on Angus Campbell and Howard Shuman, *Racial Attitudes in Fifteen American Cities* (Ann Arbor: Social Science Archive, 1973). Reprinted with the permission of the Institute for Social Research, Center for Political Studies, University of Michigan.

Exhibit 13.1 from Inter-university Consortium for Political and Social Research, *Guide to Resources and Services, 1994–1995* (Ann Arbor: University of Michigan, Institute for Social Research, Center for Political Studies, 1994), p. xxiii. Reprinted with the permission of ICPSR.

Table 14.1 from Paul F. Lazarsfeld and Alan Barton, "Qualitative Measurement in the Social Sciences: Classification, Typologies, and Indices" in *The Policy Sciences*, edited by Daniel Lerner and Harold D. Lasswell (Stanford, Calif.: Stanford University Press, 1951), p. 161. Reprinted with the permission of Stanford University Press.

Exhibit 14.1 from the General Social Survey, 1996, from the National Opinion Research Center, University of Chicago. Reprinted with permission of the NORC.

Figure 14.1 from James L. Gibson and Richard D. Bingham, *Civil Liberties and the Nazis*. Copyright © 1985 by Praeger Publishers. Reprinted with the permission of the publishers.

Tables 15.1 through 15.12 and Figures 15.1 through 15.4 adapted from the General Social Survey, 1996, from the National Opinion Research Center, University of Chicago. Reprinted with permission of the NORC.

Tables 16.5, 16.6, 16.10, and 16.11 adapted from the General Social Survey, 1996, from the National Opinion Research Center, University of Chicago. Reprinted with permission of the NORC.

Table 16.7 adapted from Elizabeth Addel Cook, Ted G. Jelen, and Clyde Wilcox, "The Social Bases of Abortion Attitudes" from *Between Two Absolutes: Public Opinions and the Politics of Abortion* (Boulder, Colo.: Westview Press, 1992). Copyright © 1992 by Westview Press. Reprinted with the permission of the publishers.

Table 18.7 based on Jules J. Wanderer, "An Index of Riot Severity and Some Correlates," *American Journal of Sociology,* 74 (1969): 503. Reprinted with the permission of The University of Chicago Press.

Table 19.6 adapted from Jane Riblett Wilkie, "Changes in U.S. Men's Attitudes Toward the Family Provider Role, 1972–1989," *Gender and Society,* 7, no. 2 (June 1993): 261–279. Copyright © 1993 by Sage Publications, Inc. Reprinted with permission of the publishers.

Figures A.1 through A.40 (all generated figures from SPSS for Windows Release 9.0). Reprinted with the permission of SPSS Inc.

Appendix B (guidelines for preparing tables) adapted from classroom handout prepared by David Wegge of St. Norbert College. Reprinted with the permission of the author.

Appendix D abridged from William H. Beyer, editor, *Handbook of Tables for Probability and Statistics, Second Edition* (Cleveland: Chemical Rubber Company, 1968). Copyright © 1968 The Chemical Rubber Company, CRC Press, Inc. Reprinted with the permission of the publishers.

Appendix E from Harold O. Rugg, *Statistical Methods Applied to Education* (Boston: Houghton Mifflin Company, 1917), pp. 389–390. Reprinted with the permission of the publishers.

Appendices F and H abridged from Ronald A. Fisher and Frank Yates, *Statistical Tables for Biological, Agricultural, and Medical Research, Sixth Edition,* Tables III and IV. Reprinted with the permission of Longman Group, Ltd., on behalf of the Literary Executor of the late Sir Ronald A. Fisher, F.R.S., and Dr. Frank Yates, F.R.S.

Appendix G from George W. Snedecor and William G. Cochran, *Statistical Methods, Seventh Edition.* Copyright © 1980 by Iowa State University Press. Reprinted with the permission of the publisher.

AUTHOR INDEX

SUBJECT INDEX

WORLD OF CULTURE

MUSIC

by Frederic V. Grunfeld

Newsweek Books, New York

NEWSWEEK BOOKS

Joseph L. Gardner, Editor

Janet Czarnetzki, Art Director
Edwin D. Bayrd, Jr., Associate Editor
Ellen Kavier, Researcher-Writer
Elaine Andrews, Copy Editor

S. Arthur Dembner, President

ARNOLDO MONDADORI EDITORE

Giuliana Nannicini, Editor

Mariella De Battisti, Picture Researcher
Marisa Melis, Editorial Secretary
Enrico Segré, Designer
Giovanni Adamoli, Production Coordinator

Contents

1

The Family of Music

WHEN A MODERN MINSTREL like Paul McCartney picks up his electric guitar, steps to the microphone, and sings "My Love," he is adding yet another link to a chain of musical tradition that stretches back to the dawn of mankind. The guitar he holds in his hands is the latest mutation of an instrument whose shape can be seen on 3,000-year-old Hittite bas-reliefs and whose name goes back to a still older Middle Eastern word, *si-tar*—"three strings"—which indicates that other strings have been added at later stages of its evolution into the "Spanish guitar" and thence into the mainstay of blues and pop music.

The melody McCartney sings contains reminiscences of both African and European folksongs. It owes its lithe, elastic shape partly to the African-descended blues and partly to English and Scotch-Irish ballads that reveal their age by using ancient five-note scales or the Dorian and Aeolian modes of the Middle Ages. The underlying beat of the rhythm has come out of Africa, a continent preeminent in matters of the drum and the dance, although it has lost most of its African subtleties in the process of being adapted to a ballad beat. The chords with which he harmonizes his melody are a specifically European contribution to this alloy. They had to undergo an elaborate evolution at the courts of Burgundy, in Johann Sebastian Bach's organ loft, and in George Gershwin's Tin Pan Alley before arriving at their present state.

As for the words, they too belong to a great tradition, and it is not difficult to find comparable examples in every part of the world, whether among the Berbers of North Africa,

> Do not trample down the furrows, little gazelle.
> I am ready now to show you
> The path that you do not know.

or the headhunters of Borneo,

> The seashell is transparent,
> The banana is good to eat.
> You are beautiful, girl!
> And your breasts are still soft.

or among the Eskimos of Greenland,

> My betrothed, my beloved,
> I leave you now.
> Do not sorrow too much for me.
> I cannot forget you . . .

The Baulé tribesmen of Africa's Ivory Coast still play the simple instruments of their remote forebears, thus perpetuating a form of musicmaking that is millennia old. African rhythms have been a major influence on modern music.

7

All who love one another
Find it hard to part . . .

The musical means that are used to express these sentiments vary enormously from Greenland to Tierra del Fuego. But the basic kinetic and emotional impulse is the same, and the acoustical laws that govern their expression are immutable. In that sense, music is, if not a universal language, at least a universal means of communication between human beings. And it is not only the love song that is ubiquitous, but also the work song. The fishermen of Greece, the sailors of Japan, the Maoris of New Zealand, and the men who ply the Nile and Brahmaputra rivers all have their boat songs. A Navajo Indian silversmith sings in rhythm to the tap-tap of his hammer; a Spanish olive farmer, riding to his orchard in Andalusia, sings a long, mellow chant in rhythm to the hoofbeats of his mule—a song that floats out over the surrounding countryside like smoke rising and curling on a breeze.

In the cities of the industrial world, the rise of the discothèque, taking over from the far more pretentious night club, has restored the dance to at least a vestige of its ancient place at the center of tribal social life. As an arena in which to unleash one's dance instincts, a discothèque floor is not so different from a jungle clearing, and the rites that are performed in both places serve very much the same function. Once, in the jungles of Orissa in central India, I observed a dance on a full-moon night when a whole village of naked aborigines of the Saora tribe had worked themselves up to a frenzied dance pitch. Then the drums began beating, and the young women turned up en masse and formed a long row, linking arms, their breasts bobbing jauntily as they surged backward and forward, while the young men pranced wildly in

Stringed instruments, creations of infinite variety and almost universal appeal, represent a major advance over the simple resonating chambers of early neolithic times. Primitive harps such as the Mesopotamian model featured on the terra-cotta relief at right were the forerunners of more refined stringed instruments. Among the latter are, from left to right below: an Abyssinian lyre, an Arabian rebab, an Indian sarangi carved from a single piece of wood, a sinuous Russian guitar, a double-keyboard guitar, and a classic Spanish guitar.

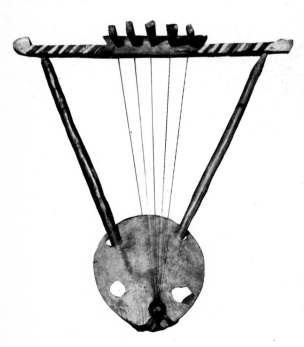

front of them, beating all sorts of percussion instruments and letting out blood-curdling cries of sheer happiness. Only after everyone had reached a state of near exhaustion, what with all the laughing and wriggling and the brandishing of spears and sticks, did the two groups finally merge and the dancers wander off into the night in convenient couples.

On the walls of their adobe huts, the Saora tribesmen paint pictures of these dance sessions that illustrate their importance in the tribal scheme of things. In a flat, fluent style that resembles prehistoric cave painting, they depict the highlight of the festival—a dozen women dancing with linked arms, shoulder to shoulder, so that the smallest ones are left kicking the air because their legs are not long enough to reach the ground. These pictures are not unlike the dance figures that occur in the caves of southern Europe—some of them dating back to the ice age—except that these dancers are usually dressed in animal skins, and their function seems to have been to impersonate wild animals in the dance, to give the hunter magic powers over his prey.

Paintings of this sort furnish the earliest evidence of human musical activity. In southern France, for example, in the cave of Trois Frères in Ariège, there is a rude drawing of a man impersonating a bison, and in his mouth he holds a musical bow—an instrument he supports with his left hand and twangs with his right. The painting is thought to be seventeen thousand years old. Yet this same instrument, essentially a one-string "guitar" using the mouth and skull as sounding board and resonating cavity, can still be heard in some parts of Africa as the "okongo" as well as among the American Indians. It is the original ancestor of all stringed instruments, and its acoustic principles are iden-

tical with those of the other chordophones that can be heard around
the world in the form of gourds strung with gut strings, or turtle shells
strung with fiber chords, or silken chords mounted on wooden bowls
—Persian lutes, Greek lyres, the African kora, the Italian violin, the
Indian sitar.

Each of the world's peoples has developed the musical potential of
such instruments in its own distinctive fashion. The sitar, for example,
has been the king of Indian court music since the fourteenth century,
and it, in turn, is a modification of an earlier instrument, the veena
(sacred to Saraswathi, the Hindu goddess of art and learning), which
has a documented history of some four thousand years. The sitar is
made of teak, jackwood (a kind of breadfruit tree), and a seasoned
gourd. Its long neck towers above the player's head when he sits cross-
legged in the customary playing position. It has six or seven main playing strings running above the frets and, below them, a dozen or so sympathetic strings that set up a steady humming "echo" when the rest are
plucked. The sitarist plucks the main strings with a wire plectrum
worn on the forefinger of his right hand. Occasionally he reaches out
with his little finger and runs it across the sympathetic strings, which
give off a sound like a row of broken icicles. Four to twenty arched
metal frets are clamped to the neck of the instrument, and these are
moved fractionally up or down for each performance, to suit the particular intervals of the raga, or melodic pattern, being played.

The sitar's music is a world in itself, of which most westerners can
gain only the most superficial understanding. Learning to play the
instrument with any degree of proficiency is a matter of ten or twelve
years of intensive study with a guru. Only about ten percent of the
music is written down; the vital ninety percent consists of improvisation, when the player can explore an infinite range of melodic possibilities within the strictest limits of tradition. The rhythmic and melodic
patterns of Indian music are prescribed by ancient usage and passed

10

The nobles of ancient Egypt took the music of the harp with them everywhere—even into the Valley of the Dead, the great necropolis at Thebes—as the wall painting at left indicates. In time, the harp's popularity was to decline in the Eastern Mediterranean as public taste shifted to more sophisticated instruments. The ivory detail at right, which once adorned a Mesopotamian casket, shows men playing early versions of the guitar (top) and the recorder (bottom).

from generation to generation via the chain of playing and listening known as *guruparampara*—the all-important master-to-pupil succession that is essential to Indian musical life (and, for that matter, equally important to Polish pianists, or Nigerian drummers, or Japanese koto players; music always has to be learned by hearing someone play it).

To be a sitarist requires both the stamina of an athlete—concerts regularly last into the small hours of the morning—and the spiritual preparation of a monk, for this is an exercise in philosophy as much as in muscular coordination. The raga on which the sitarist decides to improvise must be wholly in harmony with the mood and circumstances of the occasion. And there is a vast range of ragas from which to choose: Kedara, for instance, is meant for "early night, active, confident, joyful and intense"; Kanada is ideal for the "second part of the night, deep happiness and passion"; Hindola is intended for "springtime, bursting life, violence and no softness"; and Megha Mallar is associated with "rainy season, commanding and happy." There are many other possibilities, which Indian artists have depicted in the *raga-mala* ("garland of ragas") paintings, and the number of possible permutations reaches into the hundreds.

During the opening alap ("invocation") of his performance, the sitar player lingers caressingly over each note of the ascending and descending melody—a gradual exposition, full of hesitations and repetitions, that has been compared to the unfolding of a lotus. The tempo speeds up, and the patterns grow more intricate as the tabla drums pick up the thread. The climax is reached anywhere from twenty minutes to two hours later, when the sitarist has accelerated to a dazzling explosion of virtuosity, his fingers flying over frets and strings until the hand is quicker than the ear, and the raga seems to dissolve into a blur of sound.

This highly complex and sophisticated way of organizing the raw material of music is, of course, very different from that of the European tradition. It is a connoisseur's music, although in recent years it has attracted more and more western admirers who are fascinated by the precision and elasticity of the Indian approach. It reflects the historic preference of most of the world's cultures for an elaboration of melody and rhythm, in all of their finest nuances.

Within the worlds of Asian and African music there are, of course, many other equally valid alternatives to the western tradition epitomized by the hundred-man symphony orchestra. The musicians of West Africa form themselves into *ad hoc* orchestras of drums, balaphons, flutes, harps, and miscellaneous percussion instruments that produce a magnificent welter of sounds without requiring written music or rehearsals. Everyone simply knows instinctively and from long experience how to fit his own sounds into the overall pattern. At the same time the dancers move in perfect rhythm to the drums, improvising their steps—shaking, shimmying, with elbows revolving, hips gyrating, heads thrown back, bare heels stamping the ground. And the dancing, like the music, is only a step away from pure acrobatics. I have seen a Senegalese dancer who could turn cartwheels while balancing a glass of water without spilling a drop, and another who could revolve rhythmi-

Using the sitar, an instrument so ancient that its name antedates any known representations of stringed musical devices, Indian musicians created the endlessly improvised raga, a musical pattern with no western equivalent. The Indian dancing girl seen in silhouette above plays a hand drum. In the eighteenth-century miniature at right, a sari-clad woman is shown (lower right) playing an identical drum. Before her sits the ensemble's principal musician, whose veena is a precursor of the modern sitar.

cally atop a free-standing thirty-foot pole, and a third who could do an unconcerned jig on stools while three pairs of assistants twirled ropes over and all around him. The music never seems to stop, for left to itself, a balaphon orchestra may go on all day and all night, and perhaps into the next day, until the last drummer is ready to drop with exhaustion.

The music of Bali suggests another significant alternative to the symphonic way of organizing the tonal substance of music. Virtually the whole island is alive with the music of the percussion groups known as gamelan orchestras. Every village has two or three of them, consisting of twenty or more players presiding over an astonishing assemblage of gongs, drums, and various kinds of metallophones. Some players have only a single note to play; others have a range of three to five notes. They strike their instruments with light wooden hammers in a steady up-down, up-down rhythm that interlocks with, but does not duplicate, that of their neighbors. The result sounds like the jangle of a thousand bells and anvils—organized, however, into very precise rhythmic patterns, sometimes loud, sometimes delicate, with sudden bursts of silence to underscore the unanimity of the effort. Each man is independent yet wholly coordinated with the rest, for they practice constantly and have been playing all their lives. When the gamelan performs, even four- and five-year-olds are allowed to sit next to their brothers and learn how to play the gongs.

There is a fierceness in this percussion music that has its roots in an ancient warrior culture, now softened by centuries of a gentler, more

feminine civilization. The gamelan is used for accompanying all of the village ceremonials. It plays all day when the women take food to the temples to be blessed by the gods, carrying on their heads pyramids of fruits and delicacies piled two or three feet high. (The Balinese are practical people. They take the food home again, after it has all been duly admired and bathed in a sea of music and prayer, so that it can be eaten by the people who produced it.)

The musicians will play all day for a wedding and all night for a dance drama presented at the entrance to one of the temples. There are groups with portable gamelan gongs who take part in the festive cremation ceremonies that are one of the highlights of the Balinese social calendar; they also march in the funeral processions that carry the ashes of the dead down to the beaches in enormous bamboo towers, so that they can be consecrated and carried away by the sea. The towers, carried on the backs of fifteen or twenty young men, are paraded through other villages en route and whirled around in circles every now and then, for the soul of the departed must be prevented from finding its way home, and spinning it around is supposed to make the spirit so dizzy that it will lose its bearings. Meanwhile, the marching sound of the gongs and drums goes on, spreading its invitation throughout the surrounding countryside, so that increasingly large crowds are drawn into the procession.

This is precisely how music was used in the early Mediterranean civilizations, including the Greek and the Roman. Although only a few fragments of classical Greek music have survived, musicologists are certain that Greek songs sounded "Oriental," and that originally the various types of Greek music were as carefully classified as the Indian ragas. "Among us," explains Plato in the *Laws*, "music was divided into various classes and styles; one class of song was that of prayers to the gods, which bore the name of 'hymns'; contrasted with this was another class, best called 'dirges'; 'paeans' formed another; and yet another was the 'dithyramb,' named, I fancy, after Dionysus. 'Nomes' also were so called as being a distinct class of song; and these were further described as 'citharoedic nomes.' So these and other kinds being classified and fixed, it was forbidden to set one kind of words to a different class of tune. . . ." Later, these divisions were disregarded, when, as Plato says, the composers "mixed dirges with hymns and paeans with dithyrambs . . . and blended every kind of music with every other."

Greek life abounded in musical occasions. There were choral songs accompanied by dancing in honor of Apollo and the magical cure dances (like those still practiced by the Sufi dervishes of Persia, in which the patient, placed in the middle of the dance circle, receives the positive vibrations and curative good wishes of those who are dancing around him). There were also the *pyrriche*, or sword dances for young warriors; the *gymnopaidai*, or wrestlinglike dances for unclothed athletes; the *parthenia*, for Spartan virgins; and the choruses and solo songs presented during performances of the great tragedies by Aeschylus, Sophocles, and Euripides and the comedies of Aristophanes (a passage in Aeschylus mentions a chorus of fifty voices).

Besides these ceremonial functions, Greek music also served more

15

humble purposes. The Greeks had work songs for threshing barley, treading grapes, spinning wool, making rope, and drawing water—in fact, music for all the essential peasant tasks. Some of these songs have come down over the centuries almost unscathed, since the need for music and rhythm with such activities never ceases. In many parts of the Mediterranean today, fields cannot be plowed, nor grain threshed, nor almonds gathered except to the accompaniment of work songs whose melodies are at least collateral descendants of those used by the Greeks. In much the same way, the ancient round dances shown on Greek vase paintings survive today, in only slightly modified form, both in Greece itself and in Catalonia, where the Greeks established colonies. Greek and Greco-Roman ceremonial songs were also absorbed into the chants of the Christian Church, and vestiges of them are still sung as part of the Catholic liturgy.

The music of the early Christian Church, however, had its origins not only in the Greek temples but also in the Jewish synagogues, with their ancient tradition of "song in the house of the Lord, with cymbals, psalteries, and harps" (1 Chron. 25, mentions a total of 228 skilled musicians in the service of Solomon's temple). Portions of the Jewish sacred service—including the "Hallelujah" ("Praise ye the Lord," in Hebrew) and the "Holy, Holy, Holy"—were taken over bodily into the Chris-

Combining myth and music in equal portions, the ancient Romans created bas-reliefs such as the one shown below, which records an imaginary parade of satyrs playing double flutes led by a maenad carrying a tambourine. The gold figurine at right, thought to be Greek in origin, also depicts a double-flute player.

tian liturgy; in other cases, traditional synagogue chants were altered to suit Latin texts. Apparently the early Christians also adopted the practices of some of the Hellenistic Jewish sects, such as the antiphonal singing described in the first century A.D. by Philo of Alexandria: "They all stand up together, and . . . two choruses are formed . . . the one of men and the other of women, and for each chorus there is a leader . . . who is the most honorable and most excellent of the band. Then they sing hymns which have been composed in honor of God in many metres and tunes, at one time all singing together, and at another answering one another in a skillful manner."

Many of the early Christian writers mention the importance of singing to the new Church. "The Greeks use Greek, the Romans Latin," writes the third-century theologian Origen. "Everyone prays and sings praises to God as best he can." Saint John Chrysostom, bishop of Constantinople in A.D. 400, wrote that "when God saw that many men were indolent" and too lazy to read the Scriptures, he gave them the music of the Psalms in addition to the words of King David, so that everyone could learn their message by singing joyful hymns: "For nothing so uplifts the mind, giving it wings and freeing it from the earth . . . as modulated melody and the divine chant. . . ."

The remarks of Saint John Chrysostom on the Psalms suggest that at that time there were no great musical differences between Church chants and the songs of everyday life, for he compares them to the lullabies with which infants are rocked to sleep and to the songs that travelers sing, "driving at noon the yoked animals," to lighten the hardships of the journey. He goes on to describe these everyday songs:

And not only travelers, but also peasants often sing as they tread the grapes in the wine press, gather the vintage, tend the vine, and perform their other tasks. Sailors do likewise, pulling at the oars. Women, too, weaving and parting the tangled threads with the shuttle, often sing a certain melody, sometimes individually and to themselves, sometimes all together in concert. This they do, the women, travelers, peasants and sailors, striving to lighten with a chant the labor endured in working, for the mind suffers hardships and difficulties more easily when it hears songs and chants.

Hebrew, classic Greek, Roman, and Byzantine melodies all helped to form the great body of plain-song liturgy known as Gregorian chant, which, according to tradition, was collected and edited by Pope (afterward Saint) Gregory the Great in the sixth century. It includes more than six hundred compositions for various parts of the Mass, and some three thousand antiphons and responds for the Daily Hours of divine service. In the early Middle Ages, Gregorian chant represented only one of several branches of liturgical tradition within the Western Church. There was the so-called Ambrosian chant of Milan, named for Saint Ambrose; the Visigothic, or Mozarabic, chant of Spain; and the Gallican chant of medieval France. Gradually, however, these others were replaced by the Gregorian liturgy of Rome, with only the Ambrosian chant retaining some of its independence. In the case of the Mozarabic chant, however, the musicologist-monks of the Benedictine monastery of Santo Domingo de Silos, near Burgos, have recently revived the Visigothic rite and restored it to active use for the first time in nearly a thousand years.

Known and sung in all the churches, schools, and monasteries of western Christendom, the Gregorian chant was to have an incalculable influence on subsequent musical developments. It was, indeed, one of the cornerstones on which the whole edifice of European music was to be constructed. Yet the evolution of western music is equally indebted to the profane tradition of folk music and dance—to the "lascivious songs" that Saint John Chrysostom deplored as being the work of "comedians, dancers and harlots," and which, he said, made the mind "softer and weaker." Although these dances and love songs have often drawn the fire of the moralists, they have contributed an incalculable number of new ideas and precedents to the mainstream of music.

Over and over again, the lowliest and most despised beginnings have led to the most magnificent musical developments. The passacaglia form, for example, which Bach used for one of his most resplendent organ works, began life as a popular Spanish dance step whose rhythms were strummed by strolling musicians (and, it is reported, especially by barbers) while passing through the *calles* ("streets")—hence the name. The catchy rhythm of passacaille, as the French called it, soon attracted the attention of serious composers and became the basis of an increasingly complex contrapuntal form employed by some of the foremost baroque masters. A hundred similar examples could be cited. During the nineteenth century, the waltz was at first denounced as the

Church chants, a musical form as ancient as Jerusalem's second Temple, were not collected and systematized until the sixth century A.D. That achievement is traditionally attributed to Pope Gregory; hence the three-voiced chorus featured on the miniature above is said to be singing Gregorian chants. A cappella chanting was ultimately replaced in popularity by more elaborate modes of liturgical accompaniment, including bells, stringed instruments, and bellows organs—all depicted in the thirteenth-century miniature at left, below.

devil's work for placing ladies' waists in the "lewd grasp" of their male partners. Yet Chopin composed some of his most poetic music in "voluptuary" waltz time, and it was to account not only for Richard Strauss's finest operatic moments but also for some of the most powerful episodes in Gustav Mahler's symphonies. Jazz, too, has had a comparable history. In making the long voyage from the brothels of New Orleans to Carnegie Hall, jazz lent its rhythm to a nation and its name to an entire era.

At every stage of history, this glorious pageant of musical invention has fascinated the practitioners of the other arts—the poets and novelists, painters and sculptors. From Geoffrey Chaucer to Thomas Mann, literary men have written vivid pages about musical people. But the most persistent music lovers of all have been the artists who have recorded the visual aspects of the musical life. The results of this love affair can be seen in Egyptian bas-reliefs, Roman mosaics, medieval book illustrations, Italian Renaissance frescoes, French baroque paintings, and countless other works of art in every conceivable medium. Matthias Grünewald paints a concert of angels, and Velásquez the musicians of a Spanish tavern; Veronese paints his self-portrait as a viol player; Rembrandt has the young David playing a harp; Vermeer shows his ladies at the harpsichord; Watteau's gentlemen play lutes; Goya's dandies sing to the guitar; Delacroix portrays Chopin at the piano; Picasso draws a jazz trio as a sheet-music cover for Stravinsky.

Clearly, there is something about music that perpetually appeals to the eye as well as the ear. For one thing, many instruments are very beautiful, since most of them are splendid examples of form following function. But beyond that, the act of making music still retains some of the magic it held for the stone-age dancer playing the mouthbow in the cave of Trois Frères.

Music has become such a piece of everyday magic that one may be hardly conscious of the human and technological miracle that is represented by a phenomenon such as Arthur Rubinstein playing a Liszt sonata or Isaac Stern performing the Beethoven Violin Concerto. As the music-loving Bishop Joseph Hall wrote about lute playing in the seventeenth century:

> Had we lived in some rude and remote part of the world, and should have been told, that it is possible, only by a hollow piece of wood, and the guts of beasts stirred by the fingers of men, to make so sweet and melodious a noise, we should have thought it utterly incredible; yet now that we see and hear it ordinarily done, we make it no wonder.

2

A Royal Road to Song

THE TROUBADOURS CAME RIDING out of the hilltop castles of southern France in the twelfth century, twanging their lutes, fiddling on their viols, and singing magnificent songs that brought several new kinds of civilized pleasure to the courts of Aquitaine and Provence. The times were prosperous and relatively peaceful; trade routes were open, and travel on the highways was no longer a suicidal affair. It was a propitious moment to begin a new movement in the arts of music and poetry.

To be a troubadour was to be both a poet and a composer (the word comes from the verb *trobar*, to compose), for no one ever considered one without the other. As the troubadour Folquet de Marseilles says in one of his songs, "A verse without music is a mill without water." Their language was that form of medieval Romance spoken throughout southern France and now known as Provençal. In this very supple and expressive idiom they wrote songs about things that were too personal, too passionate to be phrased in monkish Latin—and thus they created the first lyric poetry in any modern European language. They sang about love, sex, and politics, about the physical and mental pleasures to be derived from courtship in accordance with the rules of the *ars amatoria*, the "arts of love." A "pleasant fever" is what Guillaume de Cabestaing calls it in his song *Li dous cossire*:

> That pleasant fever
> That love doth often bring
> Lady, doth ever
> Attune the songs I sing
> Where I endeavor
> To catch again your chaste
> Sweet body's savor
> I crave but may not taste.

To the troubadours, love was an experience to be cultivated, prolonged, intensified, and cherished as one of the great gifts of civilization. It was not, as has sometimes been claimed, that the woman's inaccessibility had to be taken for granted. On the contrary, most of the troubadour songs contain declarations of intent couched in much stronger terms than the Beatles' "I Want to Hold Your Hand." The great troubadour Arnaud Daniel, for example, looks forward to being with his lady so that he can feel "the great joy of having her, amid kisses and laughter, disclose her fair body that I may gaze at it beneath the lamplight." Bernart de Ventadour expresses the hope that his love will have the courage "to have me come one night there where she undresses and make me a necklace of her arms." Duke William of Aquitaine, who is considered the first of the troubadours, describes himself as an "infallible master," not on account of his songs but because "there is no woman who, after a night with me, will not want me back the next day." And Bertrand de Born, Viscount of Hautefort, describes his mistress—and the twelfth century's feminine ideal—as a lady "delicate and fair, charming, gay and young; her hair is blond

Ferrara, the ducal seat of the Este family, was one of Renaissance Italy's notable musical milieus. The Este palace itself was decorated with elaborate allegorical frescoes, each devoted to a given month and each built upon a musical theme. April's delights are arrayed below.

with a ruby tint, her body white as hawthorne, with soft arms and firm breasts and a rabbit's suppleness in her back."

Besides singing of love, the troubadours also served as the news commentators of their day. Since the printing press was not to be invented for another three hundred years, there was virtually no other way of disseminating the latest news. In the songs known as sirventés, the troubadours discussed current affairs, politics, personalities, the latest fashions and scandals, and the "joyful season" of war, when the knights had a chance to test their training and equipment on the field of battle. Bertrand de Born became famous for writing warmongering songs that stirred up the barons and provoked kings into going to war

with one another. To Bertrand, war was the continuation of poetry by other means:

> I love to see the press of shields
> With their hues of red and blue
> Of ensigns and of banners
> manycolored in the wind,
> and the sight of tents and rich pavilions pitched,
> lances shattered, shields pierced, shining
> helmets split, and blows exchanged in battle.

In theory, troubadours were supposed to be belted knights, but in practice they came from all walks of life. Like the pop composers of the twentieth century, many of them became rich and famous by taking their songs from court to court, where the great princes might reward them with horses, armor, or feudal privileges. The ideal patron of the arts was someone like Blacatz, Lord of Aups in the early thirteenth century, who also enjoyed a considerable reputation as a troubadour: "And he delighted in ladies, and love, and war, and spending, and feasting, and tumult, and music, and song, and play, and all such things as give a good man worth and fame. Never was there a man who loved better to take than he to give."

Like composers of a later day, some of the troubadours hired professional singers and entertainers (*jongleurs*) to perform their works,

Originally written to celebrate such wholly secular occasions as the jousting tournament seen above, the songs of the troubadours were subsequently adapted for exclusively religious purposes. The renowned Cantigas de Santa Maria, *which were produced under the supervision of Alfonso the Wise of Castile, recorded those songs for posterity. And as the illustrations at left, below, and at right indicate, the* Cantigas *also provided graphic evidence of the extraordinary range of instruments available to thirteenth-century musicians.*

since their own voices were often unequal to the task of displaying their songs to advantage. What their music was like no one knows for certain. It has been preserved in a handful of early manuscripts that indicate only the melodic outline of each song, but not the rhythm or accompaniment. Some of the miniatures of this period, however, show troubadours and minstrels accompanying themselves on lutes, viols, or early forerunners of the guitar. In any case, a well-equipped thirteenth-century castle was apt to have a music room full of instruments with which to accompany songs, dances, and ceremonials.

The richest source of pictures of·medieval musicmaking is one of the manuscripts of the *Cantigas de Santa Maria*, produced at the court of Alfonso the Wise, a thirteenth-century ruler of Castile. He was one of the last to cultivate troubadour poetry, and one of the first to adapt it to religious purposes, calling himself a "troubadour of Saint Mary." The miniatures of the *Cantigas* show the whole incredible range of instruments available to a great court in the Middle Ages. There are musicians playing metal trumpets and ivory horns, lutes of all sizes, vielles plucked and bowed, gitterns, rebecs, psalteries, harps, mandolas, organistra (hurdy-gurdies), chime bells, cymbals, castanets, tabors and tabor-pipes, bagpipes, recorders, flutes, shawms and double-shawms (two primitive clarinets with their mouthpieces bound together), and a great many others whose precise names are no longer known. These instruments are the ancestors of those in the modern symphony orchestra. Their function, however, was not to play together to produce a pattern of harmonies (that idea had not yet occurred to anyone) but to play singly, in pairs, or in small groups to punctuate the rhythm of a dance or to accompany the solo voice in unison and at the octave, supporting the melody and supplying a sort of drone for it.

Most of these instruments had originated in the Near East and had

come to Europe via the Moorish kingdoms of southern Spain, which had been under Arab domination since the eighth century. In the course of their conquests, the Arabs had taken over the ancient civilization of Persia and had imported it, in turn, into their magnificent courts at Córdoba, Seville, and Granada. Their culture was so obviously superior to the rude life-style of the Christian kingdoms in northern Spain that, despite the incessant warfare between them, the Christian kings soon felt obliged to match the Moslem emirs in music, literature, and the visual arts. Indeed, the illustrations of Alfonso's songs in honor of Saint Mary show that Moorish minstrels were among the musicians of his court; perhaps as many as fifty percent of his musicians were of Moorish origin. Spain thus served as the gateway through which much of Persian and Arabic culture entered Europe—an influence that included every sort of eastern instrument from kettledrums to lutes.

But the musical culture of Europe was destined to follow its own unique path of development, which was to produce an art that had very little in common with musical styles from other parts of the world. It was a royal road that led from the monody of Gregorian chant to the complex polyphony of the Renaissance masters; from the troubadours with their lute accompaniments to the great choral and instrumental aggregations of the baroque era.

In Europe, far more than anywhere else, music became a matter of social organization and applied technology. For the consecration of Salzburg Cathedral in 1628, for example, the Italian composer Orazio Benevoli wrote a festival Mass that almost rivals the architecture of the cathedral in the intricacies of its colossal plan. It has two eight-part

choruses, each with two solo quartets and an organ, and each accompanied by an instrumental ensemble. One of these orchestras consists of a six-part body of violins and violas, an eight-part wind band of oboes, flutes, and trumpets, and another section of two trumpets and three trombones. The second chorus is accompanied by comparable forces, among them eight trumpeters and four kettledrummers. The immense group that provides the thorough bass includes cellos, contrabasses, bassoons, harpsichords, harps, and lutes. The individual parts of the Mass total fifty-three, necessitating a score page nearly three feet long. It is as though Bernini's gigantic colonnades in St. Peter's Square had been transformed into music.

The key to such a vast sound-producing enterprise is the score, which provides the only practical means by which the work can be planned and executed. Other cultures have sometimes brought together great numbers of voices and instruments for temple rituals, but they have had to do without the master plan that directs the activities of the symphony orchestra. It is the "script culture" of the West that determines the essential distinction between a Balinese gamelan orchestra and

the Vienna Philharmonic. The fifty-three separate melodic strands of Benevoli's Mass had to be charted visually before they could be coordinated aurally. For that matter, even the relative simplicity of a four-voiced Bach fugue could never have come about without the prior existence of a system of notation, unique to the West, that enables a composer to express his musical ideas on paper, in a graph that can be read and executed by any well-trained musician.

This system is responsible not only for some of the stylistic differences between the Eastern and Western approaches to music; it also accounts for a vital philosophical distinction. An Indian sitar player must be adept at choosing the raga for the particular moment of his performance, and his choice will reflect the season of the year, the time of day, and his own mood as well as that of his listeners. He improvises, of course, and he perceives music as a transitory phenomenon that lives

and dies with each performance. To a composer in the Western tradition, his score is a kind of permanent monument that will outlive him and which exists forever in an ideal, Platonic dimension. Any particular performance can only be an approximation of the theoretical perfection of the score. As a result, many composers have written at least some of their music, as did Beethoven or Anton von Webern, not for their own time but "for a future age." This idea would never occur to an Oriental musician, whose medium is the here and now.

The long road from the troubadours to the baroque era is a thoroughly international one, leading through every country of Western Europe and touching all levels of culture. Around the year 1200, to coincide with the beginnings of great cathedrals like those of Notre Dame in Paris, and at Rheims and Rouen, the first two- and three-voiced church music began to make its appearance. This school of primitive polyphony was known as organum, and its earliest representatives were Magister Leoninus of Notre Dame and his successor, the choir-

The Renaissance produced scores of great composers, among them (from left to right) Orlando di Lasso, known throughout Europe as "the prince of musicians"; Giovanni Pierluigi da Palestrina, renowned composer of religious music; Giovanni Battista Lully, royal composer to Louis XIV; François Couperin, noted scion of a famous musical family; Jean Philippe Rameau, supreme musical theorist; and Claudio Monteverdi, progenitor of opera.

master Perotinus. A century later, at about the time Dante was at work on *La Vita Nuova* and the *Divine Comedy*, the rigid discipline of this dissonant style (the *ars antiqua*) gave way to the freedom of the *ars nova*, brilliantly propounded by the French poet and musician Guillaume de Machaut, who discovered many new ways of setting note against note and point *contra* point.

The 1380's—the age of Geoffrey Chaucer's *Canterbury Tales* in England—saw the first flowering of the Italian madrigal in Florence (the word comes from *matricale*, a pastoral in the mother tongue as opposed to Latin) and the beginnings of the Meistersinger movement in Germany (five hundred years later, Richard Wagner was to make this the subject of his only comic opera). In 1415, when Henry V of England defeated the French at Agincourt, the English school of composers, headed by John Dunstable and Lionel Power, was at work on the

first musically unified choral Masses, together with motets (sacred compositions for several voices) and French chansons. A generation later, as the Flemish brothers Hubert and Jan van Eyck were producing their famous musical altar painting for the cathedral at Ghent, a new school of counterpoint arose in Burgundy under Guillaume Dufay, a technical innovator who wrote sacred and secular music in a great variety of styles.

Around 1500, while Leonardo da Vinci was painting the *Mona Lisa* and Michelangelo the Sistine ceiling, the great Flemish composer Josquin Des Prés was active in Italy. (His first book of Masses was published in Venice in 1503.) Josquin has been called the Raphael of music, for both he and the great Italian painter prepared the way for the baroque age. Before Josquin, music was primarily concerned with structural principles, but it was his example that shifted the emphasis to emotional expressiveness and "the passions of the soul in music."

In Germany, around 1530, the Protestant Reformation brought the

Overleaf: The lute and the virginal are said to have been the most popular instruments in sixteenth-century Venice, where music lessons such as this one were a part of every gentlewoman's upbringing.

Lutheran chorale—and with it, a new folk spirit—into church music. Italy, at about the same time, witnessed the second golden age of the madrigal; literally thousands of such songs were produced by native Italian and visiting Flemish composers. Among the Netherlanders in Italy were Adrien Willaert (who established a school in Venice), Cipriano de Rore, Philippe de Monte, and Roland de Lassus, alias Orlando di Lasso, known throughout Europe as "the prince of musicians." From Italy, Lassus went on to Munich to become music director to the Duke of Bavaria. He wrote two thousand works in Latin, Italian, German, and French, received a patent of nobility from the Emperor Maximilian, and was decorated with the Order of the Golden Spur by Pope Gregory XIII.

Another master of the madrigal was Giovanni Pierluigi da Palestrina, foremost of the composers who served at the papal court in Rome. His

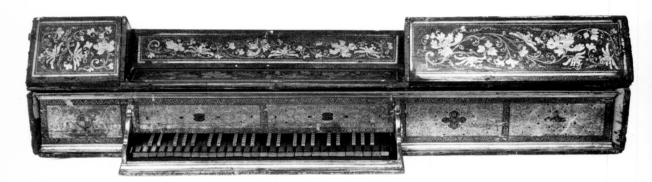

secular achievements are overshadowed by his work in perfecting the great a cappella Masses with their smoothly flowing counterpoint and harmonic buoyancy. In Spain, meanwhile, Luis Milan, Alonso de Mudarra, and several other virtuosos on the guitarlike vihuela created the first truly instrumental idiom that was not simply a translation from the vocal style. During the age of Cervantes, in the latter part of the sixteenth century, the greatest of Spanish composers was Tomás Luis de Victoria, who succeeded Palestrina in the pontifical chapel. In England, Shakespeare's musical contemporaries were William Byrd, Thomas Morley, and John Bull, all of them devoted to writing pavanes and other dances for the virginals (an early form of harpsichord) as well as the more conventional vocal forms.

Instrumental music had been steadily gaining in importance during this period and began coming into its own about 1600. Freed from the necessity of accompanying words, music now moved to dance rhythms rather than speech rhythms; the sound of viol consorts and other chamber ensembles was heard in the land. Claudio Monteverdi, the first of the great Italian operatic composers (and the last madrigalist) was also the first to explore the tone-color resources of the orchestra. He revolutionized performing techniques with such devices as the tremolo and pizzicato in the strings.

The golden age of baroque instrumental music really begins with

The virginal at lower left once belonged to Elizabeth I, and the instrument's name may well derive from its association with the Virgin Queen. In any case, the virginal enjoyed immense popularity in sixteenth-century England—a fact reflected in the publication of music books (left) especially for that instrument. Music was also a vital dimension of French court life, as the contemporary portrait below of Louis XIV surrounded by court musicians indicates. The Sun King himself was reputed to be a skilled dancer and guitarist.

Overleaf: Venice became the pleasure capital of eighteenth-century Europe, and scores of international visitors crowded the lagoon city to hear concerts such as the one depicted in Francesco Guardi's painting.

orchestral combinations such as the one Monteverdi employed in the first performance of his opera *Orfeo*, presented to celebrate the wedding of the Duke of Mantua in 1607. It consisted of two harpsichords, two contrabasses, twelve members of the violin family, a double harp, two archlutes, two organs with wooden pipes, a small portable organ, three viola da gambas, four trombones, two cornets, a small flute, a clarino trumpet, three muted trumpets, and further assistance from harp, flute, and zither. With these Monteverdi dramatized his characters and situations: a shepherd is accompanied by the high flute and a small violin; the underworld is suggested by brasses and organ music; Orpheus' entreaties are underscored by the strains of a harp; the spirits of the netherworld whisper in Flemish counterpoint.

Thirty years later, while the young Rembrandt was at work in Amsterdam and the aged Galileo went before the Inquisition in Rome for advocating the idea that the earth revolves around the sun, the German composer Heinrich Schütz created a brilliant series of dramatic oratorios on biblical themes—although the development of his gifts was hampered by the disastrous effects of the Thirty Years' War. In France, the son of a poor Italian miller, Giovanni Battista Lully, became viceroy of music at the court of that redoubtable monarch Louis XIV, for whom Lully produced a steady stream of operas, ballets, and ceremonial suites.

Louis himself was a skilled guitarist and dancer (for twenty-two years he took daily lessons from his dancing master, Pierre Beauchamps), and he took an active interest in the musical affairs of Versailles. In 1693 he personally presided over a competition to select a new organist for the royal chapel. A young and unknown organist was chosen when Louis commented to the other judges, "I shall be glad to know your opinion; in my own judgment, it is this young man I never heard of before who played best and seems to me the most worthy." It was François Couperin, afterwards known as "Le Grand" to distinguish him from the rest of the very numerous clan of musical Couperins. Louis soon knighted him for his services to the Crown in creating a brilliant and distinctive style of French keyboard music—a task that was to be completed after his death by another ingenious clavecinist, Jean Philippe Rameau.

In Restoration England, meanwhile, musical life under Charles II and his immediate successors was dominated by Henry Purcell, who became organist of Westminster Abbey at the age of twenty. His church and ceremonial music was so expressive that some of his listen-

The word concerto *is Italian in origin, reflecting the fact that musical history's most prolific writer of concertos was a Venetian named Antonio Vivaldi (above). The intimate musical performance at left was captured by Venetian painter Pietro Longhi.*

ers were moved to wonder whether "they ever heard any thing so rapturously fine and solemn and Heavenly in Operation." But Purcell also composed the catchiest theater music of the time and some of the most ribald songs ever written.

In Italy, where the great violin makers were concentrated, chiefly in Verona, it was the violin virtuosos who were perfecting new forms and styles of instrumental music. (The terms *concerto*, *sinfonia*, and *sonata* all arose out of Italian usage, although their precise "classical" meanings were not to be defined until the latter part of the eighteenth century.) Among the violinist-composers were Giovanni Vitali, Giuseppe Torelli, Arcangelo Corelli, and Giuseppe Tartini. But the one destined to become best known was Antonio Vivaldi, the musical director of the orphanage-conservatory of the Ospedale della Pietà in Venice. It was here, in the early eighteenth century, with an all-girl orchestra, that Vivaldi wrote most of his five hundred concertos, the majority of them scored for violin or various combinations of strings. The girls gave a public concert every Sunday, and their programs were constantly changed; hence the need for such vast amounts of new music. The French traveler Charles de Brosses described the ensemble:

> They sing like angels and play the violin, the flute, the organ, the cello, and the bassoon; in short, there is no instrument, however unwieldy, that can frighten them. They are cloistered like nuns. It is they alone who perform, and about forty girls take part in each concert. I vow to you that there is nothing so diverting as the sight of a young and pretty nun in a white habit, with a bunch of pomegranate blossoms over her ear, conducting the orchestra and beating time with all the grace and precision imaginable.

Certainly the art of music had come a long way in the five hundred years since the troubadours; only the underlying motives for music-making had remained unchanged. Above all it was still a feast for aural sensualists. As Samuel Pepys confided to his diary, "music is all the pleasure that I live for in the world, and the greatest I can ever expect in the best of my life." It would have been difficult to find a cultivated man in the baroque era who would have disagreed with him. The fact that music now possessed an enormous arsenal of ways and means, of forms and effects, only increased the power that it exerted on men's minds. Perhaps it never stood higher in prestige than at that moment in history, when it had acquired an almost magical ability to enthrall the sedulous ear with gorgeous instrumental colors and magnificent harmonies. When Pepys went to see a musical performance in 1688, he observed afterward that the sounds had taken "real command" of his soul, and that he had remained in transports of delight the whole night through. "That which did please me beyond anything in the whole world was the wind-musique when the angel comes down, which is so sweet that it ravished me, and indeed, in a word, did wrap up my soul so that it made me really sick, just as I have formerly been when in love with my wife."

3

The Splendor of Bach

HE WAS A STRANGER in the town and struck up an acquaintance with the local organist, explaining that he belonged to the same profession. Since the local organist was known to be a musician of considerable ability, and his church was one of those which contained two organs, it seemed only natural that the stranger should suggest a trial of skills. They would improvise on the two organs in question-and-answer fashion, playing the game known as "leading each other astray" while extemporizing fantasias in various styles of counterpoint.

For a time the contest sounded like an equal match. The two organists took turns, each picking up where the other had left off, tossing musical challenges back and forth. It seemed at first as if the four hands and four feet were directed by a single head. But gradually the visiting virtuoso began to employ the more recondite arts of counter-. point and modulation. He stretched out his fugue subjects by augmentation and compressed them by diminution; he turned them upside down and right side up again; he made them suddenly overlap or combined them with seemingly unrelated themes in a complex web of sound, as he discovered ingenious ways of slipping into unexpected keys. The local organist observed what the other man was doing and tried to imitate him, but soon he could no longer keep up the pace. Whenever he faltered, the visitor would help him recover his equilibrium. Then he would lead the way into new mazes of harmony from which the host, in the end, could no longer extricate himself. At last he jumped up from the keyboard and ran over to the stranger, conceding himself beaten but entreating his guest to go on playing as long as he might, for "You must be either Sebastian Bach or an angel from heaven!"

It was indeed the great Johann Sebastian Bach, with whom the local organist would not have attempted to match wits had he known his identity. This is one of the stories told about Bach by the theorist F. W. Marpurg, who knew the composer personally and may have heard the tale from Bach himself. To engage in a keyboard duel with Bach was something few virtuosos of the day were rash enough to try— hence the need for incognito and subterfuge in looking for a sparring partner. Some of his rivals had been known to leave town in a hurry rather than face the prospect of a public confrontation with him. A great deal of prestige was at stake in these contests, for to excel in the art of improvisation was a matter of particular pride among baroque

Baroque organs were not designed to produce the diminishing and swelling tones familiar to us, but rather were known for clarity, lightness, and contrast. The organ at left is in Bologna's Church of San Michele.

43

Johann Sebastian Bach (left, in Elias G. Haussmann's 1741 portrait) was born in the quiet Thuringian town of Eisenach, shown opposite, below. He heard himself lauded as a virtuoso organist rather than finding acclaim during his lifetime for the hundreds of works he produced; a page from one of his violin sonatas is at right.

organists; they considered it the highest test of their musicianship. And Bach was acknowledged to be the master of them all.

His fame as "the greatest organ and harpsichord player we have ever seen" brought him a great many invitations to serve as official examiner of the splendid organs that were being built throughout northern Germany in the early eighteenth century. On the social calendar of a sleepy Saxon town like Naumburg or Halle it was always a major event when Bach arrived to inaugurate a new organ. In those pious days virtually everyone went to church, and an organ was often their only source of Sunday entertainment, besides being as advanced and impressive a piece of precision machinery as anyone was ever apt to see.

In putting the instrument through its paces, Bach would give a breathtaking demonstration of fingerwork on the manuals and footwork on the pedals. His earliest biographer, J. N. Forkel, describes how, after seating himself at the organ, Bach would

   . . . choose some one theme and develop it in the various forms of organ composition, but in such a way that his material was always based on

this same subject, even when he played uninterruptedly for two hours or more. First he would use this theme for a prelude and fugue with full organ. Then he would display his art of using the stops, for a trio, quartet, etc., still on the same subject. Afterward followed a chorale, whose melody was again playfully surrounded ... with a fugue on the full organ, in which either another treatment of only the first subject might predominate, or, depending on its nature, one or two other subjects might be mixed with it.

When Bach played like this on a visit to Hamburg in 1720, improvising for half an hour on the chorale *By the Waters of Babylon*, the ninety-seven-year-old organ master Adam Reinken said to him, "I thought this art was dead, but I see that it still lives, in you."

It was true, however, that Bach was the representative of a dying art. He had the misfortune to be born thirty years too late, for counterpoint was going out of style, and his contemporaries were far more fascinated with the lighter, less polyphonic music of the Italian opera. His music was considered old fashioned, if not actually obsolete. "This great man would be the admiration of whole nations if he had more charm," wrote a Hamburg critic in 1737, "and if he did not diminish the natural quality of his pieces with his turgid and confused style, darkening their beauty with all-too-excessive art." Although some of his admirers rushed to his defense, none of them would have denied that he was the last of a vanishing race of great contrapuntalists. And no one at the time could have foreseen that within a hundred years every serious composer would come to regard Bach as the "founding father" of music and "the demigod of our art," as Schumann called him.

Tastes change, of course, and many earlier composers have since joined the pantheon, but the musical world still refers to them as the "pre-Bach" composers, in tacit recognition of his unique position at the Great Divide of music history. After more than two centuries, moreover, Bach is still pre-eminently the composer from whom the others like to borrow their ideas. Since the first Bach revival of the 1800's, he has been an inexhaustible source of inspiration to everyone from Bee-

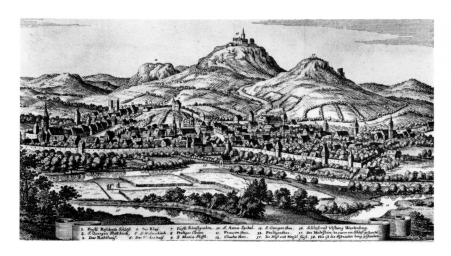

thoven and Brahms to Ferruccio Busoni, Igor Stravinsky, Dave Brubeck, and the Beatles. The Swingle Singers perform him in skat-singing style, Jacques Loussier with a jazz combo, Walter Carlos with an electronic sound synthesizer. Clearly, everyone indulges in Bach cribbing not on account of his historical importance but because his music is tremendously alive and full of harmonic surprises, or what Stravinsky called "the wonderful jolts, the sudden modulations, the unexpected harmonic changes, the deceptive cadences, that are the joy of every Bach cantata." Paradoxically, Bach the great contrapuntalist is also Bach the great harmonist. When modern jazzmen and pop groups steal from him, what they covet most are his harmonic progressions, which contain some of the most excruciatingly beautiful dissonances in the whole literature of music.

But the harmonies that now fascinate jazzmen and connoisseurs often baffled the solid Saxon burghers who constituted the bulk of his audience. In Arnstadt, for example, where Bach worked for four years as organist—it was his first job—the town consistory once lodged an official complaint against him for having "made many curious *variationes* in the chorale and mixed many strange tones into it, so that the congregation has become confused thereby." For that matter, most of the source documents for a biography of Bach are in the form of complaints of one kind or another—about the dissonances in his conduct as well as in his music. They are to be found in obscure town records or court archives, and the picture that emerges from between the lines is that of an energetic, headstrong, and rather irritable personality not even remotely resembling an angel from heaven.

In 1705 there is mention of a street brawl in which the twenty-year-old Bach was attacked by five bullies led by a member of his church choir whom he had provoked with the dreadful epithet *Zippelfaggotist*—"nanny-goat bassoonist." Another complaint was lodged against the young organist for having made his chorale prelude too long, "but after his attention had been drawn to it by the Superintendent, he had at once fallen into the other extreme and made it too short." Then there is another, more intriguing, charge that he allowed a "stranger maiden" to visit the organ loft and make music there. That would have been his second cousin Maria Barbara Bach, an organist's daughter (all the Bachs, for seven generations, were church or town musicians in Thuringia, as was Sebastian's own father, Johann Ambrosius). She was soon to become the first of two wives who bore him the now-legendary total of twenty children. What makes this a somewhat misleading statistic is that ten of his children died in infancy; of those that remained, five became well-known professional musicians.

In 1708, the year after his marriage, Bach entered the service of the Duke of Weimar, whose musical establishment included "sixteen well-disciplined musicians clad in Hungarian *haiduk* uniforms." After a decade in Weimar the court archives record a rather more serious complaint than usual: "On November 6, the former concertmeister and organist Bach was confined to the county judge's place of detention on account of the stiff-necked obstinacy with which he expressed his insistence on being dismissed, and finally on December 2 was freed

The harpsichord above was Bach's, built for him by Gottfried Silberman, who also experimented with the piano, a new instrument that never satisfied Bach —although it gradually eclipsed the harpsichord in popularity. Another popular instrument was the flute, being played at right in a portrait by Johann Hapetzky.

The Lutheran Church of Saint Thomas in Leipzig opened onto a busy street (above) from which parishoners stepped every Sunday into a vaulted interior (top). After hearing a Scripture reading, they listened to a scant choir and a dozen instrumentalists take part in one of Bach's specially composed cantatas elaborating on the Scripture; Bach himself led the music at an organ similar to the one shown opposite.

Overleaf: *Angels holding a score gaze impassively from this fresco painted in the Cathedral of Udine, Italy, by a younger contemporary of Bach's, Giovanni Battista Tiepolo.*

from arrest with notice of his unfavorable discharge." It was a forcible reminder, if he needed it, that the feudal system was still in effect.

A new post was waiting for him at the diminutive court of Anhalt-Cöthen, sixty miles away. As musical director to the young prince of Anhalt-Cöthen, he had charge of a seventeen-man orchestra largely staffed with men of solo caliber. It was for them that he wrote his great instrumental suites as well as the six *Brandenburg Concertos*, named for the Prussian prince to whom they were dedicated but modeled on the Italian concerto grosso form. Bach was acquainted with a great deal of Italian music, and the lyric, expressive melodies of composers like Vivaldi and Corelli had made a deep impression on him. Ultimately he was to bring north and south into a perfect equilibrium, spinning out a tracery of independent melodies over a solid harmonic bass. The result is a combination of logic and fantasy: the German fugue married to the Italian aria. His orchestrations were always designed to take maximum advantages of any virtuoso players who happened to be at his disposal. The second *Brandenburg Concerto*, for example, is written for a solo group of flute, oboe, violin, and trumpet who engage in animated conversation among themselves and with the main body of strings.

At Anhalt-Cöthen, Bach also composed a systematic series of keyboard studies ranging from the simplest *Two-Part Inventions* for the education of his children to the formidable bravura pieces in Book I of *The Well-Tempered Clavier*. His purpose in writing the *Clavier* was to demonstrate the advantages of his preferred method of tuning ("tempering") a harpsichord and to explore the musical characteristics of the twenty-four major and minor keys by writing a prelude and fugue appropriate to each of them. But it was destined to become the bible of keyboard playing. Even Chopin, whose style is so very different from Bach's, considered it "the highest and best school" of pianism and always warmed up for his concerts by playing the *Clavier*.

In 1723 Bach resigned his post at Anhalt-Cöthen to become cantor (music director) at St. Thomas' School in Leipzig. Here the record of complaints, both by and against him, begins again and mounts to a dissonant crescendo. He seems to have spent much of his time in a long series of squabbles with pettifogging church and town authorities to whom he was to become known as the "incorrigible" cantor. His principal duties were to direct the music for four Leipzig churches as well as the training of choirboys at St. Thomas'. But the post was not as lucrative as he had been led to expect, and Leipzig was very expensive. Besides, as he wrote to a friend, the authorities were so unmusical and uncooperative "that I must live amid almost constant vexation, envy and persecution. ... My situation here is worth about seven hundred taler, and when there are more bodies than *ordinairement*, the funeral fees rise in proportion. But when a healthy wind blows, they fall accordingly; last year, for example, I lost over one hundred taler that would ordinarily have come in from corpse fees (*Leichen accidentia*)."

Bach tried to organize an efficient musical establishment but was frustrated by the town council's refusal to appropriate sufficient funds for it. In one of his reports to the authorities he drew up a list of those choristers who were "usable," those who needed further training, and

those, alas, who were not musicians at all. The final balance sheet: seventeen usable, twenty potentials, seventeen unfit. Ideally, Bach said, he would like a chorus of sixteen trained singers for each church and an orchestra of at least eighteen men—eleven strings, two oboes, bassoon, three trumpets, and tympani—to accompany the cantata of the week, which was performed in only one church at a time. The orchestra he actually had to work with, however, was a terrible comedown from Anhalt-Cöthen: "four town pipers, three professional fiddlers and one apprentice." That meant he had to recruit volunteers from the University of Leipzig, a task made more difficult by the council's refusal to pay them the usual fees. Yet these were the forces for whom he wrote the great majority of his choral masterpieces—266 of his 295 church cantatas (only two-thirds of which have been preserved), the Magnificat in D Minor, the Mass in B Minor, and the two dramatic settings of the gospel narrative for Good Friday, *The Passion According to St. Matthew* and *The Passion According to St. John.*

Although this adds up to a vast amount of music, much of which had to be written on a clockwork schedule, Bach never treated any of these as routine assignments. Every cantata shows evidence of having been lovingly worked over, especially in the cryptic musical puns and contrapuntal allusions that were obviously meant only for the eyes and ears of the initiated. The cantata texts are full of images that are pictorially illustrated in the accompaniment: the splashing of waves, the bounding of stags on the hills, the shedding of tears in chromatic pain. In one case, where the text mentions joy, the singers burst into a twenty-five-note "paroxysm" of laughter; in another, based on the parable of the seven wise and the seven foolish virgins and their responses to the coming of the bridegroom, the orchestra maintains the steady beat of a wedding march while the chorus sings a Lutheran chorale punctuated with shouts of "Wake Up! Wake Up!"

The baroque was an age of skilled performers—from soloists like the violinist shown sitting comfortably before his score (above) to ensemble musicians (right) who could probably play one another's instruments with equally cheerful countenances. Among these virtuosos, Domenico Scarlatti (above, right, in a retrospective portrait) was often ranked as the best harpsichordist of his day.

Toward the end of his life, Bach evidently felt the need to preserve and systematize his matchless knowledge of polyphony, for the works that he composed, engraved, and privately printed during the 1740's constitute a giant compendium of the contrapuntal arts and crafts. In the *Goldberg Variations*, ostensibly written so that his pupil J. G. Goldberg could entertain Count Kayserling on sleepless nights, a simple household tune is turned into a set of thirty ingenious variations, of which every third one is based on a different sort of canon. Another demonstration of polyphonic alchemy is the dazzling set of organ variations on the Christmas chorale *Vom Himmel Hoch*, which Bach presented to a Leipzig musical society in lieu of an inaugural address. These variations culminate in a cascade of canons like a shower of stars. His visit to Frederick the Great of Prussia in 1747 produced *The Musical Offering*, in which he explored the fugal possibilities of the "right Royal theme" that Frederick had suggested to him as a subject for improvisation. Having shown what he could do with an amateur's theme, he then proceeded to subject one of his own to the same process. In *The Art of the Fugue* the basic theme is transformed into a series of increasingly complex fugues and canons to illustrate some of the limitless ways in which a fugue subject could be combined, com-

pressed, expanded, turned upside down, and run off backward.

Most of *The Art of the Fugue* was engraved under Bach's supervision, but blindness prevented him from finishing the great triple (or perhaps quadruple) fugue that introduces his four-note signature theme, B-A-C-H (a musical spelling that works only in German notation; in English practice, the notes are known as B-flat-A-C-B). Thus the last and most difficult contrapunctus of all breaks off in mid-flight at the two hundred and thirty-ninth measure. When Bach, having suffered a stroke, felt that death was near, he dictated to his son-in-law a chorale prelude on the hymn *Wenn wir in höchsten Nöten seyn* ("When We Are in Greatest Need"), but as a superscription he chose the first line of another stanza: *Vor deinen Thron tret' ich hiemit* ("With this I step before Thy Throne"). His death, at sixty-five, in 1750 "was uncommonly mourned by all true connoisseurs of music," as a Leipzig newspaper reported. But the town council merely used the occasion to complete the record by registering one last complaint about their incorrigible cantor.

Bach and his two great contemporaries George Frederick Handel and Domenico Scarlatti all happened to be born in the same year, 1685, but each represents a different facet of baroque music—let the astrologers make of that what they may. Bach, born under the sign of Aries (March 21), personifies the splendor of German Protestant church

music; he is the genius on the organ bench, adept at manipulating that technological miracle, the baroque organ, and its necessary adjunct, the church choir. Handel, born on February 23 (Pisces), embodied the theatrical spirit of the high baroque, a time when "all that impresses mankind is theatrical," as the critic Johann Mattheson wrote in 1728, "The whole world is a giant theater." As for the Scorpio, Scarlatti (born on October 26), he epitomizes the court composer, and his music is that of the Mediterranean palaces, with their baroque flourishes and arabesques.

Handel and Scarlatti became acquainted in Rome during the former's Italian journey (neither of them ever met Bach). The meeting probably took place in 1709 at the palace of Cardinal Ottoboni, who brought the two composers together for the inevitable trial of skill. "The issue of the trial on the harpsichord has been differently reported," writes Handel's first biographer, John Mainwaring. "It has been said that some gave the preference to Scarlatti. However, when it came to the organ there was not the least pretence for doubting to which of them it belonged. Scarlatti himself declared the superiority of his antagonist." Mainwaring reports that Handel often spoke of Scarlatti with great admiration, "for besides his great talents as an artist, he had the sweetest temper, and the genteelest behavior." Scarlatti, meanwhile, if complimented on his playing, "would mention Handel, and cross himself in token of veneration." Scarlatti was known for his "elegance and delicacy of expression," although he possessed a technique so formidable that one witness said it sounded as though "ten hundred

The making of music depended upon patrons, from the hundreds of aristocrats who treated their friends to concerts (left, below) to George elector of Hanover and later king of England who sponsored the compositions of George Frederick Handel, above. The reigning duke had persuaded Handel's worried father that it was perfectly acceptable to let the boy study music.

Overleaf: The elegant charm of a mid-eighteenth-century Italian concert is recreated in an engraving by Giorgio Poggiali. As noble folk stroll about a palace, an orchestra and chorus, complete with organ, provide musical diversion from the gallery above.

devils had been at the instrument." Handel is said to have had "uncommon brilliancy and command of finger, but what distinguished him from all other players who possessed these same qualities was that amazing fullness, force, and energy which he joined with them."

Scarlatti was born in Naples but went to Lisbon in his mid-thirties and then spent the rest of his life in Spain as music master and harpsichordist to Maria Barbara de Braganza, afterward queen of Spain. Following the royal family on its rounds of the great palaces from Seville to Aranjuez, he composed some 550 harpsichord sonatas that are brief, incisive, and touched with some of the rhythmic fire of Spanish folk music. He could elaborate a musical idea more brilliantly in three minutes than anyone else in thirty—not, as he said, with profound intentions but as "an ingenious jesting in art."

Handel's muse wore a more serious mien: he preferred to fill whole evenings with his operas and oratorios. Born in Halle, in Saxony, he went to London for a visit in 1710 and liked it so well that he settled there permanently two years later. As "the Orpheus of our age" he became the principal purveyor of Italian opera to the English public, writing and producing dozens of operas with various companies in which he had a financial stake. Unlike Bach, who was tied to his jobs and children, Handel remained unmarried and self-employed, risking his own capital when he could not borrow from others and riding the seesaw of free enterprise in the cutthroat theatrical world of London. When his operas suddenly went out of style, leaving him with a bankrupt theater and a deficit equivalent to 150,000 dollars, he came close to serving a term in debtor's prison. He extricated himself only when it finally dawned on him that an English public might prefer English texts to Italian ones. Oratorios like *Saul, Israel in Egypt*, and *Solomon* helped him pay off his creditors and changed him from an embattled impresario into a dignified elder statesman of music.

Essentially, Handel's oratorios were Italian operas in disguise—biblical operas in English, shorn of scenery and action. Much of the love music he had written for his amorous operas was easily transferred to this "sacred" framework, and sounds equally valid in either context. Certainly there was no doubt that he had found the ideal medium for projecting the sweep and drama of the Scriptures. "Words are wanting to express the exquisite Delight it afforded to the admiring crowded Audience," reported the Dublin press after the 1742 première of his oratorio *Messiah*. "The Sublime, the Grand and the Tender, adapted to the most elevated, majestick and moving Words, conspired to transport and charm the ravished Heart and Ear." *Messiah* earned him a lasting place in the affections of the musical world, and smoothed his way into Westminster Abbey. When he was buried there in April, 1759, "There was almost the greatest Concourse of People of all Ranks ever seen upon such, or indeed upon any other Occasion."

4

Mozart's Europe

WHEN FRANZ JOSEPH HAYDN, aged twenty-nine, became conductor of Prince Esterházy's private orchestra in 1761, his contract stipulated, among other things, that he should "conduct himself as becomes an honorable official of a princely household," appear always in the prescribed uniform and wig, and inquire twice daily "whether His Highness is pleased to order a performance of the orchestra." The idea that this kind of servitude might be incompatible with his dignity as an artist never occurred to him. He worked for the Esterházy family for thirty years, and neither he nor his employers ever had cause to regret the arrangement.

By eighteenth-century standards Haydn was an immense success, having begun his career in an unheated garret and worked his way up to the rank of princely *Kapellmeister*. As head of what one of the princes called "the music individuals," he was on a par with the master of the stables and the keeper of the silver: "My prince was always satisfied with my works; I not only had the encouragement of constant approval, but as conductor of an orchestra I could make experiments, observe what produced an effect and what weakened it, and was thus in a position to improve, alter, make additions or omissions, and be as bold as I pleased. I was cut off from the world; there was no one to confuse or torment me, and I was forced to become *original*."

Haydn's principal task was to provide the musical entertainment at Esterháza, an immense pleasure palace built by Prince Nicholas, "the Magnificent," as a Hungarian rival to Versailles. His orchestra of about twenty men soon became renowned as one of the best in all of the Habsburg domains, and with it he proceeded to create a whole new world of instrumental music. Beginning modestly with orchestral works that still took the form of serenades or divertimenti (musical "diversions"), he gradually evolved the classical symphony with its four contrasting movements: allegro, adagio, minuet, finale.

Haydn composed a hundred-odd symphonies during his lifetime, and he never stopped experimenting with the symphony's possible form and contents. Sometimes he began with a long slow movement rather than the usual brilliant allegro; sometimes he employed shock effects and trick rhythms deliberately written to throw the listener off balance; sometimes he based whole movements on Hungarian or Croation folksongs or on complex contrapuntal forms. In the Symphony No. 60, the violins are required to mistune their lowest string from G down to F, then interrupt in mock horror and re-tune raucously. The Symphony No. 73, *La Chasse*, incorporates a dashing hunting episode from one of Haydn's operas. The *Farewell Symphony* (No. 45) was composed, so the story goes, because Prince Esterházy had taken to spending too much time in his drafty summer place, to which the musicians were not permitted to bring their families. In 1772, the prince so extended his season that the players became desperate to rejoin their wives and children. Haydn solved the problem diplomatically by composing a symphonic finale in which one player after another blew out his candle and departed, leaving only two violins to carry on to the end—presumably they were played by Haydn himself and his concertmaster, Tomasini, the prince's favorite. His Highness took the hint. "Well, if they all leave we might as well leave, too," he is reported to have said, and the court departed the next day.

Esterháza had its own band-box opera theater, for which Haydn wrote Italian operas in the fashion of the day. They made a lasting impression on the Empress Maria Theresa when she paid a gala visit to the palace in 1773. "If I want to hear a good opera I shall come to Esterháza," she declared afterward, a remark that must have given considerable satisfaction to the prince, who liked to boast that he could match the emperor in everything. He was one of the richest men in Europe, and the entertainments he provided for the empress were lavish

even by court standards. The Viennese newspapers reported that her visit was marked by an almost continual succession of musical delights. First she was offered a comic opera by Haydn, then an elaborate masked ball. "Later the empress was taken to the Chinese pavilion, whose mirror-covered walls reflected countless lanterns and chandeliers flooding the room with light. On a platform sat the princely orchestra in gala uniform and played under Haydn's direction his new symphony, entitled *Maria Theresa*, together with other music. The empress then retired to her magnificent suite, while her retinue continued to enjoy the ball until dawn."

The next day an enormous banquet took place, "during which the virtuosos of the orchestra demonstrated their skill." In the afternoon the empress attended a performance of Haydn's marionette opera, *Philemon et Baucis*. After supper the guests watched a huge display of fireworks arranged by the pyrotechnician Rabel, "their variety and brilliance surpassing all expectation." The visiting monarch was then conducted to an immense open space hung with multicolored lights. "Suddenly, about a thousand peasants appeared in their beautiful Hungarian and Croation costumes [since they were serfs, this was not an expensive production number], and performed national dances to the entrancing tunes of their own folk music. The next morning the empress left, after distributing costly presents. Haydn received a valuable golden snuffbox filled with ducats. . . ."

Life at Esterháza was not always so spectacular, however, and Haydn grew rather weary of the daily routine of serving on the household staff. What he really liked were the soirées in Vienna, where he could make chamber music with "people of my own class." He sometimes felt "forsaken in the wilderness" of the prince's estates. As he wrote to a Viennese lady in an *opera buffa* letter dated February 9, 1790, "Here in Esterháza no one asks me: 'Would you like some chocolate, with milk or without; will you take some coffee, black or with cream? What may I offer you, my dear Haydn? Would you like a vanilla or a pineapple ice?' "

Only a few months later, following the death of Prince Nicholas, Haydn suddenly found himself pensioned off at full pay and free to come and go as he pleased. Rather than retire in Vienna at fifty-eight, he elected to see something of the world. His young friend Wolfgang Amadeus Mozart, who had already toured all of Europe in his child-prodigy days, is said to have wept when he heard the news that Haydn had signed a contract to appear in London. "Do not go, Papa!" he pleaded. "You are not suited to the great world, and you speak so few languages." To which Haydn is said to have replied, "But the language I speak is understood the world over!"

Not the least of Haydn's reasons for leaving home was his desperate need to escape not only his tiresome wife but also his increasingly importunate mistress, the Italian singer Loisa Polzelli. A year of separation helped to cool off what was becoming a rather difficult situation. Ultimately she had to content herself with no more than a legal option on Haydn: "I, the undersigned, promise to Signora Loisa Polzelli (in case I should consider marrying again) to take no other wife than said Loisa Polzelli. . . ."

Safely arrived in London, Haydn was able for the first time to enjoy the fruits of his international fame. "Everyone wants to know me," he reported happily. "I had to dine out six times up to now, and if I wanted, I could dine out every day; but I must first consider my health, and second my work. Except for the nobility, I admit no callers till 2 o'clock in the afternoon." For Johann Peter Salomon, the concert promoter who had guaranteed the tour, he composed the twelve symphonies that constitute the capstone of his career—and are still the most often performed of all his symphonies. "At the concerts in Hanover Square where he has presided," wrote the noted English music critic Dr. Charles Burney, "his presence seems to have awakened such a

Old enough to be Mozart's father, Haydn befriended the young virtuoso in Vienna. In the imaginative engraving at right by Francis Rigaud, Haydn plays as Mozart listens—or makes notations on a score. An 1808 performance of Haydn's oratorio The Creation *was immortalized in a watercolor painted on a golden snuff box that was presented to Haydn after the performance; the engraving below is based on that memento. All Vienna—including Beethoven—had turned out to greet the aged composer (seated at center).*

degree of enthusiasm in the audience as almost amounts to frenzy."

Only one thing marred his well-deserved triumph: the news that, during his absence, Mozart had died in Vienna. "For some time I was beside myself about his death," he wrote to a mutual friend, "and I could not believe that Providence would so soon claim the life of such an indispensable man." Haydn had always recognized that here was a composer greater than himself: "Posterity," he declared, "will not see such a talent again in a hundred years!" And although after his return to Vienna, Haydn became the teacher of the young Beethoven, it may very well be that he was right. Certainly there has never been another native talent like Mozart's; as Sacheverell Sitwell put it, he was "the most gifted human being that has ever been born."

Hardly less remarkable, however, is the fact that Haydn, unlike the rest of his colleagues, was never jealous of this phenomenal young man. Instead, he did his best to tell the world about Mozart's genius. When, in 1787, someone wrote him from Prague asking him to write a comic opera, he recommended Mozart instead: "If I could impress on the soul of every friend of music, and on high personages in particular, how inimitable are Mozart's works, how profound, how musically intelligent, how extraordinarily sensitive! (for this is how I understand them, how I feel them)—why then the nations would vie with each other to possess such a jewel within their frontiers. ... It enrages me to think that this incomparable Mozart is not yet engaged by some imperial or royal

court! Forgive me if I lose my head: but I love the man so dearly. . . ."

Haydn had first met Mozart during one of Haydn's annual visits to Vienna, probably during the winter of 1781-82, when he was fifty and Mozart exactly half that age. Haydn's schedule did not permit them to spend much time together, but from that time on, the two were on the warmest terms of mutual admiration. Musically the example of one always stimulated the other, so that both wrote their best works after the start of their friendship. Between them they established most of the sonata and symphonic precedents that account for the lasting fame of the Viennese classical school. "Mozart was able, through the peculiar gift of his genius, effortlessly and suddenly to reach a level of symphonic perfection for which Haydn had struggled for decades," writes the Haydn scholar H. C. Robbins Landon. Mozart also learned a great deal from Haydn's string quartets, and as an expression of his gratitude, he dedicated six of his own to Haydn in 1785: the inscription addresses him, with almost filial affection, as "a highly celebrated man and my dearest friend." It was while they were trying out some of these quartets in Vienna that Haydn turned to Mozart's father and said, "I tell you before God and as an honest man that your son is the greatest composer I know, either personally or by reputation. . . ."

This unsolicited testimonial must have come as balm to the elder Mozart, a man full of wise counsels and dire prophesies (usually correct, but unheeded) about the consequences of his son's easygoing ways. Leopold Mozart was assistant conductor at the court of the prince-archbishop of Salzburg. He was an earnest, dedicated musician who was very much the dominant figure in his son's life. Mozart the *Wunderkind*, the child prodigy, had been to a large extent his invention. When he realized that he had a son with incredible gifts—a child who could play the piano like an adult, who had perfect pitch and an infallible memory for music—he decided that it was his obligation (and might also be profitable) "to convince the world of this miracle."

When Wolfgang was six, he and his gifted sister Nannerl were taken on the first of a long series of concert tours that were to cover most of the major courts in Western Europe. In Vienna Wolfgang was allowed to jump into Maria Theresa's ample lap; in France he played at Versailles and was offended when Madame de Pompadour refused his kisses; in England he was warmly received by George III and played fugues with Johann Christian Bach, the youngest of Bach's sons. "His execution was amazing," reported a British music lover who heard Mozart improvise on the piano when he was nine. "He was also a great master of modulation, and his transitions from one key to another were excessively natural and judicious. . . ."

This great knack for modulation was always one of the hallmarks of Mozart's style. If he was a "master" of the art at nine, he was a sheer miracle worker in later years, after he had developed a harmonic subtlety and breadth unequaled by any other composer. It is the modulations that account for the remarkable poignance of so much of Mozart's music, but these key changes are always very subtly prepared. Not for him are the sudden shocks and *volte-face* deceptions of Haydn's symphonies, and still less the "clumsy plunging" with which some of

At right Leopold Mozart plays the violin while his gifted young son Wolfgang performs at the harpsichord and his daughter Maria Anna (nicknamed Nannerl) sings. The Mozarts lived in the house above in Salzburg.

64

his lesser contemporaries peppered their works. He was always very critical of those who did not understand this art. "He modulates in such a violent way as to make you think he is resolved to drag you with him by the scruff of the neck," he wrote to his father after hearing the Mannheim composer Joseph Vogler. And again, when he first heard the music of Friedrich Graf in 1777: "He often plunged into a new key far too brusquely and it is all quite devoid of charm." To show how it ought to be done, Mozart then proceeded to give a practical demonstration. "Herr Graf, who is director here, stood transfixed, like someone who has always imagined his wanderings from key to key are quite unusual and now finds that one can be even more unusual and yet not offend the ear. In a word, they were all astounded." This was typical of the object lessons he used to give, very nonchalantly, while cutting a swath through the musical world. And then he wondered why he had so many jealous rivals.

Of all the stopping places on Mozart's grand tour, it was operatic Italy that gave him the greatest pleasure and recognition. In Rome he was decorated with the Order of the Golden Spur, although afterward he was unable to make use of his knighthood because the genuine aristocrats would not have tolerated a title acquired by a fluke. The venerable Philharmonic Academy of Bologna elected him to membership at

Seated at the harpsichord, Mozart is shown playing in Paris for the court of Prince Conti during one of his European tours. The tour, and others like it, failed to accomplish its aim—that of providing Wolfgang with a good musical post.

fourteen—the youngest musician in its history—after he had demonstrated his ability to write the most difficult sort of counterpoint. Better yet, his operas found favor with the hypercritical Milanese. Since he spoke Italian fluently, he felt very much at home there amid the frenetic bustle of music. In 1772 he wrote to his sister, who had remained in Salzburg: "Upstairs we have a violinist, downstairs another one, in the next room a singing master who gives lessons, and in the other room opposite ours an oboist. That is good fun when you are composing! It gives you plenty of ideas!"

Most musical prodigies begin to falter sometime late in adolescence and never regain their original momentum; it seems to take a special sort of tenacity to overcome the disadvantages of a too-spectacular head start in life. It was Mozart's well-developed sense of his own worth that carried him past the danger point in the cycle, when he was no longer young enough to be a prodigy but was merely a young man with a great deal of talent and no particular prospects. "I am a composer and was born to be a *Kapellmeister*," he wrote to his father, who had suggested he might earn a living by teaching, "and I neither can nor ought to bury the talent for composition with which God in his goodness has so richly endowed me (I may say so without conceit, for I feel it now more than ever)...."

67

But under the patronage system of musicmaking it was not easy to earn a living. The nobility had a stranglehold on the arts, and there was no place in their scheme of things for an impatient genius. "I am surrounded by mere brute beasts," he wrote from the heart of fashionable Paris, relating that the Duchesse de Chabot had kept him waiting for half an hour in an ice-cold, unheated room before condescending to appear for a private recital. Then she sat down with her friends and made drawings for another hour while "not only my hands but my whole body and my feet were frozen and my head began to ache." At last it was Mozart's turn to do what he had come for: "I played on that miserable, wretched pianoforte. But what vexed me most of all was that Madame and all her gentlemen never interrupted their drawing for a moment, but went on intently, so that I had to play to the chairs, tables and walls. Under these detestable conditions I lost my patience. I therefore began to play the Fischer variations and after playing half of them I stood up. Whereupon I received a shower of compliments."

Mozart's rebellious tendencies were not exactly helpful to an office seeker in the protocol-ridden eighteenth century, and he never found the powerful patron who might have smoothed the way for him. He had too little diplomacy for Paris, too little influence in Munich, and too many rivals in Vienna. For a time a stopgap solution was found for him in Salzburg, although the archbishop took a rather dim view of the prodigal returned. He was appointed court and cathedral organist at a salary of four hundred gulden per year, just below the poverty line. Life in Salzburg, moreover, was far too confining for Mozart's taste. "I detest Salzburg," he wrote to a friend, "and not only on account of the injustices which my dear father and I have endured there. . . . Salzburg is no place for my talent. In the first place, professional musicians are not held in much consideration; and secondly, one hears nothing, there is no theater, no opera; and even if they really wanted one, who is there to sing?"

His patience finally snapped when he was made to sit at the valets' table during one of the archbishop's state visits to Vienna. Their last interview terminated (as Mozart tells it) when the composer, assuming that the archbishop was not satisfied with him, questioned the prelate. In a fury, the archbishop replied: "What, you dare to threaten me—you scoundrel? There is the door! Look out, for I will have nothing more to do with such a miserable wretch." Mozart shot back, "Nor I with you," and the archbishop, having the final word, commanded, "Well, be off!"

From then on Mozart lived in Vienna as a freelance composer, giving concerts and piano lessons, and writing music on commission. His real greatness as a composer began precisely at the point where he turned his back on rococo etiquette and struck out into the uncharted regions of a subjective, utterly personal music. It was a quiet revolution, occurring almost secretly in the inner voices of his string quartets, the long, arching andantes of his piano concertos, and the breathtaking multiplicity of his operatic ensembles, in which several different characters, each expressing his own feelings, unite to form a perfect harmonic nexus that also sums up the dramatic situation of the moment. It

The portrait of Mozart at right by Taddeo Helbling shows the renowned prodigy at the age of eleven or twelve; it is considered one of the most faithful likenesses of the composer.

Overleaf: A party of gaily dressed Florentines enjoy a musical afternoon in this scene created from precious stones.

In the romanticized watercolor at left Beethoven is shown at the piano surrounded by a group of friends in various postures of listening. Above he appears as the last and possibly the handsomest of the three musical giants of Vienna as painted by Joseph Karl Stieler, whose flattering representation of the founder of romanticism appears in detail on page 74.

Overleaf: The romantic spirit is evident in this watercolor by William Blake depicting a scene from Shakespeare's A Midsummer Night's Dream—the dance of the fairies before Oberon, Titania, and Puck. In the year 1826, still in his teens, Felix Mendelssohn wrote his overture to Shakespeare's play; nearly two decades later he composed incidental music for the entire play.

live, Ach! within my breast!"—and this implicit tension is characteristic of all of Goethe's writing. Beethoven's work, too, is Janus faced, looking backward with the logic and lucidity of the eighteenth century and forward with the heaven-storming passion of the nineteenth. Moreover, his music incorporates the whole arsenal of images and ideas that succeeding generations were to develop in their own fashion. His nine symphonies, sixteen string quartets, and thirty-two piano sonatas were to acquire a kind of canonical authority as definitive models—and unattainable ideals. "To us musicians," wrote Franz Liszt in 1852, "the work of Beethoven parallels the pillars of smoke and fire which led the Israelites through the desert, a pillar of smoke and fire to lead us by day and a pillar of fire to light the night, so that we may march ahead both day and night. His darkness and light equally trace for us the road we must follow; both the one and the other are a perpetual commandment, an infallible revelation."

It proved to be, however, an overpowering and frequently oppressive influence, although not until the end of the century did anyone dare to break the spell that Beethoven had cast over symphonic music. Claude Debussy, who was the first to do so, wrote an essay in which he suggested that Beethoven had exhausted the forms in which he worked and that his example ought therefore to be avoided. Proof of "the futility of the symphony" after Beethoven had been furnished by Robert Schumann and Felix Mendelssohn, who "did no more than respectfully repeat the same forms with less power." This is an unflattering but accurate view of what actually happened to the German tradition in the post-Beethoven era. Indeed, Mendelssohn, the "bright, pure, aspiring spirit" who wrote most of his finest music before he was eighteen, abandoned his airy Midsummer Night's Dream brilliance in order to assume the portentous attitude of the Beethoven symphonies. It was a pose so little suited to his real personality that, of his later works, only his chamber music fulfills his early promise. "He began by being a genius and ended by being a talent," was one conductor's unkind but succinct way of summing up the case.

Schumann also paid his debt to Beethoven by writing four magisterial and rather pompous symphonies, although his real genius was for small, lyrical forms like the fantasy pieces that make up the *Carnaval* suite for piano, or the *Kreisleriana* suite, inspired by a character in Hoffmann's *Tales*. If there is such a thing as a quintessential product of German musical romanticism (as opposed to the later and more radical French kind), then it is the poetry of Heinrich Heine set to music by Schumann, notably the *Dichterliebe* ("Poet's Love") and *Liederkreis* ("Garland of Songs") collections. As Schumann explained, such poems had inspired a whole new genre of music, "and thus arose that more artistic and profound style of song of which earlier composers could of course know nothing, for it was due to the new spirit of poetry reflected in music."

Of all the composers in this group, it was Franz Schubert who was best able to hold his own against the full force of the Beethoven tide—Schubert, who had lived all of his thirty-one years in Beethoven's shadow. Perhaps it was just as well that they were introduced to each other only at the very end of Beethoven's life, in 1827; had it been earlier, Schubert might have become just another one of Beethoven's many musical errand boys. As it was, he was able to develop a personal style that somehow managed to absorb the older composer's influence without being crushed by it. The generation gap had something to do with it. Schubert was twenty-seven years younger than Beethoven, and he moved in far less rarified social circles. His Viennese friends were the Bohemian poets, the young painters, the government clerks and merchants' daughters. He began his career as a schoolmaster and ended it a decade later as an unemployed composer of vast amounts of music, most of it unpublished. During his lifetime the Viennese publishers accepted only one of his nineteen quartets, only three of his twenty-one piano sonatas, one of his seven Masses, less than a third of his six hundred songs, and not a single one of his nine symphonies.

Only once in his life, in the spring of 1828, did Schubert give a concert of his own music—and it was prompted not by a petition of princes but by a letter from a friend who was a lawyer and would-be poet. "Do you want my advice?" wrote Eduard von Bauernfeld, "Every new song of yours is an event. You have composed the most glorious string quartets and trios, not to mention the symphonies. Your friends are enchanted with them, but as yet no publisher will buy them, and the public still has no idea of the beauty and grace that slumber in these works. So take a running start, master your inertia, give a concert. . . . A single evening will at least be enough to cover your expenses for a whole year." Schubert complied with the suggestion. His admirers rallied to the occasion and contributed their services, the *Musikfreunde* donated their hall free of charge, and the concert, consisting of songs, choruses, and chamber music, turned out to be a great success, netting the composer a profit of eight hundred gulden. With the proceeds he was at last able to buy himself a much-needed piano.

When it was suggested that he give a repeat performance, Schubert declined. He was not a concert virtuoso but a chamber player, a composer of choral serenades to be sung under girls' windows by moon-

The first generation of romantics after Beethoven were all principally composers for the piano: Mendelssohn (left, above), Robert Schumann (above), and Franz Schubert, seen in the idealized 1826 painting below playing at a musicale in his publisher's home. Schubert's intense admirers include Beethoven (who leans toward him over the piano), although Beethoven had long been acutely deaf; two years later both he and Schubert were dead.

light, a pianist who liked to play for his friends' parties. "He never danced," recalled his friend Leopold von Sonnleithner, "but he was always ready to sit down at the piano, where for hours he improvised the most beautiful waltzes; those he liked he repeated, in order to remember them and write them out afterwards. Mozart and especially *Beethoven* were his ideals . . . about them he became enthusiastic."

Sonnleithner testifies that Schubert was too retiring and tonguetied to venture out into the fashionable world: "He was only really animated among intimate friends. . . . He was shy and taciturn, especially in smart society, which he only frequented in order to accompany his songs, more or less as a favor. Whilst doing this his face wore the most serious expression, and as soon as it was over he withdrew into the neighboring room." Schubert was an even smaller man than Beethoven, and cut such an unprepossessing figure that his friends called him *Schwammerl*—"little mushroom." "Inwardly a poet and outwardly a kind of hedonist," he had a round face, stubby nose, short neck, bushy eyebrows, and thick curly hair—"one could have taken him for an Austrian, or more likely, a *Bavarian* peasant."

Yet there is no music that is lighter on its feet than Schubert's. And while Beethoven was at work putting the finishing touches to his epic tonal monuments, Schubert was busy inventing the German Lied, the epitome of all that was most lyrical in the romantic movement. There had been German songs before Schubert, but they lacked the unmistakable spark that, in his magnificent Lieder, is struck when the hammer of music meets the anvil of poetry. For him the text of a song often serves merely as a point of departure for some superb musical metaphors, and

many of his verses are by minor poets who would hardly rate one star in a guidebook to literary Germany. His best-known cycle, for example, *Die Schöne Müllerin* ("The Miller's Beautiful Daughter") is based on a group of sentimental verses by the otherwise undistinguished poet Wilhelm Müller. But to a composer accustomed to transcending his material, they were enough to inspire a series of brilliant character studies.

The piano always played a vital role in Schubert's songs, and in the *Müllerin* he has the accompaniment impersonating the millstream that "fumes and frets and foams" through the entire cycle, underscoring the turbulent emotions of its protagonists. Where the poet hears "a stream gushing from its rocky bed," Schubert has a flood of undulating figures in the accompaniment. And when, in the next song, the stream's power is harnessed to the mill wheel, the pages bear clusters of notes that look as if they were churning up a spray. Farther downstream is a place where, in a melancholy interlude, the hero sheds a tear or two; they can be heard splashing like raindrops in the accompaniment.

Famous for more than six hundred love songs and ballads, Schubert (left) gained inspiration from folk tunes, and as depicted in the scene at right, frequently listened to Gypsy musicmakers. In 1814 Vienna welcomed Europe's most important statesmen to a peace congress and feted them with song and dance, especially the popular waltz, as demonstrated by the willowy couple at left, below.

Beethoven, of course, never got to hear Schubert's songs, but he did get to see them when he was already in bed with his last illness. His factotum, Anton Schindler, brought him a collection of sixty Schubert Lieder, many of them still in manuscript. Schindler has described Beethoven's reaction:

> The master was amazed at the number of them, and simply could not believe that at that time [February, 1827] Schubert had already written over five hundred. But if he was amazed at their number, he was utterly astonished when he got to know their content. For several days he simply could not tear himself away from them, and he spent hours every day over *Iphigenia's Monologue, Grenzan der Menschheit, Die Allmacht, Die Junge Nonne, Viola,* the *Muller* Lieder, and others as well. With delighted enthusiasm he called out repeatedly, "Truly, in Schubert there dwells a divine spark!"

Schindler finally brought Schubert to Beethoven's bedside a week before his death. Nothing is known about what passed between them, except that when Beethoven was told that there were several visitors waiting to see him, he said, "Let Schubert come first!"

Schubert's friend Josef von Spaun has another story to tell that may help to explain why, until that moment, Schubert had always been too shy to approach Beethoven. One day, as Schubert was performing some of his songs for Spaun, he turned to his friend and asked, "Do you really think something will come of me?" Spaun was deeply moved, and as he later recalled, "I embraced him and said, 'You have done much already and time will enable you to do much more and great things, too.' Then he said quite humbly, 'Secretly, in my heart of hearts, I still hope to be able to make something out of myself, but who can do anything after Beethoven?'"

6

The Romantic Imagination

PARIS IN THE EARLY 1830's was "the capital of the nineteenth century" —a city of poets, painters, and musicians, of brilliant young men with daring ideas and abundant energies for carrying them out: Alexandre Dumas, Alfred de Musset, Théophile Gautier, Alfred de Vigny, Honoré de Balzac, Prosper Mérimée, Gérard de Nerval. At the première of Victor Hugo's play *Hernani* in 1830, the clean-shaven supporters of classical conventions had been routed by the bearded partisans of romanticism. With the success of that theatrical coup d'état, the way was suddenly open for a new freedom of expression in every branch of the arts. "We were mad with lyricism and with art," Gautier remembered afterward. "It seemed as if we had just discovered a long-lost secret; and that was true, for we had rediscovered poetry."

It was an age to compare with the Italian Renaissance, a great cultural transformation based on a revolution of human consciousness. Not only poetry had been rediscovered by the romantics, but also the uses of history and myth, the beauties of nature in the Alps and the Mediterranean, and—not least—the psychic and sexual mysteries of the self. The Baroness Aurore Dudevant, better known to literature as George Sand, launched a great campaign for woman's liberation with her novels *Valentine*, *Indiana*, and *Lélia*, soon to be followed by still other passionate revelations about the true state of a woman's heart. Among the older writers, Stendhal, "the first *modern* man," published his masterpiece, *The Red and the Black*, in 1830. It is a ruthlessly unsentimental study of ambition and sexuality in a young man who has been described as the quintessential romantic hero, "a Napoleon without a sword." Henrich Heine came to Paris from Germany in 1831 to write some of the finest poetry and some of the most biting political satires of the age—"standing all alone," as Ford Madox Ford describes him, "perhaps the most exquisite of all the world's lyricists since the great Greeks, perhaps the greatest of all the world's realistic-bitter romantics."

The young painter Eugène Delacroix, newly returned from a voyage to North Africa, was already at work on the turbulent pictures of Arab life whose dazzling colors were to change the course of modern painting. His older rival Jean Auguste Ingres, meanwhile, continued to paint his cool, restrained portraits and neoclassical nudes. Stylistically these artists were poles apart, yet each in his own fashion was a thoroughly romantic artist.

A nation of revolutionaries, the French welcomed Europe's artistic energy to Paris during the decade of the 1830's. There the opera bouffe came into its own and enjoyed a long popularity. The poster at left advertising Jacques Offenbach's satirical La Vie Parisienne *dates from 1866, when France and the rest of Europe had seen an end to revolutionary fervor.*

On the musical scene, three young titans made their debuts within a few years of one another—Hector Berlioz, Franz Liszt, and Frédéric Chopin. The twenty-seven-year-old Berlioz stood Paris on its ear in that same fateful year of revolutions and turning points, 1830, when he presented the première of his *Symphonie fantastique*, an event that proclaimed the beginning of a new musical epoch. It also marked the start of his friendship with Liszt, who expressed his admiration for the *Fantastique* by making a piano arrangement of it which he played at his concerts and undertook to publish at his own expense.

Born in Hungary, Liszt had first come to Paris as a child prodigy. Now, as a virtuoso in his early twenties, he was giving the musical world a series of breathtaking demonstrations of what could be done with ten fingers on the eighty-eight keys of a pianoforte. Chopin, in his turn, came to Paris from Poland in 1831, when he was twenty-one, to demonstrate a keyboard technique and a style of composition that was more intimate and subtle than Liszt's. "Yes, one must grant Chopin genius in the fullest sense of the word," Heine wrote. "He is not simply a technician, he is a poet and can express for us the poetry that lives in his soul; he is a poet in sound, and nothing is quite like the delights he lavishes on us when he sits at the keyboard and improvises."

It was Berlioz, the eldest and also the most energetic of the three, who pointed the way for the others. Gifted, audacious, and fiercely devoted to his art, he possessed "the most powerful musical brain in France," as Liszt observed, and at the same time one of the best literary minds in the country. He loved literature of great themes and passions —Vergil, Byron, and above all, "Shakespeare and Goethe, the mute witnesses to my torments, who have explained my whole life to me." Some of his greatest works were inspired by *Romeo and Juliet*, *Faust*, *Childe Harold*, and *The Aeneid*. Yet it was not so much a matter of "illustrating" these works as of realizing his visions of them in sound—of finding their equivalents in the metaphor of music. That meant creating new forms or putting old ones to new uses. For *Romeo and Juliet* he devised the dramatic symphony, for *Faust* the dramatic legend (a kind of opera for the imagination), and for *The Tempest* and *King Lear* the dramatic overture or fantasia, which is really a kind of tone poem in classical disguise.

Liszt and Chopin were accustomed to working out their compositions at the piano; Berlioz always conceived of his music orchestrally from the very first. As a boy in provincial France he had studied flute and guitar rather than the piano (there happened to be none in his parents' home), and in later years he realized that this circumstance had shaped his whole approach to music. "When I consider the appalling platitudes to which the piano has given birth, I give grateful thanks to the good fortune that forced me to compose freely and in silence, and delivered me from the tyranny of the fingers, so dangerous to thought."

When he went to Paris, supposedly to become a doctor like his father, his passion for music made a change of plans inevitable. Before long, much against his family's wishes, he enrolled as a student of composition at the Conservatoire. He also became notorious as a heckler at the Paris Opéra, taking it upon himself to serve as a one-man watchdog

Hector Berlioz (above, as drawn by Ingres) was born in 1803, before the poet Goethe had completed his seminal work Faust. *Twenty-five years later Berlioz had composed* Eight Scenes from Faust *and in 1846 came his fully developed "imaginary opera"* The Damnation of Faust *(the program for the first performance is above, right). Berlioz' novel technique appeared earlier in his* Symphonie fantastique, *for which he published pre-performance program notes; a page from that symphony is shown below. The drawing at right, below, is of the showman violinist Nicolò Paganini, for whom Berlioz composed* Harold in Italy.

committee on behalf of his favorite composers, Gluck and Weber. The playwright Ernest Legouvé recalled afterward how he had caught his first glimpse of Berlioz at a performance of Weber's *Der Freischütz.* "Suddenly in the middle of the ritornello of Caspar's aria, one of my neighbors leaps to his feet, leans over to the orchestra and shouts in a thundering voice: 'Not two flutes, you scoundrels! Two piccolos! Two piccolos! Oh, what brutes!'"

It was Berlioz, in the full flowering of his wrath—and surely the only man in Paris who knew or cared that the orchestra was not following the score. Legouvé gives a memorable account of how he looked at that arch-romantic moment: "a young man quivering with rage, his hands clenched, eyes flashing, and an amazing head of hair, but what a head of hair! It was like an immense umbrella of hair, overhanging and waving about the beak of a bird of prey. It was comic and diabolical at the same time."

While he was still a student at the Conservatoire, an English theatrical troupe came to Paris to perform a season of Shakespeare. Berlioz promptly fell in love, not only with the plays, but with Harriet Smithson, the Irish actress who played Juliet and Ophelia. "It prostrated me, and my heart and whole being were invaded by a cruel, maddening passion, in which the love of a great artist and the love of a great art were mingled together, each intensifying the other." For a long time this terrible passion was to remain altogether unrequited. But fortunately the romantics were always at their best in the midst of a tempestuous love affair; their whole aesthetic movement depended for its power on just such an intermingling of art and sexuality.

True to form, Berlioz poured his feelings into the *Symphonie fantastique,* with its semiautobiographical scenario about a lovesick musician who tries to poison himself with opium, and sees his beloved in a series of feverish visions. Not until the second performance, in 1832, did Berlioz have an opportunity to invite Miss Smithson to hear the work. When the actress took her seat for the concert, she may have been the only person in the audience unaware that she herself figured as the heroine of the symphony, for she had heard only rumors of Berlioz' infatuation. Still, as he writes in his memoirs, "the passionate character of the work, its burning melodies, its cries of love, its accesses of fury, and the violent vibrations of such an orchestra heard close by, were bound to produce an impression."

Indeed, the message was unmistakable. Harriet went home in a trance; within the year they were married at the British embassy, with Liszt as witness. Not that there was to be a genuine fairy-tale ending to this most romantic of love stories. In time, Harriet became an alcoholic, and Berlioz left her to live with a young singer, Marie Recio, whom he was to marry after Harriet's death. But the first years following his marriage were easily the happiest and most productive of his life. He wrote *Harold in Italy* for that formidable virtuoso Nicolò Paganini (Heine called him "a vampire with a violin"), who became one of Berlioz' greatest admirers. The day after hearing *Harold* for the first time, Paganini sent the composer a gift of 20,000 francs, together with the note: "Beethoven is dead, and only Berlioz can revive his spirit!"

Thanks to this act of generosity, Berlioz was able to compose his great symphony with voices, *Romeo and Juliet.* "I worked for seven months at my symphony, not leaving off for more than three or four days out of every thirty on any pretence whatever. And during all that time, how ardently did I live!"

This ardor is one of the hallmarks of his whole life and style. Berlioz himself said that the dominant qualities of his music were "passionate expression, inner fire, rhythmic drive and the element of surprise." All of these were elements that distinguish the romantics' ideal from the orderly, positive, and more predictable manner of the classicists who preceded them. In performance, Berlioz added, his works required a very difficult combination of "extreme precision and irresistible verve, a regulated vehemence, a dreamy tenderness and an almost morbid melancholy."

These paradoxical features of musical romanticism are nowhere more in evidence than in the great *Requiem Mass*, which the French government commissioned him to write in 1837. Alfred de Vigny, after hearing the première, called it "beautiful and bizarre, savage, convulsive and heart-rending." It also gave Berlioz an unfortunate reputation as something of a circus ringmaster specializing in colossal effects and oversize orchestrations. In the *Dies Irae* ("Days of Wrath") section of the *Mass*, where the text speaks of the Last Judgment, Berlioz harnesses the power of massed voices and brasses to conjure up a spine-chilling vision of the trumpet call that will reverberate through the tombs of the dead. Here the main orchestra and chorus are surrounded by four satellite brass bands that challenge and answer one another in furious vectors of sound. It is an arrangement requiring split-second coordination, and Berlioz was never more in his element than when he had a chance to conduct this prophecy of the Apocalypse. His memoirs contain an account that gives us an inkling of the physical sensations he could experience on such occasions:

> The chorus sustained the assault of the orchestra without flinching; the fourfold peal of trumpets broke forth from the four corners of the stage, already vibrating with the rolling of ten kettledrums and the tremolo of fifty bows; and, in the midst of this cataclysm of sinister harmonies and noise from the other world, hurled forth their terrible prediction. . . .

He always responded physically to music, and on the podium he would sometimes be overcome by a sort of rapture of the deeps, what he described as "a peal of bells in my heart, a millwheel in my head, my knees knocking against each other." The great tragedy of his life was that he could not get enough of such experiences, for the music industry of Paris had no appropriate place for a man of his genius. When both of his grand operas proved to be failures, and the main orchestras, run by his rivals, turned a deaf ear to his works, he was forced to earn his living by writing music criticism for the newspapers. It was a job he detested, although he did it brilliantly, with more style and gusto than any critic before or since. To bring his own works before the public he had to become an impresario, hiring the hall and paying the musicians

The Shakespearean actress Harriet Smithson (left) fared little better than the Juliet or Ophelia she played; eventually courted by neither the public nor her husband, Berlioz, she turned to alcohol. Berlioz is caricatured below as the rather foppish conductor of his own music.

out of his own pocket. The one advantage of this arrangement was that, while composing, he was not bound to the dimensions of any existing orchestra. He could write for any orchestral combination that suited his particular purpose, and for the acoustics of the hall in which the performance would occur.

The problem of acoustic balance is a technical question, but a highly significant one, since it arose directly out of the social and economic changes accompanying the Industrial Revolution. The nineteenth century witnessed the so-called triumph of the middle classes. Although there were still a few dukes and princes, the minor courts were fast disappearing, and the major ones no longer supported private orchestras. It was the upper middle class that now called the tune, founding publicly supported orchestras and building concert halls seating hundreds, or thousands, of people. Seventeen men may have sufficed to play Bach's *Brandenburg Concertos* in the music room at the court of Anhalt-Cöthen (particularly as the prince, for whom the concert was being given, was both player and audience); but in a bourgeois concert hall with fifteen hundred listeners, there had to be a proportionate increase in the size of the orchestra and the volume of sound it could produce.

Berlioz always insisted that the theaters of his day were too large for the standard orchestra. If the music proceeded from a point too far away from the listener, "we *hear* but do not vibrate. Now we *must vibrate* ourselves with the instruments and voices, and be made to vibrate by them in order to have true musical sensations." (One wonders whether he would have been delighted or horrified by the decibels that shake the walls of a modern discothèque.) On one occasion, when he was asked to organize a concert in the giant exhibition hall of the 1844 Paris Industrial Exhibition—an event that perfectly expressed the power of the burgeoning bourgeoisie—he filled the stage with a chorus and orchestra of 1,022 men and women, about evenly divided between singers and instrumentalists. It took six assistant conductors and chorus masters to control this vast socio-musical enterprise. But, as Berlioz declared, "... notwithstanding the acoustic defects of the place, I do not think that such an effect has often been produced." At one point, he himself was overcome by the sound. "I was seized with such a fit of nervous trembling that my teeth chattered as though I were in a violent fever ... the concert had to be stopped for some time."

Berlioz relates that the concert took in 32,000 francs, but that only 800 of them went into his pocket. That was typical of the pitiless economics that ultimately turned him against the bourgeois society of his day. "I belong to a nation that has ceased to be interested in the nobler manifestations of intelligence, and whose only deity is the golden calf," he wrote bitterly when he was fifty. "The industrialism of art, followed by all the base instincts it flatters and caresses, marches at the head of an absurd procession. ..." At the root of his difficulties lay a nineteenth-century dilemma that the twentieth has yet to resolve: since it is no longer the princes who support the artist, he must now look to the general public for a livelihood. But the public's taste is notoriously shallow and untrustworthy. It prefers commonplaces and will rarely trouble itself over complex or unfamiliar matters. This attitude is not calculated to decrease the artist's sense of estrangement from his audience.

The theme of the artist's alienation from society is hardly a nineteenth-century invention, of course, but it was with the romantics that the theme became almost an obsession. "My joys, my griefs, my passions and my powers,/ Made me a stranger," says Byron's hero Manfred, summing up the poet's own feeling of isolation from the world. Manfred is a mountain climber (Byron, with his lameness, could follow him only in his imagination). And he likes to stand poised on the edge of an alpine abyss, a typically romantic situation from which the artist-misanthrope can look down on a distant world. This is the romantic's favorite view of himself with respect to the rest of society. He takes risks but is rewarded with a vantage point like that of an eagle. High above conventional mankind, he is a solitary spectator whose figure is outlined against the sky.

The curious melancholia that accompanies this sense of unbridgeable remoteness between the artist and other people was known as *Le Spleen* among the French romantics. Berlioz describes it in his memoirs when he writes about his youthful emotions on May mornings in the meadows of his native Dauphiné:

> Silence . . . the faint rustling of the wheat, stirred by the soft morning air . . . the utter calm . . . the dull throbbing of my own heart. . . . Life was so far, far away from me. . . . On the remote horizon the Alpine glaciers flashed like gems in the light of the morning sun . . . below me, Meylan . . . and beyond the Alps, Italy, Naples, Posilippo . . . burning passions . . . and unfathomable and secret joy. . . . Oh for wings across the space! I want life and love and enthusiasm and burning kisses, I want more and fuller life!

No other musician succeeded so well as Berlioz in describing the great *Sehnsucht* ("yearning") that underlies the romantic imagination. And he was not only able to put it into words; he expressed it musically in many of his works, notably in the meadow scene of the *Symphonie fantastique*. Here his hero is in the country, thinking of his beloved as he listens to two shepherds in the distance playing a *ranz-des-vaches* (the tune used by Swiss shepherds to call their flocks). At the end of the movement, according to Berlioz' program note, "one of the shepherds resumes the melody, but the other answers him no more. . . . Sunset . . . distant rolling of thunder . . . loneliness . . . silence. . . ."

Something of this anguished mood can be found in all of the great romantics, but its most voluptuous expression occurs in the music of Chopin—in the nocturnes, préludes, and ballades, whose "despairing beauty of sound" has never been approached by any other composer. Chopin's piano music is a world in itself, and unlike Berlioz' symphonic realm, requires no literary explanations. He always avoided giving descriptive titles to his pieces, and deeply resented other people trying to do it for him (although there was no stopping the ladies who gushed "Play me your *Second Sigh*" or "I love your *Bells*!"). On rare occasions even he would resort to words. Describing his E Minor Piano

Two Delacroix portraits (below) show Frédéric Chopin and his mistress George Sand. The pair met late in the decade of the 1830's and traveled to the Mediterranean where the young but already consumptive Chopin composed some of his Twenty-Four Preludes for the piano. Romance frequently overtook susceptible pianists of the period; the young woman at right, sculpted by Jean Pierre Dantan, reflects this indulgent mood.

Concerto to a distant friend, for example, he wrote that the second movement was intended to convey "the impression you get when your eye wanders over a moonlit landscape you know well and love much" —a description that would have done credit to Heine. His real concern, however, was for the musical effect he was creating. "Have I made it haunting?" he asked. "I wonder—time will tell."

Virtually everything important that Chopin wrote is for the piano. The orchestra simply did not interest him, and his songs are a minor part of his output. His contribution to music consists of more than two hundred piano works that are, for the most part, as brief and brilliant as was his own life. He gave these works elastic forms that could express his moods of the moment: the impromptu, the scherzo, the concert waltz, the polonaise, the mazurka. In the hands of the right pianist they can still sound today as though they had just been freshly improvised.

Yet, there is much more hard work and artifice in Chopin's works than meets the ear. "His creation was spontaneous and miraculous," writes George Sand, with whom he lived for ten years. "He found it without seeking it, without foreseeing it. It came on his piano suddenly, complete, sublime, or it sang in his head during a walk, and he was impatient to play it to himself." But then, she adds, began a period of agonizing struggle, while he had second thoughts about what he had

written. "He shut himself up in his room for whole days, weeping, walking, breaking his pen, repeating and altering a bar a hundred times, writing and effacing it as many times, and recommencing the next day with a minute and desperate perseverance. He spent six weeks over a single page to write it at last as he had noted it down at the very first."

Chopin worked with a range of chromatic harmonies that were like Delacroix' palette with its reds, yellows, and grays. Often the whole structure of a Chopin piece is determined by the contrasting "colors" of his harmony, as it moves from brighter to darker levels of sound. His style is so subtle and luminous that it sounds most at home in the intimate acoustics of a drawingroom. That, rather than any inability to play fortissimo, was why Chopin hated performing in large concert halls, and why he did so only rarely during his later years. His natural habitat was the aristocratic salon of a Prince Czartoryski or a Baron Rothschild, where he could play to a small, select circle of cultivated listeners. Berlioz recalled these occasions:

> What emotions he could then call forth! In what ardent and melancholy reveries he loved to pour out his soul! It was usually towards midnight that he gave himself up with greatest abandon, when the big butterflies of the salon had left ... then, obedient to the mute petition of some beautiful, intelligent eyes, he became a poet. ...

Everyone who knew Chopin agreed that he was "the most sensitive genius in existence," and it was often remarked that in some mysterious way he resembled his music the way some people resemble their dogs. "The particular sound he drew from the piano was like the glance of his eyes," noted Ernest Legouvé. "The slightly ailing delicacy of his fingers was allied to the poetic melancholy of his nocturnes, and the careful attention he conferred on sartorial details helped explain the worldly elegance of certain parts of his work."

What was less evident in Chopin's work was the energy and concentration that he brought to his task. A composer who dies of tuberculosis at thirty-nine and yet produces as many masterpieces as Chopin

With its changing friends and lovers, the life of the romantic artist was an art unto itself. Above, George Sand entertains her friends at a country romp: Franz Liszt kneeling, Delacroix standing, and Chopin poised as a parrot on the hostess's hand. In the realistic painting below, at right, Liszt plays the piano for his kneeling mistress, the Countess d' Agoult, who later wrote novels under the name Daniel Stern, and for his friends (from left) Alexandre Dumas, Berlioz, George Sand, Paganini, and Gioacchino Rossini.

did could hardly have been "dying all his life," as Berlioz suggested. He had to possess the kind of iron discipline usually attributed to men of action rather than poets and intellectuals. For that matter, his life should be written as a success story rather than a tragedy. A young man of humble origins takes foreign capitals by storm, becomes a world figure, dines with princes, but never loses the common touch. With his indulgent mistress, George Sand, he sometimes acted the spoiled child, but essentially he was rock hard and quite unspoilable. Robert Schumann sensed as much when he heard Chopin's music; here, he decided, were "cannon buried in flowers."

Franz Liszt is known to have envied Chopin's "vaporously fluid" way of playing the piano, which, he said, made the melody undulate to and fro, "like a skiff driven over the waves." During the early years of their friendship, Liszt learned to imitate Chopin's style so successfully that one evening, playing in a darkened room at George Sand's estate, he tricked their most intimate friends into believing that it was the poetic Chopin, not the fiery Liszt, who was improvising for them. Their friendship, however, was destined to end in a falling out. Liszt was far too much the extrovert, the man of the theater, and his incessant exuberance got on Chopin's nerves. Their temperamental differences, of course, were reflected in the sounds they produced at the piano. "Chopin carried you with him into a dreamland, in which you would have liked to dwell forever," wrote Sir Charles Hallé, who first heard them in 1836. "Liszt was all sunshine and dazzling splendor, subjugating his hearers with a power that none could withstand. For him there were no difficulties of execution, the most incredible seeming child's play under his fingers."

As a composer, Liszt was far more erratic and unpredictable than Chopin. Many of his early salon pieces and bravura studies were written simply as crowd pleasers. "I am the slave of the public," he used to say rather ruefully. But his greatest works, such as the *Sonetti del Petrarca* or the *Paganini Etudes,* are stamped with an irresistible power and breadth of vision. With his hands freely ranging the keyboard, destroying the classical division of labor between right-hand treble and left-hand bass, he was prepared to take all kinds of harmonic chances. During much of his career Liszt was really an avant-gardist disguised as a matinée idol.

Liszt lived nearly twice as long as Chopin, and his career spanned virtually the whole romantic epoch. As a child prodigy he had been kissed on the forehead by Beethoven, and he had published his first music in a collection together with Schubert. Later he befriended Felix Mendelssohn and Robert Schumann as well as Chopin and Berlioz; he helped Rossini to his last success and Wagner to his first; he taught and aided two whole generations of younger musicians, including Bedřich Smetana and Edward MacDowell. And finally, in his old age, he discovered and sponsored the young Russians of the Borodin-Moussorgsky circle. Emotionally as well as musically he was always ready to try something new. "You cannot expect from an artist that he should forego love in any form whatever," he once wrote to a woman who was trying to hold him back, "neither the sort that moves the senses and emotions, nor the ascetic and mystical forms of love."

In Paris, as a young man, he was no less famed for his affairs of the heart than for his piano technique—which was, of course, entirely to be expected from a romantic artist of such Mephistophelean charm. In 1835, when he was twenty-four, he eloped to Switzerland with the blonde, blue-eyed Countess Maria d'Agoult, a married woman of great social distinction who was described by a friend as "six inches of ice over twenty feet of lava." They spent the next few years in the Alps and in Italy, where Liszt composed the miniature tone poems and landscape sketches afterward published as *Années de Pelérinage* ("Years of Pilgrimage"). The countess saw herself as "a chosen one, destined as an offering for the salvation of this divine genius," and she bore him three children (one of whom, Cosima, was destined to become the second, and decisive, wife of Richard Wagner).

Their relationship, however, lasted no longer than did that of Chopin and Sand, or of Berlioz and Harriet Smithson. Soon, Liszt was on the road again. Traveling in a horse-drawn *Reisewagen* that served as a salon by day and a boudoir by night, he lived a vagabond life that took him to every capital in Europe from Portugal to Turkey. He was the pianist of the hour and of the century. The crosses and medals he had received from kings and princes jangled rhythmically on his chest when he played in court dress. In Budapest his countrymen acclaimed him a national hero (although he never learned to speak Hungarian; German and, preferably, French, were his usual languages).

Then, in his late thirties, Liszt settled down in the town of Weimar with the Princess Carolyn Sayn-Wittgenstein, the estranged wife of a Tsarist nobleman. Here, with an orchestra at his disposal for the first

Photographed (above) but never recorded by the phonograph that was invented six years before his death in 1886, the Hungarian piano virtuoso Franz Liszt was concerned that he had not written down all the great works he carried about in his imagination. Instead, he had expended his considerable energies at the keyboard, astonishing audiences and teaching others to play, or by taking time out for the turbulent love affairs that seemed not to cease even when he donned clerical garb (caricatured at right).

time, he followed Berlioz' example and composed a long series of tone poems for orchestra, including the great *Faust* and *Dante* symphonies, and the well-known *Les Préludes* (a work based on Alphonse de Lamartine's *Méditation*: "What is life but a series of preludes to that unknown song whose first solemn note is sounded by death?").

Meanwhile an era was drawing to a close. The brave romanticism of the 1830's gave way to the frustrations and disappointments of 1848, the year when a wave of abortive revolutions swept through Europe. Mendelssohn died in 1847; Chopin in 1849; and by 1854 Schumann was incurably ill in a mental asylum. At mid-century Berlioz could write, "If not at the end of my career, I am at any rate on the last steep decline. . . ." In music as well as literature and politics, Europe was settling down to the red-plush respectability that, in England at least, became known as the Victorian Era. Yet Liszt continued to have adventures of the old school and to write music that was harmonically more audacious than ever, as though the Philistines simply did not exist.

He moved to Rome in the 1860's and took minor orders in the Catholic Church to become, at least nominally, the "Abbé" Liszt. He was not a priest, however, and (fortunately, as it turned out) did not have to take a vow of celibacy. Nor did his cassock detract in any way from his charm; "women still go perfectly crazy over him," a friend observed. One of his piano pupils in Rome, the "Cossack Countess," Olga Janina, fell in love with him and resolved, "he shall be mine or I will kill him." As she afterward told the story, he surrendered to her without much of a struggle. But the next morning, as Liszt slept, it occurred to this wild Ukrainian horsewoman that he might have regrets, that thoughts of remorse would take him from her. Armed with a poisoned dagger, she braced herself for the awakening. "One tiny puncture and he was mine for all eternity, for we would lie under the same winding sheet in the same tomb. I held the dagger in the hollow of my hand and waited for his first word. It was one of love. He was saved."

If Liszt realized how narrow had been his escape, he must have breathed a sigh of relief not only for himself but for art's sake, for by then he was the last of the great romantics. And the music that he wrote during the years before his death in 1886 was curiously dissonant and experimental, preparing the way for modernists like Claude Debussy and Béla Bartók, who were to consider him one of their most important influences. Among his own students there were none who understood the "bizarre" pieces of the seventy-year-old Liszt. "Is one allowed to write such a thing?" one of them asked about the dissonant *Csárdás Macabre*. "Is one allowed to listen to it?" But Liszt himself had lost nothing of his romantic sense of distance and detachment from an alien world. His motto had become "*Wir können warten*" ("We can wait"). "I have to accustom myself to treating my music with a sort of systematic disregard and passive resignation," he told a friend. "The fact is that 'Monsieur Litz' is welcome everywhere when he shows himself at the piano. . . . But they will not let him think and compose his own way. . . . They may be right, but . . . I am filled with the spirit of resistance and determined to follow my own path to the end without pampering or deceiving myself."

7

In Search of Musical Alternatives

DOCTOR ALEXANDER BORODIN, professor of organic chemistry at the St. Petersburg Academy of Medicine, paid a visit to the aging Abbé Liszt in Jena during the summer of 1877 and, to his delighted surprise, was welcomed with open arms. Liszt, it seemed, already knew all about the music that Borodin had been composing in his spare time; he even knew the doctor's First Symphony by heart. "Your first movement is perfect," Liszt told him as soon as the introductions were out of the way. "Your *andante* is a masterpiece. The *scherzo* is enchanting ... and then, *this* passage is so ingenious!"—and his long fingers picked out a skittish progression of distant intervals that, in the symphony, are played by pizzicato strings.

Speaking in an excited mixture of French and German, he confided to Borodin (who, in turn, recorded their conversation in a long letter to his wife) how much he admired Russian music, as opposed to the local product. "You know Germany," he said. "It is full of composers. I am lost in a sea of music that threatens to entirely submerge me; but Heavens, how insipid it all is, not one living idea! With you there exists a vitalizing stream."

This was a curious compliment, coming from a composer who was considered one of the founders of the *Neudeutsche* ("New German") movement, and the father-in-law of Richard Wagner at that. But as if to prove that this was not just a momentary lapse, Liszt carried on in this fashion for the next three weeks, until it was time for his guest to make his departure. And when Borodin returned for another visit four years later, Liszt had still more flattering things to tell him. "You Russians are indispensable to us," he insisted. "You have a quick and vital spring; the future belongs to you, while here I see nothing but lifeless stagnation all about."

In search of a native Russian idiom, Nikolai Rimsky-Korsakov looked to the folk songs and tales he had absorbed during a country childhood. Costume sketches for his satirical opera La Coq d'Or *(left, by Alexander Benois) reveal the Oriental flavor so often found in the composer's work.*

There was something almost heretical in Liszt's assessment of the musical situation. In the 1870's and 1880's it was generally taken for granted that Wagner held a patent on "the music of the future," and indeed the great Wagner festival at Bayreuth was a living monument to that idea. But Liszt, with his extraordinary perception of new values in music, was well aware that romanticism (even *post*romanticism) had run out of steam, and that serious music was now badly in need of rejuvenation. The "lifeless stagnation all about" (and Bayreuth was less than a hundred miles away) was caused primarily by the rhythmic inertia of the German symphonic tradition, whose basic rhythms tended to fall either into the ONE-two-three-four pattern of the march, or the SLIDE-two-three of the waltz, invariably punctuated with the thumping of a big bass drum. Now at last a fresh wind was blowing from the east, where the Russian composers were able to draw on sources of inspiration hitherto untapped by serious musicians—peasant songs, folkdances, the sound of shepherds' pipes and balalaikas, and the strange, haunting harmonies of the choruses that serfs sang as they worked in the fields.

This search for musical alternatives had begun with Mikhail Glinka, a gentleman composer from St. Petersburg who had learned much of what he knew about music from his uncle's orchestra—an orchestra of serfs, of which his uncle owned the players as well as the instruments. In

The music of Russian peasants was written down by gentlemen: Mikhail Glinka (below) was one of the first to use peasant tunes in operas created for the ears of the aristocracy; and it was for aristocratic eyes that P. Malyavin painted three peasants in song (left). The prerevolutionary Russian spirit was evoked in the music of an informal but pivotal group called The Mighty Five and in such views as that opposite, which illustrates a popular song concerning a troika passing through a Russian landscape.

1830 Glinka had gone to Italy and learned to imitate Vincenzo Bellini, a composer who dominated the Italian operatic scene. He was successful enough to have had some music published in Milan, but it suddenly dawned on him that he ought to be composing like a Russian instead. To accomplish this ambition he had only instinct to guide him. The term "folksong" had not yet been invented, nor the whole folklore mystique that went with it. But Glinka knew and loved the "doleful Russian songs" he had heard among the peasants, and he proceeded to incorporate such tunes into the score of his patriotic opera *A Life for the Tsar.*

When the opera was first performed in 1836, his music struck the aristocrats of St. Petersburg like a slap in the face. Countess Nesselrode, wife of the foreign minister, said it was disgraceful to put onstage the songs she heard from her serfs. It was coachmen's music—"*C'est la musique des cochers!*" Her remark made the rounds of the salons; Glinka muttered that a coachman is a more sensible person than a gentleman. In any case, the Tsar himself was moved to tears by the opera,

and it was generally agreed that Glinka had succeeded in launching a Russian national school.

It remained for a group of composers in the next generation, however, to bring his ideas to fruition. The so-called *Moguchaya Koochka* —literally "the mighty handful," but better known in English as The Mighty Five—were easily the most astonishing collection of dilettantes and geniuses ever assembled into a school of composition. There was Borodin, the illegitimate son of a Georgian prince, a chemistry professor as well as a composer; César Cui, a military engineer (later a lieutenant general) and composer; Nikolai Rimsky-Korsakov, the naval cadet turned composer and inspector of naval bands; Modeste Moussorgsky, the Imperial Guard officer turned composer; and Mili Balakirev, the only one to begin as a professional musician, although he sacrificed a promising career as a concert pianist to devote his life to the cause of a new Russian music. It was he who had brought the *Koochka* together and, as Rimsky-Korsakov wrote, "he held us absolutely spellbound by his talents, his authority, his magnetism."

Borodin was the first of the five to gain recognition in Western Europe, and then it was for his research into the properties of aldehydes as well as for his symphonies and the tone poem *In the Steppes of Central Asia*. "Borodin was an extremely cordial and cultured man, pleasant and witty to talk with," writes Rimsky-Korsakov in his memoirs. And he goes on to describe Borodin's working habits:

On visiting him I often found him working in the laboratory which adjoined his apartment. When he sat over his retorts filled with some colorless gas and distilled it by means of a tube from one vessel into another—I used to tell him that he was "transfusing emptiness into vacancy." Having finished his work, he would go with me to his apartment, where we began musical operations or conversations, in the midst of which he used to jump up, run back to the laboratory to see whether something had not burned out or boiled over; meanwhile he filled the corridor with incredible sequences from successions of ninths or sevenths.

In the end it was the chemistry that got the lion's share of Borodin's divided attention, since he rarely had time to write music, as he said, "except during my summer holiday, or when some ailment compels me to keep to my rooms." Both his magnum opus, the opera *Prince Igor*, and his Third Symphony were left unfinished at his death in 1887.

Moussorgsky, the mightiest of the five in terms of talent, had a constitutional reluctance to finish anything. "I think, think, think, think of many sensible things," he conceded, "and many plans swirl through my head; if one would only bring these to fulfillment it would be splendid." When he resigned his commission in the exclusive Preobrazhensky Guards regiment in order to do great things for Russian music, his friends were exceedingly doubtful. Vladimir Stassov, the *Koochka*'s literary mentor, called him "a perfect idiot." To Balakirev he seemed little better—"practically an idiot." Even Borodin, who was willing enough to be impressed by Moussorgsky's work (what there was of it), had to admit that "I was incredulous when he told me he intended to devote himself to serious music."

A turning point came in 1861, however, when Tsar Alexander II issued the proclamation emancipating the serfs, an edict that swept away the feudal system in Russia. The immediate effect of the edict on Moussorgsky was to send him to the provinces to straighten out his family's financial affairs. Living in the country during the summer months, he watched and listened carefully while working with the liberated peasants. "I have been raking hay, cooking jam and putting up pickles. . . . I am observing characteristic peasant women and typical peasant men—they may all come in handy. With how many fresh sides, untouched by art, the Russian nature swarms, oh, how many! and with what juicy ones, splendid ones. . . . A small part of that, which life has given to me, I have pictured in musical images. . . ."

He was collecting material and gathering strength for a creative breakthrough. "My music must be an artistic reproduction of human speech in all its finest shades, that is, the sounds of human speech, as the external manifestations of thought and feeling, must, without exaggeration or violence, become true, accurate music. . . ." This principle was applied to his opera *Boris Godunov* (with its extraordinary arias of speech heightened into song—the pleading beggar, the drunken vagabond, the storytelling priest, the exulting Tsar) as well as to a series of songs for solo voice and piano. These songs represent a milestone in the history of music: the *Sunless* cycle, the *Songs and Dances of Death*, and the astonishing cycle *The Nursery*, with texts by Moussorgsky himself illustrating episodes from child life.

A friend who was present when Liszt received a copy of *The Nursery* in 1873 and first tried it out on the piano relates that the experience was nothing short of a revelation. Liszt instantly understood what

Moussorgsky was driving at. In the first song, the time indication changes with each bar, beginning with 7/4, continuing in 6/4 and 5/4, and reaching 3/2, 3/4, and 4/4—seventeen times within twenty-four measures. Yet, Liszt played it from the page with a power of expression that took his listeners' breath away. "Hardly had Liszt played, with great simplicity, several bars of this little song which clearly overcame him, than we were swept up in his emotion. . . . You should have heard Liszt crying out at each new page: 'How interesting! . . . and how new! . . . What discoveries! . . . No one else would have said it this way. . . .' And thousands of other exclamations of satisfaction and pleasure. . . ."

Liszt usually had a kind word for young composers with new ideas, but he was not easily carried away like this. Moussorgsky's songs excited him because they pointed the way out of the rhythmic and harmonic impasse of Western music. Their variable time-scheme was the much-needed antidote to the "lifeless stagnation all about."

At first there was a great deal of resistance to this kind of music, and not only from the Establishment. In his pursuit of peasant music, Moussorgsky had gone much further toward dissonance and "barbarity" than the others of the *Koochka*. And the more conservative Russian composers, notably Peter Ilich Tchaikovsky, dismissed him simply as a talented eccentric. "He has been too easily led away by the absurd theories of his set," Tchaikovsky wrote to his patroness, Madame von Meck. "He likes what is coarse, unpolished and ugly . . . and even seems proud of his want of skill, writing just as it comes to him, believing blindly in the infallibility of his genius. As a matter of fact his very original talent flashes forth now and again."

Chemistry professor Alexander Borodin (left, above) composed his short list of twenty-one works whenever vacations or an illness gave him the leisure; his unfinished melodic opera Prince Igor *(première program at left) had to be shaped by Rimsky-Korsakov after Borodin fell dead at a masked ball. Borodin and Modeste Moussorgsky (above) were both in their twenties when* The Mighty Five *was formed in 1862; Moussorgsky's unfinished opera* Khovanshchina *(costume sketches for it are shown at right) was not performed until five years after his death.*

Overleaf: A *scene from Moussorgsky's opera* Boris Godunov *sets the stage for its protagonist, the Russian people, as represented by the opera's chorus.*

Tchaikovsky himself occupied the middle ground in the conflict between the so-called coachmen's music and the German orchestral tradition. On the whole, he regarded the *Koochka* as a group of presumptuous amateurs. "Their mockery of the schools and the classical masters, denial of authority and of the masterpieces, was nothing but ignorance. . . ." They, in turn, accused him of being too receptive to German and Italian influences instead of relying on Russian sources of inspiration.

Yet Tchaikovsky was nothing if not a truly Slavic composer. Although his symphonies and concertos conform more or less to classical German models, his style is always instantly recognizable as Russian. Indeed, his works often quote or adapt folksongs he had heard in the country: for example, the "blind beggar" tune that appears as the main theme of the first movement of the Piano Concerto No. 1 ("It is curious," he wrote, "that in Russia every blind beggar sings exactly the same tune with the same refrain"), the Polish folksong in the first movement of the Fifth Symphony, or the Ukrainian folk tune known as "The Crane," in the finale of the Second Symphony. Even the famous *andante cantabile* of the D Major String Quartet (which reduced Tolstoy to tears and is now known to popular music as "When It Is June on the Isle of May") began life as a beautiful Russian folksong that runs, "Vanya sat drinking; as he drank he thought of his sweetheart. . . ."

Even these relatively gentle (and not at all barbaric) translations of Slavic folksongs into a more international idiom were capable of rousing the guardians of the German tradition to outbursts of angry invective. Sensing that their musical hegemony was being threatened, they reacted by doing their best to discredit the challengers. When Tchaikovsky's utterly lyrical Violin Concerto was given its première in Vienna, for example, the critic Eduard Hanslick talked about the "savagery" of the first movement and railed against the finale. "It puts us in the midst of the brutal and wretched jollity of a Russian kermess. We see wild and vulgar faces, we hear curses, we smell bad brandy. . . . Tchaikovsky's Violin Concerto brings to us for the first time the horrid idea that there may be music that stinks in the ear."

Hanslick's review was written in 1881, by which time the world of serious music had split into three competing and mutually hostile camps: the nationalists on the periphery, and the feuding Wagnerians and Brahmsians at the center. The nationalists included not only the Russians but also the Czechs Bedřich Smetana and Antonín Dvořák, as well as the Norwegian Edvard Grieg—soon to be followed by Jean Sibelius in Finland and by three great Spanish composers, Isaac Albéniz, Enrique Granados, and Manuel de Falla.

In one way or another, each of these men drew on the folk traditions of his native country in order to assert his independence from classical models. "It is possible to say after a few bars: that is Mozart—that is Chopin," Smetana once explained to a friend. "If only one day it were possible to say after a few bars: that is Smetana. . . ." Although he established Prague as a Pan-Slavic musical center to rival Moscow and St. Petersburg, Smetana's brilliant career was cut short by deafness just as he reached the height of his powers. "If martyrs are still born today,

Shortly after the never-married Peter Ilich Tchaikovsky (above) came under the thirteen-year support of a wealthy widow who stipulated they never meet, he wrote his ballet Swan Lake; *a Benois scene for the famous work is shown at right. Russia's search for a national music was duplicated in all the developing nations of Europe: Richard Wagner (right, below) used German myths in an attempt to fuse poetry with music and produce a dramatic whole.*

then I am the unhappiest of all," he wrote in 1883, "for fate has sentenced me to a silent tomb where the sound of human voices is unknown; I have never heard the greater part of my poetic creations [including the great cycle of tone poems *My Country*], but I have seen many times how the majority in the audience wept as they listened to the fruits of my mind!"

The Wagnerians, centered on their festival of music-drama at Bayreuth (they never called it opera), constituted a party unto themselves. By 1880 Wagner's "music of the future" had become almost a religious cult. Indeed, at one point Catholic newspapers warned that Wagner was trying to usurp the function of the Church by substituting his theater for the Mass. His influence, moreover, was symphonic as well as operatic, since the younger symphonists were profoundly affected by his orchestral style—the continual ebb and flow of chromatic harmonies, moving through carefully planned progressions of keys; the massive, glittering sound of his orchestra, with its leitmotiv themes serving as identity tags; and the brilliant use of sonic analogies drawn from nature. This was the sort of thing that George Bernard Shaw once catalogued as "music of river and rainbow, fire and forest ... the love music, the hammer and anvil music, the clumping of the giants, the tune of the young woodsman's horn . . . the dragon music and nightmare music and thunder and lightning music."

Wagner was an ultranationalist in his own right, preaching a murky gospel of Teutonism and salvation-by-music-drama. "I am the most German of beings," he wrote to his royal patron, Ludwig II of Bavaria. "I am the German spirit. Consult the incomparable magic of my works;

hold them side by side with everything else; you have no choice but to say—this is German." Despite his phobia of the French, Wagner had nearly as many French admirers as German, and every Bayreuth festival included a large delegation of musicians from Paris who had come to "join the faithful." Two generations of French poets, from Baudelaire to Mallarmé, Valéry, and Claudel, worshiped Wagner as the symbolist par excellence. Baudelaire confessed that on hearing Wagner he had the sensation of "letting myself be penetrated and invaded—a really sensual delight that resembles rising on the air or tossing upon the sea. . . ." And Emanuel Chabrier, one of the most vivacious of French composers, burst into tears at the thrill of hearing, at long last, the Prelude to *Tristan und Isolde* at Bayreuth. "Ten years," he sobbed into the ear of his neighbor, the composer Vincent d'Indy, "ten years I've been waiting for that A on the cellos!"

Johannes Brahms, living in Vienna, represented a more sober, less theatrical side of the German tradition. He never wrote an opera, had very little to do with program music, and did his best work within the

Aubrey Beardsley depicted the modish devotion of Wagner lovers in the drawing opposite of an audience listening to Tristan und Isolde *at the Bayreuth theater Wagner and his admirers built. The unwilling champion of the anti-Wagner camp in divided Germany, Johannes Brahms (above, left, at the age of twenty), composed music for its own sake—"absolute" music as his followers called it. Brahms, in turn, did not escape caricaturization and is shown above as a plump, perhaps overly self-engrossed conductor of his own music.*

framework of forms developed by Mozart, Haydn, and Beethoven. But if the form is studiously classical, the content is glowing romantic. "One sees what can still be done with the old forms when someone comes along who knows how to handle them," remarked no less an authority than Wagner himself when the young Brahms came for a visit in 1864 and performed some of his piano music. But this adherence to old precedents ultimately proved to be more than Wagner and the futurists could bear. Even Tchaikovsky, who took a dim view of the Wagnerians, felt that Brahms' position was hopelessly outdated. "Isn't Brahms in reality a caricature of Beethoven?" he wrote to Madame von Meck. "Isn't this pretension to profundity and power detestable, because the contents that are poured into the Beethoven mould are not really of any value?"

At close range it was difficult to see that Brahms' conservatism concealed a radicalism of his own. He worked instinctively within the established order because the tightest forms provided the richest harmonic contrasts. Brahms was interested in sounding new depths, where Wagner's ambition was to reach new heights. One of Brahms' youthful notebooks contains a significant reference to the "inner sound" of music, and a reminder that "the real musician should reverberate with music within himself." This inward resonance was to become one of the hallmarks of Brahms' style, and involved the use of a rich, somber palette of instrumental colors in the middle range. Cello, French horn, and clarinet are cornerstones of his orchestral sound as well as of his chamber music. And in his vocal works, too, he often gravitates to the "serious" sound of low voices and dark chest tones.

Working within the classical tradition did not mean that he could avoid having to take musical risks. On the contrary, as Brahms pointed out, "you have no idea how it feels to hear behind you the tramp of a giant like Beethoven." And there were lessons for even the most revolutionary modernist in his four symphonies, his concertos, his vast output of chamber music, songs, and piano works. The twentieth-century innovator Arnold Schoenberg once said that Brahms' music had taught him four vital elements of style. The first was melodic asymmetry, "especially uneven numbers of measures; extension and contradiction of phrases." The second was elasticity of form, "not being stingy or cramped when clarity demands more space; carrying out each figure to the end." The third was "the systematic construction of movements," and the last was "economy, yet richness." There was, after all, much to be done with the old forms when someone came along who knew how to handle them.

8

Fin de Siècle

IN 1889 PARIS CELEBRATED the hundredth anniversary of the French Revolution by holding a great "universal exhibition" in the very heart of the city, on the Esplanade des Invalides and the Champ de Mars. No effort and expense was spared to make this the most spectacular world's fair of the century. The Eiffel Tower had been erected especially for the occasion. At 984 feet it was then the tallest structure in the world and one of the wonders of modern technology (although many leading artists and intellectuals had signed a petition against it, protesting that it would eclipse the rest of the city's monuments).

Besides the more conventional displays of commerce and industry, the exhibition provided a lavish sampling of exotic cultures from Africa and the Far East. There was a Buddhist temple, a Moroccan bazaar, a Chinese pavilion, a Senegalese village, a whole Cairo street in replica, a settlement of Congolese ivory carvers, a Vietnamese theatrical troupe, a village of Tonkinese silk weavers. For the composers who came to see them, some of these special exhibits opened the door to an utterly fascinating world of sounds they had never heard before, or had even been able to imagine, for this was, after all, long before the age of the all-hearing phonograph. Rimsky-Korsakov, for example, who came from Russia to conduct a pair of *Koochka* concerts at the Trocadéro, was intrigued by the warbling of the primitive Balkan Panpipes and by the music of the North African section. "At the Algerian café, in the dance of a little girl with a dagger, I was captivated by the sudden blows struck by a Negro on the large drum at the dancer's approach"—an effect he promptly appropriated, along with the Panpipes, for his next opera, *Mlada*.

In another part of the exhibition, the twenty-seven-year-old Claude Debussy made a discovery that was to have a decisive and lasting effect on his musical thinking. A gamelan orchestra from Java was encamped in the Dutch colonial section on the Esplanade des Invalides, and he spent many fruitful hours there listening to that astonishing barrage of rhythms and timbres, so totally unlike anything to be heard in a Western concert hall. The official review of the exhibition reported on this ensemble:

> The whole gamelan orchestra plays at once. There is the gamelan itself, a sort of "piano" of thin wooden slabs, played with wooden mallets. Then the *bonang*, a set of bronze gongs shaped like pots and arranged

Impressionism, with its emphasis on the sensuous response to tone in music and to light in art, dominated the turn of the century; it appeared in Claude Debussy's L'Aprés-midi d'un Faune, which later was used for a ballet performed by an airy Waslaw Nijinsky. The legendary dancer appears opposite in Leon Bakst's watercolor design for a poster announcing the seventh season of the Ballet Russe in Paris.

on a table, played with padded sticks; it produced two scales of full-bodied sounds. Then the *rebab*, a two-string violin; the *selumpret*, a sort of oboe; and finally the *tam-tam*. It's like living in a dream. Imagine a melody from another world, elusive and thrilling, the fluid rhythms constantly moving within a sort of ritual monotony, translated into the sonority of muffled bells, muted strings, delicate woodblocks, attenuated gongs and cymbals. . . . Yes, we are truly in Indra's paradise!

Debussy never forgot this first encounter with the music of the Orient. The Javanese gamelan, he wrote to his friend Pierre Louÿs, was able "to express every shade of meaning, even those that cannot be described in words, and which make our tonic and dominant seem like phantoms meant to impress small naughty children." And in an article written many years later, he maintained that all music should be like the Javanese: "Their conservatory is the eternal rhythm of the sea, the wind in the leaves, and the thousand little natural sounds which they understand very well without having to consult some arbitrary treatise. . . . And if one would listen without European prejudice to the charm of their percussion, one would have to admit that ours is nothing but the barbarous noise of a traveling circus."

With the sound of the gamelan still fresh in his memory, he composed the piano piece *Pagodes*, with its tinkling bell effects and Oriental scales. But it was not just a matter of borrowing a few picturesque devices. The experience of the gamelan reinforced Debussy's preoccupation with instrumental textures and supplied the basis for that shimmering *pointillisme* of sound that was to become known, much against his wishes, as impressionism. The sound of his orchestra in works like the symphonic sketches *La Mer* ("The Sea") and the two nocturnes *Nuages* ("Clouds") and *Fêtes* ("Festivals") has been described as a "stylized gamelan." It was no accident that when Debussy's String Quartet was first performed, one of the critics complained that it sounded too much like the Javanese music at the exhibition, with "bounding rhythms, violent harmonic jerks, alternating with languid melodies and pizzicato effects suggestive of guitars and mandolins."

One of the elements that attracted Debussy to Oriental music was its spontaneity; he wanted his own music to sound as though it had "not been written down." At the same time, it suggested a viable alternative to the rhythmic clichés of postromantic music. Above all, the pentatonic scales of the East influenced the coloring of his harmonies, just as Chinese painting and Japanese prints influenced the art nouveau of Paris—the veiled dancers of Toulouse-Lautrec and the fashion-plate figures of Pierre Bonnard. Debussy's art is essentially one of elusive harmonies that refuse to remain within a key, but rise and fall like the tides. He will revert to the Middle Ages for some of his effects, or to ancient Greek modes as well as pentatonic scales, using a succession of dissonances and unrelated chords that are rarely resolved in accordance with the precepts of traditional harmony.

Debussy had loved the forbidden fruits of harmony even before his Oriental enlightenment. One of his fellow students at the Paris Conservatoire, Maurice Emmanuel, remembered how Debussy's earliest improvisations used to annoy the faculty but fascinate his classmates:

118

PELLÉAS ET MÉLISANDE

CLAUDE DEBUSSY
MAURICE MAETERLINCK

Debussy's 1902 opera Pelléas et Mélisande *(program cover, above) was much admired by the impeccable Ravel (left) with whom Debussy, the more subjective composer, is often compared. Both men wrote music for the symbolist poets of their day, and both wrote ballets for Diaghilev that were danced by Nijinsky, shown in Valentine Gross's 1913 drawing at right with two ballerinas in Debussy's* Jeux.

In a curiously graphic way, this famous *volte-face* of Nijinsky's symbolizes Ravel's whole relationship to the rest of the musical world of the early twentieth century. At the time he was writing some of his best-known works, several leading contemporaries—notably Arnold Schoenberg, Igor Stravinsky, and Béla Bartók—were beginning to make the great leap forward into unrestricted dissonance and atonality. Others, like Giacomo Puccini and Richard Strauss, preferred to stay rooted to the spot where traditional harmony prevailed. Ravel, after taking a running start as an *enfant terrible* of French music, executed a deft flanking maneuver that landed him off to one side, about midway between the avant-garde and the conservatives. In the years following *Daphnis et Chloé*, the modernist procession gradually passed him by. World War I, in the last year of which Debussy died of cancer, interrupted Ravel's career. When he returned from volunteer service as an ambulance driver, he still had twenty years of work ahead of him, yet he now belonged among the Old Masters rather than the Young Turks. Although he could write "problem music" as difficult as the next man's, he neither ventured beyond the limits of tonal harmony nor into the deeper waters of theoretical speculation. "Music does not need philoso-

phy," he told the Viennese critic Paul Stefan.

But that was decidedly a French view of the matter. In Beethoven country—Vienna, Munich, Berlin—composers were accustomed to spending a good deal of time philosophizing about their art. Tradition demanded a certain amount of profundity from the serious musician, and after Wagner had established himself as a composer-intellectual of sorts, the whole German musical establishment took on an increasingly philosophical air. Sometimes, of course, the metaphysics resided chiefly in the program notes—as in Richard Strauss's *Also sprach Zarathustra*, whose Nietzschean subject serves as hardly more than a pretext for some particularly sensuous musicmaking. Characteristically, when the music revolution finally came to Vienna and Berlin, it was not just a change of styles but a whole elaborate methodology: the Schoenberg theory, supported by a school, a textbook, a manifesto, and a number of attendant interpreters.

Strauss, the leading German composer of the turn of the century, encountered most of the same problems as Debussy, especially the question of diminishing harmonic and rhythmic returns. His solutions, however, tended to be more conventional and Wagnerian. He owed his meteoric rise to fame as the "golden youth" of the 1890's to a series of richly orchestrated, excitingly illustrated tone poems, each of which represents a triumph not only of inspiration but of mechanics, acoustics, and logistics. His *Alpine Symphony*, to take an extreme example, calls for the collective and synchronous operation of at least eighteen first and sixteen second violins, twelve violas, ten cellos, eight basses, two piccolos, four flutes, three oboes, an English horn, a heckelphone, two clarinets in A-flat, two clarinets in B-flat, two clarinets in C, three bassoons, a contra bassoon, four horns, four trumpets, four trombones, four tenor tubas, two bass tubas, two harps, an organ, a wind machine, a thunder machine, a glockenspiel, cymbals, bass and side drums, a triangle, a tam-tam, a celesta, two sets of timpani, and "in the distance," a satellite band of twelve horns, two trumpets, and two trombones.

Any man capable of mobilizing and controlling so vast an apparatus for satisfying the human need for musical expression fulfilled a highly respected function in the bourgeois society of the *fin de siècle*. Nineteenth-century Germany was the one nation in the world that supported a dozen institutions of this kind, under conductors like Karl Muck, Arthur Nikisch, and Felix Weingartner. It was Strauss, doubling as composer and conductor, who devised the most successful new programs and applications for these superb musical facilities. He did not invent the tone poem any more than D. W. Griffith invented the movies, but like the latter he expanded the form to make it more meaningful and intriguing.

Both Strauss and Griffith were dream merchants of a sort, marshaling complex technical resources to stimulate and inspire audiences; to shock, soothe, uplift, and titillate. Debussy already said of Strauss's music: "It's just like cinematography." His tone poem *Till Eulenspiegel's Merry Pranks*, produced in 1895, is a typical case in point. Strauss stressed its "old-time, roughish" antecedents and its classical rondo form. But it is basically a new kind of music—an eighteen-minute comedy

Richard Strauss (above) chose to follow Wagner in developing the dramatic function of music, although he introduced modern harmonies to his works. Strauss's works, especially the lighter operas, were much loved, and in 1910 his native Munich treated him to a Strauss week, as announced in the poster at right.

RICHARD STRAUSS-WOCHE
LUDWIG HOHLWEIN MÜNCHEN
MÜNCHEN 1910
23-28 JUNI
Prospekte durch die Geschäftsstelle der Ausstellung (Musikfeste u. musikalische Veranstaltungen) München, Theatinerstr. 38, Bayer. Reisebureau Schenker & C°, München, Promenadepl. 16 u. durch alle offiziellen Auskunftsstellen

with a spectacular cast, including eight horns, six trumpets, and a bass tuba. The twenty-four subtitles suggested by the composer might have been written for a silent-film version of the same scenario: "Off for new pranks," "Just wait, you hypocrites!" "She really has made an impression on him," "A kind refusal is still a refusal," and so on. In the final scene, when the prankster has been marched off to the gallows, a seemingly breathless flute trill is said to depict "the filtering out of the last air from the man dangling at the rope."

From the late 1880's until World War I, Strauss's tone poems drew the same sort of audience, and were discussed with the same avid interest, as today's art films. Newspaper critics engaged in earnest debates over the psychology of *Don Juan*, the imagery of *Don Quixote*, the ethics of *Zarathustra* (eighty years after it was written, *Zarathustra* became the theme music for Stanley Kubrick's film *2001: A Space Odyssey*). In *Death and Transfiguration*, Strauss anticipated the modern medical drama: "the sick man on his bed" undergoes a "pain motif," "fever motif," "groaning motif,", "life-preservation motif," until the "last stroke of Death's ironhammer" brings "deliverance . . . transfiguration of the world." In his *Synfonia domestica* of 1904, a baby gurgles in

The elegant interior at left is a scenic sketch for Der Rosenkavalier, a popular Strauss opera in which the composer's bold orchestral color manifests itself. At right a seductive Salome, painted by Gustav Klimt, evokes the heroine of Oscar Wilde's verse play, the play on which Strauss based his 1905 opera Salome.

its bath, a glockenspiel chimes the hours, and a husband-and-wife argument is disguised as a double fugue.

Not long afterward, however, Strauss conceded that he no longer took pleasure in writing symphonies. The *Alpine Symphony* arrived as an epilogue to the whole series in 1915, the year of Griffith's *The Birth of a Nation*. It featured a sunrise, ascent, waterfall, view from the summit, thunderstorm, and descent (in retrograde motion). At one early performance, an assistant stood onstage and, as the *Musical Times* noted, "diligently exhibited numbers corresponding to the explanations in the programme, so that no one should mistake the glacier for the thermos flask." But by that time it was clear to everyone that the movies had usurped the aesthetic function of the tone poem. Strauss,

who had seen the handwriting on the concert-hall wall, wisely moved from there to the opera house and spent most of the next forty years of his career writing operas—among them *Salome* and *Der Rosenkavalier*. But in the last works that he wrote before his death at eighty-five, in 1949, he suddenly reverted to classical principles: his *Symphony for Winds* is dedicated to Mozart's "undying spirit, at the close of a life filled with gratitude."

Gustav Mahler was Strauss's only serious rival as a master of the post-Wagnerian orchestra. His scoring is as complex and expansive, but far more transparent in texture and less literal in its message. Mahler is a symbolist rather than a realist, and his music is fundamentally inner directed. He belongs, in fact, to the extraordinary epoch of Viennese cultural life that produced Hugo von Hofmannsthal, Karl Kraus, Egon Schiele, Oskar Kokoschka, and, above all, Gustav Klimt, whose glittering golden impastos and sinuous arabesques make the perfect visual counterpart to Mahler's symphonies.

Mahler was also a contemporary and compatriot of Sigmund Freud, and it is not too much to say that he wrote the first Freudian music—at least in the sense that he was the first to be consciously concerned with the workings of the subconscious in art. He did, in fact, have the benefit of a single psychoanalytic session with Freud during the summer of 1910, when the good doctor spent the whole of an afternoon analyzing what he diagnosed as Mahler's "mother fixation." It was a remarkably successful session. Mahler had been having trouble with his wife, Alma —had "withdrawn his libido from her," in Freud's phrase—but on the way home he already felt sufficiently recovered to write her a long love poem. Freud, for his part, was deeply impressed by Mahler's intuitive grasp of what was involved in psychoanalysis. "I had plenty of opportunity," he told Theodore Reik, "to admire the capability for psychological understanding of this man of genius."

Mahler had arrived at some Freudian insights long before he actually met the founder of psychoanalysis. Gifted with a neurotic's talent for self-analysis, he had already discovered the unconscious within himself and observed its effects on his music. "In the creative arts," he said, "virtually the only impressions that are fruitful and decisive in the long run are those that occur between the ages of four and eleven . . . anything later than that is rarely turned into art."

In his own symphonies and songs he always alluded to the tunes he had heard as a small boy. There was something fiercely compulsive about the way he kept reverting to his earliest memories as though, despite his technical perfection, he was trapped in the charmed circle of his childhood. What complicates Mahler's case is that his first impressions were of military marches and beerhall ditties, since he was brought up in a Czech garrison town where nothing else was available. As the story goes, "whenever little Gustav could not be found at home, it was certain he had gone marching off with some regiment, or else he might be standing on a coffee-house table, singing his songs for a throng of customers."

Growing up at the edge of a parade ground, he developed a lasting love-hate for the Austro-German marching band. Nearly all the Mahler

symphonies have at least one full-blown march movement—a funeral march, a mock-triumphal procession, or a march to the scaffold. At other times, often just at the most lyrical moments, he will suddenly launch into a savage parody of the old parade music, the drums lurching drunkenly, the brasses contorted into an agonized grimace. This penchant for barrack-room music was bound to annoy the critics of his day. As yet deaf to the possibilities of surrealism in music, they were almost unanimous in condemning his work as arid, banal, vulgar, derivative. "One wonders," wrote one critic, "whether indeed there has ever been a respectable composer who has utilized ideas as platitudinous [as these]...."

But Mahler's platitudes belong to a special order of banality. He can take a vulgar scrap of melody, hold it up for inspection in the trumpets, deliver an ironic commentary in the horns, and fling it aside with a stifled curse from the kettledrums. (One of his most striking innovations was the use of brasses, rather than strings, as his principal melody instruments.) Working with two such tunes against the middle, he arrives at a new harmonic principle—dissonance by collision. More recent composers have written music that is much more densely dissonant than his. But perhaps no dissonances are quite as sharp and exciting as those that result when a seemingly predictable succession of consonances is suddenly derailed.

Mahler's youth was marked by a long series of tragic experiences, some of them afterward reflected in his *Kindertotenlieder* ("Songs on the Deaths of Children"). He came from a poor Jewish family in which only three of the twelve children lived to maturity. In later years, even after his rise to fame and his conversion to Catholicism, he referred to himself as a thrice homeless man: "as a Bohemian among Austrians, as an Austrian among Germans, and as a Jew among the peoples of the whole world." His "golden decade" as artistic director of the Vienna Opera, 1897–1907, established him as the foremost conductor of the day. His orchestras, by turns "alarmed and fascinated," always played better for him than they ever had before. "Mahler, in aspect and gesture, seemed at once genius and demon," wrote the conductor Bruno Walter, who became one of his assistants when he was only eighteen. "Never had I encountered so intense a human being. . . ." He went to New York to conduct at the Metropolitan Opera, and then took over the directorship of the New York Philharmonic. But he was already suffering from a severe cardiac ailment. After he collapsed during his forty-seventh concert of the 1911 season, he was rushed to Europe for medical attention, only to die in a Viennese sanatorium.

Mahler's conducting assignments never left him time enough to write his own music. Like Borodin, he called himself a *Sommerkomponist*, for nearly all his works were written during his summer holidays, when he could escape "this terrible treadmill of the theater" and spend his days in rural Austria, "roaming over mountains and through forests, and carrying off my day's bag of sketches. . . ." Once, when Bruno Walter went to visit him in Steinbach, on the Attersee, and stopped to admire the mountain scenery, Mahler told him: "Don't bother to look—I've composed all this already."

Conducting during the winter and composing only during summer vacations, Gustav Mahler (left) struggled to find time for his large-scale symphonies and his songs; below, the cover of his most tragic cycle of songs, the Kindertotenlieder. *The symbolic painting at right, by Klimt, matches the music of Mahler in giving a sense of the period's tension.*

He drew vast, cosmic conclusions from his annual encounters with the Alps, and the symphonic results are sometimes maddeningly metaphysical. In the Second Symphony, a huge fresco of death and immortality culminates in the great choral cry "Resurrection!" The Third Symphony is a hymn to nature nearly two hours long that includes "Summer Marching In" and reveals, among other things, "What the Flowers in the Meadow Tell Me." The Fourth Symphony presents a child's-eye view of paradise, based on an old peasant rhyme about the heavenly joys. The Eighth, the so-called Symphony of a Thousand, is nothing less than a gargantuan ceremonial for up to eleven hundred singers and instrumentalists (shades of Hector Berlioz!) that combines a medieval Latin hymn with Goethe's intimations of immortality from the final scene of *Faust*. "The symphony must be like the world," he once told Jean Sibelius. "It must embrace everything."

If Mahler had done no more than this—harangue the world on the beauties of faith and nature—he would probably be a forgotten composer. But Mahler's metaphysics have become secondary and expendable. His posthumous reputation, never higher than in the 1970's, rests on the fact that modern audiences have learned to value him for other things. His sarcasm is one of the saving graces—the curious way in which his music mocks and parodies in its own highest aspirations. His greatest discovery was the possibility of a new ambivalence in music. There had never been anything like it before, this polyphony of sonic ideas, this sense of music moving on several different levels of meaning at the same time. It was surrealism: not the small-scale surrealism of the fur-lined teacup, but oversize and magnificent in scale—the stream-of-consciousness in march time. Perhaps what he said about paradise is negligible, but he spoke all the more eloquently about the life of the unconscious self and the human condition. Never was a more brilliant technique placed at the service of a more fascinating neurosis. It was fortunate that Dr. Freud came too late to cure him of it.

9

Innovation and Revolution

ON MAY 29, 1913, AT THE NEWLY inaugurated Théâtre du Champs-Elysées, Sergei Diaghilev's Ballet Russe presented the première of Igor Stravinsky's *Le Sacre du Printemps* ("The Rite of Spring") before an audience composed of the most elegant women, the most fashionable young people, the most famous artists, the richest financiers, and the most arrant snobs in Paris. They had come to see the ballet, but what they got was a battle. No sooner had the performance begun than the first skirmishes erupted in the theater. "People laughed, scoffed, whistled, hissed and imitated animal noises," wrote the poet Jean Cocteau, who was in the thick of it. "They might eventually have tired themselves out had not the crowd of aesthetes and a few musicians, carried away by their excessive zeal, insulted and even roughly handled the public in the loges. The uproar degenerated into a fight."

Standing in her box, her tiara askew, the dowager Countess de Pourtalès flourished her fan and shouted, "It's the first time in sixty years that anyone has dared to make a fool of me!" Maurice Ravel, who had come to hear his colleague's work, politely requested a resplendently dressed neighbor to be quiet and was roundly abused for his pains. But the Beautiful People were divided in their sympathies. One society woman spat in the face of a demonstrator; another slapped the face of a man who was hissing in the next box. Her escort rose, and cards were exchanged; a duel was to be arranged. "It was all incredibly fierce," reported the American writer and doyen of expatriates Gertrude Stein. "We could hear nothing. As a matter of fact, I never did hear any of the music. . . ."

Indeed, for most of the audience the noise drowned out the startling new sounds coming from the pit. The young conductor on the podium, Pierre Monteux, threw desperate glances at the director's box, but he had orders not to interrupt the performance under any circumstances. The manager of the theater, Gabriel Astruc, who had put up half a million francs to guarantee *Sacre* and the season, stood in the box shouting, "First listen, then hiss!" Beside him—and beside himself—was Diaghilev, the veteran impresario of the Ballet Russe, vainly pleading, "Please let them get on with the show!" Finally they ordered the house lights turned on in order to quiet the audience and to let the police pick out and eject the worst troublemakers.

The thirty-year-old composer of the ballet had left the auditorium

Beneath layers of civilization called technology, or nationalism, or Christianity, stands a human being with relatively standard desires and fears. He is the pagan within, studied by Sigmund Freud, placed in a new outer medium by Albert Einstein, and greeted by the artists of the twentieth century with the dance. Matched at left with fragments of Igor Stravinsky's score for Le Sacre du Printemps, *Valentino Hugo's drawings for the première show a young woman dancing herself toward death—for she is to be the pagan sacrifice in "the rite of spring."*

131

at the first sign of trouble and had gone backstage to watch the uproar from the wings. In later years, he recalled that evening:

> I have never again been that angry. The music was so familiar to me; I loved it, and I could not understand why people who had not yet heard it wanted to protest in advance. ... For the rest of the performance I stood in the wings behind Nijinsky [the choreographer] holding the tails of his *frac,* while he stood on a chair shouting numbers to the dancers, like a coxswain.

Onstage, the dancers were performing a stylized version of a primitive fertility rite based on Stravinsky's own startling vision of a pagan ceremony: "sage elders, seated in a circle, watched a young girl dance herself to death. They were sacrificing her to propitiate the god of spring."

It was a ballet without the conventional love interest, ostensibly close to the dawn of civilization. Musically, too, it reverted to those primitive sources from which the performing arts had originally sprung: nature worship, the choric dance, the rhythm of tribal drums. In many of its episodes, Stravinsky's complex and sumptuous score employed the kind of percussion that would have been more familiar to an African tribal chief than a Parisian balletomane. There were pages, like those of Moussorgsky (who was one of Stravinsky's decisive influences), consisting of constantly shifting accents—2/8, 3/16, 2/16, 3/16, 2/8, 2/16, 3/16, and so on—and these were hammered out by a pair of timpanists and an assortment of lesser percussion. Here, for the first time, was the full application of those neopagan principles that were to lead classical music out of the nineteenth-century doldrums. Like Picasso's African-inspired painting *Les Demoiselles d'Avignon,* it was one of the aesthetic milestones of the century, a work so important as to be considered the birth certificate of contemporary music. As one French critic wrote, "We were dumbfounded, overwhelmed by this hurricane that had come from the depths of the ages and which had taken life by the roots."

Both in its immediate impact and its long-range effect, *Sacre* proved to be one of the most influential works ever written. Somehow it crystallized the century's quest for a new sound, and soon there were dozens of composers who drew their own independent conclusions from Stravinsky's example. His Russian colleague Sergei Prokofiev, for example, composed a *Scythian Suite* that contains many of the same elements, including the sharp cutting edge of percussion and the pagan subject matter. "It is quite possible that I was now searching for the same images my own way," Prokofiev later admitted. Darius Milhaud, a leader of the Stravinskian French school known as *Les Six,* borrowed Brazilian jungle rhythms for his ballet *L'Homme et Son Désir* ("Man and His Desire"), for which he found the inspiration while serving in the French diplomatic service in Brazil during World War I. The chief of his mission, the poet-ambassador Paul Claudel, provided him with the ballet's scenario: "The principal character is Man, over whom the primitive forces have resumed their sway. ... And all the beasts, all the sounds of the everlasting forest come to gaze at him. ... And his dance

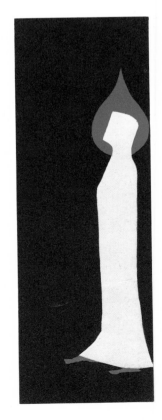

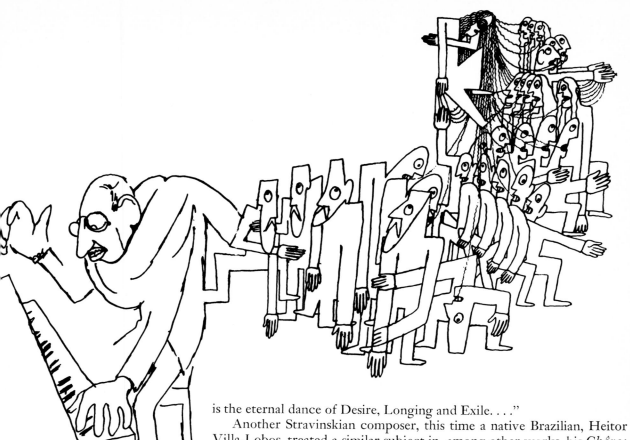

is the eternal dance of Desire, Longing and Exile. . . ."

Another Stravinskian composer, this time a native Brazilian, Heitor Villa-Lobos, treated a similar subject in, among other works, his *Chôros No. 10*, which depicts man's reaction to the valleys of the Amazon and the land of the Mato Grosso. The ballet *Appalachian Spring* by the American composer Aaron Copland is a more gentle, lyrical celebration of the same theme of the Eternal Return. Béla Bartók, who spent much of his youth hunting for primitive survivals in the peasant music of his native Hungary, perfected a "pagan" style of his own in works like *The Miraculous Mandarin* ballet or the Sonata for Two Pianos and Percussion. The piano itself turned into a sort of percussian instrument under the insistent "hammering" of his martellato style (beginning with the *Allegro Barbaro* of 1911)—an effect described by the English critic Percy Scholes as "A touch like a paving stone."

In one way or another these men all rediscovered something of the untapped energy that had previously been expressed only in works of primitive art. Yet now, in the midst of the twentieth century's aesthetic revolution, it was suddenly everywhere—in the violent colors of the Fauves, the "wild beasts" of French painting; in the jagged lines and fractured planes of the cubists; the pipeline-and-girder art of Fernand Léger; the number-and-alphabet poetry of Dada; the transposed images of the surrealists. There was a new poetry and a new prose—T. S. Eliot's *The Waste Land*, James Joyce's *Ulysses*, Guillaume Apollinaire's *Le Poète Assassiné*, Franz Kafka's *The Trial*. It was as though the release of energy in the arts was intended to keep pace with the new physics of Albert Einstein ($E = mc^2$) and the new psychiatry of Sigmund Freud.

Indeed, the throbbing rhythms of Stravinsky's work seemed just as appropriate for the machine age as for the primitive forces of pagan ritual. The Swiss composer Arthur Honegger, another prominent

It was Sergei Diaghilev who, after vowing in the 1890's to blend music, dancing, and scenery into a new whole, began to enliven Paris with commissioned works for his new company, the Ballet Russe: Stravinsky's Firebird *marked the company's second (1910) season, his* Petrouchka *its third, and his controversial* Le Sacre du Printemps *its fifth. (In the Jean Cocteau drawing above, Stravinsky plays the piano section of that work.) When Diaghilev invited Darius Milhaud to write a ballet, the French composer responded with* L'Homme et Son Désir *(for which Andrée Parr executed the costume sketch at left); Diaghilev produced it in 1921.*

Overleaf: Raoul Dufy's Grande Orchestre *epitomizes the twenty-year period between two wars when artists from all over the world thronged to Paris.*

133

10

The Once and Future Music

If music had gone as far as it could go with Stravinsky's conversion to serialism, rock fans of the second half of the century neglected to mourn and turned to their own form of rejoicing: at left a rock organist stays in electronic touch with his Mannheim, Germany, audience.

DUKE ELLINGTON, BURT BACHARACH, Loretta Lynn, Lightning Hopkins, Elvis Presley, Leonard Bernstein, Ray Charles, The Rolling Stones, Luciano Berio, Bob Dylan, B. B. King, Frank Zappa, Cat Stevens, Aretha Franklin—these are a few of the prominent musicians of the latter third of the twentieth century, and their names are symbolic of the "many mansions" that comprise the house of music in the age of electronic communication. Never before has there been so much music available to so vast an audience, or such a multiplicity of ways for human beings to express their musical impulses—jazz, folk, soul, rock, pop, country and western, symphonic and "light classical," Broadway and Hollywood, serious and trivial. This bewildering profusion of styles is evidence of a great revolution in the art of organizing sounds. The old conventions are suddenly no more. The forms and purposes of music are in a state of flux; no one seems at all certain where music might be heading next.

A generation after the introduction of the tape recorder and the LP record, the full impact of electronic technology begins to be felt both in the production and consumption of music. Now that it is no longer necessary to have a hundred-man symphony orchestra in order to produce a sound loud enough to fill an auditorium, the emphasis has shifted to individual expression by soloists and "chamber" groups, such as the pop combination of singer, guitars, organ, bass, and percussion.

No less important is the fact that music of all epochs, countries, and styles is now available on tapes or discs, so that every music lover is free to exercise his options continually, and with a far wider choice of material than even the greatest of the old music patrons of Versailles or Esterháza would ever have dreamed of. A not untypical record collection might range from Monteverdi madrigals and Corelli concertos to Bach, Berlioz, and Bartók, Tibetan monks chanting mantras, Carlos Montoya playing flamenco guitar, Erroll Garner on the piano, Muddy Waters singing the blues, Ravi Shankar playing the sitar. In short, the age of total eclecticism is upon us. By the same token there is no longer a single prevailing taste in contemporary art music, which ranges all the way from relatively traditionalist works by composers like Benjamin Britten, to the fragmentations of Karlheinz Stockhausen, the tape-loop constructions of Terry Riley, and the "indeterminacy" experiments of John Cage. The picture may appear hopelessly unfocused, yet there are forces at work to bring about an eventual reconciliation between the competing worlds of pop and avant-garde—a synthesis foreshadowed in the later Beatle records and in some of the more adventurous film scores.

Despite the fragmentation and the contradictions, there is one thing that all modern music has in common: every style, without exception, has been profoundly influenced by the convergence of the two great mainstreams, African rhythm and European harmony, which first occurred in America and has since spread to the rest of the world. This fusion of elements is probably the most significant musical development of the last hundred years, comparable in importance to the birth of counterpoint or the romantic revolution.

Yet it was a slow process that occurred spontaneously and often against determined opposition from the guardians of musical taste. Then, before anyone quite realized what was happening, a new sound welled up out of the former colonial countries where black and white had long been, if not on equal terms, at least within earshot of each other. And an astonished world suddenly found itself listening and moving to Dixieland, the blues, the foxtrot, the conga, the mambo, the Lindy Hop, be bop, bossa nova, soul, rock. "The plaintive and derisive songs of an oppressed people," noted the British anthropologist Geoffrey Gorer, "have become the background for a whole society's pleasures and distractions." But the influence went deeper than that. Within the last fifty years, Afro-American rhythms have altered the world's conception of how music ought to sound. As one European concert pianist expressed it, "Once you hear how the blacks move in music, you never want to go back to the old way."

In the United States, musical integration has been a continuous process going back to Colonial days. Although the African slaves were often denied the right to use their drums—their masters feared, perhaps rightly, that the drums would spark insurrections—they were allowed to go on singing and playing stringed instruments. Often they displayed such a genius for music that anyone with a trained ear was

Diaghilev sensed that the approach to the twentieth-century pagan was through dance, and jazz with its sophisticated African rhythms always spoke to the body and made it move. Below is Joe "King" Oliver's dance band with its witty virtuoso trumpeter, Louis Armstrong, standing at left; at right, above, gospel singers clap in a production of The Trumpets of the Lord.

bound to take notice, and many white men were deeply impressed. It was on account of the blacks' singing that the white planters were first obliged to recognize the humanity of their "savage" slaves. The slave-owning, violin-playing Thomas Jefferson even had the temerity to suggest, in his *Notes on Virginia*, that black men were superior to white men in this respect: "In music they are generally more gifted than the whites," he wrote, "with accurate ears for tune and time."

European musicians who came into contact with the slaves often reached the same conclusion. The famous English actress and singer Fanny Kemble, in her *Journal of a Residence on a Georgia Plantation*, confesses herself profoundly moved by the singing she heard among the slaves in the 1830's: "The high voices all in unison, and the admirable time and true accent with which their responses are made, make me wish that some great musical composer would hear these ... performances. With a very little skillful adaptation and instrumentation [they] would make the fortune of an opera." The great Viennese pianist Henri Herz came to America from Paris in the 1840's and fell in love with the "solemn, resonant and harmonious" notes of the black banjo players he heard during his tour of the South. Herz wrote of the music he heard:

> Negroes are very appreciative of music, and their souls are far from being closed to the beauties of poetry. A collection of their songs has been made, and a study of it reveals an uncommon tenderness and rigorous observance of the laws of rhythm, that elemental core of all music, so well known to everyone, and yet so difficult to explain. From time to time, while listening to Negro banjo players, I have pondered the mysterious law of rhythm which seems to be a universal law, since rhythm is coordinated movement, and movement is life, and life fills the universe.

Louis Moreau Gottschalk, the first American-born composer of international importance, made his reputation in the mid-nineteenth century with a series of piano pieces based on black music from Louisiana and the Caribbean, with its mixture of French, Spanish, and African elements. During the 1890's, when the Bohemian composer Antonin Dvořák came to teach at the American Conservatory in New York, it was again the Negro spirituals that made the most lasting impression on him: indeed, a paraphrase of "Swing Low, Sweet Chariot" found its way into the *New World Symphony* (it had been among the plantation songs sung for him by his black pupil, Henry Burleigh).

Dvořák told his students that "the future music of this country must be founded upon what are called the Negro melodies." And in a long article published in *Harper's* magazine, he wrote that black music was already "unconsciously recognized as their own" by most Americans: "What songs, then, belong to the American and appeal more strongly to him than any others? What melody could stop him on the street if he were in a strange land and make the home feeling well up within him, no matter how hardened he might be or how wretchedly the tune were played?" This reads like a scenario for George Gershwin's *An American in Paris*, where a blues melody is introduced to underscore the hero's homesickness. It was as though Dvořák had foreseen that thirty or forty years hence, the jazz descendants of his "plantation melodies" would in fact sound the keynote for American culture.

Gershwin, as it happens, was one of the first composers to try his hand at symphonic jazz. His best-known effort in this direction, the *Rhapsody in Blue*, was perhaps less successful in "making a lady out of jazz" (as the saying went) than in creating a concert framework for the Broadway pseudo-jazz of which he was then the world's leading exponent, and which was in itself a melange of black and white elements. Gershwin was a brilliantly gifted master of the idiom: "I Got Rhythm," "The Man I Love," "That Certain Feeling," "Someone to Watch over Me," and the rest are to the American repertoire what Franz Schubert's songs were to the German Lied. But his most successful use of black folklore was in *Porgy and Bess*, an all-black opera about the inhabitants of Catfish Row in Charleston, South Carolina.

In 1934, while Gershwin was at work on the score, he and his librettist, Dubose Heyward, spent a summer doing background research among the black farmers of the Carolina sea islands. At that time there were still some African musical survivals in these isolated communities, including the singing technique called "shouting," which Heyward described as "a complicated rhythmic pattern beaten out by feet and hands as an accompaniment to the spirituals." Gershwin, who soon learned how to take part in the "shouting," steeped himself in the local music just as Moussorgsky had when he went to live among the Russian peasants in preparation for *Boris Godunov*. Heyward recalled an experience he and Gershwin had one evening:

> ... as we were about to enter a dilapidated cabin that had been taken as a meeting house by a group of Negro Holy Rollers, George caught my arm and held me. The sound that had arrested him ... consisted of perhaps a dozen voices raised in loud rhythmic prayer. The odd thing about it was that while each had started at a different time, upon a different theme, they formed a clearly defined rhythmic pattern, and that this, with the actual words lost, and the inevitable pounding of the rhythm, produced an effect almost terrifying in its primitive intensity.

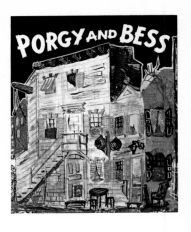

Ella, Louis—both the blues and jazz were personal, rising like easy, sometimes secret, conversations from the lives of America's blacks. Above: the cover of a Porgy and Bess *program from the works of the jazz student George Gershwin; at right, a lithograph entitled* Jazz Birth *depicts a scene from the rural South; below left, Ella Fitzgerald singing the blues, and right, Armstrong takes off on a trumpet improvisation while holding his familiar white handkerchief.*

For Gershwin this experience led directly to the storm scene of *Porgy and Bess* in which six simultaneous prayers rise above the fury of an orchestral hurricane. But the whole episode serves as a perfect illustration of the rhythmic (and melodic) inspiration that black musicians invariably brought to white music—not only at the operatic level but at every point of cultural contact.

Although Heyward, like many other writers, uses the word "primitive" to describe this music, technically speaking African rhythm is anything but that—as anyone who has ever tried to write it down will testify. It involves several highly sophisticated techniques that are evidently the product of an ancient tradition of rhythmic interplay, such as can take place only in close-knit tribal communities. The results are far more flexible and exciting than anything to be found in European rhythm. Inevitably, some of this elasticity was lost in the process of adjusting the African beat to the needs of a four-square harmonic pattern, yet enough freedom remained to lend rhythmic excitement to the early jazz styles. In most 1920's jazz, for example, a steady 1-2-3-4 beat in quick tempo supports one or two interlocking rhythms that break down the beat into smaller components and stress the offbeats; sometimes it is also instinctively "polyrhythmic," in that two or more entirely different rhythms may be moving along at the same time.

The question-and-answer character of so much Afro-American music has its origin in the antiphonal structure of African work songs

147

and tribal chants, where the lead singer is answered by the massed voices of the other participants:

> It is crying, it is crying,
>   Sihamba Ngenyanga.
> The child of the walker by moonlight,
>   Sihamba Ngenyanga.
> It was done intentionally by people whose
>   names cannot be mentioned
>   Sihamba Ngenyanga.
> They sent her for water during the day,
>   Sihamba Ngenyanga.

When the African slaves were converted to Christianity in the new world, they went on singing in the same patterns. The typical spiritual is just as antiphonal as the African work song:

> Oh, the River of Jordan is deep and wide,
>   One more river to cross.
> I don't know how to get on the other side,
>   One more river to cross.
> Oh, you got Jesus, hold him fast,
>   One more river to cross.
> Oh, better love was never told,
>   One more river to cross.

The American blues, too, have their antecedents in African chants with a similar sort of construction: a steep rise in the melody, followed by a gentle "sloping down," followed by another steep rise and gentle, step-wise descent. Blues singers follow the African tradition of "vocalizing" the sound of their accompanying instruments by "teasing" the strings of a guitar with a knife or a bottle neck, for example, so that the tone becomes very elastic and responsive. And ethnomusicologists have noted the same penchant for "gapped pentatonic" scales among Mississippi bluesmen as among the tribal singers of West Africa.

A long and complex development led from the "hollers" and blues of the southern field hands to the full-blown Dixieland jazz bands that first rose to prominence at "$1.50 a couple" picnics outside of New Orleans. Later, the sound moved north with the riverboats. The first mention of jazz in the press is in a *Variety* story dated October 27, 1916:

Chicago has added another innovation to its list of discoveries in the so-called 'Jazz Bands.' The Jazz Band is composed of three or more instruments and seldom plays regulated music. The College Inn and practically all the other high-class places of entertainment have a Jazz Band featured, while the low cost makes it possible for all the smaller places to carry their Jazz orchestra.

It was this strong, exuberant music, played by ear and bursting with vitality, that gave its name to the Jazz Age. Pure jazz, played largely by black musicians, gradually evolved into several distinct varieties, giving birth to be bop (which abandoned the old rhythmic framework) and modern jazz. Although it began as a folk idiom designed for dancing, it has developed into a complex form of instrumental "chamber music" intended simply to be listened to by audiences of connoisseurs comparable to those for classical music. In much diluted form, the jazz impulse inspired the swing bands of white musicians like Benny Goodman, as well as the swinging style of pop singers (also known as crooners) of the Bing Crosby-Frank Sinatra school. Meanwhile, jazz played an increasingly important role in serious music. Charles Ives, the Connecticut Yankee whose polytonal experiments had anticipated Stravinsky's, led the way by using ragtime rhythms at the turn of the century. Gershwin, Copland, and Bernstein were among the Americans who followed suit, while Ravel, Stravinsky, Hindemith, and Milhaud headed

From shouts in the work fields and from the tender gospel heritage of The Trumpets of the Lord *(right), black music moved through the New Orleans ensemble and the Chicago soloist style to the big band of Edward Kennedy "Duke" Ellington (below, left). The Duke's arrangements seemed more like improvisations than they actually were.*

the list of Europeans who set down their symphonic (and in some cases rather hilarious) impressions of what jazz sounded like to their ears.

The full impact of soul rhythm could be felt only after white popular music began to respond to the stimulus of "race records," alias rhythm and blues, and singers like Leadbelly (Huddie Ledbetter), Bessie Smith, and Billie Holiday. Elvis Presley and the rock 'n roll of the 1950's were part of the answer to this challenge. Then, in the 1960's, it was the Beatles' turn to launch a revolution in popular music. When they first appeared on the scene they sang like very young and energetic angels flapping wing-shaped guitars, with a hard-driving sound based on Memphis rock, British "skiffle" groups, and the Harlem blues. Only the texts of their songs belonged to the English music-hall tradition, and were thus closer to Bea Lillie than Leadbelly.

The words the Beatles sang were surprisingly bland, coming from an unruly generation whose taste for unabated high volume was blowing the roofs off the discothèques. Evidently the Beatles had got hold of some secret sorrow and made it articulate—"Don't be bad to me; hold me, love me; I call your name but you're not there; I'm a loser; did you have to treat me, oh, so bad?" (Perhaps it was the Oedipal drama of a generation that had undergone the trauma of permissive parenthood and demand feeding. When Lennon and McCartney pleaded, "don't go 'way; I'm afraid that I might miss you," they touched on the same emotional anguish that another British poet, A. A. Milne, had summed up so poignantly in the lines, "You must never go down/ to the end of the town/ without consulting me.")

In later Beatle records the focus shifted from second person accusative to third person feminine ("She's a Woman"), the accent stopped

The Beatles—John Lennon, Paul McCartney, Ringo Starr, and George Harrison—struck reverberating notes in their listeners; but there is no planned sound in 4'33" the famous silent work of John Cage (above). As the serialist composers abandon much of their control to a predetermined sequence of notes, Cage abandoned his in 4'33" to chance and to the audience, giving them only a time limit and an opened but silent piano.

coming down on the hard beats, and the twang of guitars was augmented by the palsied tones of the electronic organ. In "We Can Work It Out," echoes of a French music-hall musette broke like a thunderclap across a pop scene that had heard nothing but four-four time for a generation. It was as if the Beatles had independently invented waltz time (here disguised as triplets).

At about the same time, serious musicians made the discovery—discussed on television by Leonard Bernstein—that some of these tunes were nearly as modal as Gregorian chant. Yet it was hardly surprising that the Beatles should show the same preference for the Dorian mode and the pentatonic scale as the English folksongs and American blues from which their melodies derive. George Harrison learned to play an uncertain sitar in India and brought an Asian element into the arsenal of pop sounds. Soon they were borrowing sounds from everywhere: a horn obbligato from Schubert, a clarin trumpet from Bach (blowing fanfares for the fireman who likes to keep a clean machine), and for "Eleanor Rigby," a string accompaniment that bore a striking resemblance to the *Bachianas Brasileiras* of Villa Lobos.

"I don't like that kind of classical music. I can't stand it," McCartney explained to the underground *International Times*. "But it fitted, it was just lucky it fitted." Yet whether they wanted to or not, the Beatles had already breached the great wall between classical music and the pop world. Later, in "Sergeant Pepper," they unleashed a great orgy of free association that was related to the experiments of John Cage, the father of "random" musicmaking. Here the sound was composed of jangling harps, wheezing calliopes, Detroit soul rhythms, a choral fugato on "We shall scrimp and save," electric guitars going off like wobbly firecrackers, dogs barking, memories of Fred and Adele Astaire, and a Hindu-inspired chant about saving the world through love. There was even a forty-one-man symphony orchestra, raising a vast banshee wail and making a sound only slightly smaller than the one Mahler used in the *Symphony of a Thousand*.

Their talents were such that every record they touched turned to gold. They possessed an extraordinary power to sway the multitudes, and indeed, although the group itself has split up, their songs seem destined to go on forever. It was as if a whole society—not otherwise noted for its generosity to poets—had decided to subsidize its creative subconscious to the tune of twenty million dollars a year. And, whatever their fate as a group, the line of musical development the Beatles chose to follow is of vital importance to the further development of music. They were the first to demonstrate that pop and classical can be brought together in some musically meaningful way. If their eclecticism is pursued to its logical conclusion, it may be that the art of music will become a continuum once more instead of a series of independent and soundproof compartments. Perhaps, in the day of the "global village," that may not be too distant a prospect.

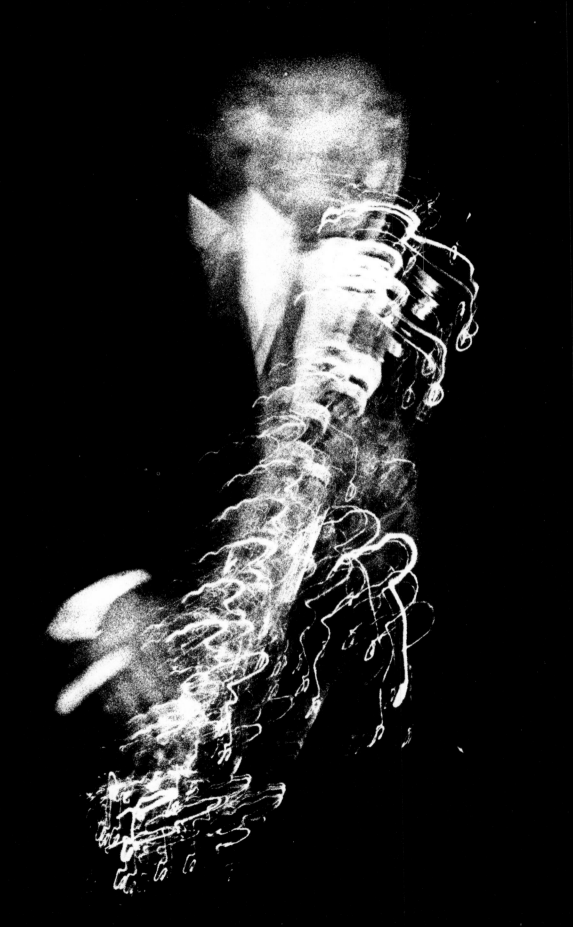

MEMOIRS OF
MUSICAL LIVES

Arturo Toscanini's concentration on the symphony orchestra began late in his career. But such was the brilliance of his technique that our perception of the conductor's role has been permanently altered as a result of his work. A profile of the maestro, written by Winthrop Sargeant while Toscanini was conductor of the NBC Symphony from 1937 to 1954, gives us an insight into his genius.

Thirty years ago, the name Arturo Toscanini referred to an able but relatively obscure and already middle-aged Italian opera conductor whose principal triumphs had been achieved in the orchestra pits at La Scala and the Metropolitan Opera House. Today, Arturo Toscanini is, without question, the most celebrated musician in the world. He is, with the possible exception of the Pope, the most famous living Italian. His reputation outshines those of nearly all the contemporary composers whose works he occasionally conducts. He is probably the highest-paid symphony conductor in the history of music. Musicians have reverently collected the splintered batons that he breaks and throws away when he is angry. One sentimental New York woman treasures a piece of ruptured paneling that he once broke when, in a temper, he thrust his fist through a door in his Carnegie Hall dressing room. Legends about his amazingly accurate ear and his phenomenal memory have approached the incredible. Not since Nicolò Paganini reputedly sold his soul to the devil for an E string has a prominent musician enjoyed such a reputation for uncanny, occult and mysterious power. In an age of virtuosos, when the symphonic conductor has become the king of virtuosos, Toscanini is the greatest virtuoso of them all.

The man thus prematurely immortalized is a sharp-eyed, white-haired, extremely wiry Italian whose bare five feet of height usually come as a surprise to those who meet him off the stage. He dresses with prim severity—nearly always in black. Socially he is surprisingly shy. He loves the company of pretty women and hugely enjoys an occasional evening at a Manhattan night club. But he always looks vaguely out of place in any gathering he cannot lead with a baton. He has a reputation for childish helplessness in practical affairs and is said to be incapable of finding his own collar buttons or getting his hair cut without the help of his sedate, capable-looking wife. But he is shrewd enough to bargain closely over his concert and broadcast fees. In private life he is alternately fussy and playful, headstrong in both his enthusiasms and hatreds, intolerant of anything in the way of opposition. To many, his celebrated encounters with Europe's Nazi and Fascist authorities have made him a symbol of democratic idealism. A fervent nationalist like most of his countrymen, he is politically an avowed and tested liberal. But Toscanini is, both professionally and by temperament, an absolute dictator. He is also deeply and matter-of-factly convinced that he is the greatest conductor in the world.

His arrival at Rockefeller Center in New York City for his weekly broadcasts is as carefully prepared as the official reception of a monarch. In his dressing room several dress suits, complete from tie to socks, are carefully laid out, awaiting his intermission rubdown and change of clothing. A bowl of watermelon balls, which he likes to eat following a concert, lies cooling for him in a refrigerator. Pictures of his wife and family and favorite composers, without which he will refuse to conduct, are tastefully arranged on his dressing table. A punctual half hour before broadcast time, Toscanini's chauffeur-driven Chevrolet arrives at the 49th Street entrance of the RCA Building from his rented home in Riverdale. Toscanini steps into an elevator and is carefully whisked to the eighth floor. The hundred men of the NBC Symphony, already seated and tuned up, are waiting in nervous silence. So is a hushed audience that has begged and bought, at fantastic black-market prices, the tickets that the National Broadcasting Company allots to a chosen few of the musical world. This audience, composed largely of connoisseurs, listens to the ensuing program with the most reverent attention, for it is, like all Toscanini programs, a unique experience. . . .

Toscanini's uncanny control of the orchestral machine rests largely on the fact that he is acutely aware of the work of each individual instrumentalist. Musicians know that the average conductor is easily satisfied with a general impression of puffed cheeks and active bow strokes. With Toscanini it is different. When a musician makes an effort he can see it register immediately on his imperious face. When the effort is not made, that fact registers also. And such is the maestro's keenness of ear that even the third double-bass player from the end feels like a goldfish in a bowl, his every groaning sixteenth-note under microscopic observation.

There are, however, compensations for the player who sweats under this omniscience. Toscanini has a way of intuitively sensing the potentialities, failings and even the momentary emotional status of the men who are playing under him. He seldom tyrannizes over a nervous man, and he never picks a flaw or throws a tantrum arbitrarily. Nor does he seek, as lesser conductors sometimes do, to bamboozle experienced orchestra players with meaningless and transparent sleight of hand in order to impress them with his knowledge. The knowledge, fortified by the famous Toscanini memory, is there. It needs no herald trumpeting to get itself noticed. Any mistake, except one due to carelessness or downright stupidity, generally meets with encouragement and patient drilling. Though he is relentless in exposing any laxity, the maestro's attitude toward the music and toward his men is one of open, almost childlike, sincerity. Moreover, orchestra players will tell you that it is actually more difficult to make a mistake under Toscanini than under any other conductor. His erratic, paddling beat is so enormously expressive that even an unimportant player who is temporarily at sea can tell, just by watching it, exactly where and how to make his entrances. . . .

Every rehearsal sees a thousand moods rise and subside in the "old man," a thousand ways of getting what he wants out of the hundred-odd men under him. Completely absorbed in his complicated task, he seems as transparent and unself-conscious as a four-year-old child gravely making mud pies. While he is conducting, he sings continuously—or rather, wails like a disembodied banshee—apparently quite oblivious to the fact that his piping, cracked-sounding voice can often be heard above the music. For a while he will play elegantly and delightedly with the delicate lacework of some Mozart or Haydn symphony. An exquisite sensual happiness will seem to permeate his whole being. Intolerant of the slightest imperfection in his toy, he will smooth out the air before him, stroking and shaping it into a symbol of elegant and polished sound. A sour note or a scratchy fiddle passage will overwhelm him with a desperate sense of disappointment which would move even a bass-drum player to remorse. For a moment anger will threaten. Unable to get what he wants by imperious methods, he will try wheedling it out of the players like a clever woman, or he will threaten to tear himself apart with hysterics if he is not appeased. Sometimes, like a possessed dervish he will take to praying and swearing, trying to bring forth a performance by a species of incantation. An obstinately repeated error will suddenly rouse him to furious sarcasm: "*Io credo . . .*" he will begin with fiery deliberation, "I think, that there is an accent over that F sharp. But," he will continue, biting off each word and glaring at the culprit, "I am only Toscanini, and I am probably wrong. *Vediamo!*" Calling for a copy of the score, he will rustle impatiently through the pages holding them within three or four inches of his nearsighted eyes. Then, finding the passage in question, he will elaborately pretend to be thunderstruck. "Ah, no *Signori*. Imagine. I am right! Mozart has written an accent there." With an impatient whip stroke and a murderous-sounding grunt, the scene will be finished and the culprit, who has been staring guiltily at the accent all the time, will thank his stars that his temporary moment in the spotlight is over. . . .

As geniuses go, Toscanini is not an enormously conceited man, and aside from moments of Napoleonic Latin imperiousness, he is certainly not a pompous one. Yet the maestro, like all authentic geniuses, has a deep sense of the importance of his extraordinary abilities. Perhaps this sense is better illustrated by another anecdote, which I can vouch for, as I was there when the event happened: Several years ago (in 1930, to be exact) on a train approaching Budapest, a cosmopolitan group of Philharmonic musicians sat in a compartment talking and drinking champagne. Their spirits were high. But their manners were respectfully restrained, and their conversation was relatively lofty. Their host was Toscanini. Usually affable and friendly in his off-duty moments, Toscanini had been smiling in his detached way, quietly discussing details of scoring and instrumental technique, gesticulating between sips with his incredibly expressive lean fingers. But, as the evening wore on, the little maestro became more and more preoccupied. Suddenly he got up and rummaged through a suitcase, returning with a carefully folded

Mozart's Der Schauspieldirektor

letter which he handed around for the inspection of his companions. It was a letter he had carried with him for many years, written to him long ago when he was a sprouting young opera conductor in Italy. It was from the great Giuseppe Verdi. An old man's letter, it spoke encouragingly to the young conductor, telling him, among other things, to take good care of Verdi's operas in the long future that lay ahead of them. The musicians handed it around, poring over it with great respect. When they were finished, the maestro returned it to his valise. But he seemed even more troubled than before. Finally, with one of his characteristic little explosive grunts, he got what was troubling him out of his system. "An immortal," he remarked sadly. "Verdi will live forever. But Toscanini?" He gestured backward at his chin with one hand as if displaying himself as a detached object for their consideration. "Toscanini will be dead like all the rest. He will never conduct orchestras again. And the worst of it is" (here a fiery glint came into the little maestro's eye), "that they will play badly—badly!"

WINTHROP SARGEANT
Geniuses, Goddesses, and People, 1949

During his years at the helm of the Philadelphia Orchestra, Leopold Stokowski held complete mastery over that superb musical instrument. However, as the orchestra's biographer Herbert Kupferberg relates, Stokowski encountered much more difficulty taming the Philadelphia audience.

Stokowski was not only determined to remake the Philadelphia Orchestra; he also set out to reform the Philadelphia audience—which was, perhaps, an even more difficult task. His especial target was the Friday afternoon gathering. The ladies for the most part doted upon the blond young man, but they had no intention of letting him alter long-established habits which went back to the days of Scheel and Pohling. They sat and knitted while the music was being played. They kept their hats fixed firmly on their heads despite requests in the programs to remove them. They talked and coughed and rustled. Most irritating of all to the new conductor, they arrived late and left early, for when there was a conflict between the running time of a Brahms symphony and the Paoli local, the train always won out.

Soon after his triumph in the Mahler *Symphony of a Thousand* had securely established his place as the city's virtual musical dictator, Stokowski, armed with a new contract running through 1921 at an estimated salary of $40,000 a year, began to turn on his feminine audience, subjecting them to a torrent of words, some as acerbic and prickly as the modern music he was now playing in increasing amounts. Of course, they adored being admonished by him for their sins of deportment, and he relished lecturing, scolding, and chiding them. . . .

The battle over arrivals and departures went on for years, and was never really resolved. Although Stokowski did shame some of the worst offenders into quiescence, the afternoon outflux never quite stopped altogether. One famous Stokowski story tells of his being greeted by a female American tourist one summer in Rome. "I recall your face, madame," said Stokowski, "but I can't quite remember who you are." "I'm one of the old ladies with bundles," replied the tourist sweetly. Reminiscing about the old days, veteran concertgoer Mary C. Smith of Haverford, Pa., recalled her grandmother, Mrs. E. Wallace Matthews, stomping up a side-aisle during an early performance of Richard Strauss' *Death and Transfiguration*, calling back over her shoulder: "When *my* time comes, I hope there won't be so much brass."

Stokowski's war on latecomers reached its climax on a Friday afternoon in April, 1926, in an incident that not only had Philadelphia talking for weeks, but was reported widely throughout the United States. The program for that day was highly unusual. It opened with a very obscure work, a Fantasie by the late nineteenth-century Belgian conductor Guillaume Lekeu, and closed with Haydn's *Farewell* Symphony. Somewhere between was Wagner's *Ride of the Valkyries*.

This was, to put it mildly, an odd combination, but its significance became apparent quickly. The Lekeu work is written for small orchestra, with only the first violin and first cello playing at the start. These were the only two players actually on the stage when Stokowski mounted the podium and began to conduct, the others drifting in just before they were due to start playing. In fact, one or two had to start while they were still walking toward their seats, so tardy were they in arriving.

When the time came for the *Ride of the Valkyries* to begin, only the small band required for the Lekeu was on the stage; the rest of the players' seats were still empty. Nevertheless, Stokowski raised his baton preparing to give the downbeat. Before he could start, a group of brass players rushed in to take their seats. Then another breathless group arrived as the conductor again lowered his baton. After several more instrumentalists hastened into their seats the full complement was finally in place and the performance began. By now the audience realized that its own habitual tardiness was being mimicked, and there were some murmurings and a few hisses. The climax of the concert came in the *Farewell* Symphony in which, of course, the score calls for the players to depart individually until only the last two violinists remain to play the concluding measures—almost the reverse of the opening Lekeu work. Stokowski embellished the *Farewell* Symphony a bit, by having the players look at their watches and stir about impatiently just prior to their departure. At the end, as he faced an empty stage, Stokowski signalled to his phantom "orchestra" to take a bow, then turned around himself and bowed solemnly to the buzzing house.

While many in the audience accepted the ribbing in good humor, a considerable number of the matinee regulars were outraged by Stokowski's behavior. The next day management officials tried to explain

Brahms' Sonata for Two Pianos, Opus 34 B, F Minor

that the Lekeu and Haydn works had simply been played as written, with no insult to the audience intended. Later on, though, it became known that Stokowski had instructed the players to imitate the actions of the latecomers in the audience. In any case, he felt that he had made his point, and that particular experiment was not repeated.

Stokowski also took to haranguing his audiences whenever he felt they were coughing or sneezing too much during performances. Many women began arming themselves with cough drops on the way in, and one subscriber suggested to the management "that booths be installed at convenient locations in the Academy lobby on concert days for the sale of cough drops and soothing syrups of diverse kinds, after the manner of sale of opera books and librettos."

But cough drops, wherever bought, didn't seem to help much. Stokowski once bid the audience cease its "disagreeable and disgusting noises," and when a sneeze occurred during Gluck's *Alceste* Overture, followed by the arrival of several stragglers, he simply stopped playing and walked out. In the spring of 1927, when it was announced he was taking a six-month furlough to travel to the Far East, he bid farewell to his Friday matinee audience with this parting shot: "Goodby for a long time. I hope when I come back your colds will be all better."

HERBERT KUPFERBERG
Those Fabulous Philadelphians, 1969

Although the Boston Symphony has always been recognized as an outstanding orchestra, it reached a peak of perfection under the leadership of Serge Koussevitzky. Harry Ellis Dickson, a violinist with the Boston Symphony during the Koussevitzky era, wrote the following affectionate portrait of the maestro.

The history of the Boston Symphony Orchestra will forever be classified into two eras: B.K. (before Koussevitzky) and A.K. (after Koussevitzky). From the time he first came to the orchestra in 1924 through the twenty-five years of his conductorship he was able to establish and maintain an aura of Olympian aloofness and royal untouchability. His sartorial splendor, his beautiful carriage, his reserved but dramatic gestures on the podium, all of these endeared him immediately to the Back Bay ladies. Serge Koussevitzky was an actor, a sincere and wonderful actor who not only portrayed a role but actually lived it and passionately believed in that role. . . .

The question of Koussevitzky's musicianship has long been debated by critics, musicologists, and players and I leave the final judgment to posterity. I am convinced he was the greatest conductor who ever lived. Whether or not he was a deeply intellectual student of music, the fact is that he made music, that he felt it through every fiber of his being. It might be said that Koussevitzky approached music first with his heart, then with his mind. He had unfailing musical instincts and instinctive good taste in everything he did. Even when he was wrong he could, through his iron will and dynamic force, convince you that he was right. I have seen him argue with composers over their own music and, with rare exceptions, prevail. It was proven time and time again that Koussevitzky could present a composer's work infinitely better than the composer himself.

To him music could not exist without great beauty of sound and he is the only conductor I have ever known who spent hours of rehearsal time practicing sound. We would play certain passages over and over again "until," as he would say, "we will have 'our' sonority." One of his constant pleadings was for "more dolce." Indeed "dolce" became for him a word signifying perfection in music. If there was bad ensemble, he would shout, "Gentlemen, it is awfully not togedder! You must play more dolce." If he thought it was too loud, he would admonish the players to play more softly and "more dolce." If it was too soft, he would say, "I cannot hear the dolce." Not sustained enough? "Gentlemen, please don't made it a low in the music ... because when you made it a low the dolce was lost!" ...

The era of Koussevitzky was an exciting and turbulent one. Almost every rehearsal was a nightmare, every concert a thrilling experience. Those were the days when it was expected of conductors to be tyrannical and temperamental, and Koussevitzky was no exception. During his reign there were in the B.S.O. one hundred and five players and one hundred and six ulcers. (One man had two.)

But the concerts with Koussevitzky were wonderful. In spite of everything, he had a way of instilling into each musician a kind of pride and self-esteem that made him play better than his own capabilities. I don't remember a concert under Koussevitzky where, at the end, each player was not as soaking wet and emotionally spent as the conductor.

Koussevitzky had an intensively subjective approach to music, all kinds of music, it didn't matter what school, what style, what period. He simply loved music, and whatever he conducted he appropriated as his own, whether it was Tchaikovsky, Beethoven, or Bartók. Whenever he conducted a new work, whether or not he understood it, he would convince himself, and us, that this was the "greatest since Beethoven," and if the audience did not agree with him, he would walk off the stage muttering, "Idiot publicum!" and perhaps never play the piece again. His way with composers was imperious. "Aaron," he would say to Copland in the balcony while we were rehearsing a new work, "vy do you write mezzo-forte? You know mezzo-forte is di most baddest nuance *qui existe*. It must be pianissimo." And Copland would nod in agreement. With other composers he would have occasional difficulties. Hindemith, for example, would not let Koussey alter even one nuance.

Serge Koussevitzky was a born leader and he found it almost impossible to take orders from anybody, musical or otherwise. He was not a good accompanist for soloists, for unless things went his way they were

Schubert's Winterreise

apt not to go at all. I remember the Prokofiev G Minor Violin Concerto with Heifetz in which we finished a half bar after Heifetz, and there were others.

During the Koussevitzky era there were comparatively few soloists with the B.S.O. The glamour of Serge Koussevitzky was great enough to maintain full houses without soloists. And in all the eleven years I played under K. I do not remember an empty seat either in Symphony Hall or any of the other halls we played throughout the country. And such were the encomiums heaped upon him and the orchestra by critics and public that he would have had to be less than human not to have been influenced by it all. No wonder when a dear old lady said to him after a concert, "Doctor Koussevitzky, to us you are God," he answered "I know my responsibility!" There is also a story that after a concert a friend said, "You know, Serge Alexandrovitch, you are not only the greatest conductor, you are the *only* conductor!"

Koussey, pulling himself up, said, "Come now, there are other fine conductors in the world."

"Who?" asked the friend.

"Well . . ." And he turned to his wife: "Natasha, who?"

HARRY ELLIS DICKSON
"Gentlemen, More Dolce Please!" 1969.

From 1939 until his death in 1971, Igor Stravinsky resided in the United States. Although much of his time and energy was spent on new compositions, Stravinsky also conducted concerts with many of the country's leading orchestras. On one such occasion in 1966, Stravinsky led the Houston Symphony Orchestra in a combined Bach-Stravinsky program. The novelist Paul Horgan, a close friend of the maestro and his wife, accompanied them to Houston and later wrote this intimate portrait of Stravinsky at work.

The hall manager received Stravinsky and led us backstage to a plaster-lined dressing room with metal make-up desk and a mirror, a black leatherette sofa, a chair, and a small bathroom. Stravinsky asked me to give over the scores to the manager who left to place them on the conductor's stand.

"How do you feel, Maestro?"

"For the moment, that is a needless question. Ask me after the rehearsal. I will now get ready—" this politely dismissive.

"I will be out front if you need me."

"Thank you," with a little bow.

I went to the auditorium. The orchestra under the work lights tuned and retuned their instruments, playing the Shah of Persia's music. . . . There was an invigorating air of tension over the stage, waiting for Stravinsky. Many looks were directed at the stage side from which he would enter. The Persian cacophony continued and then as suddenly as though a baton had wiped it out, it ceased, as Stravinsky, hobbling as little as possible with his stick, wearing a grey cardigan, with a towel folded about his neck like an ascot tie, and his left arm aloft in almost a Papal gesture of benediction and greeting, appeared in the harsh and stimulating light of a symphony rehearsal. The players rose and applauded. He made his way to the central stand, faced them, and bowed deeply to left, to center, and to right. His rehearsal etiquette was thus immediately established, to the visible pleasure of the orchestra. Then promptly to work.

In an habitual gesture, he licked the thumb and first finger of his left hand and turned the cover of the score on his desk. In a lifted voice, colored by comradely humor, he said, making a pun on the title of the Bach chorale,

"Ladies and gentlemen, we will begin by coming down from heaven to earth."

There was a ripple of appreciative amusement over the stage, and then, abruptly serious, he spread his arms, his strong square hands furled for the up-down beat, he created the new sort of silence required of the moment, and then broke it clearly and gravely.

His rehearsal manners were an effective mixture of strict professionalism and sympathetic courtesy. He was vigorous in his beat and in his cues, and he swiftly alternated his gaze from the pages of his score and the players. There was never in his conducting a flourish for its own sake. His score-indications had of course long been familiar to him and he built his fabric of sound out of the original auditory concept. His better-known works had for decades acquired a sort of "public" sound —that patina of temperament overlaid upon them by the versions of different conductors in recordings and in concerts. All such was swept away when he conducted his own works, and the result was that their anatomy emerged in their primal purity. Total logic was what he sought, never the momentary fragmental effect. . . .

In the morning [the following Monday] there was another rehearsal, much like those of Saturday and Sunday. Monday afternoon was given over to rest before the first concert. . . . The day seemed at moments to approach the evening concert with unsettling swiftness, and at others, to drag along at an exasperating and ominous pace, both conditions producing hollow nervousness even in myself, who had but to carry scores and extra towels, and a small bag containing perhaps an extra shirt, and, surely, assorted medicaments whose presence in the dressing room would be a comfort, even should no dosages be required.

The management had provided a box for Madame [Mrs. Stravinsky], Mirandi [Levy, a family friend], and myself. I went backstage with Stravinsky while Madame and Mirandi remained in the auditorium. He was somewhat abstracted, his concentration already forming for the work ahead. His movements as he adjusted his professional possessions on the make-up counter, his neatness in all things, were executed as slowly as in a dream. It was no time for small talk, but tension

Boccherini's Opera 42

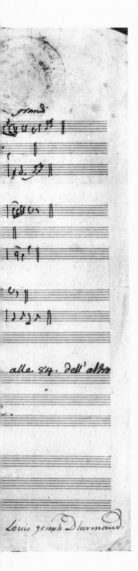

is contagious, and I relieved mine by remarking on the fine cut and fit of his tailcoat.

"Thirty-five years ago or more," he said, smiling broadly. "I had it made in London"—the same tailcoat, surely!

He wore a soft white shirt with collar turned down, and a white tie. Dimly away was the sound of the orchestra already on the stage, tuning and riffling.

"Pol," he said, "please, come back in the intermission to keep the door. Not to see anyone during the intermission." . . .

His workmanlike rehearsals had produced excellent results. The Bach variations proceeded in the stately balance he had labored for, and the ceremony between orchestra and chorus was beautiful to see as well as hear. The meeting of two masters in the work was a lesson out of *The Poetics of Music*, when in our very presence, we heard how "tradition . . . appears as an heirloom, a heritage that one receives before passing it on to one's descendants," for if Bach was there, so, too, and unmistakably, was Stravinsky.

He left the stage and it seemed to us he was gone a fairly long time, and Madame gave me an inquiring look. I was about to go to the dressing room for news when he reappeared, and it later turned out that he had needed to rearrange his hernia appliance, which had slipped—a tedious process, as it meant undressing and dressing almost entirely. But when he lifted his arm for *Orpheus*, his power was all present, and for the duration of that score I was concerned with nothing but the work itself.

He received so many calls that I was in the dressing room for many minutes before he returned. He came in, seized a towel, and began patting his face with it, while in pantomime he instructed me to lock the door. White with perspiration, he was catching his breath in long draughts through his nose. His little chest rose and fell like the top half of a pair of bellows. I believed he should lie down. I offered him a fresh towel which he took. Someone knocked and I opened the door a slit and said that Maestro Stravinsky asked to be excused from seeing anyone, and then I locked us in again. He was rapidly coming down to ordinary respiration and I suppose heartbeat. I felt it suitable to say, now,

"Well, Maestro, when I hear you conduct, I feel that not only do most conductors do things that are quite unnecessary, but are often actually harmful."

He threw down the towel. He took my shoulders and declared in a voice of high glee,

"Pol! I h-h-ate interpretation!"

I delighted in his vehemence. I laughed—I had not before heard him actually state this famous position. In the context of that dressing room, I could not fail to have a fleeting thought of its absent resident.

"The concert is wonderful," I said, "and the *Orpheus*!"

He had no need to hear superlatives from me, but he saw my excitement, and pulling me to the dressing table where duplicates of the evening's scores lay, he opened to certain pages of *Orpheus*, and began to explain to me the musical anatomy of certain passages. This inversion. That progression. Variation of a phrase prominently heard earlier in a different scoring. To the grasp of these abstract niceties I was inadequate but this did not lessen my fascination with the fact of his demonstration. His animation was as fresh as if the work had just been composed, and despite my inadequacy in technical matters, I received a direct and powerful demonstration of the primacy of form among all the elements of creation in any art. At the same time, in my hinterthought, I was nagged by other questions—the couch; a quick shower or sponging; a fresh shirt; at least attention to the 'ernia and its retainer. But before there was time for anything else, even for finishing the elucidation of the *Orpheus* score, there was a tap at the door, and the call boy said, "Ready, Mr. Stravinsky, please," and the intermission was spent. It had been spent for me, for my interest, in response to my great elation at the performance.

"Is there anything I may do for you before I go out front again?"

"No, thank you, my de-ar," he said, "but come back immediately, we will all escape."

And so we did, after a performance of *L'Oiseau de feu* which rose to a thundering climax more theatrical and audience-rousing than I had ever heard, all despite strict canons of taste against "interpretation." Stokowski could not have produced a more overpowering crescendo than that with which the composer himself closed the piece. Houston leaped to its feet, and later, backstage, crowded the cement corridors; but with self-accusing charm, Stravinsky, wearing a great fur coat (sables? martens?) like the one which had belonged to his father, the pre-Chaliapin Imperial Opera basso, made his way past hands which pulled at him, and the voices of patronesses hoping to halt him with fascinating anecdotes—"heard you conduct in Paris in 1922"—"met you and your charming wife on the *Ile de France* and we all had a drink together"—"Ah just cain't stay away tomorrow naght, Ah'm comin' again, mystro"—and we at last were encapsulated in the limousine and on our way to the Rice Hotel, and early bed. Nothing much was said in the car. Stravinsky descended into stillness and I felt that some dissatisfaction was at work in him. He would have supper sent up by room service. As we parted he politely said goodnight.

PAUL HORGAN
Encounter with Stravinsky, 1972

Handel's Messiah

In the first volume of Arthur Rubinstein's autobiography, My Younger Years, *he narrates the story of his initial concert appearance in the United States, in 1906, and the storm touched off by an innocent breach of orchestral protocol.*

Anxious to see what the tuner had done to my piano, I arrived at Carnegie Hall half an hour before rehearsal time, but I found many of the

orchestra's musicians already on the stage enjoying the familiar cacophony of tuning and trying out their respective instruments. At ten sharp, the conductor, Mr. Fritz Scheel, appeared and, without losing a second, began to rehearse the overture of Weber which was to precede my concerto.

Scheel was the typical German musician, well trained, solid, but cold. The orchestra played splendidly—it would have been a dream, I thought, to hear it under a Nikisch! When my turn came, Mr. Scheel asked me right away, "Are you related to the 'great' Rubenstein?" [The Russian pianist Anton Rubenstein] I had heard this question often before, but it irritated me this time more than ever. The piano sounded better, to my great relief; the tuner had kept his promise, so I played my long solo introduction to the concerto better than I had feared I would; after a few minutes I had the orchestra on my side. The rehearsal went very well. Mr. Scheel was efficient and indifferent, though my dynamic tempo in the last movement did stir up some reaction in him. I returned to the hotel in good spirits and spent the rest of the day in anticipation. In the evening, well ahead of time, Mr. Ulrich came to take me to the concert.

"The hall is well filled," he said with satisfaction, "and William Knabe and his brother Ernest [piano manufacturers] and their wives have arrived from Baltimore and invite you for supper after the concert." I had sat barely twenty minutes in the artists' room—the overture was short—when they called me to go up on the stage. The well-lit hall, filled with people, looked twice as big as in the morning. My appearance was greeted with a warm applause. As I made my bows I became aware of a gift which served me well through my entire concert career: the bigger the hall, the larger the audience, the more confidence and self-control I felt, and I had none of the paralyzing stage fright which afflicts so many of the best concert performers. And so I attacked my concerto with a tremendous impact. The public applauded each movement, and at the end of the brilliant finale I received a roaring ovation. I brought the conductor out, twice, to acknowledge the applause, and shook hands with the concertmaster, but the public would not give up and shouted "Bravo," and "More, more," called me back three or four times, and finally forced me to give an encore. I played the A flat Polonaise of Chopin with pride. The ovation doubled, and I had to add another piece before they calmed down. An anticlimax awaited me in the artists' room. "How dare you give encores!" Fritz Scheel screamed at me, foaming with rage. "You ruined my concert—I won't let you play again with my orchestra"; and he left the room, slamming the door behind him.

I was speechless. I hadn't known that encores were taboo at symphony concerts; in Europe they were generally accepted. Scheel's threat was a great blow; it killed the joy of my success. Suddenly the door opened, and a real crowd entered the room. Mr. Ulrich, beaming, shook my hand as if it were a pump, slapped me on the back, and shouted, "Great, you were great, you made it!" Then he introduced me to the two members of the Knabe family, who were very nice, and their wives; the two men gave me a hug, their wives kissed me. William, the elder brother, said cheerfully, "Take your time. After you have had a rest, we will take you to a good supper." At that moment Armand [a young French count and friend of Rubinstein's] appeared, followed by some friends whom he introduced to me. I, in turn, introduced him to the Knabes. His title, as usual produced a magic effect. They babbled, "Will you do us the honor and join us at supper, count?" "Count, this is a real pleasure." It was as if they were trying to learn how to pronounce "Count," they used it so often. Armand, courteous as ever, kissed the hands of the ladies and accepted the invitation. He was determined anyway to spend the evening with me.

When I told Mr. Knabe and Mr. Ulrich about Mr. Scheel's outburst, they were indignant. "He is obliged to continue the concerts with you," said Mr. Knabe. "We paid for it." Vastly relieved, I started to sign cheerfully some autographs for the waiting crowd, while my party waited patiently. Finally we were able to leave. Three hansoms, the English-styled two-wheeled cabs, took us to Delmonico's, one of the two most fashionable supper places in New York then. ... The place was packed, but the Knabes had a table reserved. Both brothers were in their early thirties, tall and rather good-looking; their wives were young and pretty. And the four of them were gay! My success was toasted at every drink, but "the Count" remained the center of their attention. They invited him to come to their home town of Baltimore, where I had my next concert, and Armand promised to come. I was well pleased with my debut in America. The critics, next morning, expressed divided opinions about my performance; two reviews were enthusiastic, one augured a great future for me, another one praised my technique and brilliance but thought less of my musicianship, and one critic, a Mr. Krehbiel, did not like me at all. ...

I seemed to be characterized as "a great talent, a fine temperament, the promise of a brilliant career, but still immature ... he has much to learn." I must admit that this was also my own opinion.

ARTHUR RUBINSTEIN
My Younger Years, 1973

Paris in the early twentieth century was no less a center for musical activity than it was for art and writing. Of the many American composers who lived and studied in Paris, the vast majority received instruction in harmony and composition from a remarkable Frenchwoman, Nadia Boulanger. Aaron Copland, one of Mlle. Boulanger's most renowned pupils, recalls the qualities which made her such a brilliant mentor.

It is almost forty years since first I rang the bell at Nadia Boulanger's Paris apartment and asked her to accept me as her composition pupil.

Chopin's Polonaise, Opus 26, No. 1

166

Any young musician may do the same thing today, for Mademoiselle Boulanger lives at the same address in the same apartment and teaches with the same formidable energy. The only difference is that she was then comparatively little known outside the Paris music world and today there are few musicians anywhere who would not concede her to be the most famous of living composition teachers.

Our initial meeting had taken place in the Palace of Fontainebleau several months before that first Paris visit. Through the initiative of Walter Damrosch a summer music school for American students was established in a wing of the palace in 1921 and Nadia Boulanger was on the staff as teacher of harmony. I arrived, fresh out of Brooklyn, aged twenty, and all agog at the prospect of studying composition in the country that had produced Debussy and Ravel. A fellow-student told me about Mademoiselle Boulanger and convinced me that a look-in on her harmony class would be worth my while. I needed convincing—after all, I had already completed my harmonic studies in New York and couldn't see how a harmony teacher could be of any help to me. What I had not foreseen was the power of Mademoiselle Boulanger's personality and the special glow that informs her every discussion of music whether on the simplest or the most exalted plane.

The teaching of harmony is one thing; the teaching of advanced composition is something else again. The reason they differ so much is that harmonic procedures are deduced from known common practice while free composition implies a subtle mixing of knowledge and instinct for the purpose of guiding the young composer toward a goal that can only be dimly perceived by both student and teacher. Béla Bartók used to claim that teaching composition was impossible to do well; he himself would have no truck with it. Mademoiselle Boulanger would undoubtedly agree that it is difficult to do well—and then go right on trying.

Actually Nadia Boulanger was quite aware that as a composition teacher she labored under two further disadvantages: she was not herself a regularly practicing composer and in so far as she composed at all she must of necessity be listed in that unenviable category of the woman composer. . . .

It would be easy to sketch a portrait of Mademoiselle Boulanger as a personality in her own right. Those who meet her or hear her talk are unlikely to forget her physical presence. Of medium height and pleasant features, she gave off, even as a young woman, a kind of objective warmth. She had none of the ascetic intensity of a Martha Graham or the toughness of a Gertrude Stein. On the contrary, in those early days she possessed an almost old-fashioned womanliness—a womanliness that seemed quite unaware of its own charm. Her low-heeled shoes and long black skirts and pince-nez glasses contrasted strangely with her bright intelligence and lively temperament. In more recent years she has become smaller and thinner. . . . But her low-pitched voice is as resonant as ever and her manner has lost none of its decisiveness. . . .

As her reputation spread, students came to her not only from America but also from Turkey, Poland, Chile, Japan, England, Norway, and many other countries. How, I wonder, would each of them describe what Mademoiselle gave him as teacher? How indeed does anyone describe adequately what is learned from a powerful teacher? I myself have never read a convincing account of the progress from student stage to that of creative maturity through a teacher's ministrations. And yet it happens: some kind of magic does indubitably rub off on the pupil. It begins, perhaps, with the conviction that one is in the presence of an exceptional musical mentality. By a process of osmosis one soaks up attitudes, principles, reflections, knowledge. That last is a key word: it is literally exhilarating to be with a teacher for whom the art one loves has no secrets.

Nadia Boulanger knew everything there was to know about music; she knew the oldest and the latest music, pre-Bach and post-Stravinsky, and knew it cold. All technical know-how was at her fingertips: harmonic transposition, the figured bass, score reading, organ registration, instrumental techniques, structural analyses, the school fugue and the free fugue, the Greek modes and Gregorian chant. Needless to say this list is far from exhaustive. She was particularly intrigued by new musical developments. I can still remember the eagerness of her curiosity concerning my jazz-derived rhythms of the early twenties, a corner of music that had somehow escaped her. Before long we were exploring polyrhythmic devices together—their cross-pulsations, their notations, and especially their difficulty of execution intrigued her. This was typical, nothing under the heading of music could possibly be thought of as foreign. I am not saying that she liked or even approved of all kinds of musical expression—far from it. But she had the teacher's consuming need to know how all music functions, and it was that kind of inquiring attitude that registered on the minds of her students.

More important to the budding composer than Mademoiselle Boulanger's technical knowledge was her way of surrounding him with an air of confidence. (The reverse—her disapproval, I am told, was annihilating in its effect.) In my own case she was able to extract from a composer of two-page songs and three-page piano pieces a full-sized ballet lasting thirty-five minutes. True, no one has ever offered to perform the completed ballet, but the composing of it proved her point—I was capable of more than I myself thought possible. This mark of confidence was again demonstrated when, at the end of my three years of study, Mademoiselle Boulanger asked me to write an organ concerto for her first American tour, knowing full well that I had only a nodding acquaintance with the king of instruments and that I had never heard a note of my own orchestration. "Do you really think I can do it?" I asked hopefully. "*Mais oui*" was the firm reply—and so I did.

Mademoiselle gave the world première of the work—a Symphony for organ and orchestra—on January 11, 1925, under the baton of Walter Damrosch. My parents, beaming, sat with me in a box. Imagine

Gluck's Orfeo

168

our surprise when the conductor, just before beginning the next work on the program, turned to his audience and said: "If a young man, at the age of twenty-three, can write a symphony like that, in five years he will be ready to commit murder!" The asperities of my harmonies had been too much for the conductor, who felt that his faithful subscribers needed reassurance that he was on their side. Mademoiselle Boulanger, however, was not to be swayed; despite her affection for Mr. Damrosch she wavered not in the slightest degree in her favorable estimate of my symphony....

Many of these observations are based, of course, on experiences of a good many years ago. Much has happened to music since that time. The last decade, in particular, cannot have been an easy time for the teacher of composition, and especially for any teacher of the older generation. The youngest composers have taken to worshiping at strange shrines....

In the meantime it must be a cause for profound satisfaction to Mademoiselle Boulanger that she has guided the musical destiny of so many gifted musicians: Igor Markevitch, Jean Françaix, and Marcelle de Manziarly in France; Americans like Walter Piston, Virgil Thomson, Roy Harris, Marc Blitzstein, among the older men, Elliott Carter, David Diamond, Irving Fine, Harold Shapero, Arthur Berger among the middle generation, and youngsters like Easley Blackwood during the fifties.

In 1959, when Harvard University conferred an honorary degree on Nadia Boulanger, a modest gesture was made toward recognition of her standing as teacher and musician. America, unfortunately, has no reward commensurate with what Nadia Boulanger has contributed to our musical development. But, in the end, the only reward she would want is the one she already has: the deep affection of her many pupils everywhere.

AARON COPLAND
Copland on Music, 1960

Marian Anderson's 1939 Easter Sunday concert in front of the Lincoln Memorial was a truly unprecedented musical event. As Miss Anderson's manager, Sol Hurok was involved in every aspect of the planning and execution of the concert. Hurok's description of those activities, as told in Impresario, *the first volume of his memoirs, gives a firsthand glimpse of Miss Anderson's artistry and grace under extreme pressure.*

The *cause célèbre* which came to its climax at the Lincoln Memorial on Easter Sunday in 1939 began with a perfectly routine request from Howard University in Washington, D.C., for a concert by Marian Anderson under the University's auspices. Arrangements were made in June, 1938, for a concert to take place in Washington the next season.

When we were scheduling Marian's tour the date we gave the University was April 9th.

Early in January, 1939, the manager of Howard University's concert series applied to Fred E. Hand, manager of Constitution Hall, to reserve the auditorium for a performance on April 9th. . . .

Mr. Hand replied to the University's manager that a clause in the rental contract of Constitution Hall prohibits the presentation of Negro artists. . . .

When the University informed us of the clause, we wrote to Mr. Hand, asking him if it would be possible to waive the restriction in the case of Miss Anderson, so as not to deny to the people of Washington a great musical experience.

Back came the reply from Mr. Hand: "I beg to advise you that Constitution Hall is not available on April 9th, 1939, because of prior commitments." In the matter of policy, he advised us to communicate with Mrs. Henry M. Robert, Jr., President General of the National Society, Daughters of the American Revolution. . . .

Marks Levine, my good friend, of National Concert and Artists Corporation, wrote to Mr. Hand at about this time asking for available dates for a concert by Ignaz Paderewski in Constitution Hall. Hand replied with a list of dates which did not include the 9th, but did mention the 8th and 10th as open. I wired the University's concert manager that the 8th and 10th were open and he promptly applied to Hand for either date.

The answer came back: "The Hall is not available for a concert by Miss Anderson."

Now the facts were clear. The 9th might very well be closed, but neither was any other date open to Marian Anderson at Constitution Hall. Indignation began to sizzle. . . .

Protesting telegrams continued to pour into the office of the DAR. Newspaper editorial pages bristled with editorials, crackled with letters to the editors.

And on February 27th Mrs. Roosevelt resigned from the DAR. . . .

On February 24th I had announced that Marian Anderson would sing in Washington, out of doors, within earshot of the Daughters and their Hall. I sent my press agent, Gerry Goode, to Washington with the intention of asking permission to use the Lincoln Memorial for the concert.

Walter White, the sparkplug president of the NAACP, was on his way to Washington too. Together they went to the Department of Interior, which has jurisdiction over the parks of the capital. Assistant Secretary Oscar L. Chapman listened, nodded, said, "Wait a minute," went into Secretary Ickes' office, and came back. In literally one minute the Secretary had granted permission for Miss Anderson to sing a concert at the Lincoln Memorial. . . .

Platform, public-address system, ropes to mark the aisles—all had to be provided. And the complicated business of the radio network, news-

Beethoven's Trio for Piano and Strings, Opus 70, No. 1, D Major

reel cameras, sound-recording devices had to be handled by an expert. My publicity staff was on hand to give the radio, newsreel and newspaper men the service they have come to expect in this highly organized modern world. . . .

We gave our services, we paid the incidental expenses, but this is one event I do not claim as a publicity stunt. Anyone who has read the record knows it was as nearly spontaneous an arising of men and women of good will in Washington as there can be in our times. Well managed, of course. No untoward events. No jarring notes.

Easter Sunday came closer. All the arrangements were made. Everything was ready. For us the excitement mounted until it was almost unbearable.

And on Saturday, at about midnight, Marian telephoned from Philadelphia, "Must we really go through with this?"

For Marian it had been a difficult time. The denial of the Hall . . . was a painful shock to begin with. And then the storm of protest that swirled about her innocent head, welcome as it was for the sake of principle, violated all her personal needs for privacy, serenity, peace. I have said it before and it bears repeating: Marian has not the instincts nor the temperament of a fighter. And when, through no fault of hers, the issue arose and the fight was on, she was as uncomfortable as one might well be at the center of a cyclone. Willingly as she did her part in the service of her people, she would far rather it had been some other, someone who could enjoy the fight.

And so on the eve of her greatest concert she telephoned in a state of actual fright to ask whether we really had to go through with it.

But when we took her from Union Station to Governor Pinchot's house, with the sirens of a police escort shrieking through the quiet Sunday-morning streets, she was calm and ready. At the Governor's, she changed to her concert gown and quietly glanced over her music once more, while the police captain stood on the sidewalk nervously counting the seconds ticking by. We drove to the Lincoln Memorial in a trance of hushed expectancy. As she walked beside me along the roped-off aisle and up the steps to the platform, where great men and women of America stood to honor her, the arm which I took to steady her was steadier than my own. She raised her eyes once to the great bronze figure with so much sorrow in the deeply lined face. Then she turned to the people who had come to hear her and to pledge by their presence there a faith in the rights of man.

There were 75,000 of them. To describe a crowd of 75,000 men and women—and children, too—standing with upturned faces, expectant, quiet, attentive, is beyond my powers. The effect of such a mass of human beings, their eyes and ears and very hearts fixed on one figure, is indescribable. Looking down at them, one feels a kind of buoyancy, as though one were floating on a sea—and it was a sea, with a tide of strong feeling flowing from them to the erect figure of a woman standing composed and ready by the piano on the platform.

When she opened her lips and sang, it was as though the tide flowed back again to them. She returned to them, with all the sincerity in her, the human goodness which they had offered her. We have come to expect of Marian and her singing not only the beautiful instrument beautifully used, but the truly great power of music. We listen, not only to be sung to, but to be exalted. On that Easter Sunday 75,000 Americans shared in that exaltation, and it shone in their faces.

A mural painting of that Easter Sunday afternoon, the work of Mitchell Jamieson, adorns a wall in the Department of Interior building. At the dedication in January, 1943, Secretary Ickes said, "Her voice and personality have come to be a symbol—a symbol of the willing acceptance of the immortal truth that 'all men are created free and equal.'"

To which Marian replied, "I am deeply touched that I can be in any way a symbol of democracy. Everyone present was a living witness to the ideals of freedom for which President Lincoln died. When I sang that day I was singing to the entire Nation."

SOL HUROK
Impresario, 1946

The annual outdoor summer concerts at Lewisohn Stadium on the campus of the City College of New York were an integral part of New York's cultural landscape for more than four decades until they were suspended in 1966. Responsibility for hiring artists, arranging schedules, raising funds, and checking the weather forecasts fell to Minnie Guggenheimer, a diminutive woman whose energy and good humor became a hallmark of the series. From a place at her mother's side, Sophie Untermeyer shared those exciting evenings at Lewisohn Stadium, as she describes in the following excerpts from Mother is Minnie.

Wagner's Das Rheingold

It has been estimated that almost as many people trek up to New York's Lewisohn Stadium on clear summer nights to chuckle over the intermission antics of Minnie Guggenheimer as to hear any of the world-famous singers, instrumental virtuosi and conductors she lines up for appearances with the Stadium Symphony Orchestra in her full-time, unsalaried job as impresaria of the world's largest-scale musical project.

Minnie's perennial tussles with such tongue twisters as Khatchaturian and Slenczynska over the Stadium loudspeakers; her persistent public confusion as to whether Moiseiwitsch is a ballet dancer, Szigeti plays the piano, or Beethoven wrote the Verdi *Requiem*; the unabashed bloopers and blithe malapropisms she perpetrates while rattling off advance programs and introducing celebrity guests; and the utter lack of inhibition with which she shares intimate household secrets and problems of dress and digestion with crowds running into the tens of thousands have become . . . a part of the New York legend. . . .

A short, busty, gray-haired dowager who might have stepped right out of a Helen Hokinson cartoon, Minnie will float from the wings of the vast outdoor stage at around 9:30 of a June or July night—in all likelihood wearing the same heavy, rubber-soled sport shoes and dowdy, five-year-old cotton dress she put on to walk the dog before breakfast, with a frumpy inverted flowerpot of a hat borrowed at the last minute from the cook—and, waving her right hand giddily in mid-air, chirp a cheery "Hello, everybody" to a motley mass that choruses its reciprocal "Hello, Minnie" in ecstatic unison. Then, planting herself behind a standing microphone and sliding her framed spectacles down the not inconsiderable length of her nose, she'll proceed to forecast the musical highlights of the week, identifying *Richard* Strauss as the composer of "The Beautiful Blue Danube" and *Pinafore* as everybody's favorite by Gilbert and *Solomon*; promising that *Anton* Rubinstein will play the Tchai-COW-sky *Violin* Con-SERT-o, Jan Peerce will sing the role of *Aida*, and *Rodger Hammerstein* "personally" will conduct a number from *South Pacific;* and interrupting herself from time to time to implore the echo of her own voice to "shut up" or exhort her listeners to "Tell everybody you know to come to the Stadium. And tell everybody you don't know too, because unless we have people in the empty seats I'll simply go bust!"

Habitual Stadiumgoers recall with particular delight the night in 1947 when she came out to herald the upcoming appearance of "one of the best-known names in the musical world," then, hesitating for an anguished moment, reached into her overstuffed pocketbook for the crumpled bank check on which she had written her notes and identified him as Ezio Pinza, *baass*." "Oh dear, that can't be right," she corrected aloud. "A bass is a kind of fish!"...

Surviving two wars, a national depression, and an endless succession of local crises, the Stadium Concerts have provided for those of us who grew up in New York in the 1920's, '30s, '40s, and '50s an endless chain of memories, of works first heard, of personalities first experienced, of evenings under the spell of stars and great music. The long and notable line of Stadium soloists has run the gamut from Rosa Ponselle and Kirsten Flagstad to Frank Sinatra and Harry Belafonte; from Fritz Kreisler and Arthur Rubinstein to Benny Goodman and Errol Garner. The roster of conductors has ranged all the way from Beecham, Mitropoulos, Reiner, and Stokowski to Paul Whiteman and Duke Ellington. Victor Herbert and Sigmund Romberg, Villa-Lobos and Leonard Bernstein, Robert Stolz and Richard Rodgers have conducted their own works at the Stadium. Alicia Markova, Argentinita, and José Greco have danced across the big stage; Carl Sandburg has recited his poetry and Ethel Barrymore Colt read Shakespeare; Larry Adler and John Sebastian have played Bach and Mozart on the harmonica, and Léon Thérémin and Lucie Rosen have plucked eeire notes from the summer air with the aid of the mysterious instrument bearing Thérémin's name.

The average member of the audience for New York's famous summer symphonic programs, according to the results of a questionnaire circulated in 1952, attends the concerts regularly for at least twelve years of his life, going at least ten times a season. Although his own musical talent and training is limited to "a little piano," he has pretty definite ideas about the kind of music he likes to hear. His favorite symphony is the Beethoven Fifth; his favorite violin concerto the Beethoven "Emperor"; his favorite opera *Carmen;* his favorite song "Kiss Me Again" . . . and his favorite soloist Jascha Heifetz (with Lily Pons in second place and Arthur Rubinstein, Yehudi Menuhin, and Nathan Milstein close runners-up). . . .

The habitual Stadiumgoer likes to think of himself as a member of a large, yet fairly close-knit family, which shares with favorite public figures their intimate problems and personal joys and sorrows. . . . He was proud that night in 1942 when a fine young pianist was given time off from the army to play at the Stadium and Captain Sam Russell came onstage at intermission to promote Private Eugene List to the rank of corporal. He suppressed a tear or two when plucky Marjorie Lawrence was rolled out in a wheel chair to sing Brünnhilde's "Immolation" in one of her first public appearances after a crippling attack of polio. He welcomed the news that lovely Roberta Peters and handsome Robert Merrill, just married in a wedding ceremony of fairy-tale splendor, would be returning from their honeymoon for a joint concert at the Stadium; then wondered what strange feelings the young baritone must have had facing his wife of only a few weeks, wearing her wedding dress onstage a day after their divorce had been made public. He shouted "bravo" for Arthur Schuller, a second violinist in the Stadium orchestra, directing his fellow players for the first time in a valiant eleventh-hour pinch hit, while holding a little silent prayer for the scheduled conductor, Miguel Sandoval, who had keeled over on the podium rehearsing the same program earlier in the day and was gasping for the last breaths of a brilliantly gifted life in a hospital a few blocks away. And if he happens to be one of the hepcats whom new concepts of programming have lured to the Stadium in increasing numbers in recent seasons, he is not likely to forget that dramatic moment, midway through the 1959 July Fourth "Jazz Jamboree," when a grand old showman who had been reported fatally ill only a week before in Italy and for whom five or six top bandleaders had volunteered at the last minute to substitute, wandered out from the wings virtually unnoticed, flashed a familiar grin to his "All-Stars," snatched a trumpet from one of them and gave forth with the first blaring reassurance that Louis Armstrong was in the groove again, while thousands burst exuberantly into "Happy Birthday, dear Satchmo" on the fifty-ninth anniversary of his coming into the world in a dismal New Orleans back alley.

Throughout Stadium Concerts' history there have been moments of thrilling new discovery to treasure. Perhaps the night in 1930 when a dance program starring Anna Duncan, adopted daughter of the illus-

Verdi's Ernani

174

trious Isadora, provided a red-headed young fiddler from the Capitol Theatre Orchestra with his first chance to wield a symphonic baton. Said the music critic of the New York *World* the next day: "His technique, sharp and incisive and peculiarly toneless, is better suited to the theater." But the Stadium audience disagreed vociferously, as have audiences (and more astute critics) all around the world in the ensuing years, hailing Eugene Ormandy as one of the giants of the podium. . . .

They still speak with special affection of a night in 1925 when a nervous young contralto no one had ever heard of till then stepped timidly before the orchestra to sing "O Mio Fernando" from Donizetti's *La Favorita* and brought the house down with her breath-taking trill at the end of the aria. She had been given her first big-time engagement as winner over three hundred and sixty contestants in a series of talent auditions held throughout the previous winter on behalf of Stadium Concerts. At a table way up in front near the stage, the work-hardened hands of Anna Anderson, a Negro laundress from Philadelphia, applauded with special pride for her daughter Marian.

On July 25, 1927, a twenty-nine-year-old composer from Brooklyn, with a number of successful Broadway show scores to his credit, was to appear for the first time at the Stadium, providing another unforgettable experience as he played his own jazz-infused piano concerto and a haunting utterance of twentieth century frustration called *Rhapsody in Blue* with the orchestra under the baton of Willem Van Hoogstraten. He made a tremendous hit with the audience and reappeared as piano soloist on varied symphonic programs in each of the four succeeding years. Then in 1932 a rush of seventeen thousand eight hundred and forty-five of his fans through the turnstiles broke all previous Stadium attendance records for the first of the memorable All-Gershwin concerts, with William Daley and Albert Coates sharing the podium, Gershwin playing the *Rhapsody in Blue* himself, and his virtually unknown young friend Oscar Levant playing the Piano Concerto. Five years later, George Gershwin, only thirty-nine, was dead in Hollywood of a brain tumor, and a vast audience, saddened by the loss of one of America's most promising musical talents, paid tribute to his memory at the Stadium. . . .

SOPHIE G. UNTERMEYER
Mother Is Minnie, 1960

During the 1930's the jazz-derived big band sound known as "swing" dominated popular music. Bands lead by Benny Goodman, Tommy and Jimmy Dorsey, and Woody Herman traveled across the country, appearing in hotels and nightclubs as well as on radio broadcasts and college campuses. Nevertheless, as Benny Goodman wrote in an informal history of this era, The Kingdom of Swing, *no one expected the frenzied adulation that greeted his band on the opening day of an appearance at the Paramount Theatre in New York City.*

By the time we finished our job in "The Big Broadcast of 1937," which was made in the summer of *1936*, we had a pretty good idea that the public for real jazz was a big one, and growing all the time. Even when we opened at the Pennsylvania, some of the people around the hotel were skeptical, saying the band was too loud. That was a big night for me. . . . After the band was set in the room and the crowds started to come and keep on coming, we didn't hear much more comment on the band being loud. But I don't think that any of us realized how strong a hold it had on the youngsters until a certain day early in March 1937.

We had undertaken to double at the Paramount Theatre in New York in addition to playing our job at the Pennsylvania, with no expectation that we would do more than fair business. After all, our only previous theater bookings had been something less than sensational. So when we arrived at the theater for an early morning rehearsal before the first show and found a couple of hundred kids lined up in front of the box-office at about 7 A.M., we couldn't help feeling that every one of our most loyal supporters in the five boroughs was already on hand.

However, this wasn't a patch on what happened even before we got on stage. All through the showing of the picture, the folks backstage said there were noises and whistling coming through from the house as Claudette Colbert did her stuff in "Maid of Salem." The theater was completely full an hour before we were supposed to go on, and when we finally came up on the rising platform, the noise sounded like Times Square on New Year's Eve. It certainly was a lot different from the days when I played on that same platform with Eddie Paul's orchestra.

The crowd quieted down a little when the band started in, but even on stage you could get an undercurrent of intense excitement that really did something to us. That reception topped anything we had known up to that time, and because we felt it was spontaneous and genuine, we got a tremendous kick out of it. It's only in these latter days, when some of the youngsters just come to cut up that it gets in our way. After all, if a fellow like Jess Stacy or Ziggy Elman or Vernon Brown gets up to play a solo, he has a right to be heard—and the people in the audience who know what they're listening to feel the same way about it.

However, we didn't know half the story until we got off the stage and were back in our dressing rooms. It seems that Willard was sitting in the mezzanine with Bob Weitman, the manager of the Paramount. They got the same thrill out of this enthusiasm that we did, up to the point where a couple of youngsters got up and started to shag in the aisles. Then a few more started to climb over the rail towards the orchestra, and Bob jumped up and rushed out, yelling:

"Somebody's going to get hurt there any minute. There'll be a panic."

He ran down the steps to the back of the orchestra, and as soon as the ushers saw him, they snapped to attention and started saluting.

"The hell with that," he shouted. "Get down there and stop those kids from killing themselves!"

As he went from aisle to aisle to get the ushers organized, he had to go through this same routine of being saluted by each one before he could get things under control.

By three o'clock in the afternoon, 11,500 people had paid their way into the theater, and the total for the first day's attendance was 21,000. Another thing about that first day which caused talk around the theater was this: The total for the day's sale at the candy counter was $900—which is some kind of a record, too.

BENNY GOODMAN
The Kingdom of Swing, 1939

In the last years of his life, illness slowed Louis Armstrong down and virtually ended his musical career. But on at least two occasions the brilliance of Armstrong's past was reawakened—at his seventieth birthday celebration in 1970, and at a nightclub appearance with Pearl Bailey. Jazz critic Leonard Feather, an admirer and friend of Armstrong's, was on hand both evenings and recorded the events that transpired.

Although tributes and celebrations had long since become his way of life, few if any were more important to Satch than the seventieth birthday celebration arranged by his old friend Floyd Levin, head of the Southern California Hot Jazz Society. Louis arrived at Los Angeles airport on the evening of June 30 and found, to his surprise, something he normally expected only at foreign airports: a big brass band, and hundreds of fans jamming the arrival area. Lucille [Mrs. Armstrong] did her best to whisk him away from the surging crowd and the Armstrongs left for their hotel after a brief press conference.

The concert was held at the Shrine Auditorium on the night of July 3, after a year of planning by a coalition of California Dixieland clubs. Almost 50 traditionalist jazzmen had been rounded up to represent various phases of the Satchmo story. I opened the proceedings by introducing the master of ceremonies, Hoagy Carmichael, who brought the guest of honor to the stage. At the sight of Louis, the crowd of 6,000 rose to its feet; the applause was as heartfelt and as long-lasting as one of Pops' high-C finales.

Seated in a rocking chair in front of a New Orleans French Quarter backdrop, Louis and Hoagy sang an unaccompanied duet—"Rockin' Chair," which they had recorded together in 1929. They then commented on a series of slides, which showed the wooden backyard building where Louis was born; thirteen-year-old Louis playing in the Waifs' Home band; the 1918 riverboat ensemble, and King Oliver's Creole band in 1923, with Louis on second cornet. As these reminders flashed on the screen, Louis reminisced freely while a succession of combos filed onstage to amplify his stories with music. (The riverboat band included, fittingly, many men who had been playing for years in a boat on a simulated Mississippi at Disneyland.)

Later, in a recreation of the Oliver band, Louis heard an old buddy, Andy Blakeney, who had replaced him with Oliver in 1924. The Armstrong Hot Five was represented by Teddy Buckner's group. Another combo, announced as the "Ambassador Satch Band," had four Armstrong alumni: Barney Bigard, Tyree Glenn, Joe Bushkin, and Red Callender.

As the midnight deadline approached, Louis reappeared to croak "Sleepy Time Down South," followed by "Blueberry Hill"; then he hypnotized the happy crowd into a sing-along, clap-along "Hello Dolly!" with Tyree Glenn up front playing the obbligato.

The evening was climaxed when an 800-pound cake, 11 feet high, was wheeled onstage. Satchmo had to climb up seven steps to take a slice off the top. In all it was a night filled with joy and love, in which the only missing element was the sound of Satchmo's horn. The question nagged at all of us: would he ever play again? "I still practice an hour a day, every evening before dinner," he told me. "Dr. Schiff says maybe I'll be ready in a couple of months."

Ready or not, his mere presence meant instant nostalgia to his fans. Everyone at the Shrine had his own private memory of Louis; perhaps a long-forgotten dance in a Depression-era ballroom; perhaps a forty-year-old Hot Five record that had triggered a career in music; perhaps the recollection of departed giants who had become part of the Armstrong legend—Joe Oliver, Jack Teagarden, Edmond Hall, Billy Kyle.

The next afternoon, on his actual birthday, Louis relaxed quietly with Tyree Glenn, Barney and Dorothe Bigard, Floyd Levin, and a few other friends in the sunlit penthouse apartment of Bobby Phillips of Associated Booking Corporation, the organization Joe Glaser had headed until his death.

Perhaps because Dr. Schiff was present, or perhaps because Louis wanted us all to know how seriously he took his doctor's injunction, he even refused to toot a note on a small toy trumpet that was handed him as a gag during the birthday party.

Looking back at the nostalgic joys of the previous evening, Louis turned to Levin and said: "Man, I've had a lot of wonderful honors in my life, but last night was the biggest thrill of all." So it had been for many of us whose pleasure was dimmed only by the belief that Louis had long since blown his final chorus.

As it turned out, the impossible took a little while. Two months later the International Hotel in Las Vegas announced: "The Pearl Bailey Show, with Louie Bellson and His Orchestra. Special Guest Attraction—Louis Armstrong." Pearl Bailey had the unprecedented pleasure of sharing her customary standing ovations with a legend brought back from limbo, and the overtones of this evening made it unforgettable.

It was not just Louis himself we applauded as he ambled onstage to the opening stanza of "Sleepy Time Down South"; it was the fact that he was once again able to play his horn, for the first time after two years of illness.

Satchmo and his combo (most of his 1968 men were back with him) cruised through their traditional show, with the usual "Indiana" for openers, followed by "Someday," "Tiger Rag," and "The Saints," among others. His horn had lost none of its incandescence. His sound might have been stronger, but we told ourselves that time would take care of that. Each note was perfectly on target and Armstrong-pure.

The teaming of Pearl and Louis was a delight as they traded choruses, from "Bill Bailey" to "Blueberry Hill." "Didn't We?" with occasional vocal murmurs from Satch, was Miss Bailey's most affecting ballad. For a finale the two of them went through a mutually stimulating series of choruses on "Exactly Like You." "There was an awful lot of love in the house tonight," Miss Bailey said later.

More than thirty-eight years had gone by since my first personal exposure to the Armstrong horn. It was just as well that nothing alerted me, during this evening of celebration, to the fact that this was, for me, the last time.

LEONARD FEATHER
From Satchmo to Miles, 1972

Mozart's Violin Sonata, K. 376

A Chronology of Music

Although song has probably always been a part of man's life, it is difficult to pinpoint dates in the history of music before the Middle Ages—and even then there are relatively few events that can accurately be cited. The reign of Pope Gregory I—Gregory the Great—from A.D. 590 to 604 saw the systemization of Church music, although it is not known how much Gregory himself had to do with the introduction of what came to be known as Gregorian chant. The Church continued to dominate music for another five hundred years—until the age of the troubadours saw the popularization of music and the development of a notation system that allowed men to record their songs permanently and accurately. Subsequently, composers, performers, and compositions can be listed in the long evolution of one of man's most important cultural expressions.

Music	Date	World Events
	1099	Soldiers of the First Crusade capture Jerusalem from the Moslems
Appearance of secular songs in Romance language (the dialect of southern France), written and performed by troubadours	1150-1200	
Leoninus of Notre Dame composes *Magnus Liber Organi*, series of musical pieces for the entire liturgical year	1160-1180	
	c.1168	Founding of Oxford University
	1183-1236	
Perotinus of Notre Dame perfects the four-part song	1194-1260	Western façade of Chartres cathedral constructed
	1215	Magna Carta signed by King John at Runnymede
Franco of Cologne explores the use of harmony in musical composition	1220	
"Sumer is icumen in," oldest English round	1226	
Stabat Mater, a part of Catholic liturgy, attributed to Jacopone da Todi	1228-1306	
Cantigas de Santa Maria produced at court of Alfonso the Wise of Castile	1250	
Life of Philippe de Vitry, theoretician and composer whose treatise *Ars Nova* ushered in a period of experimentation in musical composition	1271-95	Journey of Marco Polo to the Orient
	1291-1361	
Guillaume de Machaut, leading composer of the French *ars nova*, serves the royal house of France	1321	Dante completes *The Divine Comedy*
	1346-77	
Francesco Landino, the finest organist and composer of fourteenth-century Italy, wins a competition in Venice for organ compositions	1364	
	1368	Founding of the Ming dynasty, which ruled China for more than 200 years
	1415	Battle of Agincourt: English forces under Henry V defeat the French in a climactic battle of the Hundred Years' War
Guillaume Dufay composes *Sine nomine*, a Mass in three parts.	c.1420	
Dufay appointed conductor at the papal chapel	1428	
	1453	Fall of Constantinople to the Ottoman Turks
	c.1454	Publication of the Gutenberg Bible marks the beginning of printing from movable type
Josquin des Prés, master composer of medieval Church music, serves at papal court in Rome	1486-94	
	1492	Fall of Granada marks the end of Moorish influence in Spain; Christopher Columbus sets forth on his first voyage to the New World

Diversification of instruments: clavichord, virginal, spinet, harpsichord, violin, and lute come into common use	c.1500	
	1508	Michelangelo begins painting the ceiling of the Sistine Chapel
	1517	Martin Luther presents his "95 Theses"
	1519-22	Magellan circumnavigates the globe
	1543	Copernicus publishes his discoveries on the nature of the solar system
Book of Common Prayer, a Protestant hymn book, compiled by John Marbeck	1550	
Orlando di Lasso appointed chapelmaster at St. John Lateran in Rome	1553	
Palestrina composes *Missa Papae Marcelli* in honor of Pope Marcellus II	1565	
Giovanni Gabrieli named the organist of St. Mark's Basilica in Venice	1585	
English composer William Byrd publishes a volume of madrigals	1588	England turns back the Spanish Armada; Christopher Marlowe's *Dr. Faustus* performed
Publication of *Sacrae Symphoniae*, a collection of religious music composed by Gabrieli	1597	
More than 500 motets of Orlando di Lasso are published posthumously by his family	1604	Shakespeare's *Othello* first presented
Monteverdi's opera *Orfeo* performed in Mantua; employs first "modern" orchestra with more than 36 instruments	1607	
	1620	Pilgrims land at Plymouth Rock, Massachusetts
Samuel Scheidt writes *Tabulatura Nova*, the classic treatise on the art of organ music	1624	
Heinrich Schütz composes *Daphne*, the very earliest German opera	1627	
	1632	Galileo publishes his work supporting Copernicus' theories on the solar system, and the following year is tried for heresy by the Inquisition
	1642	Rembrandt completes his mammoth group portrait *The Night Watch*
Luigi Rossi produces *Orfeo*, the first Italian opera heard in Paris	1647	
	1666	Molière's comedy *Le Misanthrope* is performed
	1667	John Milton completes his epic poem *Paradise Lost*
Royal Academy of Music founded in Paris	1669	
Admission charged for the first time at a number of concerts held in London	1672	
Giovanni Battista Lully, considered the founder of French opera, directs the first performance of his *Alceste*	1674	
	1687	Isaac Newton publishes *Principia*, stating fundamental laws of gravity and motion
	1688	Glorious Revolution in England
Invention of the clarinet attributed to Johann Christoph Denner of Nüremberg	c.1690	
Francois Couperin becomes organist at Louis XIV's private chapel at Versailles	1693	
Alessandro Scarlatti becomes conductor at the chapel of the Polish court	1708	
Bartolomeo Cristofori develops modern pianoforte in which hammers are used to strike strings	1710	
Antonio Vivaldi composes the twelve concertos known as *Estro Armonico*	1712	
Handel writes *Te Deum* and *Jubilate* to celebrate the Peace of Utrecht	1713	Treaty of Utrecht
Violinist and composer Arcangelo Corelli composes the famous *Concerti Grossi*	1714	
Bach composes the six *Brandenburg Concertos*; one year later he completes the first volume of *The Well-Tempered Clavier*; second volume is published in 1740	1721	Publication of Montesquieu's *Lettres Persanes*

Production of John Gay's *The Beggar's Opera*	1727	
Bach's *The Passion According to Saint Matthew* is performed on Good Friday in Leipzig	1729	
Giovanni Pergolesi, a composer of religious and secular music, completes *Stabat Mater*	1736	Production of Voltaire's finest tragedy, *Zaire*
Royal Society of Musicians organized in London	1738	
First public performance of the English anthem "God Save the King"	1740	
Handel completes *Messiah*; the oratorio receives its first production the following year	1741	
	1758	Voltaire completes *Candide*
Haydn serves as *Kapellmeister* to the Esterházys	1760-90	
	1776	American Declaration of Independence; James Watt develops the steam engine; Adam Smith's classic treatise, *The Wealth of Nations*, published
First production of Mozart's *The Marriage of Figaro*; within the next five years Mozart completes *Don Giovanni, Così fan Tutte*, and *The Magic Flute*	1786	
In a three-month period Mozart composes three of his greatest symphonies: the E Flat, G Minor, and C, also known as the *Jupiter* symphony	1788	
	1789	Parisians storm the Bastille; Declaration of the Rights of Man proclaimed
French national anthem, "Le Marseillaise," is composed by Claude Rouget de Lisle	1792	
Paris Conservatory of Music opens	1795	
	1803	United States purchases Louisiana Territory
First performance of Beethoven's *Eroica* symphony	1804	
Beethoven completes the Fifth Symphony, perhaps the most popular piece of serious music ever written	1808	
Schubert writes the art song *Erl King*	1815	Napoleon defeated at Waterloo
Johann Maelzel invents the metronome	1816	
Beethoven composes his *Missa Solemnis*	1818-22	
Schubert completes Symphony No. 8 in B Minor, called the *Unfinished Symphony* because it has only two movements; Royal Academy of Music opens in London	1822	
Première performance of Beethoven's Ninth Symphony in Vienna	1824	First trade union formed in England
Mendelssohn composes *A Midsummer Night's Dream* overture; in 1843 he writes incidental music for a full-length production of the play	1826	
Initial performance of Hector Berlioz' *Symphonie fantastique*	1830	Victor Hugo writes *Notre-Dame de Paris*
Chopin settles in Paris	1831	
	1837	Accession of Queen Victoria of England
Robert Schumann writes *Dichterliebe*, a cycle of songs to poetry by Heine	1840	
New York Philharmonic Society and the Vienna Philharmonic are founded	1842	
Berlioz publishes *Treatise on Modern Instrumentation and Orchestration*, which becomes standard work on symphony orchestras	1844	
Johannes Brahms gives his first piano concert in Hamburg, Germany; publication of "Oh! Susanna," early work of American folk-music composer Stephen Foster; Franz Liszt appointed court conductor to the Grand Duke of Weimar; beginning of Liszt's friendship with Richard Wagner	1848	Revolutionary movements erupt and are quelled in Germany, Italy, Austria; abdication of Louis Philippe and proclamation of the Second Republic; Marx and Engels publish *Communist Manifesto*
	1850	Publication of Charles Dickens' *David Copperfield* and Nathaniel Hawthorne's *The Scarlet Letter*
Liszt composes *Sonata in B Minor*, considered the finest composition for the piano written in the romantic period; a year later he composes the symphonic poem *Les Préludes*	1853	
	1854	Commodore Perry secures agreements opening Japan to Western trade

Music		World Events
The Mighty Five—Russian composers Mili Balakirev, César Cui, Alexander Borodin, Nicholai Rimsky-Korsakov, and Modeste Moussorgsky—form a group dedicated to Russian national music	1859 1862	Charles Darwin's *Origin of Species* . . . published
	1863	Battle of Gettysburg, turning point of American Civil War
Peter Ilich Tchaikovsky named professor of harmony at the Moscow Conservatory	1866	Fëdor Dostoevski's *Crime and Punishment* written
Johann Strauss the younger gives first performance of his own composition, *The Blue Danube Waltz*; Moussorgsky's *Night on Bald Mountain* performed	1867	
	1870-71	Franco-Prussian War ends with capitulation of Napoleon III and formation of Third Republic
"The Internationale," anthem of the international communist movement, written by the French composer Eugene Pottier; Verdi's *Aida* receives initial performance in Egypt	1871	German Empire proclaimed; Otto von Bismarck becomes German chancellor
Smetana completes symphonic poems called *My Country*—best known of which is *The Moldau*	1874-79	
Johann Strauss the younger completes the popular operetta *Die Fledermaus*	1874	
Wagner's four-opera cycle *Der Ring des Nibelungen* presented at the first Bayreuth Festival; Tchaikovsky composes music for the ballet *Swan Lake*; Edvard Grieg writes *Peer Gynt Suites* as incidental music for the Ibsen play	1876	First telephone constructed by Alexander Graham Bell
Brahms scores his four symphonies—C Minor (1876), D Major (1877), F Major (1883), and E Minor (1885),—which rank among the most important orchestral works of the late nineteenth century	1876-85	
Gilbert and Sullivan's most popular operetta, *H.M.S. Pinafore*, presented in London	1878	Congress of Berlin convenes
Rimsky-Korsakov composes the spectacular suite *Scheherazade*	1879 1884	Ibsen's *A Doll's House* performed
Anton Bruckner, Wagner's disciple, writes *Te Deum*	1885	Louis Pasteur tests vaccine to prevent rabies
Cesar Franck's Symphony in D Minor performed	1889	
Tchaikovsky visits United States to participate in ceremonies marking the opening of Carnegie Hall	1891	
Antonin Dvorák leads the first performance of his Fifth Symphony, *From the New World*; Tchaikovsky completes his Sixth Symphony, called the *Pathétique*, and dies a few days after conducting its first performance	1893	
Claude Debussy, leader of the impressionist school of music, composes his most famous work, *L'Après-midi d'une Faun*	1894	Conviction of Dreyfus sparks controversy in France
Strauss writes the tone poem *Till Eulenspiegel's Merry Pranks*; *Also sprach Zarathustra* is produced a year later	1895	Publication of Freud's *Studies on Hysteria* marks beginning of psychoanalysis
Gustav Mahler heads Imperial Opera House, Vienna	1897-1907	
First performance of Sibelius' *Finlandia*; Symphony Hall in Boston opens	1900	Boxer Revolution in China crushed
Mahler conducts the first performance of his Third Symphony	1902	
Igor Stravinsky receives his first formal musical training as a pupil of Rimsky-Korsakov	1903	Orville and Wilbur Wright design and fly the first airplane
	1905-16	Albert Einstein formulates special and general theories of relativity
	1907	Pablo Picasso's *Les Demoiselles d'Avignon* exhibited
English composer Frederick Delius completes *In a Summer Garden*	1908	
Mahler serves as principal conductor of the New York Philharmonic	1909-10	
Gabriel Fauré completes the piano composition *Nine Préludes*	1910	Union of South Africa formed

Debut of Maurice Ravel's *Daphnis et Chloé* suite	1912	Chinese Republic proclaimed
Riotous uproar greets première performance of Stravinsky's *Le Sacre du Printemps* in Paris	1913	
	1913-28	Marcel Proust's multivolume masterpiece, *Remembrance of Things Past*, published
	1914	World War I begins; Panama Canal opens
	1917	Russian Revolution
Spanish composer Manuel de Falla writes the music for *The Three-Cornered-Hat* ballet	1919	
First performance of George Gershwin's *Rhapsody in Blue*; Arnold Schoenberg composes *Suite for Piano*, his first piece based entirely on the twelve-tone system; Arthur Honegger's *Pacific 231* has the orchestra imitating the sound of a steam locomotive; Respighi's *Pines of Rome*	1924	Sean O'Casey's *Juno and the Paycock* performed at Dublin's Abbey Playhouse
Duke Ellington organizes his first band; première performance of Aaron Copland's *Symphony for Organ and Orchestra*, commissioned by Nadia Boulanger for the New York Symphony Society	1925	
Ravel completes the popular symphonic piece *Boléro*	1928	Discovery of penicillin by Alexander Fleming
	1929	Stock market crash on Wall Street leads to world-wide economic depression
Première performance of Gershwin's *Porgy and Bess*	1935	
Sergei Prokofiev composes music to accompany the fairy tale *Peter and the Wolf*; Roy Harris' First Symphony performed	1936	Spanish Civil War begins
Dimitri Shostakovich writes the Fifth Symphony to celebrate the twentieth anniversary of the Bolshevik Revolution; Béla Bartók's *Music for String Instruments, Percussion and Celesta*	1937	
Charles Ives' *Second Piano Sonata*—written between 1904 and 1915—receives initial performance	1939	German invasion of Poland marks beginning of World War II
Paul Hindemith composes *The Four Temperaments*, theme and variations for piano and strings	1940	
Rodgers and Hammerstein's *Oklahoma!* sets a new style in American musical plays	1943	
Martha Graham choreographs an American folk ballet to Copland's *Appalachian Spring*	1944	
	1945	Allies defeat Hitler's Germany; first atomic bombs used against the Japanese to end World War II in Pacific; United Nations organized
	1947	India gains independence from Great Britain
	1948	State of Israel established
	1949	People's Republic of China proclaimed
	1950-52	Korean War
Canti di Liberazione by Luigi Dellapiccola	1951-55	
Karlheinz Stockhausen creates an electronic music composition, *Gesang der Junglinge*; opening of Lerner and Lowe's *My Fair Lady*	1956	First production of Eugene O'Neill's autobiographical play *Long Day's Journey Into Night*
Duke Ellington composes *Such Sweet Thunder*	1957	*Sputnik I* launched by Soviet Union
French composer Pierre Boulez writes *Improvisation sur Mallarmé*	1958	Charles de Gaulle elected president of France; establishment of the Fifth Republic
Igor Stravinsky composes *Movements for Piano and Orchestra*—a major work of serial music	1960	
Benjamin Britten writes *War Requiem* to mark consecration of Coventry Cathedral in England; first United States tour of the Beatles	1962	Cuban missile crisis
	1963	Assassination of President John F. Kennedy
	1967	Arab-Israeli Six Day War; first heart transplant performed by Dr. Christiaan Barnard
Nearly half a million people gather for Woodstock rock festival in Bethel, New York; première of John Cage's multimedia composition *HPSCHD*	1969	American astronauts walk on the moon
Performance of Leonard Bernstein's *Mass* opens John F. Kennedy Center in Washington, D.C.	1972	
Seiji Ozawa becomes music director of the Boston Symphony Orchestra	1973	Agreement signed to end the Vietnam War

Selected Bibliography

Barzun, Jacques. *Berlioz and the Romantic Century*. 2 Vols. New York: Columbia University Press, 1969.

Briffault, Robert. *The Troubadours*. Bloomington: Indiana University Press, 1965.

Bukofzer, Manfred F. *Music in the Baroque Era*. New York: W. W. Norton, 1947.

Calvocoressi, M.D. and Abraham, Gerald. *Masters of Russian Music*. Reprint of 1936 edition. New York: Johnson Reprint Corporation.

Chase, Gilbert. *America's Music: From the Pilgrims to the Present*. New York: McGraw-Hill, 1955.

David, Hans T. and Mendel, Arthur, eds. *The Bach Reader*. New York: W. W. Norton, 1966.

Davison, Archibald T. and Apel, Willi, eds. *Historical Anthology of Music*. Cambridge: Harvard University Press, 1949.

Lockspeiser, Edward. *Debussy: His Life and Mind*. 2 Vols. New York: Macmillan, 1962.

Malm, William P. *Music Cultures of the Pacific Near East and Asia*. Englewood Cliffs: Prentice-Hall, 1967.

Newman, Ernest. *The Man Liszt*. New York: Taplinger, 1970.

Pleasants, Henry. *Serious Music and All That Jazz*. New York: Simon & Schuster, 1969.

Reese, Gustave. *Music in the Middle Ages*. New York: W. W. Norton, 1940.

Sachs, Curt. *The History of Musical Instruments*. New York: W. W. Norton, 1940.

———. *The Rise of Music in the Ancient World*. New York: W. W. Norton, 1943.

Schenk, Erich. *Mozart and His Times*. New York: Knopf, 1959.

Schindler, Anton F. *Beethoven As I Knew Him*. Edited by Donald W. MacArdle. New York: W. W. Norton, 1972.

Slonimsky, Nicolas. *Music Since 1900*. Fourth Ed. New York: Scribner's, 1971.

Stravinsky, Igor. *An Autobiography*. New York: W. W. Norton, 1962.

Strunk, Oliver, ed. *Source Readings in Music History*. New York: W. W. Norton, 1950.

Weinstock, Herbert. *Chopin*. New York: Knopf, 1949.

Wiora, Walter. *The Four Ages of Music*. Translated by M. Herter. New York: W. W. Norton, 1965.

Acknowledgments

The author, Mr. Grunfeld, wishes to express his special appreciation to the staffs of the British Museum library, and to the librarians of the Warburg Institute of London University, whose assistance was particularly helpful during the research phase of this book. Invaluable help in preparing the manuscript was provided by Barbara Barnes, Naomi Brandel, and Catherine Doggwiler.

Picture Credits

TITLE PAGE: Louvre, Paris (Lalance)

CHAPTER 1 **6** (Folco Quilici) **8-9** Instruments: Museo del Castello Sforzesco, Milan (Archives AME) **9** Bas-relief: Louvre, Paris (Foliot) **10** Wall painting: (Hirmer Fotoarchiv) **11** Ivory casket: Museo del Bargello, Florence (Scala) **12** New Delhi Museum (Borromeo) **13** Bibliothèque Nationale, Paris (Snark International) **14-15** Museo Nazionale, Naples (Parisio) **16-17** Antiquarium del Palatino, Rome **18** Museo Nazionale, Naples (Pedone) **19** Museo Lazaro, Madrid (Manso-Mas) **20-21** Both: Museo Archeologico Nazionale, Cividale del Friuli (Ciol)

CHAPTER 2 **22** Biblioteca Estense, Modena (Scala) **24-25** Palazzo Schifanoia, Ferrara (Arborio-Mella) **26** Jousting: Musée Condé, Chantilly (Snark International) Musicians: El Escorial (Molenaer) **27** El Escorial (Mas) **28** El Escorial (Molenaer) **29** Biblioteca Laurenziana, Florence (Scala) **30** Chartres: (Garanger-Giraudon) "Practica Musicae": Biblioteca Trivulziana, Milan **31** Biblioteca Civica,

Index